MUGASHA

New Zealand Banking Law

NEW ZEALAND BANKING LAW

Alan L Tyree LLB (VUW) MSc (Ohio) PhD (Massey)
University of Sydney

Wellington
Butterworths
1987

New Zealand	Butterworths of New Zealand Ltd, 205-207 Victoria St, WELLINGTON, 1st Floor, Johns Building, 21-23 Chancery St AUCKLAND
England	Butterworth & Co (Publishers) Ltd, LONDON
Australia	Butterworths Pty Ltd, SYDNEY, MELBOURNE, BRISBANE, ADELAIDE and PERTH
Canada	Butterworth & Co (Canada) Ltd, TORONTO Butterworth & Co (Western Canada) Ltd, VANCOUVER
Singapore	Butterworth & Co (Asia) Pte Ltd, SINGAPORE
South Africa	Butterworth Publishers (Pty) Ltd, DURBAN
USA	Mason Publishing Co, ST PAUL, Minnesota Butterworth Legal Publishers, SEATTLE, Washington: BOSTON Massachusetts; and AUSTIN, Texas D & S Publishers, CLEARWATER, Florida

National Library of New Zealand
Cataloguing-in-Publication date

TYREE, Alan L.
    New Zealand banking law/Alan L. Tyree. -
Wellington [NZ]: Butterworths, 1987. -
1 v.
    ISBN 0-409-70223-4
            346.931082
    1. Banking law-New Zealand. 2. Banks and
banking-New Zealand. I. Title.

Preface

The law of banking has been a Cinderella subject in law schools for many years. If the subject was taught at all, it was as a small part of a general commercial law course. That position is changing as rapidly as the business of banking itself. Economic deregulation has opened the business of banking to a much larger number of players. We can expect the demand for banking lawyers to increase as a result of the increased economic activity and the teaching of banking law courses to increase as the demand for banking lawyers increases.

At least since the decision of the English Court of Appeal in *Joachimson v Swiss Bank Corporation* [1921] 3 KB 110 it has been well understood that the relationship between banker and customer is a contractual one. It is an unusual contract since the terms are, for the most part, implied terms. The importance of the contractual relationship has recently been reaffirmed by the Privy Council in *Tai Hing Cotton Mill Ltd v Liu Chong Hing Bank Ltd* [1986] AC 80. Because of the central importance of the contract between banker and customer, I have tried to analyse banking law problems by reference to the contract when possible. I have also used the terms of the contract to structure the book in what I hope is a logical and pleasing fashion.

I owe a debt to the writers of previous banking law texts. I have consistently relied upon *Paget's Law of Banking*, Weaver and Cragie, *The Law Relating to Banker and Customer in Australia*, and *Chorley's Law of Banking*. I owe an even greater debt to Professor EP Ellinger who taught not only the law of banking but also the beauty of the subject.

I wish to express my thanks to Butterworths of New Zealand for their help and consideration in the project. The gold medal for patience and tolerance must, however, be awarded to my wife Allison who encouraged me throughout this project.

Alan L Tyree

University of Sydney

Summary of Contents

Summary of Contents

Table of Contents

Chapter 8   The Account I   108

Chapter 9   The Account II   129

Chapter 12   Liability of the parties to a bill   182

Chapter 13   Cheques   210

Chapter 14   The collecting bank I   228

Chapter 15   The collecting bank II   246

Chapter 18   Money paid under a mistake of fact   297

Chapter 19   Other payment systems   322

Chapter 20   Consumer issues in EFT   351

Chapter 21   Credit cards   364

Chapter 22   General principles of lending   372

Table of Cases

A

B

D

H

I

J

K

L

M

N

O

T

U

V

W

Y

Z

Chapter 1

Introduction

Nature of banking law

1.1 It is somewhat misleading to speak of "banking law", for there is no extensive area of law which applies solely to bankers or to the business of banking. Bankers are, with a few notable exceptions, subject to the same law as everyone else.[1] By virtue of the special nature of banking business, this means that the complete banking lawyer should be an expert in the law of contract, in the law of agency, in the law of torts, in the law of negotiable instruments, in the law of companies and of partnerships, in the law of security interests in real and personal property and probably a dozen other areas as well.

1 One of the most important exceptions is the definition of "cheque" in the Bills of Exchange Act 1908 and the special position accorded to a "banker" within the meaning of that Act. See Chs 13-17.

1.2 The task is not hopeless however, for within each of the major legal areas there are parts which are not only accessible but which are of particular importance to bankers and to their legal advisers. As one example of this selective procedure, most books on the law of banking consider the law of agency only in so far as it applies to the banker's role in the cheque collection process.[1] Many bankers will act as agents from time to time in other capacities, but all bankers will act as agents for the collection of cheques every day of their banking life. Therefore this topic is discussed at length in every book on banking law.

1 See Chs 13 and 14. In addition, the position of the banker as agent in direct funds transfers and in letter of credit transactions is discussed: see Chs 19, 28 and 29.

1

Implied contract

1.3 One of the most salient features of "banking law", particularly the relationship between the banker and the customer, is that it is based almost entirely on the legal concept of the implied contract.[1] Although the implied contract is legally indistinguishable in its effects from any other kind of contract, it is peculiar in that it arises not from the agreement of the parties before the fact but from the perceptions of the common law Judges after a dispute arises between the parties.[2]

1 *Joachimson v Swiss Bank Corp* [1921] 3 KB 110; and see Ch 2.
2 This is so in spite of the language often used by the Courts which suggests a search for the parties' intentions. See *Liverpool City Council v Irwin* [1977] AC 239; *Tai Hing Cotton Mill Ltd v Liu Chong Hing Bank Ltd* [1985] 2 All ER 947; Ch 2.

1.4 One consequence of this is that the rights and obligations of the banker and the customer are the result of a long series of cases where the Courts have balanced the competing interests of the parties involved. In order to understand banking law it is essential to understand the common law process and to appreciate fully the legal importance of previously decided cases.[1]

1 For an elementary introduction to the common law method, see Chisholm and Nettheim, *Understanding Law*, Sydney, 1978. For more detail, Derham, Maher and Waller, *An Introduction to Law*, Sydney, 1971.

Banking practice

1.5 A second consequence is that the custom and practice of bankers become important as a means of defining the current state of the law.[1] The common law Courts have always had respect for commercial practice when considering commercial cases and this is reflected in the many examples of cases where banking practice has been admissible as evidence. However, the banker should not be misled into thinking that any practice will be accepted as valid, for the Courts have also always reserved the power to find that some existing banking practice does not meet minimum standards.[2]

1 See *United Dominions Trust Ltd v Kirkwood* [1969] 2 QB 431, particularly Lord Denning at p 454.
2 See *E B Savory & Co v Lloyds Bank Ltd* [1932] 2 KB 122 where the standard was rejected; also *Rosenhain v The Commonwealth Bank of Australia* (1922) 31 CLR 46 where the Court found that there was no existing practice.

Statute law

1.6 Although much of the law of banking is based on case law, there are some statutes which are of particular importance to bankers.

The most important of these is the Bills of Exchange Act 1908 which provides the banker with important immunities which are not enjoyed by other members of the general or the financial community. Other major Acts will be considered in this book, but the complete banking lawyer must be familiar with all of the hundreds of statutes and regulations which are of importance to any modern financial or commercial lawyer.

Regulation of banking

1.7 The modern business of banking is one with very special characteristics, for the banking system of a country is in a position to create money and thereby have a beneficial or deleterious effect on the economic policies of the government of the day.[1] For this reason, the legal system of every country treats the business of banking in some special way. It is customary to find limitations both on who may enter into the business and how the business may be conducted.

1 See Galbraith, *Money: Whence It Came, Where It Went*, London, 1975.

Traditional approach

1.8 From 1933 until 1984, the approach of various New Zealand governments was to exercise stringent controls over both the entry of companies into the banking business and over the conduct of the business of the established banks.[1] The main forms of regulation were the prohibition of the formation of a company which has as its major object the carrying on of the business of banking, the setting of interest rates and the total control of foreign currency exchange rates.

1 See Bright, *Banking Law and Practice in New Zealand*, Wellington, 1969; also The Reserve Bank of New Zealand, Financial Policy Reform, Wellington, 1986.

Recent changes

1.9 Economic and political changes forced the government to re-evaluate this policy in mid-1984. An "internationalisation" of financial markets meant that New Zealand could no longer easily remain isolated from the rest of the financial world. At the same time, the traditional lines which separated the business of banking from the business of other financial institutions began to blur so that the regulation of banking was both discriminatory and ineffective.[1]

1 The Reserve Bank of New Zealand, Financial Policy Reform, Wellington, 1986.

1.10 Although the distinction between the business of banking and other financial business remains for some purposes, a significant amount of "deregulation" of the business of banking has occurred while at the same time financial institutions which previously escaped any form of regulation have been placed on much the same footing as the banks. The Reserve Bank now has the power to recommend to both the trading banks and other financial institutions policies to be followed in relation to the level of acceptances, minimum and maximum rates of discount and interest rates and maximum charges for acceptance fees.[1] Under current government policy, these powers are now to be used only in extraordinary circumstances.

1 See Ch 10 for a discussion of the use of acceptances in modern commercial financing.

1.11 Prior to March 1985 the exchange rate of the New Zealand dollar was set from time to time by the Reserve Bank. Since that date, the dollar has "floated", ie, its value in terms of other currencies has been determined by market forces. At about the same time, controls over the exchange of New Zealand currency for foreign currency were eased to allow New Zealand residents to purchase foreign currency for investment purposes and to hold overseas accounts.

1.12 Prior to February 1985, trading banks were required to maintain a certain level of deposits and government securities with the Reserve Bank as well as holding a certain proportion of their funds in so-called public sector securities. These were abolished and replaced by a more informal system of consultation with the Reserve Bank as a method of prudential control.

The Reserve Bank

Central banks generally

1.13 In various countries during the nineteenth century, a single bank emerged which became known as the "central bank" and which fulfilled the functions of issuing government notes and acting as banker for the government. In other countries, of which New Zealand is one, the emergence of a central bank was the result of a conscious decision brought about by the financial management problems which resulted from the First World War. Still other countries delayed the introduction of a central bank until the onslaught of the great depression of the 1930s.

The Reserve Bank of New Zealand was established by the Reserve Bank of New Zealand Act 1933 and commenced operations the following year. It was given the sole right of issuing notes and was to serve as banker to the government and to other bankers.

Functions of the Reserve Bank

1.14 The Bank currently operates under the authority of the Reserve Bank of New Zealand Act 1964. The preamble of the Act indicates the purpose:

> WHEREAS it is the sovereign right of the Crown to control currency and credit in the public interest: And whereas for that purpose it is desirable to define more fully the powers and duties of the Reserve Bank of New Zealand as the central bank.

1.15 The primary functions of the Bank are enumerated in s 8. They are:

(a) To act as the central bank for New Zealand; and
(b) To ensure that the availability and conditions of credit provided by financial institutions are not inconsistent with the sovereign right of the Crown to control money and credit in the public interest; and
(c) To advise the Government on matters relating to monetary policy, banking, credit, and overseas exchange; and
(d) Within the limits of its powers, to give effect to the monetary policy of the Government . . . .

Other institutions

1.16 Recent years have seen the development of a wide range of deposit-taking and loan-arranging institutions. Some of them operate under statutory regimes but many have developed precisely for the purpose of evading regulation. The breadth of the business conducted may be seen in the new s 2 of the Reserve Bank of New Zealand Act 1964 in the definition of "Financial institution". The term means:

> . . . any body of person (including a body of persons, whether incorporated or not) who in the course of business — (a) Borrows money or accepts deposits (whether on demand or for a fixed term) or receives credit or sells any credit instrument; and also (b) lends money or grants credit or buys or discounts any credit instrument . . . .

1.17 In order to close the "loophole" of institutions known as "merchant banks" the section also includes ". . . any person . . . who acts as agent or intermediary in any of the transactions aforesaid;". The section goes on to name specific types of institutions which are included. These are trustee savings banks, private savings banks, life insurance companies, superannuation funds of certain types and building societies. There is then a catchall phrase which allows the Governor-General to declare specified persons or class of persons to be a financial institution.

5

1.18 These definitions and the powers given to the Reserve Bank go far to eliminate many of the traditional divisions between the business of banking and that of other financial institutions. "Banks" are still given a privileged position by the Bills of Exchange Act 1908 but it is expected that any further distinctions between banks and other financial institutions will be eroded in favour of distinctions which are related to the size and function of the institution rather than whether it technically qualifies as a bank or some other form of entity.[1]

1 See *New Banks and Financial Structure Reform* in The Reserve Bank of New Zealand, Financial Policy Reform, Wellington, 1986.

Chapter 2

The banker and customer relationship

2.1 If one reflects on the many services provided by the modern bank to its customer, it is apparent that the legal relationship between the banker and the customer must be a complex one. Indeed, it would seem almost impossible to fit the relationship into a single legal category. Yet, such a classification is necessary if the variety of legal disputes which arise are to be analysed and solved in a satisfactory fashion. It may surprise the reader to learn that the relationship is not defined by statute but rather by a series of common law judgments.

Possible relationships

2.2 The common law analysis of the relationship was a late development. Perhaps because modern banking had its origins with the goldsmiths of London, for many years there was the possibility that the legal relationship might be one of bailment. On the other hand, it was clear that in many transactions the banker acted in a position of trust and, in still other situations, the relationship could be considered one of agent and principal. Since it was possible right up to the mid-19th century that the Courts might have found the basic relationship to be any one of these, each will be considered in turn, for had any of the three been selected as the basic legal relationship which defines the rights and obligations of the parties, banking could not exist in the form in which we now know it.

7

Bailor and bailee

2.3 A bailment is the transfer of the possession of a chattel without the transfer of title. The transfer may be very informal as when a person leaves a lawnmower with a neighbour while on vacation, or it may be a formal contractual arrangement such as when a chattel belonging to the debtor is left with the lendor as a security for a loan. The owner of the chattel who parts with possession is known as the bailor, the person who receives the chattel is the bailee.

2.4 It is clear that there are occasions when the banker acts as the bailee of goods which are deposited by the customer for safe keeping. When the goldsmiths of London first began receiving goods for safe keeping, there is no doubt that they were doing so as bailees of those goods. However, at a later time when receipts were issued and when it was not expected that the goods, ie gold, returned would be exactly the same as those deposited, it was no longer possible to consider the relationship to be one of bailment.

2.5 The business of banking, based on receiving deposits and lending money could scarcely exist if the fundamental relationship between banker and customer were one of bailment. It would mean, for example, that when the customer deposited notes and coins into an account, the banker would be obliged to return precisely those same notes and coins rather than a sum of money equivalent to the deposit. Furthermore, the duties of a bailee are simply not directly applicable to the business of banking save where the banker is acting in the special capacity of custodian of property which has been deposited for safe keeping.

2.6 It might be thought that money is special and that there might still be a bailee/bailor relationship even though the banker is clearly not expected to return the same identical notes and coins. In legal terms, it is said that money is a "fungible". However, it seems that the concept of bailment is incompatible with that of a fungible. In *Chapman Bros v Vercos*[1] the High Court of Australia held that an arrangement whereby wheat was deposited with a company which would then sell it or, at the request of the "bailor", return an equivalent amount of wheat if the terms of sale were unacceptable, could not be a bailment precisely because the same identical grains of wheat were not to be returned.

1 (1933) 49 CLR 306.

2.7 There is one very practical consequence of the *Vercos* decision. If the relationship were one of bailment, then the property in the goods or money remains with the depositor. In the event of the insolvency of the banker, the customer would be entitled to receive the full value of the deposit in preference to other creditors of the banker. However, if the relationship is one in which the depositor loses property in the goods or money deposited, then the other creditors of the banker will rank equally and the depositor can expect only a small fraction of the original deposit to be returned.

Trustee and cestui que trust

2.8 There are clearly occasions when a banker acts in a fiduciary capacity similar to that which exists between trustee and beneficiary. Had the Courts held that the opening of an account and the deposit of money established the legal relationship of trust, then once again, modern banking simply could not exist. A trustee is severely restricted in the use to which trust funds may be put and will ordinarily be restricted in the class of investment. The freedom of investment enjoyed by bankers would be restricted with the economic consequence that financing for all but the safest of projects would of necessity come from non-banking sources. Banks would cease to be the major economic and financial force that they are now.

2.9 Had the primary relationship been found to be one of trust, then once again, the position of the depositor would have been improved in the event of the banker's insolvency. Since the beneficial, ie equitable, ownership of the money would remain with the customer, other creditors would be deferred until depositors were fully repaid.

Agent/principal

2.10 Again, it is clear that there are certain circumstances in which the banker acts as the agent of the customer. Perhaps the most common situation is the collection of cheques, a matter which is discussed at some length in Chs 14 and 15. There is no legal obstacle to the creation of an agency in which the banker would have the authority to use the customer's money at discretion. However, the law relating to the remuneration of an agent and the duty of an agent to account would severely hamper the development of modern banking practice.

Debtor and creditor

2.11 Perhaps because of the difficulties attached to the above possibilities for defining the primary legal relationship between the banker and customer, it was not until 1848 that the legal relationship was firmly established as being a relationship between debtor and creditor which arises from contract.

2.12 In the landmark case of *Foley v Hill*[1] the plaintiff had deposited a sum of money with the defendant banker many years before bringing the suit. The banker had agreed to pay 3% interest but no interest had been credited to the account for well over six years.

The problem for the plaintiff was to overcome the Statute of Limitations,[2] for if the money owed by the banker was a mere debt, then an action for its recovery was barred by the statute. However, if the relationship between the parties was one in which the banker owed the plaintiff a fiduciary duty, then the statute did not apply. Lord Cottenham said:[3]

> Money paid into a bank is money known by the principal to be placed there for the purpose of being under the control of the banker; it is then the banker's money; he is known to deal with it as his own; he makes what profit he can, which profit he retains to himself . . . . He has contracted, having received that money, to repay to the principal when demanded a sum equivalent to the paid into his hands.

It should be noted that there is still the trace of the agent/principal relationship in the language used by Lord Cottenham.

1 (1848) 2 HL Cas 28; 9 ER 1002.
2 See 2.42.
3 At 2 HL Cas 28, 35; 9 ER 1002, 1005.

2.13 Thus, when a banker receives money from a customer, or receives money from some third party for the account of a customer, the banker does so as a borrower. The ownership of the money is transferred to the banker who is then free to use the money in any way that he or she so chooses. As a consequence, the banker is also free to retain the income from or any other benefit of the money. There is no duty to hold the actual notes or coins or to keep the money segregated in any way from any other of the banker's money. He is simply a borrower with a contractual obligation to repay the money to the customer when certain conditions are met.

2.14 Approval of the debtor/creditor basis of the banker/customer relationship was given explicitly by the High Court of Australia in *Croton's* case.[1] A man and woman who were living together opened a joint bank account where each had the authority to draw cheques. Both of the parties deposited money into the account. Without the woman's authority or knowledge, the man withdrew the money from the account and deposited it in another bank account in his own name. When the woman discovered this, she complained to the police who charged the man with larceny. A majority of the High Court upheld his appeal on the basis that the correct charge should have been fraudulent misappropriation. Barwick CJ said:

> Though in a popular sense it may be said that a depositor with a bank has "money in the bank" in law he has but a chose in action, a right to recover from the bank the balance standing to his credit in the account with the bank at the date of his demand or the commencement of action.

> But the money deposited becomes an asset of the bank which it may use as it pleases. Neither the balance standing to the credit of the joint account in this case nor any part of it, as it constituted no more than a chose in action in contradistinction to a chose in possession, was

susceptible of larceny, though it might be the subject of misappropriation.[2]

1 *Croton v R* (1967) 41 ALJR 289.
2 *Croton v R* (1967) 41 ALJR 289,291.

Additional contractual incidents

2.15 Although the basic legal relationship is one of debtor and creditor, there are additional contractual terms which are necessary to facilitate the fulfilment of the parties' expectations. The first comprehensive judicial acknowledgment of the complexity of the contract entered into by the banker and customer was in *Joachimson v Swiss Bank Corpn*.[1] The case concerned the question of when the debt owed by the banker is repayable and, in particular, the need for a demand by the customer.

1 [1921] 3 KB 110.

Demand

2.16 In *Foley v Hill*, Lord Cottenham LC made it quite clear in his speech that the contractual duty to repay is slightly different from the normal debtor/creditor relationship. Ordinarily, it is for the debtor to seek out the creditor and to make repayment when due.[1] It is obviously not contemplated that the banker will seek out the customer and repay the debt since that would have the effect of closing the customer's account, a result which is not desired by either party.

1 *Walton v Mascall* (1844) 13 M & W 452, 458.

2.17 The confusion regarding the need for the customer to make a demand before the debt became due was possibly a result of the fact that the headnote of *Foley v Hill* neglected to mention Lord Cottenham's qualification to the debtor/creditor relationship. In 1921, Lord Atkin, in one of the most famous and most often quoted passages of the law of banking, undertook a more complete analysis of the banker/customer relationship.

> I think that there is only one contract made between the bank and its customer. The terms of that contract involve obligations on both sides and require careful statement. They appear upon consideration to include the following provisions. The Bank undertakes to receive money and to collect bills for its customer's account. The proceeds so received

are not to be held in trust for the customer, but the bank borrows the proceeds and undertakes to repay them. The promise to repay is to repay at the branch of the bank where the account is kept and during banking hours. It includes a promise to repay any part of the amount due, against the written order of the customer addressed to the bank at the branch, and as such written orders may be outstanding in the ordinary course of business for two or three days, it is a term of the contract that the bank will not cease to do business with the customer except upon reasonable notice. The customer on his part undertakes to exercise reasonable care in executing his written orders so as not to mislead the bank or to facilitate forgery. I think it is necessarily a term of such contract that the bank is not liable to pay the customer the full amount of his balance until he demands payment from the bank at the branch at which the current account is kept.[1]

1 *Joachimson v Swiss Bank Corpn* [1921] 3 KB 110, 127.

2.18 Recall that a term will not be implied into a contract unless it is necessary to do so and that in the absence of the implied term the whole transaction would become "futile, inefficacious, and absurd".[1] It seems likely that bankers would agree that the implied term as to demand at the branch where the account is kept is necessary, for otherwise the customer would be entitled to demand the money at any branch of the bank, irrespective of where the account was kept. Customers, in like manner, would certainly agree that the consequential need for giving notice before ceasing to do business is also necessary, for otherwise the banker would be entitled to repay the account balance at any time and to then dishonour any outstanding cheques. The contractual terms concerning the collection of bills and the payment against "written orders" are the subject-matter of Chs 13 to 15 of this book.

1 Per Lord Salmon in *Liverpool City Council v Irwin* [1977] AC 239.

2.19 The actual decision in *Joachimson's* case is somewhat confusing, for after holding that a demand is necessary for the debt from the banker to the customer to become due, the Court of Appeal held that the issue of a writ by the customer for the amount due would be sufficient demand in spite of the fact that there was no previous demand. There is, however, no right to obtain the writ unless there is a debt due and owing.

2.20 It is often said that the basic relationship is one of debtor and creditor with "superadded obligations". This expression of the relationship does no harm so long as it is understood that all it means is that there is a single contract between the banker and the customer and that the contract has many terms. Indeed, much of the subject matter of the law of banking is nothing more than the explanation and the elaboration of the terms of the contract between the banker and customer.

2.21 The Privy Council referred to some of the ways in which the banker/customer relationship differs from the normal debtor/creditor relationship in *Bank of NSW v Laing*.[1] The plaintiff alleged that a series of cheques were forged. He drew cheques totalling the amount of the cheques which he claimed were forged and presented them to the defendant bank for payment. They were dishonoured and the plaintiff sued. Unfortunately, legal practice in New South Wales at the time still retained the forms of pleading and the decision in favour of the bank turns entirely on a technicality. However, during the course of the judgment, Lord Asquith of Bishopstone commented upon the ways in which the banker/customer relationship differs from that of the ordinary debtor/creditor relationship. First, the debt does not become due until the customer makes a demand. Secondly, "a further 'peculiar incident' is that the bank is only indebted to the customer for the amount . . . standing to his credit as at the time of the demand . . . If the balance falls short of [meeting the demand], even by a penny, he [the customer] fails altogether, another distinction which distinguishes the creditor-debtor relationship in the case of customer and banker from that relationship in other cases".[2]]

1 [1954] AC 135.
2 Per Lord Asquith of Bishopstone, p 154.

Altering the relationship

2.22 One of the consequences of the relationship being contractual is that it may not be altered unilaterally by either of the parties. This can cause great inconvenience to bankers who wish to change the manner in which business is conducted. For example, in *Burnett v Westminster Bank Ltd*,[1] the customer kept accounts at two branches of the defendant bank. After Burnett opened his account, one of the branches adopted computerised accounting methods and issued cheque-books with magnetic ink character recognition (MICR) figures pre-printed on the cheques.[2] The inside cover of the cheque-books of the computerised branch contained a notice to the effect that the cheques could only be used to draw upon the account for which they had been prepared.

1 [1965] 3 All ER 81.
2 The use of MICR cheques is discussed at 19.19.

2.23 Burnett used one of the MICR cheque forms to draw a cheque in which he struck out the name of the computerised branch and wrote in the name of the non-computerised branch at which he kept his other account. He subsequently wished to stop payment on the cheque and gave notice to the non-computerised branch, the branch upon which he believed that he had drawn the cheque.

2.24 The cheque was paid in the ordinary course of the computer processing and the bank claimed the right to debit the (computerised) account. The Court held that the customer was entitled to succeed on the basis that the purported change in contractual conditions by the bank was not effective to bind the customer and consequently he was able to change the form to give instructions to the non-computerised branch. It followed that the stop order was directed to the correct branch and that Burnett was entitled to succeed. An important consideration in the decision was that the bank was unable to show that the notices in the cheque-book had been brought to Burnett's attention. Consequently, the use of the cheque-book could not be construed as an agreement by Burnett to abide by the new terms which the bank wished to insert into the contract.

2.25 Even though the relationship is contractual, it is a contract of a very unusual kind in that ordinarily all, or nearly all, of the terms are implied terms. This is just another way of saying that the terms of the contract between banker and customer state rights and obligations which have been defined by the Courts over many years. However, Burnett's case shows that it is possible that the terms may be changed or overridden by express agreement between the parties, even though the same case shows that the change may not be unilaterally made.

2.26 Long and complex written agreements are common in North America and it is no doubt tempting for bankers in other parts of the common law world to introduce terms into the contract between banker and customer which would throw more of the risks on the customer. A common term in overseas contracts is one which requires the customer to read the periodic statement and to report any irregularities within a fixed period of time. In default of so doing, the customer is to be bound by the terms of the periodic statement. Another common term is one which purports to throw the risk of forgeries onto the customer. As will be seen later,[1] the general rule is that the customer has no duty to examine the periodic statement and the risk of forgery is prima facie on the banker.

1 At 2.56ff.

2.27 A recent decision by the Privy Council indicates that clauses such as these can not be introduced without the customer being clearly informed of the changed responsibilities. In *Tai Hing Cotton Mill Ltd v Liu Chong Hing Bank Ltd*[1] a number of clauses were inserted in written agreements or were incorporated by reference.

1 [1985] 2 All ER 947.

2.28 In one instance, the customer agreed to be bound by the bank's "rules and procedures in force from time to time governing the conduct of the account". One of the rules was rule 7:

> A monthly statement for each account will be sent by the bank to the depositor by post or messenger and the balance shown therein may be deemed to be correct by the bank if the depositor does not notify the bank in writing of any error therein within ten days after the sending of such statement . . . .

The customer in fact returned a confirmation slip upon receipt of the statements, but failed to notice a number of forgeries.

2.29 In another account operated by the same customer, the terms appeared on the back of a pro forma letter which was signed by the customer. One of the terms read:

> The bank's statement of my/our account will be confirmed by me/us without delay. In case of absence of such confirmation within a fortnight, the bank may take the said statement as approved by me/us.

The customer never confirmed any of the accounts sent.

2.30 A third account was opened by request of the customer in which the customer agreed to open the account subject to the bank's rules and regulations. Rule 13 provided:

> A statement of the customer's account will be rendered once a month. Customers are desired:
>
> to examine all entries in the statement of account and to report at once to the bank any error found therein.

2.31 to return the confirmation slip duly signed.
In the absence of any objection to the statement within seven days after its receipt by the customer, the account shall be deemed to have been confirmed.

2.32 In this case, the bank never sent any confirmation slips to the company and the company never sent the bank any confirmation of the accounts.

2.33 The Privy Council held that the terms had contractual effect but that they did not prevent the customer from challenging the validity of the statements since their terms did not bring home to the customer either the intended importance of the inspection of the accounts or that they were intended to have conclusive effect against the customer in the event that no timely query is raised. In the words of the Privy Council:

> If banks wish to impose upon their customers an express obligation to examine their monthly statements and to make those statements, in the absence of query, unchallengeable by the customer after expiry of a time limit, the burden of the obligation and of the sanction imposed must be brought home to the customer . . . .The test is rigorous because the bankers would have their terms of business so construed as to exclude the rights which the customer would enjoy if they were not excluded by express agreement.[1]

It is clear that the Privy Council considered the implied contractual terms of the ordinary banker/customer relationship to be in the nature of common law rights and that express terms which purport to alter those rights will be construed strictly against the party attempting to take advantage of them. In such circumstances, the imposition of express terms becomes difficult and the banker must weigh the advantages to be gained from the terms against the possibility of frightening off customers by "bringing home" the burdens sought to be imposed. The *Tai Hing* case is discussed further at 3.65.

1 Per Lord Scarman, *Tai Hing Cotton Mill Ltd v Liu Chong Hing Bank Ltd* [1985] 2 All ER 947, 959.

Duration of the relationship

2.34 There are certain circumstances in which it becomes important to know if the banker/customer relationship is in existence between two parties to a dispute. For example, a banker is given certain statutory defences against an action for breach of contract or an action in tort provided the banker is acting on behalf of a "customer";[1] only a "customer" has any right to expect his or her cheques to be honoured by the banker. Again, the banker has a lien over certain documents belonging to a customer who is indebted to the banker.[2]

1 See the Cheques Act 1960 and the discussion in Chs 14 and 17.
2 The so-called "banker's lien"; see Ch 25.

2.35 The question of the beginning of the relationship, ie when the contract between the banker and a potential customer is formed, will be discussed later.[1] In this section, the question of termination will be considered. When and how does the banker/customer contract come to an end?

1 See 3.2ff.

The banker may not terminate without notice

2.36 Lord Atkin indicated that the banker could not terminate the relationship without notice. This is because the customer has every right to expect that, in the ordinary course of events, cheques will be met which are outstanding and for which the other preconditions for payment are satisfied. Lord Atkin referred to "reasonable notice" being required before the banker ceases to do business with the customer. What is "reasonable notice"?

2.37 In *Prosperity Ltd v Lloyds Bank Ltd*[1] a suit was commenced by the customer for declarations and an injunction against the banker on the ground that the banker had given insufficient notice of the intention to close the customer's account. The account was, at all material times, in credit. A month's notice was held to be insufficient, but there were very special circumstances and it was expressly held that the period of notice required must depend upon the particular facts of the case.

1 (1923) 39 TLR 372.

2.38 The special circumstances were that the plaintiffs ran what they called a "snowball" scheme of insurance whereby a subscriber on payment of £1 15s would receive a book containing ten application forms valid for a year. Each new subscriber obtained by the first subscriber would fill up one of the forms and go through the same process. The first subscriber would receive a 2s credit in respect of each of his "descendants". When sufficient sums had been credited, an insurance policy would be taken out with an associated company in favour of the subscriber.[1] The nature and purpose of the scheme was discussed with the bank before the account was opened. Many circulars had been sent out and many were outstanding at the time when the bank wished to close the account. Since the rules of subscription called for the subscriber to make the sum payable to Lloyds bank the promoters of the scheme required more than a month to reorganise their business.

1 The scheme is, of course, what is now known as a "pyramid" scheme and is now illegal in most jurisdictions.

Injunction

2.39 It was also held that an injunction was an inappropriate remedy since it would be functionally equivalent to making an order for specific performance of a contract for the provision of personal services and the borrowing of money by the banker. The appropriate remedy sounds in damages for the dishonour of any cheques which the customer might rightfully expect to be honoured, but which are in fact dishonoured due to the wrongful closure of the account. As will be seen later, these damages can be substantial,[1] so it behoves the banker to exercise some care in closing an account.

1 See 6.45 and 17.35.

2.40 Certain obligations of the banker/customer relationship may endure beyond the termination of the contract. Most important of these is the banker's duty to treat as confidential certain of the financial affairs of the customer. This duty of confidentiality is discussed at length elsewhere.[1]

1 See 7.2.

Consequences of the contractual relationship

2.41 This section explores some of the further consequences of the fact that the banker/customer relationship is founded in contract.

Limitations Act 1950

2.42 Since the banker/customer relationship is, inter alia, a debtor/creditor relationship which is founded on contract, the rights of recovery are limited by the time restrictions imposed by the Limitations Act 1950. The important feature of the Act is that it is merely a procedural bar, ie the debt remains in existence after the expiry of the limitations period, but the help of the Courts to recover it is no longer available. If there are other procedures for recovery available, they are not affected.

2.43 If at any time prior to the expiration of the limitation period there is a part payment of the debt or an acknowledgment of the debt then the time period begins to run afresh. It is also possible to revive the rights to seek the Courts' assistance if after the expiry date there is some promise by the debtor to pay the debt. This may be a promise which is express or which may be inferred from some act of acknowledgment of the debt.[1]

1 See *Re River Steamship Co; Mitchell's claim* (1871) LR 6 Ch App 822, 828.

2.44 As might be imagined, there is a large body of case law which considers the adequacy of various acts of acknowledgment for the purposes of revival of the procedural remedies.[1] It should be noted that it is not necessary to show any fresh consideration for the new promise to pay. It is not a new contract which is being formed, but a procedural remedy which is being revived.

1 See Lightwood, *The Time Limit On Actions* (1909).

When time begins to run

2.45 Time begins to run for the purposes of a debt when the debt is due. The particular time may depend upon the type of the account and whether the account is in credit or overdraft.

Account in credit

2.46 One of the consequences of *Joachimson's* case is that the debt owed by the banker to the customer does not become due until such time as a demand is made by the customer. It follows that when the account is in credit, time does not begin to run against the customer for the purposes of the Limitations Act 1950 until such time as that demand is made.

2.47 It would, of course, be most unusual for a bank to plead the statute as a means of resisting repayment of a credit account. However, "dormant" accounts can cause considerable inconvenience for the banker and represent a generally unproductive relationship. In order to relieve the banker from this burden and to clarify the position with regard to such accounts many jurisdictions have legislation similar to the Unclaimed Money Act 1971 which provides that dormant accounts are transferred to the Crown, but such legislation usually provides a method for the customer, or someone legitimately claiming through the customer, to reclaim the money.

2.48 The Unclaimed Money Act 1971 defines unclaimed money in s 4. For current accounts which are non-interest-bearing, money becomes unclaimed money if the customer has not operated on the account for a period of 25 years in the case of a savings bank account and six years in all other cases. For fixed term interest-bearing accounts, money is defined as unclaimed after six years from the expiry of the term. Interest-bearing accounts with no fixed term which provide for reinvestment of interest become unclaimed if the customer has not operated the account for a period of 25 years.

2.49 The Act provides that the banker shall keep a register and notify the Commissioner of Inland Revenue of any accounts which fall within the definition of "unclaimed money".[1] All such money becomes payable to the Consolidated Fund after which time the banker has no liability to the owner of the account.[2]

1 Ss 6 and 7.
2 S 8.

2.50 Any person may claim the fund by satisfying the Commissioner that he or she is the person who is entitled to it. If the Commissioner is satisfied and pays the money, then the only right of any other claimant to the fund is to recover the money from the first claimant. Neither the banker nor the Commissioner has any further liability.[1]

1 S 11.

2.51 The Unclaimed Money Act 1971 solves the "dormant account" problem if the banker follows the requirements for keeping the register and paying the unclaimed money to the Commissioner. If there is a failure to do so, the Act does not provide any guidance as to the disposition of the money. In at least one extreme case, the Court has been willing to invoke a presumption that an account had been properly repaid and closed by the banker. In *Douglass v Lloyds Bank Ltd*[1] the account had not been operated for over 20 years. One Fenwicke had deposited some £6,000 with a branch of the defendant in 1868. The account was never operated after 1868. In 1927, some of Fenwicke's survivors found a deposit receipt which showed a balance of £3,500. They claimed that amount from the bank with interest.

1 (1929) 34 Com Cas 263.

2.52 Evidence was given to show that Fenwicke was a man who was careful with his financial matters and that there was reason to believe that the £6,000 represented the proceeds from some shares which he sold during the financial crash of the 1860s. The plaintiff had no evidence of the debt other than the deposit book, but claimed that to be conclusive in the absence of any better evidence. The bank produced evidence to the effect that the books of the particular year in question had been destroyed, but that there was no evidence of any accounts which were still in credit from the period.

2.53 In the course of the judgment, Roche J said:

> . . . I recognise to the full the strength of the fact that the plaintiff produces this deposit receipt, but I cannot ignore what experience tells me, and the evidence in this case shows, that people lose or mislay their deposit receipts at the time when they want to get their money back, and that money is paid over , if they are respectable persons and are willing to give the necessary indemnity . . . .[1]

Roche J was unable to accept that Fenwicke either intentionally left the money there or forgot about it. There was some evidence that the defendant bank had treated the deposit as repaid at least from about 1873.

1 P 273.

2.54 The case is sometimes said to rest on a presumption that a debt has been repaid after a long period of time, but there is certainly no need to invent a presumption to understand the case. The plaintiffs had a strong case on the basis of the passbook, but there was other evidence to support the bank's defence. The bank could not have succeeded without the production of any evidence whatsoever.

Unsecured overdraft account: the debtor

2.55 Since it is scarcely imaginable in the ordinary course of events that a banker would attempt to rely upon the Limitations Act 1950 in order to avoid repayment of the sum standing due in a credit account, the effect of the limitations period when the account is in overdraft or where it is sought to recover from a guarantor is of far more importance.

2.56 The problem is complicated by the view of bankers that an overdraft does not become due and payable until such time as a demand is made. As a consequence, it is argued, time does not begin to run against the bank until such time as the demand is made for the overdraft to be paid. Unfortunately, there is no recent authority and the older authorities are against the proposition.

2.57 In *Parr's Banking Co Ltd v Yates*[1] the Court appeared to hold that time begins to run from the date of each advance. As a consequence, it may be that some parts of the overall debt are time barred while others are not.[2]

1 [1898] 2 QB 460.
2 See also the discussion of the rule in *Clayton's case* at 8.3.

2.58 The case was an action on a guarantee. It appeared that the defendant had guaranteed to the plaintiff payment of all moneys which might be owing to them in an account with a customer together with interest and other charges. The guarantee was a continuing one and not to be withdrawn with less than six months' notice. The bank made advances to the customer down to a period more than six years before the action, but not after that period. The customer paid sums to the plaintiff from time to time against the liability, including some payments within the six year period. The Court held that the right of action for the principal sum was barred by the Statute of Limitations but that the interest which had accrued due from the customer within the preceding six years was able to be sued upon. The rule with regard to the appropriation of payments by which interest is presumed to be paid before principal is not applicable in the case of interest on an overdrawn account which according to the practice of bankers has been from time to time converted into principal.

2.59 During the course of his judgment, Vaughan Williams LJ said:

> My view is that the cause of action on the guarantee arose as to each item of the account, whether principal, interest, commission, or other banking charge, as soon as that item became due and was not paid . . . .[1]

None of the other members of the Court was quite so explicit. The importance of the point is that if the view is correct, the banker's right of recovery might be time-barred as to part of the debt, but not others.

1 At p 467.

2.60 Bankers do not like the implications of the view expressed by Vaughan Williams LJ, for if the same logic applies to overdraft accounts then it means a very substantial increase in the bookkeeping required for such accounts if rights against the customer are not to be accidentally lost. On the other hand, it may be argued that an overdraft account, where the debt is owed by the customer to the banker, is similar to an ordinary current account in credit, that is, it does not become due until such time as a demand is made.

2.61 Unfortunately, a decision of the English Court of Appeal seems to argue against the "demand" theory. In *Bradford Old Bank v Sutcliffe*[1] it was said:

> Generally, a request for the payment of a debt is quite immaterial, unless the parties to the contract have stipulated it should be made. Even if the word "demand" is used in the case of a present debt, it is meaningless, and express demand is not necessary, as in the case of a promissory note payable on demand.[2]

1 [1918] 2 KB 833.
2 Per Scrutton LJ p 848.

2.62 Similarly, Pickford LJ said:

> It was argued on behalf of the defendant that the words "on demand" should be neglected because the money was due, and therefore a demand was unnecessary and added nothing to the liability. This proposition is true in the case of what has been called a direct liability — for example, for money lent. There the liability exists as soon as the loan is made, and a promise to pay on demand adds nothing to it, as in the case of a promissory note for the amount payable on demand, and the words "on demand" may be neglected.

2.63 Modern authors, eg Weaver and Cragie, suggest that the position may have changed over the years so that the "on demand" aspects of an overdraft have increased their importance, yet conclude that it would be most unwise for a banker to ignore these old cases. The only safe course is to presume that time begins to run at the date of each advance.

Overdraft account: the guarantor

2.64 The comments made so far relate to an action by the bank against the primary debtor, ie the account holder. When the banker is attempting to recover against a guarantor, the situation is somewhat different, for generally the guarantee will be a "continuing guarantee", ie one which is expressed to guarantee the balance of the account which is struck from time to time. In *Bradford Old Bank* itself, the action was of this kind and the Court held that the contract of surety was a collateral one so that the words "on demand" should be given their full meaning. Thus, after making the comments above concerning the lack of meaning of the words "on demand" when used in conjunction with an ordinary debt, Pickford LJ went on to say:

> It . . . has been held . . . that this doctrine does not apply to what has been called a collateral promise or collateral debt, and I think a promise by a surety to pay the original debt is such a collateral promise, or creates such a collateral debt. . . . The only question, therefore is whether, on the construction of the guarantee, the parties meant the words "on demand" to mean what they say. I cannot doubt that they did. Interest is to run from demand.

Consequently, time did not begin to run against the bank, vis a vis the guarantor, until such time as a demand was made against the guarantor.

2.65 The matter has been considered by the Court in *Wright v NZ Farmers' Co-op*,[1] in an action against a guarantor where it was claimed that the rights of the bank were barred by virtue of the dictum in *Parr's Banking Co v Yates*. Wright agreed to guarantee to the plaintiff the payment by a husband and wife

> of all goods already supplied or hereafter supplied by you to them and of all advances already made or hereafter made by you to them together with interest thereon at the current rate charged by you and together with such charges as are usually made by you.

The guarantee was expressed to be a continuing guarantee and the amount claimed on the guarantee was some £12,000; the amount of £3,255 which represented advances made by the respondent prior to July 31, 1928, being six years prior to the commencement of the action, was disputed as being outside the Statute of Limitations.

1 [1936] NZLR 157; [1939] NZLR 388.

2.66 In the Court of Appeal, the statement of Vaughan Williams LJ in *Parr's Banking Co* was doubted and it was suggested that the real ground of decision in *Parr's* case may have been that there had been no advances made to the principal debtor within six years prior to the commencement of the action. An action for the balance arising upon a series of debits and credits extending beyond a period of six years is, it was suggested, not barred by the statute if it is brought within six years from the date of the last advance. Since that was the case here, the Court distinguished *Parr's* case on that ground.

2.67 This approach treats the entire debt owed to the bank as a single debt which becomes due for the purposes of the statute at the time of the last advance. It should be noted that it does not confirm the bankers' view that the debt becomes due only upon demand. The approach used by the Court of Appeal is out of step with other parts of the law which concern the repayment of overdrawn accounts, eg, the rule in *Clayton's case*, and should be viewed as an attempt to circumvent the invidious effects of the Statute of Limitations.

2.68 The case went on appeal to the Privy Council which chose to distinguish *Parr's Banking Co* on the basis of the wording in the guarantee which was signed by Wright. Lord Russell of Killowen gave the opinion of the Judicial Board during which he said:

> It is difficult to see how effect can be given to [the terms of the guarantee] except by holding that the repayment of every debit balance is guaranteed as it is constituted from time to time, during the continuance

23

of the guarantee, by the excess of the total debits over the total credits
. . . . The question of limitation could only arise in regard to the time
which had elapsed since the balance guaranteed and sued for had been
constituted.

2.69 It is important to note that the Privy Council made it quite clear
that they were expressing no opinion on the correctness of the
decision in *Parr's* case.

2.70 The matter was considered in New Zealand by Perry J in
Commercial Union Assurance v Revell.[1] There was an express written
contract which contained the words "I hereby undertake . . . to
repay . . . on demand . . .". The document was signed by the plaintiff
in 1957. There was no demand made until mid 1967 and the sole
issue was whether the action was time barred. Perry J followed *In
re Brown's Estate*[2] and *Bradford Old Bank Ltd v Sutcliffe*[3] in holding
that the words "on demand" when used in an express contract
which does not relate to a present debt will be given their full effect
so that time does not begin to run unless and until a demand is
made.

1 [1969] NZLR 106.
2 [1893] 2 Ch 300.
3 [1918] 2 KB 833.

2.71 So far as the banker is concerned, the matter is still open, for
it is still not clear whether an overdraft account is a "present debt".

Secured overdraft account: the debtor

2.72 Although it may not be possible to sue the customer on the
debt, it may be possible to enforce securities given by the customer.
In *Brown's* case,[1] a mortgage was classified as a "collateral" debt or
promise. Consequently, the mortgage fell within the class of debts
mentioned by Pickford LJ in the *Bradford Old Bank* case which do
not fall due until a demand is made by the creditor.

1 *Re Brown's Estate; Brown v Brown* [1893] 2 Ch 300.

2.73 The rule in *Brown's* case was expressly approved in *Lloyds Bank
Ltd v Margolis*.[1] The case concerned a legal charge which was given
over a farm; the defendant objected that the claim was statute-
barred because there had been no advances made within the
limitation period. Chitty J held that on the true construction of the
charge a demand was necessary, but that in any case the charge
was collateral security and, therefore, even if no demand was
necessary to the bringing of an action of a direct present debt
payable on demand, in the present case a demand would be
necessary.

1 [1954] 1 All ER 734, 738.

2.74 Since most large overdrafts will be secured by some kind of a charge or mortgage, this line of cases would seem to be adequate to protect the banker from the worst effects of the decision in *Parr's Banking Co v Yates*.

2.75 In summary, the only safe course of action for the banker is to presume that the debt of the customer becomes due at the date of each advance so that advances made more than six years previously may be statute barred. However, properly worded guarantees may be enforced against guarantors and "collateral" debts owed by the primary debtor do not become due until a demand is made.

Savings accounts

2.76 As in the case of a current account, a savings or deposit account is a loan to the banker.[1] There is probably no right to draw cheques against a savings account, even when the account is expressed to be repayable without notice. The matter is unlikely to ever be raised in New Zealand where it is common practice to require the production of the passbook and a withdrawal receipt as one of the pre-conditions for the withdrawal of money from the account. Many accounts require a specified period of notice before general withdrawals may be made and some are for a fixed period of time. In the latter type, the customer has no right to call for the repayment before the expiry of that period, even though it is not uncommon for a banker to permit such a withdrawal, perhaps with some loss of interest.

1 *Pearce v Creswick* (1843) 2 Hare 286; 12 LJ Ch 251.

Nature of the relationship

2.77 It has been said that a savings account is one continuing contract and that no fresh contract is made with each deposit by the customer.[1] Mocatta J has expressed the opinion that there is no such thing in law as an overdrawn deposit account.[2]

1 *Hart v Sangster* [1957] 1 Ch 329.
2 *Barclays Bank Ltd v Okenarhe* [1966] 2 Lloyd's Rep 87.

2.78 Savings accounts are usually accompanied by a passbook in which deposits and withdrawals are recorded. This passbook is, or should be, essentially a copy of the customer's account in the bank's ledger. It is also usual for the passbook to contain the basic terms of the agreement between the banker and customer. It is universally a condition precedent to any withdrawal that the book must be presented together with a signed withdrawal slip. In many cases, the passbook contains a specimen of the customer's signature which is normally invisible but may be read under an ultraviolet lamp.

Role of the passbook

2.79 The English Court of Appeal has held that the passbook is in fact indicia of title to the account.[1] The result was that delivery of the passbook in the circumstances of the case was held to be a valid donatio mortis causa. The Court placed considerable weight on the fact that presentation of the book was a condition precedent to any withdrawal from the account.

1 *Birch v Treasury Solicitor* [1951] Ch 298.

2.80 It might be thought that the position could be different when the passbook itself contains a statement that it remains the property of the bank or when there is legislation to the same effect. However, the same result was reached by an Australian Court even before the *Birch* decision. In *Watts v Public Trustee*[1] it was held that a gift of a Commonwealth Savings Bank passbook was good evidence of a valid donatio mortis causa of the balance of the account despite legislation which provided that the passbook remained at all times the property of the Savings Bank.

1 (1950) 50 SR(NSW) 130.

2.81 Needless to say, a banker who paid some third party merely on the basis of the party's possession of the passbook would be taking great risks, since possession itself is certainly no indication that there has been an intended assignment.

Chapter 3

The customer

Introduction

3.1 As noted in the previous Chapter, it is important to know if the banker/customer relationship exists between two parties. The problem of the termination of the relationship has been considered. In this section, the problem of the time of formation is considered.

Forming the relationship: who is a customer?

3.2 There is no statutory definition of the term "customer". For many years, there was a body of opinion that a continuing relationship of some duration was required, that it was indeed necessary to show some "custom". At the other end of the spectrum, some thought that, by analogy with the use of the word in other businesses, that if the banker had any dealings at all with a person, then that person was a "customer".

3.3 Neither of these views is correct. The cases are primarily concerned with the meaning of "customer" for the purposes of the bank claiming statutory protection under the Cheques Act 1960 or its equivalent.[1] In this context,the cases show that a contractual relationship must exist prior to the act which gives rise to the dispute.[2] In these circumstances, it is difficult to see how a person could be a "customer" who has only casual dealings with the banker.

1 See Chs 14 to 17.
2 See 3.12.

3.4 However, it may be that a person is a "customer" for one purpose but not for another. For example, a bank collecting cheques for a "customer" is given certain statutory defences against charges of conversion when the person for whom the collection is being performed has no title, or a defective title to the cheque.[1] In *Lloyds Bank Ltd v EB Savory and Co*,[2] cheques were collected for a person who had an account with the bank, but not at the branch which performed the collection. Lawrence CJ expressed doubt that the person was a "customer" of the bank for the purposes of the then English equivalent of s 5 of the Cheques Act 1960. There is, of course, no doubt that the person was a "customer" of the bank for most other purposes.

1 Cheques Act 1960, s 5.
2 [1932] 2 KB 122; [1933] AC 201.

3.5 It is clear that even a regular established pattern of transactions does not suffice to make a person a "customer" if the transactions are not sufficient to establish a continuing duty on the part of the banker under the usual rules of contract formation. In *Great Western Railway Co v London and County Banking Co Ltd*,[1] a man, H, had for some years been in the habit of cashing cheques over the counter at the defendant bank. The cheques were crossed not negotiable which meant, inter alia, that it was necessary for them to be presented for payment by a bank.[2] H never opened an account at the defendant bank. He obtained a cheque from the plaintiffs by fraud which he cashed at the defendant bank. The plaintiffs claimed to be entitled to recover the amount of the cheque from the defendant bank; one of the issues was whether H was a customer of the defendant bank. It was held that he was not since there was no account and no intention to open an account.

1 [1901] AC 414.
2 See 13.34 for the meanings of crossings on cheques.

Duration not important

3.6 On the other hand, it is now abundantly clear that the duration of the relationship is of no significance. In *Ladbroke & Co v Todd*[1] a thief stole a cheque and took it to the defendant banker where it was used for the purpose of opening an account. The Court held that the account was opened when the cheque was collected and that the thief was a "customer" even though there was only one transaction during the entire life of the relationship.

1 (1914) 30 TLR 433.

3.7 This was followed and endorsed by the Privy Council in *Commissioners of Taxation v English, Scottish and Australian Bank Ltd*.[1] Again, the case concerned an account which had been opened with the deposit of a single cheque which had been misappropriated. The decision of the Judicial Committee was delivered by Lord Dunedin who said:

Their Lordships are of the opinion that the word "customer" signifies a relationship in which duration is not of the essence. A person whose money has been accepted by the bank, on the footing that they undertake to honour cheques up to the amount standing to his credit is, in the view of their Lordships, a customer of the bank in the sense of the statute, irrespective of whether his connection is one of short or long standing. The contrast is not between a habitue and a newcomer, but between a person for whom the bank performs a casual service, such as, for instance, cashing a cheque for a person introduced by one of their customers, and a person who has an account of his own at the bank.

1 [1920] AC 683.

Before the opening of the account

3.8 The *ES & A Bank* case shows that the existence of an account is sufficient to establish the banker/customer relationship, but it appears that there may be circumstances where the relationship is established prior to the opening of an account.

3.9 In *Woods v Martins Bank Ltd*[1] the plaintiff was a director of a company but he had no real business experience. In May 1950, he asked the manager of the Quayside branch of the defendant bank to act as his financial adviser. Subsequently the manager told the plaintiff that he might be able to obtain some preference shares on the plaintiff's behalf in a private company called Brocks Refrigeration Ltd. This company was a customer of the defendant bank, a fact known to both the plaintiff and the defendant. At all material times, BR Ltd had a large overdraft with the defendant bank and was in need of funds. On 9 May, the plaintiff authorised the defendant bank to acquire the shares on his behalf. There was no account opened until 1 June. The Court found that the advice given had been negligently given.

1 [1958] 3 All ER 166.

3.10 The defendant argued, inter alia, that the plaintiff was not a customer of the bank at the date of the first transaction in May, the time when the advice was given and that as a consequence they owed the plaintiff no duty of care.[1] Salmon J held that the plaintiff had become a customer by 9 May and that the advice given earlier in the month must be considered as being impliedly repeated at that time. But even if the plaintiff had not become a customer until later the defendant would still have been under a duty, for giving advice of the type given is part of the business of the bank. As Salmon J phrased it:

In May 1950 the plaintiff paid business, not social, calls on [the manager] in his office. The plaintiff made it plain that he was consulting [the manager] as manager of the defendant bank's Quayside branch. The plaintiff was a potential customer and one whose custom [the manager] was anxious to acquire and soon did acquire . . . . No doubt [the manager] could have refused to advise the plaintiff, but, as he chose to advise him, the law in those circumstances imposes an obligation on him to advise with reasonable care.[2]

1 Note that this argument would have no chance of success now since the duty of care may exist independently of contract. See 7.37.
2 Per Salmon J p 174.

3.11 It is also possible for another bank to be a customer. In *Importers Co v Westminster Bank*[1] a cheque which was crossed "account payee only" was stolen and paid into a foreign bank for collection. The Court held that the foreign bank was a customer of the defendant bank for the purposes of the special protective provisions of the Bills of Exchange Act 1882, but the case should not be taken to imply that a collecting bank is always a customer of a paying or further collecting bank. There were special arrangements between the banks for the collection of foreign cheques.

1 [1927] 2 KB 297.

General principle

3.12 If there is a general principle to be drawn from the cases concerning the definition of customer then it appears to be that the relationship does not exist unless the banker is contractually bound to provide at least some of the services normally provided by a banker. In determining the existence of the contract, normal principles of contract formation are used. In the *Great Western* case, it is clear that the bank could have refused at any time to collect the cheque for H. It would seem foolish to attach magical powers to the actual opening of the account, so that if a banker had agreed to accept the customer there is no reason why the relationship should not come into existence at that time, even if the account is not formally opened until later.

3.13 On the other hand, it would seem impossible to imagine a situation where the banker is contractually bound to provide banking services to someone who is not a customer.

Duties of the customer

3.14 Once the contract between customer and banker is formed, there are obligations on both of the parties. In this section, the general duties of the customer are considered. There is general agreement that there are two primary duties placed upon the customer by the contract. First, the customer is under a duty to draw his or her cheques carefully so as not to facilitate forgery which might cause a loss to the banker. Secondly, the customer is under a duty to notify the banker of any forgery of a cheque purportedly drawn on the account as soon as the customer becomes aware of it.

3.15 There is no general agreement as to the existence or extent of any further duties which may be placed on the customer, although the matter may have been laid to rest for the time being by the recent decision of the Privy Council, in the *Tai Hing Cotton Mill* case[1] which will be discussed later in this section.

1 *Tai Hing Cotton Mill Ltd v Liu Chong Hing Bank Ltd*[1985] 2 All ER 947.

Duty to write cheques carefully

3.16 It seems that the Courts in New Zealand have long assumed a duty on the part of a customer to exercise care in the drawing of cheques. In *Brown v Bennett*,[1] the Court said:

> On the whole, I am of opinion that, except in the case of banker and customer, the maker of a negotiable instrument does not owe any duty to be careful in the mode of making the complete instrument, and the maker is not, as to all who may become holders, under any obligation to anticipate, and therefore to preclude, the fraudulent interpolation of words of figures.[2]

1 (1891) 9 NZLR 487.
2 Per Prendergast CJ at p 501.

3.17 Although the duty appears to have been recognised, there are no early cases which define the extent of the duty or the consequences of its breach. It was not until *London Joint Stock Bank v Macmillan & Arthur*[1] that the House of Lords explained the precise scope of the duty. A confidential clerk was employed by the plaintiff firm of stockbrokers. As a part of his duties. the clerk prepared cheques for the signature of the partners. He drew a cheque payable to the firm or bearer. The amount of the cheque was not entered in the place for words and was entered in the place for figures as £ 2 :0:0, leaving a gap between the sterling symbol and between the first 2 and 0. He handed the cheque to one of the partners who signed it and returned it to the clerk. The clerk then added the words "one hundred and twenty pounds" in writing and then altered the amount in figures by adding a "1" before and a "0" after the 2. The cheque was presented to the defendant bank and was paid over the counter.

1 [1918] AC 777.

3.18 The firm sued the bank to recover the £118 and succeeded at first instance and in the Court of Appeal. The House of Lords, in one of the most important decisions in the law of banking, unanimously allowed the appeal. There are two distinct principles which were mentioned, either of which could support the decision. The one which appears to have been favoured by the majority is that a customer owes a duty to the bank to take care in the mode of drawing a cheque and, in the circumstances, the alteration in the amount of the cheque was the direct result of the breach of duty. The second principle which could also support the decision is that the drawer of the cheque was estopped in the circumstances from denying the authority of the clerk to complete the cheque in the way that it was actually completed.

3.19 It is important to note that the duty to draw cheques carefully arises from the banker/customer relationship, not from the relationship of various parties to a cheque. There is no corresponding duty on the drawer of a bill of exchange to see that it is carefully drawn.[1] The failure to appreciate the source of the duty led the Privy Council astray a few years before *Macmillan's* case in *Colonial Bank of Australasia Ltd v Marshall.*[2] On facts very similar to those of *Macmillan*, the Privy Council held that there was no duty to exercise care in drafting a cheque. The result was that the law of Australia was out of step with the rest of the Commonwealth on this subject until the High Court of Australia overruled the *Marshall* decision in *Commonwealth Trading Bank of Australia v Sydney Wide Stores Pty Ltd.*[3]

1 See *Scholfield v Earl of Londesborough* [1896] AC 514.
2 [1906] AC 559.
3 (1981) 55 ALJR 574.

3.20 The duty to take care in the drafting of cheques appears to extend to the normal precautions which are ordinarily taken by prudent drawers of cheques. These may vary from time to time and place to place as business practices change. In *Slingsby v District Bank Ltd*[1] the Court held that there was no breach of duty where the drawer left blank spaces after the name of the payee which were later exploited by a rogue to obtain payment of the cheque. The cheque was made payable to "John Prust & Co" and there was a blank space between those words and the printed "or order" at the end of the line. A fraudulent solicitor added the words "per Cumberbirch and Potts" in the space, indorsed the cheque on the back, cashed the cheque and misappropriated the money.

1 [1932] 1 KB 544.

3.21 As the bank had not followed the customer's mandate, they were prima facie unable to debit the account with the amount of the cheque. The bank argued that the customer was in breach of the *Macmillan* duty. That argument was rejected, the Court holding that it was not a "usual precaution" to draw lines after the payee's name. The Court clearly left open the possibility that the situation might change, and that if such precautions did become "usual" then the outcome of the case would be different.

3.22 In the *Sydney Wide* case, the drawer of the cheque carried on business with a company called Computer Accounting Services. A clerk made the cheque payable to CAS and obtained an authorised signature of the drawer. The clerk then changed the name of the payee by adding an "H" to the end of the writing already there and obtained payment of the cheque. The High Court of Australia specifically left open the question as to whether in these specific circumstances it was a breach of the contract between banker and customer to have issued the cheque in that form.

The effect of warnings

3.23 It may be that the bank can raise the standard of care which a customer must exercise. In *Varker v Commercial Banking Co of Sydney Ltd*,[1] the bank had given Varker some special warnings concerning the way in which cheques should be drawn. There was also a warning printed in the cheque-book in the following terms:

> Commence figures, and the words of the amount with a CAPITAL Letter, as near the left-hand edge as possible, leaving no blank spaces between the words.

1 [1972] 2 NSWLR 967, discussed in detail below.

3.24 The Court held that both of these factors operated to make Varker liable for negligence in circumstances where the law of Australia at the time would have excused him.[1] However, the decision in the *Tai Hing* case[2] shows that imposing a higher duty on the customer is not an easy task. It seems unlikely in view of that case that merely printing warnings in the cheque-book will have the desired effect.[3]

1 Australia did not at that time follow the *Macmillan* decision. See 3.19.
2 *Tai Hing Cotton Mill Ltd v Liu Chong Hing Bank Ltd* [1985] 2 All ER 947.
3 See also *Burnett v Westminster Bank Ltd* [1966] 1 QB 742 and the discussion at 2.22ff.

Subsequent negligence of the bank

3.25 Even when the customer has been negligent in the drawing of the cheque and the cheque has been altered as a consequence of that negligence, it may still be possible for the customer to resist the debit to the account if it can be shown that the banker was negligent in the payment of the altered cheque. The only case known to the author where this has been raised is the remarkable *Varker v Commercial Banking Co of Sydney Ltd*.[1]

1 [1972] 2 NSWLR 967.

3.26 The plaintiff was a paraplegic who had received a large sum of money as compensation for the accident which had caused his injuries. He opened a number of savings accounts with the defendant bank and a current account with an initial balance of $18,000. Varker was capable of writing cheques, but only with considerable difficulty. The assistant accountant of the bank interviewed Varker at the time of opening the account and emphasised the importance of drawing cheques carefully. It was given in evidence that Varker was told that the amount in words should commence as near as possible to the words "the sum of" and that the amount in figures should commence as near as possible to the printed dollar sign. It was also said that Varker was warned that if someone else was requested to fill in the cheques on Varker's behalf that he should take care to see that the cheque was properly drafted by that other person.

3.27 Varker drew several cheques on the account which were made payable to "Cash or bearer", none of which exceeded $200. On one occasion the assistant accountant telephoned Varker with a warning that cheques should not be drawn payable to "Cash or bearer" when they were intended for a named payee.

3.28 About two months after the opening of the account, Varker drew a cheque which was filled in by his brother-in-law, McKinnon. The cheque as filled in by McKinnon had the words "one hundred and fourty" (sic) in the space where the amount is expressed in words and there was a space of about an inch between the printed words "the sum of" and the beginning of the written words. In the space for figures, McKinnon placed "140.00", leaving a space between the printed dollar sign and the beginning of the figures. The cheque was made payable to "Cash or bearer". After Varker had signed the cheque, McKinnon altered it by placing the word "sixty" between the printed words "the sum of" and the written word "one" and placing the figure "6" between the printed dollar sign and the written figure "1". McKinnon deposited the cheque for collection with his own bank and the cheque was paid by the defendant.

3.29 The Court found that Varker had been negligent in the drawing of the cheque.[1] It was argued on behalf of the plaintiff that he should be entitled to succeed if it could be shown that the defendant bank had been guilty of contributory negligence. Macfarlane J held that that argument was substantially correct:

> . . . if, subsequently to the breach of duty by the plaintiff there had been a breach by the bank of the duty which it owed to the customer in the very same transaction . . . then the bank would not be able to maintain the debit.[2]

[1] This was a major problem at the time. Australia did not follow the *Macmillan* case until 1981 with the decision of the High Court in *Commonwealth Trading Bank of Australia v Sydney Wide Stores Pty Ltd* (1981) 55 ALJR 574.
[2] At p 976.

3.30 Macfarlane J held that the bank had paid the cheque negligently, the most important factors being the unusual appearance of the cheque, that Varker had been warned about drawing cheques in favour of "Cash or bearer", that the bank had known that Varker was a person who could easily be a victim of fraud and that the bank could easily have telephoned Varker about the cheque but did not.

3.31 It should be noted that although the words "contributory negligence" were used in the arguments, the case is not concerned with contributory negligence in the sense that it is usually used in tort cases. The true position seems to be that the banker must perform his or her contractual obligations without negligence and that failure to do so will abrogate the right of the banker to debit the customer's account. On the other hand, the fraud could not have occurred were it not for the customer's breach of contract. It would seem to be a proper situation for apportionment of damages, but that does not seem to have been argued in the *Varker* case.

3.32 The case is also unusual in that, on one view, it seems that the fact that the banker took special steps to warn Varker and to treat him as a special customer was used as an argument that an even higher degree of care should be used.[1] On the other hand, another view is that the bank realised that Varker was a special case. Had the bank ignored this, they would have been even more negligent than they were in fact. Once they learned that Varker was a special customer they were obliged to maintain a certain standard, a standard which was not reached merely by one interview and one telephone call. On this view, the fact that the banker had previously telephoned Varker with a warning is only evidence that the bank was aware of Varker's special status.

1 This is the view taken by *Weaver and Cragie*, p 350.

Duty to notify of known forgeries

3.33 The second duty of the customer is to notify the banker of any forgeries discovered by the customer. As will be seen, the banker bears the risk of a rogue forging the drawer's signature on a cheque. It would clearly be inappropriate if the customer knew of forgeries, but failed to notify the banker so as to allow the banker to exercise care to avoid losses from further forgeries. Notice that this is not a duty on the customer to discover forgeries, even if that might be done easily. It is merely a duty to notify the banker about forgeries which the customer in fact knows about.

3.34 The duty to notify is often phrased in terms of estoppel. It is said that the customer may be estopped from asserting that his signature has been forged or placed on the cheque without authority. The estoppel may arise either from an express representation that the signature is indeed that of the customer, as when the cheque is referred to the customer for verification of the signature, or it might arise by a failure to communicate to the banker in circumstances where there is an obligation to do so.

3.35 In the second case, where there has been failure to notify the bank an explanation in terms of estoppel can result in confusion. An estoppel only arises if there has been a representation which has been acted upon by the person to whom the representation was made and that person suffers from some change in position as a result of the reliance. Treating silence as a representation causes difficulty in identifying precisely what the representation is supposed to have been. If it is considered rather as a breach of a contractual duty, then it becomes clear that the banker is entitled to debit the account for forged cheques which occur after the customer obtains knowledge of a forgery, for the loss represented by the later forgeries is a direct consequence of the customer's breach of contract.

Cases defining the duty

3.36 Even when there is a direct representation, it will sometimes be difficult to determine the precise scope of the customer's liability. Thus in *Brown v Westminster Bank Ltd*[1], an elderly woman who kept an account at the defendant bank brought an action against the bank claiming some £1,200 in respect of more than 300 cheques which she claimed had been forged on her account by her servants. The bank admitted that the cheques were forgeries, but claimed to be entitled to maintain the debit due to an estoppel arising against the plaintiff. The bank manager had visited the plaintiff on several occasions to discuss the state of her account with her and had, in particular, drawn her attention to the large number of cheques which were drawn in favour of Mr Carless, a servant who lived with her. She assured the manager that the cheques were genuine.

1 [1964] 2 Lloyd's Rep 187.

3.37 The Court held that this raised an estoppel against Ms Brown, not only with regard to cheques which had been paid after the visit from the manager, but also with regard to cheques which had been paid before. With respect, the latter part is difficult to understand, since there could not have been any reliance by the bank on her representation before the representation was in fact made.

3.38 This point was argued, but rejected by the Court. The reasoning was:

> What were the facts which then existed and in relation to which the representation is then made? The facts that cheques which in truth were forged were represented as genuine . . . the plaintiff is thereafter debarred from setting up the true facts . . . by reason of the fact that the bank paid the future cheques, the bank has suffered detriment.[1]

1 At p 203.

3.39 However this analysis is incomplete. If the representation is merely that the original cheques were valid, then why is the plaintiff estopped from claiming that the later cheques were forged? In truth, there are two representations, one express and one which may be inferred. They are:
 (i) the original cheques were valid;
 (ii) future cheques will also be valid.

3.40 It is the second representation which was relied upon by the bank and which caused the bank to suffer detriment. There was no reliance on the first representation since the cheques had already been paid. This is not to say that there could never be reliance on the first representation. One common example is if the bank were to lose a right of action against the forger.[1]

1 See *Greenwood v Martin's Bank Ltd* [1933] AC 51.

3.41 The matter would have been more clearly and more satisfactorily resolved if it had been analysed as a breach of contract, for in that case the only right of the bank would be to debit the account for those "losses" which followed from the breach of contract.

3.42 *Brown v Westminster Bank Ltd*[1] was followed in the Victorian case of *Tina Motors Pty Ltd v Australian and New Zealand Banking Group Ltd.*[2] An employee of the plaintiff company had forged some 54 cheques having a total value of more than $70,000 on the company account. He presented the cheques at the drawee bank for payment which he received. It was found as a fact by the Court that on two occasions the bank had questioned the signatures on the cheques and before paying had telephoned the manager of the company. The manager informed the bank on each occasion that the cheques should be honoured. The company sought declarations that the company account should not be debited. The Court held that the bank had relied upon the oral representation and had acted to its detriment by paying the cheques. As a consequence, the company was estopped from denying the truth of the representations.

1 [1964] 2 Lloyd's Rep 187.
2 [1977] VR 205.

3.43 However, one of the cheques was paid prior to the first representation and it was argued for the plaintiff that there could be no right to debit the account with that cheque. Crockett J held that the bank was entitled to succeed with regard to this cheque as well. In so finding, he cited *Brown's* case and quoted the passage of Roskill J which is quoted above. Again, it is submitted that the correctness of that reasoning depends upon a construction and interpretation of the actual representation.

3.44 *Brown's* case is clear in that there was an express statement to the bank to the effect that the cheques were valid. It does not demonstrate decisively the duty to notify. Is it possible that mere silence can raise the estoppel against the customer?

3.45 *Greenwood v Martin's Bank Ltd*[1] provides the definitive example of a failure to notify. The plaintiff's wife had forged a series of cheques in his name. When the plaintiff discovered that this had been occurring, he threatened to notify the bank immediately, but she begged him not to, explaining that she had needed the money to assist her sister in a legal action. The plaintiff did not inform the defendant bank of the forgeries. Later he found that his wife's explanations had been lies and that she had continued to forge cheques on his account. He then said that he would inform the defendant bank. The wife committed suicide and the husband sued the defendant bank to recredit his account with the monies which had been paid on the forged cheques.

1 [1933] AC 51.

3.46 The Court held that the husband had breached his duty to notify the bank of the forgeries. Under legislation in force at that time, the plaintiff's liability for the torts of his wife came to an end upon her death, so that the defendant bank lost their right of recovery of the money as a result of the plaintiff's delay in notification. The banker was consequently entitled to maintain the debit to the account.

3.47 But it is not every delay in notifying of known forgeries that will raise an estoppel against the customer. In *Fung Kai Sun v Chan Fui Hing*[1] after discovering forgeries of mortgage documents, the plaintiff did not notify the defendant for some three weeks whereupon the writ was issued. The defendant's claim that they were prejudiced by being deprived of the opportunity to obtain restitution from the forger was dismissed by the Privy Council. Although the plaintiff was not entitled to withhold the information, the true test was whether the defendant had in fact been materially prejudiced by the delay. There was no evidence to substantiate such a claim. Again, the matter is more clearly analysed in contractual terms. Although the plaintiff was in breach of contract, the bank suffered no losses as a result of the breach.

1 [1951] AC 489.

3.48 The duty to speak is probably not confined to the case when the customer knows that cheques are forged, but probably extends to forgeries of other documents which may prejudice the bank.

3.49 In *M'Kenzie v British Linen Co*[1] the customer was aware of the fact that his name had been forged on a bill of exchange, but took no immediate action. The bank made an inquiry, but did not wait for the results before discounting the bill. Under the circumstances, the Court considered that the action of the bank did not depend upon the representation, if the silence did amount to a representation, of the customer. It was said that a person who knows that a bank is relying upon his forged signature on a bill, cannot fail to divulge the fact until he sees that the position of the bank is altered for the worse. But there is no principle on which his mere silence for a fortnight from the time when he first knew of the forgery, during which the position of the bank was in no way altered or prejudiced, can be held to be an admission or adoption of liability, or an estoppel. It seems that if the bank had relied on the "representation" or had in some way changed its position for the worse, then the customer may have been held liable.

1 (1881) 6 App Cas 82.

3.50 However, if the customer's silence is encouraged by an officer of the bank, then there can be no estoppel raised against him. In *Ogilvie v West Australian Mortgage and Agency*[1] a customer of the bank discovered that his account was debited with forgeries. He immediately brought the matter to the attention of an officer of the bank who also happened to be the son of the majority shareholder. The officer requested Ogilvie to maintain silence, explaining that the forgeries had been committed by a trusted clerk and that if the clerk were arrested then the bank would lose all chance of recovering the money. The fraudulent clerk was in fact warned and permitted to abscond. Ogilvie later requested the bank to recredit his account with the amount of the forged cheques. The bank refused, claiming that Ogilvie was estopped due to his silence. The bank also claimed that it had not ratified the actions of the officer.

1 [1896] AC 257, 270.

3.51 The Court held that Ogilvie should succeed. The main argument for the bank was the *British Linen* case which was distinguished as follows:

> The ground upon which the plea of estoppel rested in [*British Linen*] was the fact that the customer, being in the exclusive knowledge of the forgery, withheld that knowledge from the bank until its chance of recovering from the forger had been materially prejudiced. Here, an agent of the bank had earlier and better information as to the forgeries than the customer himself.[1]

1 At p 268.

3.52 This appears to be a restatement of the obvious fact that the bank did not rely upon the representation and consequently no estoppel could be supported. Phrased in contractual terms, even if Ogilvie was in breach of the contract between banker and customer, the losses suffered by the bank flowed not from the breach but from the behaviour of the bank's officer.

Other duties

3.53 From time to time there have been circumstances where it has been claimed by the banker that there are further obligations owed by the customer which arise from the contract between banker and customer. In general, it may be said that the additional obligations sought to be imposed reduce to one of two. First, it has been claimed on occasion that the customer has a duty to read the periodic statement and to detect any irregularities there which would point to forgeries. Secondly, there is the rather more vague proposition that the customer is under a duty to organise business in such a manner as to prevent the facilitation of forgery.

The duty to read the statement

3.54 In *Kepitigalla Rubber Estates Ltd v National Bank of India Ltd*[1] the question of the existence of the duty to read the statement was raised. The secretary of the company forged the signatures of two directors to a number of cheques over a period of time. At that time, the manner of conducting banking business was that the customer would from time to time collect the passbook which contained a statement of accounts and the cancelled cheques which had been paid by the bank since the last period. The customer could then examine the entries in the passbook and reconcile them with the paid cheques, returning the book to the bank when satisfied that the accounts were in order. In the *Kepitigalla* case, neither the company's own books nor the bank passbook had been examined by the directors of the company for a period of approximately two months, during which time the majority of the forgeries had occurred.

1 [1909] 2 KB 1010.

3.55 Bray J held that the customer had breached no duty owed to the bank and that the bank was consequently not entitled to debit the account for the amount of the forgeries. The case was followed a few years later in *Walker v Manchester and Liverpool District Banking Co Ltd*[1] where Channell J expressly held that the fact that the customer did not examine the passbook did not prevent him from recovering the amount of the forged cheques.

1 (1913) 29 TLR 492.

3.56 The situation with statements, as opposed to passbooks, would appear to favour the customer even more strongly since the factual situation does not demand that the customer even have physical possession of the statement. In any case, the *Kepitigalla* case was approved by the New Zealand Court of Appeal in *National Bank of New Zealand v Walpole and Patterson*[1] and appears to be firmly established.

1 [1975] 2 NZLR 7.

3.57 It should be noted further that since the obligations arise from contract, it is certainly possible that the bank could make an express term of the contract requiring the customer to examine the accounts, but the *Tai Hing case*,[1] shows that such terms must be clearly stated and brought to the customer's attention.

1 *Tai Hing Cotton Mill Ltd v Liu Chong Hing Bank Ltd* [1985] 2 All ER 947.

3.58 In Canada, such terms go under the name of "verification agreements" and have been upheld in a number of instances. A typical agreement is that in *Arrow Transfer Co Ltd v Royal Bank of Canada*[1] which reads:

> In consideration of [the bank] opening or continuing an account with the undersigned, the undersigned hereby agrees with the bank . . . to verify the correctness of each statement of account . . . and within 30 days . . . to notify the bank in writing at the branch . . . where the account is kept of any alleged omissions from or debits wrongly made to or inaccurate entries in the account . . . and at the end of the said 30 days the account as kept by the bank shall be conclusive evidence . . . that . . . all the entries therein are correct and . . . the bank shall be free from all claims in respect of the account.[2]

Only Laskin J thought that the agreement was not sufficient to cover the risk of forgery for reasons similar to that given by the Privy Council in the *Tai Hing case*. However, it must be noted that the entire Supreme Court of Canada mentioned that such agreements should be strictly construed against the bank. Further, that it is banking practice in Canada to return the paid cheques to the customer with the statement. Although it might be possible to introduce a "verification agreement" into banking practice in New Zealand, it seems likely that there would be a substantial consumer resistance and, in view of the *Tai Hing* case,[3] a number of legal problems.

1 (1972) 27 DLR (3d) 81.
2 At p 89.
3 *Tai Hing Cotton Mill Ltd v Liu Chong Hing Bank Ltd* [1985] 2 All ER 947.

The duty to organise business

3.59 The second duty often argued is that the customer should organise business in such a way as to protect the banker from forgery. Phrased in this way, the duty is vague and imprecise and it is possible that this vagueness has been its downfall, for in each of the cases where the alleged duty has been judicially considered the Court has emphasised the difficulty of determining standards by which to judge if the customer has or has not complied with the alleged duty.

3.60 One of the earliest attempts to establish a kind of "organisational" duty was in *Lewes Sanitary Steam Laundry Co Ltd* *v Barclay & Co Ltd*.[1] The company's cheques were required to be signed by the secretary and one director. The secretary of the company had been convicted of forgery some years earlier, a fact known to the chairman of the board of directors. The secretary kept the company's cheque-book and used it to forge the name of one of the directors on several cheques to which he then added his own signature and obtained payment. The defendant bank claimed the right to maintain the debit of the account on the basis of the plaintiff's negligence in hiring a known forger and entrusting him with care of the cheque-book.

1 (1906) 11 Com Cas 255.

3.61 The defence failed on the basis that the harm complained of was not caused by the conduct of the plaintiff but by the fraud of the secretary. Note that this analysis admits of the possibility that there could be "negligence", ie, a failure to comply with some contractual term, which could result in the bank being entitled to maintain the debit. However, given the facts of the case, it is difficult to imagine what conduct of the plaintiff could in fact have that result.

3.62 In *Lewes'* case, the passbook had also been seen by the directors of the company and returned by them without complaint to the bank. The company was still held entitled to succeed in accordance with the principle of *Kepitigalla*.

3.63 The question came before the Court of Appeal in *National Bank of New Zealand v Walpole and Patterson*.[1] A clerk had forged cheques over a period of six years and received payment from a branch of the defendant bank. The main issue in the case was described by the defence counsel in the following terms:

> ... the bank is entitled in the circumstances of this case to raise by way of defence the negligence of the plaintiff over a period of more than six years in relation to the drawing of cheques on its current account.

Numerous acts of "negligence" were relied upon, but the chief ones were that the periodic statement was never read and reconciled by responsible members of the company and that the method of business adopted by the company was such as to facilitate the commissions of fraud.

1 [1975] 2 NZLR 7.

3.64 The Court of Appeal held that as between banker and customer, the customer is under no duty to exercise reasonable care in the general course of his business to prevent forgeries on the part of his employees and that the only type of negligence on the part of the customer which exonerates the banker from liability for payment of a forged cheque is negligence in or immediately connected with the drawing of the cheque itself. In each case, the Court relied upon the decision of the House of Lords in *Macmillan* to support its conclusions.[1]

1 *London Joint Stock Bank v Macmillan & Arthur* [1918] AC 777.

3.65 The matter would seem settled for the immediate future by the decision of the Privy Council in *Tai Hing Cotton Mill Ltd v Liu Chong Hing Bank Ltd*[1] which has already been mentioned in the context of introducing express terms into the contract.[2] There were three defendant banks, but for the purposes of the case, the facts were essentially the same in all cases. The plaintiff company was a customer of all three defendants. The banks honoured a total of some 300 cheques having a total value of approximately HK$5.5 million. The cheques appeared to be drawn by the company and to be signed by Mr Chen, the company's managing director who was one of the company's authorised signatories. The banks in each instance debited the company's current account.

1 [1985] 2 All ER 947.
2 See 2.27ff.

3.66 The cheques were forgeries. In each case, the signature of Mr Chen had been forged by an accounts clerk employed by the company, Leung Wing Ling. The case raised squarely the issue of who should bear the losses and what is the scope of the duties owed by the customer to the banker under the terms of the contract between banker and customer. The contention of the banks was that in addition to the *Macmillan* duty[1] and the *Greenwood* duty,[2] the customer owes some further duty to the bank. The precise scope of that duty was argued in the alternative and is summarised as follows:

> . . . the relationship of banker and customer gives rise in contract and in tort to a duty owed by the customer to the bank to exercise such precautions as a reasonable customer in his position would take to prevent forged cheques being presented to the bank ("the wider duty"); or . . . at the very least to check his monthly (or other periodic) bank statements so as to be able to notify the bank of any items which were not, or may not have been, authorised by him ("the narrower duty").[3]

1 *London Joint Stock Bank v Macmillan & Arthur* [1918] AC 777.
2 *Greenwood v Martin's Bank Ltd* [1933] AC 51.
3 Per Lord Scarman at p 950.

3.67 Leung was employed as an accounts clerk by the company in late 1972. He was immediately given responsibility for the books of account of two of the five divisions of the company and he began to steal from the company almost immediately. At first he did this by opening accounts in names similar to those of real suppliers to the company, persuading Mr Chen to sign cheques in their favour by showing him forged documents as evidence of the supposed transactions. In his first year of employment with the company, he stole over HK$300,000 in this way. These cheques, and other later cheques in which Leung defrauded the company in the same way, were not the subject of the *Tai Hing* litigation, for Leung changed his modus operandi, presumably believing that it was safer to forge Mr Chen's signature entirely.

3.68 It is with these forged cheques that the litigation is concerned. Between 1972 and 1978, Leung defrauded the company of some HK$7 million. The forged cheques, as already mentioned, account for some HK$5.5 million. There were some 500 cheques of which approximately 300 were total forgeries.

3.69 The trial Judge was required to determine how such a massive fraud could remain undetected for over five years. His answer was that Leung was trusted and that the accounting system in use by the company had ineffective means of internal control. There was no division of function which might have made Leung's task more difficult. There was a failure to check or to supervise in any way Leung's reconciliation of the monthly bank statements with the cash books of the company. The frauds were uncovered in 1978 only when a newly appointed accountant "entered upon the simple, though tedious, task which had not previously been undertaken, of reconciling bank statements with the company's account books".

1 [1985] 2 All ER 947, 951.

3.70 The arguments for the banks fell into four categories. First, it was argued that the duties mentioned above arise from the implied terms of the contract between banker and customer. Secondly, that they arise in tort as a result of the banker/customer relationship. Thirdly, that the duties, or at least the narrower duty, arise from the express terms of the written contracts used. Fourthly, that the customer should in all the circumstances be estopped from asserting that the cheques were forged. The third of these has already been discussed at 2.17.

3.71 The trial Judge ruled against the banks on all issues except the estoppel where two of the banks succeeded. On appeal, the Hong Kong Court of Appeal electrified the banking community by holding that the contract between banker and customer gave rise to the wider duty which they held arose also in tort. There was disagreement concerning the effects of the express terms, but all three Judges agreed that the company was estopped by its own negligence from challenging the correctness of the bank statements.

3.72 Much of the argument centered on the need to find terms implied into the contract which would cast the named duties on the customer. The Hong Kong Court of Appeal accepted the banks' contention that the contract must contain terms which express such duties. Cons JA said:

> . . . that in the world in which we live today it is a necessary condition of the relation of the banker and customer that the customer should

take reasonable care to see that in the operation of the account the bank is not injured.[1]

1 [1984] 1 Lloyd's Rep 555, 560.

3.73 The company appealed to the Privy Council which made the following findings on each of the major arguments.

The implied terms

3.74 The Privy Council concluded that such a term was not a necessary incident of the banker/customer relationship. Citing Lord Atkin's speech in *Joachimson*, and Bray J in *Kepitigalla*, the Judicial Committee agreed that the wider duty was too vague and that even the duty to read the statement and report errors was not essential to the operation of the relationship.

Tort

3.75 While accepting that there might be duties which arise in tort between parties who are in a contractual relationship, the Privy Council did not react favourably to the idea that the tort duties could be wider than the contractual ones, particularly when the relationship is a commercial one. Lord Scarman said:

> Their Lordships do not . . . accept that the parties' mutual obligations in tort can be any greater than those to be found expressly or by necessary implication in their contract. If, therefore, as their Lordships have concluded, no duty wider than that recognised in *Macmillan* and *Greenwood* can be implied into the banking contract in the absence of express terms to that effect, the respondent banks cannot rely on the law of tort to provide them with greater protection than that for which they have contracted.[1]

1 [1985] 2 All ER 947, 957.

Estoppel

3.76 There were no express representations made by the company to the banks. Once the Privy Council held that there were neither of the duties argued by the bank, mere silence on the part of the company could not be construed as a representation. Since the company did not know of the forgeries until May 1978 and they then took action immediately there was no breach of the *Greenwood* duty.[1] Since the cheques in question were wholly forged, there could be no breach of the *Macmillan* duty.[2] Consequently, there could be no estoppel arising from either of these two duties. Similarly, since the Privy Council held that the effect of the express terms was not to impose the narrower duty, an estoppel by silence could not arise from that source.

1 *Greenwood v Martin's Bank Ltd* [1933] AC 51.
2 *London Joint Stock Bank v Macmillan & Arthur* [1918] AC 777.

3.77 The *Tai Hing* case is undoubtedly a landmark decision in the law of banking and also an unpopular one with bankers. As mentioned in 2.22, while it is certainly possible to impose the extended duties on customers by express terms of the contract, the increasingly competitive nature of banking means that such a move would not be without cost in lost custom unless the entire banking community acted in concert. The alternative is to seek legislation which would extend the protection offered to bankers in much the same way as the provisions of the Cheques Act, but the general legislative changes sought by the financial institutions have been directed toward less government regulation and it might seem opportunistic to argue in favour of increased protection at such a time.

3.78 It now seems unlikely that banks can expect any extension of the customer's duty to be implied into the contract by the Courts. The Privy Council decision was most unsympathetic:

> One can fully understand the comment of Cons JA [in the Hong Kong Court of Appeal] that the banks must today look for protection. So be it. They can increase the severity of their terms of business, and they can use their influence, as they have in the past, to seek to persuade the legislature that they should be granted by statute further protection. But it does not follow that because they may need protection as their business expands the necessary incidents of their relationship with their customer must also change. The business of banking is the business not of the customer but of the bank.[1]

1 Per Lord Scarman at p 956.

Chapter 4

Special customers

Introduction

4.1 There are certain classes of customers which call for special attention. While these customers assume the obligations imposed by the contract between banker and customer upon all customers, there are various features which call for more than normal care on the part of the banker.

Unincorporated associations

4.2 Unincorporated associations are not, strictly speaking, legal entities at all. They are groups of people who are formed for some purpose other than gain. Since there is no contemplation of profit, they are not partnerships.[1] The membership will usually be fluctuating and the members are not normally liable to the organisation in any way save to pay membership subscriptions required by the rules of the association. Such organisations are normally formed for social or sporting purposes and it is not uncommon for them to keep a current account with certain of their members authorised to sign cheques.

1 If the association is with a view towards making profits, then the organisation may be a partnership. See 4.6.

Account in credit

4.3 It seems that there is little problem with such an arrangement so long as the account is kept in credit, but the lack of a legal entity means that the banker should normally resist any pressure for the account to go into overdraft. Weaver and Cragie suggest that the authorised signatories might be answerable for the amount, but advise that as the matter is by no means clear such arrangements should be avoided.[1]

1 *Weaver and Cragie* at p 104.

Overdraft accounts

4.4 The problem of the overdraft is compounded by the fact that any property of the club which is used as security for advances may have an uncertain ownership. Property is usually held on behalf of the organisation by trustees which will frequently be the members of the governing body. Even if these parties have the full authority of each member of the club to enter into security arrangements, it has been held that they have no power to contract on behalf of those who become members after the date of the contract. These new members will not be bound unless the conditions are such that the mere fact of becoming a member may be taken to signify consent.

4.5 The problem can be illustrated by *Abbatt v Treasury Solicitor.*[1] The club ceased to operate and a question arose concerning ownership of former club property. It was held that once the club had ceased to function the interests of the existing members became fixed so that club property belonged to those individuals who were members of the club at that time.

1 [1969] 1 WLR 561.

Partnerships

4.6 A partnership is defined by s 4 of the Partnership Act 1908:

> (1) Partnership is the relation which subsists between persons carrying on a business in common with a view to profit. . . . .

4.7 But the relation between members of any company or association registered as a company under the Companies Act 1955 or any other Act of the General Assembly for the time being in force and relating to the registration of joint stock, trading, or mining companies, or formed or incorporated by or in pursuance of any other Act of the General Assembly or letters patent, or Royal Charter, is not a partnership within the meaning of the Act."

Formation of a partnership

4.8 It should be noted that a partnership is not a legal entity. It is a relation which exists between persons engaged in certain activities, but the situation is very much different from that of an unincorporated association due to the fact that the rights and obligations of the partners inter se and their relationship with third parties are specified in considerable detail in the Partnership Act 1908.

4.9 There are no formal requirements for the creation of a partnership. If the parties are in fact carrying on a business in common with a view to profit, then the partnership relationship may exist even if the parties never give any conscious thought to the formation of the partnership. The partnership may be formed without any public notice of its existence and there is no need for any public registration.[1]

1 Certain types of partnerships, so-called special partnerships, are treated separately by the Act. A special partnership does require registration.

4.10 It is often difficult to know when a partnership has been formed. Section 5 of the Act specifies a number of instances where it is not to be presumed that a partnership exists, but there is only one positive rule, namely, that the receipt by a person of a share of the profits of a business is prima facie evidence that he is a partner in the business,[1] but the rule is only prima facie evidence and the section itself goes on to provide exceptions.

1 S 5(c).

4.11 The essential feature from the banker's point of view is that each of the partners is an agent of the firm for the purpose of conducting transactions which are within the scope of the business of the firm.[1] At least when the partnership is a trading firm, each partner has the right to open an account in the name of the firm and to operate it by means of his or her own signature.

1 S 8, Partnership Act 1908.

4.12 Further, although there is a new commercial entity created, there is no new legal entity. The partners are jointly and severally liable for all of the liabilities of the firm. This liability is not limited to the personal contribution that the partner may have made, nor is it limited to his or her share in the firm's assets. A partner who is forced to pay the firm's debts from private assets is entitled to be indemnified by the firm and by the other partners, but that is a matter inter se which is of no interest or concern to outsiders.

4.13 The rights of the partners to act on behalf of the firm may be limited by the articles of partnership. Because of the wide powers which are prima facie granted to each of the partners, this power of limitation is very common, but such limitations do not bind third parties who are not aware of them. However, the practice of requiring multiple signatures to operate a bank account might be so widespread that it could be that a banker who opens a partnership account to be operated by a single signature might be held to have had constructive notice. It is common and highly recommended practice to take an express mandate as to the terms of the account operation.

Dissolution of the partnership

4.14 The dissolution of a partnership revokes the authority of each of the partners to act on behalf of the firm. Dissolution may occur by any one of the partners giving notice to the other partners of his or her intention to dissolve the firm;[1] by the completion of the single adventure or undertaking for which it was formed;[2] by the death of any one of them or by the bankruptcy of any one of them;[3] or by means of other occurrences which are mentioned in ss 35-38.

1 S 35(2).
2 S 35(1)(b).
3 S 36(1). However, the partnership agreement may provide for the continuance of the firm by the survivors.

4.15 In the event of a dissolution, it is important for the banker to note that the only authority which remains is to operate the account for the purpose of winding up the business affairs of the firm. The banker should not permit the operation of the account for any other purpose. This is clearly an onerous task for the banker, but there seems no easy solution to the problem.

Executors and trustees

4.16 When a person dies, it is necessary that burial be arranged, that outstanding debts be paid and collected, and that the property of the deceased be distributed either as dictated by his or her will or by the law of intestacy where there is no will.

4.17 Where the deceased has left a will, it will ordinarily name a person who is to undertake the duties mentioned above. Such a person is known as an executor. The executor has power to deal with the deceased's estate for the purposes mentioned above and, when those duties are complete, holds the remaining property in trust for the survivors. The executor must apply to the appropriate Court and, after complying with certain legal obligations and formalities, probate will issue. Probate is official evidence of the person's title to act as executor.

4.18 If the person has not left a will, or if the named executor has predeceased the testator or refuses to carry out the duties of an executor, a person will be appointed by the Court to carry out the duties. The appointment is by means of letters of administration which are issued by the Court and the person so appointed is known as an administrator.

4.19 From the banker's point of view, there is little difference between the executor and the administrator, save that the executor derives his title and power from the will itself; probate is merely the evidence of these powers. The administrator, on the other hand, derives his power from the letters of administration and has no rights until the issue of such.

4.20 Executors and administrators constitute a single legal entity so that any one of them is entitled to operate on the executor's account. The death or other departure of one of them is irrelevant to the course of the administration and to the operation of the account.

Power to carry on business of the deceased

4.21 Executors have the power to carry on the business of the deceased for the purposes of administration, that is, for the purpose of winding up the estate or of selling the business as a going concern. This would not be expected to continue for any length of time. The executor has no power to continue the business for the benefit of the beneficiaries unless authorised by the will or by the Court.

4.22 However, when the business of the administration is complete, the executors thereupon convert, perhaps unknowingly, into trustees who hold any remaining property in trust for the beneficiaries of the estate. In such a capacity, there would be no objection to the trustees continuing to operate the business.

4.23 The distinction between executor and trustee is very important to the banker, for once the executors become the trustees, they are no longer a single legal entity and the operation of the account is on quite different terms.[1]

1 See 8.13ff.

Position when borrowing

4.24 Since the executor always has the power to conduct the estate business for the purposes of administration, there are bound to be circumstances where the executor wishes to borrow in order to facilitate the winding up process. The lending banker must recognise that he or she does not automatically become the creditor of the estate. The true position is that the executor is personally liable to the lender but if the debt was properly contracted, ie, for the purpose of the administration of the estate, the lender may be entitled to the executor's right to indemnity from the estate.

Minors

4.25 The contractual capacity of minors is governed by the Minors Contracts Act 1969. A "minor" is a person who has not yet attained the age of 20 years.[1] The Act divides minors into different categories with varying levels of contractual incapacity. Any person who is or has been married has full contractual capacity.[2] A person who has attained the age of 18 years has full contractual capacity, save that the Court is given express power to relieve such a person from a contractual obligation where it is satisfied that the consideration for the minor's obligation was so inadequate as to be unconscionable or if the contractual term imposed a harsh or oppressive burden on the minor.[3]

1 S 4, Age of Majority Act 1970.
2 S 4.
3 S 5(1) and (2).

4.26 Contracts entered into with minors under the age of 18 are unenforceable against the minor without special consideration by a Court.[1] The contract is in all other respects valid and binding. For bankers this means that it is safe to allow minors to open accounts provided the account is not allowed to run into overdraft. If the banker does wish to lend to a minor, it is probably best to take a guarantee from some person of full contractual capacity. The guarantee is fully enforceable even if the contract with the minor is not.[2]

1 S 6(1).
2 S 10, Minors Contracts Act 1969.

4.27 Minors who become parties to bills of exchange appear to be bound by the same rules. Section 22(1) of the Bills of Exchange Act

1908 provides that capacity to incur liability as a party to a bill is co-extensive with the capacity to contract. Section 22(2) provides that the holder of a bill which is drawn or indorsed by a minor who lacks capacity is still entitled to receive payment on the bill. Consequently, a cheque drawn by a minor entitles the banker to pay the cheque and to debit the account, at least as long as the amount does not throw the account into debit.[1]

1 The problem of lending to minors is discussed further in Ch 22.

Joint accounts

4.28 There are three problems which arise with joint accounts that must concern the banker at the time of opening the account. They are, first, the means by which the account is to be operated, ie, are all signatures required on cheques or may the account be operated by means of a single signature. Secondly, it should be clear from the outset which of the account holders are to be liable and in what way for any overdraft. Thirdly, and finally, there should be an express instruction taken which will define the rights of any of the surviving account holders to give a good discharge to the banker in respect of any balance in the account in the event of one or more of the customers' deaths.

4.29 As regards the first problem, in the absence of any agreement, the liability is joint only, with the consequence that cheques must bear the signatures of all the account holders. It is most common for the banker to take an express mandate from the account owners which expresses, inter alia, that the liability is both joint and several. The problem of forged signatures on joint accounts is considered below.

Presumption of survivorship

4.30 Ordinarily, when a customer dies, the account vests immediately in his personal representative, that is, the administrator or the executor. However, when the account is a joint account and one of the parties dies, it is the surviving account holders who are entitled to the balance of the account. It is not entirely clear whether this rule is part of the general law of devolution between joint owners or is due to an implied term in the contract between banker and customer, but in either case, it is based on an implied intention of the parties which may be rebutted by evidence of a contrary intention.[1]

1 See *Paget*, p 27, *Thorpe v Jackson* (1837) 2 Y & C Ex 553; 160 ER 515.

4.31 The question of survivorship is separate from the question of the operation of the account, so that it is not relevant to the question that the mandate taken calls for all signatures on cheques or allows the account to be operated on the signature of any one of the account holders.

4.32 The question of contrary intention has arisen most often in cases where the joint account is held by husband and wife and the husband dies. There are a number of English decisions which are not easy to reconcile. Although the problem has ordinarily been between husband and wife, it arises in all cases where the funds for the account have been supplied solely or primarily by one of the account holders, for in such a case, there is a presumption that the other party or parties holds the sum in trust for the party who provided the funds. The resulting conflict between the two legal presumptions, that of survivorship and that of trust, has resulted in a confused body of case law. The matter is the subject of an Australian High Court decision.

4.33 In *Russell v Scott*[1] a joint account was opened by an aunt and her nephew by means of the transfer of a sum of money from her private account into the new joint account. The nephew assisted his aunt in all business matters, but did not himself contribute to the account directly. Indeed, all funds which went into the account were from the aunt's investments. Withdrawals from the account were used solely for the needs of the aunt although the mandate taken by the bank called for the signature of both before withdrawals could be made. It was found as a fact from statements made by the aunt that she intended that the nephew should take beneficially any balance in the account in the event of her death.

1 (1936) 55 CLR 440.

4.34 The High Court held that the nephew was entitled to the balance of the account and that the evidence of intention was sufficient to override any presumption of a resulting trust in favour of the aunt and her estate. During the course of their judgment, Dixon and Evatt JJ said:

> The right at law to the balance standing at the credit of the account on the death of the aunt was thus vested in the nephew. The claim that it forms part of her estate must depend upon equity. It must depend upon the existence of an equitable obligation making him a trustee for the estate .
> . . As a legal right exists in the nephew to this sum of money, what equity is there defeating the aunt's intention that he should enjoy the legal right beneficially? Both upon principle and upon English authority we answer,none. English authority is confined, so far as we can discover, to cases of husband and wife. But there is much authority to the effect that where a joint bank account is opened by husband and wife with the intention that the survivor shall take beneficially the balance at credit on the death of one of them that intention prevails, and, on the death

of the husband, the wife takes the balance beneficially, although the deceased husband supplied all the money paid in and during his life the account was used exclusively for his own purposes.[1]

1 At 451 and 453.

4.35 On the other hand, in *Brophy v Brophy*,[1] the Court held that where a joint bank account was operated by husband and wife but all the deposits were made from the wife's earning and there was no evidence of an intention to make a gift of the money to the husband, the balance was held by him in trust for the wife.

1 (1974) 3 ACTR 57.

4.36 The doctrine of survivorship for joint bank accounts has long been recognised in New Zealand. In *Downes v Bank of New Zealand*[1] the headnote reads:

Where moneys are deposited in a bank in the joint names of two depositors and nothing more is said when the deposits are made, the liability as between the depositors and the bank is to the two jointly, and the right to sue in respect of it inures to the surviving creditor only.[2]

1 (1895) 13 NZLR 723.
2 P 723.

4.37 The matter has been recently before the High Court in *Taylor v National Bank of New Zealand*:[1] About a week before his death W asked his wife to obtain forms for him to sign to change his trading and savings accounts to joint accounts. At first W did not sign the forms for the savings accounts because, it was said, he thought there was not much in them. The bank advised Mrs W that there was a substantial balance and that they should be converted to joint accounts if that was her husband's intention. Upon being informed of the true value of the accounts W signed the forms. The executors claimed the sums in the accounts but the bank refused to pay them out, claiming that they belonged to Mrs W by survivorship.

1 [1985] BCL 895.

4.38 The Court found that the forms did have the effect of converting the accounts to joint accounts, that W had the capacity to make the changes and that he intended the wife to be a joint account holder.[1] There was also argument on behalf of the executors that there was a presumption of undue influence which could only be rebutted by showing that the bank had discharged its fiduciary duty by ensuring that the deceased formed an independent judgment after free and informed consideration. Prichard J held that there was no evidence that suggested that W did not exercise his own free and informed judgment.[2]

1 See also *Edgar v CIR* [1978] 1 NZLR 590.
2 See also *National Westminster Bank Ltd v Morgan* [1985] 1 All ER 821 and the discussion of undue influence in Ch 26.

Forgery of one signature

4.39 There has been some confusion concerning the right of one party to recover from the bank when another party to the joint account defrauds by means of a forged signature.

4.40 Most of the problem has been caused by the decision in *Brewer v Westminster Bank Ltd*,[1] a decision of the Queen's Bench Division in England. A joint account was operated by two co-executors. One of the parties drew over 450 cheques totaling some £3,000 which he signed himself and forged the signature of the plaintiff. The plaintiff claimed that the money had been wrongly debited to the account. McNair J found in favour of the bank on the basis that no action could be maintained by the joint account holders unless each of them was in a position to sue. Since it was clear that the fraudulent party could not have sued, the action failed.

1 [1952] 2 All ER 650.

4.41 The decision was much criticised and only a few years later the Supreme Court of Victoria refused to follow *Brewer* in *Arden v Bank of New South Wales*.[1] The joint account holders were partners, but in other respects the facts appear to be identical to those of *Brewer.* Martin J held in favour of the innocent account owner apparently agreeing that when the bank contracts to honour joint drawings it is also agreeing with each party severally that it will not honour drawings which are signed by a single party.

1 [1956] VLR 569.

4.42 In the *Arden* case it was also noted that the appropriate measure of damages is half the amount of the forged cheques, since the partners in that case were entitled to equal shares in the account. When the account is a trust account, such a reasoning would not, of course, apply.

4.43 It now seems very unlikely that *Brewer* will be followed even in England. In *Catlin v Cyprus Finance Corp (London) Ltd*[1] there was a joint account held by a husband and wife where the signature of both parties was required to operate the account. The husband made representations to the bank to the effect that he had his wife's authority to operate the account on his own and the bank then paid out funds on the strength of the husband's signature alone. The wife sued the bank. Contrary to most of the cases of this type, the husband was not joined as a party to the action. The Court noted that the parties had, when opening the account, clearly expected that the bank would honour the obligation to require both signatures. The only way in which that obligation could be given legal effect is if the duty to refrain from paying on one signature was owed to both parties severally and it could therefore be enforced at the suit of the innocent account holder alone. The Court refused to follow *Brewer* and it now seems unlikely that *Brewer* retains any authority at all.

1 [1983] 1 All ER 809.

Company accounts

4.44 A company is a separate legal entity which may sue and be sued in its own name. In New Zealand, the formation of companies, their powers and responsibilities are governed by the Companies Act 1955 as amended. By far the largest number of companies arecompanies which are limited by shares, that is, the liability of the shareholders of the company is limited to the nominal value of the shares held. These are the only companies that will be dealt with in this book, but most of what is said concerning the relationship between a banker and a company customer applies to all types of company.

4.45 Although a company is a separate legal entity, it must clearly act through agents. Generally, the shareholders of a company do not have a direct say in the day to day running of the affairs of the company, but rather periodically elect a board of directors. This board of directors may, in turn, delegate many powers to individual directors or managers. It is this necessity for the company to act through agents which causes some of the difficulties which may appear in the banker/customer relationship.

Memorandum and articles of association

4.46 The other problem which may arise is that the powers of the company itself are circumscribed by the memorandum and the articles of association. Roughly speaking, the first of these documents is the more important to the banker as it sets out the objects and powers of the company and the relationship of the company with the outside world. The articles govern the internal management of the company, a matter which will usually, but not always, be a matter of less importance to the banker. It is said that in the event of a conflict between the two documents that the memorandum should dominate.[1]

1 See *Ashbury Railway Carriage & Iron Co v Riche* (1875) LR 7 HL 653.

Knowledge of powers of company

4.47 Until recently, every person who dealt with the company was deemed to know the contents of the memorandum and the articles to the extent that they regulate the company's relationships with outsiders, but persons dealing with a company were generally entitled to assume that the internal proceedings of the company have been completed in a regular fashion.[1] That position has now changed with the passage of the Law Reform (Miscellaneous Amendments) Act 1985 which inserted a new s 18B into the Companies Act 1955. That section reverses the rule that everyone is deemed to know the contents of the memorandum and articles.[2] The change in the rule is unlikely to have a significant effect on bankers since the memorandum and the articles are usually provided to the bank at the time when an account is opened.[3]

1 *Royal British Bank v Turquand* (1856) 6 E & B 327; see also Ch 22.
2 The new section does not apply to the registration of company charges.
3 Note, however, that the changes in the requirements as to the contents of the documents may have significant effect. See the Companies Amendment Act (No 2) 1983 and the discussion below in Ch 22.

Formation of a company

4.48 The formation of a company is a matter of some formality which culminates in the issue of a certificate of incorporation by the Registrar of Companies. The certificate of incorporation is in some respects similar to the birth certificate of a natural person, but is even more important to those who would have dealings with the company, for the company does not exist before the issue of the certificate and the general rule is that a company is not bound by contracts made prior to its incorporation.[1]

1 Section 42A of the Companies Act permits the Court to make orders against a company which has derived benefits from a pre-incorporation contract.

4.49 These fundamentals of company law have profound consequences for the banker who wishes to open an account for a company customer. First, any mandates taken from the company must be dated after the date of the issue of the certificate of incorporation. Secondly, the banker should inspect the relevant clauses of the memorandum and the articles of association, making copies at least of the relevant clauses. Careful note should also be taken by a banker of the borrowing powers of the company, the right to sign cheques and other negotiable instruments and the seal of the company and the correct method of affixing the seal. Thirdly, the banker should also see copies of the minutes of the directors' meeting which authorises the opening of an account and the names of the personnel who are authorised to operate the account.

The ultra vires rule

4.50 Prior to the passage of the Companies Amendment Act (No 2) 1983, the banker and everyone else who dealt with a company had to be certain that the transaction was within the powers of the company. A transaction which exceeded those powers, an ultra vires transaction, was void.

The consequences could be catastrophic: a loan made to a company which had no power to borrow was irrecoverable by the lender in an action for debt.[1] Further, the money was not recoverable in an action for money had and received.[2]

1 *Cunliffe, Brooks & Co v Blackburn and District Benefit Building Society* (1884) 9 App Cas 857.
2 *Sinclair v Brougham* [1914] AC 398.

4.51 This very unjust state of affairs is now changed so that nothing done by a company is invalid, void or unenforceable by reason only of the fact that the company was without capacity or power to do it. It should be carefully noted that it is the power of the company that is at issue here, not the power of a director or other agent which is acting on behalf of a company.

4.52 The Act preserves the rights of certain classes of persons to plead that acts or transactions of the company are ultra vires. The classes who may do so are shareholders, debenture holders and the trustees thereof, the company itself and the Registrar of Companies.

4.53 Since the ultra vires problem usually arises in the context of lending to a company, further discussion will be deferred until Ch 22.

Agency

4.54 A director of a company who engages in transactions on behalf of a company is acting as an agent for the company. How is the banker to know if the director is acting within the powers granted by the company? The matter is now primarily governed by ss 18C and 18D of the Companies Act 1955. These amendments were inserted by the Law Reform (Miscellaneous Amendments) Act 1985. Since the matter usually concerns the banker when lending to a company, discussion will be deferred until Ch 22.

Other issues when dealing with company customers

4.55 There are a number of other issues which the banker must consider when dealing with a company customer. These include forming contracts with directors who may have an interest in the

New Zealand Banking Law

transaction;[1] transactions which involve a company dealing in its own shares;[2] the winding up of a company;[3] and certain investigations which give inspectors the right to examine company accounts and override the duty of secrecy owed by a banker to the customer.[4] Each of these will be discussed in later sections.

1 Ch 22.
2 See 7.73ff.
3 See 9.71ff.
4 See 7.17ff.

Chapter 5

The Banker

Who is a banker?

5.1 Surprisingly, there is no precise definition of either a banker or the business of banking. This might be no cause for concern except that banks and bankers are given special privileges by some statutes and are subject to special duties as a result of others.

5.2 Because of the important economic function of banks they are from time to time more heavily regulated than other financial institutions. Bank records are subject to special laws regarding their production in Court and to certain regulatory bodies.[1]

1 See, for example, the Banking Act 1982, Public Finance Act 1977, Trustee Savings Bank Act 1983.

5.3 Some of the older cases where the question was important were concerned with the Moneylenders Acts. This is no longer relevant in New Zealand since the repeal of the Moneylenders Act 1908 by the Credit Contracts Act 1985.

5.4 Possibly the most important reason to determine if any particular institution is or is not a bank is the prominence given to banks and bankers in the Bills of Exchange Act 1908. A cheque is defined as a bill of exchange which is drawn on a banker.[1] Bankers are given quite privileged statutory defences to certain actions which arise when a cheque is misappropriated.[2]

1 Bills of Exchange Act 1908, s 73; see Ch 13.
2 Cheques Act 1960 and see Chs 14 to 17.

Difficulty of definition

5.5 There is an historical reason for the difficulty in defining "bank" and "the business of banking". Banking during the Middle Ages was largely the use of private fortunes in the lending and financing of trade projects. It was not until comparatively recent times that the deposit of funds by the wider community with a banker, who was then expected to use the funds at his discretion for commercial lending, was established.

5.6 This modern form of banking is said to have begun during the mid 17th century when citizens began to deposit money and valuables with goldsmiths. The practice changed slightly when the goldsmiths' receipts began to circulate as a kind of informal currency. That development combined with the trend to return only a certain amount of gold, not necessarily the same goods which were deposited in the first instance, led directly to the development of "fractional reserve" lending. The goldsmiths learned that there was most unlikely to be more than a relatively small number of demands for return of valuables at any one time. By lending through the issue of receipts, it was possible for the goldsmith, now called a banker, to lend more than the total amount which was actually held in reserve.

These banks were owned by individuals or by partnerships which often engaged in banking as a sideline to some other business. It is for this reason that the early habit was to refer to individuals as bankers and to the "business of banking", for a person carrying on such a business might be engaged in any number of enterprises.

5.7 In New Zealand, the current banking system consists of relatively few large banking corporations which carry on business through many branches. In these circumstances, it might be thought that the search for a definition is merely an academic exercise, but that would be a great mistake, for there are still a significant number of circumstances where the outcome of a dispute will be decided on the basis of whether or not one of the parties "carries on the business of banking". The most important example is the Cheques Act 1960 which provides a statutory defence against an action in conversion provided the defendant is a "banker" within the meaning of the Bills of Exchange Act 1908. As more and more financial institutions seek their customers' deposits, often in the form of cheques made payable to the customer, the matter becomes of increasing importance.

Some statutory definitions

5.8 The Bills of Exchange Act 1908 contains a number of provisions which are of immense importance to bankers. However, the definition in s 2 is most unhelpful:

"Banker" includes a body of persons, whether incorporated or not, who carry on the business of banking;

The Banking Act 1982 is no more helpful:

"Bank" means any person, partnership, corporation, or company carrying on in New Zealand the business of banking.

The Trustee Banks Act 1983 takes a very operational point of view:

"Trading bank" means any bank for the time being named in the First Schedule to the Reserve Bank of New Zealand Act 1964.

The Reserve Bank of New Zealand Act 1964 does not define bank, being interested instead in "Financial Institutions".

5.9 Unfortunately, a search of the Acts discloses no clues as to what the "business of banking" might be. It is common knowledge that banks borrow money from depositors and lend money to customers and others. It is also well known that banks deal in foreign exchange, the discounting of bills of exchange and the facilitation of international trade through the operation of the documentary letter of credit system. But other organisations accept deposits and lend money. The banks are no longer the sole method of exchanging foreign currency and there are an increasing number of financial institutions which could never be mistaken for banks but which issue and confirm letters of credit.

On the other side of the same coin, banks now seem to be branching out into businesses which have little to do with the traditional business of banking. It may be that the local branch bank also runs a travel service or acts as an agent for the collection of certain payments.

Judicial definition

5.10 The High Court of Australia considered the question in *Commissioners of the State Savings Bank of Victoria v Permewan Wright & Co Ltd*[1] where it was held, by a majority, that the Commissioners of the State Savings Bank of Victoria were "bankers" for the purposes of the (Australian) Bills of Exchange Act 1909 which has a definition which is identical to the New Zealand Act. This was in spite of the fact that the repayment of deposits was permitted only on the production of the depositor's passbook with the order for payment.[2]

1 (1914) 19 CLR 457.
2 It is to be noted that *Permewan Wright* preceded *Joachimson's* case where there seemed to be more emphasis on the operation of the cheque account.

5.11 During the course of his judgment, Isaacs J said:

The fundamental meaning of the term is not, and never has been, different in Australia from that obtaining in England . . . . The essential characteristics of the business of banking are, however, all that are necessary to bring the appellants within the scope of the enactments; and these may be described as the collection of money by receiving deposits upon loan, repayable when and as expressly or impliedly agreed upon, and the utilisation of the money so collected by lending it again in such sums as are required. These are the essential functions of a bank as an instrument of society. It is in effect a financial reservoir receiving streams of currency in every direction, and from which there issue outflowing streams where and as required to sustain and fructify or assist commercial, industrial or other enterprises or adventures. If that be the real and substantial business of a body of persons, and not merely an ancillary or incidental branch of another business, they do carry on the business of banking.

5.12 The passages cited above were quoted with approval by the High Court in Australia in *Australian Independent Distributors Ltd v Winter*.[1] One of the issues was whether the Adelaide Co-operative Society had carried on the "business of banking". The Court held that it had not since although the Society accepted deposits from their members and the deposits were recorded in a passbook, the Society lacked one of the "essential characteristics" namely the power to lend money. This was interpreted to mean a general power to lend. Since the Society was limited to the making of loans to its members rather than to the world at large, it could not be a "bank".

1 (1965) 112 CLR 443.

5.13 The English Court of Appeal has considered the "business of banking". In *United Dominions Trust Ltd v Kirkwood*[1] Lord Denning referred to the *Permewan Wright* definition of banker and said of it and some other old cases:

If that were still the law, it would mean that the building societies were all bankers. The march of time has taken us beyond those cases of fifty years ago. Money is now paid and received by cheque to such an extent that no person can be considered a banker unless he handles cheques as freely as cash. . . . Whereas in the old days it was a characteristic of a banker that he should receive money for deposit, it is nowadays a characteristic that he should receive cheques for collection on behalf of his customer. How otherwise is the customer to pay his money into the bank? It is the only practicable means, particularly in the case of crossed cheques. . . . Whereas in the old days he might withdraw [money] on production of a passbook and no cheque, it is nowadays a characteristic of a bank that the customer should be able to withdraw it by cheque, draft or order.

1 [1966] 2 QB 431.

5.14 As a consequence, Lord Denning approved of a test discussed in *Paget* for determining if a person is a "banker" in the following terms:

It is therefore a fair deduction that no one and no body, corporated or otherwise, can be a "banker" who does not: 1 conduct current accounts; 2 pay cheques drawn on himself; 3 collect cheques for his customers.[1]

1 *Paget* 8th ed, p 12.

5.15 Interestingly enough, United Dominions Trust also was found to be a banker on the basis of its reputation in the city of London as well as by the application of this three-pronged test. This might be important in the future as the "business of banking" in the commercial sense changes. For example, it may not be long before the cheque account is replaced by an account operated by means of a plastic card for the majority of non-commercial customers. It would be most unfortunate if the "business of banking" in the legal sense was unable to keep pace with such changes. The test based on commercial reputation is a valuable addition to a purely mechanical test which may soon be outdated.

Range of possible tests

5.16 The Supreme Court of Canada has provided a valuable discussion of the various tests which might be applied to determine if a person or an organisation is carrying on "the business of banking". The issue before the Court in *Canadian Pioneer Management v Labour Relations Board*[1] was whether a company fell under legislation concerning labour relations; part of the determination of that issue involved the question as to whether the company is a bank. Laskin CJC and Dickson J considered that the question is whether functionally the business of such a trust company is that of a bank. Their use of the word functionally apparently meant that the company was or was not treated like a bank by the regulatory authorities for they observed that although a trust company such as the one being considered carries on many activities also carried on by banks, it has not been brought within the federal regulating authority in relation to banking.[2]

1 (1980) 107 DLR (3d) 1.
2 Throughout the case, the so called "functional test" seems to vary from time to time; see the summary given by Beetz J below.

5.17 The other members of the Court disagreed.[1] They considered that the functional test was, in the circumstances inappropriate. They preferred what they referred to as the formal or institutional test. Under this test it is relevant to consider whether an institution holds itself out as a banker and its reputation as such, a test very similar to that proposed by Lord Denning in the *Kirkwood* case.

1 Beetz J, Martland, Ritchie, Pigeon, Estey and Mcintyre JJ.

5.18 Beetz J provides a valuable survey of the possible means of defining the business of banking. They are:

1 By a consideration of the nature of the relationship between the institution and its customers. This is the test which is implicit in the *Foley* and *Joachimson* line of cases which decide the formal legal relationship between the parties.

2 By a consideration of the function of the institution. This approach in turn breaks into two parts; the economic point of view, that banks create credit, and the legal point of view, that banks operate current accounts and pay and collect cheques. The legal functional test is represented by the formal definition of banking given by Lord Denning in the *Kirkwood* case.

3 By a consideration of the way in which the institution views itself and is viewed by other institutions. Beetz J refers to this as the formal or institutional test, "holding oneself out as a banker", or "having a reputation as a banker".

The Banking Act (UK)

5.19 The situation has been changed somewhat in England by virtue of the Banking Act 1979 (UK). The Act provides certain criteria which must be met before an institution may become a "bank". The important point is that it is solely a matter for the Bank of England to determine if an institution has fulfilled those criteria for the purposes of the Act only.

The Act specifically preserves the right of any person or organisation to claim to be a "banker" or to "carry on the business of banking" for the purposes of any other act or purpose. Consequently, what is a "bank" is largely a matter for decision by the Bank of England, but what constitutes the "business of banking" is unaffected by the Act.

Chapter 6

Duties of the Banker I

Duties with regard to cheques examined in detail

6.1 Although it is difficult in theory to define precisely the scope of the activity which constitutes the business of banking, there is much less difficulty in defining the duties of a banker to the customer which arise under the contract between banker and customer. Aside from the duties related to the current account which were mentioned by Lord Atkin, there are more recently defined duties of trust and care in the conduct of the customer's account and the long understood duty of confidentiality about the customer's affairs.

The duty to pay cheques

6.2 In *Joachimson*, Lord Atkin observed that the banker's obligations under the contract ". . . includes a promise to repay any part of the amount due against the written order of the customer addressed to the bank at the branch . . ."[1] Although Lord Atkin spoke of "written orders", it seems clear that he had in mind the cheque since he observed that the written orders might be outstanding for several days.

1 *Joachimson v Swiss Bank Corpn* [1921] 3 KB 110, 127.

6.3 It is unclear if the banker has any obligation to repay the money owed to the customer when the demand is in a form other than a written one. Most authors seem to think that the banker would be so obliged, but there does not appear to be any judicial pronouncement on the subject. Weaver and Cragie argue that even if there is an obligation to repay against an oral demand, there is no obligation to make a third party payment against the oral orders of the customer.[1]

1 Weaver and Cragie, *The Law Relating to Banker and Customer in Australia*, Sydney, 1975, p 333.

6.4 Weaver and Cragie also suggest that if the customer sends a written order to the bank, as opposed to sending it to the ultimate recipient of the funds, then the bank is probably obliged to make the payment ordered irrespective of the actual terms in which the order is written, provided only that it is clear and unequivocal.[1]

1 Op cit p 333; see also the discussion of the GIRO system in Ch 19.

6.5 If Lord Atkin intended "written order" to be co-extensive with "cheque" it is unfortunate that he did not say so, for a cheque is a very special sort of instrument. It is something of an historical accident that the cheque is a particular form of a bill of exchange; it is an accident which has given rise to a considerable amount of difficulty, for the relationships of the parties to a typical trade or finance bill are substantially different from that of the parties to a cheque. It is for this reason that the cheque is an instrument sui generis in most civil law countries, and some common law countries, most notably Australia.[1]

1 See now the Cheques and Payment Orders Act 1986.

6.6 The legal aspects of a cheque as a bill of exchange will be considered further in Ch 13. In this section, the cheque will be treated primarily as a written order addressed to a banker. Note, however, that the ordinary path of a cheque is from the drawer (the customer) to the payee to the payee's banker, through the clearing house, finally arriving at the banker to whom the order is addressed.

This seems a strange path for a piece of paper which is an order from the customer to his or her banker, but is a result of the cheque being derived from the bill of exchange. There are payment systems where the customer sends the written order directly to the paying banker. Such systems are known as GIRO payment systems and are a common form of payment system in European countries and in England. In Australasia, it seems likely that a similar form of payment system may be introduced, but with electronic messages replacing the piece of paper. Such systems are known as electronic funds transfer systems (EFTS). Both the GIRO and EFTS will be discussed in Ch 19.

When the duty to pay arises

6.7 When the order is in the form of a cheque, there are several preconditions to the bank's contractual duty to pay. Indeed, if these preliminary conditions are not met, there will be times when the banker's duty is to refuse to make the payment. The duty to pay arises when:

1 the cheque is drawn in a proper form and signed by a person who is authorised to draw on the account, ie, the cheque is a proper mandate;

2 there are funds which are available to meet the cheque;

3 there are no legal impediments to the bank's honouring the cheque; and

4 the cheque is presented for payment at the branch on which it is drawn. This will in nearly all cases be the branch at which the customer keeps the account.

Each of these four conditions requires elaboration.

Proper mandate

6.8 It must be recognised that the cheque is more than an authority from the customer to the banker to make a payment. It is a mandate, that is, an order to make the payment. The obligation of the banker is to follow the mandate strictly. The banker must, if certain preconditions are satisfied, pay the correct amount to the correct person. If the banker does anything different, then there is prima facie a breach of the banker/customer relationship.

6.9 As a direct consequence of the fact that the duties imposed on the banker are strict, there is a duty on the customer to express the mandate carefully and clearly. Thus, in the *Macmillan* case,[1] Viscount Haldane said:

> The customer contracts reciprocally that in drawing his cheques he will draw them in such a form as will enable the banker to fulfil his obligations, and therefore in a form which is clear and free from ambiguity.[2]

and:

> The banker, as a mandatory, has a right to insist on having his mandate in a form which does not leave room for misgiving as to what he is called upon to do.[3]

1 *London Joint Stock Bank v Macmillan & Arthur* [1918] AC 777.
2 At p 816.
3 At p 814.

6.10 The extent of the customer's obligation to draw the cheque carefully and the consequences of failing to do so have been discussed above at 3.16ff. So far as the banker is concerned, it would seem that if the mandate is ambiguous, that the banker is entitled to refuse payment. This may ordinarily be the most prudent course. If, however, the banker does decide to pay the cheque, it would seem that the action would incur no liability provided the interpretation placed on the ambiguous mandate is a reasonable one. This is a general rule of agency; what is reasonable depends, of course, upon all the facts of the situation.[1] Unless there is some very special reason to do so, it would seem foolish for a banker to risk interpreting an ambiguous mandate, for if the interpretation is not what the customer intended there will almost certainly be a dispute as to the "reasonableness" of the banker's action.

1 See *Ireland v Livingstone* (1872) LR 5 HL 395.

Funds must be available

6.11 Even if the account is in credit, the bank may refuse to pay a cheque if the balance falls short of the amount of the cheque by even a small amount. In *Bank of New South Wales v Laing*,[1] Laing claimed that cheques had been forged to an amount in excess of £19,000. He drew a cheque on the account for the amount which he claimed had been paid out on the allegedly forged cheques. The bank dishonoured the cheque, whereupon he brought this action. Unfortunately, New South Wales at that time retained the old forms of pleading and the case turned on a point of pleading, not on the merits. Although Laing had made the necessary demand by drawing the fresh cheque, he failed to plead and to prove that there were funds in the account which were sufficient to meet the cheques which he had drawn. During the course of the judgment of the Privy Council, Their Lordships observed that:

> . . . where the creditor is a customer and the debtor a bank on current account, the "peculiar incidents" of that relationship govern the legal position and determine what the plaintiff must prove. . . . If the "balance" falls short of [meeting the cheque] he fails altogether, another distinction which distinguishes the creditor-debtor relationship in the case of a customer and banker from that relationship in other cases.

1 [1954] AC 135.

6.12 When money in the form of notes and coins is paid into the account, it is not immediately available for payment of cheques. It has been sensibly held that there must be a certain amount of time allowed for the bank to complete the necessary internal bookkeeping operations.[1]

1 *Marzetti v Williams* (1830) 1 B & Ad 415.

6.13 When cheques are paid in, it is customary for the deposit slips to contain a note to the effect that the proceeds are not available for drawing upon until such time as the cheque has been cleared. In *Westminster Bank v Zang*,[1] both the Court of Appeal and the House of Lords held that such a notice was sufficient to negate any possible implied term to the contrary.

1 [1966] AC 182.

6.14 Some caution on the part of bankers is necessary here, for it is by no means clear that an express agreement to allow drawing will override the notice on the deposit slip and it is by no means clear, in spite of the comments in *Zang's* case, that the notice will protect the bank if there has been a course of dealing established whereby the customer has in fact been permitted to draw against uncleared effects over a period of time.

6.15 If the banker has agreed to allow the customer to go into overdraft, then there is a duty to pay cheques provided that they are within the limit of the overdraft agreed upon.[1] Although there is no general obligation to allow an overdraft, it has been held that the presentment of a cheque for payment which would take the account into overdraft may be treated by the banker as a request by the customer for an overdraft.[2] Presumably a banker who habitually honours a customer's cheques which result in an overdrawn account may establish a course of dealing whereby it would become obligatory to continue to honour such cheques until such time as the customer is formally notified that the practice is to change.

1 See, for example, *Fleming v Bank of New Zealand* [1900] AC 577.
2 *Cuthbert v Roberts, Lubbock & Co* [1909] 2 Ch 226.

Proper branch

6.16 For many purposes a bank is a single institution, but for the purposes of presenting cheques and receiving payment for them, each branch is considered a separate and individual bank.

6.17 Most cheques are presented for payment not by the payee or the holder of the cheque directly, but by being collected through the clearing house system by another banker acting as agent for the payee or holder. For present purposes, there is no difference in how the cheque arrives at the drawee branch. Only when the cheque is crossed is the manner of presentment relevant.[1]

1 See 13.30 for a discussion of crossed cheques.

6.18 But it is not only the cheque which must be presented at the proper branch. It appears that the debt owed by the bank is localised at the branch where the account is kept and may not be recovered at any other location. There are times when the customer may wish to demand repayment at a branch of the bank other than that at which the account is kept.

6.19 The House of Lords considered such a situation in *Arab Bank v Barclays Bank DCO*.[1] When the British mandate in Palestine expired, the new state of Israel passed laws which related to the ownership of "absentee property". This was defined to be property which belonged to any person who had left Israel after a certain date. Such property vested immediately in a custodian. The Arab Bank held an account with the Jerusalem branch of Barclays and, following the creation of Israel, had moved their offices to Amman. The plaintiffs contended, inter alia, that they had the right to claim the balance of the account, some £580,000, from any branch of the defendant bank. The House of Lords affirmed the decisions of the lower Courts which had held that there was no such right even though there had been an outbreak of war which made repayment impossible at a time before the account vested in the custodian.

1 [1954] AC 495.

Legal impediments

6.20 Certain legal impediments may exist which will prevent the banker from paying a cheque even though the other conditions for payment are satisfied. An example of this is a garnishee order. Such an order "freezes" the entire account, even if there is more than enough money in the account to cover the amount of the order unless the order is specifically worded to attach only a limited sum. Garnishee orders are discussed in more detail at 9.82ff.

6.21 Another important situation in which the banker must refuse to pay cheques otherwise in order is when the bank has notice of a Mareva injunction issued against its customer. The Mareva injunction is a recent development of the greatest importance to bankers. It is discussed in more detail in Ch 27.

6.22 Perhaps the most serious situation for the banker is when he or she should know that the mandate, although proper in form, is being used to misappropriate funds which belong to some third person. This difficult matter is discussed at 7.73ff.

When payment is complete

6.23 Surprisingly, there are circumstances where it may not be clear whether or not the bank has in fact finally paid the cheque.

Payment over the counter

6.24 Payment of a cheque over the counter will ordinarily be in cash, the cheque being relinquished by the holder and the cash by the teller concurrently. In such a circumstance, payment will ordinarily be completed when the money passes into the possession of the holder.

6.25 Thus, in *Chambers v Miller*[4] the teller had paid over the money to the holder of the cheque. The holder was still counting the money when the teller realised that a mistake had been made since the drawer's account was overdrawn. The teller demanded the return of the money. The holder not unreasonably refused. The teller then seized the holder and took the money from him by force. The holder sued for false imprisonment and assault. He succeeded, the Court noting that when the teller chose to pay the cheque, the money became that of the person presenting the cheque from the time he put his hand upon the money.

1 (1862) 13 CB(NS) 125; 143 ER 50.

6.26 This case does not stand for the proposition that the bank can never recover money paid under a mistake of fact, only that in the circumstances the payment was complete and that any recovery would need to be by legal action rather than by physical violence.[1]

1 See Ch 18 concerning the right of the banker to recover money which has been paid under a mistake of fact.

6.27 *Chambers* was applied in *Balmoral Supermarket Ltd v Bank of New Zealand*.[1] A bank robbery occurred where money was stolen not only from the bank but from customers who were in the bank. The money in question had been emptied out of a bag and onto the counter midway between the customer and the bank teller. The cheques which were part of the same deposit were placed to one side. The teller had taken a small bundle of notes and counted $100 which was placed to one side on the teller's side of the counter. The Court held that the money belonged to the customer at the time of the theft, not to the bank. Until such time as the money has been checked and the bank has signified its acceptance thereof, the money has not been deposited and the bank has not become the debtor of the customer in respect of the money.

1 [1974] 2 NZLR 155.

6.28 These decisions may also be seen as merely applications of a general principle that property in money generally passes with possession.[1]

1 *Sinclair v Brougham* [1914] AC 398.

Payment through a clearing house

6.29 The vast majority of cheques are paid through the Databank clearing system. The question of the time of payment will be discussed at 19.77ff.

Stopping the cheque

6.30 Stopping the cheque refers to the withdrawal of the banker's authority to pay the cheque when it is presented by the holder. The banker has well defined duties when a cheque is stopped, but because it is an occurrence outside the normal run of business it often happens that the duties may be overlooked.

The right to stop: s 75

6.31 Section 75 of the Bills of Exchange Act 1908 provides, inter alia, that the

> . . . duty and authority of a banker to pay a cheque drawn on him by his customer are determined [terminated] by — (a) countermand of payment: (b) notice of the customer's death.

6.32 The section goes on to allow the banker to pay certain cheques which have been drawn after the customer's death since it was found that considerable inconvenience was caused by the former more strict rule.

6.33 It is important to note that the customer has a right to countermand payment, commonly called "stopping" the cheque, and that no special means of notifying the banker are specified. It is further important to note that the right is one exercisable against the bank, that is, the consequences of stopping a cheque so far as the payee and other third parties are concerned is an entirely different question. The rights of the payee and other parties are derived primarily from the provisions of the Bills of Exchange Act. These are discussed in Ch 12.

Method of stopping

6.34 A countermand need not be in writing, but it must be brought to the attention of the banker. It is in all cases a question of fact whether or not a particular cheque has been stopped. It would seem that a telephone call or a telegram would, even if identification is not positive, be cause for the banker to make further inquiries. This is not a happy position for the banker to be in, for on one hand there is the duty to the customer to comply with the mandate and on the other the uncertain possibility that the mandate has been withdrawn. The course recommended by the authorities in such a circumstance is to return the cheque with an answer which is calculated to cause the least injury to the customer's credit should the supposed countermand turn out to be false.

6.35 As noted, the question of countermand is one of fact. There are few general principles. It is worth examining a few of the cases.

6.36 There is no duty to act on an unauthenticated telegram even though the banker might wish to do so and would be protected from an action for breach of contract if the payment of the cheque is delayed while inquiries are made. In *Curtice v London City &*

Midland Bank Ltd[1] the plaintiff drew a cheque and on the same day, but after business hours, he telegraphed the bank with an instruction to countermand payment of the cheque. The telegram was delivered on the evening of the same day, being placed in the bank's letterbox. By oversight, and probably negligence on the part of the bank, it was not brought to the notice of the manager until two days later, during which time the cheque was paid. Cozens-Hardy MR held that the cheque was not effectively countermanded, reaffirming that "countermand is really a matter of fact".[2] This does not mean that the customer had no rights at all against the bank, for the bank might be liable in negligence but the measure of damage would be by no means the same as in an action for the wrongful payment of the cheque. In *Curtice* itself, it would seem likely that any losses suffered by the customer would have been at least partially due to his own negligence.

1 [1908] 1 KB 293.
2 At p 298.

6.37 If the customer has effected a countermand, then there is no obligation to pursue the payee of the cheque in order to prevent the debit of the account, nor is there any requirement that the payee of the cheque be legally entitled to the funds. In *Reade v Royal Bank of Ireland Ltd*,[1] the plaintiff wrote a cheque and later the same day sent a telegram which the jury found to be an effective countermand. The cheque was a part payment of a gambling debt and may not have been recoverable had the payee wished to sue upon it. It was argued that Reade was unable to prevent the debit to the account since he had taken no action to show that he had attempted to recover the money from the payee of the cheque. The Court held that the defendant bank was guilty of a breach of contract, that there was no need for Reade to attempt to recover the money paid by the bank and that the damages for the breach were the amount of the cheque.

1 [1922] 2 IR 22.

6.38 The outcome of *Reade's* case is obviously correct, but the matter would never have gone on appeal but for the argument based on breach of contract since the appeal was concerned solely with questions concerning the measure of damages flowing from a contractual breach. The true position is that the bank had no right to debit the account since their mandate had been effectively withdrawn.

6.39 *Commonwealth Trading Bank v Reno Auto Sales Pty Ltd*[1] provides an example of an ineffective countermand. The plaintiff bank was attempting to recover money from the payee of a cheque which had been paid. The bank claimed that the payment had been mistakenly made because the cheque had been effectively countermanded.[2] Part of the defence was that the cheque had not in fact been countermanded.

1 [1967] VR 790.

2 The right of a bank to recover in such circumstances will be discussed in Ch 18.

6.40 The cheque in question had been given to the payee during a weekend as payment on a secondhand motorcar; the customer changed his mind concerning the transaction and asked his wife to telephone the branch early on the following Monday and to place a stop payment order on the cheque. The wife spoke to an employee of the bank to whom she gave the message that the cheque should be stopped. The employee misunderstood, apparently believing that the customer would call in to sign a stop payment notice before the cheque could be presented. As a consequence, neither the manager nor any officer of the bank was notified as to the telephone message. The cheque was presented later in the morning and was paid after being referred to the manager on the question of adequacy of funds.

6.41 The Court held that there had not been an effective countermand. The employee was little more than a switchboard operator and the Court held that communication to her was not communication to the bank. At least when the stop payment instruction is given orally, it must be given to an officer of the bank of appropriate status and responsibility. Even if given to the proper person, the instructions in the *Reno* case may have been ambiguous. If that were so, then the result of the case could still have been the same.

Time for stopping

6.42 A customer may countermand payment of the cheque at any time before it has been paid by the drawee branch. This raises difficult questions concerning the time for payment, questions which will be discussed at 19.77ff. However, there have been a number of cases where it has been held that the customer has the benefit of the clearing house rules on this matter. On the other hand, if the holder of a cheque presents it for collection in circumstances where it is clear that presentment will be through a clearing system, then the holder must be taken to consent to the delays which are inherent in the ordinary operation of the system.

6.43 In *HH Dimond (Rotorua 1966) Ltd v ANZ Banking Group*[1] the plaintiff was the payee of a cheque drawn on the defendant bank which he deposited with his own bank for collection. The cheque was processed by the Wellington Databank centre on 4 of February and was delivered to the defendant bank at about 9 am on the morning of 5 February. It was agreed between the parties that this delivery was the time of presentment. Sometime between 11.20 and 11.30 that same morning a receiver who had been appointed for the drawer of the cheque countermanded payment and this was brought to the notice of the defendant bank. It was said that from the place on the list which was delivered by Databank that the cheque would normally have been dealt with at about 2.30 in the afternoon. The clearing house agreement allowed for dishonour up until 3 pm following the debit in the branch bank. Following their instructions, the defendant purported to dishonour the cheque and reversed the credit in favour of the plaintiff.

1 [1979] 2 NZLR 739.

6.44 The plaintiff sued the paying bank in negligence claiming that if the cheque had been dealt with directly when it arrived it would have been paid and that in the circumstances the bank was not entitled to the full day.[1] Part of the argument for the plaintiff was the evidence of an expert banker who testified that under the old system, the procedure would have been to examine all of the cheques which had been delivered from the clearing house and to pay those which had already been "presented" by delivery. It was also argued, and acknowledged by the paying bank that if the cheque had been presented at the counter then it would have been paid. The customer should not, it was said, suffer from a system which is in place largely for the convenience of the banker.

1 The case is rather remarkable in that it is generally thought that a paying bank is under no obligation to the payee of the cheque to pay the cheque. If this is so, then it is difficult to see how there can be a duty to make the payment at a certain time. The matter is not really discussed in the case.

6.45 These arguments were rejected by Jeffries J who cited a number of authorities which suggest that when a cheque is cleared through the clearing house that the paying bank is probably given the time allowed by the rules, at least if the cheque is dealt with by the end of the day. As to the argument that the cheque would have been met if presented at the counter, the Court acknowledged that this would have been so, but observed that the method of presentment was chosen by the plaintiff. He could have chosen to present directly, but chose to use a bank as agent for collection and in such a circumstance must be taken to assent to reasonable clearing house rules.

Answers on cheques

6.46 When the banker decides to dishonour a cheque it is customary to write upon the cheque itself some indication of the reason for dishonour. Since the dishonoured cheque is then returned to the collecting bank and ultimately to the named payee, the comment on the cheque is "published" in the legal sense and the paying banker becomes exposed to a possible action in defamation. Although there have been occasional suggestions that the banker can plead qualified privilege as a defence, it is most unlikely that such a plea will succeed.[1] It should be noted that if the answer is not published, then no action in defamation will lie. Consequently, when the customer who had drawn the cheque presented it himself for payment over the counter and the bank refused to pay, it was held that there was no defamation since there was no publication to a third party.[2]

1 See Tyree, "Wrongful Dishonour, Defamation and Qualified Privilege" (1980) 8 Aust Bus L Rev 220.
2 *Kinlan v Ulster Bank Ltd* [1928] IR 171.

6.47 There are several different reasons why a banker might dishonour a cheque. Probably the most common is that the cheque has been stopped by the drawer, but if a cheque is carelessly or ambiguously drawn it will usually be in the banker's interest to refuse to pay it. Provided the answer given on the cheque is correct in these cases, there seems little scope for the customer to claim that he or she has been defamed.

6.48 The category of cheque dishonour which does raise the problem of defamation is where the cheque is dishonoured for lack of funds. Banks have sought for a formula which conveys the correct reason for the dishonour, but which is incapable of defamatory meaning. Words have a defamatory meaning if they "tend to lower the customer in the estimation of right thinking members of society generally".[1]

1 Per Atkin LJ in *Sim v Stretch* [1936] 2 All ER 1237, 1240.

6.49 In *Baker v Australia and New Zealand Bank Ltd*[1] the words "present again" were placed on cheques which were wrongfully dishonoured by the defendant bank. It was argued by the bank that the words were incapable of a defamatory meaning. During the course of his judgment, Shorland J said:

> ... the answer "Present again" marked on a cheque conveys the meaning, inter alia, that the customer has insufficient credit in his account to meet the cheque on original presentation ... Whatever the answer "Present again" may imply as to prospects of future or later payments, it surely imports the clear intimation that the maker of the cheque so answered has defaulted as to time for performance of the legal and ethical obligation to provide for payment by the bank on presentation of a cheque issued for immediate payment. Written words which convey such meaning must, to my mind, tend to lower a person in the estimation of right minded members of society generally.

Consequently, he held the words defamatory and awarded substantial damages on the basis that there were three libels touching the reputation of financial solvency of a woman engaged in commercial business. The Court also noted that there had been no apology or retraction, the bank instead choosing to defend the case vigorously.

1 [1958] NZLR 907.

6.50 In *Jayson v Midland Bank Ltd*[1] the bank dishonoured two of the plaintiff's cheques in spite of the fact that the plaintiff claimed that there were funds available under an agreement with the bank which gave the plaintiff overdraft facilities. The answer on the returned cheques was "Refer to drawer". In spite of views expressed to the contrary by Scrutton J in *Flach v London and South-Western Bank Ltd*[2] that the words amounted to a statement by the bank "We are not paying; go back to the drawer and ask why", the jury found the words to be defamatory. However, the jury found that the bank had not in fact agreed to honour cheques to the amount specified.

1 [1968] 1 Lloyd's Rep 409.
2 (1915) 31 TLR 334.

6.51 In *Hill v National Bank of New Zealand Ltd*[1] several cheques were returned with the symbol "R/D". Eichelbaum J held that the marking was defamatory. During the course of the judgment, he said:

> One is conscious of changes since *Baker* was decided and I would have liked to have heard more evidence and argument on today's banking conditions since all regular users of cheque accounts must be conscious of the large volume of cheques and the variety of types of accounts. There is also the computerised nature of cheque processing . . . . To the casual observer it might seem that these changes in banking practice have led to greater opportunity for innocent error but that evidence might be dispelled by evidence to the effect that in fact the current systems are more efficient . . . I have concluded that dishonour of a cheque remains a serious matter and that the majority of reasonable people would think that in all probability the bank had done so on good grounds founded of some circumstance discreditable to the drawer of the cheque.[2]

The purpose of this passage is somewhat confusing. The innocence or otherwise of the defamation is not material. If, however, Eichelbaum J meant that the changes in practice have made error and wrongful dishonour so commonplace that there is no longer any damage to reputation, then it is scarcely likely that a banker would give evidence to that effect.

1 [1985] 1 NZLR 736.
2 At pp 749-750.

Summary: answers on cheques

6.52 Unfortunately, it is in the nature of the law of defamation that words which may appear innocent can in fact be defamatory if there is an "innuendo", that is, a meaning of the words beyond their simple meaning. It is for this reason that it is most unlikely that a formula will be found which is safe. If the meaning is conveyed to the collecting banker that the cheque is being dishonoured for lack of funds, then there is at least the possibility that the words used, no matter how innocent on the face of them, will convey the defamatory meaning expressed so clearly by Shorland J in the *Baker* case. Yet, if the words do not convey that meaning, why use them at all?

6.53 The libel action can only succeed if the meaning conveyed is untrue, that is, the cheque has been wrongfully dishonoured. Yet, it is not every instance of wrongful dishonour which will result in substantial damages being awarded, for the gist of the defamation action is that there should be damage to the reputation of the plaintiff. If the reputation of the customer is such that it cannot be damaged by the words used, then the banker may escape liability for substantial damages even if the reply is defamatory. In *Ellaw Co Ltd v Lloyds Bank Ltd*,[1] the account of the plaintiff was said to be used for kiting operations and that on many occasions cheques had been quite properly dishonoured. Although the dishonour was held to have been proper in the *Ellaw* case, the Court commented that even if it had been wrongful the damages would have been nominal.

1 (1934) 4 LDAB 455.

6.54 If a banker finds that a customer's cheque has been wrongfully dishonoured, it follows from the result in *Baker's* case that subsequent conduct will be relevant in the determination of damages. Weaver and Cragie note that the usual course of action is to contact the payee of the cheque and explain that a mistake has been made.[1] The drawer of the cheque should be offered a full apology as soon as possible, preferably in writing and public. It follows from this that an attempt to plead the customer's reputation, or lack of it, in an attempt to reduce damages is a very risky tactic. The banker should mount a vigorous defence only in those circumstances where he or she is absolutely certain of their position.

1 Weaver and Cragie, *The Law Relating to Banker and Customer in Australia*, Sydney, 1975, pp 380-381.

The duty to collect cheques and bills

6.55 One of the duties of the banker is that "[t]he bank undertakes to receive money, and to collect bills for its customer's account".[1] When the bill in question is a cheque, the banker is acting primarily as an agent for the customer for the purposes of presenting the cheque to the paying bank for payment. In this role as agent, the banker is exposed to one very serious danger, namely, the possibility that the customer has no title or a defective title to the cheque. In such a circumstance, the fact that the banker is entirely "innocent" is no defence to an action in conversion brought by the person who is entitled to the cheque.[2]

1 Per Atkin LJ in *Joachimson v Swiss Bank Corpn* [1921] 3 KB 110, 127.
2 Although "innocence" is not relevant, the banker is given certain privileged statutory defences in the Cheques Act 1960; see Chs 14 and 15.

6.56 A collecting banker is, like any other agent, under a duty to the principal to carry out the task with proper skill and care, taking all reasonable steps to safeguard the interest of the principal.

Duties with regard to presentment

6.57 The most important duty in this context is the prompt presentment of cheques and bills lodged by the customer for collection.
If the presentment is not timely, there can be little doubt that the banker will be responsible for any losses suffered by the customer as a result of the delay.

6.58 The method of presentment is not, however, fixed and will depend upon a number of surrounding circumstances. "Promptness" is thus a matter of fact which will depend upon all of the surrounding circumstances. The rules may be different for cheques than for other bills of exchange.

6.59 The presentment of bills of exchange for payment is governed by s 45(d):

> A bill is presented at the proper place — (i) Where a place of payment is specified in the bill, and the bill is there presented: (ii) Where no place of payment is specified, but the address of the drawee or acceptor is given in the bill, and the bill is there presented: (iii) Where no place of payment is specified and no address given, and the bill is presented at the drawee's or acceptor's place of business . . .

Through clearing house

6.60 Although these rules should be followed by a banker for all bills other than cheques, the clearing system introduces special considerations. For cheques it has long been accepted that presentment through the clearing house is a satisfactory method of performing the collecting bank's duty to its customer. The legal basis for this is not entirely clear, but there can be no doubt that it is a correct statement of the law. If it were put to the test, it could clearly be justified as an implied term in the contract between banker and customer that cheques will be so presented.[1]

1 Although the case was not one of contract, that would seem to have been the attitude adopted by Jeffries J in *HH Dimond (Rotorua 1966) Ltd v ANZ Banking Group* [1979] 2 NZLR 739.

6.61 Therefore as long as the collecting banker complies with the clearing house rules and as long as the cheque is forwarded to the clearing house promptly, the customer can have no cause for complaint. There are a number of English and Australian authorities on the time when the cheque must be presented, but it is thought that these cases are no longer relevant to the modern clearing house and that the time for presentment is prima facie that specified in the clearing house rules.

Liability for delay

6.62 In the event that the collecting banker does not fulfil the duty to present promptly, the customer may hold the banker liable for any resulting loss. Chorley suggests that there are three main risks of loss faced by the tardy banker.[1] First, the risk that the acceptor of the bill or the drawer of the cheque might become insolvent; if it appears that it would have been paid had presentment been made at the proper time, then the banker would be liable. Secondly, the bank's failure to make a timely presentment may have the result of discharging indorsers from their obligations.[2] Finally, in the case of a cheque, there is the risk that the drawer's bank may become insolvent during the interval; the customer of the collecting bank will lose the amount by which the failed bank is unable to meet its obligations and the holder will be entitled to recover that amount from the collecting bank.

1 *Chorley*, p 143.
2 See s 45, Bills of Exchange Act.

6.63 There is also authority that the collecting banker will be liable to the customer in the event that any of the customer's cheques are dishonoured which would not have been dishonoured had the bank acted promptly on the collection.[1]

1 See *Forman v Bank of England* (1902) 18 TLR 339.

Duties with respect to dishonour

6.64 When a bill or a cheque is dishonoured, notice of the dishonour must be given to indorsers and the drawer. Failure to do so will ordinarily mean that they are discharged from any liability on the instrument, although in the case of a cheque s 50(2)(c)(iv) will often operate to dispense with the requirement for notice to the drawer. That section provides that as regards the drawer, notice is dispensed with "where the drawee . . . is as between himself and the drawer under no obligation to accept or pay the bill". Thus there is no need for notice to the drawer when the drawer stops the cheque or when the cheque is dishonoured for insufficient funds. If the cheque is indorsed, notice to the indorsers is required in order to maintain their liability on the instrument. Neither the holder of the cheque nor the collecting banker will be in a position to know, at the time of dishonour, whether or not the section excuses notice to the drawer.

Notice

6.65 Section 49 of the Bills of Exchange Act sets out the rules for giving a valid and effectual notice of dishonour. Of particular interest to collecting bankers is para (o):

> Where a bill when dishonoured is in the hands of an agent, he may either himself give notice to the parties liable on the bill, or he may give notice to his principal. If he gives notice to his principal, he must do so within the same time as if he were the holder . . . .

6.66 It is clear that it is in the interests of the collecting banker to give notice directly to the customer. Any other course of action involves risks that the strict rules of s 49 might not be observed, with the result of attracting possible liability to the customer.[1]

1 See 12.63ff concerning the rules for giving notice of dishonour.

Return to customer

6.67 Section 49(f) provides that "The return of a dishonoured bill to the drawer or an indorser is in point of form deemed a sufficient notice of dishonour". The common method is, however, to return the dishonoured instrument not to the drawer or the indorser, but to the customer/holder of the instrument. It seems likely that such a return must necessarily amount to notice to the customer of the dishonour.

6.68 The Act contemplates notice being given either in writing or by personal communication. It would seem obvious that a notice by telephone would be within the realm of "personal communication", but there are English dicta which casts doubt on that. In *Lombard Banking Ltd v Central Garage and Engineering Co Ltd*[1] Scarman J said:

> In the present case the prior oral or telephonic communication of the Westminster Bank to its principal was a warning of what was in the post and not the substantive notice of dishonour.[2]

1 [1963] 1 QB 220.
2 At p 232.

6.69 With respect, there seems little sense in disqualifying telephone communication, or indeed any other type of communication provided only that the notice has the required content and the sender of the notice is reasonably identifiable.

Chapter 7

Duties of the Banker II

Duty of secrecy — Duties to third parties — Bailment

The duty of secrecy

7.1 One of the terms of the contract between banker and customer is that the banker is under a duty of secrecy in respect, at least, of the transactions which go through the account and any of the securities taken by the banker. The leading case is *Tournier v National Provincial & Union Bank of England*.[1] The facts were that the plaintiff had banked with the defendant for some time. His account became overdrawn and he agreed with the branch manager to repay the overdraft by weekly instalments of £1. His address was given as that of a firm with which he was about to enter employment.

1 [1924] 1 KB 461.

7.2 Unfortunately, he failed to maintain the weekly payments. The manager telephoned the employer, ostensibly to obtain the home address of the plaintiff, but in the course of the conversation the manager informed the employer of the reason for attempting to contact the plaintiff. Just for good measure, he added that the bank suspected the plaintiff of gambling since several cheques had named a bookmaker as payee.

7.3 As a result of this information, it was alleged the employer refused to renew the employment. The plaintiff claimed damages from the bank for breach of contract. He succeeded, the Court holding that there was the duty of confidentiality mentioned above.

Several members of the Court suggested that the duty went further. For example, Lord Atkin said:

> I further think that the obligation extends to information obtained from other sources than the customer's actual account, if the occasion upon which the information was obtained arose out of the banking relations of the bank and its customers — for example, with a view to assisting the bank in conducting the customer's business, or in coming to decisions as to its treatment of its customers.[1]

1 At p 485.

7.4 The duty of secrecy is not, of course, absolute. Bankes LJ attempted to define the major exceptions in *Tournier's* case. He said:

> There appears to be no authority on the point. On principle I think that the qualifications can be classified under four heads: (a) where disclosure is under compulsion by law; (b) where there is a duty to the public to disclose; (c) where the interests of the bank require disclosure; (d) where the disclosure is made by the express or implied consent of the customer.[1]

1 At p 473.

Exceptions to the duty of secrecy

7.5 These "qualifications" to the duty of secrecy are not as clear cut as they may first appear. There are numerous factual situations which place the banker in the difficult position of being forced to choose between the contractual duty of secrecy which is owed to the customer and some other legal or moral duty which requires disclosure of the customer's affairs. The following discussion outlines the general principles.

Disclosure under compulsion by law

7.6 There is no doubt that any contractual duty of confidentiality is overridden by the duty of both parties to submit to other legal requirements. There is little authority on the matter, but Lord Diplock made the point clearly and forcefully in *Parry-Jones v Law Society*[1] when he said:

> ... [the] duty of confidence is subject to, and overridden by, the duty of any party to that contract to comply with the law of the land. If it is the duty of such a party to a contract, whether at common law or under statute, to disclose in defined circumstances confidential information, then he must do so, and any express contract to the

contrary would be illegal and void. For example, in the case of banker and customer, the duty of confidence is subject to the overriding duty of the banker at common law to disclose and answer questions as to his customer's affairs when he is asked to give evidence on them in the witness box in a Court of law.[2]

1 [1969] 1 Ch 1.
2 At p 9.

7.7 Note however that there must be a compulsion; it is not every demand which comes from a government department which falls into the exception. There can be no doubt that the power to compel disclosures is more widely granted by various acts than was previously the case, and a complete list of the circumstances in which there is a compulsion by law would soon be out of date. There are, however, several circumstances which are common and unlikely to change in the near future.

Bankers' books

7.8 The obligation of a bank to abstain from disclosing information as to a customer's affairs is qualified by the authority of the Court to order for special cause, production of the books or the appearance of an officer of the bank.

7.9 Section 5 provides that copies of the entries in the "business records" of a bank shall be received as prima facie evidence of such an entry and of the matters, transactions, and accounts therein recorded. The section also details the matters which must be proved in order for a copy to qualify.

7.10 If the business records of a bank are sought in proceedings where the banker is not a party, then the person seeking the production of the records must seek an order of the Court:

> **6. Officer not compellable to produce business records** — An officer of a bank shall not, in any legal proceedings to which the bank is not a party, be compellable either to produce any business record of the bank the contents of which can be proved pursuant to section 5 of this Act, or to appear as a witness to prove the matters, transactions, and accounts therein recorded, unless by order of a Court made for special cause.

7.11 Further, the Court has the power to order that one of the parties to a litigation may inspect and take copies of certain banking records:

> **7. Court may order inspection** — (1) On the application of any party to a legal proceeding a Court may, on summons, order that such party be at liberty to inspect and take copies of any entries in the business records of a bank for any of the purposes of such proceeding.

7.12 Note that the section does not limit the power of the Court to make orders to inspect only accounts of parties to the litigation. The equivalent section of the old Act was considered in *James v Mabin (No 3)*[1] where Adams J was faced with a request to make an order under the Act which would allow the inspection of an account of a person who was not a party to the litigation. He refused, saying:

> . . . the power [of s 7] should seldom if ever be exercised except where the account sought to be inspected is in form or substance really the account of a party to the litigation, or is kept on his behalf, so that the entries in it would be evidence against him at the trial . . . . Further, I think that on such an application the party whose account is to be inspected ought to be heard.

1 [1929] NZLR 899.

7.13 On the other hand, an order may be made ex parte under the Act even if there is no evidence given, but it is better if notice is served on the person whose account is to be inspected. In some cases the Court may require evidence of the bona fides of the applicant and of the materiality of the inspection.[1]

1 *Arnott v Hayes* (1887) 36 Ch D 731.

7.14 When the bank is a party to the proceedings there may be an order for discovery under certain circumstances. In *Bankers Trust v Shapira*,[1] two men presented to the plaintiff bank in New York two cheques purportedly drawn on the National Commercial Bank of Saudi Arabia and made payable to one of the men. The bank paid $1,000,000 and then, on their instructions credited more than $700,000 to accounts of the two men at the London branch of the Discount Bank (Overseas) Ltd, which was the third defendant. The cheques were forged and the Saudi bank refused to pay. The plaintiff bank claimed against the Discount Bank asking for injunctions to prevent any dealings with the funds in the accounts of the Discount Bank.[2] They obtained the injunction and then sought an interlocutory order that the Discount Bank should disclose and permit the plaintiff bank to inspect and take copies of certain documents relating to the accounts of the two men.

1 [1980] 1 WLR 1274.
2 See Ch 27 for a discussion of Mareva injunctions.

7.15 At first instance, they failed on the basis of the confidential banker/customer relationship, particularly since the two men who appeared to be responsible for the fraud had not been served with notice of the motion. The Court of Appeal allowed the appeal, holding that an order was justified even at the interlocutory stages of an action where the plaintiff sought to trace funds which in equity belonged to them and of which there was strong evidence that they had been fraudulently deprived and delay might result in the dissipation of the funds before the action came to trial.

Walker LJ made the special point that the plaintiff should be bound to undertake that such information would be used only for the purposes of the action and not for any other purpose.

7.16 In *R v William Bacon & Co*[1] it was held that the manager's diary is an ordinary book of the bank and an entry made therein is made in the usual and ordinary course of business. Consequently, an order may be made directing an officer of the bank to produce the diary and to appear as a witness to prove the matters, transactions and account therein recorded. The Court also noted that the order which is made under the Act has nothing to do with admissibility of the evidence contained therein. Admissibility is governed by the usual rules of evidence.

1 [1969] NZLR 228.

Companies Act 1955

7.17 Section 6 appears to be read rather strictly. For example, there are powers given to company liquidators to use Court proceedings to obtain information about the affairs of the company.[1]

1 S 171.

7.18 In *Re Hartly & Riley Consolidated Gold Dredging*[1] the Court held that an examination held by the Court under s 210 of the Companies Act 1908 is for the information of the liquidator and the person who is questioned is not giving evidence as a witness in a legal proceeding to prove any matter. Thus, s 6 of the Banking Act 1982 does not extend to protect a banking officer from being called in a s 210 investigation.

1 [1931] NZLR 977.

Income tax

7.19 The Commissioner of Inland Revenue is given powers by the Inland Revenue Department Act 1974 which will allow an officer authorised by him to take extracts from or copies of certain records and documents. There must be a written authority specifying the information or records required, signed by the Commissioner.

Duty to the public to disclose

7.20 The author knows of no reported cases which examine the rights of a banker who has taken it upon himself to exercise the right to disclose the customer's affairs pursuant to a duty to the public. The category is by far the most ill defined of any of the four categories of exception. There have been suggested examples, eg, where in time of war the customer's dealings indicated trading with the enemy.[1]

1 Chorley, *Law of Banking* 6th ed, 1974, p 23.

7.21 The only sound advice which may be given is that the banker should exercise extreme restraint before disclosing information pursuant to any supposed duty to the public.

The interests of the bank

7.22 There are several circumstances in which the bank's own interest will justify disclosure of at least some of the customer's account information. Weaver and Cragie note that the issue of a writ whereby the bank initiates legal action against the customer will necessarily contain confidential information.[1]

1 Weaver and Cragie, *The Law Relating to Banker and Customer in Australia*, Sydney, 1975, p 169.

7.23 More common is the case of a guarantor seeking information concerning the account of the primary debtor. As will be seen later, the bank need not, and should not, volunteer information concerning the account, but if the guarantor asks questions, he or she is entitled to frank and honest answers even though the guarantor is not generally entitled to full information regarding the whole account. The precise limits of disclosure are not entirely clear. They are discussed in Ch 26.

7.24 There seems to be only one reported case. In *Sunderland v Barclays Bank*,[1] the defendant bank had dishonoured the plaintiff's cheques due to insufficient funds in the account, but the real reason was that the bank manager thought it unwise to grant her an overdraft since he was aware that the plaintiff was losing large sums through gambling. She complained to her husband. He encouraged her to telephone the bank to demand an explanation. She did so and during the course of the conversation handed the telephone to her husband. He was told during the conversation that most of the cheques drawn on the wife's account were in favour of bookmakers. She sued the bank claiming breach of the duty of secrecy.

1 (1938) 5 LDAB 163.

7.25 The Court held that the manager had impliedly or expressly received a demand to explain and that by handing the telephone to her husband the plaintiff had impliedly authorised the disclosure to him. Even if there was no implied authorisation, the fact that a demand for explanation had been made meant that it was in the bank's own interest to explain to Dr Sunderland. The reasoning and the decision are far from satisfactory, for it is perfectly clear that Mrs Sunderland would not have authorised such a disclosure and it is also difficult to see how the bank's interest in maintaining the goodwill of one customer, ie Dr Sunderland, can authorise a breach of contract with another.

7.26 The final point of the *Sunderland* case is that Du Parcq LJ went on to say that even if there had been a breach of contract by the bank, he would award only nominal damages since the plaintiff had suffered little if any damage as a result of the breach.

This latter point is important, for there are often breaches of the duty of secrecy when account information, often the balance, is given by telephone in order to verify that there are funds in the account which are sufficient to cover a cheque which is about to be written by the customer. If not expressly or impliedly authorised by the customer, there is no doubt that there is a technical breach of the duty of secrecy, but, provided the information is correct, there will seldom if ever be any damage to the customer as a result of the breach. If the funds are adequate to cover the cheque then the transaction will go ahead; if the funds are inadequate, then the customer is attempting to write a cheque for which there are inadequate funds. This is both a criminal offence and a tort upon the payee and it can scarcely be imagined that the "damage" suffered is such as to be attributable to the breach by the bank.

7.27 This should not be interpreted as condoning the giving of account information over the telephone. There may well be circumstances other than those mentioned above where real damage flows from such a breach. In such a case, there would be no doubt that the banker would be liable. Since there is no way of knowing ahead of time which type of situation is being dealt with, the only safe course of action for the banker is to refuse to give account information over the telephone unless the customer has given an express, preferably written, authorisation.

Express or implied consent by the customer

7.28 When the customer gives an express consent to the release of information, there can be no complaint provided that the banker discloses only information which is correct and within the confines of the customer's consent.

7.29 Implied consent may only be inferred when the customer knows that the information is likely to be disclosed and submits to it. In other words, there can be no consent to the giving of information unless it can be shown that the customer is aware of the banking practice which gives rise to the disclosure.

Banker's reference

7.30 The common problem which arises with implied consent is when the banker gives a "banker's reference", that is, a reference which is addressed to another banker rather than to the person who is intended to be the ultimate recipient of the knowledge. The position in law would seem to be that the fact that the reference is, in the first instance, between bankers is irrelevant and must be considered precisely as though the information were given by the banker to the ultimate inquirer.

7.31 In considering the question of the banker giving a reference concerning the customer, Bankes LJ seemed to have contemplated express consent in this circumstance when he said that the common instance of the exception "is where the customer authorises a reference to his banker"[1] and Lord Atkin said:

> I do not desire to express any final opinion on the practice of bankers to give information as to the affairs of their respective customers, except to say that if it is justified it must be upon the basis of an implied consent of the customer.[2]

1 *Tournier v National Provincial & Union Bank of England* [1924] 1 KB 461, 473.
2 At p 486.

7.32 Yet, the common opinion among bankers is that they are entitled to give a banker's reference, a reference which almost necessarily must disclose some of the confidential account information, without the express authorisation of the customer. The only way in which this practice may be justified is on the basis of implied consent and there can scarcely be any implied consent if the practice is unknown to the customer.

7.33 This in turn raises the question of whether the practice of bankers giving references is not only widespread but also notorious. Weaver and Cragie argue that the practice is probably as well known as several other practices which are undoubtedly incorporated into the contract between banker and customer, eg, that an overdrawn customer is taken to assent to the charging of interest, that a customer who lodges a cheque for collection assents to the normal delays inherent in the clearing house rules, even though in each case it is extremely unlikely that the customer is aware of the details of the arrangements to which he or she has "consented"[1]

1 Weaver and Cragie, *The Law Relating to Banker and Customer in Australia*, Sydney, 1975, p 170.

7.34 However, the argument is not entirely convincing. Even though the customer may never have had an overdraft, the general practice of charging interest on loans is well known. Similarly, although the customer may not be aware of the precise content of clearing house rules, anyone who writes cheques is aware that there are delays involved. By contrast, the practice of bankers' references is wholly unknown to the normal customer.

7.35 There is a possibility that the position of commercial customers is different in this regard from the position of the ordinary customer. It seems less likely that a commercial customer could be unaware of the practice. Further, it may be that the practice, although not well known earlier, is now becoming notorious. In *Mutual Life and Citizens' Assurance Company v Evatt*,[1] Kitto J noted "the multitudinous inquiries of this kind that everyone knows are constantly made of bankers". However, there is still room to doubt that the facts known to a High Court Judge and to lawyers generally are necessarily known to "everyone".

1 (1968) 42 ALJR 316.

7.36 Clearly, the best advice is to obtain an express consent from the customer where practicable before giving confidential information, whether to another banker or to a commercial firm.

Duty to the customer

7.37 Even if there is consent by the customer, that consent would only extend to giving a fair and accurate report of the customer's financial position. If the report is favourable, it hardly seems possible that the customer could sustain any damage regardless of the accuracy.

7.38 If the report is unfavourable but accurate, then any damage suffered by the customer would most likely not be recoverable, for the customer would be forced to argue that but for the (accurate) report a more favourable (inaccurate) impression of the customer's financial position would have been given to the inquirer. In the words of Weaver and Cragie, "it seems unlikely that a plaintiff in this position would attract a great deal of sympathy from a Court".

7.39 There remains, however, the action in defamation if the report is unfavourable. In such a circumstance, the banker would need to plead justification, if the report is accurate, and qualified privilege. The details are beyond the scope of this book.[1]

1 *Gatley on Libel*, 8th ed, London, 1981.

Duty to the ultimate inquirer

7.40 The banker who is giving a reference concerning the financial affairs of a customer also owes a duty to the ultimate inquirer. Except in those cases where the inquirer is also a customer of the same bank, or possibly the same branch, the relationship between the banker providing the opinion and the inquirer will not be one of contract. This is important in that it will permit the banker to refuse to give an opinion, for there is no non-contractual duty for the banker to give advice when asked. If, on the other hand, the banker does comply with the request for an opinion concerning one of the bank's customers, the bank is under a duty to the inquirer. The scope and range of that duty are still not clearly defined in law.

7.41 That some duty is owed is now beyond dispute, even when the ultimate inquirer makes that inquiry through another banker, as indeed will usually be the case. In *Hedley Byrne & Co Ltd v Heller & Partners Ltd*,[1] the House of Lords considered a case where a written opinion was sent by Heller & Partners to the National Provincial Bank in response to a request from that bank which was itself a response to a request from Hedley Byrne & Co concerning the financial standing of one of Heller's customers. The reference was headed "For your private use" and also contained an express disclaimer of liability. The House of Lords held that the relationship between the ultimate inquirer and the banker providing the information was such as to raise a duty on the banker to exercise care in providing the requested information.

1 [1964] AC 465.

7.42 The words "For your private use" were also considered by the High Court of Australia in *Commercial Banking Co of Sydney Ltd v R H Brown & Co*.[1] The Court rejected an argument from the bank that these words meant that no duty on the bank in favour of the ultimate inquirer could arise. This was because banking practice is such that the information was obviously sought for a customer of the inquiring bank who were proposing to deal with the subject of the reference.

1 (1972) 126 CLR 337.

The scope of the duty

7.43 Prior to *Hedley Byrne*, it was accepted law that in the absence of contract or of some very special relationship, the duty of a person who made a statement which purported to be fact or who made a statement of opinion was merely to be honest in making the statement. Such a duty was owed to those whom the maker could reasonably foresee would rely upon it in a matter affecting their economic interest. But there was thought to be no duty to be careful unless the recipient of the information was in a relationship with the maker of the statement of a sort which was classified as fiduciary. *Hedley Byrne* thus expanded the class of people to whom the duty to be careful might arise.

The duty to be careful

7.44 The duty is a duty to be careful, that is, to give an answer which is accurate and honest based on the facts which are available at the time. There is not, in the absence of special contractual terms, a duty to go outside the information which is in the possession of the bank through operation of its customer's account and financial affairs. Lord Diplock summarised the position in the Privy Council as follows:

> A banker giving a gratuitous reference is not required to do his best by, for instance, making inquiries from outside sources which are available to him, though this would make his reference more reliable. All that he is required to do is to conform to that standard of skill and competence and diligence which is generally shown by persons who carry on the business of providing references of that kind. . . . The reason why the law requires him to conform to this standard of skill and competence and diligence is that by carrying on a business which includes the giving of references of this kind he has let it be known to the recipient of the reference that he claims to possess that degree of skill and competence and is willing to apply that degree of diligence to the provision of any reference which he supplied in the course of that business . . . If he supplies the reference the law requires him to make good his claim.[1]

1 *MLC v Evatt* (1970) 122 CLR 635.

7.45 Although there have been some developments which cast doubt on the basis of the liability of parties making careless statements,[1] it would appear that by any of the tests of liability that a banker giving a gratuitous reference is under the duty of care expressed by Lord Diplock.

1 See 7.17ff.

Disclaimer of liability

7.46 The House of Lords in *Hedley Byrne* found that although the defendant had been negligent there was nevertheless no liability because of the disclaimer of liability. There seems little doubt that the disclaimer will have some effect, but it may be too soon to find that it will always be sufficient to allow the banker to escape completely. Barwick CJ in the High Court of Australia in *Mutual Life and Citizens' Assurance Co Ltd v Evatt*[1] treated the matter as one which was still open in Australian law. Further, on the matter of disclaimers, he expressly said:

> The duty of care, in my opinion, is imposed by law in the circumstances. Because it is so imposed, I doubt whether the speaker may always except himself from the performance of the duty by some express reservation at the time of his utterance. But the fact of such a reservation, particularly if acknowledged by the recipient will in many instances be one of the

circumstances to be taken into consideration in deciding whether or not a duty of care has arisen and it may be sufficiently potent in some cases to prevent the creation of the necessary relationship. Whether it is so or not must . . . depend upon all the circumstances. . . .

1 (1968) 42 ALJR 316.

When does the duty arise?

7.47 It is not every gratuitous giving of advice which will place upon the advisor the duty to take care in giving the advice. As indicated above, the important feature is that in all of the circumstances it is reasonable to find that the advisor assumed responsibility for his or her advice. In *MLC v Evatt,*[1] an insurance company gave information concerning the financial status of a fellow subsidiary company. The plaintiff, who was a policyholder with the defendant company, sought advice concerning the financial stability of the subsidiary believing that the defendant had greater information and/or better facilities for obtaining that information than had the plaintiff himself. As a result of negligently given information, the plaintiff invested in the subsidiary and lost the amount claimed in the action.

1 [1971] AC 793.

7.48 At one point in the judgment, it seemed that Lord Diplock was severely restricting the scope of the *Hedley Byrne* duty. He indicated that the principle laid down in *Hedley Byrne* should "be understood as restricted to advisers who carry on the business or profession of giving advice of the kind sought and to advice given by them in the course of that business".[1] However, he later made it clear that there was no such precise confinement of the duty:

> . . . Their Lordships would emphasise that the missing characteristic of the relationship which they consider to be essential to give rise to a duty of care in a situation of the kind in which Mr Evatt and the company found themselves when he sought their advice is not necessarily essential in other situations — such as, perhaps, where the advisor has a financial interest in the transaction upon which he gives his advice . . .[2]

1 P 807.
2 P 809.

7.49 It is certain now that in New Zealand the Courts will not permit the severe narrowing of the duty as suggested by the first passage of Lord Diplock quoted above. In recent times, the Court of Appeal has held that there is a duty of care in a number of circumstances where the loss was purely economic.

7.50 In *Meates v Attorney-General*[1] the plaintiff shareholders of Matai Industries claimed, inter alia, that they had been induced by the negligent statements of the Prime Minister and other Ministers of the Crown to establish the company to assist with the then government's regional development plans. Further, it appeared that when the company was in financial difficulties that the Minister of Trade and Industry had assured the plaintiffs that if they acquiesced in the appointment of a receiver with a view toward avoiding retrenchments that their interests would be safeguarded and they would be indemnified against losses. As a result of these representations, the plaintiffs failed to take normal commercial precautions to safeguard their own interests.

1 [1983] NZLR 308.

7.51 The Court of Appeal held that there was a sufficient proximity to establish a duty of care even though the Ministers were not in the business or profession of giving advice of the type which was given. They held themselves out as having special knowledge in the areas of their own portfolios and, in the case of the Prime Minister, of government policy. They knew that when they undertook to give advice that the advice would be relied upon. Woodhouse P and Ongley J specifically noted the second part of Lord Diplock's speech quoted above and concluded:

> Thus the presence or absence of a "business or professional" element should be regarded as but a single instance of a test in those particular situations where it has actual relevance.[1]

1 At p 334.

7.52 In other situations where the loss is purely economic the Court has shown a similar willingness to extend the traditional scope of those situations where a duty of care may be found to arise.

In *Allied Finance and Investments Ltd v Haddow & Co*[1] the plaintiff finance company lent $25,000 to one H for the purposes of purchasing a yacht over which they intended to take a security interest. A document was executed and H's solicitors wrote to the plaintiff's solicitor confirming that H was bound by the instrument by way of security over the yacht. In fact, the yacht was purchased not by H but by a company of which H was a director, a fact which H's solicitor either knew or should have known, and the instrument by way of security was wholly ineffective. Upon H's bankruptcy, the finance company was able to recover all but $7,000 and they brought a suit against H's solicitor for that amount. The Court held that in this case the solicitor owed a duty to the plaintiff, was in breach of that duty and that damages of $7,000 should be awarded to the plaintiff.

1 [1983] NZLR 22.

7.53 An even more startling example is found in *Gartside v Sheffield, Young & Ellis.*[1] An elderly woman had instructed her solicitors to draft a new will. Under the new will, but not under the old, the plaintiff would have been entitled to the residual estate which was substantial. The solicitors had not drafted the will when the woman died ten days later. Upon a suit by the plaintiff, the High Court dismissed the claim on the basis that the solicitors could owe the plaintiff no duty of care, but this was reversed by the Court of Appeal which held that a solicitor owed a potential beneficiary a duty of care to carry out the instructions with due diligence and to prepare the will for execution within a reasonable time.

1 [1983] NZLR 37.

7.54 In summary, it would seem that the duty of care will arise at any time when it is reasonable to assume that the banker is assuming responsibility for the advice given. That will always be the case when the advice is of the sort that is within the usual advice given by a banker, but the duty may arise when there are other factors which place the parties in a relationship which is close enough that the banker ought to know that his or her advice is being relied upon.

The duty to be honest

7.55 Even before the *Hedley Byrne* case, a duty to be honest was acknowledged. A failure to observe the duty leaves the person making the statement open to an action in deceit. In order to maintain an action in deceit, it must be shown that the representation was:

(1) false as a matter of fact,

(2) made knowingly or recklessly, that is, with complete disregard as to its truth or falsity,

(3) made with an intention that it should be relied upon by the recipient, and

(4) that the recipient did in fact rely upon it and suffer damage thereby.[1]

1 See *Derry v Peek* (1889) 14 App Cas 337.

7.56 It is crucial to note that actual dishonesty must be proved. It is not sufficient to establish that the person making the representation is merely careless.

There are, however, few cases where an action in deceit has been brought against a banker. Nevertheless it is clear that such an action may be sustained against a banker who has given a fraudulent banker's reference.

7.57 In *Commercial Banking Co of Sydney Ltd v RH Brown & Co*[1] the plaintiffs had for some years conducted business with a company known as Wool Exporters Pty Ltd. In late 1976, they entered into a contract with Wool Exporters to sell the clip on the sheep's back. Shortly before they were to deliver the wool, they were informed by their banker that there were rumours to the effect that Wool

Exporters were in financial difficulties. This naturally caused the
plaintiffs much concern and, at the request of the plaintiffs, their
banker wrote to Wool Exporters' banker, the Perth branch of the
Commercial Banking Co of Sydney, seeking a report on the financial
position of Wool Exporters. The request was in the following terms:

> Confidential. Kindly favour us with your opinion as to the financial
> position, character, standing and occupation of Wool Exporters Ltd and
> say whether you consider them quite safe in the way of business for
> generally . . . .

1 (1972) 126 CLR 337.

7.58 The request was signed by the manager of the plaintiffs'
bankers. In due course, the CBC of Sydney branch manager
returned a banker's reference in the following terms:

> The Company is capably managed by Directors well experienced in the
> wool trade. The Company has always met its engagements, is trading
> satisfactorily and we consider that it would be safe for its trade
> engagements generally.

There then followed an imprint of a rubber stamp which read:

> This opinion is confidential and for your private use and without
> responsibility on the part of this bank or its officers.

7.59 The document was not signed, but it was conceded that the
reply was that of the branch manager of the CBC of Sydney. The
plaintiffs delivered the wool to Wool Exporters on the faith of the
opinion. Shortly thereafter, Wool Exporters failed and the plaintiffs
brought action against both their own banker and the Commercial
Banking Co of Sydney.

7.60 As against their own bankers, the plaintiffs alleged negligence
in failing to mention that the qualifying clause was a part of the
report received from the CBC of Sydney. It was claimed that in the
absence of knowledge of the qualifications they were in no position
to assess the true value of the opinion for the purposes of making
their decision as to whether or not to deliver the wool to Wool
Exporters. In the Supreme Court of Western Australia, it was found
as a fact that the qualifications had been communicated to the
plaintiffs and so the plaintiffs' own banker had not been negligent.
There is some reason to believe that if the finding of fact had been
different then the outcome might also have been different.

7.61 As against the Commercial Banking Co of Sydney, the plaintiffs
alleged not only negligence, but also that the opinion was
fraudulently given. The Supreme Court found that this was the case,
that the manager knew or ought to have known that the request
was for one of the requesting banker's customers, that the customer
was likely to enter into business arrangements with Wool Exporters
and that the report was likely to be relied upon by the ultimate

inquirer. The Court further held that the report was made with intent to deceive and with intent that it should be acted upon both by the receiving banker and the customer who had requested the information.

7.62 The CBC of Sydney appealed to the High Court arguing that the effect of the disclaimer was to relieve it from liability and that the damages awarded were inappropriate.

As to the first, the High Court made it clear that Australian banking practice was such that when a bank requested information concerning the credit of a customer from another bank that it is understood that the inquiring bank will communicate that information to its own customer. It was considered impossible to construe the disclaimer to mean that the information is to be used only by the inquiring bank for the purpose of giving advice to its own customer without communicating the actual reply. The Court also made it clear that even if a *Hedley Byrne* type of disclaimer is adequate for shielding the bank against negligence when making a banker's reference, there is no disclaimer which will protect the giver of an opinion which is tainted by deceit.

7.63 As to the question of damages, the bank had argued that a failure of the plaintiff to deliver the wool to Wool Exporters would have been a breach of contract and that the damages awarded against the bank should reflect that fact. The Court held that such a fact (if indeed it was a fact) would not avail the bank, since the losses suffered were a direct and foreseeable consequence of the fraudulent representation.

Lord Tenterden's Act

7.64 Lord Tenterden's Act[1] is one of the peculiarities which were implemented in the English Statute of Frauds series of legislation. The Act is very badly drafted,[2] but the essence of it is that no action may be brought against a person who makes a fraudulent representation concerning another person's credit unless such a representation is made in writing and signed by the person making the representation.[3] But further, the Act only applies to those representations which are for a particular purpose, namely,". . . to the intent or purpose that such other person may obtain credit, money or goods. . ." .

1 Statute of Frauds Amendment Act 1828; 9 Geo IV c 14, s 6. The Act is in force in New Zealand: see *Diamanti v Martelli* [1923] NZLR 663.
2 See the comments of Salmon J in *Diamanti v Martelli* [1923] NZLR 663.
3 Although the Act itself merely refers to "any representation or assurance", the restriction to fraudulent representations is a judicial interpretation of long standing; see *Banbury v Bank of Montreal* [1918] AC 626.

7.65 Furthermore, since the Act requires that the representation be signed by the person to be charged, it is not possible to fix the bank with liability for a fraudulent statement which has been signed by the manager. The manager who signs is, of course, liable. It is interesting to note that the reference given in the *RH Brown* case was unsigned but the defendant bank elected not to rely upon the defence which would undoubtedly have been available to it under Lord Tenterden's Act.

7.66 Lord Tenterden's Act was considered in *Diamanti v Martelli*[1] where it was said that the Act applies only when the defendant's representations have been made for the purpose of inducing the plaintiff to give credit to the third person — that is to say, to trust the third person with the performance of some obligation towards the plaintiff, as, for example, the repayment of money lent, or payment for goods sold and delivered.[2] Therefore the Act did not apply when the plaintiff made fraudulent representations which induced the plaintiff to apply and pay for shares in a company, since in that case they did not give credit to the company.

1 [1923] NZLR 663.
2 At p 670.

Additional duties of trust and care

7.67 The banker has some additional contractual duties of care in the handling of the customer's account and financial affairs. The precise scope of these duties are not yet clearly defined.

Financial advice

7.68 In *Woods v Martins Bank Ltd*[1] the bank was held liable to the customer for giving negligent advice concerning investments. There can be little doubt that a banker owes the customer a duty to be careful in the giving of advice, at least when it is advice which is of the type which bankers would give in the ordinary course of the business of banking.

1 [1959] 1 QB 55.

7.69 Although the banker must be careful in giving financial advice, the liability for negligent advice will be limited by the knowledge which the banker has of the financial affairs of the customer. The point is nicely illustrated by *Box v Midland Bank*[1] where the plaintiff claimed damages from the Midland Bank for more than a quarter of a million pounds but was only awarded £5,000.

The plaintiff was an engineer who was hoping to contract with a nationalised concern in Manitoba. In order to gain the contract, he sought finance from the Midland Bank where he already had an overdraft of some £20,000. At a meeting with the branch manager he was assured that the finance would be forthcoming subject only to insurance from the Export Credit Guarantee Department and approval from the Head Office, but the manager also advised that there would be no difficulty concerning either of these. On the faith of these assurances, the plaintiff proceeded to extend his overdraft and mortgaged his own house to the bank as security. The loan failed to materialise because the Export Credit Guarantee Department would not give approval.

1 [1979] 2 Lloyd's Rep 391; 1981 1 Lloyd's Rep 434.

7.70 The plaintiff argued that the advice given had been negligent and that as a result he had not only borrowed more money but he had also lost the large profit which would have accrued from the Canadian contract. Lloyd J found that the advice had been negligent, and that as a result the plaintiff had overdrawn an additional £5,000, an amount for which the bank was liable since it was an obvious consequence of the negligent advice. However, the other damages claimed by the plaintiff, and in particular the benefits of the Manitoba contract were too remote to be recoverable unless it could be shown that the banker knew or should have known of the details of the business arrangements.

7.71 In the absence of special knowledge, the banker has no duty to consider the taxation aspects of transactions. In *Schioler v Westminster Bank*[1] the plaintiff was a foreigner who was resident in England. Under the taxation laws in force at the time, she was not liable for income tax on any foreign dividends provided only that they were not received in the United Kingdom. In order to prevent this from happening, she opened an account with the defendant bank at the Guernsey branch. As a shareholder in a Malaysian company, she instructed that company to send her dividends to the Guernsey branch. For several years this arrangement proved satisfactory because the company remitted dividends in sterling. However, in mid 1968, the company began sending dividend warrants expressed in Malaysian dollars. There were no facilities in Guernsey for negotiating foreign currency drafts, and the defendant bank sent the draft to the branch office in England in accordance with the normal practice. The sum was subjected to a deduction of UK income tax and the Guernsey account credited only with the net sum.

1 [1970] 2 QB 719.

7.72 The plaintiff claimed the bank to be liable for performing the contract negligently. The Court dismissed the claim, Mocatta J saying:

Unless special arrangements were made with a customer or special instructions given by him, bankers could not, in discharge of their contractual duties in crediting an account with a dividend, be obliged to consider the tax implications to the customer or consult him before acting in accordance with their ordinary practice. To hold a bank obliged to do this would come near to holding that a bank must gratuitously give its customers tax advice. To take such a view would be to place an impossible and unreasonable burden on the banks generally.[1]

1 At p 728.

Knowledge of special circumstances

7.73 There are, however, circumstances which should alert the banker that the customer's interest will be prejudiced by certain transactions. The duty of the banker in these circumstances is, at the minimum, to make inquiries to clarify the customer's wishes. The duty may extend to questioning a properly drawn mandate from the customer. Two cases illustrate the scope of the duty, both involving the account of a company customer.

7.74 In *Selangor United Rubber Estates v Cradock (No 3)*[1] a company bank account was used to facilitate a fraudulent purchase of the company by means of using the company's own funds. In the 1960s there were a number of companies which found themselves with no business to conduct following the withdrawal of England from her former colonies. In such a situation, the company could be wound up and the assets distributed among the shareholders, but it was found that it was often slightly more profitable to sell the company as a "shell". Unfortunately, such a practice permitted the kind of fraud which was practiced in the *Selangor* case.

1 [1968] 2 All ER 1073.

7.75 Cradock had made a "takeover bid" for the company and had obtained control of 79% of the stock by making a bid of some £195,000. Cradock did not have the money to pay, but had devised a scheme whereby his agents would be elected chairman of the board of the company; following that, they could draw cheques on the company account. But in order to become chairman of the board, it was necessary to pay for the 79% interest.

7.76 As part of the takeover deal, Selangor's banker, National, drew two bank drafts totalling some £232,000 in favour of the District Bank which was Cradock's banker. The funds were to be placed in a new account in the name of the company. Directors of the plaintiff company who were working in concert with Cradock drew a cheque for almost the entire sum in favour of Woodstock Trust (with which Cradock was closely related) by way of loan; Woodstock then loaned the required sum to Cradock who paid for the shares with it. Cradock thus gained control of the company and its assets by means of using the company's own assets in contravention of s 54 of the Companies Act[1] and in breach of the duty which a director owes to the company and its shareholders.

1 The English equivalent of s 62 of the Companies Act 1955.

7.77 The fraud could not have occurred were it not for the act of the District Bank in honouring the cheque drawn in favour of Woodstock, a cheque which was obviously drawn by Cradock for purposes which were not in the best interests of the company. The Court held that the bank should have known that the transaction was not in the customer's, ie, Selangor's, best interest and should have queried the transaction. Note that this is so even though the cheque in question was properly signed by directors of the company who were authorised to sign cheques.[1]

1 Although the authority to sign cheques was, of course, restricted to those cheques which were appropriate company business.

7.78 On almost identical facts, Brightman J found the defendant bank to be liable both for breach of contract and as constructive trustee in *Karak Rubber Ltd v Burden (No 2).*[1]

1 [1972] 1 WLR 602; see 8.38 for a discussion of the trust aspects of the two cases.

7.79 In both cases the Court emphasised that although the bank was obliged to pay a cheque which was in proper form and backed by adequate funds, it did not follow that the duty was an unqualified duty to pay without inquiry. The bank is under a contractual duty to exercise such care and skill as would be exercised by a reasonable banker, a duty which included a duty to make inquiries in appropriate circumstances. In both cases, the Court indicated that the circumstances surrounding the drawing of the cheque were so out of the ordinary course of business that a reasonable banker would have been placed on notice.

7.80 Brightman J noted that it was open to the banker to show that such inquiries would have yielded no useful information or would have produced answers which would have been acceptable to the reasonable banker. This is undoubtedly correct since if the answers would have been acceptable then the losses suffered by the customers would not have flowed from the breach of contract. Note that this is an entirely different question from that of the "useless inquiry" when the bank is seeking a defence to an action in conversion, for in that situation, the bank is attempting to bring itself within the ambit of a statutory defence.

1 See 15.79 for a discussion of the "useless inquiry" when attempting to establish a defence under s 5 of the Cheques Act 1960.

7.81 The precise scope of the *Selangor* duty is far from clear, but at the very least the banker should make inquiries if asked to pay cheques drawn on a company account by directors if there is any suspicion that the money is to be channelled to uses other than those for which the directors are authorised. The *Selangor* and *Karak* cases have been criticised as placing too great a burden on the banker, a matter which will be discussed below.[1]

1 See 8.41.

7.82 Whatever the scope of the *Selangor* duty, it is a difficult one for the banker since it creates a situation in which the banker is subjected to the pressures of two conflicting duties. On the one hand, there is an obligation to pay on demand a cheque which is properly drawn and for which there are adequate funds. On the other, there is a duty to delay payment and to make inquiries if the circumstances are such as to raise doubts in the mind of a reasonable banker. It should be noted, however, that the circumstances in both cases were very unusual and that the sums involved were quite large.

Duties to third parties

7.83 As will be seen below,[1] a banker has a duty to certain third parties who are beneficiaries of trust accounts. We have already noted the duty of the banker which is owed to strangers to be careful when giving banker's references and in Ch 19 it will be suggested that a banker may owe a duty to third parties when those parties are payees in a direct debit or a direct credit transfer.[2] In these and other situations the duty of a banker to third parties would appear to be governed by ordinary tort principles. One recent case will illustrate the point.

1 See 8.13ff.
2 See 19.68 and also *HH Dimond (Rotorua 1966) Ltd v ANZ Banking Group* [1979] 2 NZLR 739.

7.84 In *Johns Period Furniture v Commonwealth Savings Bank of Australia*[1] blank bank cheque forms were stolen during a burglary of the North Adelaide post office in early February 1979. The defendant bank did not learn of the loss until about a month later. They took no steps to give any public warning about the cheque forms. In early May one of the cheque forms with a forged signature was given to the plaintiff to pay for goods. The bank refused to pay the cheque and the plaintiff brought an action in negligence claiming that the bank owed a duty to traders in the area to warn of the stolen cheques. The Court rejected the claim on the basis that the plaintiff was not a member of any clearly ascertained class as required by the decision of the High Court in *Caltex Oil (Australia) Pty Ltd v The Dredge "Willemstad"*.[2]

1 [1981] 24 SASR 224.
2 (1976) 136 CLR 529.

7.85 The Court particularly relied upon a quote from Gibbs J:

In my opinion it is still right to say that as a general rule damages are not recoverable for economic loss which is not consequential upon injury to the plaintiff's person or property. The fact that the loss was foreseeable is not enough to make it recoverable. However, there are exceptional cases in which the defendant has knowledge or means of knowledge that the plaintiff individually and not merely as a member of an unascertained class, will be likely to suffer economic loss as a consequence of his negligence, and owes the plaintiff duty to take care not to cause him such loss by his negligent act.[1]

1 At p 555.

Safe custody

7.86 Although not strictly speaking a duty of the banker, the taking of goods and documents for safe keeping is a banking service which is at least as old as the modern business of banking itself. It is the original ancillary service offered by bankers to their customers and it offers the oldest examples of the problems of defining the duty of a banker to the customer.

7.87 When valuable chattels are deposited for safe keeping, it is customary for the customer to deposit them with the banker in a locked box and for the customer to retain the key. Documents will ordinarily be placed in a sealed envelope by the customer.

Bailment

7.88 The law which defines the duty of the banker to the customer in such circumstances is a part of the law of bailment. The banker is the bailee of the goods or documents and the bailor is the customer. The essence of bailment is that the goods are deposited by the bailor with the bailee on the condition that they will be returned to the bailor in due course.

7.89 The problems that might arise with a bailment fall substantially into two categories. First, the goods might be damaged or lost while in the custody of the bailee. Secondly, the bailee might deliver the goods to the wrong person, either inadvertently or as the result of the fraudulent conduct of a servant.

7.90 In the first case, that of damage or loss, the bailee is liable to the bailor only if there has been some negligence in the keeping of the goods. However, from a very early time the law recognised that there is a wide range of circumstances in which a bailment might arise and that the standard of care required of the bailor should vary accordingly. For example, a neighbour who, as a favour, agrees to store a household item while the bailor is on holiday is as much a bailee of that item as the banker who agrees to receive very valuable items and keep them in the bank's strongroom. Yet, the average person would certainly expect very different standards of care of these two bailees.

7.91 The distinction which was drawn by the law was that between a bailee who charged for the service provided, called a bailment for reward, and the bailee who performed the service without reward, called a gratuitous bailment. Much of the discussion to be found in some case law and texts concerns the question of whether a banker who takes goods or documents for safe custody is a bailee for reward even when there is no direct charge made for the service. For reasons which will become apparent, it is thought that the distinction is no longer relevant for a banker since the standard of care required is special to the situation of the banker.

Standard of care

7.92 The first case to consider the standard of care applicable to banker bailees was *Giblin v McMullen*.[1] A customer left a box containing debentures with the bank for safe custody. The box was stored in the strong room of the bank together with boxes belonging to other customers and other securities belonging to the bank. Customers had access to the room during banking hours but were at all times accompanied by a bank clerk. The room had two iron doors which were opened by separate keys. These keys were in the charge of the cashier by day and at night one of them was left with the cashier and the other with another officer of the bank. The cashier of the bank took the debentures from the box and used them for his own purposes.

Surprisingly, the Supreme Court of Victoria and the Privy Council held that the bank had not been negligent since the bank was a gratuitous bailee and was not bound to exercise more than ordinary care.

1 (1868) LR 2 PC 317.

7.93 *Giblin's* case has been extensively criticised. There appeared to be no serious consideration of the vicarious liability of the bank, as bailee, for its servant's action, nor as a principal for the fraud of an agent acting within the scope of employment.[1] Further, although the Court held that there was no actionable negligence, the jury found expressly that the bank had been grossly negligent. In his discussion of the case, Chorley notes that " . . . it may be doubted whether the decision would be the same at the present time".[2]

1 See *Morris v Martin & Sons Ltd* [1966] 1 QB 735; *Lloyd v Grace Smith & Co* [1912] AC 716.
2 At p 246.

7.94 *Giblin's* case was distinguished in *Re United Service Co, Johnston's Claim*.[1] Johnston owned railway shares which he deposited with a banker for safe keeping. They were stolen by the manager who obtained a transfer of the shares to his own name by means of several forgeries of Johnston's signature. When Johnston learned of the transfer, he brought a suit against the railway company and succeeded in having the shares re-transferred to him, but he did not receive any costs in the action. The banker went into liquidation and Johnston sought to prove for the amount of his costs in the action.

The Court held that the banker was a bailee for reward, distinguishing *Giblin* on the basis that the banker here had received a small commission for the safe keeping of the shares. The Court also found that the banker had been negligent, but the loss claimed by Johnston was too remote.

1 (1870) 6 Ch App 212.

7.95 If the distinction between a gratuitous bailment and a bailment for reward is still relevant, then there can be little doubt that the modern banker will be a bailee for reward since a fee is invariably charged for the safe custody service. It seems more likely however that the distinction is not relevant and that the standard is that of a reasonable banker in view of all the surrounding circumstances.

Wrongful delivery to a third person

7.96 The standard of care required of the bailee in the second circumstance, that of delivering the goods to the wrong person, is on a very much different footing, for although the standard of care to be exercised in taking care of the goods might vary with the circumstances of the bailment, the very minimum required of any bailee is that the goods be returned to the correct person. Consequently, there is a very strict duty on the bailee to return the goods to the correct person. Delivery to the wrong person will result in liability in an action for conversion. In such an action, it does not matter that the wrongful delivery was made honestly and without negligence.

7.97 This problem of delivery to the wrong person is not as rare as might be thought, for when the goods are deposited in joint names or in the name of a company or a partnership, it might be difficult for the banker to establish the right of some particular person to claim re-delivery. When goods are being deposited in such circumstances, it is of the utmost importance for the banker to obtain express instructions concerning the identity of those who are authorised to collect the goods.

Chapter 8

The Account I

*Nature of current account — Overdraft account — Trust accounts —
Responsibilities to beneficiary — Tracing and third party claims —
Appropriation — Combination*

Nature of the current account

8.1 There is no precise definition of a current account even though
the vast majority of banking transactions, both by number and by
volume, are those which are through a current account. Chorley
says that

> The principal feature of such an account is the fact that the customer
> gets his money repaid from it, or any advances which he is receiving
> from his banker by way of loan; and this is so whether the repayment
> is to himself or to a third party.[1]

1 Chorley, p 167.

8.2 Indeed, probably the salient feature of the current account is
that it may be used for third party payments by means of the
cheque. Traditionally the account has been non-interest bearing,
but recent increases in competition between banks and other
financial institutions are making inroads into this tradition both
in New Zealand and overseas.

8.3 The basic nature of a current account raises some legal
problems. Since money is from time to time deposited into the
account and, at the same time, regularly drawn upon by cheques,
it is sometimes necessary to determine which of several competing
claims will have priority when the account is not sufficient to satisfy
all. The starting point for the discussion is *Clayton's case*.[1]Clayton

had a current account with a firm of bankers in which the accounts were kept in the ordinary way, that is, transactions were recorded chronologically. One of the bankers died and the bank soon afterward failed. At the time of the partner's death, Clayton's account was in credit some £1,700, ie, the firm of bankers owed him that amount of money. Between the time of the death and the failure of the firm, Clayton had continued to operate the account, drawing out more than the sum which had stood to his credit, but paying in an even larger sum than that withdrawn.

1 *Devaynes v Noble, Clayton's case* (1816) 1 Mer 529, 572; 35 ER 767, 781.

8.4 The issue in the case was whether or not Clayton could recover anything from the estate of the deceased partner. If the drawings and deposits which occurred after the death could be treated separately, then the debt of £1,700 was owed to Clayton jointly and severally by all of the partners and he could recover. If, however, the deposits had the effect of extinguishing by repayment the earlier debt, then Clayton could only prove in bankruptcy.

8.5 The Court held that each payment in went to pay off the earliest payment out. During the course of the judgment, Sir William Grant MR said:

> . . . this is the case of a banking account, where all the sums paid in form one blended fund, the parts of which have no longer any distinct existence. Neither banker nor customer ever think of saying, "this draft is to be placed to the account of the £500 paid in on Monday, and this other to the account of the £500 paid in on Tuesday". There is a fund of £1,000 to draw upon, and that is enough. In such a case, there is no room for any other appropriation than that which arises from the order in which the receipts and payments take place, and are carried into the account. Presumably, it is the sum first paid in, that is first drawn out. It is the first item on the debit side of the account, that is discharged, or reduced, by the first item on the credit side. The appropriation is made by the very act of setting the two items against each other. Upon that principle, all accounts current are settled, and particularly cash accounts.[1]

1 (1816) 1 Mer 529, 608; 35 ER 781, 783.

8.6 The reference to appropriation is to the right of the debtor to determine which debt is to be discharged or reduced by a payment to a creditor when the creditor is one in respect of more than one debt.[1]

1 See *Deeley v Lloyds Bank Ltd* [1912] AC 756 and the discussion at 8.57.

8.7 *Clayton's case* has been described as a presumption rather than a rule of law. In the case of *In re Diplock*,[1] it was said that the rule in *Clayton's case* is a "rule of convenience based upon so-called intention". In the same case, Lord Greene MR said that the rule does not extend beyond the case of a bank account, but that proposition should be considered with caution since the rule has in fact been applied to running accounts where neither of the parties is a banker.

1 [1948] Ch 465, 554.

8.8 The rule only applies when there is a current account between the parties. It does not apply when the accounts rendered make it clear that the creditor intended to reserve the right to appropriate the payment to a different account. Finally, it is said that the rule does not apply to transactions which are effected on the same day, for in that case, the order of the transactions in the books is wholly accidental.[1] Even though the Tasmanian case *In re Laughton*[2] followed this "same day" exception to the rule in *Clayton's case*, it may not necessarily be a general exception. After all, it is still necessary to appropriate the payments to the discharge of some obligation, and the rule in *Clayton's case* is not illogical if the parties have expressed no actual or implied intention as to appropriation.

1 Per Lord Halsbury LC in *The Mecca* [1897] AC 286.
2 [1962] Tas SR 300.

8.9 Thus, in *Laughton's* case, a solicitor had become a bankrupt and the issue in the case concerned the trust account which contained money belonging to clients. The rule in *Clayton's case* was applied in order to determine the order in which the money belonging to various clients had been withdrawn, but concerning entries on any one day, the order of the entries was said not to be relevant. Consequently, if the balance was insufficient to meet the claims of these clients, their claims were met on a basis of proportionality. In the circumstances of the case, this seems like a fair enough division of the account, but it can scarcely be said to be any more logical than the rule in *Clayton's case*. The departure from the rule could have been justified by an appeal to the presumed intention of the parties, rather than elevating to a general principle that some other rule of appropriation necessarily applies when the transactions are same day.

8.10 The rule does not operate so as to affect the rights of third parties. The classic example is a trustee who has mixed his own money with that which he holds on trust. The presumption then is that any money withdrawn by the trustee is the money of the trustee, not that of the beneficial owner.[1]

1 See *Re Hallett's Estate* (1880) 13 Ch D 696.

Overdraft account

8.11 It is possible for a current account to have a debit balance; when that is the case, it is called an overdraft. It is still a common method of bank lending to meet business credit needs.

When the overdraft is intended to be for a relatively long term, it will be customary for the banker to take a security interest from the customer. The use of overdrafts for lending and the taking of securities is discussed in Chs 23 and 24.

8.12 There are often informal overdrafts which are not secured and may not even be arranged ahead of time. Although the banker is not bound to pay a cheque if there are insufficient funds in the account, he or she may choose to do so. The drawing of a cheque by the customer when there are insufficient funds to meet it is an implied request to the banker to grant overdraft facilities.[1] It would seem in such a circumstance that the banker is entitled to charge interest even if no formal arrangements have been made.[2]

1 *Cuthbert v Robarts, Lubbock & Co* [1909] 2 Ch 226.
2 At least simple interest: *Deutsche Bank v Banque des Marchands de Moscou* (1931) 4 LDAB 293; and probably compound interest according to the commercial custom of the time: *National Bank of Australasia v United Hand in Hand Band of Hope Co* (1879) 4 App Cas 391, 409.

Trust accounts

Definition of a trust account

8.13 A trust account is an account which is held by one party who is bound by law to exercise his or her rights over the account for the benefit of some other person or persons. The person who holds the account is known as the trustee and the person for whose benefit it is held is the beneficiary or cestui que trust. There are also certain circumstances where the person holding the account is not strictly speaking a trustee, but there is nevertheless a duty similar to that owed by a trustee arising in favour of some other person. Such a duty is known as a fiduciary duty and may arise in a variety of circumstances.

8.14 An example of a trustee-like relationship is an agency relationship. The situation was described by Lord Cottenham in *Foley v Hill:*[1]

Partaking of the character of a trustee, the [agent] — as the trustee for the particular matter in which he is employed as [agent] — sells the principal's goods, and accounts to him for the money. The goods, however, remain the goods of the owner or principal until the sale takes place, and the moment that money is received the money remains the property of the principal. So it is with regard to an agent dealing with any property; he obtains no interest himself in the subject-matter beyond his remuneration; he is dealing throughout for another, and though he is not a trustee according to the strict technical meaning of the word, he is quasi a trustee for that particular transaction for which he is engaged . . . .

1 (1848) 2 HLC 28, 35.

8.15 The reason that trust accounts are important to the banker is that the banker owes certain duties of care to the beneficiary. As regards the relationship between the account holder and the banker and between the banker and the third party, there is no reason to distinguish between trustees properly so called and those who owe a fiduciary duty similar to that of a trustee. All cases will be referred to as trust accounts.

8.16 There is one common case that bankers must be aware of, namely, that of executors and administrators of deceased estates. Such people are not initially trustees, but they become so after the completion of their administrative duties if they are still holding property to be distributed to survivors of the deceased. Weaver and Cragie suggest that bankers should treat all such accounts as trust accounts since the banker has no way of knowing when an executor or administrator has been converted into a trustee.[1]

1 Weaver and Cragie, *The Law Relating to Banker and Customer in Australia*, Sydney, 1975, p 109.

Trust accounts and the banker

8.17 When an account is headed "trust account", there is little difficulty in fixing the banker with knowledge that the account is indeed a trust account. The real problems arise when the account is not described as a trust account, but where the banker learns that the customer holds some or all of the money in the account on trust.

8.18 When the account is described in other terms, the question is whether the facts are such that the banker should have been aware that the funds were held in trust. In one of the leading cases, *Re Gross, ex parte Kingston*,[1] a county treasurer had two accounts at the bank, one of which was headed "Police Account". The Court held that the heading on the account, together with the knowledge that the treasurer was a public official, was sufficient to make it clear to the bank that the account was a trust account.

1 (1871) 6 Ch App 632.

Responsibilities to the beneficiary

8.19 Once the banker knows that the account is a trust account, it is necessary to bear in mind several conflicting duties which can make the banker's lot an unhappy one. On the one hand, it is beyond question that there is a duty owed to the beneficiary. On the other hand, it is equally beyond question that the banker owes the customer the usual duty to honour cheques. Undue zeal in pursuing one of these duties will lead inexorably to a breach of the other.

8.20 The precise scope of the duty owed to the beneficiary is far from clear. It is said that the banker does not have a duty to supervise the account, but the cases are not always easy to reconcile. Although the business of banking exposes the banker to circumstances which are unique, it seems that the duty of a banker with regard to trust funds is the same as that of any other person. There are, broadly speaking, two situations in which the banker may be liable to the beneficial owner of the account. The first is when the banker receives a benefit, usually a payment or a reduction in an overdraft of the customer, from the trust account with the knowledge that the benefit is trust property. The second is when the banker knowingly assists in the misappropriation of the trust property whether or not receiving any direct benefit as a result. The first is often referred to as "knowing receipt", the second as "knowing assistance".

Knowing receipt

8.21 Merely receiving money from an account which may be a trust account or even from an account which the banker knows is used for the deposit of trust funds is not enough to fix the banker with liability if the banker does not know that the money is a part of the trust fund.

8.22 In *Thomson v Clydesdale Bank Ltd*[1] a stockbroker deposited into his own account a cheque payable to himself which represented the proceeds of sale of shares sold on behalf of clients. The clients had instructed the broker to pay the proceeds into certain other banks, so the action by the stockbroker was a breach of his fiduciary duty to his customers. At the time of the deposit, the broker's account was overdrawn. The broker became insolvent and his clients claimed to be entitled to have the amount of the cheque repaid to them by the bank.

The bank was aware that the cheque represented the proceeds of the sale of shares but did not know whether the money was in the brokers's hands as agent or otherwise. Lord Herschell LC said:

> No doubt if the person receiving the money has reason to believe that the payment is being made in fraud of a third person, and that the person making the payment is handing over in discharge of his debt money which he has no right to hand over, then the person taking such

payment would not be entitled to retain the money, upon ordinary principles which I need not dwell upon.[2]

1 [1893] AC 282.
2 At p 288.

8.23 There was no evidence in the case that the banker had reason to believe that the money was being improperly dealt with. The mere fact that the customer was a stockbroker and that the cheque represented proceeds from the sale of shares was not sufficient to fix the bank with liability, for it is well known that a broker may make advances to his clients in anticipation of the amounts that will be received from the sale of shares. In such a case, it would be perfectly legitimate for the broker to pay the cheque into his own account.

8.24 It is not necessary for the banker to make inquiries as to the title of the money being paid into the account. Indeed, Lord Herschell also said:

> It cannot, I think, be questioned that under ordinary circumstances a person, be he banker or other, who takes money from his debtor in discharge of a debt is not bound to inquire into the manner in which the person so paying the debt acquired the money with which he pays it. However that money may have been acquired by the person making the payment, the person taking that payment is entitled to retain it in discharge of the debt which is due to him.[1]

1 At p 287.

Type of knowledge required

8.25 The type of knowledge which is required to fix liability was considered in *Westpac v Savin*.[1] A company called Aqua Marine carried on a business of selling boats. It was found as a fact that three out of four boats sold were sold by Aqua Marine acting as agents on behalf of individual non-commercial boat owners. One of the boats sold belonged to Savin. Proceeds from the sale of the boat were paid by Aqua Marine into its trading account with Westpac at a time when the company was in difficulties and its account was heavily overdrawn. Savin claimed to be entitled to recover the amount from Westpac, arguing that Westpac knew that the money was held by Aqua Marine on trust for the owner of the boat.

1 [1985] 2 NZLR 41.

8.26 There were actually two facts which were required in order for the plaintiff to win:
(1) that the bank "knew" that the money it received was the property of the plaintiff and

(2) that the payment of the money into the overdrawn account of Aqua Marine was a breach of fiduciary duty on that company's part.

8.27 The Court cited with approval a judgment of Peter Gibson J in *Baden, Delvaux and Lecuit v Societe Generale pour Favouriser le Developpement du commerce et de l'Industrie en France SAF*[1] where he itemised five separate types of knowledge:

(1) actual knowledge;

(2) knowledge which is obtainable but for shutting one's eyes to the obvious;

(3) knowledge obtainable but for wilfully and recklessly failing to make such inquiries as an honest and reasonable person would make;

(4) knowledge of circumstances which would indicate the facts to an honest and reasonable person; and

(5) knowledge obtainable from inquiries which an honest and reasonable person would feel obliged to make, being put on inquiry as a result of his or her knowledge of suspicious circumstances.

1 [1983] BCLC 325.

8.28 Applying this classification to the facts of the present case, Richardson J said:

> While the bank would or might not have known in respect of a particular banking whether it was in respect of a boat sold ex stock or as agent for a principal, it knew throughout that 3 out of 4 sales were in the latter category. That actual knowledge of the bank was such that in receiving those cheques and applying them in reduction of the overdraft it must be concluded that it wilfully shut its eyes to the obvious (type 2 knowledge) or, at least, that it wilfully and recklessly failed to ascertain and satisfy itself that the receipts were not in respect of "on behalf" sales (type 3 knowledge). The only reasonable conclusion is that it had constructive notice of the breach of fiduciary duty on the part of Aqua Marine and must account to the plaintiffs for their property.[1]

1 At p 54.

8.29 Richardson J, although noting that it was not strictly necessary in the present case, expressed the view that "knowledge" of any of the five types would serve to fix the bank with liability in the case where the bank has received money which is subject to a fiduciary duty.

8.30 The knowledge required, regardless of the category into which it falls, must be knowledge of an actual trust, not a claimed one. In *Carl Zeiss Stiftung v Herbert Smith & Co (No 2)*[1] an organisation referred to as the "East German foundation" commenced an action against a group known as the "West German foundation" claiming that property in England which belonged to the West German foundation was held on trust for them. The claim was by no means clear, but depended upon many disputed issues of both fact and of law. The solicitors for the West German foundation had received payments for costs and disbursements. These payments were made from the funds which the East German foundation claimed to be trust funds. The solicitors were, of course, fully aware of the allegations concerning the fund.

The East German foundation then brought the current action against the solicitors, claiming that they were constructive trustees of the amounts which they had received from the fund. The English Court of Appeal held that the action failed, since the knowledge was of an alleged trust only. It was said that notice of a "doubtful equity" could not be equated with notice of a trust.

1 [1969] 2 Ch 276.

Knowing assistance

8.31 The "knowing assistance" class of cases is more difficult for the banker, partly because of the uncertainty of what must be "known" and partly because if the banker is found liable the result is more serious than merely returning a benefit which had been previously received.

8.32 Perhaps the clearest statement of the difference between the two classes of case is that of Jacobs P in the New South Wales Court of Appeal in *DPC Estates Pty Ltd v Grey & Consul Development Pty Ltd*:[1]

> The point of difference between the person receiving trust property and the person who is made liable, even though he is not actually a recipient of trust property is that in the first place knowledge, actual or constructive, of the trust is sufficient, but in the second place ["knowing assistance"] something more is required, and that something more appears to me to be the actual knowledge of the fraudulent or dishonest design, so that the person concerned can truly be described as a participant in that fraudulent dishonest activity.[2]

The decision of the Court of Appeal in the *DPC Estates* case was overturned by the High Court of Australia[3] on the grounds that the plaintiff had not established that the defendant had actual, as opposed to constructive, knowledge.

1 [1974] 1 NSWLR 443.
2 At p 459.
3 *Consul Development Pty Ltd v DPC Estates Ltd* (1975) 132 CLR 373.

8.33 This basic principle was established in *Barnes v Addy*[1] where the plaintiff attempted to shift losses to solicitors who advised trustees. The Court noted that the basic principle is that:

> A stranger who acts as the agent of a trustee in a transaction legally within his power, but which leads to a breach of trust, is not to be held responsible as a constructive trustee unless some of the property passes into his hands, or unless he is cognisant of a dishonest design on the part of the trustee.[2]

1 (1874) 9 Ch App 244.
2 From the headnote.

8.34 The reason as explained by Lord Selborne LC is that no one could "safely discharge the office of solicitor, of banker, or of agent of any sort to trustees" if the principles were disregarded.[1]

1 At p 252.

8.35 When the banker knows that the account is a trust account, the obligation of the banker to be on guard against dishonest design appears to be relatively high. In *Rowlandson v National Westminster Bank*[1] the plaintiffs' grandmother had drawn four cheques for £500 each one in favour of each of the plaintiffs. These were deposited with the Curzon street branch of the defendant bank. Neither the grandmother, the children nor their father had an account at that branch, but the grandmother was well known there and had an account at another branch of the bank.

Apparently on the initiative of a bank officer, an account was opened with the £2,000 in the names of the plaintiffs' uncles A and G who had accounts at the branch. The grandmother died a few weeks later. Shortly thereafter A who knew of the account, used a form from another cheque-book to draw on the account in order to pay for some shares. Later he withdrew the remainder of the sum. The plaintiffs never received any benefit from the money. They sought to recover the sum from the bank.

1 [1978] 1 WLR 798.

8.36 It was argued that the effect of the grandmother leaving the cheques at the bank was such as to make the bank itself a trustee of the gift, either under an express trust or, alternatively, an implied trust. The Court rejected these arguments, holding that there could be no inference from the grandmother's actions that the bank was made a trustee under an express trust or had become a trustee under a constructive trust. The defendant received the cheques solely in their capacity as bankers.

However, the bank had actual knowledge that the account was a trust account. Consequently, even though the bank itself was not a trustee, they owed the plaintiff a fiduciary duty and so would be liable if they assisted with knowledge in a fraudulent and dishonest design on the part of a trustee. Applying the objective standard of a reasonable banker, the Court held that the drawing of a cheque in favour of a stockbroker did not of itself give notice to the bank that there was fraud but the use of cheque forms from another account should have made a reasonable banker question or prevent the withdrawal of the money. Consequently, the bank was liable for the entire £2,000.

8.37 The Court also gave some attention to the type of evidence which had been placed before it in the case, noting with heavy humour:

> there was also a great deal of evidence to suggest that I should have regard to the fact that no banker, or nobody in the bank, could possibly make a mistake or do anything wrong.[1]

1 At p 809.

Type of knowledge required

8.38 If there is an additional fact which must be "known" by the banker in the "knowing assistance" case, then which type of "knowledge" must be shown? It is necessary to examine some of the cases to determine what precisely it is that the banker might need to "know" in order that it can be said that he or she can truly be described as a participant in that fraudulent dishonest activity.

8.39 In *Selangor United Rubber Estates v Cradock (No3)*[1] the company's account was used to facilitate a fraudulent purchase of the company by means of using the company's own funds.[2] The fraud could not have occurred were it not for the act of the District Bank in honouring the cheque drawn in favour of Woodstock, a cheque which was obviously drawn by Cradock in breach of trust. So the District Bank is a second category type of person, that is, one who has assisted in the dishonest and fraudulent design on the part of the trustee. Ungoed-Thomas J noted that in order to succeed against the District Bank that the plaintiff must prove three things: (1) assistance by a stranger; (2) with knowledge; (3) in a dishonest and fraudulent design on the part of the trustee. The only point really in contention was (2), did the District Bank have "knowledge" of the dishonest and fraudulent design of Cradock?

The Court held that the Woodstock cheque was paid in circumstances known to District before that payment and in which a reasonable banker would have concluded that the payment was to finance the purchase by Cradock of the stock in the plaintiff.

1 [1968] 2 All ER 1073.
2 See 7.73 for a fuller discussion of the facts.

8.40 The degree of knowledge required was described as follows:

> . . . knowledge of circumstances which would indicate to an honest reasonable man that such a design was being committed or would put him on inquiry, which the stranger [the District Bank] failed to make, whether it was being committed.

8.41 The decision is criticised in *Paget* (9th ed p 225ff). There it is said that:

> [t]o most bank officers no skill (in banking) or care would have prevented them in this case from obeying their mandate nor could they reasonably have done so. The standard set by the learned Judge virtually demands an understanding of finance and the disposition of a detective. It is submitted that this decision places an impossibly high burden on a bank not to be negligent, in requiring its officers to be expert in finance as well as in banking.[1]

1 At p 225.

8.42 Whether that is correct or not must surely depend upon the type of bank officer who was dealing with the account. If it was an officer of a small branch, then that is certainly correct, but it is certainly not obvious that a commercial banker at a commercial branch of the bank would have found the situation so complicated to understand. After all, in modern banking such a banker would not only understand company takeovers, but would undoubtedly be offering to advise and, in the proper circumstances, to assist in the financing of such matters.

8.43 A second criticism offered by *Paget* is that prior to the *Selangor* case,

> a paying banker was not called upon to consider whether or not he should comply with his mandate and it may be thought to be a dangerous departure to require him in the face of a clear instruction to weigh up the facts of a situation having in mind a possible breaching of his contract.[1]

1 At p 225.

8.44 This observation appears to be incorrect. One of the classic cases concerning trust accounts is *Bodenham v Hoskyn*[1] where a receiver was appointed to collect rents and profits of an estate which belonged to the plaintiff. The collector had a private account with the defendant banker and also opened an account as receiver. He then drew a cheque on the trust account and paid it into his private account, later absconding with the funds. The Court held that the plaintiff was entitled to recover from the banker. It is hard to see why the mandate in *Hoskyn's* case is any less of a "clear instruction" than that in *Selangor*.

1 (1852) 2 De G M 903.

8.45 The *Selangor* case caused a lot of consternation among bankers and there was a sense of relief when the Court of Appeal handed down its decision in *Carl Zeiss Stiftung v Herbert Smith & C (No 2)*,[1] for it was widely interpreted as mitigating the perceived harshness of the *Selangor* case. But in *Karak Rubber Co Ltd v Burden (No 2)*,[2] Brightman J agreed entirely with the conclusions of the *Selangor* case. The facts of *Karak* were virtually identical with those of *Selangor*; Brightman J concluded that the *Carl Zeiss* case was not in conflict with *Selangor*. He explained *Carl Zeiss* on the grounds mentioned above, that there the notice was only of an alleged trust.

1 [1969] 2 Ch 276.
2 [1972] 1 All ER 1210.

8.46 The "knowing assistance" class of case was also considered in *Westpac v Savin*,[1] but with inconclusive results. The Court clearly indicated that the *Savin* case was not one of "knowing assistance", so the statements are, strictly speaking, obiter. Even so, only Richardson J made a reasonably clear and unequivocal statement concerning the type of knowledge which is required to fix liability.

1 [1985] 2 NZLR 41.

8.47 As regards the second category type of case, Sir Clifford Richmond indicated that "my present view is . . . strongly in favour of that which has been taken by the Court of Appeal in England".[1] He said:

> In principle I cannot see any adequate justification for excluding categories (4) and (5) at least in the "knowing receipt" class of case . . . .

It is not clear from his judgment if he would extend the same consideration to the second class, "knowing assistance" or not.
McMullin J said:

> I agree with their analyses of [the cases on constructive trust] and am content to state in relatively short form what I perceive to be the principles to be distilled from the cases . . . .5 A banker as a stranger to a trust becomes a constructive trustee if he has knowledge of circumstances that would put an honest, reasonable man on inquiry.

For the last proposition, he cites *Paget*, pp 91,92 and Peter Gibson J in the case mentioned above. But it is not wholly clear that he is talking about the "knowing assistance" category of cases.

1 Semble, in *Belmont Finance Ltd v Williams Furniture Ltd (No 2)* [1980] 1 All ER 393.

8.48 There have been some doubts as to the position of agents of trustees, the suggestion being that they may be in some way specially privileged when compared with those who deal as strangers with trustees. Sir Clifford Richmond suggested in the *Savin* case that this might be so in cases where agents act in relation to trust property purely in their capacity as agents. He said:

> So it can be argued that an agent who receives trust funds from the trustee will be within the first category ["knowing receipt"] only if he is setting up a title of his own to the funds which he has received and is not acting as a mere depository or . . . merely as a channel through which money is passed to other persons.

8.49 This would, of course, be relevant to the banker who is collecting a cheque for his customer when the customer is acting in breach of trust, but can be of no assistance to the banker who receives trust funds in reduction of an overdraft or to the banker who knowingly assists in the misappropriation of the account funds.

Tracing moneys in the account: third party claims

8.50 There are circumstances where there is no question of the banker being directly liable as constructive trustee but where there is a claim by a third party that the money in the account actually belongs to them and not to the customer of the bank. There are procedures which may be followed by the claimant to "trace" the money into the account in certain circumstances. These procedures are of only marginal interest to the banker in the ordinary course of things, since the dispute is really between the customer and the third party. In such a case, the usual course for the banker is to avoid the dispute entirely by interpleading, that is, paying the money into Court and leaving the customer and third party to fight it out.

8.51 If for some reason, the banker chooses to become involved in the dispute, the conflict mentioned above is faced in its barest form, for on one hand there is the contractual duty to the customer to obey mandates and on the other hand the danger that by so doing the banker will become liable to the third party under the principles discussed above.

8.52 Often the question is whether or not the money which is claimed is actually in the account. Assuming that it can be traced into the account and that it then becomes mixed with the customer's own money, under what conditions can it be said that the money has not been withdrawn by the customer and dispersed elsewhere? The outlines of the law on tracing may be summarised by consideration of two cases.

8.53 In *Re Hallett's Estate; Knatchbull v Hallett*[1] Hallett was a solicitor who had mixed money which he held in a fiduciary capacity in an account with his own money. He had operated the account as a personal account for some time after depositing the "trust" money. The Court held that he must be treated as having made all of his drawings on the account from his own money since it would be contrary to his duty as a fiduciary to draw on the other funds. Thus the rule in *Clayton's case* is displaced when the account consists partly of private funds and partly of funds held in a fiduciary capacity.

1 (1880) 13 Ch D 696.

8.54 However, when there is more than one beneficiary, as indeed there were in *Hallett's* case, then as between the beneficiaries, the rule in *Clayton's case* is applied to determine which of them is entitled to the "trust" funds in the event that the account is not sufficient to cover all claims.[1]

1 See also *In re Laughton* [1962] Tas SR 300.

8.55 It is possible to follow misappropriated funds through several transactions. In *Banque Belge pour L'Etranger v Hambrouck*[1] an employee of a customer of the bank obtained sums of money by fraud from his employer's bank account. He then paid them into his own account with another bank. Later, he withdrew sums of money from that account and made gifts of the amount to a friend. She in turn paid the money into an account with the London City and Midland Bank. The Banque Belge had been obliged to restore its customer's account to its original condition and now claimed to be entitled to the sums in the London City account. The London City bank interpleaded. The Court of Appeal held that the money could be followed through each of the transactions. Note that if the friend, who received the money innocently, had paid it away then she could not have been made liable to repay it unless she could be shown to have taken the money with knowledge that it was impressed with a trust.

1 [1921] 1 KB 321.

Banker as trustee

8.56 In the cases we have been considering, the combination of accounts would have resulted in a breach of trust. There is no protection for the customer when there is not a breach of trust but the customer nevertheless loses his or her money. An example is *Space Investments Ltd v Canadian Imperial Bank Space Investments.*[1] The bank itself was a trustee of funds with powers, indeed duties, of investment. The bank had trust power to deposit with itself as banker and did so in good faith. The bank then unfortunately went into liquidation and the beneficiaries of the trust claimed priority over the general creditors of the bank. The Court held that when the bank went into liquidation the beneficiaries were entitled to obtain the appointment of a new trustee, but on the insolvency of the bank which lawfully appropriated trust money to itself and credited the moneys to a trust deposit account, the new trustee could only rank as an unsecured creditor on behalf of the trust.

1 [1986] 3 All ER 289.

Combining accounts

Appropriation

8.57 The word "appropriation" refers to two different situations. First, it describes the situation in which a particular entry in an account is set against or matched with a transaction on the other side of the same account. Secondly, when there are several different accounts, it describes the process whereby the transaction is ascribed to one account or the other.

8.58 The law as to the appropriation of payments is described in the following passage from *Deeley v Lloyds Bank Ltd*:[1]

> According to the law of England, the person paying the money has the primary right to say to what account it shall be appropriated; the creditor, if the debtor makes no appropriation, has the right to appropriate; and if neither exercises the right of appropriation, one can look on the matter as a matter of account and see how the creditor has dealt with the payment in order to ascertain how in fact he did appropriate it. And if there is nothing more than a current account kept by the creditor, or a particular account kept by the creditor and he carries the money to that particular account, then the Court concludes that the appropriation has been made; and having been made, it is made once for all, and it does not lie in the mouth of the creditor afterwards to seek to vary that appropriation.

1 [1912] AC 756, 783.

8.59 Although the passage assumes that it is the debtor who is making the payment, it is clear that it is the paying person who has the primary right of appropriation. Even when the customer's accounts are all in credit, so that it is the customer who is the creditor and the banker who is the debtor, it is the customer which has the right to appropriate the payments of money in.[1]

1 *Clayton's case.*

8.60 Weaver and Cragie question whether it is necessary for the bank to accept certain types of appropriation. For example, a customer indicates that a certain sum is to be paid in and is to be used only for meeting a specified cheque. There is no doubt that if the banker accepts this order, or if the banker merely fails to dissent, then any use of the deposit for any purpose other than the meeting of that cheque would be improper and would expose the banker to an action in damages. However, such an appropriation is very inconvenient for the banker since the normal banking operation is simply not organised to deal with such an appropriation. Unfortunately, Weaver and Cragie can only suggest that the banker threaten the customer with closure of the account if the customer insists on exercising the right to appropriate payments.[1]

1 Weaver and Cragie, *The Law Relating to Banker and Customer in Australia*, Sydney, 1975, p 215.

Combination

8.61 Although the customer has no right to demand that the banker take all of his accounts into consideration when deciding to honour or dishonour a cheque, the law has been settled for some time that the banker has a general right to combine two of the customer's current accounts in a number of circumstances. What is not clear is the extent of this right when the accounts are not of the same type, eg, if one of the accounts is a normal cheque account and the other is, say, an account which is only used in connection with a credit card. Nor is the extent of the banker's right clear with regard to certain express or implied agreements.

8.62 The right to treat all of the customer's accounts as a single sum for some purposes is known variously as the right of combination, the right of set off, the right of consolidation and, erroneously, as the exercise of the banker's lien. The source of the right is *Garnett v M'Kewan*.[1]The plaintiff banked with the London and County Banking Company where he kept accounts at two different branches. One of the accounts was overdrawn by £42.15.11, the other was in credit some £42.18.10. The plaintiff drew three cheques on the account which was in credit, the cheques totalling slightly more than £23. The cheques were dishonoured and the plaintiff received a letter informing him that the account in credit had been debited with the amount necessary to pay the overdraft at the branch which was overdrawn. The plaintiff sued for wrongful dishonour.

1 (1872) LR 8 Ex 10.

8.63 The Court held that the bank was entitled to combine the accounts in that fashion without notice to the customer. It noted that there was no special agreement to keep the accounts separate, nor could the customer show that there was any course of business upon which he could rely to show an implied agreement in spite of the fact that the overdrawn account had been "closed", that is, inoperative, for some four months before the bank took action.

8.64 The judgments make it clear that the position would have been different had there been an agreement to keep the accounts separate and three of the four judgments suggested that the position could be different if the customer's debt to the bank had been incurred through some business other than banking. As there are an increasing number of activities carried on by bankers, this last point could be significant. Weaver and Cragie suggest that a debt to a bank in relation to travel services might not be recoverable by combination of accounts.[1]

1 Weaver and Cragie, *The Law Relating to Banker and Customer in Australia*, Sydney, 1975, p 217.

8.65 In the course of the judgment, Kelly CB said:

In general it might be proper or considerate to give notice to that effect, but there is no legal obligation on the bankers to do so, arising either from express contract or the course of dealing between the parties. The customer must be taken to know the state of each account and if the balance on the whole is against him or does not equal the cheques he draws, he has no right to expect more cheques to be cashed.[1]

1 At p 13.

8.66 Although *Garnett's* case affirms the right of the banker to combine accounts, the restrictions on the exercise of that right were ill-understood, particularly the notion that the parties might agree that the bank should have no right of combination. After all, the mere fact of opening a second account might, it was argued, be evidence to show that the parties intended that the banker should forfeit the right of combination. That argument was destroyed in the *Halesowen* case.[1]

The company maintained an account with the bank which became overdrawn. In February 1968 this account, referred to as the No 1 account, was overdrawn by more than £11,000 and the bank had discussions with officers of the company concerning the state of this account. In April of that year, it was agreed that the bank should "freeze" that account, with the result that it was to all intents and purposes a fixed loan, and should open a new account, the No 2 account, which would be maintained strictly in credit. It was agreed that the arrangement would remain in force for at least four months "in the absence of materially changed circumstances". Unfortunately, the following month the company gave notice to the bank that a meeting of creditors would be held to consider a winding up petition.

Surprisingly, the bank did not terminate the two account arrangement and the No 2 account was allowed to operate normally. On the morning of June 12, a cheque for more than £8,000 was paid into the No 2 account; that afternoon, it was resolved at the creditors' meeting that the company should be wound up and the company liquidator claimed the balance in the No 2 account. The bank argued that it was entitled to set-off the credit balance in the No 2 account against the overdrawn No 1 account.

1 *Halesowen Presswork v Westminster Bank* [1971] 1 QB 1 (CA); *National Westminster Bank Ltd v Halesowen Presswork and Assemblies Ltd* [1972] AC 785 (HL).

8.67 The claim of the bank was upheld at first instance by Roskill J, reversed by a majority in the Court of Appeal, and restored by the House of Lords. In the House of Lords, it was held that the true meaning of the agreement was that it had been intended to be operative while the relationship of banker and customer existed and the company was a going concern. Accordingly, it had come to an end when the winding up resolution had been passed and that accordingly, the bank was entitled to combine the accounts immediately.

8.68 Throughout the course of the case, there was agreement that the mere opening of two accounts could not suffice to imply an agreement. Lord Denning MR put it most succinctly: "You have to find an agreement to keep them separate. The mere opening of the two accounts does not do it".[1]

1 At p 35.

The matter of terminology

8.69 Throughout the judgment of Roskill J, he refers to the banker's lien and the exercise of that lien over a credit balance. In so doing, he was employing the terminology which had been used in many of the old cases. However, both the Court of Appeal and the House of Lords said that this use of the word "lien" is incorrect. Lord Denning MR said:

> . . . the use of the word "lien" in this context is misleading . . . when a banker has a lien over a cheque belonging to a customer or its proceeds, it means that the banker can retain the cheque or its proceeds until the customer has paid the banker the amount of his overdraft; and the banker can realise the cheque and apply the proceeds in discharge pro tanto of the overdraft . . . . Seeing that the banker's lien is no true lien, in order to avoid confusion, I think we should discard the use of the word "lien" in this context and speak simply of a banker's "right to combine accounts"; or a right to "set off" one account against the other.[1]

1 [1971] 1 QB 1, 33.

8.70 The basic facts of *Direct Acceptance Corporation v Bank of New South Wales*[1] are very similar to the *Halesowen* case. A company had an account which was overdrawn by about £35,000. The account was "frozen" by agreement with the bank and a new account opened for day to day operations. The agreement with the bank was made orally; there was, not surprisingly, a conflict of evidence over its exact terms. When a receiver was appointed to the company, the question arose as to whether the receiver was entitled to the credit balance or whether the bank was entitled to combine it with the overdrawn account.

The Court found as a fact that the agreement was to freeze the account and that there should be no right of set-off. Macfarlane J also found that the appointment of a receiver does not necessarily mean the termination of the banker/customer relationship, so that the arguments which succeeded in the *Halesowen* case would be of no avail.

1 (1968) 88 WN(NSW) (pt 1) 498.

Insolvency Act 1967, s 93

8.71 Section 93 of the Insolvency Act makes it clear that the right of set off extends beyond the customer's bankruptcy, provided only that

> . . . a person shall not be entitled under this section to claim the benefit

of any set-off against the property of a bankrupt where he had, at the time of giving credit to the bankrupt, notice of an available act of bankruptcy committed by the bankrupt . . . .[1]

1 See 9.18ff.

8.72 Indeed, the right of set off provided by the Insolvency Act might be a saving factor for the banker. If there has been an agreement to keep the accounts separate, then there is no longer an inherent right of combination. However, the best view appears to be that it is not possible to contract out of the effects of s 93, so that the right to set off will arise upon the bankruptcy of the customer by virtue of that section even if there has been an agreement to keep the accounts separate.[1] Since the section applies to the winding up of a company,[2] the same comments apply in that case.

1 *National Westminster Bank Ltd v Halesowen Presswork & Assemblies Ltd* [1972] AC 785.
2 Companies Act 1955, s 307.

8.73 On the other hand, if one of the accounts is money which is paid in for a special purpose then there is no mutuality within the meaning of s 93 and the accounts may not be combined.[1]

1 *Rolls Razor Ltd v Cox* [1967] 1 QB 552; *National Westminster Bank Ltd v Halesowen Presswork & Assemblies Ltd* [1972] AC 785.

Trust accounts

8.74 One of the important consequences of the fact that the accounts must be held by the customer in a single capacity is that there is no right to combine a customer's personal account with an account which the banker knows to be a trust account.

The matter came before the Court in *Barclays Bank Ltd v Quistclose Investments Ltd*.[1] The Rolls Razor Company was in serious financial difficulties. It had a large overdraft with Barclay's bank. In an attempt to trade out of difficulty, Rolls was attempting to borrow a sum of approximately £1,000,000. The proposed source of this loan suggested that if Rolls could obtain independent financing to pay a declared dividend of some £200,000 that the financing arrangements could go ahead. This smaller sum was obtained from Quistclose on the agreed condition that it would be used only for the purposes of paying the dividend. The amount was paid into a special account with Barclay's who knew of the loan and the purpose thereof. Unfortunately, Rolls went into liquidation before the dividend could be paid. The House of Lords held that such an arrangement made Rolls a trustee of the money for the benefit of the creditors to whom the dividend was payable. When the purpose of that trust failed, there was a resulting trust in favour of Quistclose. The consequences were that Quistclose was entitled to complete recovery of the money which Barclay's had claimed was to be combined with the overdraft account.

1 [1970] AC 567.

8.75 If, however, the banker has no notice that one of the accounts is a trust account, then the right of set off may be exercised. In *Union Bank of Australia Ltd v Murray-Aynsley*[1] the trust account was called "No 3 Account" and there was no evidence that the banker knew that it was held in trust. The banker was held justified in having exercised the right of set off.

1 [1898] AC 693.

Chapter 9

The Account II

Legal effect of statement — Stopping account — Bankruptcy — Winding up

Statements and passbooks

9.1 At one time, current account holders were furnished with a "pass book" which was a written copy of the customer's account in the bank's ledger. At certain intervals the passbook would be updated by the bank's clerks and handed to the customer for perusal. The intention was that the customer should examine the book for accuracies and inconsistencies and return it then to the banker, along with any complaint if the book showed what the customer believed to be an error.

9.2 Passbooks have been supplanted by bank statements. In modern form, these are computer-produced documents which are printed by the bank's high speed printers. They are sent to the customer at intervals but, unlike the passbook, it is not expected that they will be returned to the bank. Consequently, there is no systematic means of detecting statements which may have gone astray since there is no evidence in the hands of the banker to show that the customer ever received that statement.

9.3 There is some old authority that the passbook is the property of the customer, not of the banker. If this is correct, then a fortiori the same must be true of the statement.[1]

1 See *Akrokerri (Atlantic) Mines Ltd v Economic Bank* [1904] 2 KB 465, 470.

Legal effect of the statement

9.4 The cases on passbooks and statements are usually concerned with the legal effect that the statement has when the customer fails to note discrepancies in the account. As noted in the section on the duty of the customer,[1] the Courts have refused to impose a duty on the customer to read the account and to discover and report forgeries. The major textbook writers have been critical of this, noting that there are early authorities which appear to recognise the existence of the duty, at least to the extent that the passing to and fro of the passbook should be evidence of a stated and settled account.[2] However, given the decisions in the *Tai Hing* case and the *Walpole and Patterson* case,[3] it now seems that only legislative action could impose such a duty on the customer.

1 Ch 3.
2 See *Paget*, p 113; *Chorley*, p 178.
3 *Tai Hing Cotton Mill Ltd v Liu Chong Hing Bank Ltd* [1985] 2 All ER 947; *National Bank of New Zealand v Walpole and Patterson* [1975] 2 NZLR 7.

Account stated?

9.5 An account stated is defined by *Halsbury* in the following terms:[1]

> Where parties mutually agree that a certain sum is due from one to the other an "account stated" is said to arise, and the law implies a promise on the part of the one from whom such a sum has been agreed to be due to pay the same, on which the other party may sue without being put to proof of the details or correctness of the account.

1 3rd ed, vol 8 252.

9.6 If the statement could be considered as an account stated, then it would be binding on both the parties subject to certain exceptions which need not concern us here. However, that would be the equivalent of imposing a duty on the customer to read and reconcile the statement, and this has been decisively rejected.

9.7 That is not to say that the statement is wholly without legal effect, for there are circumstances where it may be used as evidence in disputes between banker and customer.

Evidence against the bank

9.8 The bank has a duty to its customer to keep accurate accounts and if the customer relies on the statement honestly then the bank may on occasion be bound by the entries made by it. The most recent authority is *Lloyds Bank Ltd v Brooks*,[1] an action by Lloyds Bank to recover money paid by mistake.[2] Due to an error of the bank, dividends payable to her brother were wrongly credited to the defendant's account. It was found as a fact that the money had been paid under a mistake of fact and that the defendant was not aware that she was receiving additional money to which she was not entitled.

Her defence was that the bank was estopped from reclaiming the money by virtue of representations made to her through the periodic statement of account sent by the bank. If she had known that she was not entitled to the money, then there could be no effective estoppel, for she would not have been relying on the representation.

1 (1950) 6 LDAB 161.
2 See Ch 18 for a general discussion of the right to recover money which is paid under a mistake of fact or law.

9.9 The Court held that the bank had a duty to the customer to keep her correctly informed as to the position of her account and not to "authorise her or induce her by faithful representations contained in the statement of account to draw money from her account to which she was not entitled"[1] It was also held that, since the representations amounted to a breach of duty, she had spent more over a period of time than she would otherwise have done, and that this represented the change in circumstance necessary to support the estoppel.[2]

1 At p 169.
2 See Ch 18.

9.10 Not every entry in an account will bind the bank, for it is implicit in the judgment that the bank could have recovered had it discovered the error before the defendant had changed circumstances by overspending. A more enlightening example of a situation wherein the bank will not be bound is *British and North European Bank Ltd v Zalzstein*.[1] A fraudulent bank manager attempted to deceive auditors by manipulating some accounts. One of the accounts belonged to the defendant and was overdrawn; the manager credited the account with £2,000 which was debited to another account and then later debited the defendant's account with the same amount, restoring the accounts to their original position. The customer knew nothing about these entries until after the accounts had been restored to their original position, but he claimed to be entitled to claim the £2,000 credit but to disclaim the corresponding debit. In the course of the judgment, Sankey J said:

> . . . it can [not] be . . . asserted that an entry made in a pass book is in all cases conclusive and binding on the bank . . . but each case must be judged on its own particular facts, although the customer starts with the advantage that prima facie it is an admission by the bank in his favour, which cannot in some cases be refuted.[2]

1 [1927] 2 KB 92.
2 At p 97.

Evidence against the customer

9.11 For some time it was hoped that some duty to examine the statement might be imposed upon the customer, but it now seems that that hope is dead. It is hard to imagine circumstances in which the customer will be bound, or indeed, even seriously prejudiced, by the entries in the statement.

Stopping the account

9.12 English cases often talk of "closing the account", but that expression is misleading. It does not mean the termination of the banker/customer relationship, but a situation where it becomes necessary for the banker to refuse to allow any further withdrawals from the account. This includes the need for refusing to meet any cheques drawn on the account even though in all other respects the cheque is one which should be met. In some cases, the banker should even refuse to permit any further deposits into the account. The present section will follow *Weaver and Cragie* in referring to the situation as "stopping the account". However, the reader should be aware that the terminology is not fixed.

Death

9.13 Notice of the death of a customer serves as a termination of all authority which the customer has granted to the banker, save that the amendment to s 75 of the Bills of Exchange Act 1908 which was made in 1971. Subsection (2) now reads:

> . . . a banker may pay a cheque drawn on him, notwithstanding that he has notice of the death of the customer who drew it, if the cheque is presented not more than 10 days after the date of the customer's death . . .

9.14 The section does not operate if the cheque is dated after the date of the death or if there is a countermand by someone who claims either to be entitled to a grant of administration in respect of the customer's estate or to be a beneficiary of it.[1] It should be noted that there is no mention of the executor, since the executor has the power to make a countermand without the need for statutory provision.[2]

1 Subs (2)(a) and (b).
2 See 4.19.

9.15 This rule has no bearing on the situation where the deceased is not a customer but only a signatory to an account, eg, a company director. However, it would be prudent for the banker to consider taking new authorities from the customer.

9.16 The death of one of the parties to a joint account has been dealt with previously,[1] except in one respect. If the account is overdrawn, the banker should not permit further operation by the survivors, since the operation of the rule in *Clayton's case* would mean that cheques paid after the date of the death would be fresh advances for which the estate of the deceased would not be liable and any deposits would go to paying off the earlier advances, thereby having the effect of reducing the liability of the estate. The same caveat applies also to an overdrawn partnership account when one of the partners dies.

1 See 4.28.

9.17 The only person who is entitled to demand payment of the account balance of the deceased customer is the executor of the estate or the administrator, as the case may be. In theory, the executor is entitled to the balance immediately, since the powers of an executor, unlike those of an administrator, arise immediately on the death of the testator.[1] However it is clear that a banker cannot safely part with the balance of an account merely because someone comes forward claiming to be the executor or the administrator. As long ago as *Tarn v Commercial Bank of Sydney*,[2] it was said that

> Bankers are in a peculiar position and when asked to hand over large sums of money to persons claiming as executors of deceased customers, they are justified in requiring to be made safe by production of probate.

1 See 4.19.
2 (1884) 12 QBD 294.

Bankruptcy and winding up

9.18 The law of bankruptcy is that part of the law which provides for the orderly division of assets among the creditors of individuals under certain circumstances. The law of bankruptcy is wholly a creation of statute, the current governing statute in New Zealand being the Insolvency Act 1967.

9.19 The early law of bankruptcy was directed at the punishment and imprisonment of defaulting debtors. Contrary to popular opinion, imprisonment was not one of the early methods for dealing with debtors, but rather was originally a means to "encourage" the debtor to use assets which were not available to the creditor by means of the existing legal processes. Once introduced, imprisonment for debtors who would not pay their debts was quickly extended to imprisonment of those who could not pay their debts. There is no doubt that severe injustices occurred.

9.20 Even where there were legal processes available to the creditor to attach the assets of the debtor, there were no means for ensuring that the creditors were treated fairly inter se. A single creditor who was better informed or simply quicker off the mark could attach the entirety of available assets of the debtor, thereby satisfying his or her own debt and leaving nothing for the other creditors.

9.21 Modern bankruptcy law attempts to balance the interests of several competing groups. First is the desire to see that the creditors are treated equally among themselves. Secondly, there is a public interest in relieving the debtor from a hopeless financial position and returning that person to a productive life. Thirdly, the legislation retains the policy that fraudulent or dishonest debtors should be punished.

9.22 "Bankruptcy" is a term which is often used carelessly. A person may only be made a bankrupt by the completion of the strict process of law. It is a serious matter to declare that a person is a bankrupt and the banker should take care not to claim that a person is such unless very sure that the process has been completed. Failure to exercise care may result in damages for defamation.[1]

1 See 6.45ff.

9.23 "Insolvency", on the other hand, describes a state of affairs in which the debtor is unable to pay his debts as they fall due from his own money. But even here there has been a gloss on the language, for it has been said that "own money" in this context does not limit consideration to the resources immediately available but extends to those funds which the debtor might realise if given a reasonable opportunity to liquidate some assets.[1]

1 *Sandell v Porter* (1966) 115 CLR 666.

Debtor's or creditor's petitions

9.24 All bankruptcy proceedings begin with the presentation of a bankruptcy petition. The petition may be presented by the debtor personally, a debtor's petition, or it may be presented by a creditor or several creditors acting jointly, a creditor's petition. Because of the severe consequences of a bankruptcy, the right of a creditor to present a petition is limited by a requirement that certain conditions be fulfilled prior to the presentation.

9.25 Section 23 of the Act defines the conditions which are prerequisite to the filing of a creditor's petition. They are outlined in the following paragraphs.

9.26 The debt owing to the petitioning creditor, or the aggregate debt owing to the petitioners, must be at least $200. This debt must be owing at the time when the petition is filed.

9.27 The debtor must have committed an act of bankruptcy within a period of three months immediately before the petition is filed.

9.28 The debt must be for a liquidated sum which is payable either immediately or at some future time.

9.29 The first of these conditions is intended to prevent the filing of nuisance petitions by small creditors. Unfortunately, the amount has failed to be changed to take account of inflation and so is now entirely too small. The result is that the filing or threat of filing of a bankruptcy petition is, improperly, often used as a powerful device for the collection of debts.

9.30 As a further protection of the debtor, a secured creditor may not present a petition unless it may be shown that the amount of the debt owed exceeds the value of the security held in respect of the debt by at least $200.[1]

1 See Chs 23 and 24 for a discussion of secured debts.

9.31 The acts of bankruptcy are defined in s 19 of the Act. These are intended to be acts whereby it may be objectively determined that the debtor is in fact insolvent or to indicate certain acts or transactions which evidence a desire to prejudice some or all of the debtor's creditors. So, for example, departing or attempting to depart from New Zealand with an intention to defeat or delay creditors is an act of bankruptcy, as is removing or concealing property with an intent to prejudice creditors or to prefer one creditor over another.

9.32 These acts of bankruptcy might be very difficult to prove without full access to the debtor's private records. However, one act of bankruptcy is easy to prove, namely, failure to comply with a bankruptcy notice. The bankruptcy notice is a formal document which demands that the debtor pay a judgment debt or as much of it as remains unpaid. The notice must be in the prescribed form and must state the consequences of non-compliance.[1] The vast majority of creditors' petitions are based on this act of bankruptcy.

1 S 20.

9.33 A date is then set for the hearing of the petition and, provided the Court is satisfied that the basic conditions which entitle the creditor to petition are met, it will declare the debtor bankrupt. It is at this point and not before that the debtor becomes a bankrupt. The Act refers to this as adjudication, but a more common term is sequestration.

Effect of bankruptcy

9.34 Upon being adjudicated a bankrupt, the consequences for the debtor and all creditors are dramatic. Subject to a few exceptions,[1] all of the debtor's property vests immediately in another person who is known as the assignee. Furthermore, it is not just the property which is owned at the time of the adjudication, but:

> All property whatsoever and wheresoever situated belonging to or vested in the bankrupt at the commencement of the bankruptcy, or acquired by or devolving upon him before his discharge.[2]

1 The exceptions are contained in ss 47, 48, 49, 50, and 59 of the Act.
2 S 42(2)(a).

9.35 The assignee also acquires all rights and powers to take proceedings with regard to any of the bankrupt's property, again dating from the "commencement" of the bankruptcy.

Doctrine of relation back

9.36 The "commencement" of the bankruptcy is at a time which precedes adjudication and may even precede the act of bankruptcy which gave the creditor the right to file a creditor's petition. The concept of the "commencement" effectively gives a retrospective effect to the bankruptcy. Since such a retrospective effect is unusual in legal proceedings, it is worthwhile to consider the reasons for its necessity in bankruptcy proceedings.

9.37 Long before a debtor becomes bankrupt, he will be aware that his financial position is difficult at best and hopeless at worst. If the assignee could take only the property which was available at the time of the adjudication, then the debtor would have the opportunity to plan for the event and take steps to safeguard some or all of his or her assets. This might be done, for example, by transferring assets to relatives or to trusted friends. But even if there is no attempt to alienate property, the natural course of business will be that the debtor will pay the most pressing of the creditors. The result would be that some creditors would receive full satisfaction while others would receive nothing, a situation which is one that modern bankruptcy law was intended to prevent.

9.38 In order to facilitate the intent of the legislation, the basic principle is that all property vests in the assignee from the time of the earliest act of bankruptcy within a reasonable period of time. Consequently, any dealing by the debtor after that time is prima facie invalid, for the property does not belong to the debtor, but rather to the trustee. Similarly, any money which is paid to the debtor does not discharge the obligation for which it is paid, for it is paid to the wrong person; it should be paid to the assignee.

9.39 The problem with this scheme is that no one knows that the position has changed. Indeed, if no creditor takes advantage of the act of bankruptcy by filing a creditor's petition within the specified period, then the act of bankruptcy "lapses" and all dealings with the debtor are perfectly valid. Because of this "conditional" effect, there must be some provisions which save some of the normal transactions even when the debtor is later adjudicated a bankrupt.

9.40 In summary, the prima facie position is that all transactions with the debtor which occurred after the commencement of the bankruptcy are void. Some, indeed many, may be shown to be valid, but it is on the person wishing to show that the transaction is valid to establish that the transaction falls within one of the protected categories. As we shall see, bankers are given some special consideration by the legislation.

9.41 The retrospective effect of the adjudication is called the doctrine of relation back. It is found in s 42(4) of the Insolvency Act 1967. The commencement of the bankruptcy is calculated as follows:

9.42 If the debtor has committed only one act of bankruptcy, then that must be the one which formed the basis for the creditor's petition. The bankruptcy commences at the time of that act.

9.43 If the debtor has committed more than one act of bankruptcy, then the bankruptcy commences at the time of the first act which occurred within a period of three months prior to the filing of the creditor's petition; provided that the debtor was indebted to some creditor or creditors in a sum not less than two hundred dollars.

9.44 It is important to realise that even though most creditor's petitions are based on the failure to comply with a bankruptcy notice, that the other acts of bankruptcy mentioned in s 19 are very important, for they allow the time of the commencement to be pushed back in time, possibly allowing the assignee to increase substantially the amount which is available for distribution to creditors generally.

9.45 There are other rules which allow the assignee to gain assets which the debtor disposed of before the commencement of the bankruptcy. Thus, a gift is voidable at the option of the assignee if the donor is adjudged bankrupt within two years after the making of the gift.[1] Gifts made within a five-year period before adjudication may be declared void unless the person claiming under the gift proves that the donor was not insolvent at the time of making the gift.[2] These sections are unlikely to be of great importance to bankers.

1 S 54(1).
2 S 54(2).

Exceptions to the doctrine of relation back

9.46 During the period of three months prior to the filing of a creditor's petition, all transactions by the bankrupt are subject to being overturned. A banker is in the same position as anyone else who has had dealings with the debtor during this period, but the nature of the contract between banker and customer makes the banker even more exposed, for in theory, all cheques written by the debtor which have been paid by the banker might have been paid improperly.

9.47 It is clearly intolerable that all such transactions should be overturned and the Act makes provision for saving transactions in ss 47 and 48. Section 47 deals primarily with payments or other dispositions of assets made by the debtor and is expressly made subject to the sections which deal with the giving of preferences. Provided however, that the transaction does not fall into one of those categories, it will be safe from the assignee provided that:

(e) The person (other than the bankrupt) to, by, or with whom the payment, disposition, contract, dealing, or transaction was made, executed, or entered into, had not at the time of the payment, disposition, contract, dealing, or transaction notice of any available act of bankruptcy committed by the bankrupt before that time and otherwise acts in good faith; and

(f) The payment, disposition, contract, dealing, or transaction takes place before the adjudication . . .

9.48 It seems that the notice of the act of bankruptcy which would preclude protection need not be express notice nor need it be very precise. Thus:

Where an act of bankruptcy has been in fact committed any communication which brings to the knowledge of the execution creditor before the sale the alleged fact, that an act of bankruptcy has been committed, in a way which ought to induce him as a reasonable man to believe that the notification was true, is in our judgment a sufficient notice.[1]

1 Per Parke, B in *Hope v Meek* (1855) 10 Ex 829, 845; 156 ER 676, 683.

9.49 The section probably does not protect the banker who pays a cheque of the person who later becomes a bankrupt. It is unlikely that the banker could be considered as the agent of the debtor who is making a payment to the creditor. On the other hand, it is clear that a payment by the customer to the banker by way of a reduction of an overdraft would be protected by the section.

9.50 The way in which the section may be used by the banker is illustrated by *Re Keever (a bankrupt), ex parte Trustee of Property of Bankrupt v Midland Bank Ltd*.[1] K had an account with the defendant bank which was overdrawn. After she had committed an act of bankruptcy, she received a cheque for an amount which was in excess of the overdraft. She paid the cheque into her account for collection. The cheque cleared on the day when K was adjudicated a bankrupt. The trustee in bankruptcy claimed the proceeds. The bank argued that it had a lien on the cheque on the day when it was paid in and that at that time the bank had no notice of the act of bankruptcy. The bank was held entitled to succeed.

1 [1967] Ch 182.

9.51 Section 48 concerns the position of those who make payments to a debtor who later becomes bankrupt. There is no need to make s 48 subject to the later sections since they concern only dispositions by the bankrupt:

> **48. Validity of certain other transactions with bankrupt** — A payment of money . . . to or to the order of a person who has been or subsequently is adjudged bankrupt, or to or to the order of a person claiming by assignment from him, shall, notwithstanding anything in this Act, be a good discharge to the person paying the money . . . if payment . . . was made before the adjudication was advertised and the person making the payment . . . satisfies the Court that he had no knowledge of the adjudication of the presentation of a bankruptcy petition and that the payment . . . was either in the ordinary course of business or otherwise in good faith.

9.52 The section is of the utmost importance to bankers, for in its absence, a banker who paid a cheque of a person who became bankrupt would be unable to debit the account if the payment was made after the commencement of the bankruptcy. Although it is widely thought that the section does provide such protection, there is some cause for concern. When the banker pays a customer's cheque which is in favour of a third party payee, it is not a payment to the customer. But neither is it a payment to a person "claiming by assignment" from the customer, for a cheque is not an assignment of the funds held by the banker.[1] However, the Court in *Re Dalton, ex parte Herrington and Carmichael v Trustee*[2] said that payments made by the bankrupt's solicitor on his behalf in settlement of the bankrupt's debts were "payments made to the bankrupt" under the equivalent English section.[3]

1 Section 53 of the Bills of Exchange Act 1908 specifically provides that a bill of exchange does not operate as an assignment of funds. Were it otherwise, a drawee who held funds of the drawer could be liable on a bill which was never accepted.
2 [1963] Ch 336.
3 Ibid, 354.

Voidable preferences

9.53 Of more importance to bankers is the right of the assignee to recover assets which were used by the debtor to give a preference to one or more creditors. Section 56 of the Act allows recovery of such payments made within a period of two years of being adjudicated bankrupt:

> **56. Voidable preferences** — (1) Every conveyance or transfer of property, every charge made on any property, every obligation incurred, every execution under any judicial proceeding suffered, and every

payment made (including any payment made in pursuance of a judgment or order of a Court), by any person unable to pay his debts as they become due from his own money, shall be voidable as against the Assignee, if —

(a) It is in favour of any creditor or any person in trust for any creditor with a view to giving that creditor or any surety or guarantor for the debt due to that creditor a preference over the other creditors; and

(b) The person making, suffering, paying, or incurring the same is adjudged bankrupt within two years after the making, suffering, paying, or incurring of the same.

9.54 The only difficult part of the section is the requirement to show that there was an intention to give a preference. It is not necessary that the giving of a preference should be the sole intention.[1] There is English authority to the effect that a payment made "under pressure" will be unlikely to be one which is made with the intention of giving the creditor a preference. It is said that payment made from a sense of moral obligation is not one which is made "under pressure", but that one which is made from fear of prosecution for breach of trust would amount to payment "under pressure".

1 *In re Aston* [1956] NZLR 703.

9.55 Section 56(2) avoids the same kind of transactions, but there is no requirement that the debtor have an intention and that the payment is made within one month of adjudication or before adjudication but after the filing of the creditor's petition, whichever is longer.[1] Showing that the debtor was insolvent at that time is unlikely to be difficult, so most such payments are likely to be voidable.

1 S 56(3).

Securities given by the bankrupt

9.56 Section 57 also extends the reach of the assignee beyond the commencement of the bankruptcy and is of special interest to bankers. The section makes voidable every security or charge given by the debtor within a period of 12 months immediately preceding the filing of a creditor's petition which leads to adjudication, but subject to some savings in the remainder of the section.

9.57 Section 57(2) is of the utmost importance to bankers:

Subsection (1) of this section shall not affect any security or charge in so far as it relates to —
Money actually advanced or paid, or the actual price or value of property sold or supplied, or any other valuable consideration given in good faith, by the grantee of the security or charge to the grantor at the time of or at any time after the execution thereof; . . .

9.58 The section is clearly designed to prevent a creditor from taking a security to cover past indebtedness, thereby gaining a priority over other creditors, while at the same time allowing the debtor access to continuing funds by permitting a security to be given for present and future advances. This section combines with the rule in *Clayton's case* to place bankers in a very privileged position. A security taken by a banker on Day 1 will, of course, only secure advances made on or after that day. But if the debt is by way of overdraft, then continued operation of the account will have, by virtue of the rule in *Clayton's case*, the effect of reducing the prior debt with the result that the debt is gradually converted from an unsecured to a secured debt.[1] Of course, the general rule is that the appropriation of payments is at the option of the debtor or, if the debtor makes no appropriation, at the option of the creditor. It might be thought that all creditors would wish to appropriate payments to the earlier debt. This was foreseen and foreclosed by the legislation in s 57(3), but trading banks were explicitly exempted from the rule, at least for payments made in good faith and in the ordinary course of its business and without negligence.

1 That this is indeed the effect was confirmed in *Re Yeovil Glove Co Ltd* [1965] Ch 148; but see now s 311(4), Companies Act 1955 and 9.70.

9.59 There are other security arrangements which may be attacked by the assignee. An unregistered instrument by way of security which falls within the scope of the Chattels Transfer Act 1924 is void as against the assignee.[1]

1 S 18(1)(a), Chattels Transfer Act 1924.

Fraudulent conveyances

9.60 There is one category of transaction which is voidable no matter when it occurs. Section 60(1) of the Property Law Act 1952 provides that every alienation of property which is made with an intent to defraud creditors is voidable at the instance of any person who is thereby prejudiced. It should be noted that such a conveyance amounts to an act of bankruptcy.[1]

1 S 19(b), Insolvency Act 1967.

9.61 The assignee may recover the property or its value when there has been a voidable disposition even when the person who takes the property has done so in good faith and for valuable consideration.[1] If, however, the property has passed on to other parties, the assignee has no rights against them directly.[2] In order to prevent gross injustices, the Court is given the discretion to deny the assignee recovery, provided the person who dealt with the bankrupt received the property in good faith and has altered his or her position in the reasonably held belief that the transaction was validly made or if the Court is of the opinion that it is inequitable to order recovery in part or in full.[3]

1 S 58(5).
2 S 58(5).
3 S 58(6).

After-acquired property

9.62 It is not only the property held by the debtor at the commencement of the bankruptcy which vests in the assignee, but also any property which is acquired by the bankrupt before discharge.[1] One of the consequences of this is that dealings by the debtor with the property are prima facie invalid. However, it is clearly necessary for the debtor to continue living and working and the Act makes provision for saving certain transactions provided that they are completed prior to an active intervention by the assignee. Most importantly, a transaction is valid if the person dealing with the bankrupt does so in good faith and for value and the transaction involves after-acquired property.[2]

1 S 42(2)(a).
2 S 49(1).

9.63 Perhaps because it is expected that the bankrupt will continue a fruitful relationship with a banker, the banker is given special treatment in s 49. Section 49(3) deems certain transactions to be for value:

> For the purposes of subsection (1) of this section, the receipt of any money, security, or negotiable instrument from, or by the order or direction of, a bankrupt by his banker, and any payment and any delivery of any security or negotiable instrument made to, or by the order or direction of, a bankrupt by his banker, shall be deemed to be a transaction by the bankrupt with that banker dealing with him for value.

9.64 But the banker also has a duty with regard to accounts kept by undischarged bankrupts:

> (5) Where a banker has ascertained that a person having an account with him is an undischarged bankrupt, then, unless the banker is satisfied that the account is on behalf of some other person, it shall be his duty forthwith to inform the Assignee of the existence of the account, and thereafter he shall not make any payments out of the account, except under an order of the Court, or in accordance with instructions from the Assignee, unless by the expiration of one month from the date of giving the information no instructions have been received from the Assignee.

9.65 It must be emphasised that there is nothing necessarily improper in an undischarged bankrupt carrying on a current account. One of the exceptions to the rule that the property vests in the assignee is that the bankrupt is entitled to use personal earnings for his own benefit. This is thought to be so even though the language of s 42 appears wide enough to include personal earnings. At common law, the bankrupt was permitted to keep all personal earnings; s 45 seems to confirm this rule by implication, for it provides that the Court may make an order that the bankrupt contribute towards the payment of his debts providedthe Court is satisfied

> that, having regard to all the circumstances of the bankruptcy and the bankrupt's conduct, earning power, responsibilities, and prospects, and after making a reasonable allowance for the maintenance of the bankrupt and his wife and family, the bankrupt is or will be able to meet the payments ordered . . . .[1]

1 S 45(1).

Set off and mutual debts

9.66 The other section which is of special importance to bankers is s 93 which makes it clear that the banker's right of combination of accounts,[1] survives the customer's bankruptcy provided that the banker does not extend further credit to the bankrupt after receiving notice of an act of bankruptcy.

1 See 8.71.

Winding up

9.67 The winding up of a company is similar to the bankruptcy of an individual, but there are some differences which are of concern to a banker. First, the property of the company does not automatically vest in a trustee as in the case of an individual. The winding up of the company begins at the time of the presentation of a winding up petition and the disposition of the property of the company is governed by the Act. In most respects, the disposition of property is under restrictions similar to those suffered by an individual upon the commencement of bankruptcy.

9.68 Thus, s 309 of the Companies Act 1955 provides that all payments made to a creditor at a time when the company was insolvent within a period of two years from the commencement of the winding up are voidable as against the liquidator if made with a view to giving the creditor a preference over other creditors.

9.69 The winding up also has an effect on certain charges given by the company. Section 311 invalidates charges given by a company within 12 months prior to the commencement of the winding up. There are, as in the case of a bankruptcy, some exceptions. The security may be saved if the banker can show that the company was solvent at the time when the charge was given, or if the charge is merely a direct substitution for one which was previously held. Finally, the charge will be good to the extent that it is security for advances given at the time or after the giving of the charge.

9.70 This last section could work in conjunction with the rule in *Clayton's case* to give an unfair advantage to bankers over other creditor's when the charge secured an overdraft.[1] This has been changed by the operation of s 311(4):

> For the purposes of subsection (3) of this section, where any security or charge was given by the company within the period specified in subsection (1) . . . all payments received by the grantee of the security or charge after it was given shall be deemed to have been appropriated so far as may be necessary towards repayment of money actually advanced or paid by the grantee to the company on or after the giving of the security or charge . . . .

1 See 9.59 and *Re Yeovil Glove Co Ltd* [1965] Ch 148.

9.71 Upon the commencement of a winding up, any disposition of the property of the company is void unless the Court makes an order to the contrary, usually known as a validating order.[1] Note that this section says "void" and not "voidable". The position of the banker who allows the operation of a company's bank account after the commencement of the winding up has received attention in several cases, with somewhat inconsistent views.

1 S 222; s 309(1A).

9.72 In *Re Mal Bower's Macquarie Electrical Centre Pty Ltd*[1] the Australian equivalent of the section was considered. The bank had paid cheques drawn by the company in favour of a third party and the issue was whether the bank could sustain a debit to the account for the amount of the cheques. Street CJ said:

> There is, in my view, great force in the bank's argument that the paying by a bank of a company's cheque, presented by a stranger, does not involve the bank in a disposition of the property of the company so as to disentitle the bank to debit the amount of the cheque to the company's account. The word "disposition" connotes in my view both a disponor and a disponee. The section operates to render the disposition void so far as concerns the disponee. It does not operate to affect the agencies interposing between the company, as disponor, and the recipient of the property, as disponee . . . . The intermediary functions fulfilled by the bank in respect of paying cheques drawn by a company in favour of and presented on behalf of a third party do not implicate the bank in the consequences of the statutory avoidance prescribed by section 227.[2]

1 [1974] 1 NSWLR 254.
2 At 258.

9.73 The English Court of Appeal has taken a somewhat different view of the corresponding English provision. In *Re Gray's Inn*

Construction Co Ltd[1] a payment by the company into its overdrawn account was held to be a disposition since it had the effect of discharging a part of the company's indebtedness to the bank.

1 [1980] 1 WLR 711.

9.74 The only safe course which may be followed by the banker is to stop all operations on the company's accounts following the presentation of the winding up petition pending the obtaining of a validation order.

9.75 Winding up of a company differs from the bankruptcy of an individual in one final respect. At the termination of the winding up, the company ceases to exist.

Receiver

9.76 A receiver is a person appointed either by the Court or by a debenture holder out of Court. The second is by far the most common and is the only kind which will be considered in this section. Such a person derives his or her powers almost exclusively from the terms of the debenture.

The function of a receiver who is appointed by a debenture holder is to exercise the powers given by the debenture to realise assets over which he has control in order to satisfy the debts owed to the secured creditors who were responsible for the appointment. The powers given may range from the mere power to sell the property over which the charge is given to, more commonly, wide powers of management of the business of the mortgagor company. In the older cases, only the first type is known as a receiver, the other being referred to as a receiver and manager or sometimes simply as a manager. In more modern cases, the term receiver covers the field.

9.77 The appointment of a receiver is not a winding up.[1] The structure of the company remains intact and the directors remain in office with full powers and duties save that the disposition of the assets covered by the debenture and which are within the powers granted to the receiver is within the control of the receiver. In a modern debenture, the actual assets available to the directors following the appointment of a receiver will be virtually nil.

1 *Moss SS Co Ltd v Whinney* [1912] AC 254.

9.78 The debenture commonly contains a clause which provides that in carrying out his duties, the receiver shall be the agent of the company and that the company/mortgagor alone shall be responsible for the acts and defaults of the receiver. Since the company has absolutely no say in the appointment of a receiver or of the acts performed by the receiver once appointed, the situation seems slightly strange, but the effect of the clauses has been upheld so that there is no liability at all on the appointing mortgagee for acts or defaults of the receiver.[1] Furthermore, as agent for the company the receiver may dispose of assets of the company in the name of the company. Failure to include an express clause in the debenture will result in the receiver being deemed the agent of the appointing mortgagee.[2]

1 *Gosling v Gaskell* [1896] 1 QB 669; this is not to say that the receiver will have no liability to the company: s 345B(2)(a).
2 *Albert Del Fabbro Pty Ltd v Wilckens and Burnsiae Pty Ltd* [1971] SASR 121.

9.79 A receiver is personally liable on any contract made in the performance of his or her duties unless the contract is made on terms which expressly exclude such liability. The receiver is entitled to an indemnity from the company with respect to such liability.[1]

1 S 345(2).

9.80 There is a statutory duty on receivers to exercise reasonable care in realising property of the company.[1] It would seem that this duty is no more than the common law duty imposed upon mortgagees, in particular, there is no obligation to obtain the best price available.[2]

1 S 345B.
2 See *Cuckmere Brick Co Ltd v Mutual Finance Ltd* [1971] Ch 949.

9.81 A winding up order has consequences for the receiver. If the receiver is the agent of the company, the agency will cease and the receiver will thus no longer be able to make contracts or convey property in the name of the company.[1] In such a circumstance it appears that the receiver does not automatically revert to being an agent of the mortgagee but instead becomes and assumes the responsibilities of a principal.[2] As a result of this, a receiver who purports to be making a contract without personal liability but following a winding up order will have no principal and cannot be held liable on the contract, but would be liable in damages for breach of warranty of authority. If the receiver does not disclaim personal liability then he will be personally liable on the contract. Since the damages in either case are likely to be the same, it is clear that a receiver would be well advised to cease activities on the winding up or, alternatively, obtain an indemnity from the mortgagee on whose behalf appointment was made.[3]

1 *Gosling v Gaskell* [1897] AC 575.
2 Ibid, at 581, 592.
3 See *Weaver and Cragie*, p 667.

Garnishee orders

9.82 Garnishment orders allow a creditor to attach a debt which is owed to his own judgment debtor by a third party. Since every

customer of a bank who has an account in credit is a creditor of
the bank, it will be clear that bankers must be familiar with the
consequences of garnishment proceedings. The usual form of
garnishment proceedings is in two stages. A garnishee order nisi
will be addressed to the third party debtor, the banker in the case
we are concerned with, ordering that debtor to show cause why
the amount owing by that debtor to the judgment debtor should
not be made available for the purposes of satisfaction of the
judgment debt. The order nisi is granted on the affidavit of the
judgment creditor that he believes that there are moneys owing by
the garnishee to the judgment debtor.

9.83 Provided that the garnishee does not show cause, the Court
will issue an order absolute which directs the garnishee to pay the
judgment creditor directly rather than the original debtor.
Garnishee orders issued by the High Court are known formally as
charging orders, those issued by the District Court are attachment
orders.

Debt due and owing

9.84 A garnishee order nisi is expressed to attach debts owing or
accruing due to the judgment debtor. A debt which is owing is one
for which the creditor could have immediately sued. An accruing
debt is one which is not yet actually payable but which is
represented by an existing obligation.

9.85 When the order is phrased merely in these terms, it may not
be easy to know if the entire account should be frozen or only the
amount of the judgment debt. The matter came before the House
of Lords in *Rogers v Whiteley*.[1] Whiteley ran a banking business and
Rogers had an account there which was in credit some £6,800.
Rogers lost an action and became a judgment debtor for some
£6,000; the judgment creditor obtained a garnishee order nisi
ordering that "all debts owing or accruing due" to Rogers should
be attached and the order was served on Whiteley. Meanwhile,
Rogers had drawn a number of small cheques which totalled less
than £800. The cheques were dishonoured and Rogers sued
Whiteley for wrongful dishonour. The sole issue in the case was
whether the order nisi attached the whole of the account, or only
enough to cover the judgment debt. The House of Lords held that
it was the entire balance that was attached. When the order nisi
states the precise sum which is to be attached, the position is
thought to be different.[2]

1 [1892] AC 118.
2 See *Weaver and Cragie*, p 160.

The need for a demand

9.86 *Rogers* case clearly assumed that the relationship between the banker and customer was the ordinary debtor and creditor relationship. Following the decision of the English Court of Appeal in *Joachimson v Swiss Bank Corp*,[1] doubts were cast upon the availability of garnishment procedures against current accounts. The argument was that Lord Atkin had made it clear beyond argument that the debt owing from a banker to the customer was not "due and owing", but required a demand in order to become so. The case was not a garnishee case, but the Court addressed the matter, arguing that a garnishee order nisi would itself amount to a demand sufficient to allow attachment. While that is a very practical solution, it is one which is singularly lacking in logic, a point observed by Atkin LJ.

1 [1921] 3 KB 110.

9.87 Most authors consider that current accounts have been the subject matter of garnishee proceedings for so long that it is extremely unlikely that the view of the majority in *Joachimson* would not be followed. However, in *Re ANZ Savings Bank Ltd, Mellas v Evriniadis*,[1] the Victorian Full Court doubted that the proposition is correct. They observed that the dicta in *Joachimson* which held that the order nisi itself could be the demand necessary to make the debt "due and owing" were ". . . at the most obiter because in the *Joachimson* case, their Lordships were not dealing with garnishee proceedings". However, the Court expressly left open the question since it was not then necessary to decide it.

1 [1972] VR 690.

9.88 Weerasooria and Coops criticise this decision and argue that it failed to consider other authority.[1] It would seem that regardless of the logic of the position, the better view is that current accounts are subject to garnishee proceedings.

1 At p 328.

Savings accounts

9.89 Although the garnishee order nisi might serve as a substitute for the customer's demand when there is an attempt to garnish a current account, it does not seem that this order can similarly substitute as a customer's demand where there are certain conditions precedent relating to withdrawal from an account. The matter has been considered on several occasions with regard to savings accounts.

9.90 Savings accounts ordinarily require that a passbook must be presented together with a signed withdrawal slip before the customer is entitled to withdraw money from the account. In addition, some accounts have a requirement that a period of notice be given before withdrawal or before withdrawal of sums in excess of a certain amount. The question is whether the service of a garnishee order nisi may be treated as a substitute for these requirements.

9.91 After a series of false starts, it now seems clear that unless the terms and conditions of the deposit account are complied with concurrently and together with the service of the garnishee order nisi, then the balance in the account cannot be attached. It has been so held by the Full Courts of three Australian States and this also represents the position in England prior to legislative intervention.[1]

1 See *Bank of NSW Savings Bank Ltd (Garnishee) v Fremantle Auto Centre Pty Ltd (Judgment Creditor) and Poland (Judgment Debtor)* [1973] WAR 161; *Music Masters Pty Ltd v Minelle and the Bank of NSW Savings Bank Ltd* [1968] Qd R 326; *Re ANZ Saving Bank Ltd; Mellas v Evriniadis* [1972] VR 690; *Bagley v Winsome and National Provincial Bank Ltd* [1952] 2 QB 236.

9.92 The position is now different in New South Wales and in England. The Supreme Court Rules 1970 (NSW) specify that a sum shall be "due and accruing" for the purposes of garnishee orders notwithstanding that conditions concerning notice of withdrawal or production of the passbook have not been complied with; Pt 46. There is a similar section in the English Administration of Justice Act 1956.

Money credited after service

9.93 Money which is deposited by the judgment debtor following the service of the order nisi increases the debt owed by the banker to the customer, but can it be said that such moneys were "owing or accruing" due? The question was considered in England by the Court in *Heppenstall v Jackson.*[1] The bank had been served with a garnishee order nisi in respect of a customer's account. Money had been deposited into the account following this service and the issue in the case was whether these after deposited funds were attached by the order. The Court reviewed the earlier cases and came to the conclusion that it was clear that a garnishee order attaches only those debts which exist at the time that the order is made and served. Consequently, money deposited into the account after the service of the order is not attached.

1 [1939] 1 KB 585.

9.94 Unfortunately, the case does not make clear the fate of money which might be deposited after the order is made but before it is served or the status of money which might be paid out by the bank between the time of making and service of the order. Perhaps some guidance may be taken from *Bank of NSW v Barlex Investments Pty Ltd.*[1] The issue concerned the fate of a cheque for some £400 which had been deposited prior to the making of the garnishee order nisi, but which had remained uncleared at that time. There was a credit for the amount in the customer's account, but the deposit had been accepted with the customary condition that uncleared effects could not be drawn upon. The Court held that the sum was not part of the debt owed by the bank at the time when the order was made and so was not attached by it.

1 (1963-1964) 64 SR(NSW) 274.

9.95 Unfortunately, there is no information concerning the situation at the time of the service of the garnishee order nisi. As a practical matter, if the banker wishes to continue with a current account for the customer, the prudent course would be to open a new account to which outstanding cheques and new deposits would be credited. It is then clear that the new account is not affected by the order nisi.

Multiple accounts

9.96 When there is an overdraft account and a current account in credit, it appears to be ordinary banking practice for the banker to combine the accounts and to treat as attached only the surplus balance if any. It appears that this practice is followed irrespective of any agreement with the customer concerning notice.

9.97 Weaver and Cragie consider the position where one of the accounts is a fixed loan account.[1] There appears to be no definitive authority on the matter. Those authors suggest that the matter is probably governed by the terms of the fixed loan agreement which related to the banker's right to combine.

1 Weaver and Cragie, *The Law Relating to Banker and Customer in Australia*, Sydney, 1975 p 220.

Accounts in which third parties have an interest

9.98 The money in the account must belong to the judgment debtor in order to be attachable. Since the judgment creditor takes subject to all equitable interests, this means that it is not merely sufficient that the account be in the name of the judgment debtor. For example, if the money is held in trust, or if there has been a valid assignment of the account to some other party, even if the assignment is equitable only, then the account is not attachable by the garnishment procedure. In *Harrods Ltd v Tester*[1] the account of a married woman was garnished. Her husband brought evidence to the effect that he had supplied all of the money in the account and that the wife only signed cheques with her husband's consent. It was held that there was indeed a resulting trust in the husband's favour and the account could not be attached by the wife's creditors even though it stood in her name.

1 [1937] 2 All ER 236.

9.99 Following on from the same principle, it seems that a joint account cannot be attached in respect of a debt owed by one only of the account holders, and this applies equally to partnership accounts. In *Hirschorn v Evans*[1] the Court of Appeal held that the joint account of a husband and wife was prima facie the property of both and that as a consequence it was not available for attachment in respect of the husband's debt.

1 [1938] 2 KB 801.

Chapter 10

Bills of Exchange

10.1 The law of negotiable instruments is sometimes considered difficult, but usually that is because the commercial uses and needs which gave rise to the instruments are not understood. Once the function of a negotiable instrument is perceived, many of the legal problems can be understood and solved merely by a consideration of that function.

The problem: the need to transfer debts

10.2 In a remarkable range of commercial situations, it is necessary and/or desirable for one of the parties to be able to transfer a debt which is owed to him. As an example of such an occasion, the party to whom the debt is owed might wish or need to have the money in advance of the time when payment is due. This can be achieved if there is a reliable and inexpensive method of legally "selling" the debt to a third party. Unlike an ordinary sale of a chattel, the sale of a debt inevitably involves at least three parties, namely, the person who owes the debt, the original creditor and the transferee of the debt.

10.3 The original common law rules concerning the transfer of a debt were very simple: it was not allowed.[1] A debt was treated in much the same way as any other contract so that the obligations were considered to be personal to the contracting parties and neither the benefits nor the obligations of the contract had anything to do with outsiders.

1 *Lampet's Case* (1613) 10 Rep 46b; 77 ER 994.

10.4 However, a debt is not like any other contract. The obligation to pay money is impersonal in the sense that generally speaking the debtor will be indifferent to the identity of the recipient of the money so long as the debt is discharged by the payment. Similarly, the creditor is only interested in obtaining payment; its source is usually a matter of the greatest indifference. This impersonal nature of a contract of debt is particularly apparent in commercial contracts.

A sample trade situation

10.5 The earliest examples of the need to transfer debts arose in the international sale of goods. A seller wishes to receive payment as soon as possible. The buyer is obliged to pay the price at the time when the goods are shipped,[1] but clearly wishes to postpone payment until as late a date as possible. From the time of shipment, the seller is owed a debt by the buyer. If it were possible to transfer that debt to a local financier or bank, then the seller could receive payment immediately and the debt could be collected from the buyer by the intermediary at a time agreed upon. The costs of financing would, of course, be shared in some manner to be negotiated in the contract of sale between the buyer and seller.

1 More precisely, at the time when the shipping documents are tendered in a cif contract. See Schmitthoff, *The Export Trade*, 7th ed, London, 1980.

10.6 The trade example illustrates another commercial advantage of having an efficient legal method of transferring debts. The financier involved in the transaction will ordinarily be a banker. If it is a banker with an overseas branch located in the place of the buyer, then when the time for payment is due, the buyer/debtor may pay in that place. The need for the payment to be physically transferred from one place to another is eliminated.

10.7 It is not even necessary for the local banker to have an overseas branch in order for this benefit to accrue. It is only necessary for there to be a "correspondent" banker with which the first banker does a volume of business of this type. In order to facilitate the discussion, call the seller's banker SB and the buyer's banker BB. The seller S transfers the debt to SB and receives payment immediately. SB then transfers the debt to BB who collects it from B when due. If the transaction between SB and BB were the only one of its type, nothing would be gained so far as the transfer of funds was concerned, for BB would have to pay SB for the debt.

10.8 But if SB and BB do a volume of business in both directions, that is, if SB regularly buys debts from BB as well as sells debts to BB, then only a very small proportion of the total amount traded need ever be physically transferred. In an ideal world, the amounts bought and sold would balance perfectly and there would be no need at all to transfer actual money.

10.9 Even when the amounts do not balance precisely, it may not be necessary to transfer sums. One of the parties, say SB, ends by owing an amount to the other. SB could pay this by the physical transfer of money, but it might be that some third party, TB, owes SB a debt. It would then be possible for the obligation between SB and BB to be satisfied by the transfer to BB of the debt owed by TB.

Basic requirements of a good transfer

10.10 In order for the transfer of debts to function efficiently and commercially, it is necessary that there be a legal framework which makes it advantageous to the parties to transfer the debts rather than to insist upon payment of the money.

10.11 To understand this more fully, consider the situation between the parties when a chattel is sold. The rule in such a circumstance, subject to many exceptions, is nemo dat quod non habet, ie, the seller cannot give a better title than that which he has to give. It is therefore necessary for the buyer to assure himself that the seller has a good title to give or to take the risk that the purchase will yield a defective title or no title at all.

10.12 The nemo dat quod non habet rule is only just acceptable in the law relating to the transfer of chattels, but it would be crippling as a part of the law relating to the transfer of debts. First, the "title" to debts is much more difficult to investigate since the original debtor may have a wide variety of defences against the original creditor. Secondly, the would-be transferee of the debt may be in a physical position far removed from that of the original debtor, so that it is either impossible or prohibitively expensive to contemplate the investigation of the "title" to the debt.

Reliance on transferor

10.13 A second requirement is that the transferee must be able ultimately to rely upon the credit of the transferor. Again, the reason for this requirement is simply one of investigative costs. The person who owes the debt may be unknown to the transferee or, if known, may be of an uncertain credit risk. The transferor is the person with whom the transferee does business and whose credit the transferee is in a position to evaluate.

Enforceability

10.14 Thirdly, the debt must be simply and cheaply enforceable by the transferee. It should not be necessary to join the transferor either as plaintiff or as defendant. It is desirable if the procedures for the enforcement of the debt require as little evidence, and consequently as little expense, as possible.

10.15 As a consequence of the enforceability criteria, it is further desirable that the debt be transferable free from equities which attach to previous "owners" of the debt. If, as in the case of assignments of debts, the transferee takes subject to equities, then it is almost certainly necessary that the previous "owners" of the debt should be joined as parties to the action, for it is only in that way that all accounts may be settled by a single judicial decision.

Negotiability

10.16 As mentioned, the early common law did not allow for the transfer of a debt. Early merchants began to use documents which were honoured by merchants everywhere as containing obligations which were subject to usage which was not always in conformity with strict law. The usages which were observed by merchants came to be known as the law merchant and was enforced by special trade Courts that were, in a sense, international in outlook. The law merchant was absorbed into the common law and the bill of exchange, as these documents were known, came to be recognised as choses in action which possessed special legal characteristics.

10.17 These characteristics are precisely those required to make transferability of debts a valuable commercial item. They are:

1 the instruments are freely transferable, by indorsement and delivery if made payable to a named person or order, by delivery only if made payable to bearer;

2 the transferee may sue on it in his own name. It is not necessary to join any prior party either as plaintiff or defendant;

3 enforcement procedures are inexpensive; consideration and certain other matters which would normally need to be pleaded and proved are presumed;

4 the transferee may, in certain circumstances, take free of any title defects which may have affected the transferor. This includes, again in certain circumstances, the possibility of taking a good title when the transferor has no title at all. It is said that the instrument may be "transferred free of equities".

10.18 An instrument which has these qualities is referred to as a negotiable instrument, but care must be taken with the word "negotiable", for even within the Bills of Exchange Act 1908[1] it is used in several different senses. Sometimes the word is merely a substitute for "transferable". Sometimes it means transferable with

the additional quality that the transferee may sue upon it in his or
her own name. Some authors, however, use the word only for
instruments which satisfy all four of the above requirements,
placing particular emphasis on the fourth item.

1 Hereinafter referred to as the Act.

Uses of bills

10.19 The original use of bills of exchange was, as indicated above,
as a means to facilitate international trade. They are still used in
that role, although their importance in that respect has declined
considerably in the years following the crash of 1929. However, their
adaptation for providing the legal foundation for modern financing
has meant that bills are more important to the banker today than
at any time in history.

International trade

10.20 The importance of the bill in international trade today is
difficult to assess. On the one hand, it has virtually died out as a
means of the supplier providing short term credit to the buyer. This
is as a result of the changes in world markets. Whereas international
trade was a "seller's market" for many years with goods in short
supply, since the mid-1950s the tide has changed and it is now the
buyers who call the tune. The bill of exchange provides very little
advantage to the buyer over other forms of credit. Indeed, as will
be seen when considering the defences available to an action on
the bill, the use of a bill imposes considerable legal disadvantages
for the buyer when there is a contractual dispute concerning the
performance of the contract.

10.21 However, there has been a dramatic increase in the use of
documentary letters of credit in the financing of international trade
and, in the common law world, a documentary credit is nearly
always accompanied by a bill of exchange drawn on the banker
issuing the credit. As will be seen in Chs 28 and 29, this use of the
bill of exchange may cause more problems than it solves, but it is
firmly established in commercial banking practice.

Accommodation financing

10.22 It is in the role of "accommodation finance" that the bill has
achieved a most remarkable "revival". In this financial context, a

common form of arrangement is that the borrower B wishes to obtain finance for some project. B approaches a lending institution L (which may or may not be a bank). The two arrangements which are most common are:

1 the "acceptance credit";
2 the "bill option" clause.

Acceptance credits

10.23 The acceptance credit is perhaps the easier of the two arrangements to understand. For various reasons, the lending institution may wish to do business with B, but would prefer not to advance funds directly. The solution is that the institution L "lends its credit" to B in the form of accepting a bill of exchange drawn on L by B with B as the payee. B may then negotiate the bill of exchange to a third party who is content to rely upon the credit of L. The taker of the bill also has the credit of B to rely upon, but by the very nature of things the credit of L will usually be the predominant motivation for taking the bill.

10.24 However, B does not receive the full face value of the bill. The difference between the amount that B receives and the face value of the bill represents the interest that is paid for the use of the money between the time of discounting and the time of maturity. B will also expect to pay a percentage fee to L which represents, from B's point of view, additional interest. This fee is known as the acceptance fee.

10.25 Although L appears as the party primarily liable on the bill, the contract between L and B will require B to put L in funds when the bill reaches maturity. This contract between B and L is of the utmost importance to the two parties and, provided both remain solvent, establishes that B is ultimately responsible to repay the sum. The contract is, however, entirely irrelevant to outside parties who may become holders of the bill. They are entitled to rely entirely on the bill and to treat L as being the party who is primarily responsible.

The bill option

10.26 In the bill option, the institution L is prepared to advance the sums directly to B. However, particularly in times of large interest rate fluctuations, L may wish to retain the option of re-liquefying. Contractually, this could be done by stipulating that the loan was repayable by B on demand, but this might be commercially unacceptable to both L and B. The solution is the "bill option" whereby there is a clause in the contract which allows the institution to call upon B at any time during the currency of the loan agreement to draw a bill upon L which is then accepted by

L and discounted in the bill market. The face value of the bill will ordinarily be for the amount of the loan. L will not receive that sum for the bill on the market, of course, but depending upon the movement of interest rates, it may be profitable for L to market the bill quite apart from any desirability to increase liquidity.

Rolling over bills

10.27 In each of the above cases, the financing appears to be relatively short term, since the bill market generally deals only in bills with 90 to 180 days usance. The solution is to be found in the "rolling over" of bills. When the bill reaches maturity, it is paid by L and a new bill with the same face value is issued. In this way, the finance may be extended indefinitely. Of course, it is B who pays for any charges involved in the rolling over exercise. These charges again represent a part of the interest rate that B is paying for the finance.

The chain of liabilities

10.28 In order to make an effective legal structure which will facilitate the transfer of the original debt which is embodied in the bill of exchange, it is necessary that a person who is considering taking a bill should be able to evaluate its worth with as little investigation as possible. To this end, every person who has signed a bill of exchange makes, by the act of signature, certain promises to all future holders of the bill and also undertakes certain liabilities to future parties.

10.29 In this section, it is proposed to give a brief illustration of the way in which the Act imposes these undertakings and liabilities. The details will wait until later; the illustrations here are for a bill which passes through its normal life with no legal difficulties, that is to say, the vast majority of bills traded.

Ultimate liability: the drawer

10.30 The bill normally begins life when it is drawn by the drawer. It may be important that the bill be traded before it is accepted by the drawee; bills used in international trade nearly always are negotiated before acceptance. In order to facilitate this process, the Act provides that by the act of signing, the drawer promises that the bill will be accepted and paid.[1] Furthermore, in the event of the bill being dishonoured either by non-acceptance or by non-payment, the drawer promises that he or she will make it good to any holder of the bill or to any later indorser who has been compelled to pay.

1 See s 55.

10.31 The form of these promises means that a person who is contemplating the taking of the bill may rely upon the credit of the drawer of the bill. This will be of importance in the situation where the bill is the traditional trade bill. The drawer is the seller of goods who wishes to receive funds prior to the time when the buyer will pay. The drawer may discount the bill with his own bank. This bank, the seller's bank, is in an excellent position to evaluate the seller's credit; s 55 of the Act says in essence that the bank may take the bill knowing that it may rely on that credit.

Primary liability: the acceptor

10.32 Once the bill has been accepted, it is to be expected that the holder of the bill should look to the acceptor for payment. After all, it is the debt owed by the acceptor to the drawer which is being transferred when the bill is negotiated from hand to hand. Indeed, the Act does provide that the acceptor shall assume primary responsibility for paying the bill.[1] In addition to promising payment, the acceptor is estopped from making certain claims which might invalidate the bill, again adding to the currency and value of the bill.

1 See s 54.

Secondary liability: the indorser

10.33 A bill of exchange may pass through many hands during its lifetime. Suppose that a would be buyer of the bill B is considering taking the bill from the current holder H. B may not know the acceptor of the bill, may not know the drawer of the bill, may not know any of the previous parties to the bill, but B knows H and wishes to be able to rely upon the credit of H in order to evaluate the worth of the bill.

10.34 Assuming that the bill is an order bill, it can only be transferred by indorsement, so that H will indorse the bill to B should B decide to take it. Section 55(2) of the Act provides the necessary promises: by signing as indorser, H promises not only B but also any later holder that the bill will be paid and, if not yet accepted, that it will be accepted. Just as in the case of the other parties to the bill, H is also precluded from asserting certain facts that would make the bill invalid. If the promises are unfulfilled, then H promises to pay the holder himself.[1]

1 See s 55(2)(c).

The "chain" of liabilities

10.35 The result of these sections is the so-called "chain of liabilities": a person who takes the bill may rely upon the credit of any party who has already signed as drawer or indorser as well as the credit of the acceptor if the bill has been accepted at the time of negotiation. If the bill is dishonoured upon presentment, the holder may look not only to the person from whom the bill was taken, but to any person who signed prior to the time when the holder took the bill.

10.36 This chain of liabilities greatly facilitates the transfer of bills. When coupled with the extremely limited defences available to any of the parties to a bill, it means that the worth of a bill may be evaluated with as little cost as possible. A bill that is accepted by one of the major trading banks is thus a very valuable document which will be traded at a small discount, for any taker of the bill knows that it has the credit of the bank behind it. Bills with lesser known names will be traded at a higher discount.

History of bills and the Bills of Exchange Act 1908

10.37 Instruments similar to bills of exchange are very old. They were used by Arab traders during the eighth century and there are examples of bills which still survive from the 14th century.[1] By 1758 the law was sufficiently developed for a precise judicial definition to be given to the term "negotiable instrument".[2]

1 Holdsworth, *A History of English Law*, 2nd ed, vol viii, London, gives an example dated 1339. Street, *The Foundations of Legal Liability*, Northport, 1906 mentions bills dated 1304 and 1325.
2 *Miller v Race* (1758) 1 Burr 452; 97 ER 398, cited almost 100 years later by Blackburn J in *Crouch v Credit Foncier of England Ltd* (1873) LR 8 QB 374.

10.38 In 1878, Mackenzie Chalmers published a digest of case law on bills of exchange which contained more than 2,500 cases. As a result of this Digest, he was instructed to prepare a draft bill which was intended, for the most part, to formalise and codify the existing law. The result became the Bills of Exchange Act 1882. The Act was promptly adopted by virtually the entire English speaking world.

Nature and scope of the Act

10.39 The Act was intended to codify the existing law, but not in the sense of a code in civil law countries which completely states the law and which is the ultimate source of all law on the subject. Indeed, the rules of the common law are preserved in so far as they are not inconsistent with the express provisions of the Act. In the New Zealand Act, this is made explicit in s 98:

> **98. Saving** — (1) The rules of common law, including the law merchant, save in so far as they are inconsistent with the express provisions of this Act, shall continue to apply to bills of exchange, promissory notes, and cheques.

10.40 The method for interpreting the Act was laid down in definitive terms by Lord Herschell in *Bank of England v Vagliano Bros*[1] in one of the most widely quoted passages in all of English law:

> (a) The proper course is in the first instance to examine the language of the statute and to ask what is its natural meaning, uninfluenced by any considerations derived from the previous state of the law.
> (b) It is incorrect to start with inquiring how the law previously stood, and then, assuming that it was probably intended to leave it unaltered, to see if the words of the enactment will bear an interpretation in conformity with this view.
> (c) Resort may be had to the previous state of the law for the purpose of aiding in the construction of the provisions of the code if, for example, a provision is of doubtful import, or words are found in the code which have previously acquired a technical meaning or been used in a sense other than their ordinary one. These are examples only, and do not exhaust the category, but an appeal to earlier decisions can be justified only on some special ground.

1 [1891] AC 409, 419.

Chapter 11

Legal definition of bills

11.1 The legal definition of a bill of exchange focuses entirely upon the form of the bill. In the past, many difficulties have been caused by the fact that many instruments were handwritten and varied greatly in form. With the advent of standard printed forms and typewritten instruments, the problem seems to have lessened, but it has not disappeared.

11.2 This preoccupation with form is characteristic of the law of negotiable instruments and is firmly rooted in commercial practice. The purpose of a negotiable instrument is that, in so far as possible, it should be possible to determine the value of an instrument quickly and inexpensively. It should not be necessary to "go behind the instrument", that is, to go beyond the form of the instrument itself. It is not possible to implement this policy in all respects, but it enables better understanding of the law of negotiable instruments if the policy is kept firmly in mind.

11.3 Although it is the form which is important in deciding whether or not a particular document is a bill, the consequences are far from formal. The defences available when being sued on a bill of exchange are very limited.[1] However, if the document is not a bill, then it is at most an assignment of the original debt with the consequence that any of the defences which the "acceptor" might have raised against the drawer of the document will be allowed.[2]

1 See 11.48.
2 As an example of the importance of this to the "acceptor" see *Rosenhain v Commonwealth Bank of Australia* (1922) 31 CLR 46.

Section 3

11.4 In order for an instrument to be governed by the Act and to have the automatic benefits which flow from negotiability, it is necessary that the form of the instrument conform with the definition given in s 3 of the Act:

> **3. Bill of exchange defined** — (1) A bill of exchange is an unconditional order in writing, addressed by one person to another, signed by the person giving it, requiring the person to whom it is addressed to pay on demand, or at a fixed or determinable future time, a sum certain in money to or to the order of a specified person, or to bearer.
>
> (2) An instrument that does not comply with these conditions, or that orders any act to be done in addition to the payment of money, is not a bill of exchange.

Unconditional

11.5 Perhaps the most fundamental requirement is that the order to pay should be unconditional. The reasons for this have been explained thus:

> It would perplex the commercial transactions of mankind, if paper securities of this kind ẇere issued out into the world encumbered with conditions and contingencies, and if the persons to whom they were offered in negotiation were obliged to enquire when these uncertain events would probably be reduced to certainty.[1]

1 *Carlos v Fancourt* (1794) 5 TR 482, 485.

11.6 Section 3 of the Act gives the first example of orders which are not "unconditional":

> (3) An order to pay out of a particular fund is not unconditional within the meaning of this section; but an unqualified order to pay, coupled with
> (a) an indication of a particular fund out of which the drawee is to reimburse himself or a particular account to be debited with the amount, or
> (b) a statement of the transaction giving rise to the bill, is unconditional.

11.7 Some of the cases have concerned instruments which have receipts attached to them. In such cases, it has been held that when the instruction is addressed to the drawee, then the order to pay is conditional; when the instruction concerning the receipt is addressed to the holder or to the world at large, the order to pay is unconditional. So "Pay X on completion of the attached receipt" is a conditional order, but "Pay X" together with a notice on the bottom of the instrument which says "The attached receipt must be completed" is an unconditional order.[1]

1 See *Bavins Junr & Sims v London & South Western Bank Ltd* [1900] 1 QB 270; *Nathan v Ogdens Ltd* (1905) 94 LT 126; *Capital & Counties Bank Ltd v Gordon* [1903] AC 240.

11.8 Additional words may make it difficult to predict whether a Court will find the order to be "unconditional". This uncertainty is such that it must be considered very bad practice to include any words which might conceivably be interpreted as qualifying the order. Several cases will illustrate the kind of words that are so often unnecessarily added.

11.9 In *Peacock v Williams*[1] there was a document that the defendant claimed was a conditional order. The document read "Dear Sir — Please pay to Messrs H J Peacocke & Co the sum of one hundred and fifty pounds (£150) and deduct same from moneys coming due me on account of contract for Mrs Williams residence, Whataupoko". The Court held that the document was a bill of exchange, the direction being nothing more than an indication of the particular fund from which the drawer was to reimburse himself.

1 (1909) 28 NZLR 354.

11.10 In *Guaranty Trust Co of New York v Hannay & Co*[1] the bill was drawn by American sellers of cotton on the defendant's bank in Liverpool. The form of the bill was "Sixty days after sight this first bill of exchange (second unpaid) pay to the order of ourselves £1,464 9s 0d value received, and charge the same to account of 100/RSMI bales of cotton". The Court held that the indication of the account was not such as to make the order unconditional.

1 [1918] 2 KB 623.

Order

11.11 It is clear that the words must amount to an order and not merely a request. It is said that the inclusion of words of courtesy will not invalidate an expression which is in all other respects an order to pay, but it must be said that the cases are by no means easy to reconcile. In *Little v Slackford*[1] an instrument bearing the words "Please let the bearer have £7 and place it to my account and you will much oblige me" was held not to be a bill of exchange, whereas one drawn "[The drawee] will much oblige [the drawer] by paying to the order of [the payee]" was held to be a bill.[2] Once again, it is to be hoped that the more standardised forms currently in use will prevent the problem from being a modern one.

1 (1828) 1 Mood & M 171; 173 ER 1120.
2 *Ruff v Webb* (1794) 1 Esp 129; 170 ER 301.

In writing

11.12 Writing includes printed or copied material.[1] In the case of cheques,[2] the banks now issue printed forms with magnetic ink character recognition symbols printed on them to facilitate computer processing.[3] It would be a great inconvenience to the clearing system if other forms were used. It may be that there is an implied term in the contract between banker and customer which limits the rights of the customer to draw cheques on some other medium, but given the difficulty of establishing implied terms which derogate from the rights of the customer,[4] a banker would be well advised to pay cheques drawn by the customer on other forms. If the problem becomes significant, then steps should be taken to incorporate the term explicitly into the contract.

1 Acts Interpretation Act 1924, s 4.
2 A cheque is a special form of a bill of exchange. See s 73 of the Act and Ch 13.
3 See 19.19.
4 See *Tai Hing Cotton Mill Ltd v Liu Chong Hing Bank Ltd* [1985] 2 All ER 947 and the discussion at 2.22.

Addressed by one person to another

11.13 The person to whom the order to pay is addressed is known as the drawee. Section 6 of the Act deals with the requirements of this part of the definition:

> **6. Address to drawee** — (1) The drawee must be named or otherwise indicated in a bill with reasonable certainty.
>
> (2) A bill may be addressed to 2 or more drawees, whether they are partners or not; but an order addressed to 2 drawees in the alternative, or to 2 or more drawees in succession, is not a bill of exchange.

11.14 Thus, a bill addressed to "A and B" is valid, but an instrument ordering payment by "A or B" is not a bill of exchange, nor is one addressed "To A, but failing payment, to B".

Bank drafts

11.15 Since the bill must be addressed by one person to another, it follows that a bank draft is not a bill of exchange. However, s 5(2) provides that:

> Where in a bill drawer and drawee are the same person, or where the drawee is a fictitious person or a person not having capacity to contract, the holder may treat the instrument, at his option, either as a bill of exchange or as a promissory note.

11.16 The rights of the holder of the instrument are consequently not prejudiced by the technical irregularity in form of the instrument.

Signed by person giving

11.17 The Act does not define the meaning of "signature", but s 92 provides that it is not necessary that the instrument be signed by the hand of the person as long as it is written there by someone with the authority to do so.

11.18 It is perfectly possible that the bill is accepted prior to the signature of the drawer being affixed, a possibility recognised by the Act in s 18(1). Such a circumstance might arise, for example, when the debtor is the person who is actually the author of a bill, accepting it and sending it to the creditor for the signature of the creditor as drawer of the bill.

11.19 The drawer's signature must, however, be on the bill prior to payment. If the drawer's signature is forged it is "wholly inoperative, and no right to retain the bill or to give a discharge therefore or to enforce payment thereof against any party thereto can be acquired through or under that signature . . . ": see s 24.

On demand

11.20 Section 10 sets out the conditions when a bill is payable on demand:

> (1) A bill is payable on demand —
> (a) if it is expressed to be payable on demand, or at sight, or on presentation; or
> (b) If no time for payment is expressed therein.
>
> (2) Where a bill is accepted or indorsed when it is overdue, it shall, as regards the acceptor who so accepts, or any indorser who so indorses it, be deemed a bill payable on demand.

11.21 The most common form of a demand bill is, of course, the cheque: see s 73. Demand bills, including cheques, are often used as "security" for a loan. Such a bill is not a security in the proper sense, but it does allow the holder of the bill to make use of the summary procedures available for suing on the bill rather than the more complex action of suing on the contract of loan.

Future times

11.22 Problems sometimes arise with bills which are expressed to be payable at some future time which is not a fixed date but rather dependent on the occurrence of some event. The beginning point is s 11:

> (1) A bill is payable at a determinable future time within the meaning of this Act if it is expressed to be payable —
> (a) At a fixed period after date or sight:

(b) On or at a fixed period after the occurrence of a specified event that is certain to happen, though the time of happening may be uncertain.

(2) An instrument expressed to be payable on a contingency is not a bill, and the happening of the event does not cure the defect.

11.23 The problem, of course, is in distinguishing between events which are certain to happen and those which are mere "contingencies". It seems that "Pay A forty days after the death of B" would be a valid bill since the death of B is inevitable. On the other hand, a document expressed to be payable "six days after the ship *Childers* clears the Port Phillip Heads" is not a bill of exchange.[1] Further the second document is incapable of being a bill even if the *Childers* clears the Port Phillip Heads; the happening of the event does not cure the deficiency.

1 *Baker v Efford* (1873) 4 AJR 161.

Dating the bill

11.24 It is not necessary to date a bill of exchange, but later holders of the bill may fill in the date. In some cases this may be necessary. For example, in a bill payable at a fixed period after date, the date is necessary in order to fix the time of maturity. The drawer should enter the date, but the Act provides for the omission:

> **12. Omission of date in a bill payable after date** — Where a bill expressed to be payable at a fixed period after date is issued undated, or where the acceptance of a bill payable at a fixed period after sight is undated, any holder may insert therein the true date of issue or acceptance, and the bill shall be payable accordingly. . . .

11.25 A proviso to the section protects a holder in due course from the consequences of a wrongful date being inserted. In such a case, the bill is payable as if the inserted date were the true one.

11.26 For other bills, the holder may complete by virtue of s 20 which deals with inchoate instruments.

A sum certain in money

11.27 The exact amount to be paid must be ascertainable at the time when payment is to be made. Consequently, a document is not a bill if the sum ordered to be paid is dependent upon something which depends upon facts which may occur after the date of payment. As an example, in *Rosenhain's* case, the Court found that a document which purported to be a bill of exchange payable 60 days after sight was not a bill because it ordered the payment of a sum of money "with interest at the rate of eight per cent per annum until arrival of payment in London to cover". Since the time of arrival in London could not be ascertained at the time of payment, the amount was not a "sum certain"[1]

1 *Rosenhain v Commonwealth Bank of Australia* (1922) 31 CLR 46.

11.28 Some expressions have been in use so long that the Act allows them even though to most of us the amounts would not seem to be certain at the time of payment. Thus, s 9 provides that the sum is certain even though it is required to be paid with interest, or by stated instalments, or according to an indicated rate of exchange or a rate of exchange which is to be ascertained in some specific manner as directed by the bill. Note that the instalment requirement is that they be stated. This is thought to mean that a document which merely says "payable in instalments" is not a bill, but one which says "payable in two equal instalments due June 1 and July 1" would be a bill.

11.29 Rather surprisingly, it has been held that it is not necessary for the bill to express a particular rate of interest, ie, "pay $500 with interest" appears to be a valid sum certain. The rate of interest then payable then depends upon the law of the place where the bill was negotiated.[1]

1 See s 72.

11.30 Bills generally express the amount to be payable in both words and figures. This leads to the possibility that there might be a discrepancy between the two. In such a case, s 9(2) directs that the amount denoted by the words is the amount payable. There is no reason why this section should not also apply to cheques, but a paying banker should probably refuse to pay the cheque on the basis that the order from the customer is ambiguous.[1]

1 See 6.8.

Bearer bills

11.31 A bill is payable to bearer if it is expressed to be so payable, or if the only or the last indorsement thereon is an indorsement in blank.[1] An indorsement in blank is one where the holder merely signs his or her name but does not name an indorsee.[2]

1 S 8(3).
2 S 34(1).

11.32 The importance of being a bearer bill is, as will be seen in para 11.77, that the bill may be negotiated by delivery only. Bearer bills may circulate in much the same way as cash.

Order bills

11.33 Section 7(1) provides that:

> Where a bill is not payable to bearer, the payee must be named or otherwise indicated therein with reasonable certainty.

11.34 The definition itself contemplates a non-bearer bill in two different forms, namely, "Pay A" and "Pay to the order of A". This latter type is also commonly written as "Pay A or order". In fact, there is no significant difference between the two forms, since s 8 states:

> (4) A bill is payable to order if it is expressed to be so payable, or if it is expressed to be payable to a particular person, and does not contain words prohibiting transfer or indicating an intention that it is not transferable.
>
> (5) Where a bill, either originally or by indorsement, is expressed to be payable to the order of a specified person, and not to him or his order, it is nevertheless payable to him or his order at his option.

Parties to a bill

11.35 A party to a bill is a person who has signed the bill. By the act of signing, a party to a bill assumes certain liabilities and duties which depend upon the capacity in which the person has signed.

Holder

11.36 The holder of a bill is the person who, for the time being, has the right to collect the bill when it falls due. The holder is to be thought of as the person who "owns" the bill, although as will be seen, the rights of the holder will depend upon the circumstances under which the bill was taken.

11.37 The meaning of "holder" is defined in s 2:

> "Holder" means the payee or indorsee of a bill or note who is in possession of it, or the bearer thereof:

11.38 Although the definition is poorly worded, it is actually in two parts. The first defines the holder of an order bill as the payee or indorsee of the bill who has possession of it. The second part defines the holder of a bearer bill as the person in possession.

Rights of holder for value

11.39 The rights of a holder depend on which of three categories the holder falls into. Holders may be described as mere holders, holders for value, and holders in due course. Although the Act discusses holders for value, the term is not defined. The rights of a mere holder are set out in s 38:

> **38. Rights of the holder** — The rights and powers of the holder of a bill are as follows:
> (a) He may sue on the bill in his own name:

11.40 The effect of this section is not as far-reaching as it at first appears. It does not confer upon the holder a right of action, rather it enables a holder to conduct an action in his own name without the necessity of joining other parties either as plaintiff or defendant. The holder may not maintain the action unless it is possible to fulfil the requirements of the rules regarding consideration. There is, however, some assistance from the Act, for the rules regarding the need for consideration are extended somewhat by it.

Consideration for a bill

11.41 It seems that to enforce a bill, the holder must be a holder for value as the term is used, but not defined, by the Act. As against an immediate party, ie, a party from whom the holder took the bill, this requires that the holder has given consideration for the bill. Even in this context, the Act somewhat extends the contractual meaning of consideration by s 27(1):

> **27. Value, and holder for value** — (1) Valuable consideration for a bill may be constituted by —
> (a) Any consideration sufficient to support a simple contract:
> (b) An antecedent debt or liability. Such a debt or liability is deemed valuable consideration whether the bill is payable on demand or at a future time.

Past consideration

11.42 The extension to past consideration is an exception to the general rule in contract. However, it must be appreciated that this antecedent debt or liability must have been one owed by the plaintiff; third party debts or liabilities are not within the scope of the section unless the discharge of this liability may be taken to imply some obligation on the part of the plaintiff, eg, some forbearance to sue or a promise to forbear. Phrased another way, an antecedent debt or a liability can constitute valuable consideration for a bill if and only if there is some relationship between the receipt of the bill and the antecedent debt or liability.[1]

1 *Oliver v Davis* [1949] 2 KB 727.

11.43 There are times when it seems that the Courts are very willing to find consideration has been given. Thus, in *Bonior v A Siery Ltd*[1] a company director had drawn a cheque on a company account and given it to one of his personal creditors. The company itself was in debt to the director for a sum greater than the value of the cheque. The Court held that by drawing the cheque on the company account the director was requesting the company to pay the payee of the cheque a part of the sum due him. It was argued by the company that the payee was seeking to treat the antecedent debt of the director as consideration for the cheque. This argument was rejected. The company received benefit in two ways. First, the company would have been embarrassed had the managing director been harassed by the debtor but by issuing the cheque this harassment was prevented. Secondly, the company became entitled to offset the amount of the cheque against the amount which was owed the director.

1 [1968] NZLR 254.

11.44 Again, it was held in *Spencer v Crowther* [1] that the acceptance of a cheque in place of legal tender was good consideration. Thus, a cheque which was given as a deposit and then negotiated could be sued upon by the transferee.[2]

1 [1986] BCL 422.
2 Even though the transferee had not given value for the cheque. See below 11.45. The decision in *Spencer* followed *Pollway Ltd v Abdullah* [1974] 1 WLR 493.

Value given by some previous holder

11.45 Section 27(2) extends the notion of giving value even further. Consider the position of a holder of a dishonoured bill who wishes to enforce the bill not as against the party from whom the bill was taken, but from some party further back in the "chain". Is it possible that the holder can be met with the defence of no consideration? In order to forestall such a possibility, the Act provides:

> (2) Where value has at any time been given for a bill, the holder is deemed to be a holder for value as regards the acceptor and all parties to the bill who became parties prior to that time.

11.46 In order to understand the operation of the section, it may help to consider the following transactions. P is the payee in possession of a bill. For consideration, P negotiates the bill to X for valuable consideration who makes a gift of it to Y. The bill has been accepted by A and drawn by D. Y is a holder of the bill, but cannot enforce it against X. However, since value was given by X, Y is deemed to be a holder for value against all who became parties to the bill prior to the time when X gave value for it; consequently, the bill is enforceable by Y against P, A, and D.

Presumption of value

11.47 The Act also makes the action of the holder easier in that the giving of consideration is presumed. Section 30(1) states:

> **30. Presumption of value and good faith** — (1) Every party whose signature appears on a bill is prima facie deemed to have become a party thereto for value.

Holder in due course

11.48 It is the so-called holder in due course who receives the full benefit of the negotiability of a bill. The situation of a holder in due course is set out in s 38(b) and (c):

> **38. Rights of the holder** — The rights and powers of the holder of a bill are as follows:
> . . .
> (b) Where he is a holder in due course, he holds the bill free from any defect of title of prior parties, as well as from mere personal defences available to prior parties among themselves, and may enforce payment against all parties liable on the bill:
> (c) Where [the title of a holder] is defective, —
>
> > (i) If he negotiates the bill to a holder in due course, that holder obtains a good and complete title to the bill . . .

11.49 The "defect" in title may include the situation where the prior party had no title at all, such as a thief in possession of a bearer bill. The exact scope of "mere personal defences" is not defined by the Act, but includes such matters as rights of contractual counterclaim and set-off.

Section 29

11.50 Section 29(1) of the Act sets out the conditions under which a person can be a holder in due course of a bill of exchange. In effect, the holder in due course is a bona fide purchaser for value without notice of title defects:

> **29. Holder in due course** — (1) A holder in due course is a holder who has taken a bill, complete and regular on the face of it, under the following conditions, namely:
> (a) That he became the holder of it before it was overdue, and without notice that it had been previously dishonoured, if such was the fact:
> (b) That he took the bill in good faith and for value, and that at the time the bill was negotiated to him he had no notice of any defect in the title of the person who negotiated it.

Presumption that holder is in due course

11.51 Section 30(2) has been amended by s 50 of the Credit Contracts Act 1981. It provides that there is a presumption that every holder is prima facie deemed to be a holder in due course, but . . .

> . . . if in an action on a bill it is admitted or proved —
>
> (a) That the acceptance, issue, or subsequent negotiation of the bill is affected with fraud, duress, or force and fear, or illegality; or
>
> (b) That the bill was drawn as part of, or pursuant to, a credit contract and that one or more of the provisions of the Credit Contract Act 1981 have not been complied with, or that any of paragraphs (a) to (c) of section 10(1) of that Act apply, in respect of the contract — the burden of proof is shifted, unless and until the holder proves that, —
>
> (c) In any case to which paragraph (a) of this subsection applies, subsequent to the alleged fraud or illegality, value has in good faith been given for the bill; and
>
> (d) In any case to which paragraph (b) of this subsection applies, value has been given for the bill in good faith and without knowledge of the non-compliance or any oppressiveness.

11.52 It seems that the intention of the amendment was to prevent the avoidance of the Credit Contracts Act by the use of bills of exchange,[1] but if that is the case, then it is poorly drafted for it is generally thought that it is not necessary for the holder to rely on the presumption of s 30. Consider the situation where a holder has taken a bill on the basis of past consideration which was given before the fraud or illegality. It is still possible for such a holder to plead and prove that the requirements of s 29 are satisfied without reliance on s 30(2).[2] Perhaps the answer is that a person taking a bill who knows of the non-compliance or oppressiveness in respect of the underlying credit contract cannot be said to be taking in good faith, but if that is the correct solution then the amendment is unnecessary. It is a pity that the draftsman did not alter directly the requirements for a holder of the bill to prove that he or she is a holder in due course.

1 See Ch 26 for a discussion of the Credit Contracts Act 1981.
2 See Jones, *The Gilbart Lectures on Banking*, 1949, p 33.

11.53 The section was applied in a rather strange way in *Bank of Australasia v Curtis*.[1] A teller had stolen £645 from the plaintiff bank. He obtained a cheque from the defendant by means of fraud. The cheque was made payable "Self or bearer" and was uncrossed. The teller placed the cheque in among the cash and credits of the bank, but did not make out a pay-in slip. The cheque was not credited to the account of any customer. No director or officer of the bank was aware of the cheque until after presentment for payment. The defendant apparently had second thoughts about the transaction and placed a stop payment order on the cheque. The plaintiff bank sued as holder of the cheque.

1 [1927] NZLR 247.

11.54 There was no doubt that the plaintiff bank was a holder, but by virtue of the fraud being raised, was obliged to prove that they had taken it for value and in good faith. The Court held that the teller had handed the cheque to the plaintiff bank in fulfilment of his obligation to repay the stolen money; consequently, the plaintiff was a holder for value. It was clearly impossible for the plaintiff to prove honesty affirmatively, but as there was nothing to justify a suspicion of dishonesty, the plaintiff ought to be treated as having proved honesty in the circumstances.[1]

1 This part of the judgment seems quite unsatisfactory, for in essence it presumes that the bank took in good faith, precisely what the statute says must be affirmatively shown by the bank. It would be better to have based the conclusion on evidence of banking practice.

Taken a bill

11.55 Section 29 provides in its first part that in order to be a holder in due course the holder must have "taken" the bill and in para (b) there is also the implication that the bill was negotiated to him. So although the payee of an order bill who is in possession is a holder, the bill has not been negotiated and it follows that the payee cannot be a holder in due course.[1]

1 See *RE Jones Ltd v Waring & Gillow Ltd* [1926] AC 670.

11.56 However, it may be that the original payee later becomes the holder of the bill in a different capacity. This was the situation in *Jade International Steel Stahl & Eisen GmbH v Robert Nicholas (Steels) Ltd*.[1] The Court held that the party could be a holder in due course even though they were the original payees of the bill.

1 [1978] 3 WLR 39.

Complete and regular

11.57 If there is some irregularity in the bill itself, then the holder, however honest, cannot achieve the status of a holder in due course. The face of a bill includes the back,[1] with the consequence that the indorsements must be "regular". The requirement of completeness is reasonably self explanatory.

1 *Arab Bank v Ross* [1952] 2 QB 216.

11.58 The meaning of "regular" was considered by the English Court of Appeal in *Arab Bank v Ross*.[1] The defendant had made two promissory notes payable to "Fathi and Faysal Nabulsy Company" as a part payment for some shares. The notes had been indorsed over to the plaintiff bank. The defendant later learned that the bank had a charge over the shares which ranked prior to his claim. He alleged fraud, partly on the basis that the payees of the notes were directors of the bank. Fraud could only be raised against the plaintiff bank if they were not holders in due course of the notes.

1 [1952] 2 QB 216.

11.59 The indorsement was in the form "Fathi and Faysal Nabulsy" with the word "Company" omitted. The Court held that the indorsement was valid in the sense that it could be effective to negotiate the notes and constitute the bank a holder, but that the indorsement was irregular since the omission of the word "Company" was sufficient to give rise to reasonable doubt whether the payees and the indorsers were the same entity. Since the indorsements were irregular, the bank could not be a holder in due course and the defence of fraud could be raised.[1]

1 The defence was raised and defeated on the facts.

11.60 Lord Denning discussed the difference between regularity, validity and liability:

> Regularity is a different thing from validity . . . . On the one hand an indorsement which is quite invalid may be regular on the face of it. Thus the indorsement may be forged or unauthorised and, therefore, invalid under section 24 of the Act, but nevertheless there may be nothing about it to give rise to any suspicion . . . . Conversely, an indorsement which is quite irregular may nevertheless be valid. Thus, by a misnomer, a payee may be described on the face of the bill by the wrong name, nevertheless, if it is quite plain that the drawer intended him as payee, then an indorsement on the back by the payee in his own true name is valid and sufficient to pass the property in the bill . . . . Regularity is also different from liability . . . . Thus, if a payee, who is wrongly described on the front of the bill, indorses it in his own true name, the indorsement is irregular, but he is liable to any subsequent holder . . . . Conversely, a regular indorsement will not impose liability if it is forged or unauthorised.

11.61 It will be seen that regularity is solely a matter of form. An indorsement will be irregular if it is such as to give rise to doubt whether it is the indorsement of the named payee. It is likely that the practice of bankers is good evidence as to when an indorsement is such as to give rise to the doubt.[1]

1 Per Lord Denning at pp 226-227.

Overdue

11.62 In order to be a holder in due course, the holder must take the bill before it is overdue. Where a bill is payable other than on demand, then the date on which it falls due is calculated according to the specifications of s 14 which defines which days are to be included, the allowance of days of grace, the meaning of "month" and so on.

11.63 When a bill is payable on demand, it is overdue when it appears on the face of it to have been in circulation for an unreasonable length of time; "unreasonable" is a question of fact.[1]

1 S 36(2).

Good faith and value

11.64 A thing is deemed to be done in good faith within the meaning of the Bills of Exchange Act where it is in fact done honestly, whether it is done negligently or not.

11.65 It seems the requirement that the holder take for value is met if the holder is a holder for value within the meaning of s 27.[1]

1 *Barclays Bank Ltd v Astley Industrial Trust Ltd* [1970] 1 All ER 719.

Defects of title

11.66 The phrase "defect in title" was introduced into the Act as a substitute for the older expression "subject to equities". The principles of equity are foreign to the law of Scotland and the phrase was an attempt to make the Act intelligible to both the common law and the civil law. The meaning of the phrase is amplified in s 29(2):

> In particular, the title of a person who negotiates a bill is defective within the meaning of this Act when he obtained the bill, or the acceptance thereof, by fraud, duress, or force and fear, or other unlawful means, or for an illegal consideration, or when he negotiates it in breach of faith, or under such circumstances as amount to a fraud.

Duties of holder

11.67 The Act requires the holder to perform certain duties. Subject to many exceptions, they are set out in the following paragraphs.

Section 40 : presentment for acceptance

11.68 Section 40 requires the holder of a bill payable after sight either to present the bill for acceptance or to negotiate it to another holder within a reasonable time. Failure to do so results in the discharge from all liability of the drawer and all indorsers prior to the holder. "Reasonable" time is determined by having regard to the nature of the bill, the usage of the trade and the facts of the particular case.

11.69 Section 41 sets out the rules which define what is a proper presentment for acceptance and, in s 41(2), circumstances where the duty of the holder to present for acceptance is excused.

Section 45 : presentment for payment

11.70 Section 45 requires that, subject to certain exceptions, the holder must present the bill for payment.[1] Failure to do so results in the discharge of the drawer and all indorsers. Section 45(2) sets out the rules which define the way in which a bill is to be presented for payment and s 46 sets out excuses for delay or failure to present for payment.

1 Discussed in more detail below at paras 12.54ff.

Sections 42, 48 : notice of dishonour

11.71 When a bill is dishonoured either by the drawee refusing to accept the bill when properly presented for acceptance or by non-payment when the bill has been properly presented for payment, the person presenting the bill must treat it as dishonoured.[1] Failure to do so results in the loss of the right of recourse against the drawer and all indorsers.

1 There are exceptions. The details of notice of dishonour are discussed further at para 12.63.

11.72 The primary duty of the holder when a bill is dishonoured is to give notice to all parties of the dishonour. Failure to give proper notice to any drawer or indorser results in the discharge of liability.[1] Section 49 sets out the rules as to notice of dishonour. It is crucial to note that the time allowed for giving notice of dishonour is lamentably short and the consequences of failure to do so disastrously severe. Section 50 provides for some situations in which delay or failure to give notice is excused.

1 See ss 42, 48.

11.73 In certain circumstances, it may be necessary or desirable that the "noting" or the "protesting" of a bill be done. This is discussed in para 12.76.

Negotiation of bills

11.74 The key concept in the Act is that of negotiation. Negotiation is the means whereby a bill is transferred so that the transferee receives the benefits of being a holder of a bill of exchange. Section 31 is the key section:

New Zealand Banking Law

31. Negotiation of a bill — (1) A bill is negotiated when it is transferred from one person to another in such a manner as to constitute the transferee the holder of the bill.

11.75 Section 31 then continues to detail the procedure in which bills may be negotiated. The Act considers bearer bills first, but it is better to look first at the negotiation of order bills:

(3) A bill payable to order is negotiated by the indorsement of the holder completed by delivery.

11.76 It should be noted that the indorsement must be by the holder; consequently, a person who takes a bill under a forged indorsement does not have the bill negotiated to him and so does not become a holder of the bill. As a further consequence, the party who takes the bill next does not become a holder and so on. When a forgery intervenes, none of the later parties are holders of an order bill no matter how honest or innocent they may have been when taking the bill.

11.77 Subsection (2) which explains the negotiation of a bearer bill is different: "(2) A bill payable to bearer is negotiated by delivery".

11.78 The section does not say delivery by the holder. Consequently, a person to whom a bearer bill is transferred becomes a holder of the bill. Indeed, even the thief is a holder of the bill, since the holder of a bearer bill is merely the person in possession. However, the thief will have no rights which are enforceable, but as will be seen, the party who takes the bill from the thief may well have very significant rights as holder.

Indorsement

11.79 Order bills must be indorsed in order to be negotiated and s 32 sets out the requisites of a valid indorsement. The main requirement is that the indorsement be written on the bill itself. Paragraph (f) explicitly provides that the indorsement may be either special or in blank and it may contain terms that make it restrictive. A special indorsement names the person to whom the bill is to be payable.[1] A blank indorsement specifies no indorsee and a bill so indorsed becomes payable to bearer.[2]

1 S 34(2).
2 S 34(1).

11.80 A somewhat peculiar provision of the Act is that a bill which has been "converted" into a bearer bill by means of an indorsement in blank may be converted back into an order bill by the holder. Section 34(4) authorises the holder to convert the blank indorsement into a special indorsement by writing above the indorser's signature a direction to pay the bill to or to the order either of himself or some other person. Note that when the holder specifies some other person and delivers the bill to that person, the transferor is not liable on the bill since he or she has not signed it.

Conditional indorsements

11.81 There are times when an indorsement is added to a bill with a condition attached. Section 33 provides that where such an indorsement appears, the condition may be disregarded by the payor of the bill and the payment is valid whether the condition has been fulfilled or not.

11.82 It seems likely however, that the condition is good as between the indorser and the immediate indorsee. Thus an indorsee who receives payment under a conditional indorsement when the condition has not been satisfied would hold the proceeds in trust for the indorser.[1]

1 See Weaver and Cragie, *The Law Relating to Banker and Customer in Australia*, Sydney, 1975, pp 309-310.

Restrictive indorsements

11.83 A restrictive indorsement is one which either prohibits the further negotiation of the bill or indicates that the holder has authority merely to deal with the bill for a certain purpose and that the indorsement is not intended to be a transfer of the ownership of the bill. Examples given in s 35(1) are "Pay D only", "Pay D for the account of X" or "Pay D or order for collection".

11.84 Subsection (2) states the rights of the indorsee under a restrictive indorsement:

> A restrictive indorsement gives the indorsee the right to receive payment of the bill, and to sue any party thereto that his indorser could have sued, but gives him no power to transfer his rights as indorsee unless it expressly authorises him to do so.

11.85 In the event that a restrictive indorsement does authorise further transfer, subsequent indorsees take the bill subject to all of the conditions imposed upon the first indorsee under the restrictive indorsement.[1]

1 S 35(3).

Dual role of indorsements

11.86 Indorsements play a dual role in the Act. On the one hand, they are necessary for the negotiation of an order instrument. On the other hand, the act of indorsing a bill gives rise to certain obligations and liabilities which are expressed in s 55(2) and which will be discussed in para 12.10.

11.87 It will often happen that a bearer bill is indorsed by the transferor. It is important to note that the indorsement is irrelevant to the question of whether or not the new holder is a holder in due course. The signature is merely there to add currency to the bill. Of course, if the holder strikes out the "or bearer" part of the bill and converts the last indorsement to a special indorsement, then the result is probably such as to convert the bill into an order bill.

Acceptor

11.88 The acceptor is the person who is primarily liable on the bill. The acceptance may be given before the bill has been signed by the drawer or even if it is overdue and previously dishonoured,[1] although in the latter case, the holder is entitled to have the bill accepted as on the date of its first presentment for acceptance.[2]

1 S 18(1).
2 S 18(2).

11.89 If the acceptor accepts the bill as drawn, then it is known as a general acceptance. However, an acceptor may express acceptance in terms that vary the terms of the bill, in which case the acceptance is known as a qualified acceptance.[1] The holder of a bill may, and in most cases should, refuse a qualified acceptance and if the acceptor still refuses to give a general acceptance, the holder may treat the bill as dishonoured by non-acceptance.[2]

1 S 19(1) and (2).
2 S 44(1).

Referee in case of need

11.90 Section 15 of the Act defines a person who may be important in certain practical situations even though not strictly speaking a party to the bill:

> **15. Referee in case of need** — The drawer of a bill and any indorser may insert therein the name of a person to whom the holder may resort in case of need — that is to say, in case the bill is dishonoured by non-acceptance or non-payment. Such person is called the referee in case of need. It is in the option of the holder to resort to the referee in case of need or not, as he thinks fit.

11.91 Overseas bills often name a local representative as a referee in case of need, but unless the referee has full power to act on behalf of the drawee his ability to settle disputes is very limited.

The referee in case of need has not signed the bill and is not a party to it, although it will sometimes happen that the referee in case of need is expected to accept the bill on behalf of the person who named him.

11.92 The requisite formal procedures on dishonour must be followed before resort to the referee.[1] It should be noted also that it is at the holder's option as to whether or not to resort to the referee in case of need. It may be to the holder's advantage to ignore the referee in case of need and instead take immediate action against prior indorsers, particularly if it is known that they will act promptly on making good the bill.

1 See ss 65-68.

Chapter 12

Liability of the parties to a bill

Signature essential to liability

12.1 As discussed in Ch 11, the fundamental principle concerning liability on a bill is that the person to be charged must have signed the bill. Section 23 is in plain terms:

> **23. Signature essential to liability** — No person is liable as drawer, indorser, or acceptor of a bill unless he has signed it as such: . . . .

12.2 There then follows limited exceptions concerning signatures in trade names and signatures of firms, ie, partnerships.

12.3 Section 24(1) is complementary:

> **24. Forged or unauthorised signature** — (1) Subject to the provisions of this Act, where a signature on a bill is forged, or is placed thereon without the authority of the person whose signature it purports to be, the forged or unauthorised signature is wholly inoperative, and no right to retain the bill or to give a discharge therefor or to enforce payment thereof against any party thereto can be acquired through or under that signature, unless the party against whom it is sought to retain or enforce payment of the bill is precluded from setting up the forgery or want of authority.

12.4 One of the exceptions is given in s 60 of the Act which provides certain defences and benefits to a banker who has paid an order bill which is payable on demand.[1]

1 See 17.18.

12.5 Consequently, it is the person who takes a bill from a forger who will bear the loss, not the person who is the holder of the bill at the time when it is misappropriated. This is somewhat of an arbitrary solution to the problem of allocating losses due to forgeries. It is one of the few areas of the law where the solution is different in other countries. The general solution in the civil law countries is that the holder is the person who bears the loss, on the theory that it is the carelessness of that holder which allowed the bill to fall into the hands of the forger. Our solution to the problem is clearly based on a property concept which holds that the owner has no duty to take care of his or her own property.

12.6 All of this is not to say that parties who take following a forged indorsement have no rights at all. The effect of a forgery on the "chain of liabilities" will be discussed in 12.46ff.

The role of delivery

12.7 The definition of "indorsement" in the definition section is "indorsement completed by delivery" and that "delivery" means "transfer of possession, actual or constructive, from one person to another". Further, delivery is necessary in order for a bill to be negotiated.

12.8 Section 21 of the Act deals with the general question of delivery. The important part is s 21(1):

> Every contract on a bill, whether it is the drawer's, the acceptor's, or an indorser's, is incomplete and revocable until delivery of the instrument in order to give effect thereto:
> Provided that where an acceptance is written on a bill, and the drawee gives notice to or according to the directions of the person entitled to the bill that he has accepted it, the acceptance then becomes complete and irrevocable.

12.9 Failure to make a delivery cannot be used as a defence if the bill has come into the hands of a holder in due course, for in such a case s 21(3) provides that there is a conclusive presumption of valid delivery of the bill by all parties prior to the time when the bill came into the hands of the holder in due course.

Liability of the acceptor

12.10 As mentioned previously, the acceptor is the person who is primarily and ultimately responsible for the payment of the bill. This liability to pay is a general promise whereas the promises of the drawer and indorsers are conditional since they promise to pay only in the event that the acceptor does not. The relationship is similar to that of a principal debtor (the acceptor) and sureties (the drawer and indorsers). The analogy is close enough that an indorser who is obliged to pay is entitled to the benefit of any securities which may have been deposited by the acceptor with the holder for the purposes of securing the payment of the bill.[1]

1 See *Duncan, Fox & Co v North & South Wales Bank* (1880) 6 App Cas 1; but there must be some connection between the taking of the securities and the transaction which gave rise to the bill; see *Scholefield Goodman and Sons Ltd v Zyngier* (1985) 63 ALR 43.

12.11 If the holder of the bill who has presented it for acceptance has been content with a qualified acceptance, then the acceptors liability is limited by the qualifications of the acceptance.

Estoppel

12.12 Section 54(b) provides that certain estoppels may be raised against the acceptor by a person who is a holder in due course. The estoppels relate to certain facts which would invalidate the bill, but which must be taken to amount to representations by the acceptor at the time when the acceptor's signature was added to the bill.

12.13 For example, the acceptor is estopped from denying the existence of the drawer, the genuineness of the drawer's signature and the capacity and authority of the drawer to have drawn the bill. This will be of the utmost importance when the drawer's signature is forged: the section guarantees that the risk of the drawer's signature being forged falls upon the acceptor and not on a later holder in due course.

12.14 There is a logical difficulty in this case: since the drawer's signature is forged, the document is not strictly speaking a bill of exchange at all. How can there be a holder in due course, a concept which requires the application of the Act which, by its own terms, applies only to bills? The answer is that where there are genuine signatures mixed with forgeries, the parties who have signed the document in the belief that it is a valid bill will be held to their actions. "Holder in due course" in this context will refer to a person who has taken the bill under a genuine indorsement and has satisfied the conditions laid down in s 29(1).[1]

1 See *Bank of England v Vagliano Bros* [1891] AC 107.

12.15 The signature of the drawer will ordinarily be on the bill when accepted by the drawee, so that it makes sense to preclude the acceptor from arguing that the drawer's signature is forged. However, with regard to the remainder of the bill, the only other essential is that the payee be named; generally speaking, the payee will not have signed the bill as indorser at the time when the acceptance is placed on the bill. Consequently, the estoppels against the acceptor with regard to the payee are slightly different from those concerning the drawer. The acceptor may not assert that the payee does not exist or that the payee has capacity to indorse, but it is possible for the acceptor to plead by way of defence that the indorsement of the payee is forged or unauthorised.

12.16 The right to challenge the validity of the indorsement will not assist the acceptor in the event that the payee is fictitious or non-existent, for in that case the bill is payable to bearer and does not require a valid indorsement for negotiation.

Liability of the drawer

12.17 The drawer engages that the bill will be accepted and paid provided it is duly presented. If it is dishonoured, then the drawer is liable to compensate the holder of the bill or any indorser who is compelled to pay it provided the requisite proceedings on dishonour are duly taken.[1] There is no liability on the drawer prior to dishonour; it is a conditional liability only.

1 S 55(1)(a).

12.18 The drawer is also estopped from making certain assertions which are related to the condition of the bill when it leaves his hands. Section 55(1)(b) precludes the drawer from denying to a holder in due course the existence of the payee and his then capacity to indorse but not from disputing the validity of the payee's indorsement.

Liability of the indorsers

12.19 The indorser's liability like that of the drawer is conditional only. If the bill is dishonoured the indorser promises to compensate the holder of the bill or any subsequent indorser who is compelled to pay it, again provided that the necessary proceedings on dishonour are taken.[1] The only difference between the liability of the indorser and that of the drawer is that the indorser promises to compensate only those indorsers who are later parties to the bill. The drawer promises to compensate all indorsers.

1 S 55(2)(b).

12.20 It should not seem surprising that the indorser is precluded from denying to a holder in due course the genuineness and regularity in all respects of the drawer's signature and all previous indorsements. The indorser is also precluded from denying to all later indorsers that the bill was at the time of his indorsement a valid and subsisting bill and that he had good title thereto.

Backing bills

12.21 There are times when it is desirable to "add the credit" of some person who is not a party to the bill. The most common example involves the loan of money to a small company. It may be desirable that a bill of exchange be involved as a part of the loan and that the company be the acceptor of the bill. However, the lender will often wish to have the directors or major shareholders of such a company guarantee repayment by the company. One mechanism for achieving this has traditionally been to require the director to "back" the bill.

12.22 The difficulty is that the signature of the director on the bill is not strictly speaking an indorsement since the director has never been a party to the bill in any way. It is common to call such a signature a "quasi-indorsement", although the Act does not use the term.

12.23 "Backing the bill" is considered in s 56:

> **56. Stranger signing bill liable as indorser** — Where a person signs a bill otherwise than as drawer or acceptor, he thereby incurs the liabilities of an indorser to a holder in due course.

12.24 This section presents several problems from the lender's point of view. First, the liability only extends to a holder in due course.[1] Many bills are irregular in the technical sense so that no holder may become a holder in due course. Secondly, by the very nature of things, the order in which signatures are placed on a bill may not necessarily achieve the results that are desired.

1 This strict reading of the section was confirmed by the Court in *H Rowe & Co Pty Ltd v Pitts* [1973] 2 NSWLR 159.

12.25 The type of problem which may occur is illustrated by *H Rowe & Co Pty Ltd v Pitts*.[1] The defendant was the director of a company called C & S Electrics Pty Ltd which owed sums to the plaintiff company. At the urging of the plaintiffs, a bill was drawn on C & S Electrics and accepted on its behalf by the defendant. The payee of the bill was the plaintiffs. The plaintiffs also wished to have the defendant "back" the bill. This was done by the defendant "indorsing" the bill, his signature appearing after the signature of the plaintiffs who appeared as the first indorser.[2] The plaintiffs later indorsed the bill to a merchant bank. When the bill reached maturity, it was dishonoured by C & S Electrics.

1 [1973] 2 NSWLR 159.
2 The defendant was not a true indorser, since he never had any title in the bill.

12.26 The plaintiffs made good the dishonour as they were obliged to do as indorsers of the bill and then sought to recover from the defendant. The defendant argued, inter alia, that he could not be liable to previous indorsers. The Court held that the Australian equivalent of s 56 could not assist the plaintiffs since they were not holders in due course.[1] However, in the case of immediate parties such as this, the Court held that it was entitled to hear evidence as to the intention of the parties. Since the intention was clearly that the defendant should be liable in the event that the company was unable to pay, the plaintiff succeeded.

1 They had taken the bill after knowing that it had been dishonoured.

12.27 The litigation could have been easily avoided had the bill been drawn in a different form. The intention of the parties was that C & S Electrics should be primarily liable and that the director should act as a guarantor, that is, the director would be the second in the chain of liabilities. That is easily accomplished if C & S Electrics is the drawee/acceptor and the director is the drawer of the bill. The plaintiff could have been named as payee or, better, the director named as payee and then indorse the bill over to the plaintiff company.[1]

1 The second form is better since the plaintiff company is then eligible to be a holder in due course. The payee of a bill, although a holder, cannot be a holder in due course. See *RE Jones Ltd v Waring & Gillow Ltd* [1926] AC 670 and the discussion at 11.55.

The aval

12.28 The law of the civil law countries on bills is governed by the Geneva Conventions.[1] Articles 30 to 32 provide for a person known as an aval. The aval is a stranger to the bill who signs it as a surety for some specific party to the bill, most often the acceptor. The aval assumes the same liability as the person for whom he guarantees. If there is no indication of the party for whom the aval is acting as surety, there is a presumption that it is for the drawer of the bill.

1 League of Nations Conventions No 3313, 3314, 3315 and 3316.

12.29 The existence of the aval would easily solve the problems which occur with parties "backing" a bill, but unfortunately decisions of the English Courts in *Jackson v Hudson*[1] and *Steele v M'Kinlay*[2] have precluded this simple and straightforward approach.

1 (1810) 2 Camp 447; 170 ER 1213.
2 (1850) 5 App Cas 754.

Material alterations

12.30 The commercial importance of negotiable instruments is based upon a legal regime which allows their value to be determined quickly, and therefore cheaply, merely by examination of the instrument itself. In such a circumstance, it is clear that an unauthorised alteration of the instrument has the most serious consequences. Parties to the bill will either incur liabilities which they did not intend, or later takers of the bill will be deceived as to its value.

12.31 In New Zealand law, it is the later takers who bear the risk of unauthorised alterations. Section 64 of the Act states the basic rule: when a bill is materially altered without the assent of all parties liable on the bill, the bill is avoided except as against a party who has himself made, authorised, or assented to the alteration and subsequent indorsers.

12.32 This was the common law rule prior to the codification. There are several points about it. First, it is only material alterations which avoid the bill. Secondly, the bill is still good against certain parties, namely, the person who made the alteration, any party who in fact authorised it and subsequent indorsers. There is no injustice in holding subsequent indorsers liable, for they believed that they were dealing with a bill in the altered form and incurring liabilities accordingly.

12.33 As to the question of what is a material alteration, s 64(2) gives some specific examples of alterations which are deemed to be material: the date, the sum payable, the time of payment, the place of payment. If the bill has been accepted generally, then the addition of a place of payment without the assent of the acceptor is deemed to be a material alteration of the bill. Further the Act itself provides that a crossing on a cheque is a material part of the cheque.[1]

1 See s 78 which refers only to crossings which are authorised by the Act. It seems to be an open question as to whether "crossings" which are not authorised by the Act could be considered as a material part of the cheque.

12.34 The examples mentioned in subs (2) are not exclusive, as suggested by the words "in particular" with which the section begins. Although not every alteration is material, those which result in a change in the business effect of the instrument or which have the effect of varying the rights or liabilities of the parties to the bill are.

12.35 Before the passing of the Act, a material alteration was a complete defence. The bill was avoided and discharged except as against the party who made the alteration or who assented to it.[1] Section 64 has the effect of changing the common law rule by virtue of the proviso to subs (1):

> Provided that, where a bill has been materially altered, but the alteration is not apparent, and the bill is in the hands of a holder in due course, such holder may avail himself of the bill as if it had not been altered, and may enforce payment of it according to its original tenor.

1 *Scholfield v Earl of Londesborough* [1896] AC 514; note that this is not relevant when considering the relationship between a banker and customer when a cheque has been altered through the carelessness of the customer in drawing the cheque.

12.36 First, it should be noted that the proviso will often be small comfort to the holder of an altered instrument. The most common form of alteration is, after all, the "raising" of a bill. So if a bill for ten dollars is raised to one for a thousand, the holder may, if the alteration is not apparent, enforce the cheque according to its original tenor, that is, for ten dollars. On the other hand, if the alteration involves a change in the name of the payee or of some other party, then the right to enforce according to the original tenor might still be a valuable one.

12.37 What meaning attaches to "the alteration should be not apparent"? Few people are likely to take a bill which has obviously been altered in the amount or where the names of the parties have obviously been changed. The English test is:

> An alteration in a bill is apparent within s 64 if it is of such a kind that it would be observed and noticed by an intending holder scrutinising the document, which he contemplated taking, with reasonable care.[1]

1 *Woollatt v Stanley* (1928) 138 LT 620.

12.38 The High Court of Australia seems to have taken a different view. In *Automobile Finance Co of Australia Ltd v Law*[1] a promissory note was made on a printed form. The handwriting which filled in the form was not that of the maker of the note and, at the time of making the note, nothing was written after the words "Payable at" which were printed at the side of the space for the maker's signature. The payee, without authority, filled in the place of payment in handwriting which was clearly different from that on the remainder of the note and was in a different colour ink. The note was then negotiated to the appellant who was a holder in due course. In a suit on the note, the maker claimed that the note was avoided by the operation of the Australian equivalent of s 64.

1 (1933) 49 CLR 1.

12.39 The High Court held that there was no apparent alteration. According to the High Court, an alteration is apparent only if the document itself shows that some revision of the text has taken place and its appearance must be consistent with the revision having occurred after completion or issue. The Court observed that the test mentioned above "does not mean merely that what has been substituted or added should be visible to him upon reasonable examination, but that the fact that it was put there as an addition or substitution will thus be seen". The alteration must

> be visible or apparent, as an alteration or change in the very words or figures originally written or printed in the document . . . . It is not enough to say that a prudent businessman would be put upon inquiry, or that his suspicions would be aroused by the form of the document. The alteration may be by addition, interlineation, or otherwise, but it must be visible as an alteration, upon inspection.[1]

1 Per Starke J at p 12.

12.40 It may be that the effect of the two differing formulations is not all that great, for if the form is such as to put a "prudent businessman" on inquiry, then it is at least possible that the holder could be shown not to be a holder in due course.

Taking a bill with a forged indorsement

12.41 As mentioned before, the legal regime of negotiable instruments is designed to facilitate the assessment of the value of an instrument merely by examining the instrument itself. It is generally not necessary to trace the title of the person offering the instrument nor need the taker be concerned that unseen equitable interests may return to haunt him at the time when the instrument is to be realised.

12.42 One of the unavoidable dangers of such a scheme is the danger of forgery. The legal problem is then to allocate the risks of forgeries. Only two possibilities present themselves. The first is that the risk of forgery should be on the holder of the bill, that is, the person who was the holder of the bill before it was misappropriated by the forger. The argument in favour is that this would encourage holders of instruments to be careful in their keeping of the instrument. Since most forgeries appear to be the work of clerks and others who are inside the establishment of the holder, placing the risk of such forgeries on the holder of the instrument would, it is argued, reduce the incidence of such forgeries.

12.43 The second possibility is to place the risk of forgery on the party who takes from the forger. The argument in favour is that commercial reality often demands an assessment of the credit and the honesty of the person with whom one is dealing and the person taking the instrument is obviously the person who is in the best position to make this assessment. Consequently, it is that person who should bear the risk of an error in judgment. Further, it is argued that the best way to reduce the incidence of forgery is to make life more difficult for the forger and that the best way of achieving that is to throw the risk of forgery on the taker of the instrument, for then it will be more difficult for the forger to pass off the instrument.

12.44 New Zealand law chooses the second solution. Under s 24 of the Act, a signature which is placed on the bill and which is forged or unauthorised is wholly inoperative. The person whose signature it purports to be cannot be held liable, and no right to retain the bill or to give a discharge or enforce the payment can be acquired by virtue of the forged or unauthorised signature.

12.45 The rule does not apply when the person against whom enforcement is sought is precluded from asserting the true facts. For example, a person who indorses a bill is precluded from denying to a holder in due course the genuineness and regularity in all respects of the drawer's signature and all previous indorsements.[1] Furthermore, the indorser is precluded from denying to his immediate or a subsequent indorsee that the bill was at the time of his indorsement a valid and subsisting bill, and that he had then a good title thereto.[2]

1 See s 55(2)(d).
2 See s 55(2)(e).

The chain of liabilities when there is a forged indorsement

12.46 To see how these sections work in the event of a forged indorsement on an order instrument, an example will be considered. Suppose a bill is drawn by B, accepted by A and that C is the payee and first holder of the bill. C indorses the bill to D who then becomes the holder. Suppose now that the bill is taken by a thief who "negotiates" the bill to E, necessarily forging D's signature. E indorses the bill to F and F indorses the bill to G. The position of G will be considered.

12.47 G is not a holder of the bill, much less a holder in due course. This is because G can only become a holder of an order bill by the indorsement of the bill by a holder. The bill was indorsed to G by F. But F is not a holder because F took from E and E is not a holder because the bill was indorsed to him not by a holder but by a thief. It is clear that there can be no holder of the bill who takes after the forged indorsement of the thief. None of the parties E, F, or G has any right to enforce the bill or to retain it. Indeed, if D, the last proper holder of the bill, can find it, D is entitled to demand the return of the bill.

12.48 This does not mean that G is without rights. Suppose G wishes to sue F. G is not a holder, but F is precluded from arguing this since to do so would be to argue that he had no valid title to the bill at the time when it was indorsed. Since it is assumed that G satisfies all of the other requirements of s 29, G may claim to be a holder in due course so that F may not deny the validity of any of the previous indorsements. So far as F is concerned it may be established that G is entitled to enforce the bill against F as an indorser. The same argument shows that G may enforce the bill against E.

12.49 But when G attempts to enforce the bill against D, the situation is quite different, for D is not precluded from asserting any of these things. D is not an indorser of the bill and is not bound by any of the estoppels which flow from an indorsement.

12.50 The effect of these sections is, then, that the ultimate risk of forgery is placed on the party who took from the forger, for in the above example, F and G may both have recourse against E, but E has no rights against anyone.

Forged drawer's signatures and acceptances

12.51 When the drawer's signature is forged, then the apparent drawer has not signed the instrument and so cannot be liable on it. If such an instrument is accepted, then the instrument will be treated as a bill of exchange as far as the acceptor is concerned and he or she will be subject to the liabilities and the estoppels of s 54.[1]

1 The instrument is not a bill of exchange since it has not been signed by the person giving the order. There is a certain circularity here, since if it is not a bill then the Act does not apply. Good sense has triumphed over logic, however, and parties who sign the instruments in the belief that they

are bills of exchange will find themselves with the rights and liabilities imposed by the Act. See the discussion in *Bank of England v Vagliano Bros* [1891] AC 107.

12.52 When the acceptor's signature is forged, then the bill is avoided since the addition of the acceptor's name is a material alteration to the bill, but once again, the bill will be treated as a valid and subsisting bill against all those who signed it in the belief that it was genuine. The acceptor will not be liable, but in all other respects the rights and liabilities of the parties will be the same as if the bill had been a normal unaccepted bill. In the unusual event that the acceptor pays the bill in the mistaken belief that the acceptance is genuine, then there are special rules which regulate his right to recover the money as money paid under a mistake of fact.[1]

1 See *Price v Neal* (1762) 3 Burr 1354; *National Westminster Bank Ltd v Barclays Bank International Ltd* [1974] 3 All ER 834; *Barclay's Bank Ltd v W J Simms, Son & Cooke (Southern) Ltd* [1980] 1 QB 677 and the discussion in Ch 18.

Duties of the holder

12.53 The Act imposes certain duties on the holder of a bill. Chief among these are the need to present the bill for acceptance, if not yet accepted, and to present it for payment at the proper time.

Presentment for acceptance

12.54 Not all bills need be presented for acceptance, although all may be if the holder so chooses. Those which must be presented are described in s 39, the most common of these being a bill which is payable "after sight", that is a fixed number of days after acceptance. It is clear that such a bill must be presented for acceptance in order to fix the maturity date.[1] Less common, but equally as clear, is where a bill expressly stipulates that it must be presented for acceptance. The third category of bill which must be presented for acceptance is "a bill . . . drawn payable elsewhere than at the residence or place of business of the drawee".[2] However, there is a special provision for this last kind of bill. Section 39(4):

> Where the holder of a bill drawn payable elsewhere than at the place of business or residence of the drawee has not time . . . to present the bill for acceptance before presenting it for payment on the day that it

falls due, the delay caused by presenting the bill for acceptance before presenting it for payment is excused, and does not discharge the drawer and indorsers.

1 See s 39(1).
2 S 39(2).

12.55 This does not eliminate the need for presentment for acceptance; it only provides an excuse for late presentment for payment.

12.56 In no other case is a bill required to be presented for acceptance.[1] It must be understood that a drawee of a bill who does not accept it will not be liable on the bill. This is so whether the bill is presented for acceptance which is refused, or whether it is presented for payment where acceptance is not necessary and that payment is refused.

1 S 39(3).

12.57 The holder of a bill which is payable after sight may not simply hold the bill and do nothing, for that would unreasonably delay the time of payment and perhaps prejudice earlier parties to the bill. For this reason, the holder is required either to present the bill for acceptance or to negotiate it within a reasonable period of time.[1]

1 S 40(1). "Reasonable time" depends upon the nature of the bill, the usage of trade and the facts of the particular case; s 40(3).

12.58 This is an extremely important requirement, for the failure to obey this duty has dire consequences: the drawer and all prior indorsers are discharged.[1] The Act specifies a series of rules as to when the bill has been properly presented for acceptance, as well as those conditions under which presentment is excused.[2] In this regard, it is important to note that it is not an excuse that the holder has reason to believe that the bill will be dishonoured.[3]

1 S 40(2).
2 S 41.
3 S 41(3).

Presentment for payment

12.59 With only a few exceptions, every bill of exchange must be presented for payment; failure to do so in accordance with the rules laid down in the Act will have the effect of discharging the drawer and indorsers of the bill, a catastrophic result for the holder if the bill is dishonoured.[1] There are circumstances where a delay in presentment may be excused:

46. Excuses for delay or non-presentment for payment — (1) Delay in making presentment for payment is excused when the delay is caused by circumstances beyond the control of the holder, and not imputable to his default, misconduct, or negligence. When the cause of delay ceases to operate, presentment must be made with reasonable diligence.

1 S 45.

12.60 Subsection (2) lists circumstances which will dispense entirely with the need to present for payment. Again, it is of the utmost importance to note that the fact that the holder has reason to believe that the bill will, on presentment, be dishonoured, does not dispense with the necessity for presentment.[1]

1 S 46(2)(a).

12.61 As in the case of dishonour by non-acceptance, if the bill is dishonoured when presented for payment, the holder has a duty to notify the drawer and indorsers of the bill. Failure to do so will, in general, result in the discharge of any party not receiving such notice.[1]

1 S 48.

12.62 Presentment for payment must be made by a proper person, at the correct place and to the proper person. Section 45(2)(c):

> Presentment must be made by the holder, or by some person authorised to receive payment on his behalf, at a reasonable hour on a business day, at the proper place . . . either to the person designated by the bill as payer, or to some person authorised to pay or refuse payment on his behalf, if by the exercise of reasonable diligence such person can be found.

Duties on dishonour: the duty to give notice

12.63 With only two exceptions, when a bill is dishonoured either by non-acceptance or by non-payment, the holder has a duty to give notice of such dishonour to the drawer and each indorser. Failure to give notice to a person entitled to it will result in the discharge of the party even if the party suffers no actual prejudice from the failure.[1] The exceptions are set out in the following paragraphs.

1 S 48.

12.64 Where a bill is dishonoured by non-acceptance, and notice of dishonour is not given, the rights of a holder in due course subsequent to the omission will not be prejudiced by the omission.[1] However, the later holder cannot be a holder in due course if he or she has notice of the fact that the bill has been dishonoured by non-acceptance.[2]

1 S 48(a).
2 S 29(1)(a).

12.65 Where a bill is dishonoured by non-acceptance, and due notice of dishonour is given, it shall not be necessary to give notice of a subsequent dishonour by non-payment unless the bill has in the meantime been accepted.[1] This is an extremely unusual sequence of events.

1 S 48(b).

12.66 It is never necessary to give the acceptor notice of dishonour, since that is precisely the person who has dishonoured it. The Act includes this obvious conclusion as s 52(3).

12.67 There are a number of specific circumstances which dispense with the need to give notice. Notice to the drawer of a dishonoured bill is unnecessary when:
   (i) the drawer and the drawee are the same person;
   (ii) the drawee is a fictitious person or a person who does not have the capacity to contract;
   (iii) the drawer is the person to whom the bill is presented for payment;
   (iv) the drawee or acceptor is as between himself and the drawer under no obligation to accept or pay the bill;
   (v) the drawer has countermanded payment.[1]

1 S 50(2)(c); (iv) and (v) cover the two most common situations where a cheque is dishonoured.

12.68 It is not necessary to give notice to an indorser when:
   (i) the drawee is a fictitious person or a person who lacks contractual capacity and the indorser was aware of the fact at the time when the bill was indorsed;
   (ii) the indorser is the person on whom the bill is presented for payment;
   (iii) the bill was accepted and made for the accommodation of the indorser.[1]

1 S 50(2)(d).

12.69 Needless to say, the wisest choice for the holder is to give notice to all of the indorsers and the drawer whenever possible. The time permitted for investigation is too short to determine if any of the parties fall within the exceptions and the consequences of failing to give notice are too severe. The exceptions only really come into play when it is desired to hold a party liable who has, for whatever reason, not been given notice.

Form and time of notice

12.70 Notice does not mean merely that the party knows of the dishonour. It means actual notification; even if a party entitled to notice knows for a fact that the bill is going to be dishonoured, he is still entitled to be given notice. The form of notice is not crucial; it may be given in writing or in personal communication and need only communicate enough information so that the recipient may identify the particular instrument and know that it has been dishonoured either by non-payment or non-acceptance.

12.71 Notice may be given as soon as the bill is dishonoured, and must be given within a reasonable time thereafter.[1] In the absence of special circumstances, notice is not deemed to have been given within a reasonable time unless the person giving the notice complies with s 49, rule (n). This is in two parts and depends upon whether the party giving the notice and the party receiving it reside in the same or different places. Where the parties reside in the same place, the notice must be given or sent off in time to reach the recipient on the day after the dishonour of the bill.[2] When the parties reside in different places, the notice must be sent off on the day after the dishonour if there is a convenient post on that day, otherwise by the next post.[3]

1 S 49, rule (m).
2 S 49, rule (n)(i).
3 S 49, rule (n)(ii).

12.72 The rules concerning notification are clearly anachronistic in terms of modern communication systems. In *Lombard Banking Ltd v Central Garage and Engineering Co Ltd*,[1] the bank advised the holder of a bill by telephone that the bill had been dishonoured and that the bills were being returned by post. The holder did not notify the drawer and indorsers of the dishonour until such time as the bills were actually received. The Court held that the telephone communication was, in the particular circumstances of the case, not notice of the dishonour, but merely "a warning of what was in the post and not the substantive notice of dishonour"[2] so that the holder's notice to the other parties was not out of time.

1 [1963] 1 QB 220.
2 At p 232.

12.73 The rules have also caused difficulty when notification is by post. In *Eaglehill Ltd v J Needham Builders Ltd*[1] it was clear to all of the parties that the bill in question was going to be dishonoured. The holder prepared a notice of dishonour which was dated 1 January 1971, the day after the bill was due to be paid. Through inadvertence, the letter was in fact posted on 30 December, the day before the bill reached maturity. The letter reached the defendants on the following day, the day on which the bill was in fact dishonoured. The House of Lords held that the notice was good since notice sent by post is not "given" until such time as it is received. In the absence of evidence, the House was willing to presume that the dishonour and the giving of notice had occurred in the proper order.

1 [1972] 3 All ER 895.

12.74 It may be that the holder will only give notice to some, but not all, of the indorsers. To cover this possibility and to allow those indorsers who have received notice to preserve their rights against all prior indorsers, the Act provides that notice may be given not only by the holder, but by or on behalf of an indorser who, at the time of giving the notice, is himself liable on the bill.[1] Further, notice given by the holder to an indorser preserves the rights not only of the holder, but also any indorser who has a right of recourse against the party who has received the notice.[2] Similarly, notice given by an indorser preserves the rights of the holder and all intervening indorsers.[3]

1 S 49, rule (a).
2 S 49, rule (c).
3 S 49, rule (d).

12.75 In all cases, the party giving the notice is allowed time which is similar to the time allowed the holder following the dishonour of the bill.[1] Finally, the sender of a notice which has been duly addressed and posted is deemed to have given due notice notwithstanding any miscarriage by the post office.[2]

1 S 49, rule (p).
2 S 49, rule (q).

Noting and protesting

12.76 In certain cases, it is desirable or necessary to follow a formal procedure upon the dishonour of a bill. The procedure is known as a "protest" and provides formal evidence of both the dishonour and the time of dishonour.

12.77 The procedure is that the holder of the bill takes it to a notary public who then makes a formal demand for payment or acceptance as the case may be. Upon the refusal, the notary makes a copy of the bill in the "protest book", notes the answer which was given to the demand and "notes" the bill, ie, writes on the bill itself a note which identifies the notary, the date of dishonour, any noting charges and a cross-reference to the entry in the protest book. The notary also attaches to the bill a ticket on which is written the essence of the answer given to the demand for payment or acceptance. The "protest" itself is a formal notarial certificate which need not be drawn up immediately. It is the document which is used as evidence at the trial should matters come to that. There is no prescribed form for a protest, but it must contain the information set out in s 51(9).

12.78 Most countries of the world require a protest upon dishonour in order to fix the parties with liability. New Zealand law does not, for ss 43(2) and 47(2) state the general rule that an immediate right of recourse accrues to the holder upon dishonour. In a bid for international uniformity, "foreign" bills must be protested; failure to do so results in the discharge of the drawer and indorsers.[1] Other bills may be protested, but it is not necessary to do so in order to preserve the right of recourse against the drawer and indorsers.[2]

1 S 51(2).
2 S 51(1).

12.79 The definition of "foreign bill" is in s 4:

> **4. Inland and foreign bills** — (1) An "inland bill" is a bill that is, or on the face of it purports to be, —
> (a) Both drawn and payable in any of the Australasian colonies; or
> (b) Drawn in any of the Australasian colonies upon some person resident therein. Any other bill is a "foreign bill".
>
> (2) Unless the contrary appears on the face of the bill the holder may treat it as an inland bill.

12.80 There are, as might be expected, some circumstances which excuse delay or dispense with the need for protest. Any circumstance which would dispense with the need to give notice of dishonour will dispense also with the need for protest.[1] Delay is excused when it is caused by circumstances beyond the control of the holder, and not imputable to his default, misconduct, or negligence; when the cause of the delay ceases to operate the bill must then be protested with reasonable diligence.[2]

1 S 51(11).
2 S 51(12).

12.81 Subject to those excuses for delay, the time available for noting is short: the bill must be noted on the day of its dishonour.[1] However, the formal protest may be issued much later and antedated so as to take effect from the date of noting.[2]

1 S 51(5).
2 S 51(6).

12.82 It is not necessary that a bill be protested in order to hold the acceptor liable.[1]

1 S 52(3).

Discharge of a bill

12.83 A bill is discharged when all rights of action on the bill are extinguished. The most common way in which a bill is discharged is by "payment in due course", but there are other possibilities. One of these has already been discussed, namely discharge by virtue of a material alteration.[1] Other, less common situations which may lead to a discharge are the acceptor becoming the holder of the bill at the time of maturity, a holder waiving his rights and the cancellation of the bill.

1 See 12.30 and s 64.

12.84 Discharge of the bill must be distinguished from discharge of one or more of the parties which will leave the bill alive and the obligations of the remaining parties otherwise intact.

Discharge by payment in due course

12.85 A bill is discharged by payment in due course by or on behalf of the drawee or acceptor. "Payment in due course" means payment to the holder of the bill made at or after the maturity thereof in good faith and without notice that the holder's title is defective.[1]

1 S 59(1) and (2).

12.86 The payment must be made by or on behalf of the drawee or the acceptor. When a bill is payable at a bank, the banker must take care to obtain the authority of the acceptor before paying on a bill which is overdue.

12.87 Payment made to a person in possession of an order bill under a forged indorsement is not payment in due course, since the person cannot be a holder.[1] This fundamental rule has an exception when the drawee is a banker and the bill is payable on demand:

> **60. Banker paying on demand draft bearing forged indorsement** — (1) Where a bill payable to order on demand is drawn on a banker, and the banker on whom it is drawn pays the bill in good faith and in the ordinary course of business, it is not incumbent on the banker to show that the indorsement of the payee or any subsequent indorsement was made by or under the authority of the person whose indorsement it purports to be, and the banker is deemed to have paid the bill in due course, although such indorsement has been forged or made without authority.[2]

1 See 12.41 and s 31.
2 See also the discussion at 17.18.

12.88 When the bill is paid by a drawer or an indorser, it is not discharged, but there are certain alterations in the rights of the parties. Where an order bill is payable to a third party and is paid by the drawer, the drawer retains a right of action against the acceptor, but may not re-issue the bill.[1] It is said that further negotiation of the bill in this case is prohibited because the effect would be to vary the contract by the drawer substituting himself for the payee.[2]

1 S 59(3)(a).
2 *Riley's Bill of Exchange*, 3rd ed, Sydney 1976, p 161.

12.89 When a bill is paid by an indorser, or when a bill payable to the drawer's own order is paid by the drawer, the party paying the bill "is remitted to his former rights as regards the acceptor or antecedent parties, and may, if he thinks fit, strike out his own and subsequent indorsements, and again negotiate the bill".[1] In this circumstance, the drawer is also the first indorser of the bill and it makes sense that he or she should be placed in the same position as any other indorser. There can be no objection to the bill being placed in circulation, since those who could conceivably be prejudiced by such an action will no longer be liable on the bill, the section providing that their names be struck out.

1 S 59(3)(b).

12.90 An accommodation bill stands on a slightly different footing.[1] It is the person accommodated who is "really" the person responsible for the bill, and there can be no objection if that person pays the bill. Consequently, s 59(4) provides that payment in due course by the person accommodated will discharge the bill.

1 See 12.21 for a discussion of accommodation bills.

Acceptor becoming holder at maturity

12.91 It may happen that the acceptor becomes a holder of a bill. If he or she remains the holder at the time of maturity of the bill, it seems absurd to demand that the holder present the bill for payment. Section 61 deals with the matter:

> **61. Where acceptor the holder at maturity —** Where the acceptor of a bill is or becomes the holder of it in his own right, at or after its maturity, the bill is discharged.

12.92 The position contemplated by the section is likely to be rare, but if it does occur then the person with primary liability on the bill, the acceptor, owes that liability to the holder, himself. There can be no possible reason to keep any of the other rights alive.

12.93 On the other hand, it must be appreciated that the acceptor must become the holder "in his own right". This means that the rights of the holder must not be subject to those of any other person. So, for example, if the acceptor becomes the holder in his or her capacity as a trustee or an executor, the section would not apply.[1]

1 *Nash v De Freville* [1900] 2 QB 72.

Holder waives rights

12.94 If the holder genuinely renounces all rights against the acceptor, there would seem to be no point in allowing the bill to continue its life. The step is such a drastic one, however, that the Act demands that it be in writing and that it be unequivocal.

> **62. Holder may waive his rights** — (1) Where the holder of a bill at or after its maturity absolutely and unconditionally renounces his rights against the acceptor the bill is discharged. The renunciation must be in writing, unless the bill is delivered up to the acceptor.

12.95 Although the section is not happily worded, it is clear that if the holder purports to retain any rights against any of the other parties to the bill, then the acceptor remains liable to these other parties even if the liability to the holder is discharged.[1]

1 *Muir v Crawford* (1875) LR 2 Sc & Div 456; *Jones & Co v Whitaker* (1887) 3 TLR 723.

12.96 If the holder takes such an action and then purports to negotiate the bill further, it would be unreasonable to hold that later parties are bound by the renunciation if they are unaware of it. Strangely, the section appears to protect later holders only if they are holders in due course.[1] Since "technical" deficiencies in the bill may prevent a holder from being a holder in due course, this seems unfortunate.[2]

1 S 62(3).
2 See *Arab Bank v Ross* [1952] 2 QB 216 and the discussion at 11.57.

Cancellation of a bill

12.97 Analogous to a waiver of rights, there is no reason to prevent a holder from cancelling the bill in its entirety or simply discharging one of the parties to the bill, provided the rights of the other parties are not adversely affected. The Act approaches the problem in the following section:

> **63. Cancellation** — (1) Where a bill is intentionally cancelled by the holder or his agent, and the cancellation is apparent thereon, the bill is discharged.
> (2) Any party liable on a bill may in like manner be discharged by the intentional cancellation of his signature by the holder or his agent. In such case an indorser who would have had a right of recourse against the party whose signature has been cancelled is also discharged.

12.98 There is no prescribed method of cancelling a bill, although it is clear from the section that the cancellation must be apparent on the face of the bill. Certainly writing "Cancelled" in prominent letters across the face of the bill would do the job. It might be thought that tearing the bill would be a good form of cancellation, but in *Ingham v Primrose*[1] the Court held that a bill which had been torn into two parts and thrown into the street had not been cancelled. It will be appreciated that tearing a bill into two parts and posting them separately was a widely used method of security.

1 (1859) 7 CBNS 82; 141 ER 745.

12.99 A cancellation which is made unintentionally or without authority or by mistake is inoperative, but the Act places a burden of proof on the party who alleges that the apparent cancellation was so made.[1]

1 S 63(3).

Acceptance for honour and payment supra protest

12.100 A bill which is dishonoured is an embarrassment to every person who is a party to it. No matter how innocent the parties might be, their credit will be damaged. One of the mechanisms to prevent this is the acceptance or payment supra protest. It has been said that the purpose of this mechanism is twofold: first to preserve the rights of the holder which he would have enjoyed had the bill been properly accepted or paid and secondly to save the credit of the parties to the bill and to prevent them from being sued.[1]

1 See *Riley's Bill of Exchange*, 3rd ed, Sydney 1976, p 175.

12.101 In many cases where the bill is dishonoured, it will simply be passed back along the line of indorsements to the drawer. This will particularly be the case when the indorsers are in reality only intermediaries whose purpose is to move the bill from the drawer to the drawee. Such a situation is common when the bill is an international trade bill and the intermediaries are bankers.

12.102 If a bill which is not overdue has been dishonoured by non-acceptance and has been protested, then any person who is not already a party to the bill may, with the consent of the holder, accept the bill supra protest for the honour of any party liable on the bill or for the honour of the person for whose account the bill is drawn.[1] The acceptance for honour supra protest must be written on the bill, indicate that it is an acceptance for honour and be signed by the acceptor for honour.[2]

1 S 65(1).
2 S 65(3).

12.103 The acceptance for honour supra protest is a conditional promise. Section 66:

> (1) The acceptor for honour of a bill by accepting it engages that he will, on due presentment, pay the bill according to the tenor of his acceptance, if it is not paid by the drawee, provided that it has been duly presented for payment and protested for non-payment, and that he receives notice of these facts.
> (2) The acceptor for honour is liable to the holder and to all parties to the bill subsequent to the party for whose honour he has accepted.

12.104 It seems that the acceptor for honour stands in the shoes of the party for whom he has intervened and so is bound by the same estoppels which bound that party. The acceptor for honour also has the same rights against prior parties as had the party on whose behalf the intervention occurred.[1] However, the acceptor for honour also has rights of recovery against the party for whose honour the intervention occurred.

1 *Williams v Germaine* (1827) 7 B & C 468; *Hoare v Cazenove* (1812) 16 East 391.

12.105 The second form of intervention is payment for honour supra protest.[1] The conditions under which intervention may occur differ from those of acceptance for honour in three ways. First, the bill may be overdue. Secondly, the person who pays for honour may be an existing party to the bill or a stranger. Thirdly, the consent of the holder is not necessary; indeed, if the holder of the bill refuses to receive payment supra protest then he or she loses any right of recourse against any party who would have been discharged by the payment.[2] This could be disastrous, for it is not only the party for whose honour the payment is made who is discharged, but all parties subsequent to that party.[3]

1 S 68.
2 S 68(7).
3 S 68(5).

12.106 In order to be effective, payment for honour supra protest must be attested by a notarial act of honour. This is a certificate given by a notary public to the effect that the original bill had been duly protested and that the payer has declared his intention to pay the bill for honour and for whose honour it is being paid.[1]

1 S 68(3) and (4).

12.107 The consequences of a payment for honour supra protest are that the payor is entitled to receive the bill from the holder and is then entitled to all the rights of that holder save that the parties which are subsequent to the party on whose behalf the intervention occurred are discharged.[1]

1 S 68(5) and (6).

Miscellaneous

Lost bills

12.108 Bills of exchange are only pieces of paper, albeit very valuable ones. It is inevitable that they will occasionally be lost or accidentally destroyed. When a bill which is not overdue is lost, the Act provides that the person who was the holder of the bill may demand a replacement from the drawer of the bill. Since this procedure has obvious dangers, particularly in the case of a bearer bill which might resurface to the great detriment of the drawer, the Act also permits the drawer of the bill to require the former holder to give security to the drawer as a means of indemnifying him against any claim in case the original bill is found again.[1] If the drawer does not comply with the request for a replacement, he may be compelled to do so.[2]

1 S 69(1).
2 S 69(2).

12.109 Rather surprisingly, the section has been held not to apply in the case of a destroyed note.[1] Further, note that there is no provision in the Act to compel the former indorsers or even the acceptor to add their names to the replacement instrument. The section also apparently fails to give the holder of a lost note the right to a replacement, for under the scheme of translation provided in s 90(2) the maker of a note corresponds not with the drawer but with the acceptor of a bill.[2] The person who corresponds to the drawer, the first indorser of a note, can scarcely be compelled to make a note, nor can it be demanded that he indorse a non-existent note.

1 *Ex parte Walker* (1892) 9 WN (NSW) 1.
2 See the discussion of promissory notes below at 12.115.

12.110 The inability to obtain a replacement is not as calamitous as it first appears, for the Act also provides for the possibility of bringing an action on a lost instrument:

> **70. Action on lost bill** — In any action or proceeding upon a bill, the Court or a Judge may order that the loss of the instrument shall not be set up, provided an indemnity is given to the satisfaction of the Court or Judge against the claims of any other person upon the instrument in question.

Bills in a set

12.111 It is common for foreign bills to be drawn "in a set", that is, more than one copy of the same bill is made. Each of the parts is then sent separately as a security against the loss or delay of the bill in transit. In order to constitute a set, each image of the bill must be numbered and contain a reference to the other parts. When that is done, the set is considered to be a single bill.[1]

1 See s 71(1).

12.112 The rules concerning bills in a set are designed to treat the set as nearly as possible as a single bill while still protecting innocent parties from the obvious danger that when the set is separated there is an opportunity for fraud. Thus, if a holder chooses to write an indorsement on two or more parts of the bill, he or she will be liable on each part indorsed and subsequent indorsers will be liable as if the parts were separate.[1]

1 S 71(2).

12.113 The possibility of having two or more holders in due course is dealt with by s 71(3):

> Where 2 or more parts of a set are negotiated to different holders in due course, the holder whose title first accrues is, as between such holders, deemed the true owner of the bill; but nothing in this subsection shall affect the rights of a person who in due course accepts or pays the part first presented to him.

12.114 The proviso to that section relates to the fact that the drawee should accept only one part,[1] although if more than one part is accepted, the acceptor is liable on each part to a holder in due course.[2] When the acceptor pays the bill, he or she should demand that the part with the written acceptance be handed over. Failure to do so will render the acceptor liable to a holder in due course of the part with the written acceptance on it.[3] Subject to all of these protections for innocent parties, when any one part of the bill is discharged, whether by payment or otherwise, the whole bill is discharged.[4]

1 S 71(4).
2 S 71(5). It seems overly restrictive to provide protection only to a holder in due course.
3 S 71(6). Again, the restriction of the protection to a holder in due course seems unnecessarily harsh.
4 S 71(7).

Promissory notes

12.115 The definition of a promissory note is similar to that of a bill of exchange except that the order to pay is replaced by a promise to pay. Thus, a promissory note has only two primary parties, the person who makes the promise, known as the maker, and the promisee, who is known as the payee. A note may be made payable to order or to bearer.

12.116 The operation of notes is so similar to that of bills that the Act provides a scheme of translation rather than repeat all of the rules related to bills. The person who is primarily liable on the note is the maker who must therefore correspond to the acceptor of a bill. The party who is secondarily liable, if there is such a party, must be the first indorser of the note who therefore corresponds to the drawer of a bill.

12.117 This is formalised in the Act in s 90:

> **90. Application of Part I to notes** — (1) Subject to the provisions in this Part of this Act and except as provided by this section, the provision of this Act relating to bills of exchange apply, with the necessary modifications, to promissory notes.
>
> (2) In applying those provisions the maker of a note shall be deemed to correspond with the acceptor of a bill, and the first indorser of a note shall be deemed to correspond with the drawer of an accepted bill payable to the drawer's order.

12.118 The parts of the Act which do not apply by virtue of s 90(3) are those sections which deal with rules related to acceptance and bills in a set. Further, by s 90(4) where a foreign note is dishonoured, protest thereof is unnecessary.

12.119 No particular words are necessary in the making of a promissory note, but the words must amount to a promise to pay, not merely some undertaking which has to be inferred from the words used. Thus, it has been held that an IOU is merely an acknowledgment of a debt and not a promissory note.[1]

1 *Akbar Khan v Attar Singh* [1936] 2 All ER 545.

12.120 As to the time for payment, the Court of Appeal in England has held that a promise to pay "on or before" a particular date is outside the requirement of a fixed or determinable future time since the option to pay before the specified date created an uncertainty in the time for payment so that the instrument was not payable at a "fixed" future time.[1]

1 *Williamson v Rider* [1963] 1 QB 89.

Liability of maker

12.121 The liability undertaken by a party who makes a note is set out in s 89 and holds no particular surprises. He undertakes to pay the note according to its tenor and is precluded from denying to a holder in due course the existence of the payee and the then capacity to indorse.

12.122 There is no objection to a note being made by two or more makers and the liability may be joint or several or both according to the tenor of the note. But the Act provides that when the words merely say "I promise to pay" and the note is signed by two or more parties, then it is deemed to be their joint and several note.[1]

1 S 86(2).

Liability of indorsers

12.123 Notes payable on demand receive a special treatment in Part III of the Act. The reason for this is that demand notes are often taken by lenders as a continuing security for the loan.[1] The rights of the lender might be merely to hold the note so as to gain the procedural advantages of the borrower's liability on a negotiable instrument, or it might be that the lender has the right to negotiate the note further in order to regain liquidity.

1 This is not, of course, a security in the sense of a property interest.

12.124 Thus, s 87(1) places upon the holder of an indorsed demand note the duty to present the note for payment within a reasonable time of the indorsement. Failure to do so discharges the indorser, but in determining what is a reasonable time regard shall be had to the nature of the instrument, the usage of the trade, and the facts of the particular case.[1] This latter consideration would include a consideration of the reason why the note was made in the first place.

1 S 87(2).

12.125 It is in s 87(3) that the real departure occurs:

> Where a note payable on demand is negotiated, it is not deemed to be overdue, for the purposes of affecting the holder with defects of title of which he had no notice, by reason that it appears that a reasonable time for presenting it for payment has elapsed since its issue.

12.126 When an overdue bill is negotiated that it may only be taken subject to any defect of title affecting it at its maturity and that, by s 36(3), a bill payable on demand is deemed to be overdue when it appears on the face of it to have been in circulation for an unreasonable length of time. "Unreasonable time" is a question of fact.[1]

1 S 36(3).

12.127 The reason for this difference is, as mentioned, the different uses to which notes are typically put. There is no reason to be suspicious of an event, eg the negotiation of a demand note which has been outstanding for a long time, when in the experience of commercial people this is not a suspicious event.

Chapter 13

Cheques

13.1 Lord Atkin spoke of the promise of the banker "to repay any part of the amount due against the written order of the customer addressed to the bank at the branch [where the account is kept]". Although he does not refer to the requirement that the written order be a cheque, it is in fact the cheque which is by far the most widely used instrument for this purpose. Indeed, the banker probably has no duty to pay some third party if the order is not a cheque.[1]

1 See *Chorley*, p 41; *Weaver and Cragie*, p 333.

13.2 In law, the cheque is more than a written order; it is a mandate, both an order to make the payment indicated in the cheque and an authorisation to debit the account for the amount so paid. As already noted in Ch 6, the duty of the banker is to follow the order of the customer, a duty which gives rise to certain obligations on both sides of the banker/customer relationship.

13.3 There is no particular reason why the cheque should be a bill of exchange, but for historical reasons this is the case. In order to be a cheque, an instrument must comply with the definition in s 73 of the Bills of Exchange Act 1908:

> (1) A cheque is a bill of exchange drawn on a banker payable on demand.
> (2) Except as otherwise provided in this Part of this Act, the provisions of this Act applicable to a bill of exchange payable on demand apply to a cheque.

13.4 This identification of a cheque as a certain type of bill of exchange has had some unfortunate consequences in the law of banking. One example which has already been noted[1] is that the relationship between the customer drawing a cheque and the banker/drawee was obscured, for the duties required of a person drawing a cheque are by no means the same as those of a person

209

drawing a bill of exchange. There is, for example, no duty on the drawer of a bill of exchange to guard against the possibility of a rogue altering the instrument by filling in blanks.[2]

1 See Ch 3.
2 See *Scholfield v Earl of Londesborough* [1896] AC 514; *Colonial Bank of Australasia Ltd v Marshall* [1906] AC 559.

Dual role of a cheque

13.5 In considering problems concerning cheques, it must always be kept in mind that the cheque has a dual role. On the one hand, it is a bill of exchange, and the relationship of the parties one to another who have signed the cheque as drawer or indorser and the relationship of these parties to the holder of the cheque will be governed by the Bills of Exchange Act 1908.

13.6 On the other hand, the cheque is the mandate from the customer to the banker which requires certain obligations to be performed as part of the banker's undertaking in the contract between banker and customer.

The economic function of cheques

13.7 The main problem with the identification of the cheque as a species of bill of exchange arises from the completely different economic and commercial functions of the two instruments. The bill was originally used to facilitate the extension of credit in international trade and has now been adapted to serve as a useful instrument for short-term financing even where there is no underlying commercial transaction. The cheque is and always has been primarily an instrument of payment.

13.8 The difference has significant practical consequences. The vast majority of cheques are never negotiated. They are handed or posted directly to the payee who then hands it to his banker for collection. Not only is the quality of negotiability seldom used in practice, it is often not desired by the drawer of the cheque, for the possibility of the cheque being misappropriated is a danger which far outweighs any advantage which is ordinarily gained from the qualities of negotiability. For this reason, methods were developed for drawing cheques so that although they were still transferable they lacked the essential feature of negotiability, ie, that a holder in due course takes free of title defects. Several other features of cheques, most notably crossings,[1] were developed to provide more protection for the true owner of the cheque.

1 See 13.34ff.

13.9 The action for conversion which is available to the holder of a bill of exchange meant that banks were exposed to such claims when handling cheques deposited by their customers when the customer had no title or a defective title. Although the misappropriation of cheques is something that is inherent in the system and there are arguments that the costs of such misappropriations should be spread to all users of the cheque system, legislation adopted by the various jurisdictions has taken a different view, so that a "banker" is provided with a statutory defence to conversion in certain circumstances.[1]

1 Cheques Act 1960.

13.10 Finally, the sheer volume of cheques written presented problems in itself. In the early days, each bank would sort the cheques which it had received for collection and send clerks to the various paying banks for presentment. The clerks themselves, it is said, recognised the futility of the arrangement and began to meet at a certain point in the city and exchange cheques, thus giving rise to the first "clearing house". The modern clearing house is a far cry from this, but the principle of operation remains the same. Cheques may be exchanged between collecting and paying banks at a central location; the clearing house also provides the accounting facilities which mean that actual payment between banks need only be for the excess amount of cheques drawn on the one over the amount of cheques which that same one has for collection from the other.

13.11 Other forms of payment are beginning to make an inroad into the cheque system of payments, but only in the sense that the volume of cheques used is no longer growing as rapidly as it was during previous decades. In spite of the introduction of new systems of payment, it will be many years before the banker no longer needs a close familiarity with the cheque system and with his or her legal obligations when dealing with cheques.

Bill of exchange

13.12 The requirement that a cheque be a bill of exchange has caused some problems in the past although it is thought that these are unlikely to be of much significance in the future because of the universal use of pre-printed forms in cheque-books. However, there is nothing in the basic contract between banker and customer which prevents the customer from writing out a cheque on a sheet of notepaper unless, of course, there is an express term in the contract which forbids the customer from so doing.[1]

1 See *Burnett v Westminster Bank Ltd* [1966] 1 QB 742; *Roberts & Co v Marsh* [1915] 1 KB 42.

13.13 There is nothing in the definition of a cheque which requires that the drawer of the cheque be a customer of the banker upon whom it is drawn, but it seems impossible to imagine a situation in practice where such a cheque would be drawn and, if drawn, why the drawee banker would honour it. Chorley suggests that a fraudulent person might steal a cheque-book and issue cheques.[1] If drawn in the thief's own name, these would be valid cheques and would, of course, confer rights on holders, but no rights would accrue against the banker by virtue of the fact that the banker never accepts a cheque and there is no contractual relationship between the banker and the thief.

1 *Chorley*, p 44.

Cheques not accepted

13.14 Although there seems to be no legal obstacle, it is unknown in modern New Zealand banking practice for a banker to accept a cheque. Consequently, the banker has no liability to the holder of the cheque. The only liability of the bank to pay the cheque is the contractual liability to its customer.[1]

1 But see *HH Dimond (Rotorua 1966) Ltd v ANZ Banking Group* [1979] 2 NZLR 739.

13.15 Cheques are sometimes "marked" by the drawee bank. This is an indication that the customer's account contains funds sufficient to meet the cheque. A marked cheque is not an acceptance by the bank; at most it appears that it is a representation to the holder as to the state of the drawer's account at the time when the cheque was marked.[1]

1 See *Bank of Baroda Ltd v Punjab National Bank Ltd* [1944] AC 176.

13.16 The position is different in Canada and the United States where the "marking" of the cheque acts as a type of acceptance. In *Gaden v Newfoundland Savings Bank*[1] it was said that:

> The only effect of the certifying is to give the cheque additional currency by showing on the face that it is drawn in good faith on funds sufficient to meet its payment, and by adding to the credit of the drawer that of the bank on which it is drawn.

1 [1899] AC 281.

13.17 The Court in *Shapera v Toronto Dominion Bank*[1] also considered the effect of certification of the cheque in a passage which seems to be somewhat different from the *Gaden* dictum, apparently reflecting a change in banking practice:

> In Canadian custom and theory certification of a cheque at the request of the holder is equivalent to payment . . . a bank has the right to certify and, having done so, becomes liable to the holder. A refusal without

cause to certify a cheque could result in the same kind of damage to the reputation of a customer as a refusal to pay.[2]

1 17 DLR (3d) 122 (1970).
2 At p 125.

13.18 It appears to be common practice when certifying a cheque to withdraw the money from the customer's account and transfer it to the bank's trust account.[1]

1 See *Royal Bank of Canada v Huber* (1971) 23 DLR (3d) 209.

13.19 The word "certifying" is the North American term for marking of a cheque, although as the passage shows, the effect is also different. The practical effect of the difference is that "certified" cheques are in wide use in North America but are virtually unknown in other common law countries. The function served by the North American certification is here met by the use of bank cheques.

13.20 That the paying banker is not liable to the holder on the cheque is correct, but in *HH Dimond (Rotorua 1966) Ltd v ANZ Banking Group*[1] it was suggested that there may be some duty owed by the paying banker to the holder. The facts of the case have been discussed elsewhere, but for present purposes the important feature of the case is that the action was one in negligence brought by the payee of the cheque against the drawee bank. It seems to have been accepted by the parties and by the Court that a duty of care was owed, although in the circumstances of the case, compliance with the clearing house rules by the bank was held to be no breach of the duty.

1 [1979] 2 NZLR 739.

Unconditional order

13.21 Since the cheque must be a bill of exchange, it must be an unconditional order to pay.[1] It is not uncommon for the drawer or some other party to add comments onto a cheque to indicate the purpose for which it is drawn. One common annotation concerns an indication of the account which is to be debited. The Act provides in s3(3) that:

> An order to pay out of a particular fund is not unconditional within the meaning of this section; but an unqualified order to pay, coupled with (a) an indication of a particular fund out of which the drawee is to reimburse himself or a particular account to be debited with the amount, or (b) a statement of the transaction giving rise to the bill, is unconditional.

1 S 3, Bills of Exchange Act 1908.

13.22 The difference is an order which says "Pay from No 2 account . . ." and one which says "Pay . . .", but with an indication somewhere else on the paper which account is to be debited.

13.23 Case law problems have arisen from the desire of drawers to obtain receipts from the payee. A convenient way is to have the cheque itself serve as a receipt, but care must be taken in the way that such an instrument is drawn.

13.24 In *Bavins Junr and Simms v London & South Western Bank*[1] the plaintiff was the payee of an instrument which read "Pay J Bavins the sum of sixty-nine pounds. Provided the receipt form at foot hereof is duly signed, stamped and dated". While the receipt form was still unsigned, the form was stolen from the plaintiff and paid into the defendant bank for collection. The instrument had been indorsed and the receipt form signed, but both were forgeries. It was held that the instrument was not a cheque since the order to pay was not unconditional.

1 [1900] 1 QB 270.

13.25 The Court also had some words to say concerning the possibility of bringing an action in conversion on an instrument which is not a negotiable one. As noted in 14.16, this is a matter which is still far from resolved. During the course of his judgment, AL Smith LJ indicated that in his view the form of the action was not the deciding factor, but other members of the Court were slightly more reluctant to hold that the damages could be awarded in conversion. All agreed that the plaintiff could recover on money had and received.[1]

1 See 14.16ff.

13.26 The *Bavins* case should be compared with *Nathan v Ogdens Ltd.*[1] The form in *Nathan's* case appeared to be in the form of a cheque, but at the bottom of the form was printed "the receipt at back hereof must be signed which signature will be taken as an indorsement of this cheque". On the back of the form was a printed form of receipt. The Court expressed its opinion that the instrument was a cheque because the clause was not a part of the order.

1 (1905) 93 LT 553; (1905) 94 LT 126.

Section 4: Cheques Act

13.27 The desire to have a receipt is, of course, to provide evidence in the event of a dispute over whether payment has in fact been made. The need for a separate form has been greatly reduced by s 4 of the Cheques Act which provides:

An unindorsed cheque which appears to have been paid by a banker on whom it is drawn shall, in the absence of proof to the contrary, be sufficient evidence of the receipt by the payee of the sum payable by the cheque.

13.28 The section is restricted to unindorsed cheques since a paid indorsed cheque has always been treated as evidence of payment.[1]

1 See *Egg v Barnett* (1800) 3 Esp 196; 170 ER 586.

Payer and payee

13.29 The drawing and delivery of a cheque is ordinarily done because the drawer of the cheque owes a debt to the payee. The general rule is that the debt is not discharged by delivery of the cheque, the presumption being that the cheque is accepted only by way of conditional satisfaction of the debt. The condition is a condition subsequent, namely that the cheque will be paid upon due presentment. Other remedies for the recovery of the debt will ordinarily be suspended until such time as the cheque is dishonoured. In the event of dishonour of the cheque, the normal situation will be that the payee will have two causes of action against the drawer of the cheque, one on the cheque itself and one on the contract which gave rise to the debt.

Restricting the negotiability of cheques

13.30 As noted above, the drawer of a cheque may be more interested in safety than in the ease with which the instrument may pass from holder to holder. Several methods of securing protection for the drawer against the misappropriation of the cheque have been developed. These go under the collective, and misleading, name of "crossings".

13.31 It is said that the practice of crossing cheques began in the clearing house for the purpose of maintaining records. According to Chorley,[1] the name of the banker whose claim was cleared, ie, the name of the collecting banker, was written across the face of the cheque between parallel lines. Chorley also says that the custom spread outside the clearing house in the early 19th century and gradually acquired a precise legal meaning.[2] The meaning to be attributed to crossings now is, with one exception, governed by the Bills of Exchange Act 1908.

1 At p 59.
2 See *Bellamy v Marjoribanks* (1852) 7 Exch 389.

13.32 Although there are several types of crossings which are authorised by s 76 of the Act, each serves as an instruction to the paying banker to effect payment of the cheque only by payment to another banker. Consequently, in order to obtain payment, the holder of a crossed cheque must have a bank account in his or her own right, have a banker willing to collect the cheque even though the holder is not a customer, or have another person willing to act as agent who has such an account. For reasons which will become apparent, the second of these options is very unlikely.

13.33 The consequence for the drawer of a cheque is a substantially increased level of protection against theft and fraud. In the old days, this was enhanced by the care which bankers took on opening bank accounts, ensuring that persons with bank accounts were likely to be of relatively good character and reputation. In more modern times when bank accounts are much more widely spread, the procedure still provides a means of tracing a cheque which has been fraudulently misappropriated.

Crossings authorised by the Act

13.34 Cheques which are not crossed are said to be "open" cheques. Those cheques which are crossed are defined by s 76 of the Act:

(1) Where a cheque bears across its face an addition of —
(a) The words "and company", or "bank", or any abbreviation thereof, between 2 parallel transverse lines, either with or without the words "Not negotiable"; or
(b) Two parallel transverse lines simply, either with or without the words "Not negotiable", —
that addition constitutes a crossing, and the cheque is crossed generally.
(2) Where a cheque bears across its face an addition of the name of a banker, either with or without the words "Not negotiable", that addition constitutes a crossing, and the cheque is crossed specially and to that banker.

13.35 The general crossing requires two transverse parallel lines. These lines must lie transversely but there is no requirement that they lie at perfect right angles to the body of the cheque nor that they run across the full width of the face. It is said to be a question of fact in each case whether the markings can be fairly said to be a crossing within the meaning of the Act and an indication to the banker that the cheque is intended to be crossed.[1]

1 See *Mather v Bank of New Zealand* (1918) 18 SR (NSW) 49, 52.

13.36 It is most uncommon to find any of the words permitted in the general crossing with the exception of "Not negotiable". Special crossings, although recognised by the Act, are very rarely seen in practice. The Manning Committee report recommended that special crossings be abolished and the Australian Cheques and Payment Orders Act 1986 allows only general crossings.

General crossing

13.37 The meaning of a general crossing is found in s 79 which defines the duty of a banker with regard to crossed cheques. The section is badly drafted, but s 79(2) can be "parsed" into pieces that define the duty. So far as the general crossing is concerned, this produces:

> Where the banker on whom a cheque [is drawn] . . . pays [the] cheque crossed generally otherwise than to a banker . . . . He is liable to the true owner of the cheque for any loss he may sustain owing to the cheque having been so paid.

Special crossing

13.38 In a like fashion, the same section provides that it is the duty of the banker to pay a specially crossed cheque to the banker named in the crossing. Failure to do so has the same consequence of making the banker liable to the true owner of the cheque for any losses which flow from the cheque being paid in some other way.

13.39 The nature of the crossing was first established in *Smith v Union Bank of London*.[1] The plaintiff was payee of a cheque drawn on the defendant bank. It was crossed specially by the payee to the London and County Bank and indorsed in blank, thereby becoming a bearer cheque.[2] It was stolen and came into the hands of a holder who took it for value and in good faith and who paid it into his account with the London and Westminster bank for collection. It was paid by the defendant bank notwithstanding the special crossing and the plaintiff sued in conversion. The plaintiff argued that the crossing had the effect of preventing the holder from taking good title, but the action failed, since it was held that the cheque was fully negotiable. The statutory force given to the "not negotiable" marking was a consequence of this case.

1 (1875) 1 QBD 31.
2 See s 34, Bills of Exchange Act 1908 and 11.79.

The true owner

13.40 The banker who pays a cheque in contravention of the instructions given in a crossing is made liable to the "true owner", a concept which is not defined in the Act. It is thought that the adjective "true" is added to the word "owner" in order to emphasise that the cheque is not to be treated merely as any other chattel, but that its negotiability should be recognised and the title of an owner determined by reference to the relevant sections of the Bills of Exchange Act 1908. Paget suggests that the "true owner of a cheque must be the party with an unassailable title to it whether in possession of it or not . . ." .[1] Consequently, the "true owner" is not necessarily the last transferee of the cheque who is in possession of it, for in the case of a forgery, the "true owner" would be the person who was the holder of the cheque at the time when the forged indorsement was made. The concept of the "true owner" is discussed in more detail in Ch 16.

1 At p 198.

Double jeopardy under s 79

13.41 It is possible that the bank may be responsible twice over if payment is made in contravention of the crossing. Section 79 makes the banker liable to losses incurred by the true owner of the cheque, but it may also be that the drawer of the cheque will have a claim against the bank. Although the drawer may be the true owner, there will be some cases where the two are different; in such a case, the paying banker may be forced to pay twice for the indiscretion.

13.42 When a cheque is paid in contravention of the crossing, the drawer of the cheque may claim that the bank is unable to maintain the debit to the account on grounds either of negligence or of failure to follow the mandate. There seems little doubt that failure to observe the crossing is negligence on the part of the paying banker, but in an action for negligence, the customer must prove that there was damage suffered.

13.43 If the drawer bases the claim on the failure of the bank to follow the mandate, it is at least possible that the bank will be unable to debit the account even if the drawer has suffered no losses as a result of the failure. This follows from *Bobbett v Pinkett*[1] where a banker erroneously and negligently paid a cheque to a banker other than the one named in the special crossing. Bramwell B said:

> It is certain that the present plaintiff might have refused to allow [the drawee bank] to debit his account with the amount of the cheque . . . .[2]

Amphlett B said:

> It cannot be denied that the crossing operated as a mandate to the drawee to pay the cheque to the bankers named and to no one else, and that the plaintiff might . . . have declined to allow his account to be debited with the amount so paid contrary to his orders . . . .[3]

1 (1876) 1 Exch D 368.
2 At p 372.
3 At p 374.

13.44 However, *Bobbett v Pinkett* was decided before crossings received statutory recognition. Weaver and Cragie suggest that it may be possible to argue that the paying banker is not invariably precluded from debiting the customer's account with the amount of a cheque which has been paid contrary to the customer's mandate, at any rate when the failure to follow the mandate is only a failure to observe a crossing on a cheque.[1] However, it is clear that the banker will need to mount some fairly strong legal arguments. Weaver and Cragie suggest some of these arguments, but admit that ". . . in this field . . . the law appears to require a much higher degree of refinement than at present exists".[1]

1 *Weaver and Cragie*, p 287.

"Not negotiable"

13.45 The words "not negotiable" which are authorised by s 76 have an effect which is quite different from the general or special crossings. Section 81 provides:

> Where a person takes a crossed cheque bearing on it the words "Not negotiable", he shall not have and shall not be capable of giving a better title to the cheque than that which the person from whom he took it had.

13.46 There is a problem in the language of the Act, for in some sections the Act uses the word "negotiable" to mean merely transferable.[1] However, in the sections dealing with cheques, the meaning is generally that the instrument is transferable free from equities.

1 See, for example, s 8 which seems to identify negotiability and transferability.

13.47 Further, the section, although requiring the cheque to be crossed, does not require that the words lie between the transverse lines. The common form of adding the words is, of course, to place them between the two lines.

Effect on the transferee

13.48 An aspect of the "Not negotiable" crossing that is often misunderstood is that the crossing in no way restricts the transferability of the cheque. It may still pass from hand to hand in the usual way; the crossing does not obliterate the distinction between bearer cheques and order cheques and the rules concerning "negotiation", ie, transfer, remain exactly the same.

13.49 What is changed by the addition of the crossing is the title which may be obtained by the transferee. The substantive effect of the "not negotiable" words being placed on a cheque is that the transferee is unable to take free of equities; any defect in title, no matter how far back it might have occurred in the chain of transfers will be transmitted to the current holder of the cheque since no transferor can have or be capable of giving a better title than that from whom he or she took the cheque. The section has the effect of reinstating the nemo dat quod non habet rule to its fullest possible force.

13.50 The section is not necessary for protection against the immediate transferee, since in that case the usual defences and remedies are available to the transferor.

13.51 An example of the situation in which the "not negotiable" crossing may have an effect is the following:

In *Wilson & Meeson v Pickering*[1] a partner in the plaintiff firm signed a cheque on behalf of the firm. The cheque was signed while still blank, but the form had a crossing with the words "not negotiable" printed on it. The signed form was handed to the secretary with instructions to fill it in for £2 and make it payable to the Commissioners of Inland Revenue. The secretary fraudulently wrote out the cheque for an amount in excess of £50 and made it payable to the defendant, handing it to him in payment of a debt which she owed him. The defendant obtained payment of the cheque through the secretary's banker; the plaintiff sought to recover the sum from the payee. The Court held that the matter fell within the English equivalent of s 81; since the cheque was marked "not negotiable", the defendant could have no better title than that of the secretary from whom he took it, that is to say, none at all.

1 [1946] 1 KB 422.

13.52 Furthermore, although there was some early doubt, it is now clear that the section applies to the proceeds of the cheque as well as to the cheque itself. In *Great Western Railway Co v London and County Banking Co Ltd*[1] Huggins had obtained by fraud a cheque in his favour from the plaintiff and had persuaded the defendant bank to collect it for him even though he was not a customer of the bank. It was argued that the section applied only to the cheque and not to the proceeds thereof. Lord Halsbury LC said:

> The supposed distinction between the title to the cheque itself and the title to the money obtained or represented by it seems to me to be absolutely illusory. The language of the statute seems to me to be clear enough. It would be absolutely defeated by holding that a fraudulent holder of the cheque could give a title either to the cheque or to the money.[2]

1 [1901] AC 414.
2 At p 418.

13.53 The same case also settled another point concerning the application of the section. It was argued that Huggins' title was only voidable, not void, and consequently could not be avoided after a bona fide transfer without notice. This is, of course, the normal rule as applied to chattels.[1] However, the House of Lords held that the operation of the section was not merely to destroy the full negotiability of a cheque which is crossed "not negotiable", but to re-establish the full force of the nemo dat quod non habet rule.

1 See s 60, Sale of Goods Act 1908.

Effect on the banker

13.54 It has been said that the words "not negotiable" on a cheque have a warning effect, so that a person taking the cheque is put on notice that the transferor of the cheque may have a defective title.[1] If this is so, then it applies equally to a banker who is collecting the cheque for a customer with the result that a banker collecting such a cheque for other than the named payee may be acting negligently and so be unable to rely upon the statutory defences in the event that the customer has no title or a defective title to the cheque.

1 *Commissioners of the State Savings Bank of Victoria v Permewan Wright & Co Ltd* (1914) 19 CLR 457; and see 15.7ff.

13.55 The notion that the word have a warning effect apparently originated with statements made by Griffith CJ in *Commissioners of the State Savings Bank of Victoria v Permewan Wright & Co Ltd*.[1] He said:

> The words "Not negotiable" on a crossed cheque are a danger signal held out before every person invited to deal with it, and are equivalent to saying "Take care; this cheque may be stolen".[2]

1 (1914) 19 CLR 457.
2 At p 467.

13.56 There is nothing in the Act to suggest such an interpretation and the statement has been criticised by textbook writers. When the statement is applied to the transferee of a cheque it has no effect, for if the cheque is not stolen the transferee gets a good title, and if it is stolen or has some other title defect, then the transferee gets only what the transferor had by virtue of s 81. The "warning" has nothing whatsoever to do with it. It is only when the person "invited to deal" with the cheque is a collecting banker that the warning acquires practical significance.[1]

1 See 15.7ff.

"Not negotiable" on open cheques

13.57 The Act, as already noted, authorises the addition of the words "not negotiable" to a crossed cheque and only gives them meaning when they are a part of a crossed cheque (s 81). What, if any, is the effect of the words on a cheque which is not crossed?

13.58 When the words are written on a bill of exchange which is not a cheque, the bill becomes non-transferable, at least if *Hibernian Bank Ltd v Gysin and Hanson*[1] is good law. In such a circumstance, their effect does not depend upon any express statutory provision.

1 [1939] 1 KB 483.

13.59 Some textbook writers argue that the inclusion of the sections in the Act which deal with the addition of the words "not negotiable" must be interpreted to mean that words which are not authorised by the Act must have no meaning at all, but that argument is very doubtful. Chorley notes that:

> A person placing these words upon a cheque presumably intends them to have a meaning and it is difficult to see that it could be any other meaning than that given to them by section 81. To give them a narrower meaning would deprive them of all effect, while it would be contrary to common sense to give them a wider effect.[1]

1 At p 57.

13.60 The Manning Committee summarised the arguments on both sides:

> It has been said on the one hand that these words if written on an uncrossed cheque are a nullity and have no effect on the instrument. On the other hand it has been said that a cheque begins as a mandate and the words "not negotiable" appearing on an uncrossed cheque may be a direction to the bank in the literal meaning and that it is not to pay anyone other than the payee.[1]

1 At para 88.

13.61 If the words are ambiguous, as they appear to be when the above two comments are compared, then it would probably be safe for the paying banker to refuse to pay the cheque if it is being collected for the account of anyone other than the named payee.[1]

1 See 6.8ff.

Summary of advantages to the drawer of "not negotiable"

13.62 A crossed cheque even without the words "not negotiable" must be collected through a bank account so that the true owner of the cheque will at least be able to learn the name of the person for whom the cheque was collected. If it is also marked "not negotiable" then the true owner retains all rights to the cheque and its proceeds. If the person for whom the cheque has been collected is found to be insolvent, then there is still the possibility of an action against the collecting bank.[1]

1 See Ch 14.

13.63 Finally, if it is learned that the cheque has gone astray, the drawer may wish to put a stop payment order on the cheque. This will have the result that the paying bank will refuse payment, but if the cheque has come into the hands of a holder in due course, the drawer might still find that he is liable on the cheque. This possibility is eliminated if the cheque is crossed "not negotiable". Since such a large number of personal cheques are bearer cheques, this is a significant advantage to the drawer.

Account payee only

13.64 The words "account payee" and variants such as "a'cct p'ee", "account payee only" and "account John Smith" are often added to cheques. Most often the cheques will be crossed cheques within the meaning of the Act, but the words may also appear on open cheques.

13.65 The addition of the words is not authorised by the Act, nor are they given any statutory recognition by any other Act. There is, however, no doubt that the addition of the words does have a legal effect although the exact scope of that effect is still not entirely clear.

13.66 On the face of it, one would have thought that the words were originally placed there by the drawer in an attempt to create a non-transferable instrument. Whether that is so or not, it is now clear that the words do not prohibit the transfer of the cheque, nor do they destroy the full negotiability of the cheque if the cheque is not also marked "not negotiable".[1]

1 See *National Bank v Silke* [1891] 1 QB 435.

13.67 But if the words do not mean that, what do they mean? There have been a number of cases that have held that the words are an instruction to the collecting bank, "a mere direction to the receiving bank as to how the money was to be dealt with after receipt".[1] As such, it is a most peculiar instruction, for generally speaking, the person who is giving the instruction, the drawer, will not be in a contractual relationship with the collecting bank so why should the collecting bank be under any obligation to pay attention to the words?

1 Per Bingham J in *Akrokerri (Atlantic) Mines Ltd v Economic Bank* [1904] 2 KB 465.

13.68 Weaver and Cragie argue that the words have acquired legal effect at least in part by the practice of bankers.[1] They suggest that the inherent ambiguity of the words means that bankers could have, in the early days, refused to pay cheques so drawn. Instead, early collecting bankers exhibited a high degree of caution when dealing with such cheques with the effect that in *Ladbroke & Co v Todd*[2] the Court held that a collecting bank was negligent for failing to maintain the high level of care.

1 *Weaver and Cragie,* p 297.
2 (1914) 30 TLR 433.

13.69 On their face, the words could also be an instruction to the paying bank, but it would be an instruction which would be extraordinarily difficult for the paying bank to follow, for the paying bank will not ordinarily know for whom the cheque is being collected. The entire machinery of the clearing system for the payment of cheques makes it virtually impossible for the paying bank to make such inquiries. As a result, the law is that the words do not require the paying bank to inquire as to the name of the person for whom the cheque is being collected:

> These words do not cast on the bank paying the cheque to a banker, any additional obligation to satisfy itself that the collecting bank is collecting it on behalf of the named payee. That is entirely the responsibility of the collecting bank.[1]

1 Per Lord Upjohn in *Universal Guarantee Pty Ltd v National Bank of Australasia Ltd* [1965] NSWR 342.

13.70 Perhaps because the instruction to the collecting bank is given by someone who is not in a contractual relation with it, the Courts have not given the fullest possible effect to the words. It is possible for the collecting bank to collect the cheque for someone other than the named payee without incurring any liability to the true owner. The precise scope of the collecting banker's duty vis-a-vis the "account payee" crossing is discussed in Ch 15.

Who may cross

13.71 Section 77 of the Act allows crossings to be "built up" in the sense that a holder of a cheque may add to the crossing, so converting a simple general crossing into a special crossing or into a crossing with the addition of the "not negotiable" protection.

13.72 There is no authorisation in the Act for the addition of a crossing by any person other than the drawer or the holder. Paget suggests that an innocent holder of a cheque through a forged indorsement could not effectively add to a crossing since such a person is not a holder.[1] This is probably correct, since s 78 deems the crossing to be a material part of the cheque and provides that no person may add to or alter the crossing except as authorised by the Act.

1 See *Paget,* p 201.

13.73 On the other hand, there is authority for the proposition that the meaning of the word "holder" is somewhat wider in this context than it is in the other parts of the Act. In *Akrokerri (Atlantic) Mines*

Ltd v Economic Bank[1] the argument was expressed that the bank could not rely upon the protecting provisions by virtue of the fact that the collecting bank had converted a general crossing into a special crossing before presentment for payment. By s 78, the crossing is a material part of the cheque; by s 64 the alteration of a material part of the cheque by an unauthorised person avoids the instrument. It was argued that the alteration was unauthorised by virtue of the fact that the collecting bank was not a holder of the cheque.

1 [1904] 2 KB 465, 472.

13.74 The argument was rejected by Bingham J:

Holder does not necessarily mean a holder for value. The expression includes every person who is in lawful possession of the instrument, and therefore includes an agent for collection.[1]

1 Per Bingham J at p 472.

13.75 Because of some doubts raised by *Capital & Counties Bank Ltd v Gordon*[1] Bingham J went on to make it clear that the banker is entitled to the protection of the section even if the account has been credited:

Where the customer of a bank delivers to the banker for collection a crossed cheque to which he has not title, the fact that the banker credits the customer in the bank ledger with the amount of the cheque before it is cleared does not deprive the banker of the protection afforded by s 82 of the Bills of Exchange Act 1882.[2]

1 [1903] AC 240; see the discussion at 14.22ff.
2 Per the headnote.

Opening the crossing on cheques

13.76 There are an increasing number of cheques which are printed with a crossing as a part of the form. However, occasionally the payee of the cheque wishes to obtain cash for it, and a custom has arisen of "opening" the crossing by means of a short note saying "pay cash" or some similar phrase written on the cheque and initialled by the payee. The Act gives no authority for such a procedure; indeed s 78 of the Act forbids the obliteration or the alteration except as authorised by the Act.

13.77 Paget suggests that when the opening is done by the customer and the banker then pays cash across the counter that the banker would be indemnified by the customer.[1] In such a circumstance, it is hard to see how the customer or the banker could ever suffer any loss provided that payment is made to the customer; if the "opening" is done by a forger then it is not a part of the mandate and is wholly ineffective.

1 At p 202.

13.78 The safest practice would be to refuse to allow the cheque to be paid across the counter except when initialled by the drawer and where the payment is to made directly to him.

Post-dated cheques

13.79 Since s 73 requires that a "cheque" be payable on demand, there is a significant problem with the so called post-dated cheque, that is, a cheque which is marked with a date which is after the time when the cheque is drawn. Unfortunately for bankers, s 13(2) of the Act provides that "A bill is not invalid by reason only that it is antedated or post-dated . . . ."

13.80 Once again the dual nature of the cheque as a bill of exchange and a mandate to the banker causes difficulty, for if the banker pays the cheque before the date on it, it is most likely that the payment will be construed as a breach of mandate.

13.81 The position of the banker who pays a post-dated cheque early was considered by the Full Court in *Pollock v BNZ*.[1] On 6 December 1900 the plaintiff drew a cheque for about £15 which was dated 15 December of the same year. The cheque was presented for payment on 12 December and it was paid by the defendant bank notwithstanding that it was post-dated. The plaintiff drew another cheque on 13 December which was presented for payment on the same day. This cheque was dishonoured for insufficient funds.

1 (1901) 20 NZLR 174.

13.82 The account would have had sufficient funds but for the payment of the cheque which was post-dated. The plaintiff sued for wrongful dishonour. It was held that the defendant bank was not entitled to pay the post-dated cheque prior to the date which appears on it, nor was it entitled to consider the cheque as a bill of exchange which had been presented for acceptance, thereby entitling the bank to hold the customer's funds sufficient to meet it at maturity.[1] The customer was entitled to damages measured in the usual way.[2]

1 It appears that this was the position at common law, but a Queensland decision had held that the Act changed the nature of a post-dated cheque; *Magill v Bank of North Queensland* (1895) 6 QLJ 262.
2 See 6.45ff.

13.83 In the course of the judgment, Williams J said:

> To arrive at a different conclusion it would be necessary to decide that a post-dated cheque was payable on a demand made by the holder at any time before the date, and that the holder could sue upon it if not then paid. This is entirely contrary to mercantile custom. A person who gives a post-dated cheque gives it with the intention that it shall not be presented before the date, and the person who receives the cheque from

the drawer knows that it is given with such an intention. Everyone to whose hands the cheque comes before the date of it, including the banker upon whom it is drawn, has by the fact of the date on the cheque notice of the intention with which it was given by the drawer and received by the original holder.[1]

1 At p 181.

13.84 The matter arose before the High Court of Australia in *Brien v Dwyer.*[1] A contract for the purchase of land called for the purchaser to make an immediate payment of the purchase price. No payment was made at the time of signing the contract, but later the purchaser gave the estate agent a post-dated cheque. It was held that the purchaser was in breach of the requirements of the contract and that the vendor was entitled to rescind the contract. In the course of the judgments, Gibbs and Aickin JJ offered some views on the nature of a post-dated cheque. Gibbs J said:

> In my opinion a bank is not entitled to pay a post-dated cheque before the date which it bears and to charge the amount to the customer's account. In my respectful opinion the view expressed in *Pollack v Bank of New Zealand* (1901) 20 NZLR 174 and *Deyes v The Royal Bank of Canada* [1947] SCR 377 at 382-383, 386-387 is to be preferred to that taken by the Full Court of Queensland in *Magill v Bank of North Queensland* (1895) 6 QLJ 262.[2]

1 (1979) 53 ALJR 123.
2 At p 128.

13.85 Aicken J expressed a somewhat different view, one which, if correct, would make post-dated cheques even more of a problem for bankers than they are at present :

> . . . it is not a "cheque" within the meaning of the Bills of Exchange Act which by s 78(1) defines a cheque as a "bill of exchange drawn on a banker payable on demand". . . . It is, I think, clear that a post-dated cheque is a bill of exchange payable at a future date. There is no authority for the proposition that it becomes a cheque properly so-called when the date which it bears arrives.[1]

1 At p 134.

13.86 If that view is correct, then paying and collecting bankers may be deprived of the statutory protections which they are given when dealing with cheques or when dealing with bills which are payable on demand. This seems harsh, since if the holder of a post-dated cheque does not present it for payment until after the date on the cheque, then there is no way for the banker or any other third party to know that the instrument began life as a post-dated cheque.

13.87 The New South Wales Court of Appeal considered the Aicken dictum in *Hodgson & Lee Pty Ltd v Mardonius Pty Ltd.*[1] The Court rejected the argument that a post-dated cheque was not a cheque, relying on the decision of the New Zealand Court in *Pollack.*

1 [1986] 5 NSWLR 496.

Chapter 14

The collecting bank I

Defences of — Duties of — Actions against — Negligence

14.1 A bank is under a contractual duty to its customer to collect cheques and bills for the account of the customer.[1] In the performance of that duty, the banker must act with an appropriate level of care and diligence and will face the prospect of being liable to the customer for any losses sustained by the customer which flow from a breach of that duty.

1 *Joachimson v Swiss Bank Corp* [1921] 3 KB 110.

14.2 However, perhaps the greatest risk to which the collecting banker is exposed is that the customer for whom the cheque or bill is being collected has no title or a faulty title to the cheque or bill. In such a case, the collecting banker by assisting with the collection of the cheque is himself liable for an action in conversion by the true owner of the cheque.

14.3 With the statutory recognition of crossings and the general growth of the cheque system, it was thought to be onerous on the collecting bank to be exposed to conversion actions in situations where the collecting bank acted "innocently". Consequently, a series of statutory provisions have given the collecting banker a statutory defence to an action in conversion. This defence is currently contained in the Cheques Act 1960, s 5.

Duties of the collecting bank

The duty to present cheques for payment

14.4 The duty of a collecting bank to make prompt presentment of cheques and bills has been discussed briefly in Ch 6. The mode of presentment will depend upon factors such as location and all other circumstances. For example, an ordinary cheque drawn on another New Zealand bank will ordinarily be presented through the clearing house. A cheque drawn on an overseas bank would probably be presented by post.

14.5 Current practice is to transport the physical piece of paper which is the cheque to the bank branch on which it is drawn. As noted elsewhere,[1] the information which is necessary for the drawee branch to make its decision has arrived perhaps as much as 24 hours ahead of the paper. What purpose is served by the expensive process of transporting the paper? The answer usually given is that the Act requires presentment of the cheque and that "presentment" means "physical presentment".

1 See Ch 19.

14.6 Schemes have been suggested which would allow the banking system to dispense with the expensive movement of paper. Such schemes go under the generic name of "truncation". In a truncation scheme, it is necessary to reach agreement on a number of issues such as:
 (1) circumstances, if any, when the paying bank is entitled to call for the physical presentment of the cheque,
 (2) what information must be transmitted and in what form for there to be a valid presentment,
 (3) what procedures should be followed on dishonour.
 As well as these major issues, there will be a host of operational details which must be agreed upon.

14.7 It is generally thought that there must be legislation enacted to allow for the introduction of a truncation scheme. Australia has recently introduced the Cheques Act 1986 which incorporates a reasonably detailed yet flexible set of provisions for a truncation scheme.

When collecting bank also paying bank

14.8 In *Carpenters of City of London (Worshipful Co of) v British Mutual Banking Co*[1] the defendant bank acted both as a collecting bank and as a paying bank. A clerk in the plaintiff company misappropriated cheques which were drawn on the defendant bank. The clerk forged indorsements and requested that the defendant bank credit his private account with the proceeds. It was found as a fact that the defendant had not acted without negligence, but that they had paid the cheques in good faith and in the ordinary course of business. The Court of Appeal held in effect that the bank was required to satisfy the provisions of the equivalent of s 4 when acting as a collecting bank and the equivalent of s 5 when acting as a paying bank. It is as though at some stage of the process the bank ceases to act as a collecting bank and begins to act as a paying bank. It must act properly in both roles.

1 [1938] 1 KB 511.

14.9 It is possible for circumstances to arise where the dual role may benefit the banker. In *Boyd v Emmerson*[1] the plaintiff was the payee of a cheque drawn on the defendant banker. The plaintiff kept accounts at the same bank. He handed the cheque to a teller and said "Place this to my account". The account of the drawer was overdrawn at the time and the banker did not pay the cheque immediately but instead made some inquiries about the drawer. The plaintiff was notified the next day that the cheque would be dishonoured. The Court held that the notice was timely since the banker was receiving the cheque as agent and not as a paying banker. Presumably the outcome would have been different if the plaintiff had made it clear that the cheque was being presented for payment instead of collection.

1 (1834) 2 Ad & E 184; 111 ER 71.

Actions against the collecting bank

14.10 When a collecting banker breaches the duty associated with the presentment of cheques or of giving notice of dishonour, then the proper action by the customer is breach of contract.

14.11 However the banker may unwittingly co-operate in the collection of a cheque which does not belong to the customer. In such cases, the "true owner" of the cheque will have an action against the collecting bank. The concept of the "true owner" of the cheque is discussed in 16.35ff.

Conversion

14.12 Conversion is:

> An intentional exercise of control over a chattel which so seriously

interferes with the right of another to control it that the intermeddler may justly be required to pay its full value.[1]

1 Fleming, *Law of Torts*, 6th ed, Sydney, p 49.

14.13 The "intention" spoken of is merely the intention to exercise control. In order to sustain an action for conversion, it is not necessary for the plaintiff to establish that the defendant intended to deprive the plaintiff of any rights over the chattel. The defendant may be quite "innocent" in that he or she did not know and had no way of learning that the plaintiff had an interest in the chattel with which the defendant was interfering.

14.14 Also note that there is no requirement that the defendant profited in any way from the interference. It is enough that the interference took place and is serious enough for the law to impose what amounts to a compulsory purchase by the defendant of the chattel.

14.15 The tort of conversion is primarily concerned with the rights of individuals over chattels, but a series of decisions last century has applied the tort to bills of exchange and other instruments

by treating the conversion as of the chattel, the piece of paper, the cheque under which the money was collected, and the value of the chattel converted as the money received under it.[1]

1 Per Scrutton J in *Lloyds Bank Ltd v Chartered Bank of India, Australia and China* [1929] 1 KB 40, 55.

14.16 There is Canadian authority to the effect that an instrument on which the drawer's signature has been forged cannot be the subject of an action in conversion against the collecting bank since the paper does not give rise to a valid chose in action.[1] The decision has been approved and followed in the Supreme Court of South Australia in *Koster's Premier Pottery v Bank of Adelaide*.[2] However, the reasoning in the cases is not free from difficulty and the matter is by no means settled.[3]

1 See *Arrow Transfer Co Ltd v Royal Bank of Canada* (1972) 27 DLR (3d) 81.
2 (1981) 28 SASR 355.
3 See Tyree, "The Liability of Banks Collecting Forged Cheques" (1983) 11 Aust Bus L Rev 236 and see 14.14.

Money had and received

14.17 The action for money had and received is an action which is independent of conversion, but in the context of conversion of cheques is usually sued upon in the alternative. The action allows the recovery of money which has been paid to the defendant in circumstances where the law deems that it is to be held by the defendant for the plaintiff's use. Common situations are where money has been paid to the defendant by mistake, or money paid when the consideration for it has wholly failed.

14.18 It is said that plaintiff may succeed in the action for money had and received where he or she might fail in the action for conversion. In *Bavins Junr & Sims v London & South Western Bank Ltd*[1] the instrument required that a receipt be signed before payment could be made and the Court held that it was not a cheque. It was argued that the action in conversion would entitle the plaintiff to only nominal damages as the instrument was not a negotiable instrument.[2] While not necessarily accepting that argument, the Court said:

> ... But in any case it seems to me to be clear that the plaintiffs are entitled to recover the amount received by the defendants upon the document as money had and received. Having received money by presenting the document which belonged to the plaintiffs they cannot in my opinion, if the plaintiffs choose to waive the tort, say that they did not receive the money on account of the plaintiffs; or at any rate they cannot say so after they have knowledge of the plaintiffs' title, unless before obtaining that knowledge they have altered their position for the worse so as to bring themselves within the doctrine [of change of position].[3]

1 [1900] 1 QB 270.
2 See 14.16.
3 Per Vaughan Williams LJ at p 278.

14.19 On the other hand, *Arrow Transfer Co Ltd v Royal Bank of Canada*[1] and *Koster's Premier Pottery v Bank of Adelaide*[2] both held that the action for money had and received must fail if the action for conversion fails.

1 (1972) 27 DLR (3d) 81.
2 (1981) 28 SASR 355.

Defences of collecting bank

14.20 Just because the plaintiff has an action against the collecting bank does not mean that he or she will win the action, for there are a number of defences which might be raised by the collecting bank. Some of these are defences that are available to anyone in the position of the defendant bank, others are statutory defences which are available only tobankers.

Common law defences

14.21 The banker is not, by being a banker, disqualified from any of the defences which could be used by an ordinary person being sued in conversion. However, as noted above, conversion is a tort of very strict liability and very few defences are available. One such defence is to show that the title of the defendant is, in fact, better than the title of the plaintiff. In the context of negotiable instruments, this usually means showing that the defendant is a holder in due course of the instrument.

Holder for value

14.22 The collecting banker who has become a holder in due course of a cheque is in the same position as anyone else, that is, the holder in due course is the true owner and may use that position as a defence against the action in conversion or for money had and received.

14.23 The problems which have arisen concern the circumstances under which it can be said that the collecting banker has given value for the cheque.

14.24 The confusion stems from the decision in *Capital and Counties Bank Ltd v Gordon*.[1] A fraudulent clerk stole cheques which were drawn in favour of his employer, forged indorsements on them and paid them into his own accounts. Immediately the cheques were deposited, the clerk's accounts were credited with the amounts and he was in fact allowed to draw on the amounts so credited. The true owner of the cheques, Gordon, sued the collecting bank.

1 [1903] AC 240.

14.25 In the course of the judgments, it was necessary to decide if the bank had been collecting for itself or for its customer, the Court believing that it was impossible that the answer could be "both". Weaver and Cragie express it well in saying that the House of Lords decision in holding that the bank was collecting for itself involved two propositions:[1]

1 A bank is not collecting a cheque for a customer in any case where the bank is a holder for value of the cheque.

2 A bank is a holder for value of a cheque if it credits the account of its customer with the amount thereof before the proceeds of the cheque have been collected from the paying banker and this position prevails even though the fact of crediting the account has not been communicated to the customer.

1 *Weaver and Cragie*, p 477.

14.26 The true position with regard to crediting the account is now accepted to be that given by the Court in *AL Underwood Ltd v*

Barclays Bank Ltd.[1] A managing director misappropriated cheques payable to the company by paying them into his own account which was credited immediately with the proceeds although the director did not in fact draw upon the funds until the cheques were cleared. The Court of Appeal held that the bank was not a holder for value of the cheques, Scrutton LJ summarising the reasoning concisely:

> The cases where an agent for collection becomes a holder for value must turn on an express or implied agreement between bank and customer that the latter may draw against the cheques before they are cleared.[2]

1 [1924] 1 KB 775.
2 At p 804.

Consequences

14.27 The consequence for banks in New Zealand is that the crediting of the account will be largely irrelevant in the determination of whether the collecting bank is or is not a holder for value. The reason for this is that

(1) there will seldom be an express contract that the customer may draw against uncleared effects and

(2) since deposit slips carry warnings that the customer may not draw on uncleared effects it will not be possible to find an implied contract that he or she may do so.

14.28 This result seems correct in principle. The accounting which the bank chooses to adopt is purely an internal matter and should have no relevance to the question of whether the banker is or is not a holder for value. If the accounting methods are to be evidence of this, then it is likely that the bank will be inviting legislative interference in the accounting procedures, a situation which exists in the United States.

14.29 There are circumstances where by virtue of the banker's lien or for some other reason that the banker might be a holder for value in his or her own right. Such was the situation in *Barclays Bank Ltd v Astley Industrial Trust Ltd.*[1] M Ltd had a large overdraft with the plaintiff bank. The plaintiff received 5 cheques totalling £2,850 for collection to M's account and, on the faith of those cheques, paid two of M's cheques to an amount of £345. The cheques made payable to M were drawn by the defendant in respect of hire purchase transactions which were later found to be fraudulent. The defendant stopped payment on the cheques and the plaintiff sued on the cheques, claiming to be holders in due course. It was held that the plaintiff had given value for the cheques by virtue of the banker's lien[2] and by virtue of the fact that they had honoured two cheques which would otherwise have been dishonoured. Even though the cheques were delivered for collection, the bank still became a holder for value and could sue on the cheques.

1 [1970] 2 QB 527.
2 See s 27, Bills of Exchange Act 1908 and Ch 25.

Statutory defences: the Cheques Act 1960

14.30 The Cheques Act 1960 is the latest in a long line of statutory provisions which have provided a defence for the collecting banker when faced with an action in conversion or in money had and received.

14.31 So far as the collecting banker is concerned, the essential part of the Act is s 5(1):

> Where a banker in good faith and without negligence —
> (a) Receives payment for a customer of an instrument to which this section applies; or
> (b) Having credited a customer's account with the amount of any such instrument receives payment thereof for himself —
>
> and the customer has no title, or a defective title, to the instrument, the banker shall not incur any liability to the true owner of the instrument by reason only of having received payment thereof.

14.32 Subsection (2) of the section defines the instruments to which the section applies and includes cheques and others although it clearly excludes bills of exchange other than cheques.[1]

1 See 15.87ff.

14.33 Although the matter is still not entirely free from difficulty, it is thought that the wording of the section makes the first proposition of the *Gordon* case inapplicable so that the collecting banker may take advantage of the section even though also a holder for value of the cheque. The point arose in the *Astley Industrial Trust* case where Milmo J said:

> I am unable to accept the contention that a banker cannot at one and the same time be an agent for collection of a cheque and a holder of that cheque for value. It seems to me that the language of section 2 of the Cheques Act 1957 negatives this proposition since it presupposes that a banker who has been given a cheque for collection may nevertheless have given value for it.[1]

1 At p 538.

Nature of the section

14.34 Much confusion will be avoided if it is recognised that the Cheques Act 1960 places no new duty on the collecting banker. Quite the contrary, the collecting banker like everyone else is under a duty imposed by law to refrain from interfering with chattels and goods belonging to other people. The effect of s 4 is to provide a collecting banker with a defence which is not available to the general public.

14.35 This position requires some comment, for a number of influential textbooks and not a few judgments are in different terms. Thus, Paget comments that:

> The importation of negligence into this section is . . . an anomaly; there can be no negligence without a duty. There is no contractual relation between the collecting banker and the true owner which gives rise to a duty on the part of the former to the latter . . . .The true exposition is that given by Denman J and the Court of Appeal in *Bissell & Co v Fox Bros & Co* [(1884) 51 LT 663]; the duty is a purely statutory one imposed on the banker in favour of the true owner and the negligence consists in the disregard of his interests. The assumption of this duty and liability to a stranger must be regarded as the price paid by bankers for protection under statute.[1]

1 At p 330.

14.36 The truth is that the word "negligence" in the statute is indeed an anomaly, but it is wrong to say that the statute imposes a duty. Without the statute the duty would still exist, but the banker would have no defence at all.

14.37 The use of the word "negligence" has, however, undoubtedly had its effect. As will be seen below, the cases tend to analyse the behaviour of the bank in terms of a duty owed by a reasonable banker to the true owner of a cheque. On the other hand, in a true negligence action, the plaintiff must prove the negligence. When suing in conversion, the plaintiff need only prove that the conversion occurred; if the banker wishes to rely upon the section, it is up to the banker to prove that the collection was "without negligence".

14.38 The true position is stated by Weaver and Cragie:

> In short, "negligence" is equivalent to "carelessness". Liability in conversion is normally absolute, ie, if a conversion has occurred the defendant is liable even if he acted with all the care in the world. Section 88D[1] gives the collecting banker an additional defence which is available to no-one else but, not unnaturally, the onus of proving the necessary elements of the defence, and notably that he acted without negligence, has to be undertaken by the banker as the party seeking to invoke the defence.[2]

1 The Australian section analogous to s 4.
2 At p 491.

14.39 The question of whether the defendant bank acted without negligence is a question of fact for the jury.

Payment received

14.40 It is important to note that the defence is available only when the banker "receives payment for a customer". The meaning of "customer" has been discussed in Ch 3, and it is clear from the *Astley* case that it is possible for a banker to be a holder for value and at the same time be receiving payment for a customer.

14.41 However, if the bank is acting as a discounter, that is, is actually purchasing the cheque or bill, then the statute will provide no defence if the banker takes under a forged indorsement. It will, of course, be an unusual circumstance for a banker to discount a cheque.

"Good faith"

14.42 Section 91 of the Act is:

> A thing is deemed to be done in good faith within the meaning of this Act where it is in fact done honestly, whether it is done negligently or not.

14.43 Section 1 of the Cheques Act 1960 is:

> (1) This Act may be cited as the Cheques Act 1960, and shall be read together with and deemed part of the Bills of Exchange Act 1908 . . . .

14.44 There is a paucity of cases in which the good faith of the banker has been questioned. Indeed, it is generally pleaded by the banker but its existence is essentially assumed by the Court.

14.45 Blundering and carelessness are not in themselves a lack of good faith, but the facts could be so bizarre that the Court could infer a lack of honesty. Lord Blackburn said:

> [a person who] honestly blundering and careless, and so took a bill of exchange or a bank-note when he ought not to have taken it, still he would be entitled to recover. But if the facts and circumstances are such that a jury, or whoever has to try the question, came to the conclusion that he was not honestly blundering and careless, but that he must have had a suspicion that there was something wrong, and that he refrained from asking questions, not because he was an honest blunderer or a stupid man, but because he thought in his own secret mind "I suspect there is something wrong, and if I ask questions and make farther inquiry, it will no longer be my suspecting it, but my knowing it, and then I shall not be able to recover", I think that is dishonesty.[1]

1 *Jones v Gordon* (1877) 2 App Cas 616, 628-629.

14.46 One of the few times that there has been a serious challenge to the good faith of a bank was in *Lawrie v Commonwealth Trading Bank of Australia*.[1] A fraudulent senior bank interviewing and investigating officer obtained a cheque from the plaintiff made payable to "B T Clifford or bearer" and crossed "Bank payee only". The fraudulent officer had the cheque credited to the named account which was operated by him. The officer disposed of the proceeds of the cheque and the amount was debited to the plaintiff's account. The defendant bank relied upon ss 86 and 88 of the Australian Bills of Exchange Act. The jury found that the officer had not acted within the scope of his apparent duty when he represented to the plaintiff that "B T Clifford" was a customer of the bank who required a loan for bridging finance. As a result, the fraudulent conduct of the officer could not be attributed to the bank and it was held that the bank had acted in good faith. If the decision is correct, it is difficult to see how the bank could ever act otherwise than in good faith.

1 [1970] Qd R 373.

Meaning of negligence

14.47 Although the question of whether a banker has collected without negligence is a question of fact for the jury, there are a large number of cases where there are judicial pronouncements on the meaning of the expression. And, although it is often said that it is incapable of a precise definition, there are a surprisingly large number of cases where the Court has attempted to do just that. However, it seems that the statement of the Privy Council in *Commissioners of Taxation v English, Scottish and Australian Bank Ltd*[1] has become the classic pronouncement on the subject.

1 [1920] AC 683.

14.48 In that case, a man who called himself Thallon wished to open an account with the defendant bank. He gave as his address a well known address in Sydney and signed the signature book. The account was opened with £20 in bank notes and Thallon was given a cheque-book. No inquiries were made to check the authenticity of the address. On the following day, Thallon deposited a crossed bearer cheque for more than £750 which the bank collected for him. He withdrew the entire amount from his account soon thereafter and disappeared. The cheque turned out to be stolen, "Thallon" was an assumed name and no such person lived at the address given.

14.49 The true owner of the cheque sued the bank for conversion of the cheque. During the course of the judgment given by the Privy Council, Lord Dunedin gave what has become the classic definition of "negligence" for the purposes of s 4 of the Cheques Act:

> The test of negligence is whether the transaction of paying in any given cheque (coupled with the circumstances antecedent and present) was so out of the ordinary course that it ought to have aroused doubts in the bankers' mind, and caused them to make inquiry.[1]

1 Per Lord Dunedin at p 688.

Factors in determining negligence

14.50 Although it is difficult to give general rules concerning the circumstances under which a banker will succeed in establishing that a collection was "without negligence" for the purposes of s 5, it seems that it is possible to identify factors which have influenced the Courts in various cases. This is facilitated if the cases are classified according to the type of negligence considered. There are essentially three such categories, namely, negligence connected with the opening of the account, negligence which results from factors which are apparent on the face of the cheque, and negligence connected with facts known by the banker about the customer.

Practice of bankers

14.51 The practice of bankers has always been influential in determining whether the particular banker has acted without negligence, but it has never been guaranteed to bring the banker automatically within the protective provisions of the Act.

14.52 For example, in *EB Savory & Co v Lloyds Bank Ltd*[1] there was evidence available that it was the practice of bankers which had a head office in London and branch offices elsewhere to accept cheques paid in at any branch for the credit of an account at any other branch. It was said that this was practice which had been established for over 40 years. The House of Lords found the practice to be inconsistent with prudent precautions against known risks, Lawrence LJ referring to cases "where bankers, solely for the convenience of their customers, have adopted a system with an inherent and obvious defect which no reasonably careful banker could fail to observe".[2]

1 [1932] 2 KB 122.
2 At p 144.

14.53 This approach by the Courts is often criticised by commercial interests, but when a case has come before the Court it is one in which the commercial system demonstrably has failed to work and someone must then bear the losses. There is perhaps a natural tendency for the Courts to shift losses to the party who is in the position to make changes in the way in which the practice is carried on rather than to let it fall on a party who must simply take the system as it is or leave it.

14.54 A further difficulty which is often experienced is that the "practice of bankers" is often not as uniform as is thought. If the Court is faced with conflicting evidence as to the practice of bankers, then there is little that can be done other than to base a decision on other principles.[1] It is not just the practice of an individual bank which is relevant, but the practice of bankers generally.

1 See, for example, *Ladbroke & Co v Todd* (1914) 30 TLR 433; *Rosenhain v Commonwealth Bank of Australia* (1922) 31 CLR 46.

Bank rules

14.55 Banks have books of instructions to staff which lay down procedures to be followed in various situations. It might be thought that a banker who has not followed the procedures laid down by the bank might have an uphill battle to establish that a cheque has been collected without negligence. While that is indeed the case, it is by no means true that a failure to follow internal rules and procedures will necessarily be fatal to the s5 defence.

14.56 In *Motor Traders Guarantee Corp Ltd v Midland Bank Ltd*,[1] Goddard J considered that the rules were evidence upon which the plaintiffs could rely, but that they were not entitled to demand literal performance. He said:

> The bank does not owe a duty to [the plaintiffs] to carry out this rule, that rule, or the other rule. Indeed, I doubt whether they owe their own customers the duty of carrying out all the rules which they may lay down as counsels of perfection. The question in every case is . . . whether the particular acts which are done are enough to discharge the onus which is upon the bank . . . .[2]

1 [1937] 4 All ER 90.
2 At p 96.

14.57 On the other hand, as already stated, the rules do offer some evidence of what may reasonably be expected. In *Orbit Mining & Trading Co Ltd v Westminster Bank Ltd*,[1] Harman LJ noted that even though the failure to comply with the rules "does not convict the bank of negligence [sic] . . . where the rules are not kept the matter needs close attention".

1 [1963] 1 QB 794.

Amateur detective

14.58 In *Lloyds Bank Ltd v Chartered Bank of India, Australia & China*,[1] Sankey LJ said:

> In my view, a bank cannot be held liable for negligence merely because they have not subjected an account to a microscopic examination. It is not to be expected that the officials of banks should also be amateur detectives.[2]

1 [1929] 1 KB 40.
2 At p 73.

14.59 On the other hand:

> If banks for fear of offending their customers will not make inquiry into unusual circumstances, they must take with the benefit of not annoying those customers the risk of liability because they do not inquire.[1]

1 Per Scrutton LJ in *AL Underwood Ltd v Bank of Liverpool* [1924] 1 KB 775.

14.60 When a case actually goes as far as litigation, there is undoubtedly a tendency to apply rather stricter rules, so that it is at the banker's peril if he or she does not examine cheques which are paid in for collection. Again, it must be noted that this is not some new and onerous duty which has been placed upon the banking community, but rather is the pre-condition for taking advantage of a defence which no other part of the community may use.

Consideration of each cheque separately

14.61 It is clear that the bank must establish that it collected each and every cheque without negligence. So, for example, when a large number of cheques were misappropriated and collected for the rogue by the State Savings Bank of Victoria, the High Court considered differences in the way in which the cheques were drawn, their amount and other details, holding that some of them had been collected "without negligence" while others had not.[1]

1 *Commissioners of the State Savings Bank of Victoria v Permewan Wright & Co Ltd* (1914) 19 CLR 457 and post 15.40.

Negligence in opening of account

14.62 The banker has an obligation to make certain inquiries concerning the customer at the time when an account is opened and if these inquiries are not made it may prove impossible for the banker to rely upon the s 5 defence. Unfortunately, the scope of these requirements is by no means clear. Banking practice will be relevant but in this area more than any other it is difficult to identify a uniform practice among bankers or to ascertain that the practice is stable over time.

14.63 At first sight, it might seem that the circumstances of opening an account are far removed from later misappropriations of cheques. Indeed, that would be true when a customer has operated an account honestly for a period of years but then begins to misappropriate cheques. On the other hand, cheque frauds are almost impossible to perpetrate without access to a bank account and there are certain situations in which care taken in the opening of the account will prevent the frauds from occurring.

14.64 As an example of the latter situation, even a perfunctory inquiry by the bank when opening the account for "Thallon" would have revealed that he was not what he claimed to be in *Commissioners of Taxation v English, Scottish & Australian Bank Ltd.*[1] Surprisingly, the Privy Council found that the bank was entitled to rely upon the defence in that case, a case which has been criticised and upon which it would be very foolish for a modern banker to rely.

1 [1920] AC 683.

14.65 It is likely that the decision in *London Bank of Australia Ltd v Kendall*[1] is a better guide to current practice. A man calling himself "Howard" went to the head office of the defendant bank in Sydney, introduced himself to the assistant accountant and indicated that he wished to open an account. He claimed to be an indent agent from Adelaide and, in response to questions from the accountant, said that he had never had a banking account in Sydney but that he had been banking in Adelaide. The accountant made no further inquiries concerning the banking activities of the man, the accountant believing that such inquiries were unnecessary because "the man appeared to be about 36 or 37 years of age, looked quite respectable and had the appearance of a businessman and spoke like an educated man".

1 (1920) 28 CLR 401.

14.66 The account was opened, with the approval of the bank manager, with £5 in notes and four crossed bearer cheques. The cheques were stolen and the plaintiff, who was the true owner of one of the cheques sued in conversion. The High Court of Australia held that the circumstance surrounding the opening of the account was one of the "antecedent circumstances" to be taken into account for the purposes of deciding if the defendant bank had collected without negligence.

14.67 The Court held that the bank did not collect without negligence. The customer was unknown to the bank, he had no credentials, he offered no information concerning his banking activities and opened the account with cheques that needed explanation. So far as his appearance was concerned, the Court noted that it was plainly insufficient as a basis for opening an account. The transaction was such as to arouse doubts in the mind of an ordinary banker.

14.68 In *Ladbroke & Co v Todd*[1] the plaintiffs were bookmakers who had drawn a cheque in favour of a client payee. The cheque was crossed and marked "account of payee only". It was mailed to the client, but intercepted by a rogue who apparently forged an indorsement. The cheque was taken to the defendant bank where the rogue requested that an account be opened with the proceeds of the cheque. He explained that he had an account with another bank but that since the cheque represented the proceeds of gambling, he did not wish to pass it through that account as he feared that it would come to the attention of the authorities of the college at which he was an undergraduate.

1 (1914) 30 TLR 433.

14.69 The banker asked the rogue to sign the signature book and compared the signature with the indorsement on the cheque, but neither asked for referees nor checked the rogue's story with the other bank. The cheque was cleared specially the same day at the rogue's request and the proceeds withdrawn soon after. The Court held that although the cheque had been collected for a customer that the bank had not collected without negligence and so were liable for the proceeds of the cheque.

What inquiries are necessary?

14.70 Since it is clear that failure to exercise care when opening an account may lead to a situation where the banker cannot rely upon the s 5 defence, it is necessary to ask what is required. On the one hand, we have the comments made above that the banker is not required to act as an amateur detective, but on the other that the banker must evidently make some inquiries.

14.71 The latest, and probably the most definitive, statement of the banker's obligation to make inquiries and the scope that those inquiries must take if the banker is to be assured of the benefit of the s 5 defence, is the judgment of Diplock LJ in *Marfani & Co Ltd v Midland Bank Ltd.*[1] One Kureshy was in possession of a cheque for some £3,000 which had been drawn by his employer in favour of Eliaszade. Kureshy went to the defendant bank where he pretended to be Eliaszade and sought to open an account in the name of Eliaszade. Kureshy, pretending to be Eliaszade, gave the name of two referees and opened the account with a small cash deposit. The bank wrote to the referees, receiving a reply from only one of them, who was also a customer of the bank, and that reply was favourable. It was later learned that Kureshy had introduced himself to the referee as Eliaszade. The referee had in fact known Kureshy, under the name of Eliaszade, for only a short time.

1 [1968] 1 WLR 968.

14.72 On the day after opening the account, Kureshy paid in the cheque which was then collected by the defendant bank. Kureshy later withdrew all of the funds and left England. On the question of whether the bank had been negligent in opening the account, it was argued for the plaintiff that the bank should have taken steps to ascertain the true identity of Kureshy. This might have been done by asking for his passport or other documents of identification, by seeking the name of his employer or of previous bank accounts.

14.73 The Court held that it was probably desirable that a banker should seek documentary identification of a new customer, but that in the present case where the customer was introduced by an "apparently trustworthy referee" it is not always necessary. There was no point in asking about employment, for Kureshy had said that he was self-employed and there is no requirement that the banker should cross-examine the potential customer on such a matter.

14.74 It was also argued that the bank had been negligent in failing to obtain both referees' reports and that in fact the bank had collected the cheque before receiving the one favourable report.

14.75 This latter point was a difficult one for the bank, primarily because of a statement made by Bankes LJ in *AL Underwood Ltd v Barclays Bank Ltd*:[1]

> I feel satisfied that the obvious inquiry whether the company had not got its own banking account would have put a stop to the fraudulent system adopted by Underwood, and I do not think that it lies in the mouth of the appellants to say that an inquiry would have been useless.

1 [1924] 1 KB 775, 789.

14.76 In the *Marfani* case, it is clear that the fact that the cheque was collected before the receipt of the referee's report made no difference whatsoever to the collection of the cheque, but it was not certain that seeking the second referee's report would have been pointless. All that could be said is that in all likelihood, the rogue would have made arrangements so that the report of the second referee would have been as good as that of the first. Cairns J said:

> In my opinion, if the bank can show that in all probability a particular precaution would have been unavailing, the failure to take that precaution is not such negligence as deprives them of the protection [of s 5]. The burden of proof on the bank is no doubt heavy, but I do not think that it can be so heavy as to require them to prove with certainty that the precaution would have been useless.[1]

1 At p 977.

14.77 The matter of the need to pursue "useless" precautions normally arises in the context of the banker failing to make inquiries which are indicated in the circumstances. The matter is discussed in more detail at 15.79ff.

Summary: negligence on opening the account

14.78 The apparently favourable opinion in the *Marfani* case should not cause bankers to believe that they may neglect the making of inquiries when opening an account, for a careful look at the judgments will convince the reader of how close the decision came to being for the plaintiff. Yet the standard of care exercised by the banker was considerably higher than is often the case. It is also important to note that there is not the slightest hint in *Marfani* that the circumstance surrounding the opening of the account is an inappropriate factor to consider when determining if the banker has collected without negligence.

14.79 On the other hand, the *Marfani* case is to be welcomed for its increased attention to the actual practice of bankers. Diplock LJ said:

> What facts ought to be known to the banker, ie, what inquiries he should make and what facts are sufficient to cause him reasonably to suspect that the customer is not the true owner, must depend upon current

banking practice and change as that practice changes. Cases decided thirty years ago, when the use by the general public of banking facilities was much less widespread may not be a reliable guide to what the duty of a careful banker, in relation to inquiries and as to facts which should give rise to suspicion, is today.[1]

1 At p 972.

Chapter 15

The collecting bank II

Cheques — Holder of and other parties — Circumstances of account

This chapter continues the examination of the requirement that the collecting bank act "without negligence" as a prerequisite to taking advantage of the statutory defence to an action in conversion.

Face of the cheque

15.1 Certain features of the cheque itself should put a collecting banker on inquiry. This includes not only the information which is directly discoverable from the cheque itself, such as apparent alterations in the cheque, but also information which may be combined with other information known to the banker which would then indicate that the transaction is outside the ordinary course of business. Examples of this latter kind of information might be that the cheque is drawn in favour of the customer's employer.

15.2 It is not possible to state the exact metes and bounds of conduct which will disentitle the banker from relying upon the s 5 defence, but by examining a number of cases which have come before the Court it is possible to establish some broad principles.

Indorsements

15.3 One consequence of the identification of a cheque as a species of bill of exchange is that the cheque is negotiated by means of indorsement. However, the majority of cheques are never negotiated, but are sent directly to the payee and deposited directly into an account for collection. It was the practice of banks to require that the holder of the cheque indorse it, usually in blank, upon paying in. It is not clear why this practice began or precisely what advantage the banks believed that they were obtaining, for it was held in more than one case that the application of the signature of the holder to the back of the cheque at the request of a bank teller did not amount to an indorsement.[1]

1 See *Smith v Commercial Banking Co of Sydney Ltd* (1910) 11 CLR 667.

15.4 This practice of requiring "indorsements" upon paying in extended to the case where the cheque had not been negotiated. The consequential waste of time was a nuisance to all concerned and seemed to serve little purpose when the cheque had not been negotiated.

15.5 Prior to the passing of the Cheques Act 1960, collection of an unindorsed or irregularly indorsed cheque for anyone other than the payee was virtually conclusive evidence that the collection was not without negligence. Now, s 4(3) is in the following terms:

> A banker shall not be treated for the purposes of this section as having been negligent by reason only of his failure to concern himself with the absence of, or irregularity in, indorsement of an instrument.

15.6 The section is identical to a section in the UK Act. There was debate in the House of Lords at the time of passing the Act as to whether the section applied where the cheque was being collected for someone other than the named payee. The House of Lords seemed to indicate that the plain words of the statute should be given effect so that the banker need not be concerned with indorsements in any case.[1] The reader should note that the Australian equivalent, s 88D, makes it quite clear that the collecting banker must be concerned with indorsements when collecting a cheque for the account of someone other than the named payee.

1 See *Westminster Bank Ltd v Zang* [1966] AC 182.

"Not negotiable"

15.7 Is the mere fact that a banker collects for someone other than the payee a cheque which is crossed "not negotiable" without making inquiries sufficient to disentitle the banker from reliance on the s 4 defence? The simple answer would seem to be "no" since it is clear that such a cheque remains transferable.

15.8 However, doubt was first cast upon the simple answer by Lord Brampton in *Great Western Railway Co v London & County Banking Co Ltd*[1] when he said:

> I am not, however, quite so sure that it was altogether without negligence, for I must assume the manager at Wantage knew the meaning and legal effect of the crossing with the words "not negotiable". This point, however, does not appear to have been raised, and certainly there was no finding upon it at the trial.[2]

1 [1901] AC 414.
2 At p 422.

15.9 Although the point was made obiter and with some diffidence, it seems clear that Lord Brampton thought that collection of a crossed "not negotiable" cheque for a third party without inquiry might not be a collection which was made without negligence.

15.10 The notion has gained some currency in Australia. Griffith CJ in *Commissioners of the State Savings Bank of Victoria v Permewan Wright & Co Ltd*[1] said:

> In my opinion the words "not negotiable" on a crossed cheque are a danger signal held out before every person invited to deal with it, and are equivalent to saying "Take care: this cheque may be stolen". I think, further, that they indicate that the drawer of the cheque . . . intended that the person to whom it was to be handed or sent should apply it to some specific purpose and no other. A reasonably careful man to whom such a cheque is tendered should therefore examine the cheque to see whether there is anything upon its face to indicate such a purpose. If there is not, it may be that he may safely rely on the honesty of the bearer; but, if there is, it is his duty to make inquiries and if he fails to do so he cannot claim to have acted without negligence.[2]

1 (1914) 19 CLR 457.
2 At p 467.

15.11 Although this speech is often cited as reflecting the same views as those of Lord Brampton, it must be noted that the Chief Justice said something quite different. It is not just the crossing which should put the banker on inquiry, but the crossing together with some indication of a special purpose. In the *Permewan Wright* case the cheques in question were for the payment of customs duty and that many of them had "duty" marked upon them.

15.12 Indeed the joint judgment of Gavan Duffy and Rich JJ reflect this distinction:

> When we remember that such cheques are crossed cheques within the meaning of the protecting sections, we have difficulty in appreciating the suggestion that the banker should prima facie be more suspicious of customers paying in such cheques than of those paying in cheques crossed without the words "not negotiable", though circumstances might call for suspicion in the case of one class of crossed cheque which would not call for it in another.[1]

1 At p 484.

15.13 It seems that there are few who would argue that if a "special purpose" is apparent on the face of the cheque, then the banker ignores that purpose at the risk of being unable to rely upon the statutory defence. On the other hand, the "pure" argument of Lord Brampton that the "not negotiable" marking itself should preclude the collection without inquiry of the cheque for a third party has been severely criticised and seems to have little merit.[1]

1 See *Paget*, p 347.

15.14 As a final point on the "not negotiable" cheque, it may well be that the banker who collects such a cheque as the first transaction on an account might be well advised to take a higher degree of care. The High Court of Australia has considered the matter in *Savings Bank of South Australia v Wallman*.[1] In a joint judgment, Rich, Dixon, Evatt and McTiernan JJ said:

> There is, of course, no doubt that special vigilance is demanded when a new account is opened and a crossed cheque is tendered, particularly when it is marked "not negotiable". For it is evident that the purpose of opening a new account may be to obtain payment of a cheque dishonestly come by, and experience has shown that frauds are not uncommonly perpetrated in this manner.[2]

1 (1935) 52 CLR 688.
2 At p 695.

"Account payee only"

15.15 If the foregoing is correct, it is not every collection of a "not negotiable" cheque for a third party which should put the banker on inquiry. When however, the cheque is marked "account payee only" or some similar phrase, there is no doubt that both banking practice and the decided cases indicate that a different approach is called for. Paget states the position very strongly but quite correctly:

> Conclusive evidence of negligence in the collecting banker is, without inquiry, to take a cheque marked with the words "account payee", or "account so and so", for an account other that that indicated . . . . The only exception hitherto recognised is where the customer was a foreign bank, and the marking "account payee" . . . referred to the foreign banker's customer, as to whom it was obviously impossible for the English bank to know or find out anything.[1]

1 At p 348.

15.16 If the facts of *Ladbroke & Co v Todd*[1] are recalled,[2] it will be seen that the words apparently have a broader effect at the time when the account is being opened. Then the words should put the banker on inquiry even when the customer represents that he or she is the named payee.

1 [1914-15] All ER 1134.
2 See 14.68.

15.17 Further, there is an apparent inconsistency in a cheque which is drawn "Pay X or bearer" yet which is crossed "account payee". However, in *House Property Co of London v London County & Westminster Bank*,[1] Rowlatt J considered the collection without inquiry of such a cheque for the account of a third party to disentitle the bank from reliance on the statutory defence. The argument for the bank, dismissed as "shallow" by the Court, was that as the cheque was made payable to "bearer" they had complied with the instruction to collect for the payee.

1 (1915) 84 LJKB 1846.

15.18 A recent decision of the High Court has flown in the face of the perceived settled state of the law. In *New Zealand Law Society v ANZ Banking Group Ltd*[1] one Calkin, a solicitor who was also a director of a company called Tina Colliery Ltd, obtained finance from a finance company for the purposes of purchasing two trucks by the company. Under the arrangement, the finance company was to become the owner of the trucks and let them to Tina Colliery under a hire purchase agreement. The trucks were to be purchased from another company of which Calkin was also a director.

1 [1985] 1 NZLR 280.

15.19 Calkin completed the hire purchase proposals and turned them over to the finance company in return for two cheques representing the purchase price of the trucks. The cheques were drawn in favour of "Tina Colliery Ltd or order", crossed "not negotiable" and "account payee only". Calkin paid the cheques into his solicitor trust account and misappropriated the proceeds. The trucks were in fact owned by another finance company and Calkin had no authority or power to make the sale. The finance company made a claim against the Solicitors' Fidelity Guarantee Fund which was settled by the Law Society who were then subrogated to whatever rights the finance company might have had against the collecting banker.

15.20 In spite of the fact that there had been no inquiries made by the collecting banker, the Court held that the collection had been without negligence. This appeared to be for the sole reason that there was evidence which established that current banking practice is to collect the proceeds of cheques for the credit of solicitor's trust accounts without making inquiries. During the course of the judgment, the Court said:

> Further, as Calkin was a director of the payee company, the company's solicitor and the person who had organised the transaction with Broadlands, it was unlikely that any inquiry from the bank would have led to the detection of Calkin's dishonest purpose. . . [I]n deciding whether or not there was a foreseeable risk . . . it is relevant to take into account:
>
> 1 The general practice of bankers in New Zealand to accept third party cheques for payment to solicitors' trust accounts.
>
> 2 The fact that payments to a solicitor's trust account should have been received by the solicitor to the credit of the person entitled . . . .

3 . . . the moneys . . . are held on behalf of the person entitled to be disposed of by the direction or on the instruction of such person.

4 . . . solicitors' trust accounts are strictly controlled . . . .

5 In considering the likelihood of loss — the existence of the Solicitors' Fidelity Guarantee Fund.

6 [The manager's] belief . . . of the personal integrity and honesty of Mr Calkin.

7 [The manager's] knowledge that Mr Calkin . . . was also a director of ["the payee"].[1]

I would say in the present case that it did not constitute lack of reasonable care to refrain from making inquiries in circumstances where it was improbable that they would have led to detection of Mr Calkin's dishonest purpose. There was no evidence of his dishonesty at that stage.[2]

1 At p 292.
2 At p 293. As to the position of the banker when the inquiries would be unlikely to yield useful information, see 15.79 for a recent alternative view.

15.21 With respect, the decision is out of step with settled law. It would be very risky indeed for bankers to rely upon it as authority for continuing the practice even with regard to solicitors' trust accounts, much less as a temptation to extend the practice of ignoring the very clear meaning of the words "account payee" in other circumstances.

Relationship between the holder and other parties to the cheque

15.22 There are a number of cases where the relationship between the customer/holder and some other party on the cheque has been such as to raise the need for inquiry by the collecting banker. The most obvious of these is when the customer is the employee of the drawer or, even more dramatically, the payee of the cheque which is being deposited. The matter is so serious for the banker that Weaver and Cragie recommend that when the cheque is drawn by the employer in favour of a third party or when drawn by some third party in favour of the employer that the situation is so unsatisfactory that the banker should simply refuse to accept such cheques.

15.23 The cases are not restricted to employer/employee relationships. There are problems whenever the relationship is one which makes it possible for the customer to be misappropriating cheques and where the circumstances are such that the customer would not ordinarily be expected to be depositing cheques of that particular form.

Employer

15.24 When a banker is collecting cheques for the personal account of a person who is known to be an employee, there is an obligation to make inquiries when the cheque shows on its face that the employer may have a legal interest in the cheque. Such a situation may arise when the employer is the original payee of the cheque, an indorsee, or even when the employer is the drawer of the cheque, particularly when the drawing is done by the employee with authority from the employer.

15.25 "Employee" and "employer" here are to be interpreted broadly, for the same duty is upon the collecting banker whether the customer be a clerk or a director or an agent of the party claiming an interest in the cheque.

15.26 The position is exemplified by *Orbit Mining & Trading Co Ltd v Westminster Bank Ltd*.[1] The customer of the bank was one of the signatories of instruments which were made payable to "cash or order". The mandate from the plaintiff company called for two signatures to each cheque. The customer's co-signatory was going to be abroad for a period of time and was persuaded to leave a number of forms pre-signed. The customer deposited the instruments into his own account with the defendant bank.[2] The Court of Appeal held that there was nothing to put the bank on inquiry since the banker did not know and, in the view of the Court, could not be expected to know that the customer was employed by the plaintiff company.

1 [1963] 1 QB 794.
2 The instruments were held not to be cheques. See 16.68.

15.27 It was also relevant that the instruments were drawn payable to "cash" and so did not require an indorsement even though the customer had in fact indorsed the cheques on the back. Had the form been such that an indorsement was required, it seemed that the bank might have been put on inquiry since in that case the bank would have recognised that the customer and one of the co-signatories were one and the same.

15.28 A similar situation arose in *Morison v London County & Westminster Bank Ltd*.[1] A clerk by the name of Abbott was authorised to draw cheques on the company's account. He drew some 50 cheques in fraud upon his employer Morison who was an insurance broker who carried on business under the name Bruce Morison and Co. The cheques totalled more than £1,800 and were all signed by Abbott in the form "per pro Bruce Morison & Co, H Abbott".

1 [1914] 3 KB 356.

15.29 The Court at first instance held that the bank could not rely upon the statutory defence since the bank knew that Abbott was the manager for the firm and that, on their face, the cheques showed that there should be inquiries before collecting them for Abbott.[1] The Court of Appeal reversed the findings on grounds that are now considered to be incorrect.[2]

1 Lord Coleridge [1913] WN 84.
2 See 15.62 and the doctrine of "lulling to sleep".

Director

15.30 The position of a director of a company is, in some respects, similar to that of an employee. When a director is depositing what appears to be a company cheque into a private account, matters precisely similar to those which obtain for the employee situation must be considered.

15.31 This can be a matter of particular difficulty when the company is essentially a "one man" company since it is so easy in such cases for the banker to overlook the legal distinction between the person and the company. Further, in such cases, there is no person to whom inquiries may be addressed since the director/owner of the company who is depositing the cheque into a personal account is unlikely to shed any light on the circumstances and the drawer of such a cheque, if in favour of the company, will be equally unlikely to interfere in the personal financial arrangements between the director and the company.

15.32 The difficulty is exemplified by *Underwood's* case,[1] where the sole active director of a "one man company" appropriated company cheques for his own account. If the collecting banker had made the inquiry suggested by the Court, it could only have been directed to the sole director of the company and there seems little doubt as to the nature of the reply.

1 *AL Underwood Ltd v Barclays Bank Ltd* [1924] 1 KB 775. See the further comments at 15.80.

Fiduciary

15.33 When the customer of the bank is known to be in a fiduciary relationship with another party, great care must be taken in the collection of cheques made payable to the principal or where the cheque is signed by the fiduciary on behalf of the principal. The standard example is *Midland Bank Ltd v Reckitt.*[1]

1 [1933] AC 1.

15.34 Lord Terrington was the plaintiff's solicitor and authorised by an express power of attorney to draw cheques on the account of the plaintiff for the purposes of the plaintiff's financial affairs.

The form of the document which conferred the power of attorney was broader than the actual authority: it authorised Lord Terrington to draw "without restriction".

15.35 Lord Terrington signed several cheques in the plaintiff's name and used them to reduce his own overdraft at the Midland Bank. The House of Lords held that the form of the cheque was sufficient to put the Midland Bank on inquiry and to give them notice that the cheque may not have belonged to their client. In this case, an inquiry to the paying bank to discover the form of the authority would probably have satisfied the collecting bank's responsibility.

"Pay A and B or bearer"

15.36 It has already been noted that a cheque which is crossed "account payee" and made payable to more than one person should not be collected for the account of only one of the named payees.[1] It would seem dangerous to collect an order cheque for the account of one of a number of payees, but if the cheque is made payable in the form "Pay A and B or bearer" then there is at least an argument that the collecting bank may safely collect for the account of either A or B.[2]

1 See 15.15.
2 Note that there would be no breach of contract by the paying bank in paying the cheque to either one of the parties. Indeed, the paying bank would probably be safe in paying to any bearer provided it has no external reasons to believe that the cheque is being used to defraud its customer. See the discussion of *Selangor United Rubber Estates Ltd v Cradock (No 3)*[1967] 2 All ER 1255 at 7.73ff.

15.37 The question was before the Court in *Moser v Commercial Banking Corp of Sydney*.[1] A cheque was made payable "J & A Moser or bearer" and was crossed "Bank Not Negotiable". The plaintiff was at the time married to J Moser who took the cheque to the defendant bank and had it collected for his private account. Franki J held that the bank had been negligent in collecting the cheque for the account of only one of the payees without making inquiries,

> because unless there is some evidence to the contrary it seems clear that one payee was entitled to no more than a joint interest in the cheque . . . it seems clear that the mere addition of the words "or bearer" is not sufficient to justify the bank regarding the details concerning the payee or payees as of little or no consequence.[2]

1 (1973) 22 FLR 123.
2 At p 126.

15.38 On the other hand, the fact that the cheque is a bearer cheque is not irrelevant to the question of whether the collecting bank has been negligent. In *Day v Bank of NSW*[1] there were two cheques which were misappropriated by a fraudulent real estate agent and collected by the defendant bank. The circumstances of the collection were similar for both cheques, save that the first was made payable "F L Day or bearer" and the second was to "Frank L Day" and the words "or bearer" were struck out. Both cheques were crossed "not negotiable". The Supreme Court of South Australia found that the collection of the first cheque was not negligent, but that the banker should have questioned the indorsement of the order cheque and sought proof of authority. Note that the Australian statute specifically addresses the problem of third party cheques so that a finding of negligence would be easier, but it is thought that the same principles would apply under the New Zealand statute.[2]

1 (1978) 19 ALR 32.
2 The Court also expressed its opinion that contributory negligence is not a defence to an action for conversion. See 15.71.

Public officials

15.39 There are a large number of cases where cheques have been collected for the customer's private account when the cheques name a public authority as payee or when there is some other indication on the cheques that they are intended for such a purpose.

15.40 One example already considered is *Commissioners of the State Savings Bank of Victoria v Permewan Wright & Co Ltd*.[1] There were 58 cheques in all. Thirty-six of the cheques showed clearly that they were to be payable to the Customs Department; the remaining 22 were marked "duty" or some such similar phrase. The High Court held that the banker had, by failing to make adequate inquiries, failed to establish the statutory defence with regard to the first class of cheque, but by a bare majority held that the second class of cheque did not sufficiently identify the intended purpose or payee and that the bank did collect these cheques without negligence.

1 (1914) 19 CLR 457.

15.41 In *Ross v London County, Westminster & Parr's Bank Ltd*[1] the cheques which were converted were stolen by a quartermaster employed by an office established to collect the estates of soldiers killed in the war. The cheques were paid into the rogue's private account. Each cheque was drawn in favour of "The Officer in Charge, Estates Office, Canadian Overseas Military Forces". The cheques were properly indorsed by the payee and then stolen by the rogue. The Court held that the bank did not collect without negligence on the grounds that:

> It is not in accordance with the ordinary course of business that a cheque so drawn and endorsed should be used for the purpose of paying the debt of a private individual. It was highly improbable that the officer in charge of the Estates Office would hand to "the quartermaster" cheques in this form with the intention that the latter should pay them into his private account. It therefore seems to me that when "the quartermaster" presented these cheques with a view to having them

credited to his private account a cashier of ordinary intelligence and experience should have been put on inquiry whether or not the credit ought to be made.

1 [1919] 1 KB 678.

15.42 Merely asking the customer for an explanation in such a case is unlikely to discharge the duty of the banker, for "to rely exclusively upon the agent's own explanation of his use of such a cheque is to encounter the risk, not to exercise care to avoid it".[1]

1 Per Dixon J in *Commercial Bank of Australia Ltd v Flannagan* (1932) 47 CLR 461, 467.

Partnerships

15.43 A cheque made payable to a partnership should not be collected for the private account of one of the partners. The arguments which have been used to support the proposition are similar to those which concern the paying in of a company cheque to the private account of a director. In some ways, the banker is more exposed in the partnership context because it may be more difficult to know what inquiries to make and of whom. For example, in the situation encountered in *Baker v Barclays Bank Ltd*,[1] it seems almost impossible to recommend an appropriate action on the part of the banker.

1 [1955] 1 WLR 822.

15.44 The plaintiff was in a partnership with Bainbridge. They operated a couple of confectionary shops under the name Modern Confections. Although it was a partnership, each of the partners was more or less responsible for the running of one of the shops. There was no written partnership agreement.

15.45 Bainbridge misappropriated some cheques worth some £1,160 which were payable to Modern Confections. They were paid into a personal bank account by Jeffcott who was innocently assisting Bainbridge in the commission of his frauds. The cheques were indorsed "Modern Confections, pp G Bainbridge" and also indorsed by Jeffcott.

15.46 The manager of the defendant bank noticed one of the cheques which had Modern Confections as payee and asked Jeffcott to see him. Jeffcott said that Bainbridge was the sole proprietor of Modern Confections and that Jeffcott was assisting him in the financial side. Jeffcott also said that Bainbridge owed him £450 and that he hoped, by running the financial side that that debt could be reduced. The manager did not ask to see Bainbridge.

15.47 One of the arguments of the bank was that they were a holder in due course since Jeffcott had an overdraft with the bank.[1] Devlin

J held that the bank could not be a holder for value since Jeffcott's explanation to the manager was inconsistent with his having given value for the cheques and the bank believed the cheques to be Bainbridge's money, so they could not be applied to reduce Jeffcott's overdraft.

1 See *Barclays Bank Ltd v Astley Industrial Trust Ltd* [1970] 2 QB 527 and the discussion at 14.22ff.

15.48 As to the statutory defence, Devlin J held that the bank had not made sufficient inquiries. There was, one might have thought, little to be gained from further question of Jeffcott, but the Court held that this was not necessarily the case, for the focus of the inquiry could broaden during the course of an interview.

15.49 Also, it seems that the Court considered that the bank should treat Bainbridge as a prospective customer since it was known that the money belonged to Bainbridge. In that case, the bank had a duty to interview Bainbridge. Again concerning the futility of such a discussion so far as learning of the misappropriation of the cheques, Devlin J thought that "discussions of this sort may very well roam more widely".

15.50 Although it was open to the bank to prove that nothing further could have been learned, they had not done so:

> . . . if a bank manager fails to make inquiries which he should have made, there is at the very least a heavy burden upon him to show that such inquiries could not have led to any action which could have protected the interests of the true owner.[1]

1 At p 838. As to the need to pursue fruitless inquiries, see 15.79.

Circumstances of the account

15.51 When should "unusual" account activity place the banker on inquiry concerning collection of a customer's cheques? In the *Permewan Wright* case, Griffith CJ said:

> . . . what might pass in the case of an account current in a commercial bank pass as an ordinary payment in of a cheque, subject to a business adjustment between the depositor and the drawer of the cheque, might well be so far out of the ordinary course of a savings bank deposit as to excite suspicion or raise a demand for inquiry in the minds of the officials.[1]

1 At p 479.

15.52 It seems unlikely that the history of the account would ever be the sole factor which disentitled a banker from reliance on the s 5 defence, but it has often been mentioned as one of the circumstances to be considered. So, for example, in *Lumsden v London Trustee Savings Bank*,[1] the customer built an account to just under £900 during the first two months but there followed deposits totalling more than £5,000 during the following five weeks. In view of the fact that the bank had failed to make proper inquiries concerning the customer's credentials at the time of the opening of the account, the Court considered that this movement of the account should have put the bank on inquiry.

1 [1971] Lloyd's Rep 114.

15.53 The timing of the deposits may also be a matter for concern. When a customer opens an account with a small cash deposit which is then followed swiftly by large deposits by cheques drawn in favour of third parties, then that is a factor which should put a collecting banker on inquiry.

15.54 The operation of the account was one of the factors considered in *Crumplin v London Joint Stock Bank Ltd*.[1] The plaintiff was a stockbroker whose manager misappropriated cheques over a period of time. The cheques were all made payable to Davies, a customer with whom the plaintiff had done a few transactions. The clerk wished to speculate but, knowing that he could not do so in his own name, he fraudulently used the account of Davies. The clerk forged the indorsements on cheques which were then collected for his account by the defendant bank. Until the use of the account by the clerk, there had not been a large number of transactions on the account and nearly all of those transactions involved amounts of less than £30.

1 (1913) 109 LT 856; 19 Come Cas 69.

15.55 On the question of the general operation of the account the Court said:

> The question in this case in my opinion comes down to a very narrow one — whether having regard to the nature and number of the cheques of this description that were paid into Rands' account and to the large proportion which the amount of those cheques bore to the amount of other cheques which were paid in to the credit of the account, those circumstances were such as ought to have put the bank on inquiry? In my opinion this case is very near the line.[1]

1 At p 78.

15.56 The activity of the account was also a significant factor in *Nu-Stilo Footwear Ltd v Lloyds Bank Ltd*.[1] M was the secretary of the plaintiff company who opened an account under the name of "E Bauer" with the defendant bank. When opening the account, M described himself as a "free lance agent" who was only beginning in the business. He named himself under his real name as a referee and gave "Bauer" favourable references when telephoned by the bank. He also wrote to the bank describing "Bauer" as a fit and proper person.

1 (1956) 7 LDAB 121.

15.57 M misappropriated some nine cheques which were drawn on the plaintiff's account and made payable either to himself or to third parties. The first cheque was for £172 and was deposited with the bank on the day following the opening of the account. There were no further deposits for a month when a cheque for more than £550 was deposited.

15.58 The case is interesting because the Court found that there was no negligence in opening the account and that the first cheque was collected without negligence. However, the further cheques were "out of harmony with the description of [M's] trade or prospects as revealed by him to the bank". Because of this, the bank could not establish that the cheques had been collected without negligence.

15.59 The case was strongly criticised by the editors of the report and Weaver and Cragie observe that it implies that the banker has a perfect, or at least a very long, memory and to "engage in speculation as to the likely turnover and profitability of any businessman who may become a customer . . . "!

1 *Weaver and Cragie*, pp 505, 506.

15.60 Although the banker should be concerned with the occupation of the customer, there is clearly no general duty to be informed of changes in employment or in status.[1]

1 *Orbit Mining & Trading Co Ltd v Westminster Bank Ltd* [1963] 1 QB 794 per Harman LJ.

Some possible defences relevant to negligence

15.61 There have been a number of cases where the collecting bank has argued that even though the collection has not been made without negligence, that nevertheless the behaviour of the customer has been such that they should be entitled to the statutory defence or to some form of defence analogous to the defence of contributory negligence in a tort action based on negligence.

"Lulling to sleep"

15.62 The argument that the banker may be "lulled to sleep" by the customer began with the decision in *Morison v London County & Westminster Bank Ltd*.[1] The frauds committed by the clerk Abbott had extended over a number of years. Some of them were known to the owner, others to the staff employed by Morison. Indeed, some of the cheques had been the subject of an arrangement between Abbott and Morison whereby Abbott agreed to repay the sums involved. Abbott had been re-employed after the earliest frauds had been discovered. None of this had been communicated to the defendant bank. It should be noted that this is not the *Greenwood* type of case,[2] for the defendant here is the collecting, not the paying bank. Morison owed no contractual duties to the collecting banker.

1 [1914] 3 KB 356.
2 *Greenwood v Martins Bank Ltd* [1933] AC 51.

15.63 The Court recognised that there was no contractual duty to notify the collecting bank, but nevertheless found in favour of the bank with regard to cheques which had been misappropriated later in the series of frauds. Buckley LJ in discussing these later frauds said:

> . . . any suspicion which they ought to have had would have been lulled to sleep by the action of Morison himself. Such a sufficient time had then elapsed during which the customer had received back his passbook and his cheques, and had raised no question as to the validity of the cheques, as that the defendants were entitled to assume that there was no cause for suspicion or inquiry.[1]

1 At p 377.

15.64 Further, the Court seemed to consider that the bank should be entitled to the statutory defence with regard to the later cheques since the circumstances there were merely repetitions of earlier ones which had gone unchallenged.

15.65 The "lulling to sleep" doctrine did not survive for long. In *Lloyds Bank Ltd v Chartered Bank of India, Australia and China*,[1] Scrutton LJ doubted the grounds of the decision in *Morison's* case noting that it was inconsistent with the doctrine

> . . . that in order to act as an estoppel negligence must be the proximate cause of the loss. If my butler for a year has been selling my vintage wines cheap to a small wine-merchant, I do not understand how my negligence in not periodically checking my wine book will be an answer to my action against the wine-merchant for conversion.[2]

1 [1929] 1 KB 40.
2 At p 60.

15.66 The matter was taken beyond all doubt in *Bank of Montreal v Dominion Gresham Guarantee & Casualty Co*[1] when Lord Tomlin said:

> Neglect of duty does not cease by repetition to be neglect of duty. If there be any doctrine of lulling to sleep it must depend upon and can only be another way of expressing estoppel or ratification.[2]

1 [1930] AC 659.
2 At p 666.

15.67 Chorley describes the situation best of all:

> This theory of "lulling to sleep" is . . . not without its difficulties, since if the banker was already asleep during the earlier period it is really more a case of failure to awaken him than of lulling him to sleep.[1]

1 At p 136.

Exigencies of business

15.68 Generally speaking, it will not be open to the bank to plead that staffing problems or inadequacies are an excuse for a failure to consider the interests of the true owner of a cheque. The "hard line" position on this is summarised by the statement of Pickford J in *Crumplin v London Joint Stock Bank Ltd*:[1]

> It is no defence for a bank to say that they were so busy and had such a small staff that they could not make inquiries when necessary; they must take the consequences.

1 (1913) 109 LT 856.

15.69 A slightly softer line is taken by Bailhache J in *Ross v London County Westminster & Parr's Bank Ltd*[1] in a statement which recognises that the standard to be applied may vary between various classes of employees of a bank:

> I recognise that the same degree of intelligence and care cannot be looked for in a cashier as in an official higher in authority . . . I must, however, attribute to the cashiers and clerks of the department the degree of intelligence and knowledge ordinarily required of persons in their positions to fit them for the discharge of their duties.

1 [1919] 1 KB 678.

15.70 Weaver and Cragie criticise this line of cases, noting that under modern conditions and pressures the Courts' attitude is somewhat unreal when compared with the duties required of the customers. However, that once again seems to overlook that the statutory protection offered by s 5 is a privilege which is extended to bankers and to no other person. It scarcely seems unreasonable for the

Courts to require a relatively high standard for any banker who is seeking to throw the loss caused by the banker's own conversion onto the innocent owner.

Contributory negligence by the customer

15.71 At common law liability for conversion was very strict. Carelessness on the part of the person whose property was converted was simply not relevant to the question. Phrased another way, there was no obligation on an owner of property to take care of that property. Anyone interfering with the property did so at their peril.[1] The above identifies "owner" with the person who has the immediate right to possession.

1 *Lloyds Bank Ltd v EB Savory & Co* [1932] 2 KB 122.

15.72 On the other hand, in a tort action for negligence, if the defendant could prove that the plaintiff had also been negligent in a way which contributed to the losses suffered by the plaintiff, then the defendant had a complete defence, the defence of contributory negligence. Even when the defendant had been grossly negligent and the plaintiff only slightly negligent, the defence was complete.

15.73 This unsatisfactory state of affairs was changed in New Zealand by the Contributory Negligence Act 1947 which changed contributory negligence from a complete defence to a partial defence. The amount of damages to be awarded is reduced according to the degree of contribution from the plaintiff's own contributory negligence.

15.74 Although the Act was thought to apply only in tort actions for negligence, the Court of Appeal held that it applied also to other tort actions. In *Helson v McKenzies Ltd*[1] the plaintiff had carelessly left her handbag lying on a counter on the premises of the defendant shop. It was found by the staff who then passed it on to an impostor claiming to be the plaintiff. There was no doubt that the handing of the handbag to a stranger was conversion, but the amount of damages was reduced by virtue of the contributory negligence of the plaintiff.

1 [1950] NZLR 878.

15.75 The matter does not seem to have been tested in an action for the conversion of a cheque until the English decision in *Lumsden v London Trustee Savings Bank*.[1] A fraudulent employee of the plaintiff firm of stockbrokers altered the employers' cheques and paid them into the account of the defendant bank. The fraud was made possible by the careless drawing of the cheques.[2] Donaldson J took the view that *Helson v McKenzies Ltd*[3] correctly stated the law and that the contributory negligence of the plaintiffs, which was assessed at 10%, could be the basis for a reduction in the damages awarded.

1 [1971] 1 Lloyd's Rep 114.
2 Note that the careless drawing of the cheque may preclude an action against the paying bank, but there is no contractual obligation owed the collecting bank. See *London Joint Stock Bank v Macmillan & Arthur* [1918] AC 777 and the discussion in Ch 3.
3 [1950] NZLR 878.

15.76 *Lumsden's* case has not been very enthusiastically received. Chorley observes that the decision "cannot necessarily be regarded as correctly stating the position unless and until confirmed by a higher Court",[1] a confirmation which was placed on a statutory footing in the UK by the Banking Act 1979.[2]

1 *Chorley*, p 136.
2 S 47.

15.77 In Australia, the Court considered the matter in *Wilton v Commonwealth Trading Bank.*[1] The case again concerned a fraudulent clerk who misappropriated cheques which were collected by the defendant bank. Samuels J examined the *Helson* and *Lumsden* cases in some detail and found that the reasons given were "far from compelling" and refused to follow them. More recently, apportionment based on contributory negligence when the action is for the conversion of a cheque has been refused in Australia in *Tina Motors Pty Ltd v ANZ Banking Group*[2] and in *Day v Bank of NSW.*[3]

1 [1973] 2 NSWLR 644.
2 [1977] VR 205, 208.
3 (1978) 19 ALR 32, 42.

15.78 It might be thought that the *Helson* case settles the matter in New Zealand, but it may be that interference with goods is to be treated differently from conversion of a negotiable instrument. An English decision has held that the Act does not provide defences for all torts.[1]

1 *Bank Russo-Iran v Gordon, Woodroffe & Co Ltd* (1972) 116 SJ 921; The Times 4 October 1972.

Inquiries which would have yielded nothing

15.79 Suppose that the circumstances are such as to put the collecting bank on inquiry, but that the only inquiries which it is reasonable to make are such that it can be shown that no further information would have been gained. Is it possible for the bank to use this fact as a substitute for making the inquiries? Or, put another way, has the bank collected the cheque without negligence if it can be shown that the only reasonable inquiries which could have been made would have yielded nothing?

15.80 There have been differing judicial views on the question. On one hand, there are views similar to that expressed by Bankes LJ in *AL Underwood Ltd v Barclays Bank Ltd*:[1]

> I feel satisfied that the obvious inquiry whether the company had not got its own banking account would have put a stop to the fraudulent system adopted by Underwood, and I do not think that it lies in the mouth of the appellants to say that an inquiry would have been useless.[2]

1 [1924] 1 KB 775.
2 At p 789. See also *EB Savory & Co v Lloyds Bank Ltd* [1932] 2 KB 122; *Baker v Barclays Bank Ltd* [1955] 1 WLR 822; *Lumsden v London Trustee Savings Bank* [1971] 1 Lloyd's Rep 114.

15.81 The other view is that there must be some demonstrable connection between the failure to make inquiries and the loss suffered by the customer. Thus, Diplock LJ in *Marfani & Co Ltd v Midland Bank Ltd*[1] said:

> It does not constitute any lack of reasonable care to refrain from making inquiries which it is improbable will lead to detection of the potential customer's dishonest purpose if he is dishonest, and which are calculated to offend him and maybe drive away his custom if he is honest.[2]

1 [1968] 1 WLR 968.
2 At p 977. See also similar comments by Cairns J at 980.

15.82 The latest opinion expressed on the subject appears to be that of the English Court in *Thackwell v Barclays Bank plc*.[1] While acknowledging the view expressed by Diplock LJ in *Marfani*, the Court relied on authority mentioned above to express the view that:

> . . . I would hold that as a matter of law it is no answer for a bank who have been guilty of negligence in the collection of a cheque to prove that, even had the question the omission to ask which constitutes such negligence been asked, a reassuring answer would have been given.[2]

1 [1986] 1 All ER 676.
2 At p 684.

15.83 Weaver and Cragie express the view that the *Marfani* approach is to be preferred as "the more rational and less draconian of the two alternatives" and believe that it is the view which will prevail in Australia.[1] By less "draconian" they appear to mean that it favours the banker, for it is the other view which is less draconian to the customer whose cheque has been converted. In truth, it is submitted that the argument for a causal connection between the negligence and the loss is simply a confusion caused by the words "without negligence" in the statutory defence. The tort is conversion, not negligence, and the defence is a privilege which is extended to bankers only at the expense of customers.

1 At p 323.

Reduction of damages in conversion

15.84 Just as the "equitable defence" may protect the banker in certain circumstances where payments have been made to the plaintiff's benefit, so it may be possible to obtain a reduction in damages if it may be shown that part of the sums obtained by the conversion went to the plaintiff's use. However, it will not usually be easy to establish that the precise money which went to the plaintiff was the money which was obtained from the misappropriated cheques.

15.85 The problem for the banker is stated precisely by Scrutton J:[1]

> It seems to me clear that damages in conversion may be reduced by the return of the chattel converted; . . . . But when you come to the conversion of a cheque, it is not at all clear how the fact that one of the persons converting has after conversion paid to the plaintiff not the cheque converted, but some currency, not necessarily the currency derived from the cheque converted, can be treated without more as a reduction of the damages for the original conversion . . . . But whether any particular payment to the plaintiff by one of the wrongdoers reduces the damages for conversion must depend on the facts of each case, and cannot be settled by mere proof of receipt without more.

1 *Lloyds Bank v Chartered Bank of India, Australia and China* [1929] 1 KB 40, 61.

15.86 This was cited by Sellers J in *Nu-Stilo Footwear* to deny a reduction in damages when the bank argued that M had drawn on the account to make some payments to the plaintiff.[1]

1 *Nu-Stilo Footwear Ltd v Lloyds Bank Ltd* (1956) 7 LDAB 121.

Instruments to which the defence applies

15.87 The s 5 defence is available to the banker when instruments are collected which are not strictly speaking cheques. So, for example, the Court found that the instrument in *Orbit Mining & Trading Co Ltd v Westminster Bank Ltd*[1] which was in the form of a cheque but made payable to "cash or order" was not a cheque. It was nevertheless possible for the collecting bank to rely on the equivalent of s 5 under s 5(2)(b), that is

> Any document issued by a customer of a banker which, though not a bill of exchange, is intended to enable a person to obtain payment from that banker of the sum mentioned in the document.

1 [1963] 1 QB 794.

15.88 This section, incidentally, shows that the legislature believed that it is possible that a banker may be sued in conversion even though the instrument is not a negotiable instrument.[1]

1 See *Arrow Transfer Co Ltd v Royal Bank of Canada* (1972) 27 DLR (3d) 81; *Koster's Premier Pottery v Bank of Adelaide* (1981) 28 SASR 355 and 14.16.

15.89 The section also applies to a variety of other instruments which might be collected by a banker. Of particular importance is s 5(2)(e):

> Any draft payable on demand drawn by a banker upon himself, whether payable at the head office or some other office of his bank.

This places beyond doubt the position of the "bank cheque".

15.90 The section also relieves the New Zealand banker from a problem which was caused by a number of judicial decisions which suggested that an altered cheque ceased to be a cheque by virtue of s 64 with the consequences that the protective provisions in force at the time, which related only to "cheques", were not available to the banker as a defence.[1]

1 See *Slingsby v Westminster Bank Ltd (No 2)* [1931] 2 KB 583, 586; *Bank of Ceylon v Kulatilleke* (1957) 59 Ceylon NLR 188.

Chapter 16

The paying bank I

Wrongful payment — Conversion — Meaning of payment — Breach of duty of care

16.1 A paying banker may be exposed to liability in two ways: (1) by making a payment when the payment should not have been made, eg paying out on a cheque after it has been countermanded; or (2) by failing to make a payment which should have been made, the most common example is failing to pay a cheque which is in order because of a mistaken opinion that there are inadequate funds in the drawer's account. In each case, the banker has prima facie done the wrong thing, but there may be defences available. In this chapter, we will explore the possible circumstances which may expose a paying banker to liability and the defences which may be open to him in different circumstances. The situation of wrongful payment of a cheque will be examined first, that of wrongful dishonour later.

Wrongful payment

16.2 The paying banker is exposed to both contractual liability and tort liability in circumstances where the banker pays either the wrong person or pays the wrong amount. The circumstances when this might happen are many and varied, but there are some that are common. For example, when an indorsement is forged, the person who appears to be the holder of the cheque is not the true owner it.[1] If the banker pays the apparent holder of the instrument, it may be that the banker has assisted in a conversion and is, prima facie, liable to the true owner. But equally, the mandate from the customer who drew the cheque was to pay the payee or the payee's order. In paying someone holding under a forged indorsement, the banker has paid someone other than the person ordered and authorised by the customer, and so will possibly be unable to debit the account under the terms of the contract between banker and customer.

1 See 12.41ff.

16.3 Again, when a rogue "raises" a cheque, the paying banker will have paid the wrong amount, again a breach of the contract for which the banker will be prima facie unable to debit the account.

16.4 But the liability is only prima facie. In certain cases, the banker will have defences against actions either in contract or in tort. Some of these defences are statutory defences which are available to bankers alone; others are general defences which arise by virtue of the relationship between the parties.

Breach of mandate

16.5 When the customer writes a cheque, he or she gives the banker an order to pay a certain person a certain amount. If crossings are added to the cheque, there may be instructions to the effect that the payment is to be made in a certain way. If the banker pays the wrong person or the wrong amount, or if the cheque is crossed, pays in the wrong way, then there is a breach of the mandate and the banker has prima facie done the wrong thing, even if there is no way that he or she could have discovered the true mandate.

16.6 The customer is under a duty to express the mandate clearly so as to guard against the possibility of the cheque being easily altered. If the customer has breached this duty then the banker may debit the account even if the payment was not in accord with the actual mandate of the customer.[1]

1 *London Joint Stock Bank v Macmillan & Arthur* [1918] AC 777.

16.7 If the banker has paid contrary to the mandate, then there is prima facie no right to debit the customer's account. This can result in an unfair situation where the customer has received a benefit from the payment of the cheque. Under certain circumstances, it may be possible for the banker to rely upon this benefit to the customer in order to maintain the debit.[1]

1 See below, 17.23.

Crossings as a part of the mandate

16.8 The question of breach of mandate is particularly difficult when the claim is that a cheque has been paid contrary to a general or special crossing. In such a case, the customer may claim that the banker is prohibited from debiting the account on one of two separate grounds, namely, negligence in having paid contrary to the crossing and/or breach of mandate.[1]

1 See *Paget*, p 199, *Weaver and Cragie*, pp 286ff. "Negligence" in this case is not the tort, but rather negligent performance of the contract.

16.9 If the customer wishes to bar the debit on the grounds of negligence, then he must show that the banker's action has caused a loss to the customer. There was no difficulty for the customer in maintaining such an action even before the introduction of the Bills of Exchange Act 1882. In *Bellamy v Marjoribanks*[1] the Court considered the issue. At the time, there was no legislation concerning crossed cheques, only evidence as to the custom of bankers. The Court said:

> If the banker disregarded the customer, and paid the cheque to a private individual, that circumstance would be strong evidence against him in the event of his seeking to charge his customer with the payment, if the person actually presenting it was not the lawful holder and bearer of the cheque.[2]

1 (1852) 7 Exch 389; 155 ER 999.
2 At 404; 1006.

16.10 Given that there is now a statutory duty on the banker to pay the cheque in accordance with the terms of the crossing, there should be little or no difficulty in proving negligence on the part of a banker who paid contrary to a crossing.

16.11 When the customer has not suffered any loss, it is still true that the bank has paid contrary to the instructions on the face of the cheque. It would appear that, subject to the equitable defence to be discussed below,[1] the banker is precluded from debiting the account. However, this view is challenged by Weaver and Cragie.[2]

1 See 17.23.
2 P 287ff.

16.12 Weaver and Cragie argue that there are two problems with the action for a breach of mandate when the customer has suffered no loss. First, the so-called mandate is artificial since the Act gives any holder the right to build up the crossings and the banker has no way of knowing which of the crossings represent the orders of the customer and which were added by some other party to the cheque.[1] It was suggested by Lord Cairns in *Smith v Union Bank of London*[2] that the additions to a crossing by later parties may be taken to be done with the authority of the drawer or, alternatively, that the authority of the Act is sufficient to alter the customer's mandate.[3]

1 S 77.
2 (1875) 1 QBD 31.
3 This argument seems to be accepted in another context: when a cheque is indorsed in blank, it would seem that the "mandate" is to pay the bearer. See s 34 and 16.63.

16.13 Secondly, Weaver and Cragie argue that it might be possible to maintain the debit if the customer has not actually suffered any loss. The problem is in overcoming the decision in *Smith v Union Bank of London*[1] where it was stated quite plainly that when the bank paid contrary to the crossing "the drawers might refuse to be debited with it as having been paid contrary to their mandate . . .". Weaver and Cragie observe that there are two reasons why the rule might need qualification:

> (i) The case was decided at a time when there was a statutory prohibition upon the payment of cheques contrary to crossing and may be considered to be of doubtful authority at the present time when the bill of exchange legislation contains no such prohibition;
>
> (ii) Lord Cairns does not ultimately suggest that a drawer who has suffered no loss by the payment of the cheque . . . can insist that the amount of the cheque be not debited to his account.[2]

1 (1875) 1 QBD 31.
2 *Weaver and Cragie*, p 288.

16.14 Rather than some tortuous circumvention of *Smith*, it would seem more straightforward to accept that there has been a breach of mandate, that prima facie the banker is not entitled to debit the drawer's account, but then to rely upon the development of equitable rules to allow the banker to maintain a debit in those circumstances when the customer has not in fact suffered any loss by virtue of the payment of the cheque.[1]

1 See 17.23.

Materially altered cheque

16.15 When a banker pays a cheque in apparent conformity with the mandate, but in fact the cheque has been materially altered, the right to debit the account would appear to depend to some extent upon the nature and effect of the alteration. In *Imperial Bank of Canada v Bank of Hamilton*[1] the Privy Council held that a cheque which had been raised in amount from $5 to $500 was treated as being a valid cheque for $5 and the paying bank was permitted to debit the account for that amount. It should be noted that the provisions of the Act relating to the rights of a holder of an altered bill are not relevant here[2] since the banker is attempting to set up the cheque as an authority, not as a bill of exchange.

1 [1903] AC 49.
2 In particular, the proviso to s 64(1).

16.16 On the other hand, although the date is a material part of the cheque and an alteration of the date will avoid it as a bill of exchange,[1] it would seem wholly unreasonable to prohibit the debit of the customer's account when the date has been altered and the cheque paid at some time after the original date, at least if the cheque has not been in circulation for an unreasonable period of time.[2]

1 S 64(2); see also *Vance v Lowther* (1876) 1 Ex D 176.
2 No authority is known for this proposition.

16.17 The above remarks apply to alterations which are skilfully done. If the alteration is carelessly done, it might be that the bank would be performing its contract negligently. If the customer suffered loss, then damages would be available.

16.18 The banker may have a defence if the alteration was facilitated by the customer's negligence in drawing the cheque. In such a case, the bank could maintain the debit under the principle in *London Joint Stock Bank v Macmillan & Arthur.*[1]

1 [1918] AC 777; see Ch 3.

Forged indorsement

16.19 When there is a forged essential indorsement of an order cheque, then payment to some person holding under the forged indorsement is not payment according to mandate, for the mandate was "pay X or order" and the forged indorsement means that some unauthorised "order" is being followed. However, the banker will often, even usually, be able to rely upon the statutory defences provided by the Bills of Exchange Act.[1]

1 See below, 17.18.

16.20 When the cheque is payable to bearer, then it is likely that there is no breach of contract even if the bank pays a thief in possession of the cheque. In this circumstance, the banker has followed the mandate and there is no need to rely upon the statutory defences.

Forged signature of drawer

16.21 If the banker pays on a cheque where the drawer's signature is forged, then the customer's account may not be debited unless there is some reason why the customer is precluded from denying the validity of the signature. There is no statutory shifting of responsibility in this case. Under certain circumstances, it would seem that the banker may recover the money from the payee as money paid under a mistake of fact.[1]

1 See Ch 18.

16.22 At one time it was supposed that this was because there was a duty on the banker to know the customer's signature, but this misconception was dispelled by Kerr J in *National Westminster Bank Ltd v Barclays Bank International Ltd:*[1]

> The common aphorism that a banker is under a duty to know his customer's signature is in fact incorrect even as between the banker and his customer. The principle is simply that a banker cannot debit his customer's account on the basis of a forged signature, since he has in that event no mandate from the customer for doing so.[2]

1 [1975] QB 654.
2 Per Kerr J at 666.

Determination of authority

16.23 The other common case of "wrongful payment" is where the banker pays in strict conformity with the mandate of the customer, but that mandate has already been withdrawn either by some act of the customer or by some extraneous event. Again, the prima facie position is that the banker will be unable to debit the account.

16.24 In some cases of payment after the authority has been determined, the banker may be able to recover payment from the recipient as money paid under a mistake of fact.[1] On other occasions, it may be possible for the banker to rely upon the so-called "equitable defence".[2]

1 See Ch 18.
2 See 17.23.

16.25 Perhaps the most common situation here is when the customer has countermanded payment of the cheque before the banker has paid it. The right of countermand is given by s 75 of the Act. The steps necessary to effect a countermand have been discussed at 6.33ff.

16.26 The authority to pay cheques is determined by notice of the customer's death, although the banker may pay cheques drawn before the customer's death and presented for payment not more than ten days after the death provided the personal representative and/or beneficiaries of the deceased estate do not countermand payment of the cheque.[1]

1 S 75(2), Bills of Exchange Act 1908.

16.27 If the customer becomes mentally incapacitated or if he or she loses contractual capacity in any other way, then the banker should not pay on cheques drawn by that customer. Such a customer is unable to give a mandate and any existing mandates are withdrawn.

16.28 It is not at always apparent when a banker should refuse to honour cheques on the basis that the customer has lost contractual capacity, particularly if it is alleged that the capacity is lost through mental illness. If a person has become a "protected person" under the Mental Health Act 1969, then there is no problem for the banker, for both the person and property, including bank accounts, come under the control provided by the Act. If the customer has not come under the terms of the Act, there is authority which suggests that if the bank has actual notice of a customer's condition and the condition is such that the customer is so seriously affected that he or she would be subject to being defrauded by unscrupulous people, then the bank should cease to honour the customer's cheques.[1]

1 *Drew v Nunn* (1879) 4 QBD 661; *Daily Telegraph Newspaper Co v McLaughlin* [1904] AC 776.

16.29 This is scarcely a satisfactory position for a banker. The refusal to pay cheques on such a ground would seem to be an open invitation for a defamation action if the banker is wrong, yet if the banker turns a blind eye to the matter then the banker may eventually be called upon to recredit all sums paid on cheques should the customer eventually come under official control.

16.30 It seems that if a banker pays cheques which are used for meeting necessary expenditures of a mentally incapacitated person or to pay legitimate debts incurred by that person, then the bank may be able to debit the account by relying on equitable principles to be discussed below.[1]

1 See 17.23.

16.31 The banker should refrain from paying cheques when certain legal orders are made against the customer. This is not precisely the termination of the customer's authority, but rather the overriding of it by other legal process.

16.32 The primary orders are garnishee orders nisi, winding up orders when the customer is a company, and Mareva injunctions. Failure to stop payment on cheques when these orders are served against a customer may not only prejudice the banker's right to debit the account, but may also expose the banker to other legal consequences.[1]

1 See Ch 27.

Conversion

16.33 The preceding paragraphs have been concerned with the situation where a paying banker pays a cheque contrary to the customer's mandate; it is generally thought that the prima facie position is that the customer's account cannot be debited with the amount of the cheque. But that is not the end of the matter as far as the banker is concerned, for it may happen that the payment of the cheque is to the wrong person in the sense that the true owner of the cheque is neither the person paid nor the drawer of the cheque. In such a case, the true owner of the cheque may have an action in conversion against the paying banker as well as against the collecting banker.

16.34 This is a serious position for the banker, for it is possible that the banker has paid the cheque to the rogue, then finds that the account may not be debited, and that there is liability for the same sum to the true owner of the cheque. Fortunately for the paying banker, there will very often be an available defence.[1]

1 See Ch 17.

The true owner of a cheque

16.35 Although the phrase "true owner" is used several times in the Act, it is not defined either in the Act or in any judicial decision. There seems, at first sight, a redundancy in the expression, for how can an owner be anything but the "true owner"? It has been suggested that the adjective is used to emphasise the dual nature of a cheque as both a piece of paper, the chattel, and the right to the funds represented by the cheque, the chose in action. Since the physical piece of paper is the subordinate part of the instrument, the "true" indicates that we are to look not merely to the right to the piece of paper, but rather to the rights given to the parties under the bills of exchange legislation.

16.36 Thus, it has been said that:

> . . . the true owner, in the sense of the person who can support conversion for a bill, note, or cheque is the person who, taking into consideration the provisions of the Bills of Exchange Act, and recognising that the negotiable character of the instrument overrides the mere property in the chattel, is on that basis entitled to the property in and possession of the piece of paper.[1]

1 *Paget*, 8th ed, p 348. This passage, which is widely quoted in this connection, appears to be absent from the 9th edition.

16.37 There are some circumstances where it is clear, either on principle or on authority, who is the true owner of a bill. Thus, if the drawer of a cheque, in the absence of fraud, hands the cheque to the payee, then the payee becomes the true owner. If the cheque is indorsed, again in the absence of fraud, the indorsee becomes the true owner upon delivery of the cheque.

16.38 If the delivery to the payee is by post, then the time at which the payee becomes the true owner depends upon the agreement between the parties. If the payee has expressly or by implication requested the delivery by post, then the post office is the agent of the payee and the payee becomes the true owner of the cheque at the time of delivery to the post. On the other hand, if there is no request, then the presumption is that the post office is the agent of the sender and the drawer remains the true owner of the cheque until such time as it is actually delivered to the payee.[1] An implied request will not be found merely from the fact that the drawer has customarily sent cheques by mail, nor from the fact that it is customary for cheques to be sent in that way.[1]

1 *Channon v English, Scottish and Australian Bank Ltd* (1918) 18 SR (NSW) 30.

16.39 If a creditor agrees to accept a cheque in payment of a debt provided it is drawn in a certain form, then the drawer remains the true owner of a cheque which is drawn in another form until such time as it is accepted by the payee. Thus, in *London Bank of Australia Ltd v Kendall*[1] cheques were left at the office of the Commissioner of Taxation by the plaintiff. They were evidently misappropriated from that office and collected by the defendant bank. Since the cheques were not drawn in a form required by the Commissioner, the plaintiff was still the true owner and entitled to maintain an action in conversion.

1 (1920) 28 CLR 401.

16.40 In *Smith v Union Bank of London*[1] a cheque which was delivered to the payee was indorsed by him in blank and crossed specially to his bank. The cheque was stolen and negotiated to a person who took the cheque for value and in good faith. It was held that this holder was the "true owner" of the cheque even though his title was derived through a theft. This is a clear example of the workings of the Bills of Exchange Act to override ordinary ownership principles.[2]

1 (1875) 1 QBD 31.
2 Weaver and Cragie suggest that the outcome might be different following the passing of the Act since the concept of holder in due course is more precisely defined. They argue that the presence of a special crossing might displace the presumption of good faith.

16.41 There may be difficulties in establishing the identity of the true owner when there is an agent involved in the drawing or as a party to the instrument. In *Marquess of Bute v Barclays Bank Ltd*[1] instruments were drawn payable to Mr D McGaw who was the farm manager of the plaintiff. However, on the same instrument appeared the words "for the Marquess of Bute". The Court held that the words were an essential part of the description of the payee and that consequently the intention of the drawer was that the plaintiff should be the true owner and that McGaw was merely an agent who was accountable to the Marquess.

1 [1955] 1 QB 202.

16.42 When there is no indication on the face of the cheque that the named payee is being given the cheque as agent for a third party, it is still true that the principal is the owner of the cheque. Thus, in *Great Western Railway Co v London & County Banking Co Ltd*[1] the cheque was made payable to Huggins who was a tax collector. Huggins misappropriated the cheque. During the course of the judgment, Lord Davey said:

> I am of opinion that Huggins never had any property in the cheque, which was handed to him only as the collector and agent of the overseers in payment of a debt alleged to be due to them. The appellants never intended to vest any property in him for his own benefit, but the property in the cheque was intended to be passed to his employer, the overseers, notwithstanding that it was made payable to Huggins' order. Huggins therefore had no real title to the cheque.[2]

1 [1901] AC 414.
2 At p 417.

16.43 When the cheque bears no indication on its face that the payee is an agent, then even though the principal or the drawer remains the true owner, a claim in conversion by either of them might be defeated depending upon other circumstances. If the defendant were a collecting bank, then it will be a question of whether the bank collected without negligence.[1] If the defendant is a later holder, then it will depend upon whether the holder is a holder in due course and if the cheque has been marked "not negotiable".[2]

1 See Ch 14.
2 See Ch 13.

16.44 If an agent is drawing a cheque and performs his duty fraudulently or if the drawing of the cheque has been induced by fraud, then the innocent principal, not the fraudulent agent, is the true owner of the cheque.[1] However, if the fraudulent agent is able to exchange the cheque for a bank cheque which he has not the actual authority to receive, then the bank cheque belongs to the agent, not to the principal. Presumably the same result would follow if the cheque were exchanged for a chattel.

1 *Smith and Baldwin v Barclays Bank Ltd* (1944) 5 LDAB 370; *Midland Bank Ltd v Reckitt* [1933] AC 1; *Morison v London County & Westminster Bank Ltd* [1914] 3 KB 356.

16.45 The situation with the fraudulent agent is well illustrated by two cases where the agent managed to exchange the misappropriated cheques for bank cheques. In *Union Bank of*

Australia Ltd v McClintlock[1] the defendant was the manager of the plaintiff company and had authority to be a co-signatory on cheques. There was evidence given to the effect that a common method of making payments was for the company to draw cheques payable to its own banker and to receive a bank cheque in exchange. By such a course of action, account could be paid by cheque even when the company's creditors would not accept the company's cheques. It was found as a fact that McClintlock's authority to exchange company cheques for bank cheques extended only so far as to obtain cheques for the company's legitimate business. By a series of frauds, McClintlock obtained cheques drawn on the company account in favour of the company's bank and exchanged them for bank cheques which he then misappropriated by depositing them in his account with the defendant bank. The company sued the defendant bank for conversion and money had and received.

1 [1922] 1 AC 240.

16.46 The action failed. The bank cheques did not belong to the plaintiff at the time of issue, since it was not within the manager's general authority to obtain bank cheques. Nor could the plaintiff claim title by ratification, for they could not choose to ratify the action of the manager in obtaining the cheques and then claim that he was not so entitled.

16.47 *McClintlock* was followed in *Commercial Banking Co of Sydney Ltd v Mann*[1] on facts which are virtually indistinguishable. A fraudulent partner in a firm of solicitors drew cheques in favour of "Pay bank cheque" and took them to the ANZ bank where the partnership account was kept. That bank issued bank cheques in favour of W according to the directions of the fraudulent partner. The cheques were paid into an account with the defendant bank. The plaintiff sued for conversion and for money had and received. The Privy Council held that the claim must fail. The authority of the fraudulent partner extended only as far as to enable him to obtain bank cheques for the purpose of the partnership. Therefore the property in the bank cheques did not belong to the plaintiff. Nor could the plaintiff obtain title by attempting to ratify the partner's action for if he ratified at all, he ratified the dealing by the fraudulent partner and the appellant bank with the cheques, and, if he did not ratify, nothing had ever been converted that belonged to him.

1 [1961] AC 1.

Waiver of tort

16.48 Whenever there is an action in conversion, it is customary for the plaintiff to make an alternative claim for a like amount as money had and received to the use of the plaintiff. The joinder of a claim for money had and received does not operate as a waiver of the tort so as to prejudice the claim in conversion. The plaintiff is free to recover on either ground and defences appropriate to each of the actions are open to the defendant.[1]

1 *United Australia Ltd v Barclays Bank Ltd* [1941] AC 1.

16.49 The action for money had and received is a separate action. There may be times when it is in the interests of the plaintiff to waive the tort and proceed with the action for money had and received. If it is correct that an instrument which is not a negotiable instrument can only attract nominal damages in an action for conversion,[1] then it may benefit the plaintiff to waive the tort. Thus, in *Bavins Junr & Sims v London and South Western Bank*[2] the instrument was not a cheque due to technical deficiencies of form. After referring to the argument that only nominal damages would be available, the Court said:

> . . . in any case it seems to me to be clear that the plaintiffs are entitled to recover the amount received by the defendants upon the document as money had and received. Having received money by presenting the document which belonged to the plaintiffs they cannot in my opinion, if the plaintiffs choose to waive the tort, say that they did not receive the money on account of the plaintiffs . . . .[3]

1 See 14.16 for references and arguments that this is not correct.
2 [1901] 1 QB 270.
3 Per Vaughan Williams LJ at 278; but see *Arrow Transfer Co Ltd v Royal Bank of Canada* (1972) 27 DLR (3d) 81 and *Koster's Premier Pottery v Bank of Adelaide* (1981) 28 SASR 355.

16.50 But there will be no waiver of tort unless the plaintiff clearly intends to make such a waiver. In *United Australia Ltd v Barclays Bank Ltd*[1] a cheque payable to the appellants was converted by M Co and collected by Barclays. United Australia brought an action in debt against M Co but discontinued. A proof of debt lodged in the winding up of M Co was also rejected. United Australia then brought an action for conversion against the collecting bank. Barclays claimed that the bringing of the original action against M Co must be considered a waiver of tort. The House of Lords rejected the argument, holding that merely bringing an action is not waiver of tort. It is judgment and satisfaction in the first action which is a bar to the second.

1 [1941] AC 1.

16.51 Three members of the House of Lords indicated that in their view even if the tort had been waived as against M Co that would not have the effect of waiving the separate action in conversion against the bank.[1]

1 Per Lord Atkin, Lord Porter and Viscount Simon LC.

16.52 However, in *Clarkson Booker Ltd v Andjel*[1] the Court of Appeal considered Lord Atkin's dictum and noted that it is always a matter of fact if the tort has been waived. It was said concerning election that the initiation of proceedings against one party is strong evidence of an election, although not conclusive.

1 [1964] 2 QB 775.

Meaning of payment

16.53 It is not necessary that "payment" be in the form of money or even in the form of a credit to the account of the holder or of some other person. In *Meyer & Co Ltd v Sze Hai Tong Banking & Insurance Co Ltd*[1] the bank had paid a crossed cheque across the counter by giving its own cheque drawn on another bank. The Privy Council held that this was payment of the cheque within the meaning of the equivalent of s 80.

1 [1913] AC 847.

16.54 Although a communication between bankers in which the paying bank intimates that the cheque will be paid is generally considered to be binding, there seems little chance that the communication itself could be considered to be payment for the purposes of the Act. The communication is referred to as notifying the fate of the cheque.

16.55 The most common means of making a payment is by means of the clearing system. The actual time when payment is complete is a matter of some complexity which will be considered later.[1]

1 See 19.77.

Payment in breach of duty of care to customer

16.56 Even when the mandate is properly drawn, the banker may have a duty to make inquiries before making the payment. This is a source of considerable difficulty for the banker, since the duty is on the one hand to pay the cheque promptly and on the other to make inquiries concerning what is in all respects a properly drawn mandate. The problem is discussed fully at 7.73.

Defences in cases of wrongful payment

Common law defences

16.57 As in the case of a collecting bank, a paying bank has available the same defences as everyone else. They remain available to the paying bank in addition to the privileged status and statutory defence which are provided to breach of contract and conversion actions.

Customer's breach of contract

16.58 The situation where the wrongful payment has been made by virtue of the customer's breach of the duty to draw cheques carefully has already been discussed. In such a case, provided the wrongful payment is a consequence of the customer's breach, it would appear that the banker can maintain the debit.[1]

1 *London Joint Stock Bank v Macmillan & Arthur* [1918] AC 777. See Ch 3.

16.59 This has only been applied in cases where the wrong amount has been paid by virtue of the fact that the cheque has been "raised." Theoretically nothing would prevent the defence from applying when the wrong person is paid, but it would appear that the banker will have a more difficult time establishing that the cheque is carelessly drawn merely by virtue of the fact that the blank spaces after the name of the payee are not filled in.[1]

1 See *Slingsby v Westminster Bank Ltd (No 2)* [1931] 2 KB 583; *Commonwealth Trading Bank of Australia v Sydney Wide Stores Pty Ltd* (1981) 55 ALJR 574.

16.60 Similarly, if the customer breaches the duty to notify of known forgeries, then the banker will be able to maintain the debit even though there was no mandate at all from the customer.[1]

1 *Greenwood v Martins Bank Ltd* [1933] AC 51.

16.61 The defence may be defeated if the bank has been negligent in the payment of the cheque even though the fraud could not have happened but for the negligence of the customer. This is the consequence of the *Varker* case when the breach of contract by the customer is the breach of the *Macmillan* duty.[1] It would seem that this same principle would hold when the customer's breach of duty is the failure of the *Greenwood* duty, although there seems to be no authority on the matter.

1 *Varker v Commercial Banking Co of Sydney Ltd* [1972] 2 NSWLR 967; see 3.25ff.

Bearer cheques

16.62 If the banker pays a bearer cheque to the person in possession of it, then the mandate has been followed precisely if the proper amount is also paid. Notice that this is true even if the payment is made to the thief or the finder of the cheque. Although such a person would not be a holder in due course and would have no right to enforce the cheque, if the banker pays without knowledge of the deficiency in title then the customer's mandate has been followed.

Fictitious payee

16.63 There are certain occasions where a cheque may be drawn in favour of a person who is fictitious in some sense. This might particularly be done when a fraud is being planned, a circumstance which could leave the banker in an exposed position, for the drawer of the cheque, in so far as it is intended that anyone will be paid, most certainly does not direct the banker to pay the person who is most likely the one claiming the payment.

16.64 There is a possible defence for the paying banker in such a circumstance. Section 7 of the Act is generally concerned with the problem of identification of the payee. Subsection (3) is as follows:

> Where the payee is a fictitious or non-existing person the bill may be treated as payable to bearer.

16.65 The way in which s 7(3) may be used as a defence is illustrated by *Clutton v Attenboroug & Sonh*.[1] A clerk in the accounts department of the appellant firm caused cheques to be drawn payable to the order of George Brett and signed by members of the appellant firm. The clerk intercepted the cheques, indorsed them in the name of George Brett and cashed them with the respondents. The cheques were then collected for the account of the respondent. There was no such person as George Brett. The action was brought by the appellants as an action in conversion or, alternatively, money paid under a mistake of fact. The Court held that the action failed since the cheques are to be treated as payable to bearer.

Consequently, the respondents became holders in due course of the cheques, for the indorsement was not necessary for their negotiation.

1 [1897] AC 1.

16.66 The advantage to the paying banker is that it is nearly always the "bearer" who will be paid and so on the face of it the banker has followed the customer's mandate. The advantage to the collecting banker is not quite as great owing to the fact that it may be difficult to establish that the banker is a holder in due course.[1]

1 See 14.22.

16.67 The section is not as clear as might be hoped. If one leaves aside philosophical difficulties, it is relatively clear what a "non-existent" person is, but what is a "fictitious" person, particularly since the fictitious person must be something different from the non-existent one? The matter has troubled the Courts on several occasions.

Impersonal payees

16.68 Several cases may be disposed of rather quickly. In the *Orbit Mining & Trading Co Ltd v Westminster Bank Ltd*[1] it was argued that the payee "cash or order" could be treated as a fictitious or non-existing person. The argument was rejected, the Court holding that a purpose or impersonal "payee" could not be a person and therefore could not be a person with the quality of being either non-existing or fictitious.

1 [1963] 1 QB 794.

16.69 In *Bank of England v Vagliano Bros*[1] a clerk named Glyka forged bills of exchange. The instruments purported to be drawn by Vucina, a foreign agent of Vagliano's. The instruments were made payable to Petridi and were accepted payable at the Bank of England by Vagliano. Vagliano often accepted bills made payable to Petridi as they conducted a fair amount of business together. Glyka then forged an indorsement and presented the bills at the bank for payment which he obtained across the counter.

1 [1891] AC 107.

16.70 The case was simply disposed of on the basis of estoppel: by accepting the instruments payable at the Bank of England, Vagliano must be taken to be representing that the bills were genuine. Alternatively, the bank is acting as Vagliano's agent for payment and when the agent is misled by the actions of the principal then the agent is entitled to an indemnity from the principal for any losses which he, the agent, might sustain.

16.71 However, a great deal of the argument in *Vagliano's* case concerned the question of whether the payee was fictitious. Obviously there was a real person named Petridi; he was not non-existent. The House of Lords held that the payee was "fictitious" in the sense that, although real, he

> has not and never was intended by the drawer to have any right upon [the bill] or arising out of it; and this is so though the bill (so called) is not in reality a bill but is in fact a document in the form of a bill manufactured by a person who forges the signature of the named drawer, obtains by fraud the signature of the acceptor, forges the signature of the named payee, and presents the document for payment . . . .[1]

1 From the headnote.

16.72 In spite of that rather clear summary, it was thought for some time that *Vagliano's* case had decided that a payee was "fictitious" if he had no right to enforce the instrument.[1]

1 *City Bank v Rowan* (1893) 14 NSWLR 127; *Rutherford Copper Mining Co v Ogier* (1905) 1 Tas LR 156.

16.73 That misconception was laid to rest in *Vinden v Hughes*.[1] A clerk who was employed by the plaintiffs had as a part of his duties the drawing of cheques in favour of trade creditors. On a number of occasions he drew cheques in favour of known traders even though the plaintiffs owed these people no debt. After obtaining the signature of the plaintiff, the clerk would forge the indorsement of the named payee and passed them on to the defendant who took them in good faith. They were then collected through the defendant's account and paid by the drawer's bank.

1 [1905] 1 KB 795.

16.74 It should be noted that there would be no hope of the drawer preventing the debit of his account and there appears to be no reason on the facts of the case to suppose that the collecting bank could not rely upon the statutory defence, a defence which was not, of course, available to the non-banker defendant. Further, the defendant was not a holder of the cheque since he took through a forged indorsement, unless it could be argued that the cheques were bearer cheques.

16.75 Once again, it is clear that the payee was not a non-existent person, but could he be treated as fictitious under the rule in the *Vagliano* case? The argument for the defendant was that the fraudulent clerk here was the "drawer" in precisely the same way that Glyka was and that there was similarly no intention that the named (real) payee should ever obtain the money. The argument was rejected by the Court. The "intention" is the intention of the drawer of the cheque, that is, the plaintiff. Since it was clearly the intention of the plaintiff that the named payee should receive the proceeds of the cheque, the payee was not fictitious.

Summary: "fictitious payee"

16.76 Byles sums up the effect of these cases as follows:

> . . . in determining whether a payee is fictitious or not, the intention of the drawer of the bill is decisive. If he inserted the name as a mere pretense, to give colour to the instrument, the payer is fictitious, notwithstanding that he in fact exists . . . . If on the other hand, the drawer intended his named payee to receive his money, the payee is not fictitious . . . .

16.77 This begs the question of who is the "drawer" since in both *Vagliano* and *Hughes* the fraudulent clerk "authored" the instrument and in each case one of the signatures was real even though obtained by fraud. It seems that if the drawer's signature is forged, we are to look to the intention of the "author"; but if the drawer's signature is real, we look to the intention of the drawer and the intention of the author is irrelevant. This scarcely has any logic to it and one can only deplore the state of the law in this situation.

16.78 There is one thing that is clear from the cases and which is of the utmost importance to a banker who would rely upon the section. When the section applies, the bill may be treated as payable to bearer not merely by the holder but by all who have any dealings with it. It is this feature which provides the defence for a banker who has wrongfully paid the bill or cheque by reason of a forged indorsement.

Ratification and adoption

16.79 The paying bank is acting as an agent for the customer when the cheque is paid. It follows that when the mandate is not strictly followed that the customer may if he so chooses ratify the payment. Note that s 24(2) of the Act says "Nothing in this section shall affect the ratification of an unauthorised signature not amounting to a forgery". The reason for the exclusion of forgeries is that a forged document is illegal and void and so is incapable of ratification.[1]

1 *Greenwood v Martins Bank Ltd* [1933] AC 51.

16.80 It is, however, possible for the customer to adopt the signature, but this will be an unusual state of affairs since adoption requires fresh valuable consideration. In the typical case where the bank has paid on a forgery, it is difficult to imagine situations where the bank will be giving fresh consideration in exchange for the customer's adoption of the forged signature.

Chapter 17

The paying bank II

Defences of — Wrongful dishonour

17.1 This chapter continues to examine the defences available to a paying banker when he or she has paid a cheque in breach of mandate or has dishonoured a cheque which should have been paid.

Statutory defences

17.2 The statutory defences available to a paying banker have undergone considerable development over the years. The original protective provisions were introduced at the same time as statutory recognition was given to crossings. The effect of recognising crossings was intended to impose upon bankers an obligation to the community to open accounts and to collect and pay cheques which were crossed, for this was the only way that the payee of a crossed cheque could obtain payment. As compensation for this extended community obligation, it seemed fair that a banker who paid a crossed cheque in accordance with the requirements of the crossing should be protected from actions by members of the community being served.

17.3 Although the statutory defence thus provided was originally confined to crossed cheques, there was soon lobbying by the banks to extend this protection to all cheques, the argument being that it was anomalous that they should have a defence when a breach of contract or conversion involved crossed cheques but not when the cheque was uncrossed.

17.4 These arguments prevailed, but the additional protection in the case of the paying banker seems merely to have been added to the existing provisions with the result that there are three separate, but overlapping, sections which are, or may be, relevant to a banker who has paid a customer's cheque in breach of mandate: ss 60, 80 of the Bills of Exchange Act 1908 and s 2 of the Cheques Act 1961. Although the sections overlap, the pre-conditions to their application and the consequences differ slightly.

Cheques Act, s 2

17.5 The broadest protection is given by s 2 of the Cheques Act:

> (1) Where a banker in good faith and in the ordinary course of business pays a cheque drawn on him which is not indorsed or is irregularly indorsed, he shall not, in doing so, incur any liability by reason only of the absence of, or irregularity in, indorsement, and he shall be deemed to have paid it in due course.

17.6 There are several preliminary points. First there is no restriction upon the form of the cheque: the section applies to crossed and uncrossed cheques and includes bearer as well as order cheques.

17.7 Secondly, subs (2) of the section extends the class of instruments to which the section applies to bank cheques and documents

> issued by a customer [of the paying bank] which, though not a bill of exchange, is intended to enable a person to obtain payment . . . of the sum mentioned in the document.

This last class would include, for example, instruments made payable to "cash or order".[1]

1 See *Orbit Mining & Trading Co Ltd v Westminster Bank Ltd* [1963] 1 QB 794.

17.8 Thirdly, the precondition for application of the section is that the banker in good faith and in the ordinary course of business pays a cheque drawn on him. There has always been some question as to the meaning of "in the ordinary course of business" in this section, particularly when regard is had to s 4 which requires that the banker collect "without negligence". It is the opinion of bankers that the "ordinary course of business" test is to be determined by evidence of banking practice and is thus a less rigid test than the "without negligence" test which may demand a higher standard than current banking practice.

17.9 The argument seems to have been accepted by some members of the Court of Appeal in *Carpenters' Co v British Mutual Banking Co.*[1] Mackinnon LJ said:

> A thing that is done not in the ordinary course of business may be done negligently; but I do not think the converse is necessarily true. A thing may be done negligently and yet be done in the ordinary course of business.

However, Ellinger has suggested that the two standards are in fact the same and that a negligent course of business could not be "ordinary" even if universal since part of the "ordinary course of business" must include acting with due care.[2]

1 [1938] 1 KB 511.
2 See Ellinger, "Collection and Payment of Cheques" (1969) 9 WA L Rev 101.

17.10 The "ordinary course of business" must be the usage of the banking community at large, not of any particular bank or group of banks.

17.11 The consequence of the section is that the banker does not incur any liability by reason only of the absence of, or irregularity in, indorsement. One of the main problems faced by the paying banker in the days before legislative protection was the situation where the indorsement was forged. Does the section cover forged indorsements?

17.12 Paget is of the opinion that "payment of a cheque with a forged indorsement does not constitute payment or a discharge of the instrument, or relieve the banker from liability to conversion at the suit of the true owner, or entitle him to debit the true owner".[1]

1 At p 263.

17.13 A similar section was considered in *Bank of New South Wales v Derham.*[1] The Australian section talks of a cheque which is "not indorsed, is irregularly indorsed or has been indorsed without authority". Although not finally deciding the matter, the Court was of the opinion that the section did cover the case of a forged indorsement, but the reasoning relied to some extent on the words "without authority" which are absent from the New Zealand section.

1 (1979) 25 ACTR 25.

17.14 Part of the argument that the section does not apply to forged indorsements is that the wording of s 60 of the Act specifically mentions forged indorsements.

"Deemed to have paid in due course"

17.15 The effect of the section is that the banker shall be deemed to have paid the cheque in due course. The effect of payment in due course is to discharge the cheque so that it is no longer possible for the true owner of the cheque, or anyone else, to bring an action on it. It might be thought that this is precisely the complaint of the true owner of the cheque and that it forms the basis for the action in conversion. Technically this is correct, but in *Charles v Blackwell*[1] it was held that if the cheque has been paid in due course conversion would not lie against the banker.[2]

1 (1877) 2 CPD 151.
2 Ellinger argues that the right of conversion may still be open to the true owner of the cheque. Perhaps the answer is that there is no true owner of a cheque which has been discharged by payment in due course. But see Tyree, "The Liability of Banks Collecting Forged Cheques" (1983) 11 Aust Bus L Rev 236.

17.16 The case also decided a very important point in respect the holder and drawer of the misappropriated cheque. Before the cheque is dishonoured, the holder is not entitled to sue either for the underlying contract or on the cheque. Assuming the banker is deemed to have paid the cheque in due course, the cheque cannot now be dishonoured, it has been paid. That is what the payee is complaining of, for it has been paid to the wrong person.

17.17 According to *Charles v Blackwell* the payee agreed to take an instrument which would be discharged if the banker paid it in accordance with existing law. Since that is what has happened when the banker is deemed to have paid in due course by s 2, the payee cannot be heard to complain. The result is that the section operates to discharge the debt for which the drawer drew the cheque, provided that the cheque has reached the hands of the payee prior to its misappropriation or there are special circumstances which place the risk of the loss on the payee. It seems clear that any indorsee is in exactly the same position.

Bills of Exchange Act, s 60

17.18 Section 2 of the Cheques Act provides a defence for the banker when paying cheques and certain other instruments which are not bills of exchange. It does not provide any protection for bills and, if the argument concerning indorsements is correct, it may fail to provide for protection when there is a forged indorsement. Section 60 of the Bills of Exchange Act may come to the rescue in such a circumstance:

(1) Where a bill payable to order on demand is drawn on a banker, and the banker on whom it is drawn pays the bill in good faith and in the ordinary course of business, it is not incumbent on the banker to show that the indorsement of the payee or any subsequent indorsement was made by or under the authority of the person whose indorsement it purports to be, and the banker is deemed to have paid the bill in due course, although such indorsement has been forged or made without authority.

17.19 Subsection (2) extends the provision to certain bank drafts.

17.20 The section requires that the bill be drawn on the banker. It is not applicable to bills which are merely accepted as payable at the bank. For such bills and for all bills which are payable after sight, the banker is in the same exposed position as everyone else who is in a position of having to pay a bill. In particular, there may be no practical means of verifying if the indorsements are genuine. There is no time for searching inquiries because a bill presented for payment must be paid promptly as long as it is complete and regular on its face: *Bank of England v Vagliano Bros* .[1] The section confers no special privilege on the banker if the bill has been materially altered or if the drawer's signature has been forged.[2]

1 [1891] AC 107, 157.
2 *Carpenters' Co v British Mutual Banking Co* [1938] 1 KB 511; *Bank of England v Vagliano Bros* [1891] AC 107, 157.

Indorsements and s 60

17.21 The banker is only protected if the bill has been negotiated by indorsement. If the bill bears no indorsement when presented to the banker, then the fact that the banker requests the person in possession of the bill to add a signature to the back of the bill will not bring the bill within the section, for the signature so added will not be an indorsement in the sense that it is added for the purposes of negotiating the bill; the signature is being added for the purposes of identification and/or receipt. In *Smith v Commercial Bank Co of Sydney Ltd*[1] O'Connon J said:

> The reason of the protection conferred by the section is the obligation of the banker to pay on indorsements which come to him in the ordinary course of business under circumstances in which it is in most cases impossible to test their genuineness. Where payment is made to the holder, as holder, and not as indorsee, where he is not bound to indorse before obtaining payment, and he is asked to put his name on the back merely as a receipt, or as a test of identity, the reason for the protection is at an end. In such a case the bank pays because it is satisfied as to the identity of the payee, and not because it is satisfied as to the genuineness of the indorsement.[2]

There may still be protection under one of the other statutory provisions.

1 (1910) 11 CLR 667.
2 P 678.

Crossed cheques: s 80

17.22 Section 80 of the Bills of Exchange Act provides that when a banker pays a crossed cheque in good faith and without negligence then he

> shall . . . be entitled to the same rights and be placed in the same position as if payment of the cheque had been made to the true owner thereof.

The section seems redundant in view of the broader protection offered by s 2 of the Cheques Act. In the *Derham* case[1] McGregor J noted that the negligence referred to could not be negligence connected with the improper indorsement on the cheque since the clear aim of the legislation was to relieve the paying banker from the need to concern himself with indorsements. The section also explicitly protects the rights of the drawer of the cheque provided that the cheque has come into the hands of the payee, but case law has extended the same protection to the drawer when the banker has a defence under s 2 of the Cheques Act.

1 *Bank of NSW v Derham* (1979) 25 ACTR 25.

The equitable defence

17.23 The law is intolerant of meddlers in other people's affairs. For example, a person who, without the authority of the debtor, pays another's debts will find that the debt is not discharged.Tthe meddler will not be able to claim any repayment from the person whose debt has been "paid" and may not even be able to recover the amount paid. The reason for this is that the debtor might dispute the debt, or wishes to set it off against a countervailing debt owed to him or would prefer to use limited assets to discharge other debts.

17.24 The rule does have exceptions. Under certain circumstances, a person who pays the debts of another without the authority of the person concerned may nevertheless take advantage of the payment. For example, money lent by a bank to meet the necessities for a mentally disordered person's household might be recovered by the banker under a right of subrogation.[1]

1 See *Re Beavan, Davies, Banks & Co v Beavan* [1912] 1 Ch 196.

17.25 In certain cases, the banker may take advantage of this "equitable defence" in order to justify the debiting of an account for payment of cheques which are, strictly speaking, paid in circumstances where the banker has no mandate.

17.26 The operation of the principle may be seen in *B Liggett (Liverpool) Ltd v Barclays Bank*.[1] The defendants negligently and contrary to instructions paid cheques of their customers, the plaintiff company, which had been signed by one director only. The cheques were drawn in favour of trade creditors of the company in payment for goods supplied to the company in its business. The Court held that as the liabilities of the company had not been increased by the payments the defendants were protected from liability on equitable grounds and were entitled to stand in the place of the creditors whom they had paid.

1 [1928] 1 KB 48.

17.27 The scope of the principle is not entirely clear. In *Re Cleandon Trust* a director had paid some debts of subsidiary companies at the request of the secretary. The payment discharged a liability of the company, as the company was guarantor of the debts owed by the subsidiaries. There was a meeting which purported to confirm the arrangement, but it was invalid. All of the companies went into liquidation and the director sought to recover the amounts advanced arguing that he was so entitled under the *Liggett* principle. The Court held that there was no knowledge or acquiescence on the part of the company which would make it liable at common law under an implied contract. There was no equitable principle which imposed a liability on the company, in as much as it had never had anything to do with the transactions.

1 [1939] Ch 286.

17.28 The equitable defence was allowed in a slightly different context in *Shapera v Toronto Dominion Bank*.[1] The plaintiff made an attempt to stop a cheque, but although his description of the cheque which he wished to stop gave the correct payee and amount, the date described was 27 January instead of 26 January. The Court held that it was not a valid countermand. Even if it had been, since the cheque went to discharge a valid legal obligation of the customer it would be inequitable to permit the customer to recover its value and leave the bank in the position of having paid the customer's debt.

1 17 DLR (3d) 122 (1970).

17.29 *Shapera* was followed in *Royal Bank of Canada v Huber*.[1] The Court of Appeal in Saskatchewan held that where a bank mistakenly certifies a corporation's cheque at the request of the payee, and subsequently pays the instrument, overlooking a stop-payment order, it cannot recover its payment where the corporation has not requested reimbursement of its account, and it is shown that the payee was, as between himself and the corporation justly entitled to receive the money represented by the cheque. Huber had been notified of the stop payment order before depositing the cheques with the Toronto Dominion bank. They were collected for his account and paid by mistake by the plaintiff bank. For some reason not entirely apparent from the report, the company had not asked that its account be recredited, nor did the bank show any intention to do so. The Court said:

> It is not difficult to understand why the Bank has not admitted liability. There is no dispute, but that the moneys which Huber received were in payment of wages — a debt owed to him. Under these circumstances, if a claim were made by the Company against the bank for payment to it of the money paid out in contravention of the "stop payment" order, it may be that the bank would be entitled to equitable relief: see *Shapera v Toronto Dominion Bank* 17 DLR (3d) 122 . . . .[2]

1 (1971) 23 DLR (3d) 209.
2 At p 211.

17.30 The Court held that the defendant was entitled to retain the money, but the reasons are obscure:

> . . . I am satisfied that the facts fully establish that it would be against equity and good conscience to insist that the defendant return the money . . .¹

1 At p 212.

17.31 After a careful consideration of the cases, Ellinger and Lee conclude that in order to make out the *Liggett* defence it must be shown that the customer owed a valid debt to the payee of the cheque, that this debt was discharged by the wrongful payment and that it would be unconscionable for the customer to retain the benefit of the payment.¹

1 Ellinger and Lee, "The *Liggett* Defence: a banker's last resort", [1984] 1 LMCLQ 459.

Wrongful dishonour

17.32 A paying banker who dishonours a cheque which satisfies all of the conditions necessary to raise the duty of payment commits a breach of contract thereby and will be liable for damages according to the principles of contract law. The banker may also face an action in defamation with regard to answers written on the cheque giving the reasons for dishonour.¹ This section is confined to liability in contract.

1 See 6.45.

17.33 Wrongful dishonour ordinarily occurs when the banker has omitted to credit deposits made by the customer, where the banker is confused by customers with similar names or as a result of overlooking overdraft arrangements. In each case, the usual problem is that the customer has funds in the account which are adequate to meet the cheque, but the banker mistakenly believes that the account is inadequate.

17.34 It does not matter that the oversight of the banker is innocent. The action is for breach of contract and the contract does not call merely for the banker to be careful, although it does call for that as well, but for the banker to pay when the pre-conditions for payment are met. Failure to do so may well mean damage to the customer and it is this damage for which the banker is responsible.

Liable for damage to credit

17.35 In accordance with well settled contractual principles, the banker will be liable for all damage which is foreseeable as a consequence of the failure to carry out the contractual promise. According to the rule in *Hadley v Baxendale*,[1] the party in breach must pay for damage which flows directly and naturally from the failure to perform the contract. Furthermore, if there are special circumstances known to the party in breach which will lead to other damage which might not necessarily be in the contemplation of ordinary parties to the contract, then there will be liability for that damage as well.

1 (1854) 9 Exch 341; 156 ER 145.

17.36 As an example, it is clear that the failure to pay a cheque will result in damage to the customer's credit. Indeed, that is the fundamental loss which the customer will suffer and there is no doubt that the banker will be liable to any such damage that is proved. Indeed, the loss to credit is so naturally and directly a result of the breach of the contract that in certain circumstances the damage need not even be pleaded.

17.37 In *Evra Corp v Swiss Banking Corp*,[1] the plaintiff was required to make a payment of $26,000. In failing to make that payment, he lost the benefit of a charterparty, ie a lease of a ship. As a consequence, the report records that his losses were assessed at more than $2,000,000. Should the banker in breach of contract be liable for that amount? Under the rule in *Hadley v Baxendale*,[2] the answer depends upon the knowledge of the banker. In the ordinary case where the banker is merely paying, or rather failing to pay, just another cheque, the answer is that there is no liability for the greater losses. In the language of contract, the losses were too remote.[3] However, if the banker knew of the importance of the payment and still failed, then it might be that there would be liability for the larger amount.

1 522 F Supp 820, rev 673 F 2d 951.
2 (1854) 9 Exch 341; 156 ER 145.
3 When the payment is one which is specially ordered, the result might be different; see 19.68.

Trader

17.38 It was mentioned above that in certain cases the loss to credit is so inevitable that it is not even necessary for the plaintiff to plead the loss. This occurs when the plaintiff is a "trader"; the rule is an exception to the general rule concerning the measure of damages for breach of contract.

17.39 In *Rolin v Steward*[1] several cheques were wrongfully dishonoured. The plaintiff was a merchant and shipowner; no special damages were pleaded. Indeed there were no special damages as the cheques were met the next day and it seems as though the plaintiff lost nothing at all. The jury awarded the plaintiff £500. That sum was held on appeal to be excessive and was reduced to £200.

1 (1854) 14 CB 595.

17.40 The basis of this exception to the general rule of contract is that a trader suffers damage to credit almost as a matter of course when a cheque is dishonoured. It is even worse when a small cheque is dishonoured, for the suspicion of insolvency is even greater.

17.41 It is open to the banker to show that the customer's reputation and credit were already in tatters and that the dishonour caused no actual damage. However, for the reasons discussed when considering an action in defamation, such a course is fraught with dangers.[1]

1 See 6.45ff.

Non-trader

17.42 When the customer is not a trader, the ordinary rules apply and damage must be pleaded and proved in the ordinary manner. It is not easy to quantify such damage, but it is likely that the assessment would be similar to that in a defamation action.

17.43 In *Gibbons v Westminster Bank Ltd*[1] the plaintiff, a non-trader, drew a cheque for about £19 in favour of her landlord. The cheque was wrongfully dishonoured by the bank since they had erroneously paid one of her deposits into another customer's account. She did not prove any actual damage and it was held that she was entitled only to nominal damages of 40 shillings.

1 [1939] 2 KB 882.

17.44 Although doubts have from time to time been expressed concerning the validity of the trader/non-trader distinction for the purposes of awarding contractual damages, the most recently reported New Zealand case has maintained the distinction. In *Baker v ANZ Bank Ltd*[1] the Court held that a woman who was a substantial shareholder and a director of a company was not a trader for these purposes. In the absence of pleading and proving special damages, she was awarded only £2 for each cheque which was wrongfully dishonoured.[2]

1 [1958] NZLR 907.
2 See also *Hill v National Bank of New Zealand Ltd* [1985] 1 NZLR 736.

Other special classes?

17.45 The most common view is that traders are the only class of customers who are entitled to substantial damages in contract without proof of actual damage. However, Chorley suggests that there are other members of the community to which the principle might apply. He mentions military and naval officers and professionals for whom the consequences of a dishonoured cheque may be no less disastrous than to the trader. He suggests, rightly, that it seems unjust to limit the right to recover damages to traders.

17.46 There is also some reason to believe that the Court in *Rolin v Steward* was not necessarily considering traders to be a class apart, but rather that they were just one class where the damage was so inevitable as to be treated in this special way. Certainly that is the interpretation put on the case by Lord Birkenhead LC in the House of Lords in *Wilson v United Counties Bank Ltd*:[1]

> On principle [*Rolin v Steward*] seems to me to belong to that very special class of cases in which a banker, though his customer's account is in funds, nevertheless dishonours his cheque. The ratio decidendi in such cases is that the refusal to meet the cheque, under such circumstances, is so obviously injurious to the credit of a trader that the latter can recover, without allegation of special damage, reasonable compensation for the injury done to his credit.

1 [1920] AC 102, 112.

Defamation

17.47 The matter of obtaining contractual damages without the need to prove actual damage is less important than it might be because bankers habitually place answers on cheques which communicate the reason for the withdrawal. Such answers may be, and often are, defamatory. The plaintiff in such a case if he is in any way dependent upon a good credit reputation is in a position very similar to that of a trader. The plaintiff in *Baker* was awarded £100 for each cheque as damages for defamation. The question of liability for defamation has been discussed at 6.45ff.

Defences in cases of wrongful dishonour

The dishonour must cause damage

17.48 Not every wrongful dishonour which will result in damages being awarded. Whether the action is framed in contract or in defamation, it is always open to the bank to show that there was no damage. Even in the case of a trader, it seems theoretically possible to show that there was in fact no damage to the trader's credit: see also *Ellaw Co Ltd v Lloyds Bank Ltd*[1] where the Court remarked that even if the dishonour had been wrongful only nominal damages would have been awarded as the plaintiffs were engaged in shady operations.

1 (1934) 4 LDAB 455.

Only the customer has a right of action

17.49 It is only the customer who has a right of action against the bank for wrongful dishonour. The payee has no contractual rights against the bank; the payee's remedy is against the drawer on the cheque.[1] To this must be added an apparent right of action in negligence against the paying bank if the cheque has not been promptly paid.[2]

1 *Schroeder v Central Bank of London Ltd* (1876) 34 LT 735.
2 *HH Dimond (Rotorua 1966) Ltd v ANZ Banking Group* [1979] 2 NZLR 739.

17.50 It would seem that there is no right against the paying bank when the cheque is presented for payment by the payee himself. There clearly is no right in defamation, since the gist of an action in defamation is that the defendant has published the defamatory material to a third party. There would be a technical action in contract, but it is difficult to imagine situations where there would be any actual damage, and in the absence of actual damage pleaded and proved there could be only nominal damages awarded. If there were actual damage, on the other hand, there seems no reason why substantial damages should not be awarded.

Statutory defences

17.51 There are no statutory defences available to the paying banker in the event of a wrongful dishonour. The Manning committee recommended that a defence should be provided where the bank has acted honestly and reasonably and ought fairly to be excused,[1] but this suggestion was not implemented in the final Cheques Act 1986 (Aust).

1 Cl 74 of the draft bill.

Chapter 18

Money paid under a mistake of fact

18.1 Where a banker mistakenly pays a cheque after the customer has withdrawn the authority, the banker will, generally, be unable to debit the account. Should the banker be able to recover the money paid from the payee? Or again, the cheque is paid in the mistaken belief that there are sufficient funds to meet it. Should the banker be able to recover?

18.2 These are just two common examples of a wide variety of situations where one person pays another a sum which would not have been paid had the payer known the true facts. Of these situations and the legal framework which deals with them, Lord Wright said:

> It is clear that any civilised system of law is bound to provide remedies for cases of what has been called unjust enrichment or unjust benefit, that is to prevent a man from retaining the money or some benefit derived from another which it is against conscience that he should keep. Such remedies in English law are generally different from remedies in contract or in tort and are now recognised to fall within a third category of the common law which has been called quasi-contract or restitution .... Payment under a mistake of fact is only one head of this category of the law ... the gist of the action is a debt or obligation implied or, more accurately, imposed by law.[1]

1 Per Lord Wright in *Fibrosa Spolka v Alcyjna Fairbairn Lawson Combe Barbour Ltd* [1943] AC 32, 61.

18.3 Unfortunately, such a broad brush does little to help with the basic principles. When is it "against conscience" that a payee should keep the sum? The only way to clarify these matters is a consideration of the case law. We shall consider some of the essential elements which must be present before it is "against conscience" for the payee to retain money which has been paid under a mistake.

The elements of the cause of action

The essential feature of the action is that the payment would not have been made save for the mistake. There is some uncertainty concerning the position of "voluntary" payments and the range of defences available.

Mistake must be operative cause of payment

18.4 In the first place, the mistake must be the cause of the payment. If the payer intended that the payment be made whether the mistaken facts were true or not, then it can scarcely be against conscience for the payee to retain the payment. This rather obvious principle is one of the oldest and most certain. In *Kelly v Solari*[1] an executrix received the proceeds of a life assurance policy from the plaintiff company. The company had overlooked the fact that the life policy had been allowed to lapse by the deceased by reason of a failure to maintain premium payments. Upon discovery of the true facts, the Court of Exchequer allowed the recovery of the money.

1 (1841) 9 M & W 54; 152 ER 24; 11 LJ Ex 10.

18.5 In so doing, it dismissed arguments that the company should not be allowed to recover by virtue of its own carelessness, since it had the means of ascertaining the true position but failed to do so. The Court indicated that, had the company made an intentional decision to decline to investigate the currency of the policy, the position would have been different, for then it would appear that the company intended to make the payment no matter what the true state of the facts might be.

18.6 During the course of the judgment as reported in 9 M & W, Parke B discusses the nature of the mistake which will allow recovery of the money. It is one which

> ... upon the supposition that a specific fact is true, ... would entitle the [payee] to the money ... and the money would not have been paid if it had been known to the payer that the fact was untrue ....

18.7 It is to be noted that in the particular case if the supposed fact had been true, ie that the policy was current, the executrix would have been entitled to receive the money from the company, not from some third party. However, in the *Law Journal* report there is no mention of the need for the mistake to be such as to entitle the payee to claim payment, only that the payment is made on the supposition that the fact is true.

18.8 There is also a passage in the judgment of Rolfe B which seems to indicate that the mistake need only have been the cause of the payment:

> . . . it seems to me that wherever [money] is paid under a mistake of fact, and the party would not have paid it if the fact had been known to him, it cannot be otherwise than unconscientious to retain it.[1]

1 9 M & W 54, 59; 152 ER 24, 26.

18.9 It is clear from *Kelly v Solari* that negligence on the part of the payer will not bar recovery, but it is also clear that had the company made a conscious decision to conduct no investigation into the state of the premiums, then it would have been barred, for in that case it is clear that the mistake would not have been the operative cause of the payment. This was reaffirmed in *National Westminster Bank Ltd v Barclays Bank International Ltd*:[1]

> [The plaintiff's argument] was based on a long line of authorities of which *Kelly v Solari* is a leading case, to the effect that a plaintiff is entitled to recover money paid under a mistake which operated as between him and the payee even if he had the means of discovering the mistake and even though the status quo of the defendant cannot be restored.[2]

1 [1975] QB 654.
2 Per Kerr J at 675.

Voluntary payments

18.10 It is often said that if the payment is "voluntary" then there can be no recovery. "Voluntary" means that, assuming the mistaken facts to be true, the payer is under no legal obligation to make the payment. The cases are not always clear or consistent in identifying to whom the legal obligation is owed. It may be that a supposed obligation owed to the payee places the plaintiff in a stronger position than one supposedly owed to a third party.

18.11 The problem of the voluntary payment arose in *Aiken v Short*[1] where the plaintiff bankers had taken an assignment of an interest in an estate as security for advances made to one Carter. They later learned that Carter was also indebted to the defendant who held an assignment of the interest as security. The plaintiffs advanced further sums for the express purpose of buying out the defendant, only to learn later that Carter had no interest in the estate. The plaintiffs claimed the right to recover as money paid under a mistake of fact. It was held that the plaintiff must fail, partly on grounds suggested by the following passage from Bramwell B:

> In order to entitle a person to recover back money paid under a mistake of fact, the mistake must be as to a fact which, if true, would make the

person paying liable to pay the money; not where, if true, it would merely make it desirable that he should pay the money.[2]

1 (1856) 1 H & N 210; 156 ER 1180; 25 LJ Ex 321.
2 156 ER 1180, 1182. This case too is bedevilled by discrepancies between two different reports. In the *Law Journal* report the reference is to a fact "which if true, would have given the person receiving a right against the person paying". See *Weaver and Cragie*, p 433 for a very full discussion.

18.12 The meaning of "voluntary" was taken further with the decision in *Morgan v Ashcroft*.[1] A bookmaker claimed that one of his clients had been overpaid and was seeking to recover the money as money paid under a mistake of fact. Under the gaming law of the time, gambling debts were not legally recoverable. The Court held that the plaintiff's claim must fail. In the course of the judgment, Sir Wilfrid Greene MR appeared to accept the above remarks from *Aiken v Short* when he said:

[The plaintiff] thought that a wagering debt was due from himself to the [defendant], whereas in fact it was not. But if the supposed fact had been true, the [plaintiff] would have been under no liability to make the payment which therefore was intended to be a voluntary payment. Upon the true facts the payment was still a voluntary payment; and there is in my opinion no such fundamental or basic distinction between the one voluntary payment and the other that the law can for present purposes differentiate between them and say that there was no intention to make the one because the intention was to make the other.

1 [1938] 1 KB 49.

18.13 However, the members of the Court left it open as to what mistakes there might be which, although not inducing a belief in the mind of the payer that the payment is a legal liability which must be discharged, will still be of such a nature as to allow for recovery.

18.14 In both *Aiken v Short* and *Morgan v Ashcroft*, the mistake was the operative cause of the payment in the sense that, had the payer known the truth the payment would not have been made.

18.15 A more recent expression of the law is in a dissenting judgment by Kitto J in *Porter v Latec Finance (Qld) Pty Ltd*,[1] where he said:

. . . the view must, I think, be accepted that a mistake of fact enables a payer of money to recover it if the mistake was fundamental to the payment, even though the payer would not have been liable to pay it if the supposed fact had existed.

1 (1964) 111 CLR 177, 190.

18.16 In the same case, Barwick CJ said:

There is some possibility of confusion when dealing with the subject matter of the recovery of payments said to have been made under mistake in speaking, as some of the cases do, of the payments being "voluntary", as if a voluntary payment made to the wrong person could never be recovered. It is preferable in my opinion to test the matter by determining whether the mistake is fundamental to the transaction, properly identifying the transaction and the relationship of the mistake to it. Such a course is, I think, universally valid although as yet the subject of money paid under mistake is not fully exhausted by decision.[1]

1 At p 187. These comments were followed in *Commercial Bank of Australia v Younis* [1979] 1 NSWLR 444.

18.17 These views of the High Court were based primarily on the decision of the Court of Appeal in England in *Larner v London City Council*.[1] The council was authorised, but not required, by the Local Government Staffs (War Service) Act 1939 to make payments to employees who were serving in the armed forces to supplement their service pay. The council claimed that too much had been paid as a result of clerical errors.

1 [1949] 2 KB 683.

18.18 The argument for the defendant was that the payments were voluntary and so could not be recovered. The Court of Appeal held that recovery was possible since although the payments were voluntary the promise to pay was made for good reasons of national policy which the council was bound to fulfil. The force of the case is diminished by an earlier holding by the House of Lords that such payments, once promised, became a contractual term of the employee's service. Thus the pronouncement that the payments in *Larner's* case that the payments were voluntary may not be strictly correct.

Summary: voluntary payments

18.19 The problem with the requirement of "legal obligation" as a precondition to allowing the recovery of money paid under a mistake of fact is twofold. First, it simply does not make any sense to base recovery on such a criterion. Why is the mistake more "fundamental" in any sense if the payer believes himself to be under a legal obligation to the payee instead of, as in the *Reno* case,[1] under a legal obligation to a third party to make the very same payment or, as in *Aiken v Short*, under no legal obligation at all? All other things being equal, it is hard to see why one payer should be able to recover and the other not. Secondly, the requirement is at odds with some of the decided cases, a matter which need not concern us here.[2]

1 See 18.75.
2 See *Weaver and Cragie*, p 450.

18.20 A more rational analysis has been given by Luntz that the real question is to find evidence of the payer's intention.[1] He argues that the fact that the payer believes himself to be under a legal obligation to the payee is good evidence that he did not intend the payee to receive the money if the circumstances were different. If that is correct, then the mistaken belief that he is under an obligation to some third party is similarly good evidence.

1 Luntz "The Bank's Right to Recover on Cheques Paid by Mistake" 6 Melbourne University Law Review 308.

18.21 The question of when a "voluntary" payment may be recovered is still not satisfactorily resolved, but the modern cases all seem to be in accord with the proposition that the mere fact that the payer is not, assuming the fact to be true, under a legal obligation to the payee or to some third party, will not alone prevent recovery. The most common case which has caused trouble in the past is that of a banker paying on a cheque under a mistake of fact and then attempting to recover from the holder. As will be seen below,[1] this case is now resolved. Other cases of voluntary payment may be expected to cause problems.

1 See 18.69.

Mistake of fact and mistake of law

18.22 At common law, it was only a mistake of fact which could entitle the plaintiff to recover, presumably on the basis that everyone must be taken to know the law. The principle derived from a statement in *Kelly v Solari*:[1]

> The safest rule however is that if the party makes the payment with full knowledge of the facts, although in ignorance of the law, there being no fraud on the other side, he cannot recover it back again.[2]

1 (1841) 9 M & W 54.
2 Per Lord Abinger at p 58.

18.23 Whatever the scope of the common law rule,[1] it is quite unsatisfactory because of the difficulty and artificiality in distinguishing when a mistake is one of law and when one of fact. Even more fundamental, why should a payee who would otherwise be required to return a payment be allowed to keep it merely because the payer's mistake was one of law? After all, the situations under discussion are those where the payee has no right to the payment.

1 See *Kiriri Cotton Co Ltd v Dewani* [1960] AC 192, especially Lord Denning at p 204.

18.24 For these reasons, the Judicature Amendment Act 1958 amended the Judicature Act 1908 by the insertion of a new section which overruled the old law:

> **94A. Recovery of payments made under mistake of law** — (1) Subject to the provisions of this section, where relief in respect of any payment that has been made under mistake is sought in any Court,

whether in an action or other proceeding or by way of defence, set off, counterclaim, or otherwise, and that relief could be granted if the mistake was wholly one of fact, that relief shall not be denied by reason only that the mistake is one of law whether or not it is in any degree also one of fact.

(2) Nothing in this section shall enable relief to be given in respect of any payment made at a time when the law requires or allows, or is commonly understood to require or allow, the payment to be made or enforced, by reason only that the law is subsequently changed or shown not to have been as it was commonly understood to be at the time of the payment.

18.25 Subsection (2) of s 94A is not very clearly drafted, but it presumably is intended to prevent the re-opening of a transaction on the basis of a subsequent change in the law or a re-interpretation by the Court of an existing rule of law.

Whose mistake?

18.26 It seems that the mistake must be on the part of the payer and that it is not material that the recipient was or was not mistaken. This is not to say that the knowledge of the recipient is irrelevant, for if the recipient's knowledge is such as to make the receipt of the money fraudulent, then he or she will not be able to retain the money no matter what defence might otherwise be available.

18.27 The matter is expressed very succinctly in *Lloyds Bank Ltd v Brooks*:[1]

> If the hand that pays the money, even though it is only that of an agent, is acting under a mistake of fact, that payment is a payment made under a mistake of fact.[2]

1 (1950) 6 LDAB 161.
2 Per Lynskey J at p 164.

Defences

18.28 There are some circumstances where the payment has been made under a mistake of fact which would ordinarily be recoverable, but extraneous events provide the payee with a defence. Payment by mistake on a negotiable instrument is a special case which will be treated more fully at 18.86ff.

18.29 The matter of defences was discussed by the Court of Appeal in *Thomas v Houston Corbett & Co*:[1] The Court said:

The right to recover money paid under a mistake of fact arises from the payment and receipt of the money. It does not depend on any previous relationship between the parties and whatever privity may be necessary is established (1) by proof of the payment of the money and (2) proof that the money would not have been paid but for the mistake of fact made by the payer. When the parties have placed themselves in the necessary relation to each other, an obligation to repay is implied as a matter of law. The only available defences to such an action are true estoppel and s 94B of the Judicature Act . . . .[2]

1 [1969] NZLR 151. The facts of this case are discussed in detail below at 18.45.
2 From the headnote.

18.30 To the list of defences must be added certain factual situations where the mistaken payment is made not to a principal, but to an agent. The position of such an agent is of the utmost importance for a banker who will act as an agent to receive payment for a customer. Assuming that the banker is acting merely as a "conduit", then the payer of money under a mistake of fact will not be able to recover from the banker once the banker has accounted to the payee.[1] For various reasons, payment which has been made on a negotiable instrument is in a very special category and there are somewhat different considerations which apply. These matters will be discussed more fully in 18.86ff.

1 See 18.31ff.

Payment to an agent

18.31 When money is paid by mistake not to the principal in the transaction but to an agent, the agent will not be obliged to refund the money if it has been paid over to the principal or if the agent has, in reliance on the payment, done something which has otherwise altered the relationship between the agent and principal. But this applies only if the agent receives the money purely as a "conduit" to the principal; it has no application if the money is received by the agent payee as principal in his or her own right, nor if the receipt is in consequence of some wrongdoing to which the agent was a party. In these latter cases, liability to the payer will remain even if the agent has already accounted to the principal.

18.32 The principles may be illustrated by a consideration of *Gowers v Lloyds & National Provincial Foreign Bank Ltd*.[1] The plaintiffs were agents of the Crown who were charged with, inter alia, the payment of pensions to retired officers of the British colonial civil service. In order to collect the sums due, the pensioner would fill in forms which included a witnessed certificate to the effect that the pensioner was still alive. These forms were provided by the plaintiffs; the pensioner would present the completed witnessed form for payment. In most cases, this presentment would be through the pensioner's bank.

1 [1938] 1 All ER 766.

18.33 The defendant bank had collected the pension of a customer named Gibson. For a period of more than five years, forged receipts and certificates had been forwarded through the defendant bank and paid by the plaintiffs. Neither of the parties was aware that Gibson had been dead for at least that amount of time. Upon discovery, the plaintiffs sued to recover the payments, amounting to some £3,500, from the defendant bank.

18.34 The Court of Appeal held that the plaintiffs must fail since the defendant bank was innocently acting for a principal to whom they had passed on the money. Note that the actual principal was the rogue, not the person with whom the bank thought that it was dealing, but that did not alter the application of the general principle.

Payment by an agent

18.35 Many payments are made by agents. In the case of a company payer, the payment must be made by an agent. It appears that the principal plaintiff may be able to recover a payment provided that both the payment and the mistake were made by the same agent. But suppose that some agents of the company know the true facts; to what extent is the knowledge of these other agents to be attributed to the agent making the payment or to the principal? The answer, for this purpose, appears to be that only actual knowledge of the parties making the payment is relevant:

> ... [when a payment is made by a company] ... and payments are made under a bona fide mistake of fact by an authorised agent of the company, the fact that some other agent of the company may have had full knowledge of all the facts does not disentitle the company to recover the money so paid provided that the agent with the full knowledge does not know that the payments are being made on an erroneous basis.[1]

1 Per Pilcher J in *Turvey v Dentons (1923) Ltd* [1953] 1 QB 218, 224.

Change of position

18.36 The general rule of the common law is that a person who has changed his or her position detrimentally does not by that reason alone have a defence which will allow the retention of money which has been paid under a mistake of fact, unless in so doing there was reliance on some representation made by the payer beyond the mere fact of payment. Phrased in a slightly different way, the payment of money by the payer is not a representation that the payee is entitled to receive it and to treat it as his own.

Jones v Waring & Gillow Ltd

18.37 This general proposition is thought to follow from the result of *Jones v Waring & Gillow Ltd*.[1] In that case a rogue by the name of Bodenham had purchased furniture from the defendants under a hire purchase arrangement. He was indebted to them for some £5,000 and the furniture was seized by them when Bodenham failed to maintain the repayments.

1 [1926] AC 670.

18.38 Bodenham told Jones that he, Bodenham, was an agent of a firm of motorcar manufacturers who were about to put a new car on the market. He persuaded Jones to sign an agreement which purported to appoint Jones as agent for the sale of the car. Under the agreement, Jones was to purchase 500 cars by means of an initial payment of £5,000. Jones sensibly was reluctant to pay this amount of money to an unknown firm. In order to convince Jones to pay, Bodenham falsely told him that Waring & Gillow were financing the operation and that the cheque could be sent to them.

18.39 Jones made the cheque for £5,000 payable to Waring & Gillow, whereupon it was delivered to them by Bodenham and the furniture which had been seized was returned.

18.40 Part of the argument in the case concerned the defence that Waring & Gillow had changed their position on the faith of the payment. A majority of the House of Lords rejected the argument, finding that there had been no representation on the part of the plaintiff which had been acted upon by the defendant. It is not enough that the payment was made and position altered on the basis of the payment. There must be some independent act or representation of the payer or a breach of some duty owed by the payer to the payee.

Judicature Amendment Act 1958

18.41 The decision in *Jones v Waring & Gillow Ltd* seems somewhat unfair. Why should the payee in that case bear all of the losses when both of the parties were swindled by the rogue? Indeed, if it could be said that there was fault or negligence in that case, it would seem that it was more with the gullible Jones than with the payees.

18.42 It is not just the outcome of *Jones'* case which is unsatisfactory, for a close reading of the judgments reveals that the ratio decidendi of the case is by no means as clear as the above statements might lead the reader to suppose. The result is that the general law is still unsettled, so that it is possible for Paget to say:

> It must be submitted that where a payee has changed his position the question of recovery is still in doubt, dependent upon the whole circumstances of the matter.[1]

1 At p 308.

18.43 For these reasons, the Judicature Act 1908 was amended to make the situation clear in New Zealand. The Judicature Amendment Act 1958 amends the 1908 Act by inserting ss 94A and 94B. Section 94A has already been discussed.[1] Section 94B is as follows:

> **94B. Payments made under mistake of law or fact not always recoverable** — Relief, whether under section 94A or in equity or otherwise, in respect of any payment made under mistake, whether of law or of fact, shall be denied wholly or in part if the person from whom relief is sought received the payment in good faith and has so altered his position in reliance on the validity of the payment that in the opinion of the Court, having regard to all possible implications in respect of other persons, it is inequitable to grant relief, or to grant relief in full, as the case may be.

1 See 18.24.

Scope of s 94B

18.44 Section 94B clearly allows for a total or a partial defence by virtue of a change in position induced solely by the fact of payment, although it is not at all clear what range of factors the Court should consider when applying the section.

18.45 The Court of Appeal considered the application of s 94B in *Thomas v Houston Corbett & Co.*[1] The Court observed that when applying the section, it is entitled to look at the equities from both sides and not just from the side of the payer.

1 [1969] NZLR 151.

18.46 The facts were that one Cook was a law clerk with the plaintiff firm. The defendant was a friend of Cook and was a young doctor with "no worldly knowledge" of financial matters. The defendant had an amount of cash available which he intended to use for the purchase of a car, but was advised that the car could not be delivered for some time. He sought advice from Cook as to worthwhile investments.

18.47 Cook advised the defendant to make certain investments which the defendant did. Through a series of devious manoeuvres, Cook convinced the defendant that the money had been invested and that the speculation had been quite successful. As part of this deception, he tricked his firm into making a payment to the defendant and convinced the defendant on the basis of that payment to write a cheque to him, Cook, for some £840. The plaintiffs sought the recovery of the payment as money made under a mistake of fact. The main issue concerned that application of s 94B.

18.48 The Court of Appeal considered the equities, found that each of the parties had trusted Cook equally and that neither had been more to blame than the other. The Court thought that it was irrelevant that the defendant was speculating with the money, a matter which had seemed to weigh heavily with the Supreme Court Judge. In the end result, the Court found the equities to be about equal and considered that the two parties should bear the loss equally.

Estoppel and ratification

18.49 The Court of Appeal noted in the *Houston Corbett* case that there were only two defences, namely the statutory defence of s 94B and the defence of estoppel. Estoppel is a rule of evidence and does not itself amount to a cause of action. Under certain circumstances, a person will not be able to argue that certain facts are true. Paget describes the circumstances thus:

> When a man, by his words or conduct, has led another to believe in a particular state of affairs, he will not be allowed to go back on it when it would be unjust or inequitable for him to do so.[1]

1 At p 298.

18.50 As a statement of general principle, that is correct enough, but it leads to a number of questions concerning the circumstances under which one person leads another to believe that a certain state of affairs is true and when it would be "unjust or inequitable" for the first person to repudiate the former words or conduct.

18.51 It has already been noted that the mere fact of payment is not to be taken as a representation that the payee is irrevocably entitled to the money. In order to raise an estoppel, there must be some further representation by the payer, either by express action or by conduct. As usual, silence may amount to a representation provided the person remaining silent is under some duty to speak.[1]

1 *Greenwood v Martins Bank Ltd* [1932] 1 KB 371. See Ch 3.

18.52 So far as the circumstances under which it would be unjust or inequitable for the representor to repudiate the words or conduct, it is usually said that there are two requirements. First, the representee must have relied upon the representation. Secondly, in reliance upon the representation, the representee has changed his or her position detrimentally.

Merely spending money not change of position

18.53 It might be thought that the fact that the recipient has spent the money might amount to a change in position, at least if the money is spent with no suspicion by the recipient that he or she was not entitled to it. Indeed, there has been some judicial recognition of this commonsense position. In *Lloyds Bank Ltd v Brooks*[1] Lynskey J said:

> If as a result of a misstatement by a bank a person is induced to spend more money than they have got to spend then it seems to me in the ordinary sense, from the factual point of view apart from the legal point of view, they are certainly acting to their detriment . . . .[2]

1 (1950) 6 LDAB 161.
2 At p 169.

18.54 From the legal point of view, however, such a general statement does not represent the true position.

> Speaking generally the fact that a recipient has spent the money beyond recall is no defence unless there was some fault — as, for instance, breach of duty — on the part of the paymaster and none on the part of the recipient.[1]

1 Per Lord Denning in *Larner v London City Council* [1949] 2 KB 683.

18.55 One matter of importance to bankers arises from this description, for in the case where a banker mistakenly overpays a customer in circumstances where the customer may successfully raise an estoppel, it may well be that the mere spending of money will amount to a change of position. In *Lloyds Bank Ltd v Brooks*[1] the Court found that there was some "fault" on the part of the banker, namely the fact that the banker failed over a period of time to keep the customer informed. Since the banker is under a duty to keep accurate accounts, a misstatement of accounts will amount to a representation upon which the customer may rely. The Court found that the defendant had relied upon the representation, had honestly believed that she was entitled to the money and that

> . . . the defendant because of this increased credit which she apparently was receiving did in fact spend more money on matters for her own purposes than she otherwise would have done.

1 (1950) 6 LDAB 161.

18.56 An instructive contrast is provided by the decision in *United Overseas Bank v Jiwani*.[1] Jiwani's account had mistakenly been credited twice and he had used the extra funds for the purposes of financing a hotel purchase. Mackenna J set out the requirements for establishing a defence in the following terms:

> First [the defendant] must show that either the plaintiffs were under a duty to give him accurate information about the state of his account and that in breach of this duty they gave him inaccurate information or that in some other way there was a misrepresentation made to him about the state of the account, for which the plaintiffs are responsible. Secondly he must show that this inaccurate information misled him about the state of the account and caused him to believe that the plaintiffs were his debtors for a larger sum than was the case and to make the transfer to Mr Pirani in that mistaken belief. Thirdly he must

show that because of his mistaken belief he changed his position in a way which would make it inequitable to require him to repay the money.[2]

1 [1976] 1 WLR 964.
2 At p 968.

18.57 The Court was clearly of the opinion that Jiwani was not misled by the erroneous accounts, but even supposing that he was, the Court considered that there was no detriment. Mackenna J considered the the fact that Jiwani had spent the money and said:

> Undoubtedly there are cases in which the customer who has spent the money in ignorance that he was being overpaid will not be required to repay . . . . There was reason for believing in each of those cases that the defendant would have acted differently if he had not mistakenly believed that he was richer than he was, that because of his mistake, he had . . . altered his mode of living . . . . There is in the present case . . . no reason for thinking that Mr Jiwani would have acted differently in the matter of purchase . . . . He would still have completed the purchase of the hotel by a further borrowing . . . .

The fact that the further borrowing would not have been as easy for Mr Jiwani was not considered to be a detriment.

18.58 The most recent judicial consideration of spending money as a change of position is in *Avon County Council v Howlett*.[1] The defendant was injured in the course of his employment and was away from work for nearly two years. The plaintiff employer subsequently discovered that due to a computer error, the defendant had been overpaid some £1,007. It was found that it was payment under a mistake of fact, not of law.[2]

1 [1983] 1 All ER 1073.
2 A matter which is not relevant in the New Zealand context. See 18.24.

18.59 It was also found by the trial Judge that the plaintiff had made representations to the defendant and that the defendant had changed his position by losing a claim for a social security benefit and by spending a sum which he would not otherwise have spent.

18.60 Much of the argument concerned the right of the payer to recover money which was unspent at the time of the demand for repayment. It was argued that even if the estoppel be established, this money should be recoverable, for otherwise the defendant is unjustly enriched. The Court rejected the argument, holding that if there was a balance remaining that it could not be recovered, provided that the estoppel is made out.

> . . . one has to postulate a situation in which the defendant was perfectly entitled to conduct his business affairs on the assumption that the relevant representations were true . . . a defendant in the situation of the defendant in the present case may . . . have either altered his general mode of living or undertaken commitments or incurred expenditure or entered into other transactions which it may be very difficult for him

subsequently to recall . . . . He may even have done so, while leaving some of the particular moneys paid to him by the plaintiff untouched.[1]

1 Per Slade LJ at p 1086.

Fault on the part of the defendant

18.61 Even if the other elements of an estoppel are made out, the defence will fail if there is some fault or some misrepresentation or concealment on the part of the defendant. For example, in the *National Westminster* case,[1] Kerr J found that even if all the other elements of estoppel had been established, which in his view they had not, Ismail would still have failed in his effort to retain the money by virtue of the suspicious circumstances under which he obtained the cheque. There can be no doubt that this is correct, for doubtless the paying bank would have considered the cheque very much more closely had it known of the suspicious circumstances.

1 The facts of this case are discussed at 18.98.

18.62 The matter was stated precisely by Lord Brampton in *George Whitechurch v Cananagh*:[1]

> . . . no representations can be relied on as estoppels if they have been induced by the concealment of any material fact on the part of those who seek to use them as such; and if the person to whom they are made knows something which, if revealed, would have been calculated to influence the other to hesitate or seek for further information before speaking positively, and that something has been withheld, the representation ought not to be treated as an estoppel.

1 [1902] AC 117, 145.

Delay in making claim

18.63 Although negligence in making the payment may not result in a defence by the payee, there is no doubt that undue delay in making the claim for the return of money paid under a mistake of fact will allow the defendant to resist, whether the delay is caused by negligence or by some other circumstance, at least in the case where the defendant has changed his or her position.

18.64 The point is illustrated in *General Accident v National Bank of New Zealand*.[1] An insurance company paid an insurance claim which arose from the destruction of a truck by fire. The truck was owned by a company, but the payment was made to the beneficiary bank which held a mortgage over the truck. In October 1929, six months after payment, the plaintiff insurance company discovered that there were false statements in the proposal and that as a result of these, the policy was void. However, they made no claim on the

bank until November 1930, at which time the position of the
company was such that the bank could not have recovered. The
Court held that the plaintiffs must fail since it had with full
knowledge stood by while the bank's chance of recovery vanished,
the money was not recoverable.[2]

1 (1932) 51 NZLR 1289.
2 These facts might today provide a defence under s 94B.

Payment made for good consideration

18.65 The decision in *Aiken v Short*[1] also provides the basis for a
third defence to a claim to recover money paid under a mistake
of fact. There the plaintiff paid money to the defendant in order
to "buy out" the rights of the defendant in the estate in which all
parties mistakenly believed Carter had an interest. Rather than state
the ratio of the case in terms of the "voluntary" nature of the
payment,[2] it is possible to argue that the decision was based on the
fact that the plaintiff paid Carter's debt which was due to the
defendant, and that since the plaintiff had the authority of Carter
to make such a payment the debt was discharged. In such a
circumstance, the defendant gave good consideration for the
payment and it could not be against "good conscience" for the
defendant to retain the money so paid. Robert Goff J notes that
several of the judgments contain explanations of the case which
make this a more attractive basis for the decision than the
"voluntary payment" theory, particularly since the case must simply
be considered wrong if based on the voluntary payment theory.
He quotes Pollack CB who said:

> The Bank had paid the money in one sense without any consideration,
> but the defendant had a perfect right to receive the money from Carter,
> and the bankers paid for him . . . . The money was, in fact, paid by the
> Bank, as agents of Carter.[3]

1 (1856) 1 H & N 210; 156 ER 1180; 25 LJ Ex 321.
2 Discussed above, 18.11ff.
3 *Aiken v Short* (1856) 1 H & N 210, 214, cited by Robert Goff J in *Barclays
Bank Ltd v WJ Simms Son & Cooke (Southern) Ltd* [1979] 3 All ER 522, 529.

18.66 Platt B said:

> Carter referred [the defendant] to the Bank, who paid the debt, and the
> bond was satisfied. The money which the defendant got from her debtor
> was actually due to her, and there can be no obligation to refund it.[1]

1 *Aiken v Short* (1856) 1 H & N 210, 215, cited by Robert Goff J in *Barclays
Bank Ltd v WJ Simms Son & Cooke (Southern) Ltd* [1979] 3 All ER 522, 529.

Summary

18.67 A complete review of the cases concerning the recovery of
money paid under a mistake of fact was undertaken by Robert Goff

J in *Barclays Bank Ltd v W J Simms, Son and Cooke (Southern) Ltd.*[1] Robert Goff J considered that the authorities established the following principles:

> (1) if a person pays money to another under a mistake of fact which causes him to make the payment he is prima facie entitled to recover it as money paid under a mistake of fact.
>
> (2) his claim may, however, fail if
>
> (a) the payer intends that the payee shall have the money at all events, whether the fact be true or false or is deemed in law so to intend;
>
> (b) the payment is made for good consideration, in particular if the money is paid to discharge, and does discharge, a debt owed to the payee (or a principal on whose behalf he is authorised to receive the payment) by the payer or by a third party by whom he is authorised to discharge the debt;
>
> (c) the payee has changed his position in good faith, or is deemed in law to have done so.

1 [1980] QB 677; [1979] 3 All ER 522.

18.68 Part (c) of the defence, although somewhat contentious at common law, is covered in New Zealand by the Judicature Amendment Act 1958.

Where the bank mistakenly pays a cheque: recovery by the bank

18.69 A banker who pays a cheque under a mistake of fact may wish to recover the money from the payee. This may be because the banker is for some reason unable to maintain the debit to the customer's account or, although able to maintain the debit the right is of no value because of the customer's insolvency. There are four situations which seem to cover the cases:

1 the bank pays a cheque mistakenly believing the account of the customer to be adequate to cover the cheque;

2 the banker pays a cheque mistakenly believing that there is authorisation to do so when in fact the cheque has been validly stopped by the customer;

3 the banker pays a cheque believing it to be a cheque of the customer when in fact the cheque has a forged signature; and

4 the banker pays one of his own cheques which has been obtained by fraud.

18.70 The problems in this area have always been complicated by the existence of two quite different views on the recoverability of money paid by mistake on a negotiable instrument to a person who is entirely innocent of the mistake. On the one hand, the need for certainty when dealing with negotiable instruments has tended toward a view that payment should be final, at least if there is any possibility that the payee's position might be altered. The opposing view would bring the law concerning payment on a negotiable instrument more into line with the general law of money paid under a mistake of fact. This view would allow recovery unless the recipient had lost the right of action against some previous party by virtue of the lapse of time for giving notice.

18.71 Throughout the long history of the argument, matters have been clouded by an inability to define the conditions whereby the payee has "changed position" so as to make the money irrecoverable. As will be seen, that confusion remains to this day.

Customer has insufficient funds

18.72 When the banker pays a customer's cheque in the mistaken belief that there are funds available in the account to cover the cheque, the money is not recoverable by the banker, for when the cheque is presented for payment the banker has the authority on the part of his customer to pay the amount and to debit the account, the writing of the cheque being treated in law as a request for an overdraft.[1] The facts thus fall squarely within the second category mentioned by Robert Goff J where the payer is not entitled to recover the sums paid.

1 *Cuthbert v Roberts, Lubbock & Co* [1909] 2 Ch 226.

18.73 Even if there were a complete lack of authority, there would be little reason in policy to allow the bank to recover in this circumstance. The bank is entitled to debit the customer's account since it has in fact followed a valid mandate. The debt owed to the holder of the cheque will have been discharged by the payment. If it turns out that the drawer is insolvent, there would seem no good reason to throw that loss on the recipient of the money instead of upon the banker who made the payment.

Cheque stopped

18.74 The second common mistake which may result in a payment of a cheque which the banker might otherwise not have paid is when a stop payment order by the customer is inadvertently overlooked. In such a circumstance, the general rule will be that the banker is unable to debit the account of the customer since there is no mandate for the making of the payment. The question arises as to whether the banker may recover from the payee.

18.75 A typical example is provided by *Commonwealth Trading Bank v Reno Auto Sales Pty Ltd.*[1] During a weekend a customer of the bank drew a cheque for some £250 and gave it to the defendant company as a down payment on a motor vehicle. The following day he evidently changed his mind concerning the desirability of the car.

He requested his wife to contact the bank early on Monday morning and to "cancel" the cheque. She telephoned the bank on Monday morning and spoke to a woman member of the banking staff. The manager was not informed of the conversation. The Court held, on the evidence before it, that the cheque had not in fact been stopped.[2]

1 [1967] VR 790.
2 See 6.38.

18.76 However, assuming that the cheque had been stopped, the Court considered that the payment by the bank was not one that the bank could recover, seemingly because the defendant was never, even had the mistaken fact been true, under a legal obligation to the defendant to pay the cheque even though there was, of course, an obligation to the bank's own customer. This reasoning is clearly based on the notion that it is necessary that the mistake be of a nature whereby the payer would, if the facts were as believed, be under a legal obligation to pay the money.

18.77 There were almost identical facts in *Southland Savings Bank v Anderson*.[1] A customer of the appellant bank had drawn a cheque for some $400 which had been "marked" by the bank as good for payment. The customer then countermanded payment, but the bank mistakenly paid the cheque. Part of the argument centered on the meaning of "marking" which Quilliam J believed to be:

> . . . no more than the practice which is generally followed in trading banks of notifying the teller that there are sufficient funds at that time to meet the cheque which is presented for payment.[2]

1 [1974] 1 NZLR 118.
2 At p 121.

18.78 Consequently, it was possible for the customer to have countermanded the cheque and in the circumstances it was found that he had done so. The Court found that the mistake was one which was within the principle of *Kelly v Solari*. There was apparently no reference to the decision in *Reno Auto Sales*. The matter was then remitted to the Magistrate for a determination of whether there had been a change of position that would bar the right of recovery under ss 94A or 94B of the Judicature Act.

18.79 In *Barclays Bank Ltd v W J Simms Son & Cooke (Southern) Ltd*[1] a housing association drew a cheque on its account with the plaintiff bank in favour of a building company. There were adequate funds in the account to cover the cheque. The following day a receiver was appointed to the payee company. As a consequence of this appointment, the association gave instructions to stop the cheque, but by mistake the payment was made when the cheque was presented by the receiver for payment. The bank subsequently sought recovery from the receiver as money paid on a mistake of fact.

1 [1980] QB 677.

18.80 By application of the principles outlined above, Robert Goff J held that the bank was entitled to recover. There was clearly no intention that the payee should receive the money if the true facts were known. Further,

> . . . since the drawer had in fact countermanded payment, the bank was acting without mandate and so the payment was not effective to discharge the drawer's obligation on the cheque; from this it follows that the payee gave no consideration for the payment, and the claim cannot be defeated on [the second] ground.[1]

1 At p 542.

18.81 Nor was there any change of position:

> . . . there is no evidence of any actual change of position on the part of either of the defendants or on the part of the [collecting bank]; and, since notice of dishonour is not required in a case such as this, the payee is not deemed to have changed his position by reason of lapse of time in notifying them of Barclays' error and claiming repayment.[1]

1 At p 542.

Summary

18.82 It is rather hard to understand the comments of the Court in *Simms'* case that the payee has not changed his position. The payee was originally in possession of a cheque, but following the recovery of the money by the bank there is only the original consideration to sue upon. As already noted, a claim on a negotiable instrument is a far more advantageous one than the claim in contract. It scarcely seems possible to argue that the payee may still sue on the cheque, for the bank paid it to a holder in good faith and without notice that the title was in any way defective, which indeed it was not in the *Simms* case. Since the cheque was paid in due course,[1] it is discharged and there is no provision in the Act for any doctrine of "revival" of a bill.

1 See s 59, Bills of Exchange Act 1908.

18.83 The problem with the logic of the *Simms* decision seems to revolve around the Court's argument that payment in contravention of the countermand did not discharge the debt owed to the payee. But this can be questioned when the payee honestly presents the cheque, the bank has apparent authority to make the payment, so there is no reason why the payee cannot treat the debt as discharged and hold the drawer bound by the act of the agent. The bank in this situation is scarcely in the position of an officious third party who intervenes to make a payment.

18.84 If that is correct, then the payee is not, as argued by the Court, a person who has received the payment without having given value for it, and consequently could resist the claim for repayment.

18.85 Does it follow that the bank cannot maintain the debit with the result that the drawer receives a windfall? Weaver and Cragie suggest that there is no reason in principle why the bank should not seek to be subrogated to the benefit enjoyed by the drawer on the principle of *Liggett's* case. The same suggestion is made by Goode.[1]

1 "The Bank's Right to Recover Money Paid on a Stopped Cheque" (1981) 97 LQR 254.

Payment on a forgery

18.86 When one or more of the signatures on an instrument are forged, then payment would not be made by the person liable if he or she knew the true facts. At one time it was thought that the person making the payment might be taken to be making a representation to the holder that the signatures were genuine and thereby forming the basis for an estoppel. It would seem, however, that the trend is to assimilating the rules of such payment to those of the general position. In order to understand the present position, it is necessary to consider some of the older cases which form the basis of the modern position.

18.87 In *Price v Neal*[1] the plaintiff was the drawee of two bills of exchange of which the defendant was an indorsee and holder. The first bill was presented to Price for payment and it was promptly paid. The second bill was accepted by Price and indorsed to the defendant and, again, subsequently paid. It turned out that the bills had been forged by a third party; it was found that the defendant had acted throughout in good faith and without any knowledge of the forgeries. Price sought to recover the amounts so paid as money paid under a mistake of fact.

1 (1762) 3 Burr 1354; 97 ER 871.

18.88 The Court held that the action failed, but unfortunately for later applications gave a multiplicity of reasons. Lord Mansfield said that it would not be unconscionable to retain money received as holder for value of a bill of exchange when there is no knowledge of the forgery. He also said that the duty was on the drawee to make sure that the bills were valid before paying or accepting. Finally, if there was any fault or negligence on the part of either of the parties to the transaction it was that of the plaintiff, not of the defendant.

18.89 *Price v Neal* was considered in *Cocks v Masterman*[1] where a bill was genuinely indorsed, but the acceptor's signature had been forged. The plaintiffs were bankers of Sewell and Cross, the apparent acceptors of the bill. The defendants were the holders of the bill which was paid upon presentment. The Court refused to allow recovery. During the course of the judgment, Bayley J said:

The holder of a bill is entitled to know, on the day when it becomes due, whether it is an honoured or dishonoured bill, and that, if he receive the money and is suffered to retain it during the whole of that day, the parties who paid it cannot recover it back. The holder, indeed, is not bound by law (if the bill be dishonoured by the acceptor) to take any steps against the other parties to the bill till the day after it is dishonoured. But he is entitled so to do if he thinks fit, and the parties who pay the bill ought not by their negligence to deprive the holder of any right or privilege.[2]

1 (1829) 9 B & C 902; 109 ER 335.
2 At p 908.

18.90 The entire doctrine was reviewed and expanded in *London and River Plate Bank v Bank of Liverpool.*[1] A bill which was drawn in Montevideo on the London plaintiffs was paid by them to the defendants. The plaintiffs learned that some of the indorsements were forged. When the fact of the forgeries was discovered, the plaintiffs sought to recover the money as money paid under a mistake of fact. It was agreed that the plaintiff bank had no means of verifying the indorsements and that there was no negligence on its part.

1 [1896] 1 QB 7.

18.91 Mathew J refused to allow recovery. He said:

In *Cocks v Masterman* the simple rule was laid down in clear language for the first time that, when a bill becomes due and is presented for payment, the holder ought to know at once whether the bill is going to be paid or not. If the mistake is discovered at once, it may be the money can be recovered aback; but if it be not, and the money is paid in good faith and is received in good faith, and there is an interval of time in which the position of the holder may be altered, the principle seems to apply that money once paid cannot be recovered back. That rule is obviously, as it seems to me, indispensable for the conduct of business . . . . It is one of the few rules of business which is perfectly clear and distinct at present, and, as it seems to me, is unimpeachable.[1]

1 At p 11.

18.92 Consequently, neither the loss of the opportunity of giving notice nor any actual prejudice or damage to the innocent payee is required to allow the holder to keep the money paid under a negotiable instrument. It is only necessary that the amount of time which has elapsed is such that the holder's position may have, not necessarily has, been affected.

18.93 On the other hand, Mathew J seemed to argue that the money is irrecoverable merely because the holder has a right to know at the time of presentment whether or not the instrument is to be paid. If that view were correct, then money paid under a mistake of fact would be irrecoverable even if paid on an unindorsed cheque to the holder/payee.

18.94 The full consequences of the dictum in the *London and River Plate Bank* case were rejected by the Privy Council in *Imperial Bank* *of Canada v Bank of Hamilton.*[1] A customer of the Bank of Hamilton drew a cheque for $5 in which he left spaces after the writing and after the figures. He took the cheque to the Bank of Hamilton where the bank "marked" or "certified" the cheque. The customer then raised the amount of the cheque by writing in "hundred" after the written part and inserting the appropriate figures so that the cheque appeared to be drawn for $500. He then used the cheque to open an account with the Imperial Bank of Canada.

1 [1903] AC 49.

18.95 The cheque was presented through the clearing house to the Bank of Hamilton. It was paid immediately without reference to the customer's account. This was said to be the usual course of business with a cheque which had been certified. A reference to the account would have showed that the account was insufficient to meet the cheque. When the fraud was discovered the next day, the Bank of Hamilton demanded the return of $495.

18.96 The Privy Council allowed recovery of the money and in so doing refused to accept the full strength of Mathew J's argument in the *River Plate* case. The basis of the decision is that

> There were no indorsers to whom notice of dishonour had to be given. The law as to the necessity of giving notice of dishonour has therefore no application. The rule laid down in *Cocks v Masterman*, and recently reasserted in even wider language by Mathew J in *London and River Plate Bank v Bank of Liverpool*, has reference to negotiable instruments, on the dishonour of which notice has to be given to some one, namely, to some drawer or indorser, who would be discharged from liability unless such notice were given in proper time. Their Lordships are not aware of any authority for applying so stringent a rule to any other cases . . . their Lordships are not prepared to extend it to other cases where notice of the mistake is given in reasonable time and no loss has been occasioned by the delay in giving it.[1]

1 At p 58.

18.97 The Privy Council also, and somewhat confusingly, held that the cheque was a "forgery" for the amount of $500, but was a genuine cheque for $5. This was relevant, for it was said that the cheque as drawn and certified was never dishonoured and so no question could arise about that, but that the cheque for the larger amount was a simple forgery.

18.98 This was the confusing state of the law when Kerr J considered *National Westminster Bank Ltd v Barclays Bank International Ltd.*[1] A customer of the plaintiff bank lived in Nigeria. In late 1971, while he was away, his house was broken into and various items taken. It was not noticed at the time that a cheque from the middle of a spare chequebook was one of the items taken. The matter first came to his attention when a debit of £8,000 appeared on the statement of account. He notified the plaintiff immediately of the forgery.

1 [1975] QB 654.

18.99 The money had been collected by the first defendant bank for the account of the second defendant, a Mr Ismail. The money was still in the account and Barclays took no active part in the defence.

18.100 Mr Ismail was a businessman who wished to transfer some Nigerian currency out of the country in contravention of the Nigerian currency laws. He was approached by a person who offered to sell him the cheque in question at a price quoted in Nigerian currency which, of course, far exceeded the official exchange rate. Mr Ismail was cautious and refused to pay until such time as the cheque was cleared.

18.101 Mr Ismail relied on three grounds for his defence:

1 estoppel by representation, in that by paying the cheque (which was specially presented) the plaintiff represented that the signature was genuine;

2 change of position; Mr Ismail claimed that on the faith of the payment he had changed his position by virtue of paying for the bad cheque;

3 the plaintiff owes a duty of care when paying cheques and the payment breached this duty.

18.102 The Court (Kerr J) held that the plaintiff bank was not negligent in their payment of the cheque. Part of this argument was based on a supposed duty of the plaintiff bank to know its own customer's signature. Kerr J provided an extremely valuable statement of the role of the signature:

> The common aphorism that a banker is under a duty to know his customer's signature is in fact incorrect even as between the banker and the customer. The principle is simply that a banker cannot debit his customer's account on the basis of a forged signature, since he has in that event no mandate from the customer for doing so.[1]

1 At p 666.

18.103 It was noted that the defence of change of position requires that the defendant establish all of the requirements of an estoppel. The matter of the estoppel was dealt with by Kerr J in the following terms:

> It seems to me . . . that Mr Ismail can in the present case only succeed in raising an estoppel against the plaintiffs if the mere fact of a banker honouring a cheque on which his customer's signature has been undetectably forged carries with it an implied representation that the signature is genuine. I cannot see any logical basis for this. At most . . . the paying banker is thereby representing no more than that he believes the signature to be genuine.[1]

1 At p 674.

18.104 It was argued strongly that although that might be the case for normal presentment through the clearing house, that the situation is surely different when it is presented specially. The Court held that the same rule applies, since the reason for special presentment is to find if there are funds available, not if there is a forgery.

18.105 Kerr J also noted briefly that even if there had been a representation, Mr Ismail could not rely upon it since it had been induced at least partly by Ismail himself when taking a cheque that was clearly suspect. This is merely an application of the general rule noted above at 18.61.

Summary: payment on a forgery or a stopped cheque

18.106 The end result of this line of cases appears to be that the law concerning the recovery of money paid by mistake on a negotiable instrument is the same as the general law of recovery of money paid under a mistake of fact except in the case where the holder of the instrument would be obliged to give notice to previous parties in the event of dishonour. In that special case, the resulting detriment is thought to be so obvious that it will be presumed, at least if repayment is not claimed immediately by the mistake payer.

18.107 Consequently, when payment is on a forged cheque which bears no valid indorsements, then recovery may be made. Similarly, when the payment is made on a stopped cheque which is unindorsed. The second of these conclusions is based on the assumptions, questioned above, that Robert Goff J is correct in the assertion that the payee of a stopped cheque suffers no change of position and that the payment by the bank does not have the effect of discharging the debt owed by the drawer to the payee.

Chapter 19

Other payment systems

19.1 If the legal nature of a cheque is reconsidered for a moment, it will be recalled that it is an order from the drawer of the cheque to his or her banker, to make a payment to a named person or to that person's order. When considered as such, it must be viewed as somewhat peculiar that the cheque, ie, the order, is then sent not to the banker, but rather to the intended recipient of the funds. Of course, the reason for this is the historical identification of the cheque as a species of negotiable instrument which is valuable in its own right quite apart from its value as an order to the banker.

19.2 If the order could be given directly to the banker, then many of the opportunities for frauds would simply disappear, for a significant number of cheque frauds involve the interception of the cheque between the time it leaves the drawer and the time when it should be received by the payee.

19.3 This simple idea of directing the order to the banker directly rather than through the payee is the basis for a system of payment which has been used successfully in European countries for some years. The system, which has also been successfully introduced into the United Kingdom, is known as the GIRO. Since the GIRO system is particularly easy to implement in a totally electronic form, it is expected that more and more payments will be made by GIRO-type payment orders. The Databank system already handles a significant number of such payments and the number may be expected to grow as the handling of cheques becomes more and more expensive.

GIRO systems generally

19.4 It is probably easier to describe the paper based system of GIRO payments at the outset. Once the paper system is understood, the electronic form presents few new problems.

Basic description

19.5 A typical GIRO payment requires the person who wishes to make the payment, the payer, to instruct his or her bank concerning the details of the payment to be made. In the typical implementation of the GIRO system, this is done by writing on a printed form the amount of the payment to be made, the account which is to be debited, the bank which is to receive the payment and the details of the account at that bank which is to be credited.

19.6 The terminology which is used in describing GIRO systems varies somewhat. The bank at which the transaction is initiated is usually called the paying bank or the transferring bank. The bank at which the account is to be credited is called the recipient bank. The person initiating the transfer of the type described in the preceding paragraph is called the payer and the person whose account is to be credited is the payee.

19.7 There are some variations on the basic transfer described above. In the UK, there are two separate GIROs in operation, one, the National Girobank, operated by the Post Office and a bank giro which is operated by the major trading banks. By agreement between the parties, it is possible to initiate the transfer from any one of the institutions participating in either of the GIROs. Further, the payment may be initiated by a person who does not maintain a bank account by lodging the appropriate sum with the transferring bank. This is a valuable feature for low income earning families who traditionally had to resort to more expensive forms of payment.

19.8 A further variation on the basic theme is the use of magnetic media to give instructions to the bank. This may be done, for example, by larger institutions which have a large number of relatively small payments to make on a periodic basis. The instructions for the transfers are encoded in a computer readable format on the magnetic media and delivered to the institution's bank whiichthen makes the payments in accordance with the instructions. The use of such payment mechanisms to meet payroll obligations results in a substantial reduction in the number of cheques which must be used.

19.9 A more significant departure from the transactions described above is the possibility of the payee initiating the transaction. The obvious possibility for abuse means that strict controls must be implemented, but provided that this is done, the procedure may result in substantial savings in system costs. A typical use of this system of "direct debit" is the payment of insurance premiums or of other regular payments which are likely to be of varying amounts. In such a situation, the standing order is not appropriate but the institutional payee may prepare instructions on magnetic media which are then delivered to the recipient bank.

19.10 Note that a GIRO system requires a system of clearing. It would be prohibitively expensive to arrange for actual cash movements to accompany each transfer order. Further, in a GIRO system, the method of settlement will almost certainly be by accounts held by the participating institutions with the central bank of the country.

Credit transfers

19.11 When there is a GIRO system in place there may be a very large number of payments made by the above system. However, the principles are not limited to GIRO systems. Many payments are made both domestically and internationally by forms which have the same functional and legal structure.

19.12 The basic transaction described above is called a "credit transfer". The transaction is initiated by the payer and is often described as "pushing" the funds from the transferor to the transferee. The transferring bank advises, possibly with the assistance of an intermediary bank or other institution, the recipient bank of the transfer. The recipient bank then credits the account of the payee and notifies the payee of that fact.

19.13 The feature which distinguishes the general credit transfer from the corresponding transaction in a GIRO system is that it is not necessary to have an existing clearing system. Further, in many circumstances the method of settlement between the banks may be decided on a case by case basis.

19.14 In an international transfer, the recipient bank must be reimbursed in some way for the amount which is to be credited to the account of the payee. The most common way for this to be done is either through the crediting and debiting of accounts held by the transferring bank and the recipient bank on behalf of the other. Thus, a New Zealand bank may keep an account in American dollars with a New York bank. When a credit transfer is arranged on behalf of a New Zealand payer and a New York payee, the New Zealand bank will send the appropriate credit order to the New York bank but will also include an indication that the account held by the New York bank is to be debited. Alternatively, the New Zealand bank may indicate that the account held by it on behalf of the New York bank will be credited. In the language of international banking, the first arrangement is a debit of the "nostro" account, the second is a credit to the "vostro" account.

19.15 If the banks do not hold mutual nostro/vostro accounts then settlement will necessarily involve a third bank. This could be a bank at which both the transferring and the recipient banks hold accounts or it could be a more complex arrangement.

Debit transfers

19.16 In a debit transfer, the transaction is initiated by the payee. In international transactions, the debit transfer will nearly always be accompanied by a bill of exchange or other negotiable instrument and the legal aspects of the transfer tend to be dominated by the law applicable to the instrument. However, there is no logical need for the instrument and a debit transfer may follow the general principles of the GIRO direct debit. Again, means of settlement between the participating institutions will need to be identified and agreed upon.

19.17 One of the reasons that the debit transfer is usually accompanied by a negotiable instrument is that there is a fundamental commercial difference between the credit and the debit transfer. In the credit transfer, there is no need for any institution to concern themselves with the solvency of the payer. When the advice is received to credit the account of the payee, the payer has either placed the money with the transferring bank or that bank is willing to grant credit to the payer. In either case, the recipient bank is unconcerned with the financial position of the payer. Another way of putting it is that the solvency of the payer is relevant only to the initiation of the transaction. By contrast, the direct debit transaction relies upon the solvency of the payer to be completed. Until that time, it is possible that the participants may need to "unwind" the transaction and so to rely upon the credit and the liability of prior parties to the transaction. When that occurs, the law relating to negotiable instruments makes the procedures much more reliable.

EFT systems

19.18 The term "electronic funds transfer" refers to a number of related systems which have as their common characteristic the use of computer technology and as their common effect a reduction in the growth of the amount of paper which is involved in the payments system.

Domestic EFT systems

MICR cheques

19.19 The earliest use of computers in the payment system was concerned not with the elimination of paper but with the efficient handling of cheques. Cheques are printed on forms which contain information which may be read by machines and processed by computers. The cheques are known as MICR cheques, the adjective being an acronym for magnetic ink character recognition, the strangely shaped numbers and letters which are now familiar to all bank customers.

19.20 When the MICR chequebook is issued to the customer, the MICR figures already on the cheque contain information which identifies the drawee bank and branch and the account information of the customer. In order to make possible machine handling and accounting, other information must be added to the cheque after it has been drawn. Consequently, the collecting bank adds MICR figures which identify the amount of the cheque, the branch of the collecting bank and the account for which the cheque is being collected. Because of the consequences of a mistake when this information is added, it is to all intents and purposes added twice and the results compared for conformity.

19.21 Since the deposit slips are also MICR coded, the procedure supplies enough information for the accounting and the clearing process to be completed by the computer processes. There is little doubt that the cheque system could not have achieved anything like the volume of cheques now processed without the aid of the MICR system.

Money transfers

19.22 On the other hand, processing the paper in the cheque system remains one of the most costly features of the system. In those circumstances where it is possible to dispense with the paper there are substantial opportunities for saving transaction costs. The Databank system which serves New Zealand banks permits and encourages the use of credit transfers in those situations where the payer is likely to have a large number of payments to make. Similarly, debit transfers are used when it is possible to make the appropriate safeguards against abuse.

POS

19.23 The final stage of development in an EFT system is to remove the need for cash entirely. In the point of service (POS) system, there is a computer terminal at the retail or service outlet which is connected directly with the computers of the bank or other service organisation which operates the system. By means of the card/PIN combination, the customer is able to order immediate payment to be made for the goods or services. The retailer or other service provider is assured of same day payment.

19.24 POS systems make large computing and communications demands and so are expensive to install. They are likely to be preferred by financial institutions because of the elimination of the float and they may be preferred by retailers if the cost of the transaction is not too large. It is difficult to see why they should be preferred by customers unless the costs of credit cards are increased so as to make the customer bear the costs of the extended credit which is now available for free.

International transfers

19.25 In the international transfer of funds, electronic devices are used in ways which are slightly different from the domestic applications. In many transactions, the computers and other communications equipment function solely as a message transmission system. They may replace telex or postal messages only because of their speed or because it is widely believed that the possibilities and chances of error are much smaller with the electronic systems.

SWIFT

19.26 By far the most significant of these message systems is that operated by the Society for Worldwide Interbank Financial Telecommunications (SWIFT). All SWIFT messages are passed first to a regional "condenser" and then by satellite to the central "switch" in Brussels where they are stored (if required) and re-routed to their destination. They are received, again by a regional centre and then forwarded to the destination bank. Messages must contain prescribed information and be in a prescribed format.

Electronic clearing systems

19.27 There are several large EFT systems which function as clearing and settlement mechanisms for certain types of international payments. Payments handled by these systems are typically very large and are restricted to bank to bank payments.

CHIPS/CHAPS

19.28 The best known of these systems is the CHIPS system in New York. CHIPS is an acronym for Clearing House for Interbank Payments System. The operation of the CHIPS system was described in some detail in *Delbrueck v Manufacturers Hanover Trust Co.*[1]

Delbrueck sent a telex message to Manufacturers which was tested and verified according to standard "answer back" procedures. The essence of the message was that Manufacturers was to pay a sum to Chase for the account of one of Delbrueck's clients, Herstatt.

1 464 F Supp 989 (SDNY 1979); affd 609 F 2d 1047 (2d Cir 1979).

19.29 After verification of the telex, staff at Manufacturers keyed into a computer terminal connected to the CHIPS computer all of the relevant identifying codes for each of the parties and details of the payment to be made. The message was then stored by the CHIPS computer awaiting the time when the payment was to be made, but in the meantime all of the relevant accounting records were retrieved and a "sending form" was sent to the sending branch of Manufacturers. This sending form is printed and contains a written record of the transaction ordered. The sending form must be approved by an appropriate officer of the bank.

19.30 When this approval is obtained, the message may be "released" by the officer keying in special (and secret) key sequences. When this occurs, a credit ticket is printed at Chase, a debit ticket at Manufacturers and the accounts held by the clearing house by the two banks are adjusted accordingly. Settlement is made at the end of each banking day by accounts held with the Federal Reserve Bank.

19.31 The CHIPS system has a curious rule which will be discussed in more detail below. In certain circumstances, the transferring bank is entitled to call back an ordered credit transfer. The effect is to "unwind" certain transactions. In such circumstances, the parties must consider that the effect of a CHIPS transfer is conditional until the time allowed for revocation has expired.

19.32 The CHAPS system in London operates in a fashion which is quite similar to the CHIPS operation, but the rules consider a credit transfer to be irrevocable once communicated.

Legal questions arising

19.33 Regardless of the medium used to facilitate credit and debit transfers, the fundamental legal problems remain the same. Whether an international transfer is ordered by telex or by SWIFT, it may still be important to know the legal relationships between the payer and the various banks involved in the transfer. Some of the cases are concerned with the very difficult problem of determining precisely when it can be said that the payment is complete.

19.34 Although the legal problems are the same, the method of transfer used has made a difference to the importance the problem is likely to assume in a dispute. A postal transfer is probably used when the parties are not very concerned about the time of payment. However, with the recently prevalent high interest rates, a payer who is obliged to make a large payment may wish to retain the benefit of the amount until the last minute and so may choose to use a SWIFT transfer with the expectation that the payment may be made quickly once ordered. With a tighter timetable comes the occasional error and a legal problem which was at one time mainly of academic interest becomes one of considerable practical importance.

Preliminary legal observations

19.35 Before considering the particular legal problems involved in funds transfers, it is worth considering a few general comments concerning the relationships in a credit or debit transfer.

Agency

19.36 The first is that the law of agency is likely to be of overwhelming importance in the solution of any of the legal problems. Thus, in a credit transfer, it is clear that the transferring bank is acting as an agent for the payer. The transferring bank may then instruct the recipient bank directly or by means of some intermediary bank. It is difficult to see how the direct contractual relationships involved can be anything other than agencies. The difficulties will usually be to determine the scope of the agency and whether two particular parties are or are not in a contractual relationship. It will not always be easy to determine on whose behalf a bank may be acting in a particular transaction.

Transfer of balances

19.37 A second preliminary point is to note what should by now be obvious. The "payment" that we are concerned with is not the transfer of cash. In all cases, the resulting changes effected by the transaction will be a change in institutional liabilities.

19.38 Thus, in the simplest case of the payer and the payee having accounts at the same bank, a credit transfer amounts merely to debiting the payer's account and crediting the payee's account with the same amount. The effect of the transfer has been to change the liabilities of the banker.

19.39 When the transfer is more complex, there may be several such changes. In the international transfer where settlement is by accounts held by a third bank, then the institutional liabilities of all of the participating institutions are changed. The transferring bank's liability to the payer is reduced by the amount of the transfer, the recipient bank becomes liable to the payee for the amount and the third bank reduces its liability to the transferring bank and increases its liability to the recipient bank by the same amount.

19.40 It is important to keep the point in mind when discussing the time at which payment is made, for the answer to the question may depend upon the form of settlement and the identity of the parties to the dispute. That is, the time of payment between the payer and the payee might not necessarily be the time of payment as between the transferring bank and the recipient bank.

Legal nature of the transfers

19.41 A transfer of funds may be initiated in several ways. The payer may instruct his or her bank by means of a written or a printed form, by means of instructions coded on a magnetic medium, by means of direct input from a computer terminal using identifying codes or by means of direct input from an ATM using the plastic card and PIN. In all cases this amounts to a mandate to the banker and there seems little doubt that the banker is obliged to follow the mandate strictly and having done so has the authority to debit the account of the customer for the amount of the transfer. The fact is, then, that the order to make a transfer looks very much like a cheque and the question arises whether an order to make a transfer may be a negotiable instrument.

Negotiable instruments?

19.42 There is no reason to suppose that transfer orders are treated as negotiable instruments by commercial custom. Consequently, the only way in which they could be considered as such is if they were to fall within the definition of a bill of exchange. Since a bill of exchange must be in writing, that would seem to exclude all those orders which are transmitted electronically or by means of a magnetic medium.

19.43 As to those instructions which are in writing, the document must be an unconditional order. This will depend upon the actual form of the words used. It is said that the forms used in the United Kingdom cannot be construed as a formal order to the banker.[1]

1 Ellinger "The Giro System and Electronic Transfers of Funds" [1986] 2 LMCLQ 178.

19.44 When the order is in the form of a telex, the Court of Appeal in England was prepared to hold that mere receipt of the telex message did not constitute payment since to do so would be to elevate the telex to the status of a negotiable instrument.[1] Perhaps the best approach is simply to note that none of the parties conceive of the orders to be negotiable instruments, that is, they are not negotiable instruments because of commercial custom regardless of whether they fit the formal definition of a bill of exchange. There is certainly no danger of a transfer order being mistaken for a bill even if the order fulfils the formal definition.

1 *The Brimnes* [1976] QB 835. The decision of the Court of Appeal was reversed by the House of Lords [1977] AC 850, but the principles relating to the time of payment do not seem to have been altered.

19.45 The matter is of more than mere academic interest, for if a transfer order is fraudulently issued or altered then the rights of the parties will depend solely on the law of agency and contract.

Assignments

19.46 Chorley argues that the legal nature of the direct credit transaction is one of assignment of a debt.[1] The argument is a natural one on a functional view of the transaction: at the beginning, a debtor D owes a debt to a creditor C; at the termination of the transaction, the recipient banker owes a debt to C, but D does not. At a functional level, a debt appears to have been transferred; in our law, the means of transferring a debt are limited. Since the entire transaction occurs by the issuing of instructions, it is natural to attempt the conceptual analysis by resort to the law of assignment.

1 Chorley, *The Law of Banking* (6th ed London, 1974).

19.47 An assignment may be either an equitable assignment or a statutory assignment as prescribed in s 130 of the Property Law Act 1952. The effect of an assignment is to transfer to the assignee all rights of the assignor.[1] An equitable assignment need not take any special form so long as the intent to assign is clear, but for the present purposes it is essential to note that a mandate to pay is different from an assignment.[2]

1 See Ch 24.
2 The difference is clear as regards the legal concepts though the distinction may not always be an easy one to draw from the facts in a given case; compare *Ex parte Hall* (1878) 10 Ch D 615 with *Re Williams* [1917] 1 Ch 1.

19.48 There are compelling arguments against considering the direct credit transaction as an assignment, the most telling of these being the contrast between the parties' intentions and expectations and the results of the assignment model. First, the payee would be in a stronger position than if he accepted a cheque, for he would be able to maintain an action directly against the banker in the case of a failure to credit. Secondly, the instructions to the paying banker would be irrevocable once the payee had notice of such instructions, for it is then that the assignment is complete; that this result cannot be contemplated by the paying banker is evidenced by the warning at the bottom of the monthly statement which warns that indicated credits may be later reversed. There is an additional argument against it being a statutory assignment. Section 130 of the Property Law Act 1952 has been held to be inapplicable to the assignment of part of a debt.[1] Yet the transfer of the whole account would be an extremely rare occurrence.

1 *Williams v Atlantic Assurance Co* [1933] KB 81, *Walter & Sullivan Ltd v J Murphy & Sons Ltd* [1955] 2 QB 584.

19.49 These results, clearly not contemplated by any of the parties to the transfer scheme, seem to show conclusively that a credit transfer is neither an equitable nor a statutory assignment of funds. In truth, the law of assignments is not necessary to explain the credit transfer system. Much more in accord with the expectations of the parties is the simple agency model.

19.50 This view seems to have been accepted by Webster J in *Royal Products Ltd v Midland Bank Ltd.*[1] He said:

> [Credit transfers] are to be regarded simply as an authority and instruction, from a customer to its bank, to transfer an amount standing to the credit of that customer with that bank to the credit of its account with another bank, that other bank being impliedly authorised by the customer to accept that credit by virtue of the fact that the customer has a current account with it, no consent to the receipt of the credit being expected from or required of that other bank, by virtue of the same fact. It is, in other words, a banking operation, of a kind which is often carried out internally, that is to say, within the same bank or between two branches of the same bank and which, at least from the point of view of the customer, is no different in nature or quality when, as in the present case, it is carried out between different banks.[2]

1 [1981] 2 Lloyd's Rep 147.
2 At p 198.

Trust

19.51 The position of a customer or some stranger who places money or effects with the banker together with a request that the funds be transferred will be considered. Is the money or effects impressed with a trust? It is certainly true that moneys which are placed with a bank for a specific purpose may be impressed with a trust to the extent that if the purpose fails then the moneys are held in trust by the banker for the customer. When that happens, the moneys may not be retained against any amount owed by the customer to the banker.[1]

1 See, for example, *Re Kayford Ltd (in liquidation)* [1975] 1 WLR 279 and the discussion in Ch 8.

19.52 However, it is thought that these cases depend on the fact that the funds originated not with the customer but with some other party who was intended to remain the beneficial owners of the funds even though the customer of the banker was the legal depositor. In *Re Kayford*, for example, the funds originated with customers of the company who paid for goods which were not then delivered. The funds so received by the company had been placed to the credit of a dormant deposit account.

19.53 Although the matter cannot be considered free from doubt, it is thought that the banker does not hold as trustee, but rather in the ordinary way is a debtor to the customer for the amount of the funds so deposited. Should the transfer fail for some reason, then the customer/payer is in the position of any other creditor of the bank.

Legal position of the participants

19.54 When considering the legal position of the participating banks in a funds transfer, it will be assumed that the foregoing is correct and that the order to transfer funds is neither a negotiable instrument nor an assignment of funds held by the banker on behalf of the customer.

Transferring bank

19.55 As agent for the customer, the transferring bank is obliged to carry out its duties with an appropriate level of care and skill. Since it is following a mandate from the customer, it is obliged to follow the mandate strictly and will be prima facie unable to debit the account of the customer if it acts otherwise. Of course, it also follows that the customer is under an obligation to give clear and unambiguous instructions. Although there does not appear to be any case law directly on the point, it would seem that if the transfer order is drawn in such a way as to facilitate a fraud to be perpetrated on the banker, then the customer would be liable under the principles of *London Joint Stock Bank Ltd v Macmillan and Arthur.*[1]

1 [1918] AC 777; and see the discussion in Ch 3.

Strict compliance with mandate

19.56 When it is said that the banker must follow the mandate strictly, this must be taken to mean that the banker must transfer the amount which is specified in the mandate and the transfer must be to the proper person. It is not generally relevant how the transferring banker effects the transfer, provided only that it is done with the required degree of care and skill.

19.57 The point is illustrated by *Royal Products Ltd v Midland Bank Ltd.*[1] The plaintiffs instructed the defendant bank to transfer funds to one of their own accounts with the B bank in Malta. It was their intention later to transfer the funds on to the N bank in Malta. The defendant bank effected the transfer by using their correspondent in Malta which happened to be the N bank.

1 [1981] 2 Lloyds Rep 194.

19.58 One of the issues in the case was whether the defendant bank was precluded from debiting the account by virtue of the fact that they did not follow the mandate given by the customer, namely to transfer the funds to the B bank. The Court held that the defendant bank had not been in breach of its mandate. In so holding, Webster J indicated that when construing instructions for a money transfer it is not necessary to give a legal implication to each detail of the order.

19.59 This is undoubtedly correct, but it should not be supposed that the customer is precluded from ordering that a transfer should occur in a particular way. If the plaintiffs had indicated to the defendant bank that they wished the funds to be transferred to the B bank without the use of correspondents or with the use of some particular method, there seems little doubt that the wishes would be respected by the Court. In the *Royal Products* case, the real point is that it is not necessary to read each order in an attempt to divine some special wishes on the part of the payer, since in the ordinary course of events the precise path taken by the payment is quite irrelevant to the payer. It is, of course, open to the bank to decline a request for a transfer which it considers to be too onerous or which it cannot carry out.

The duty of care and skill

19.60 The fact that the way in which the mandate is carried out will usually be at the discretion of the bank means that these functions must be carried out with due care and skill. The essential steps involved in carrying out the mandate are that it must be timely and that if a correspondent is used, then that correspondent must be a choice which is both reasonable and reliable.

Transfer must be timely

19.61 What amounts to a timely transfer will depend upon the circumstances. If the customer specifies a particular time then the bank would be prima facie in breach of its duties if the transfer is not made at that time. If there is no time specified, then the transfer must be made in a reasonable time, a time which will very likely depend upon the mode of transfer specified by the customer if any.

Reliable correspondent

19.62 The duty to provide a reasonable and reliable correspondent is expressed in part by the rule that the bank is liable for the default of its correspondent. The principle was originally developed and expressed in the context of documentary letters of credit. Whatever the scope of the duty when applied to funds transfers, it is unlikely to be a matter of practical consideration, for the contract between banker and customer is ry likely to contain a term which provides that the correspondent bank is employed at the risk and the expense of the customer. It seems unlikely that these kind of exemption clauses could be successfully challenged by a customer.

Correspondent bank

19.63 Although there seems to be no direct authority as to the position of the correspondent bank in a direct funds transfer, it seems that it would be the same as that of a bank which agrees to present a foreign bill for acceptance or for payment. If that is the case, then under the common law there is no privity of contract between the correspondent bank and the payer for whom the transfer is being made. In other words, the correspondent is the agent only of the transferring bank and not of the customer of that bank. The point may be of importance when the payer suffers losses caused by the negligence of the correspondent bank, for although the transferring bank is liable for the negligence of its agent, it is a liability which may be, and nearly always is, excluded by contract.

19.64 The situation may be illustrated by a consideration of the decision in *Calico Printers' Association v Barclays Bank Ltd.*[1] Barclays acted on behalf of the plaintiff for the purposes of presenting a bill of exchange to the buyers of goods. Barclays in turn employed the AP bank as a correspondent for the purpose. The bill was dishonoured and the AP bank arranged for the goods to be stored in a warehouse but was guilty of "a gross breach of the most elementary business precautions"[2] in failing to have them insured. Barclays escaped liability by means of an exclusion clause and the AP bank was held not to be liable since there was no privity of contract with the plaintiff.[3]

1 (1930) 36 Com Cas 71.
2 (1931) 4 LDAB 262, 263.
3 This does not, of course, exclude the possibility that the correspondent bank may be liable in tort. The matter will be discussed below at 19.68.

The recipient bank

19.65 It is clear that the recipient bank is acting as an agent in a funds transfer, but it may not be clear for whom the bank is acting. As will be seen below, it is important that the recipient bank have the authority to receive the funds on behalf of the payee and in the absence of such authority the payment may remain incomplete.

19.66 In the "standard" credit transfer where the payee nominates the recipient bank and the payer requests the transferring bank to make the transfer to that recipient bank, it is thought that the principles discussed above in relation to the correspondent bank apply and that there is no privity of contract between the payer and the recipient bank.

19.67 It is hard to see what facts could arise to change this basic conclusion. Even in the case where the payer requests the transfer without the consent of the payee, perhaps in the hope that the payee will accept the payment as timely even though the recipient bank is not authorised to receive it on the payee's behalf, there is no reason to suppose that the recipient bank is acting in any way on behalf of the payer. However, it must be acknowledged that the situation is less certain than might be hoped. We can only agree with Paget: "It is unwise to generalise, for much depends upon the whole circumstances of the credit transaction".[1]

1 *Paget*, p 571.

Liability to payer: consequential damage

19.68 As we have already noted, there is unlikely to be any contractual privity between the payer and any of the participating banks other than the transferring bank. This assures the banks that there can be no contractual liability to the payer, but at the same time assures the payer that the banks may not rely upon contractual exclusion clauses in order to escape tort liability. This section examines the possibility that there could be such a liability.

19.69 It is useful to consider briefly the types of losses which may occur when a funds transfer fails to go as expected by all of the parties. UNCITRAL has classified the nature of the losses which may occur into four categories: loss of principle, loss of interest, losses due to exchange rate fluctuations in international transfers, and consequential losses.[1] Any system of funds transfer must adopt rules which allocate losses of the first three types among the participating institutions. While these rules might be important for an individual institution, the actual liability rule merely shifts losses around within the system and so may not be particularly important in the long run.

1 UNCITRAL, Electronic Funds Transfers, A/CN 9/221, 1982.

19.70 Consequential damage is in class all of its own. Much of the litigation as to the time of payment has concerned late payment made under contracts of hire which have a clause which makes time of payment of the essence of the contract. In such a circumstance, a late payment which may result in no losses at all of the first three types may result in substantial contractual disadvantages to the party who was required to make the payment. In charterparties, these losses may be very high and the issue of liability of the system for such losses is an important one.

19.71 An example is *Evra Corp v Swiss Banking Corp.*[1] The Court at first instance allowed the plaintiff damages on the order of $2 million when the defendant bank negligently failed to make a $27,000 payment on the value date. The decision was reversed by the Court of Appeal on the grounds that the loss was not "foreseeable".

1 522 F Supp 820; rev 673 F 2d 951.

19.72 A reading of the *Evra* case shows that it will not automatically be resolved in the same way in New Zealand. The essence of the Court's reasoning was twofold: a strict interpretation of the requirements of the second limb of *Hadley v Baxendale*[1] and an acceptance of the proposition that the standard of foreseeability in tort is the same as that required in contract. In the current state of law, both limbs of the argument are likely to fail in a New Zealand Court.

1 (1854) 9 Exch 341.

19.73 The strict interpretation of the requirements of foreseeability in *Hadley v Baxendale* is probably precluded by the House of Lords decision in the *Heron II*[1] which imposed a test of "not unlikely" having regard to the knowledge of the parties at the time the contract was made as the measure of foreseeability required to impose liability. It is instructive to consider the factual situation in the *Heron II*: owing to a contractual breach a cargo of sugar was delivered nine days late to the port of Basrah. The shipowner knew that the other party was a sugar merchant, but did not know that it was intended to sell the cargo immediately. The market dropped and the shipowner was held liable for the amount of the loss. Are the losses which were suffered in *Evra* less foreseeable than the losses in the *Heron II*?

1 *Koufos v Carnikow Ltd (Heron II)* [1969] 1 AC 350.

19.74 The second limb of the *Evra* argument would have little chance in New Zealand where it is generally accepted that whatever the tort test is for foreseeability, it is undoubtedly less demanding than the contractual test.[1] Recent English cases have extended the duty and the foreseeability concept to a point which would seem to easily encompass the *Evra* loss. For example, in *Dove v Banhams Patent Locks Ltd*,[2] the defendants negligently installed a security door in a private home. The home was sold to the plaintiff. Twelve years following the installation of the door, burglars entered the house through the door and stole some antique silver. The plaintiff succeeded in recovering the loss.

1 *The Wagon Mound* [1961] AC 388; *Shirt v Wyong Shire Council* [1978] 1 NSWLR 631; *Mount Isa Mines v Pusey* (1970) 125 CLR 383.
2 [1983] 2 All ER 833.

19.75 Further, there is no problem which arises from the loss being purely economic, since it is clear that the problem fits comfortably within the *Caltex* test.[1]

1 *Caltex Oil (Australia) Pty Ltd v The Dredge "Willemstad"* (1976) 136 CLR 529.

19.76 If this is correct, then it is not necessarily a very desirable outcome. Although it is right that there should be a duty on banks to use all care and skill in making the transfer, it is not obvious that the transfer system should bear all of the costs of mistakes, even when the mistake is caused by carelessness. If the payer chooses to become a party to a contract where such a minor default can have such major consequences, there is no obvious reason why that risk should then effectively be transferred to a banker who has no real relationship with the payer.

Time of payment

19.77 The actual time at which payment is completed may be of importance in a number of circumstances. The customer may require that a transfer be completed at a particular time; failure to do so may result in financial losses to the customer. One of the participants in the EFT system may fail; how are the losses to be spread throughout the system? The account of a customer may be attached or frozen in some way; which transactions have been completed?

19.78 As a preliminary point, it is well to note that even in a domestic EFT system there will be many transactions which are not "instantaneous" for the purposes of this discussion. There are a number of transactions such as monthly credits or debits for payroll transactions and the like which are obviously delayed, but even in "on-line" systems, the transactions may be held in suspense until some previously defined settlement or clearing time.[1]

1 In the jargon, the machines may be "on-line" but the transactions are not "real time".

19.79 A further point to note in this context is that the problems are not all amenable to solution through the legal medium of contract. While inter-institutional problems may be solved by a multi-lateral agreement similar to the present clearing house rules for cheques and while conflict between institution and customer may be regulated by the conditions of use imposed by the institution (subject to such vagaries as the Credit Contracts Act 1981 and other consumer legislation), some of the issues involve parties who are not in direct contractual proximity. This is obvious in the context of international transfers, but is no less true in domestic transfers.

19.80 As a final preliminary comment, note that there are at least two distinct problems. The first is to determine the time of payment as between the institutions. The second is to determine the time of payment as between the payer and the payee. These two problems may have different solutions.

19.81 Some of the fundamental terminology should be recalled. "Clearing" is essentially a bookkeeping process whereby relatively large numbers of transactions between relatively few financial institutions are amalgamated and set-off against each other to minimise the required transfer of funds between the institutions.[1] In an ideal world, transfers from institution A to institution B would be exactly matched by transfers in the opposite direction so that no funds at all would need to be exchanged. In the real world, such perfect symmetry fails to occur: the required periodic transfer of funds is known as "settlement".

1 The terminology is taken from UNCITRAL, Electronic Funds Transfers, A/CN 9/221, 1982.

19.82 It is not generally appreciated that the "exposure" of a financial institution in a payments system may be substantial. The CHIPS system in New York handles (1981 figures) more than 55,000 transactions a day with an average value in excess of $3 million[1] with the result that participants regularly clear items having a value well in excess of their total worth.[2] Comparable figures do not seem to be available for a consumer oriented EFT system, but since the obvious aim is to replace the paper based system, the amounts will be large. As more and smaller institutions enter the payments system, failures must be expected and the time of payment becomes a question of fundamental importance.

1 Mayer, "The Settlements Revolution" [1981] Institutional Investor 358.
2 Revell, *Banking and Electronic Funds Transfers*, OECD 1983.

19.83 At some point in time, the transfer of funds from the transferring bank to the recipient bank must be considered as final in the sense that the transferring bank can no longer stop or recall the transfer. It seems sensible to call this time the time of payment. Although there is no logical reason why the time of payment as between the transferor and the ultimate transferee need be the same, it is clear that the time of payment as between these parties cannot be earlier than the time of payment as between the two institutions. And, if the transferring bank cannot recall the transfer, it would seem that the same time might be the prima facie time of payment between the transferor and transferee. There may, however, be circumstances which would delay the time of payment as between the end parties.[1]

1 Such as those which occurred in *The Chikuma* [1981] 1 WLR 314; see 19.115.

Institutions

19.84 The existing law on the time of payment between institutions is concerned almost exclusively with credit transfers. The English

Courts appear to have established the rule that a credit transfer is complete when the recipient bank decides to accept the transferring bank's instructions to credit the account and the accounting processes (usually computer processes) are set in motion for so crediting. The case law is unsatisfactory and the proposition is offered with considerable hesitation; it cannot be said to be the ratio of any of the decided cases.

19.85 This rule is to be understood to apply only when there are no express contractual provisions which apply between the institutions. It is certainly possible to alter the basic rule by contract in much the same way that the clearing house rules determine the rights of participating institutions. The possible contractual alternatives will be discussed below.

19.86 Since the rule is so uncertain, it is worth looking at several of the cases in detail. The cases arise in two quite different contexts. In the first, the payer wishes to stop the payment, usually because of some information concerning the solvency of the payee or because of some contractual dispute. In the second type of case, the matter arises because it is alleged that the payment has not been made in time with the result that the payer has lost some contractual benefit or has suffered some contractual loss.

19.87 The reason for the distinction between the two types of case is that the first is concerned with the time of payment as between institutions. As agent for the payer, the transferring bank will reverse the transfer order if it can do so, that is, if the time of payment as between the institutions has not yet arrived. The second type of case concerns the time of payment as between the payer and the payee. In this section, we are concerned primarily with the first type of case.

Time of payment: case law

19.88 In *Momm v Barclays Bank International Ltd*[1] the plaintiffs were a German banking partnership. They entered into a contract with another German bank, Herstatt, which provided, inter alia, that Herstatt transfer to the plaintiff's account at the defendant's bank some £120,000 in sterling. The transfer was to be on the basis of "value 26 June 1974" which meant that the payment had to be made on that date.

1 [1977] QB 79.

19.89 It happened that Herstatt also had an account with the defendant bank and intended to make the payment from that account, but that was not part of the contract between Herstatt and the plaintiff. Herstatt ordered the defendant to transfer the sum from Herstatt's account to the account of the plaintiff on 26 June.

19.90 The defendants approved the alteration of accounts on 26 June, even though this placed Herstatt's account in an overdrawn position. The decision to do so was made by an appropriate officer of the defendant bank. The accounts were processed by the defendant bank's computer that night. The next morning the defendant bank became aware that Herstatt had ceased trading. Upon receipt of this information, they informed the plaintiff, in response to an inquiry, that the transfer had not been made, "due to the present position of Herstatt's accounts", and they took steps which resulted in the computer reversing the accounts.

19.91 When the plaintiffs learned of the bank's actions they sued, claiming a wrongful debiting of their account of the amount in question; the defendants claimed that the transfer would only have been complete upon the plaintiffs receiving notice of it, and that account entries do not constitute such notice.[1]

1 The defence was based on an interpretation of *Rekstin v Severo Sibersko Gosvdarstvennoe Akcionernoe* [1933] 1 KB 47; see 19.98.

19.92 The sole issue in the case was whether the payment had become final. Kerr J thought that, as a matter of principle, when a credit transfer is to be effected by a bank on a given "value date", then the position at the end of the day must be certain, that the bank could not delay its decision to credit until the next day. That principle, which is merely an application of the general principle that the banker must follow his instructions strictly, does not settle the matter, for the question still remains as to whether the bank in fact followed the instructions, in which case the plaintiff would win, or whether the bank did not do so, in which case the plaintiff could have no claim against the bank.[1]

1 If the bank failed to follow Herstatt's instructions, Herstatt as customer may have a claim against them but it by no means follows that the current plaintiff has such a claim.

19.93 Kerr J found for the plaintiff on the basis of the old case of *Eyles v Ellis*.[1] He then went on to distinguish and explain *Rekstin v Severo Sibersko Gosvdarstvennoe Akcionernoe*,[2] the main case relied upon by the defendant, reinforcing his view of that case by reference to recent Court of Appeal decisions in two shipping cases, *The Brimnes*[3] and *Mardorf Peach and Co Ltd v Attica Carriers Corporation of Liberia (The Laconia)*.[4] Each of these cases, together with the analysis of Kerr J and comment upon that analysis, will be discussed in turn.

1 (1827) 4 Bing 112.
2 [1933] 1 KB 47.
3 [1975] QB 929.
4 [1976] QB 835. The decision of the Court of Appeal was reversed by the House of Lords [1977] AC 850, but the principles relating to the time of payment do not seem to have been altered by the House of Lords.

19.94 However this is a case which falls into the category of an institution attempting to reverse a transfer order. Although it is the payee who is the plaintiff in this case, the argument for the payee really concerns the right of the transferring bank to reverse the transfer order. As between the payer (Herstatt) and the payee, the precise time of payment is a matter of the utmost indifference.

19.95 Also note that this is a so called "in-house" payment, that is, the transferring and the recipient bank is one and the same. It may be that different principles are to be applied when there are different transferring and recipient banks, but some good reason must be made out for the difference.

19.96 In *Eyles v Ellis* the plaintiff was a creditor of the defendant. Both parties kept accounts at the same bank. On a Friday, the defendant debtor instructed the banker to transfer the sum owed to the account of the plaintiff. The banker did this by making the appropriate entry in his books, even though the defendant's account was then overdrawn. On that same day, the defendant wrote to the plaintiff to inform him that the transfer had been ordered, but the letter did not reach the plaintiff until Sunday.[1] Meanwhile, on the Saturday the banker had failed. The Court found for the defendant, observing that the plaintiff could have drawn for the sum and the banker could not have refused his draft.

1 Kerr J observes, rightly it is submitted, that the sending of the letter cannot be notice. It is actual notice which is required.

19.97 Kerr J observes that "the important feature of the case is that the payment was held to be complete when the payee's account was credited and before the payee had had any notice that this had happened". He held that, on the facts, *Eyles v Ellis* was indistinguishable from *Momm*. It is not to be supposed that Kerr J was suggesting the above statement to be the ratio of *Eyles v Ellis*. It is important to notice a further feature of the case: the judgment of the Court, given by Best CJ, clearly assumed that the bank had been given explicit authority to receive the money on behalf of the plaintiff. That this was indeed the case is evidenced by the fact that the transfer in question was a result of a complaint by the plaintiff that an earlier transfer had not taken place as it was supposed to have. Also note that Kerr J refers only to the crediting of the payee's account. This in itself is not decisive of the time of final payment, since it has long been the custom of banks to credit the account of a payee of a cheque upon deposit while reserving the right to debit the account if the cheque is dishonoured upon presentment to the paying bank. Such a practice was held to be valid in *AL Underwood Ltd v Bank of Liverpool*.[1]

1 [1924] 1 KB 775: in order to be a holder for value, the bank must show that the customer had a contractual right to draw upon the account; mere practice of allowing the customer to draw is not sufficient; see 14.22ff.

19.98 There were two defendants in the *Rekstin* case. The first was a Russian trading organisation commonly referred to as "Severo". The second was a bank at which Severo had an account. The plaintiff was a judgment creditor of Severo. Severo devised a scheme to protect the contents of their bank account from a garnishee order. Severo ordered the bank to transfer the contents of their account to the account of the Russian Trade Delegation, who had an account with the same bank. The Trade Delegation had diplomatic immunity. The order was made without the knowledge or consent of the Trade Delegation. Upon receipt of the order, a clerk of the bank made the necessary book entries to close the Severo account, and prepared a "credit slip" which was preparatory to crediting the Delegation's account with the same sum. Before such a credit entry was made, the plaintiff served the bank with a garnishee order nisi in respect of the judgment against Severo.

19.99 The Court held, inter alia, that the mandate from Severo to the bank to transfer the money to the account of the Trade Delegation was, in the circumstances, still revocable and was, in fact, revoked by operation of law upon receipt of the garnishee order nisi.

19.100 Counsel for Barclays in the *Momm* case attempted to define the ratio of the *Rekstin* case in terms of notice, asserting that transfer is incomplete until actual notice is received by the transferee. He might be forgiven for supposing that the line of argument would be readily accepted, for that seems to have been the accepted interpretation ever since the Court explained the matter in those terms in *Continental Cauoutchouc and Gutta Percha Co v Kleinwort Sons & Co.*[1] Kerr J, however, rejected this statement as the ratio of *Rekstin* on the grounds that it is inconsistent with the decision in *Eyles v Ellis*. He further observed that *Eyles v Ellis* was not mentioned in either the *Rekstin* case or the *Continental Cauoutchouc* case.

1 (1904) 90 LT 474.

19.101 Kerr J suggests that the basis of the *Rekstin* decision is one of two propositions. First, that there had been no final appropriation of the money to the credit of the Trade Delegation. Secondly "the fact that the Trade Delegation knew nothing of the proposed transfer, that there was no transaction between Severo and the delegation underlying it, and that the delegation had accordingly never assented to its account being credited with these moneys".

19.102 With respect, the first of these begs the question in that finality of the transaction is what the Court had to decide in *Rekstin*. It is, on its own, wrong, or at least misleading, in that subsequent cases, as observed by Kerr J later on, clearly indicate that payment may be complete prior to the completion of internal accounting procedures when the bank has authority to receive the payment.[1]

1 In particular, the clerk had decided to act on the order. Payment would have been complete had the bank been authorised to receive the sum on behalf of the Trade Delegation.

19.103 The second basis given by Kerr J might be summarised by the proposition that the bank was not the agent of the Trade Delegation for the purposes of receiving this payment. As will be noted below, the House of Lords decision in *Mardorf Peach" shows that payment is not completed in such a situation. Indeed, on a common sense approach, the bank in Rekstin* was a complete stranger to the Trade Delegation in so far as this particular transfer was concerned. It is as though Severo had ordered a new account to be opened in the name of the Trade Delegation in some far off bank. That the Trade Delegation might have an account at the bank is clearly irrelevant.

19.104 There seem to be three principles which may be drawn from *Momm's* case:

1 If the receiving bank has no authority to receive the money on behalf of the payee, then the transfer may be recalled at any time prior to the recipient bank receiving that authority or actually parting with the funds to the payee.[1]

2 If the transfer order actually comes to the attention of the bank, semble in its role as receiving bank, then the transfer will be irrevocable from the time that it is decided to accept the transfer and, possibly, takes some steps to credit the account of the payee. Although the transfer in *Momm* was in-house, the decisions which Kerr J considered to be of importance are decisions which would be made by the recipient bank when the transfer involved more than one bank.

3 When a value date is specified, then the transfer may be recalled at any time prior to the value date; this is merely a consequence of the fact that the order is not one to transfer funds, simpliciter, but rather to transfer on a particular date.[2] If the transfer does not actually come to the attention of officers of the recipient bank then the transfer will be irrevocable from the close of business on the value date; this would be the situation when the transfer is the result of a routine direct credit operation in a domestic EFT system.

1 *Rekstin.*
2 There may be situations where an estoppel could be raised against the transferring bank, but that is another question entirely.

19.105 It should be emphasised that the *Momm* rule is the rule which is applied when there are no contractual terms which prevent the transferring bank from recalling the order. Again, the important feature here is that the transferring bank is acting as agent. If the agent acts reasonably on the instructions of the principle, the payer, then the payer cannot change the instructions once the agent is committed.

19.106 This is illustrated admirably by the decision in *Delbrueck v Manufacturers Hanover Trust Co*[1] American litigation which also resulted from the Herstatt collapse. The plaintiff had an account with the defendant bank in the United States. On 25 June the plaintiffs sent a telex to the defendant bank ordering them to transfer some $12.5 million, value date 26 June, to Herstatt's account with the Chase Manhatten Bank. Herstatt was closed by the German banking authorities at about 10.30 am (New York time) on 26 June.

About an hour later the defendant bank made the ordered transfers by keying the appropriate transfer instructions into the CHIPS computer which then credited the clearing house account of Chase and debited that of the defendant.[2] About one half hour after that, the plaintiffs telephoned and telexed the defendants in an attempt to halt the payment.

1 464 F Supp 989 (1979).
2 See 19.27 for a discussion of the CHIPS system; the rules concerning reversals were changed as a result of this case.

19.107 The plaintiffs sought to revoke the order and to recover the amount from Chase, but according to the CHIPS rules in operation at the time, the transfers were irrevocable once processed through the CHIPS system and Chase refused to return the funds. The plaintiffs sued in both negligence and in contract, but failed due to the fact that the transfer was irrevocable under the CHIPS rules. It was simply irrelevant for this purpose that the Herstatt account with Chase had not been debited until 9 pm on the evening of the 26th. Note that if the question had been the time at which Herstatt was actually paid, then the time of crediting the Herstatt account may well be relevant.

Determination by contract

19.108 When all of the parties have agreed to some basic set of rules the time of payment may be determined by contract. There are, however, some fundamental conflicts which make such agreement difficult. In a credit transfer, the recipient bank will wish to delay acceptance of the item until such time as it is certain that the order is genuine and that it will be reimbursed for the payment order which it accepts. Consequently, it is in the interests of the recipient bank to delay the time of payment until there remains only a minimal risk that the bank will not actually receive settlement. On the other hand, a rule which gave effect to that policy would have the consequential effect of delaying the time of payment for all other purposes. The funds would presumably still belong to the transferor and not to the transferee and would be subject to legal process by the transferor's creditors. Since the transferor and the transferee may well be using an EFT system because of the speed and certainty of transfer, their desire will be that the time of payment should be as early as possible.

19.109 Probably the earliest time when payment might be considered complete is when notice of the transfer is received by the recipient bank. This is the rule used in the American FEDWIRE system, but there are certain features of that system which make the rule workable. Settlement between participants in a FEDWIRE transaction is made by the transfer of funds between the appropriate accounts held by the Federal Reserve and is guaranteed by that body. Consequently, both certainty of settlement and acceptability of the mode of settlement are assured. Furthermore, the FEDWIRE protocol authenticates the message before its receipt by the recipient bank.[1]

1 Penney and Baker, *The Law of Electronic Funds Transfer Systems*, Boston, 1980.

19.110 The next logical candidate is the time when the recipient bank makes the decision to accept the transfer. This is, of course, close to the rule which has been suggested in the English cases and may be appropriate for transfers when the mode of settlement is uncertain. One of the disadvantages of this rule is that evidence of the time of payment may be difficult to acquire. Further, the source of the evidence would be within the control of the recipient institution and that institution may have an interest in advancing or delaying the time of payment.[1] In a system with such a rule, "acceptance" would be deemed to have accrued at some fixed time, probably the close of business for those payment orders which never actually receive consideration by bank personnel.

1 Such was the case in *Momm* itself: Barclay's wished to "undo" an overnight transfer that left the Herstatt account substantially overdrawn. Herstatt ceased trading during the night.

19.111 Some legal systems attach importance to the time of posting the account.[1] But the time of posting is, in the absence of legislative control, a matter solely for the internal bookkeeping of the institution. Consequently, time of payment rules which are based on the posting process must be accompanied by rules as to the practice of posting itself.

1 The Uniform Commercial Code takes this approach.

19.112 It will be immediately apparent that the form of any electronic clearing house rules as to the time of payment will depend very much on the financial integrity of the participants involved and the method of settlement proposed. In a system where settlement is virtually guaranteed, transmission or receipt of the payment message is an acceptable time for agreed payment. If either of these preconditions is weakened, the conflict mentioned above will tend to be resolved more in favour of some later time.

19.113 As between the transferor and transferee, it has already been noted that payment cannot be said to have occurred if the funds are not readily available to the transferee. There have been suggestions to the effect that payment is not complete until the transferee receives notice of the transfer.[1] Such a suggestion seems to be based on the notion that a credit transfer is some form of assignment of funds and has little to recommend it.

1 Chorley, *The Law of Banking*, 6th ed, London, 1974.

19.114 When the transaction is a debit transfer, a similar set of possibilities exists, but it is the transferring bank which must make the appropriate verification and decisions. The rules for time of payment are modified by substituting the decisions and the acts of the transferring bank.

As between payer and payee

19.115 As between the transferee and transferor, the *Momm* rule must be further qualified by two fundamental principles. The first is that a debt owed cannot be discharged by means of a third party payment unless the party making the payment has the authority, either actual or ostensible, of the debtor to make the payment or unless the debtor subsequently ratifies the payment.[1] The second principle is that the payment cannot be considered as complete until such time as the payee can utilise them without restriction.[2]

1 For a detailed discussion, see Birks and Beatson "Unrequested Payment of Another's Debt" (1976) 92 LQR 188.
2 See *Tenax Steamship v Brimnes (Owners of)* [1975] QB 929 and the discussion below.

19.116 In general, payment cannot be complete unless it is shown that the recipient bank is the agent of the payee with authority to receive the payment. A good example of the principle in operation is *Mardorf Peach & Co Ltd v Attica Carriers Corporation of Liberia (The Laconia)*.[1] Payment was made by means of a bank "payment order", a system of inter-bank accounting which banks considered the equivalent of cash transfers. The debtor's bank was distinct from the creditor's bank, ie, it was an "out-house" payment. The Court of Appeal held that payment was complete when the receiving bank accepted the payment order and decided to act upon it, irrespective of the time required to complete the receiving bank's internal accounting processes. This decision was reversed by the House of Lords who found that the bank had authority only to receive payments which were within the contractual time. Since the payment was out of time and the owners rejected the payment as soon as it came to their notice, the payment was not effective.

1 [1977] AC 850.

19.117 The case shows dramatically the importance of identifying the parties when the time of payment is being discussed. There is no doubt that the payment as between the institutions was complete in the sense that the transferring bank could not recall the payment order, yet the payment to the payee could not have been completed at that time because of the lack of authority of the recipient bank.

19.118 A second principle is that when payment is made by a funds transfer, the payment to the payee cannot be considered complete until such time as the payee has the unconditional right to the immediate use of the funds.[1] The effect of this principle is most effectively shown by the decision in *The Chikuma*.[2]

1 See Edmund Davies LJ in *Tenax Steamship v Brimnes (Owners of)* [1975] QB 929.

2 *A/S Awilco of Oslo v Fulvia SpA di Navigazione of Cagliari (The Chikuma)*
[1981] 1 WLR 314.

19.119 Payment was due on 22 January and the day before the
payers instructed the transferring bank to make the transfer. A telex
message was sent on the due date and funds were remitted to the
recipient bank but for some reason the "value date" was shown as
26 January. Under Italian law the transfer was irrevocable and it
was even possible for the payees to draw on the money on 22
January, but the importance of the value date was that no interest
could accrue to the payees until the 26th; indeed, if they had
exercised their right to draw on the fund, they would have been
required to pay the recipient bank interest.

19.120 The House of Lords held that payment was not complete on
the 22nd. Although payment by credit transfer was permissible even
though the charterparty appeared to call for cash, the transfer had
to be such that the payee had the equivalent of cash. A transfer
which prohibited the payee from using the funds for investment
purposes could hardly be said to be the equivalent of cash.[1] Note
also that the same result would probably have been reached had
the transfer been governed entirely by New Zealand law, for the
transfer would be revocable by the transferring bank until the
"value date" and so could not be the equivalent of cash.
Furthermore, the recipient bank may well lack the authority to
receive the payment as a discharge of the contractual obligation
when the "value date" is later than the date on which payment is
due.

1 See also Tyree "Electronic Funds Transfer in New Zealand" (1978) NZUL
Rev 139; "Payment by Direct Credit" (1982) 10 Aust Bus L Rev 149.

Confidentiality

19.121 The banks' duty of secrecy concerning their customers'
affairs does not depend upon the type of transaction or the
accounting medium, so it would seem that the duties imposed by
Tournier's case would guarantee the customer some degree of
privacy in an EFT system.[1] There are, however, a number of different
considerations which come into play in a fully computerised
payments system and there are fears that the *Tournier* duty may
not be sufficient to guard against what is seen as a wider social
problem. Since bankers are directly involved with the creation of
large data banks, it is imperative that they understand the
fundamentals of the social debate.

1 *Tournier v National Provincial and Union Bank of England* [1924] 1 KB 461,
and see 7.1ff.

19.122 Although privacy issues tend to dominate the discussion of
the social impact of computers, it is in the EFT context that the full
invasive potential is most threatening. The extreme sensitivity of

financial records may be combined with the immense power of cross referencing to provide a complete surveillance system.[1]

1 See Van Tassel "Daily Surveillance Sheet, 1987, From a Nationwide Databank" 24 Computers and People 31 for an entertaining and frightening example of what might be done in a full scale EFT surveillance.

19.123 The importance of financial records in the discussion of privacy may be illustrated by a comment of an American Judge:

> In a sense a person is defined by the checks he writes. By examining them, the agents get to know his doctors, lawyers, creditors, political allies, social connections, religious affiliations, education interests, the papers and magazines he reads and so on ad infinitum.[1]

1 Per Douglas J in *California Bankers Association v Schultz* 416 US 21, 85 (1975).

19.124 The American National Committee on Electronic Funds Transfers identified five ways in which EFT systems may pose a threat to privacy:[1]

1 Each transaction gives rise to financial records which the use of cash would not create. At a minimum, an EFT record will provide information concerning the payee, the amount the location and the time. In a large scale point of sale system, these records could provide substantial information on the movements and habits of an individual.

2 EFT systems would normally store more information about each transaction than a paper based system. Consider the information contained on a salary payment cheque with that of an advice of a direct credit payment. Also note that there are good consumer reasons why the EFT record should contain more information.

3 Centralisation of records is the rule in an electronic system with the result that cross-file correlation is facilitated.

4 On-line transactions may be used to pinpoint the location and movement of the card holder.

5 Sharing of systems seems an economically desirable feature of point of sale systems. The result may exacerbate the problem of providing systems security.

1 *EFT in the United States; The Final Report of the National Commission on Electronic Fund Transfers*, 1977.

19.125 One of the most difficult problems of privacy is the unstable nature of the political opposition to privacy invasion. It is commonplace to note that privacy cannot be absolute and that there will always be legitimate violations of the right to privacy. When translated into action, this commonplace observation seems to result in a kind of ad hoc approach to records.

19.126 It is impossible to know what the political situation in any country will be in ten years. When systems such as real time EFT systems exist, the temptation to use them must be overwhelming for government departments who have an interest in the financial or other affairs of citizens. Whether such access is desirable or not will inevitably vary with the individual's perception of the circumstances. So, for example, access to financial records during the recent "bottom of the harbour" investigations would appear to have received the approval of a large portion of that very segment of the community which would, in other contexts, be the most vociferous in their objections to government surveillance.

19.127 When the criteria for access are so ill-defined, the fears which are engendered by the mere existence of EFT systems are by no means unfounded.

19.128 The United Kingdom has responded to this problem by passing the Data Protection Act 1984 which establishes a Registrar of Data Protection with whom certain users and bureaux must register. There is no doubt that each bank would qualify as a "data user" within the meaning of s 1(5) of the Act and that Databank would be a "computer bureau" under s 1(6). The Act prohibits the disclosure of information to any person who is not authorised to receive it under the registration process.

19.129 It is unlikely that the Act imposes duties on bankers which go beyond the *Tournier* duty, but it would have the effect of protecting the customer from disclosures by Databank or any other computer service provider who is not in a direct contractual relationship with the customer.

Chapter 20

Consumer issues in EFT

20.1 The introduction of Electronic Funds Transfer Systems has raised a number of issues which are loosely described as "consumer" issues. Whereas the rights and obligations of the parties using the cheque system have been worked out over many years by decisions of the Courts, the corresponding rights and obligations of the participants in an EFT system are determined almost entirely by the contract prepared by the card issuer and known as the "Conditions of Use". Concern has been expressed in New Zealand and overseas that these Conditions are unduly favourable to the card issuer.

20.2 In addition to these contractual issues, there are issues of a more public nature. These would include the dissemination of unsolicited cards, the possibility of collecting information on the financial habits of the customer which could be used to infringe the customer's privacy and the effect that the introduction of EFT might have on lower socio-economic groups.

20.3 These concerns have led to a significant amount of public debate over recent years. On the one hand, groups concerned with consumers' rights argued that legislation was necessary in order to redress the imbalance of bargaining powers between the customer and the card issuers; on the other hand, the card issuers argued that to introduce legislation prematurely would stifle the development of EFT.

20.4 After a lengthy period of discussions with all interested groups, the Ministry of Consumer Affairs prepared a Code of Practice to Cover the Issue and Use of Electronic Funds Transfer Cards within New Zealand. The Code is voluntary, but it seems clear that the major card issuers have become signatories to the Code. As will be seen, the Code gives significant new rights to cardholders so that signatories to the Code should be expected to enjoy a substantial competitive advantage over non-signatories when soliciting new cardholders.

20.5 The process leading to the establishment of a more equitable sharing of the risks in an EFT system has been a long one. The likely reason for this is the belief by the card issuers that the electronic systems are totally reliable while the consumer groups tend to see only the failures. In one sense, it is the reliability of the systems which has delayed agreement on a Code.

Reliability of payment systems

20.6 A payment system must be extremely reliable, for otherwise it would cease to exist as a payment system. As an example, consider the Databank system for clearing cheques, a system which clears many hundreds of millions of payments each year.

20.7 It is not obvious how many of these go wrong in any way, but the number is surely negligible as a percentage of the total number of transactions. Three or four reported cases make the year a good one for the teachers of commercial law; even if there are several thousand times that number which go wrong, the system must be said to be working very well by most business standards.

20.8 Somewhat paradoxically, it is this extreme reliability which causes some of the consumer problems, for the natural inclination of most of us is to meet a consumer claim of system malfunction with disbelief.

20.9 The purpose of this chapter is to identify those legal issues associated with the introduction of EFT and to indicate the solutions adopted by the Code.

Liability for unauthorised use

20.10 The current means of transaction authentication in consumer EFT systems is the card/PIN combination.[1] On one view, the card/PIN combination is really just the substitution of one form of identification for another and in a sense this is correct when the transaction proceeds according to the expectation of the parties, but the situation is very much different when the transaction goes wrong, usually because of a misappropriation in the means of identification.

1 "PIN" is the acronym for "personal identification number".

Legal status of signature

20.11 The legal status of the signature on a cheque is not that it is a means of identification, but rather the mechanism whereby authority is granted to the banker to make a payment and to debit the account. Thus,

> The common aphorism that a banker is under a duty to know his customer's signature is in fact incorrect even as between the banker and his customer. The principle is simply that a banker cannot debit his customer's account on the basis of a forged signature, since he has in that event no mandate from the customer for doing so.[1]

1 Per Kerr J in *National Westminster Bank Ltd v Barclays Bank International Ltd* [1975] 1 QB 654.

20.12 It seems likely that the use of the card/PIN combination has the same legal effect when used by the rightful owner.[1] However, when the card/PIN is misappropriated by a rogue, the consequences to the customer are very much different. Until the untroduction of the Code, the usual conditions of use issued by the financial institutions threw the risk of all unauthorised use onto the customer at least until such time as the customer notified the institution of the loss of the card/PIN.[2]

1 Strictly speaking, the customer does not ever become the owner of the card. Most conditions of use reserve the property in the card to the institution, the customer being entitled to the possession of the card only so long as the conditions of use permit.
2 A typical condition read "If the Card and PIN is lost or stolen the Customer must immediately notify the Bank. Until the Bank receives such notification the Customer shall be liable for all transactions conducted with the Card and PIN".

Change in allocation of risks

20.13 The change in the position of the customer under the pre-code regime may be illustrated by considering the analogous situation of a drawer's signature forged on a cheque: the bank may not debit the account of the customer even if the customer has been careless in the keeping of the cheque-book.[1] The customer has no duty to discover forgeries or, generally speaking, to organise business affairs in such a manner as to guard against them.[2]

1 *Kepitigalla Rubber Estates Ltd v National Bank of India Ltd* [1909] 2 KB 1010 and see the discussion in Ch 3.
2 *National Bank of New Zealand Ltd v Walpole & Patterson Ltd* [1975] 2 NZLR

7; *Tai Hing Cotton Mill Ltd v Liu Chong Hing Bank Ltd* [1985] 2 All ER 947 and see the discussion in Ch 3.

20.14 The Code provides for a limited cardholder liability for unauthorised use of the card. If the cardholder has not been "careless" in the sense defined below, then the liability is limited to $50, the balance of the account (including any prearranged credit) or the actual loss at the time of notification, whichever is the lesser.

20.15 The cardholder may be "careless" in two ways. First, he or she may mishandle the PIN by voluntarily disclosing to another person, by indicating the PIN on the card or by keeping with the card (without making a reasonable attempt to disguise the PIN) a record of the PIN. Secondly, the cardholder may be careless by failing to notify promptly the issuer of known misuse of the card or that the PIN has become known to another person or that the card has been stolen.

20.16 When the customer has been careless he or she may be liable for substantially more than $50. When there is carelessness of the first type, the cardholder is liable for all loss not exceeding the lesser of:
— the actual loss at the time the card issuer is notified of the loss or theft of the card, or that the PIN has become known to someone else; or
— the maximum amount the cardholder would have been entitled to access over the relevant period prior to notification of the loss or theft of the card calculated in accordance with the periodic transaction limit applicable to that cardholder's card or account(s); or
— the balance of the nominated account(s) (including any prearranged credit).

20.17 When the cardholder has been careless in notifying, the liability is similar save that the first limit is changed to:
— the actual losses, which could otherwise have been prevented from occurring, in the period between when the cardholder became aware of the events described above (or should reasonably have become aware in the case [that the PIN has become known to another party or that the card has been lost or stolen]) and when the card issuer was actually notified.

20.18 The card issuer is liable for all other losses, including losses which arise from system malfunction. The Code specifically makes the card issuer liable for any direct loss caused by a malfunction within the EFT system. In addition, the Code forbids the card issuer from denying "a right to the cardholder to make claims for consequential loss or damage which may arise as a result of a technical malfunction, however caused."

Dispute resolution procedures

20.19 Merely reciting rights of cardholders is of no value if the relative strength of the parties disadvantages consumers when there is a complaint of malfunction. The amounts will often be too small to justify recourse to the normal Court system. It has long been argued that some formalised method of dispute resolution must be adopted which would restore more of a balance between the parties.

20.20 There have been several suggestions for doing this. The establishment of the English "Banking Ombudsman" is a noteworthy development.[1] The Ombudsman is funded by the clearing banks and the expressed intention is that the banks will be bound by decisions of the Ombudsman which are not in excess of a ceiling to be defined from time to time.

1 Reported in *The Times*, 19 October, 1985.

The American EFT Act

20.21 A second method of dispute resolution is that adopted by the American EFT Act. The Act like the New Zealand Code, provides for a structured system of customer liability for unauthorised use, the level of liability depending on the level of the customer's "culpability" and upon the speed with which the customer notifies the institution of the unauthorised use.[1] At the lowest level, when the customer has not been negligent in the keeping of the card/PIN combination and notifies the institution promptly, the liability is limited to the actual loss or $50, whichever is less. At the other extreme, when the customer has been grossly negligent in the keeping of the means of identification or completely ignores the legitimate interests of the institution in being notified of the loss, the liability may extend to all losses.

1 The Financial Institutions Regulatory and Interest Rate Control Act of 1978 Pub L No 95-360 s 2001, 92 Stat 3641 (1978).

20.22 The solution to the problem of resolving disputes between the institution and the customer begins by noting that it is only the institution which has access to the information which can resolve the dispute. Consequently, in the first instance, the onus should be on the institution to justify the disputed transaction. The EFT Act provides that the institution must investigate and report promptly in writing to the customer in the event of a dispute.[1] If the customer does not find the determination acceptable, he or she is entitled to certain documents which were used by the institution in reaching the finding. These documents may then be used as evidence in Court proceedings.

1 The institution is given a choice of meanings of "promptly": it may report within ten business days or it may immediately recredit the account and report within 45 days.

20.23 The New Zealand Code follows the EFT Act in requiring the institution to investigate complaints and to notify the customer in writing of the outcome of the investigation. Under the Code, this notification must be done within 30 days if possible. If it is not possible, the customer must be notified of both the extent of the delay and the reasons for it. There appears to be no obligation to recredit the customer's account even if the delay is substantial.

20.24 When the card issuer determines that no error has occurred, it must advise the cardholder accordingly and is obliged to supply the cardholder on request with copies of material on which the finding was based, subject only to respecting the security and confidentiality obligations of the issuer.

20.25 If the customer is not satisfied with the outcome of the investigation, he or she may have recourse to an independent referee. The establishment of this referee appears to be a system which is unique to New Zealand and is a development to be welcomed by all parties. Signatories to the Code have agreed to meet the standing costs of the referee system including the first hour of the referee's time in any particular dispute. Although this system has been agreed to in principle, the details are not available at the time of writing.

20.26 The effectiveness of the system will in part depend upon the attitude of referees to the question of the burden of proof, for when the case comes to the referee the card issuer will already have determined, presumably on documentary evidence, that no error occurred. The Code places an obligation on the card issuer to ensure that their systems provide records which are adequate for the purpose of tracing transactions and to detect and correct errors.

20.27 Of course, some disputes will be concerned with whether a particular keeping of the PIN was "reasonable". Such disputes should cause no particular problems. However, when the dispute is one over the existence of a system error, the burden of proof virtually defines the outcome. The customer is ordinarily in no position to provide proof that an error occurred and the card issuer would find it very difficult to prove that the system used is capable of detecting all errors.

20.28 There is no easy answer to this problem of evidence in an EFT system. It is here that the forged cheque provides another striking contrast with the misappropriated card/PIN problem. The paper itself provides the evidence for resolving the dispute between the bank and its customer. The paper is retrieved, the signature is examined and that will, in the majority of cases, be an end of the matter since it will ordinarily be obvious that the signature was or was not forged. By comparison, the only evidence usually available for the EFT situation is the statement of the card issuer.[1]

1 See the discussion concerning admissibility of computer evidence in the EFT context near the end of this chapter.

Other consumer concerns

20.29 There are a number of other issues which have been of special concern to consumers and consumer organisations. Perhaps the most important of these is the general issue of information and disclosure of risks.

Disclosure

20.30 One of the major concerns of consumer representatives has been the question of information which should be brought to the attention of the consumer. By this is meant more than merely making information available, although that is important, but the more demanding question of active disclosure of information to the card holder or intending card holder.

20.31 It seems likely that few card holders have any idea of the risks which are cast upon them by the pre-Code conditions of use. Few have taken the time to read them, fewer still to understand them. In the light of the actual contents of some of the conditions, it is a remarkable expression of faith in the integrity of the financial institutions.

20.32 There is a not unreasonable opinion that it is better that card holders not be informed of all of the risks since that would undermine confidence in the EFT system. Since the probabilities of any single individual being involved in an EFT mishap are small, it seems better not to alarm the majority unnecessarily.

20.33 However sensible the argument might be in isolation, the consumer representatives have argued that it is unacceptable unless the institutions also assume the risks. If it is felt necessary to throw these risks on consumers, then it is necessary that they be informed of precisely the risks which are being undertaken. It is not enough to say that the incidence of mishaps is small, they must also be told of the possible consequences of any mishap.

20.34 The Code deals with this problem only in general terms. Card issuers agree to "issue clear and unambiguous terms and conditions of use; in particular the clauses which deal with cardholder's liabilities and responsibilities shall be clearly and simply stated and highlighted in the text."

Right to countermand

20.35 The loss of the right of stop payment, inherent in the cheque system and guaranteed by s 75 of the Bills of Exchange Act, is often mentioned as a consumer concern. Indeed, the literature of EFT is replete with calls for legislation to include a statutory right of reversal in a consumer EFT transaction. While this may be a good idea, it is hard to see how the argument can rest on the rights currently enjoyed under the cheque system. In the consumer context, the "right" of stop payment has been steadily eroded over the past 15 years, first with the faster clearing of cheques and later with the introduction of Bankcard. Indeed, payment by personal cheque in a consumer transaction would now be a rather unusual event, yet the cheque is the only payment instrument which has a right of stop payment. It may be that the case for a statutory right of reversal can be made out, but it must rest on grounds other than the replacement of the cheque system by EFT. The Code does not implement any right of reversal or of stop payment.

Access by lower socio-economic groups

20.36 Another consumer issue is access to the system by the poorer members of the community. The argument is that access to the EFT payment system necessitates a bank account and that this will preclude the disadvantaged. Studies in the USA have found that 25% of all families live entirely on a cash flow basis; for such families, an account of any kind is a major and unnecessary expense.[1] In Australia, it has been estimated that only about 50% of all individuals have bank accounts, but if accounts with other institutions are included, there is no doubt that the proportion would rise substantially.

1 Penny and Baker, *The Law of Electronic Funds Transfer Systems*, Boston, 1980; Leymaster, "Electronic Banking and the Poor: the Short End of an Expensive Stick" 14 Clearinghouse Review 721 (1980).

20.37 There is an argument that the introduction of EFT might actually increase the possibility of participation by the poor since the institution is exposed to fewer risks with an account which is operated by a debit card. Participation might prove to be an expensive burden for many families unless some form of credit education and control is provided. "Automatic" overdrafts should probably be prohibited.

Security

20.38 Security of computer systems is a complex and technical subject which has been attracting a substantial amount of public interest since the recent achievements of young American hobbyists have come under public scrutiny. If it is possible for "hackers" with small home computers to infiltrate Defence Department computers, then it is difficult to believe that any computer system can be entirely secure against the determined onslaught of professionals with large scale computer facilities.

20.39 When the nature of an EFT network is considered, it will be seen that the security problem is substantially more difficult than the problem of securing a single computer. By its very nature, an EFT network must have a large number of access points and be connected to terminals in remote areas through extended lines of communication, lines which will very likely be owned and operated by another party and thus compounding the security problem.[1] With such large sums at stake, it would be surprising if dishonest elements failed to attempt to break the system and make unauthorised transfers.

1 For example, Westpac's Handyway system has terminals connected by Telecom's Austpac network to the Westpac computer.

20.40 Computer security in an EFT system is further confused by the moral attitudes of the community towards computer "theft". It is generally looked upon with some approval and admiration for the person who is clever enough to "break the system".[1] In the EFT context, this combines with a generally unsympathetic view of the banks and other financial institutions to produce a climate which will promote attempted EFT thefts. The results can already be seen in America where individuals like Stanley Rifkin, who was arrested for transferring some $10 million from the Security Pacific National Bank to his own private accounts, are already on the road to becoming contemporary folk heroes.[2]

1 Parker, *Crime by Computer*, New York, 1976.
2 *Time Magazine*, 20 November 1978.

20.41 Security generally is broken into two distinct facets: physical security and software security. Physical security is well understood, but is still a weak point due to the number of people who must have access to an EFT system. Aside from the obvious need to monitor access to terminals and to change access codes and routines regularly, there is the need to protect the main computers from physical attack by terrorists or other elements who might stand to gain from a major disruption of the payments system. The Bank for International Settlements has published guidelines for physical security of EFT systems.[1]

1 *Security and Reliability in Electronic Systems for Payments*, 2nd ed, 1982, Bank for International Settlements.

20.42 Software security is a very much more difficult topic. As recently as 1981 it was possible for a computer security specialist to write that "all known operating systems have been penetrated at a distance by a person with no more information about the computer than the telephone number".[1] The software must contain monitoring systems which will advise of attempted unauthorised access. One scenario, by no means fanciful, is that a dishonest systems programmer could build "trapdoors" in the EFT software which would be invisible during ordinary operation of the system but which would allow later unauthorised access to anyone with the key to the "trapdoor".

1 Gait, "Security of EFT Systems" 32 J Systems Management 6 (1981). See also Comer, "How to Prevent Computer Fraud" (1982) Asian Banking 35; Nycum, "Security for Electronic Funds Transfer Systems" 37 U Pitt L Rev 709 (1976).

20.43 Security of data being transmitted to and from remote sites is a matter which calls for attention. Phone lines can be tapped and data transmission intercepted. An English computer journal ran a competition which was won by a hobbyist who showed how it is possible to intercept EFT messages and, with the aid of a small home computer, transpose digits so as to result in substantial unauthorised credits.[1] The code in use by the London banks at that time was the so-called STK code which is not a particularly sophisticated code, but any code used in data transmission must represent a trade off between the security needed and the costs, both in time and equipment, needed to encrypt and decrypt data.

1 *Computer Fraud and Security Bulletin*, 1978; more complex (and expensive) codes are now in use: Computer Security and the Data Encryption Standard, National Bureau of Standards Special Publication 500-27.

20.44 The magnitude of the data security problem may be gauged by recent developments in the United States. Recent advances in cryptography have led to government intervention to attempt to classify as defence secrets recent work in number theory. This work was previously thought to be of the purest and most harmless sort of mathematical work. Although there is still considerable conflict between the universities and the government on the matter, it is noteworthy that the American Association of Computing Machinery has recommended a scheme of pre-publication vetting of potentially sensitive results.[1] In a country where freedom from pre-publication restraint is often elevated to the status of a fundamental freedom, this move must reflect the importance which is attached to the work.

1 "Report of the Public Cryptography Study Group" 24 Comm of ACM 434 (1981).

20.45 There is another aspect of security which is closely related to the problem of consumer liability for unauthorised use. In an EFT network the remote terminals must be secured against unauthorised access to the system. The present method of authorisation is, of course, the card/PIN combination. The card contains a magnetic stripe which contains information concerning the customer's account and (in some systems) the PIN. The system will not operate if the PIN entered at the terminal does not match the assigned PIN. Most terminals are now programmed to destroy the card if there are multiple unsuccessful attempts to enter a PIN which does not match the card being used.[1]

1 But the machines have not always functioned as designed. In this regard, note the conditions of use which purport to relieve the bank of any liability for malfunction.

20.46 There is the obvious problem that a person standing near a terminal could observe the correct PIN being entered by the customer and later use it with a stolen card to access the account. For this reason, some American terminals are now completely enclosed, but it would appear that Australian practice is to continue mounting terminals in exposed walls.

20.47 There is a further danger that methods may be developed for reading the details from the magnetic stripe, decoding the information found there and thereby gaining access to accounts through the use of the card only. Such a development would greatly increase the risk of carrying the plastic cards and would probably lead to a significantly increased underworld trade in cards. It might also facilitate the forgery of cards, already a growing industry in the United States.

20.48 Needless to say, the security of the card/PIN system is severely compromised if the PIN is carried near the card or written on it. It is easy to have sympathy with the tiered standard form of conditions of use issued by the financial institutions which purports to throw unlimited liability on the customer when the PIN is treated in such a cavalier fashion. Yet, customer surveys in the United States have shown that approximately 50% of all cardholders either write the PIN on the debit card or keep it uncoded on a slip of paper in their wallet or purse thereby making it easy for a mugger to gain complete access to the account.[1]

1 Revell, *Banking and Electronic Funds Transfers*, OECD, 1983.

20.49 While it may be easy to argue that such customers are foolish, there seems little hope that there will be a spontaneous change in their habits or that improved advertising programmes will significantly reduce the incidence of carelessness in the handling of the card/PIN combination. If this is correct, then there will continue to be a significant "consumer problem" under the regime of liability imposed by the Code.

20.50 The truth of the matter is that the card/PIN combination is a very poor form of customer identification and authorisation which will likely be replaced by alternative methods once the necessary technology is in place at a cost-effective level. Various "warmbody" devices are being developed which will use some distinctive physical characteristic of the individual to provide identification at an error level comparable with that now achieved by fingerprints. Whether such procedures would be met with other objections and resistance remains to be seen although the traditional resistance in western countries to the use of fingerprints and/or photographs on official documents such as drivers' licences does not lead one to be too optimistic.

Evidence

20.51 There is a general legal problem concerned with the admissibility of computer records. The usual proposal for admissibility is that the printout be entered as evidence and supported by expert evidence which describes the operation of the computer and of the software which led to the printout. Such a scheme may be adequate for admissibility in most cases, but in the EFT problem such rules would mean that the person alleging the mistake will automatically lose.

20.52 The kind of case that is being considered here means that ex hypothesi the consumer is complaining about a mistake being made. It will always be the case that the printout and bank records will show that a mistake has not been made for otherwise the bank would adjust the account. An expert will describe the operation of a program which is in all respects incapable of making mistakes. Indeed, as noted at the beginning of this paper, a successful payments system will have a most impressive success record.

20.53 In an American case where such records were in evidence, a customer of a bank complained about a wrongful debit.[1] She was able to succeed in spite of the admissibility of computer records only because she was able to prove that she was in another town when the reported transfer at the automatic teller machine was initiated.

1 *Judd v Citibank* 435 NYS 2d 210 (1980).

20.54 The functional result of the usual admissibility scheme when applied in the EFT context is clearly a shifting of a very heavy burden of proof onto the consumer to show that a mistake has been made. This is probably unacceptable in a domestic EFT network. As mentioned above, the success or otherwise of the New Zealand scheme of appeal to an independent referee will probably depend upon the way in which the referee views computer evidence and the burden of proof.

Privacy

20.55 The legal concept of privacy is difficult. There is no general right to privacy, but certain aspects of privacy are protected by other mechanisms, most notably the law of defamation. In the banking context, the customer of a bank receives certain contractual protection by virtue of the banker's duty of secrecy.[1]

1 See the discussion in Ch 7.

20.56 In the EFT context, many of the card issuers are not bankers and there is some question as to whether they are under the same duty of secrecy. Consequently, it is significant that the Code defines the obligation of card issuers with regard to the duty of secrecy.

20.57 The Code provides that in respect of all EFT services offered and in respect of all accounts on which EFT transactions can be made that the duties of confidentiality and secrecy that apply to banks in respect of customer records shall apply to all card issuers. This general duty is supplemented by several specific instances which are special to electronic networks, eg, only agents and employees of the card issuer and persons authorised by the customer shall have electronic access to details of the customer's account.

Chapter 21

Credit cards

21.1 One of the most significant features of retail banking over the past ten years has been the emergence of the third party credit card as a major method of consumer payment. The third party card is a logical development of the two party cards which have been used by major retailers for many years. The two party card is little more than a token issued by the retailer which authorises the customer to purchase goods on short term credit at the particular retailers. The third party card, by contrast, represents a complex commercial arrangement between the card issuer, a significant number of merchants and a significant number of customers who are issued with the card.

21.2 The modern third party card which is issued by a bank provides not only a facility for purchasing goods on short term credit, but also the ability to borrow cash to the limit agreed upon from the card issuer without the need for any formalities.

Basic operation of third party credit cards

21.3 The basic sequence of events when a third party credit card is used for the purchase of goods or services is that the customer tenders the card as a means of payment. The merchant takes an impression of the details of the customer's card which are embossed upon the card, and fills in details of the purchase on a special form which is provided by the issuer. This form is in three parts. The customer receives a copy, one copy is retained by the retailer and one copy is delivered to the card issuer. It is usually necessary for the customer to sign the form as well as produce the card. At an agreed upon time, the merchant's account is credited with the amount of the purchase less any agreed upon discount. The cycle is closed with the periodic statement to the customer who then pays the issuer the amount of the invoices or, depending upon the terms of the contract, pays a proportion of the charges and credit charges on the outstanding balance.

21.4 There are some advantages for each of the parties. The customer need carry less cash and the loss or the destruction of the card need not represent as great a loss as the loss of cash. The customer ordinarily obtains a period of free credit and receives a certain amount of accounting in the form of the monthly statement which may assist in his or her financial planning. On the other hand, it is thought that the ready availability of the means to purchase items may lead to an increase in "impulse buying" which could have the effect of destroying any planning previously undertaken.

21.5 The merchant essentially eliminates the risks of bad debts, handles less cash which reduces the risks of theft and probably increases his sales due to the above mentioned "impulse buying" effect. The price which is paid for this is the agreed-upon discount.

21.6 The card issuer earns income from the discount agreed upon with merchants and by any interest charges paid by cardholders under revolving credit arrangements. When the issuer is a bank, there is a significant possibility of attracting customers who would not ordinarily keep a current account with the corresponding increase in low interest deposits. Against this is the large cost of establishing a scheme, for financial success of the third party credit card scheme depends upon the existence of a very large base of participating merchants and cardholders.

The legal framework: three basic contracts

21.7 A credit card is not a legal instrument in any way comparable to a bill of exchange; it does not carry with it any legal rights or obligations of itself. However, in order to use a credit card for the purchase of goods, there must be three basic contractual relationships established, namely, the contract between the issuer and the cardholder which authorises the cardholder to use the card, the contract between the issuer and the merchant which obliges the merchant to accept the card as payment for goods or services, and the contract between the merchant and the cardholder by which the merchant accepts the card as a form of payment in lieu of legal tender.

The contract between the merchant and the issuer

21.8 Although the precise terms vary, it is common for contracts to contain terms which oblige the merchant to accept valid credit cards and to sell goods or services at the same price as when accepting payment by cash. The merchant usually agrees to obtain the cardholder's signature on the invoice form and to compare it with the signature on the card itself; there is ordinarily an obligation for the merchant to obtain express authority from the issuer before accepting the card for payment in excess of some agreed amount.

21.9 The merchant agrees to deposit the invoices within a specified period and to be credited with the face value of them less an agreed upon discount. This discount will vary with the type and size of the merchant's business, but the range appears to be between 1.25% and 6%. The merchant further agrees to accept certain debits to the account. This may happen in circumstances initiated by the merchant, eg, when the merchant gives a credit for goods returned. However, the issuer usually reserves the right to make a debit to the account when there is a dispute between the cardholder and the merchant which relates to the specific transaction. The issuer also reserves the right to debit the account when the card is on a "hot list" of cards which have been stolen, where the card is counterfeit or where the signature has been forged.

The contract between the issuer and cardholder

General outline of the contract

21.10 The contract between the issuer and the cardholder is a standard form contract usually headed "conditions of use" which is unlikely to be sighted by the customer prior to receiving the card. It is thought, however, that the first use of the card represents the cardholder's assent to the conditions of use. These conditions typically contain undertakings by the customer to reimburse the issuer for payments made by the issuer to merchants on behalf of the cardholder's use of the card, to notify the issuer in the event that the card is lost or stolen and not to raise against the issuer any defence or counterclaim which might have been raised against the merchant in respect of the transaction.

21.11 The conditions of use also contain clauses whereby the cardholder gives the issuer the authority to pay the merchant in respect of purchases made using the card.

21.12 There is ordinarily also a clause which places liability for all transactions initiated with the card, whether authorised by the cardholder or not, on the cardholder provided that the cardholder has not given actual notice to the issuer that the card has been lost or stolen. Current practice is to couple that with a "ceiling" on liability, usually $50. There is also a clause which permits the issuer to vary the conditions of use without notice to the cardholder.[1]

1 It may be that the efficacy of this clause will need to be reassessed following the decision in *Tai Hing Cotton Mill Ltd v Liu Chong Hing Bank Ltd* [1985] 2 All ER 947. See 2.22ff.

Effect of Credit Contracts Act 1981

21.13 There is no doubt that the contract between the cardholder and the issuer is a revolving credit contract within the meaning of the Credit Contracts Act 1981.

Information requirements

21.14 One of the consequences of this is that the issuer must provide continuing disclosure to the cardholder as provided in Part III of the Second Schedule of the Act.

Possibility of re-opening under Part I

21.15 A second consequence of falling within the Credit Contracts Act 1981 is the possibility of the contract being re-opened by the Court.[1] It is unlikely that the current terms used would be found to be "oppressive", but any attempt to throw unlimited liability for unauthorised use of the card onto the cardholder might run foul of the re-opening provisions.[2]

1 See Ch 26.
2 This is not fanciful. Several years ago the Australian Bankcard unilaterally changed the conditions of use to make the cardholder liable for all charges which quoted the Bankcard number by telephone. The usual conditions were restored following governmental and consumer pressures.

The contract between the merchant and cardholder

21.16 There seems little change in the usual contract between the merchant and the cardholder. It remains a normal contract for the sale of goods save that the merchant looks to the card issuer for payment of the price.[1]

1 The possibility of the issuer failing to meet that obligation is discussed below.

Legal problems

21.17 There are few reported cases dealing with legal problems arising from the credit card system, probably because the system works well and when it does not the amounts are relatively small so that the disputes may be resolved without litigation or the claim simply dropped. The only reported case in English law concerns the failure of the card issuer, so that although the individual sums were small, the total sum involved justified litigation.[1]

1 *Re Charge Card Services Ltd* [1986] 2 All ER 289, discussed below.

21.18 The legal resolution of problems which do arise depends to some extent on the legal nature of the credit card transaction. There seem to be only two possibilities. The transaction may be in the nature of an assignment, or it may be similar to a letter of credit transaction.

21.19 In the assignment model, the theory is that the effect of the contractual relationships is that a debt is assigned by the merchant to the card issuer. The debt is that owed by the cardholder and which arises from the transaction in question. The argument in favour of the assignment model is that the issuer pays the merchant a discounted value as would be expected. The contract between the card issuer and the cardholder provides that the cardholder will not raise any of the defences against the issuer that he or she might raise against the merchant, a clause which would scarcely be necessary unless there is an assignment of the debt owed to the merchant by the cardholder.

21.20 The second model of the transaction is that it is similar to a letter of credit transaction. Indeed, the plastic card does seem to have many similarities with the letter of credit. It is clear that when the merchant accepts the credit card in lieu of payment that it is the credit of the card issuer which is being relied upon. There is a clear analogy of payment against documents when the invoice is presented by the merchant. If it is the "beneficiary" who pays the bank charges rather than the cardholder, that is no reason to change the legal analysis but is only a reflection of the difference between consumer and commercial practice. Similarly, it is argued that the clause which prevents the cardholder from raising contractual defences is merely a recitation of the fundamental position; in particular, it is not evidence that the true legal transaction is an assignment.

Failure of the card issuer

21.21 The nature of the legal transaction takes on importance when the card issuer does not pay. Such was the case in *Re Charge Card*

Services Ltd.[1] The card issuing company, Charge Card Services Ltd, issued cards which were available for use at garages which had entered into an agreement with the issuing company. The cards were used by cardholders in the way described above. Because Charge Card Services Ltd normally paid the participating garages well before they were themselves paid by cardholders, they entered into an arrangement with Commercial Credit Services Ltd whereby debts owing or to become owing from cardholders were assigned to Commercial Credit.

1 [1986] 3 All ER 289.

21.22 At the time of liquidation, there were some £3 million due to the company from cardholders. The liquidator was directed to collect all sums due and at the time of the litigation had collected more than £2 million after allowing for the costs of collection. The issue in the case was whether this entire sum was to go to Commercial Credit or whether the garage owners who had not been paid at the time of the liquidation were entitled to claim the sums due them.

21.23 The only way in which the garage owners could claim is if they had a right to claim directly from the cardholders. Thus, counsel for the garage owners argued that when cardholders filled their tank with petrol that they contracted to pay the price displayed on the pump and if they chose to pay by card it was conditional payment only, much as if they chose to pay by cheque. Counsel for Commercial Credit argued that the cardholder never became liable to the garage to pay for the petrol if they chose to accept the garage owner's standing offer to accept the credit card in lieu of cash and that the only obligation on the customer was to pay Charge Card. The garage owner must look to Charge Card to recover payment.

21.24 Millett J held that there was no ground for the conditional payment argument. He held that the essence of the agreement was that the supplier and the customer had for their mutual convenience each arranged to open an account with the same company, Charge Card, and agreed that any account between themselves might, if the customer wished, be settled by crediting the suppliers account and debiting the customer's account with the company. Furthermore, the Court held that the customer's liability to the garage owner was discharged at the latest when the owner's account was credited, not when he or she was paid.

21.25 These features were enough to displace any presumption which there might be that the payment by card was conditional. Quite the contrary, they supported a conclusion that it was not meant to be conditional payment only. Further, since Charge Card had undertaken to guarantee its obligation to reimburse the garage, it was clear that the garage owner considered himself to be giving credit to the company, not to the customer.

21.26 The result should be compared with the situation where an issuer of a documentary letter of credit has failed to make the payment called for. The normal position is that the seller of goods may then have recourse to the buyer, and if the buyer has already put the issuer in funds then he or she may have to pay twice.[1] The difference may be explained by the commercial differences of the two arrangements. In a letter of credit payment, it is usually the buyer who selects the paymaster and the transaction is usually a "one off" sale. There is no room in the letter of credit transaction for the argument that the buyer could choose to accept the seller's "standing offer" to be paid by tender of the card rather than in cash. Furthermore, the continuing nature of the credit card arrangement means that the merchant has a much greater say in the choice of acceptable credit card.

1 *W J Alan & Co Ltd v El Nasr Export & Import Co* [1972] 2 QB 189. See the discussion in Ch 29.

Unauthorised purchases

21.27 As noted above, the contract between the card issuer and the cardholder will most likely make the cardholder liable for all unauthorised use of the card until such time as the cardholder notifies the issuer that the card has been lost or stolen. Since the conditions of use currently place a relatively low ceiling on the liability, there is unlikely to be much scope for cases to arise.

21.28 If the conditions are changed to those similar to the conditions of use for EFT cards, then it is likely that problems of significant magnitude will arise. Apart from the possibility of challenging the imposition of unlimited liability as being "oppressive" under the Credit Contracts Act 1981, there is the possibility that the cardholder might escape liability if there is fraud or negligence on the part of the merchants involved in the unauthorised use of the cards.

21.29 In *Gulf Refining Co v Williams Roofing Co*,[1] the plaintiff was a card issuer who issued a number of cards to the defendant for use by the defendant's employees. The defendant typed across the face of the cards "Good for Truck Only", but one of the cards fell into the hands of a rogue who made over 200 purchases with the card before the unauthorised use came to the notice of the defendant who then notified the plaintiff. One of the clauses in the conditions of use purported to make the cardholder liable for all purchases made with the card prior to notification.

1 (1945) 186 SW 2d 790.

21.30 The rogue was not driving a truck at the time when the fraudulent purchases were made and there was evidence given that some at least of the merchants knew that the rogue was not entitled to the use of the card. The Court held that the plaintiff could not recover, noting that the merchants could not have recovered directly from the defendant and that the plaintiff could not then be in a better position.

21.31 The decision seems to be based on some variant of the assignment model with its consequences that the issuer takes the debt subject to equities, although the Court did not spell out the background reasoning for its findings.

Chapter 22

General principles of lending

22.1 Although lending to customers is an important part of the business of banking, the normal relationship of banker and customer does not include any contractual terms related to lending by any means other than overdraft. In general, lending by the banker to a customer is the subject of a separate and explicit contract which is more often than not evidenced in writing.

22.2 When engaged in the business of lending, the banker has few statutory or other legal privileges. Aside from the banker's lien discussed in Ch 25 and a few provisions in the Bills of Exchange Act, bankers are in the same legal position as any other credit provider.

Types of lending

22.3 Traditionally, lending by New Zealand banks has been short term loans provided by way of overdraft. Even in the case of housing finance where the parties expected that the loan would continue for a number of years, the legal form was that of an overdraft which was repayable "on demand". With the onset of deregulation as well as the other economic changes which have occurred over the last 20 years, this pattern is no longer as immutable as it once was.

22.4 This text is not concerned with the principles of good lending, although such a topic is of the utmost importance to the practising banker. We are concerned here only with the legal aspects of lending, practice being relevant only in so far as it affects or is affected by the law related to lending.

Secured and unsecured loans

22.5 One distinction which must be drawn is that between secured and unsecured loans. An unsecured loan is a contract between the lender and the borrower whereby the lender advances money and the borrower promises to repay that money together with any interest and charges which might be agreed upon terms which are agreed. The only remedy which the lender has in the event of default is the action for breach of contract, although since the amount claimed will usually be for a liquidated sum the default summons procedure may be used.

22.6 A secured loan, by contrast, requires in addition to the above that the borrower provide the lender with an interest in some property. In the event of default, the lender may seek to recover the amount due from the property rather than directly from the borrower. Since the lender has an interest in property, that interest will not be affected by the insolvency of the borrower, so that recovery might be possible even when the borrower is unable, as distinct from unwilling, to pay. The law relating to the taking of security interest is discussed in Chs 23 and 24.

Overdrafts

22.7 An overdraft facility is nothing more than a current account on which the banker has approved arrangements which allow drawings to a certain limit which will leave the account in debit. Generally, the overdraft is repayable upon demand.[1] The account is operated like a normal cheque account with interest being charged on the amount that the account is actually overdrawn. In addition, there may be establishment fees and penalty interest if the limit is exceeded.

1 See the discussion at 2.42 concerning the meaning of repayment "on demand".

22.8 Substantial overdrafts should be arranged ahead of time, but if the customer writes a cheque of a size which would, if honoured, result in the account being overdrawn, then this amounts in law to a request by the customer for an overdraft which the banker may or may not grant.[1]

1 See *Cuthbert v Roberts, Lubbock & Co* [1909] 2 Ch 226.

22.9 As noted at 8.57ff, the banker has, in the absence of any agreement to the contrary, a right to combine the overdraft account with any other current account belonging to the customer whether that credit account be with the same or a different branch. An agreement which precludes combination may be relatively easily implied but does not follow from the mere fact of more than one account being opened by the customer.[1]

1 See 8.57ff.

22.10 The banker's right to repayment "on demand" is, of course, matched by the customer's right to repay the overdraft without notice and with payment of interest to the day of repayment only.

Term loans

22.11 Although lending by way of overdraft may fit comfortably into the usual relationship between banker and customer, loans for a fixed period must be much more thoroughly documented. As mentioned above, the banker is in a position no different from any other lender for this type of transaction.

22.12 Functionally, the primary difference from an overdraft arrangement is that the loan is no longer repayable upon demand. Indeed, a demand for repayment before the contractual termination date would be a breach of contract by the bank. Further, while the loan agreement remains in force, the bank has no right to combine the loan account with any account which might be in credit.

Commercial and financial bills

22.13 In certain circumstances, the bank may be willing to lend to a customer but may not wish to advance cash by way of loan or overdraft. One method of "lending credit" to the customer is by way of a "line" of credit, usually through the mechanism of financial bills of exchange. Since 1978, New Zealand banks have operated in the commercial bills market. A bill which bears the acceptance or the indorsement of a bank is known as a "bank bill" and is obviously a very valuable item on the bill market. In establishing a bill line, the bank will agree to accept bills drawn on it by the customer up to the limit agreed upon. The customer may then discount the bank bill in the commercial market. The bank charges an "acceptance fee" which together with the discount from the face value of the bill represents the interest which the customer will pay for the funds.

22.14 This arrangement allows the bank to "lend its credit" to the customer. A related arrangement is a "discount line" in which the bank agrees to discount bills drawn by the customer. As far as the customer is concerned, this is very much like a loan in that he or she receives money directly from the bank and is obliged to repay funds to the bank at a particular time. From the banker's point of view, however, the bill provides a hedge against liquidity pressures since the banker reserves the right to sell the bill on the market at any time.

22.15 Generally speaking, bills are for periods of 90 or 180 days. Since the customer is likely to need funds for a longer period of time, the line of credit usually provides that the bills may be "rolled over", ie, new bills will be drawn at the time of maturity of the original set. In this way, the borrower is assured of longer term finance, although the interest rate will vary with the market.

Standby credits and performance bonds

22.16 A second way in which the banker might "lend credit" is through the use of standby letters of credit and/or performance bonds. These will be discussed in detail in Ch 28, but the basic idea is that the banker promises to some third party that payment will be made under certain circumstances. As an example, a foreign purchaser of New Zealand technology may be concerned that the vendor may not be able to deliver. Such a failure may expose the foreign importer to substantial expenses, either directly or by way of damages for breach of contract for further supply. One way in which the dilemma is sometimes solved is for a New Zealand bank to issue a performance bond in favour of the foreign purchaser. If there is a failure by the New Zealand supplier, the foreign purchaser may call upon the bank to pay a sum which will protect against the possible losses.

22.17 The arrangement works because the creditworthiness of the New Zealand bank, which may be easily assessed, has been substituted for the creditworthiness of the New Zealand supplier. The latter may either be difficult for the foreigner to assess or may be unsatisfactory if it has been assessed. In this sense, the bank has "lent credit". Of course the banker will treat the issuance of a performance bond in much the same way as a loan. The customer must promise to put the banker in funds should the bond be drawn upon and the banker will need to assess the ability of the customer to fulfil this promise. The banker will take appropriate securities to guard against the possibility of insolvency.

Types of borrowers

22.18 The banker must be aware of the different legal characteristics of borrowers, for different types of securities may be taken, different forms of guarantees may be needed and different loan structures may be used depending upon the class into which the individual borrower falls.

Private borrowers

22.19 In terms of numbers, the majority of bank lending is still to individual customers, either for "private" purposes such as the purchase of a house or a vehicle or for business reasons. Since it is highly unlikely that the banker would even be contemplating a loan which would be used for an illegal purpose, there is little in the way of legal problems involved in such a loan provided the borrower has contractual capacity.

22.20 Contracting with minors is subject to the Minors' Contracts Act 1969. In New Zealand, a person attains "full age" at 20 years and such a person has no age related contractual disabilities.[1] The Minors' Contracts Act divides minors into three categories with varying capacities to contract. By s 4 of the Minors' Contracts Act, a minor who is or who has been at any time married has the same contractual capacity as a person of full age.

1 S 4, Age of Majority Act 1970.

22.21 Except for certain contracts of life insurance and of service, a contract with a minor who has not attained the age of 18 years is unenforceable against the minor unless the contract has been approved by the District Court on the minor's behalf a procedure which is authorised by s 9 of the Act.

22.22 Minors who have attained the age of 18 have a special status under the New Zealand legislation. Section 5 of the Act allows contracting with such minors subject to the re-opening of the contract by the Court in two possible circumstances. First, the Court may intervene if the consideration for the minor's promise or act is so inadequate as to be unconscionable. Secondly, intervention may occur if there is any provision which imposes a obligation on a minor which is harsh or oppressive.

The intervention by the Court may take the form of cancelling the contract, declining to enforce it against the minor or to declare the contract to be unenforceable either in whole or in part. The Court may also make orders for the compensation or the restitution of property.

Business borrowers

22.23 Different forms of business association will give rise to slightly different concerns when the banker is lending for the purposes of the borrower's business activities.

Sole traders

22.24 There are no legal problems associated with lending to sole traders, although as will be seen in Ch 27, there may be a problem with obtaining proper security over stock in trade.

Partnerships

22.25 The basic legal characteristics of partnerships have been discussed above in Ch 3. A partnership is the relation that exists between persons carrying on a business in common with a view to profit.Ssuch a circumstance may arise without any formal intention on the part of the parties to become partners. A single partner may bind the firm but this is only so if the purpose is that of the firm or apparently that of the firm. The death, bankruptcy or insanity of a partner will dissolve the partnership. A partner who dies or becomes bankrupt is liable for the partnership debts, but the debts of the private estate have a prior claim.

22.26 Since the banker is not generally in a position to monitor any of these possible changes, it is wise to make express provision for liabilities for loans to partnerships. This is usually done by expressly making each of the partners jointly and severally liable for the loan and by taking joint and several guarantees from each of the partners.

22.27 Finally, when notified of any change in the partnership, the banker should rule off any overdraft account so as to prevent the operation of the rule in *Clayton's case* causing a loss of the bank's rights against any of the parties.[1] If it is desired to carry on arrangements with the newly constituted partnership, a new account should be opened and new documentation taken.

1 See 8.3ff for a discussion of the rule in *Clayton's case.*

Companies

22.28 The legal aspects of lending to a company differ from those of individual lending in only two major characteristics. First, the company may not have the power to borrow or it may lack the power to borrow for certain purposes.[1] Secondly, the securities which may be taken from a company differ from those which are taken from an individual.[2]

1 Although the importance of this exception is now much reduced; see 22.83.
2 See Ch 24.

22.29 Further, although the company is a separate legal entity, there are many companies which are virtually alter egos of one or a small number of individuals. Consequently, a loan to such a company will usually be accompanied by a taking of guarantees and/or securities from the individuals "behind" the company. Matters of security and the taking of guarantees are discussed in Chs 23 to 26.

Power to borrow

22.30 The Companies Amendment Act (No 2) 1983 inserted a new s 18A into the Companies Act 1955 which provides that nothing done by a company is invalid only on the ground that the company lacked the capacity, as defined in the memorandum and articles of association, to do the act. Indeed, s 14A obviates the necessity for a company to list its objects in the memorandum and s 15A provides that a company is to have all of the rights, powers and privileges of a natural person.

22.31 It might be thought that these welcome changes to the Companies Act mean that a banker need no longer be concerned with the power of a company to borrow. This impression is incorrect for two reasons. First, there are still privileged groups which may challenge the acts of a company on the ground that they are ultra vires.[1] Secondly, it is most likely that a banker will actually see the company's memorandum and articles and it is possible that these may contain express prohibitions and limitations. In such a case, the banker may be bound by the provisions. Consequently, the powers of companies to borrow which were established by the Courts prior to the passage of the amendments may still be relevant, although there is no doubt that they will be needed less frequently.

1 S 18A.

Implied power to borrow

22.32 Even in the absence of the amendments and of any express powers in the memorandum and articles, a trading company has an implied right to borrow and to give securities, since both activities have been held to be an essential part of the business of trading.[1] However, this implied power to borrow may be negatived by an express prohibition in either the articles of association or the memorandum of association.

1 *General Auction Estate & Monetary Co v Smith* [1891] 3 Ch 199.

22.33 The statutory amendments are of far more importance when dealing with non-trading companies, for such companies did not have an implied right to borrow. Further, the power to borrow did not entail a power to give securities, so that it was necessary that these powers be expressed in the memorandum or in the articles.[1]

1 *Re Introductions Ltd* [1970] Ch 199; *Rolled Steel Products Ltd v British Steel Corp* [1982] 3 All ER 1057.

22.34 Finally, the power to borrow or to give securities was limited to those purposes within the scope of the objects for which the company was formed. Although the objects for which the company was formed need not be stated if the company was registered after 1 January 1984, it is still possible that limitations on the power to borrow may be stated in the memorandum or the articles.

Agency problems

22.35 Even though the company has the power to borrow and to give securities and even though the loan is for a proper purpose, a banker deals with the company not as an abstract legal entity but rather with directors and other individuals who are acting as agents of the company. But these individual agents do not have unlimited power to commit the company by signing contracts on the company's behalf. Suppose that a director or other agent of the company is acting beyond his or her actual authority. Under what circumstances may the banker rely on the apparent authority of the agent in order to be certain that the company will be bound by the terms of the loan agreement?

22.36 The relationship of such directors to outside third parties is the subject of ss 18C and 18D of the Companies Act 1955 which were inserted by the Law Reform (Miscellaneous Amendments) Act 1985, but it is worth considering the position reached by the common law Courts before the passing of those amendments.

22.37 The basic position was discussed in *Royal British Bank v Turquand*[1] and is known as the rule in *Turquand's* case. There it was said that every person is deemed to have notice of the contents of the company's memorandum and articles of association but that it is not necessary for a person dealing with a company to inquire into the internal workings of the company to verify that an agent of the company is acting within the actual limits of authority.[2] Phrased another way, a company will be bound by the acts of an apparent agent if the company has represented that the person is an agent and the act is one which would have been within the scope of his or her authority had the person actually been the agent of the company.

1 (1856) 119 ER 886.
2 There is no longer a presumption that everyone knows the contents of the articles and memorandum, but the banker will often have actual knowledge.

22.38 This was not as favourable to the banker as might first be thought. For example, if the power to borrow which was granted in the memorandum or the articles was a power which could only be exercised by the passing of a general resolution, then the banker had to be certain to sight the resolution before granting the loan, for if there was no resolution then the director or other agent was not acting within the scope of the authority which they would have possessed had they been the actual agent of the company. On the other hand, if the resolution was sighted, then under the rule in *Turquand's* case, it was not necessary for the banker to inquire into the formal regularity of the resolution, as for example, ascertaining that a quorum was present at the meeting where the resolution was passed or that the proper rules of order were followed at the meeting.

22.39 For many years this remained a confused area of law, but the decision by the Court of Appeal in England in *Freeman and Lockyer v Buckhurst Park Properties (Mangal) Ltd,*[1] particularly the judgment of Diplock LJ, has clarified the matter considerably. The defendant company was formed for the purpose of buying a particular property and making a quick resale. The property was purchased, but the resale did not eventuate so that the directors of the company were concerned merely to dispose of the property as advantageously as possible.

1 [1964] 2 QB 480.

22.40 One Kapoor was a director of the company who was conducting the business of the company with the knowledge and approval of the other directors. Professing to act on behalf of the company, he instructed the plaintiffs to render certain services, namely the conduct of a planning application and appeal relating to the property. The payment for those services was the subject matter of the suit. The trial Court found that the plaintiffs had intended to contract with the company, not with Kapoor personally. It was also found that although Kapoor had never been formally appointed as managing director he had been acting as such and that this was known to the board of directors.

22.41 In a comprehensive review, Diplock LJ summarised the position by concluding that there were four conditions which must be satisfied in order to entitle a contractor to enforce the contract against the company when it was entered into on behalf of the company by an agent who lacked actual authority to do so. It must be shown that:

  1 a representation that the agent had authority to enter on behalf of the company into a contract of the kind sought to be enforced was made to the contractor;

  2 such representation was made by a person or persons who had "actual" authority to manage the business of the company either generally or in respect of those matters to which the contract relates;

  3 [the contractor] was induced by such representation to enter into the contract, that is, that he in fact relied upon it; and

  4 under its memorandum or articles of association the company was not deprived of the capacity either to enter into a contract of the kind sought to be enforced or to delegate authority to enter into a contract of that kind to the agent.[1]

1 Per Diplock LJ in *Freeman and Lockyer v Buckhurst Park Properties (Mangal) Ltd* [1964] 2 QB 480, 505-506.

Agency problems: s 18C

22.42 The question of apparent authority is now the subject of s 18C of the Companies Act 1955. The relevant parts which deal with agency are:

> **18C. Dealings between company and other persons** — (1) A company or a guarantor of an obligation of a company may not assert against a person dealing with the company or with any person who has acquired any property, rights, or interests from the company that —
> (a) The memorandum or articles of the company have not been complied with:
> (b) A person named in the particulars sent to the Registrar under section 200 of this Act as a director or secretary of the company —
>> (i) Is not a director or secretary of the company, as the case may be; or
>> (ii) Has not been duly appointed; or
>> (iii) Does not have authority to exercise a power which a director or secretary of a company carrying on business of the kind carried on by the company customarily has authority to exercise:
> (c) A person held out by the company as an officer or agent of the company —
>> (i) Has not been duly appointed; or
>> (ii) Does not have authority to exercise a power which an officer or agent of a company carrying on business of the kind carried on by the company customarily has authority to exercise:
> (d) A person held out by the company as an officer or agent of the company with authority to exercise a power which an officer or agent of a company carrying on business of the kind carried on by the company does not customarily have authority to exercise, does not have authority to exercise that power.

22.43 It is not thought that this section will make much difference when the banker has a dispute with the company. The first two of the requirements mentioned by Lord Diplock must still be shown under the most liberal reading of the section. The third will usually be a matter which is not in dispute in any case. The new law might be taken as excusing the fourth requirement, but as mentioned above, the banker will usually have an actual copy of the memorandum and articles in any case and so will be taken to know their contents. It might be thought that the simple solution is for the banker to cease calling for a copy of these documents, but that is a course which may not be open, for s 18C(1) ends with an exception:

> unless that person knows or by reason of his position with or relationship to the company ought to know of the matter referred to in [the above paragraphs] . . . of this section.

22.44 Given the duty that banks have towards their customers, the banker might be a person whose "relationship with the company" excludes him from the benefits of the section in most cases. If that is so, then the matter is right back to the basic principles established by Lord Diplock in *Freeman and Lockyer v Buckhurst Park Properties (Mangal) Ltd.*[1]

1 [1964] 2 QB 480.

22.45 The situation is complicated by the interaction of the above section with the provisions of the Companies Amendment Act (No 2) 1983. As mentioned above, s 18A abolishes the ultra vires rule by providing that nothing done by a company is invalid solely on the ground that the company was without capacity. But further, s 14A provides that a company no longer need to state its objects in the memorandum and s 15A which gives a company all the rights, powers and privileges of a natural person.[1] If a company chooses to take advantage of these sections, then there is no need for Lord Diplock's fourth requirement unless it is to be interpreted as referring to the powers possessed by a natural person.

1 The section numbers are references to the new sections inserted into the Companies Act 1955.

22.46 Since the new amendments still allow the ultra vires acts of the company to be challenged by some parties under some circumstances, it may be prudent for a lender to require that the company insert specific powers into the memorandum and articles even though it is not required by law. If such a course is followed, then the situation would not differ greatly from the common law position.

Statutory prohibitions

22.47 The banker should also be certain that there are no statutory restrictions on the company's borrowing powers. In particular, a company is generally forbidden from providing financial assistance for the purchase of its own shares.[1] Note in particular, that the rule in *Turquand's* case concerning the ostensible authority of agents of the company is of no protection when the "reasonable banker" would know or suspect that the authority is being misused by an agent. This is particularly important in the context of the possible use of company funds to purchase shares in the company itself.[2]

1 See s 62, Companies Act 1955.
2 See *Selangor United Rubber Estates v Cradock (No 3)* [1968] 2 All ER 1073; *Karak Rubber Co Ltd v Burden (No 2)* [1972] All ER 1210 and the discussion at 7.73ff.

Incorporated clubs and societies

22.48 The operation of these organisations is governed by the Incorporated Societies Act 1908 or possibly under specialised statutes which govern the specific type of organisation being dealt with. Usually, the property of such organisations is with trustees who have the power to deal with the property in a manner consistent with their terms of appointment and the rules of the society. Such terms of appointment and rules should be carefully sighted by the banker prior to agreeing to any advances.

Unincorporated associations

22.49 The problems of lending here relate directly to the previous discussion concerning the lack of a single legal identity for such organisations. There is no identity apart from the individuals, so special care must be taken that the individuals involved understand precisely the scope of their liability.[1]

1 See the discussion in Ch 4.

Chapter 23

Securities I

Security defined — Mortgage

23.1 When a loan is made, the borrower promises to repay the amount loaned together with any interest agreed upon. In the absence of unusual circumstances such a promise is enforceable in a Court of law. If the creditor is forced to take such proceedings, then, if successful, there are procedures for ultimately recovering the debt from the property of the debtor.

23.2 However, a lawsuit is both expensive and unsatisfactory and the hard truth of the matter is that most defaulting debtors would like to pay their debt but cannot. In such a circumstance, the obtaining of judgment against the debtor will usually be of no value, for there is no property left from which to satisfy the debt.

23.3 It is for this reason that creditors may prefer to take a security from the debtor as well as the contractual promise to repay. A general definition of "security" is notoriously difficult to formulate, but in all cases there is some right of the creditor to reclaim the debt, or part of it, from property which is "reserved" for that purpose.

Security

23.4 Perhaps the best formal definition of "security" is that given by Sykes:

. . . an interest, not being an interest arising from a trust, in property which is either owned by another person or in which another person has incomplete or inchoate rights capable of maturing into full ownership, by virtue of which interest certain rights are exercisable in relation to that property in order to obtain payment or performance of an obligation by that other person either consensually provided for or provided for by implication of law or validly directed by some third party to be paid or performed.[1]

1 Sykes, *The Law of Securities*, 3rd ed, Sydney, 1978, p 11.

23.5 As usual, the word "security" is used in a narrower sense by lawyers than by the commercial community as a whole. There are at least two other ways in which the word is used in commercial practice. First, "security" may refer to the property over which the security is given. Secondly, "security" may refer to documents of various kinds, including notes and bills, share certificates, bonds and a whole host of others.

23.6 A guarantee by a third party is not a security under the definition given by Sykes. A guarantee is merely a contractual promise given by some third party which makes that party liable in the event of a default by the debtor. However, because the guarantee is functionally so closely related to the concept of a security interest, the topic is covered in this section.

Legal and equitable security interests

23.7 A distinction must also be drawn between legal and equitable security interests. The definition is purely operational: a legal interest is one which, prior to the enactment of the Judicature Act (UK) 1873, would have been recognised by a Court of common law; an equitable interest is one which, at the same time, would have been recognised only by a Court of equity.

23.8 The distinction remains important for us today because of the fact that the Judicature Acts did not merge the two related legal systems into a single legal system, but rather merged the administration of each system of law into a single Court system.

Priorities when more than one interest

23.9 The distinction between legal and equitable interests has a number of consequences, but the most important for existing purposes is the problem which arises when there are competing security interests in the same item of physical property. It must be emphasised that there is nothing improper or fraudulent in this. A borrower may give a mortgage over property to lender A and then give a second mortgage over the same property to lender B.

23.10 If the borrower is unable to pay and the lenders have to realise the security, the question arises as to how the proceeds from the property should be distributed. Suppose that lender A had provided $1,000 and lender B had provided $500. If the property realises more than $1,500, then there is no problem. If it realises less, then the general rule would be that lender A takes the whole $1000 (if there is that much) and lender B takes whatever is left and is left only with an action on the contract of loan to recover what other sum is due.[1]

1 This is a very simplified example. There are matters of interest due and costs of the sale of the property to take into account.

23.11 The problem becomes more difficult when the security interests given to A and to B are of substantially different types. Suppose, for example, that the borrower gives lender A a mortgage over some jewellery, but then later pledges the jewellery to B, ie, gives B the right to possession of the jewellery until such time as the debt may be repaid. Both A and B believe that they should be entitled to the "first bite" of the money which might be realised from the sale of the jewellery in the event of the borrower's default.

23.12 There are problems in priorities between competing security interests. These problems are generally very difficult and call for expert advice, but, subject to many exceptions, the basic rules which establish priorities depend upon first identifying the nature of the security as either legal or equitable and then:

1 if both interests are legal, then the one which has been created first in time should have priority;

2 if both interests are equitable, then the rule is the same, that is, the interest created first in time should have priority;

3 if the first interest is a legal one and the second is equitable, then the legal interest has priority;

4 if the first interest is equitable and the second is legal, then the equitable interest has priority *unless* the legal interest was taken by the creditor without notice of the existence of the already existing equitable interest, in which case, the legal interest has priority.

23.13 The fourth rule is a slightly simplified version of the priority rules, for the time at which the subsequent creditor must be without notice is not the time of taking the legal title, but the time of making the advance.[1] This allows for a strange sequence of events: Suppose that A lends to B, taking an equitable interest. Later C lends to B, also secured by an equitable interest. Later C learns of A's prior interest which, of course, gives A priority if the security must be realised. C then takes steps to acquire a full legal interest in the secured property. C then has priority over A who has been "squeezed out". The effect is called a *tabula in naufragio*; it would seem to be restricted to the situation where C's equitable interest is a fixed, as opposed to a floating, interest.[2]

1 *Taylor v Russell* [1892] AC 244. It seems that this applies only to fixed equitable charges. See Goode, *Legal Problems of Credit and Security*, London, 1982.
2 See *Taylor v Russell* [1892] AC 244.

12.14 Again, it must be noted that these rules are general only and are subject to many exceptions and modifications. Nevertheless, they provide the starting point for any solution to a priority problem; consequently, the distinction between legal and equitable security interests is of great importance in priority problems.

23.15 Knowledge of the existence of equitable security interests is also important because equitable interests are relatively easy to create. It may happen that the formalities necessary to create a legal interest have not been properly completed so that the legal interest is not created, yet a similar equitable interest has been created. In some of the cases, it seems that an equitable interest has almost been created by "accident" for it is sometimes sufficient for the Court to find an "intention" in the behaviour of the parties which will create the equitable proprietary interest.

Consensual securities

23.16 Most security interests are created by the agreement of the parties. Such security interests are called consensual securities. However, it is also possible for a security interest to arise by operation of law, that is, that the proprietary interest vests in the creditor by virtue of some set of circumstances regardless of the intention or even the knowledge of the parties. Most of the security interests which are of interest to the banker will arise by agreement between the parties, but one very important interest, the banker's lien, is a non-consensual security.

23.17 Consensual securities will be examined first. The creation of these is, in contrast to so much of the relationship between banker and customer, generally a very formal process. The contract which creates the security interest is generally a pre-printed form used by the banker and containing many detailed and arcane clauses. Although they differ in detail from bank to bank, the contracts used by banks differ from those in general use in two ways. First, the contracts often call for the repayment of the loan "on demand".[1]

1 See 2.42ff.

23.18 The second peculiarity of bank forms is the detail and scope of the definition of moneys to be secured. The forms usually contain many clauses which attempt to define explicitly virtually every conceivable situation in which the banker might advance money to the borrower or to someone associated with the borrower together with any interest or charges which might be due. All are purported to be secured by the interest being granted by the borrower to the banker.

23.19 The length and scope of bank forms has been the subject of judicial criticism. In *Richard v The Commercial Bank of Australia*[1] a bank mortgage was given by a husband and wife who were referred to in the document as the mortgagor. It was argued, unsuccessfully, by the bank that the document should be interpreted so as to secure the husband's liability under a guarantee which was given by the husband alone. During the course of the judgment, Fox J said:

> It surely is a sad commentary on the operation of our legal system that a borrower should be expected to execute a document which only a person of extraordinary application and persistence would read, which, if read, is virtually incomprehensible and which, in any event, has a legal effect not disclosed by its language.[2]

1 (1971) 18 FLR 95.
2 At pp 99-100.

Security over real property

23.20 Security interests may be taken in real property, in chattels and in choses in action. Each is governed by a fundamentally different set of legal rules. The remainder of this chapter will examine the taking of security interests over real property.

Commercial classification of mortgages

23.21 As so often happens, there is a problem of terminology when dealing with mortgages. Bankers often speak of the "mortgage" when the lawyer would talk about the "loan". Although this section is concerned with the mortgage as the security interest taken by the banker to secure the loan, two common commercial usages will be noted.

Flat mortgage

23.22 The so called "flat" mortgage is one where the borrower repays only the interest during the term of the loan. At the end of the term, the principal is repaid and the security interest taken by the lender is discharged.

Table mortgage

23.23 In the table mortgage, the periodic repayments are calculated so that the interest and principal are repaid at the end of the term of the loan. Generally, the periodic repayments, known as instalments, remain at a constant level during the life of the loan. In such an arrangement, the payments made during the early life of the loan will have a very high percentage going toward the repayment of interest, while those made late in the life of the loan will have a large percentage applied to the repayment of principal. As a matter of practice, most mortgages contain a clause which allows for a periodic review of the rate of interest and a consequential adjustment in the amount of the instalments. It is also usual for the borrower to have the right to repay the outstanding principal with only a small or no penalty.

Legal aspects of mortgages over real property

23.24 The best way in which to understand the nature of a mortgage over land is to consider the form of the mortgage which existed prior to the introduction of the Torrens system of title registration. Under the so called "old system" or "deeds system", a purchaser of land could obtain valid title only by having the land conveyed by the true owner of the land. In order to determine that the seller was the true owner, it was necessary to establish that the previous seller was the true owner and so on right back to the original Crown grant. Such an investigation of ownership is expensive and uncertain, with the result that title to land was subject to attack by the discovery of some defective link in the chain of title.

Old style mortgages

23.25 In this context, a mortgage of land took the form of a conveyance of the land coupled with a contractual promise that the lender, the new owner of the land, would convey it back to the borrower when the borrower complied with the terms of repayment of the loan. To anyone who was not privy to the contract of loan, the transaction looked like a sale of property; there are still echoes of this in s 60 of the Sale of Goods Act 1908 which provides that the Act does not apply to transactions which, although in the form of a sale, are intended to be by way of security.

The right of redemption and second mortgages

23.26 One of the main problems with the old form of mortgage was the strict interpretation which the common law placed on the contractual promise to reconvey. If the borrower was in default by even a day, then the lender could no longer be held to his or her promise. Furthermore, even in the absence of default the only rights left to the borrower were contractual ones; the common law recognised no property interest remaining in the borrower following the conveyance.

23.27 This intolerable situation was remedied by the Courts of equity which recognised the "right of redemption". By ordering specific performance of the contract to reconvey, and by a willingness to make such an order even when the borrower had been in default, the Courts of equity created a new property interest which remained with the mortgagor of the property. This equitable property interest was, and is, known as the "equity of redemption".

23.28 It was soon realised that this equity of redemption was itself a valuable property right which might be mortgaged as security for advances from other lenders. When this was done, the transaction became known as a "second mortgage". The second mortgage is an equitable one since it is a conveyance of property recognised only by the Courts of equity.

23.29 These developments were not without their problems, for the rights and obligations of the parties were complex and confused, depending as they did upon two separate but interlocking systems of law. When ownership of land was put on the more certain footing of a system of registration, it was also necessary to change the form of the mortgage and to define more precisely the relationships between the mortgagor, the mortgagee and the land.

Other forms of equitable mortgages

23.30 Before considering the Torrens land registration system, it should be noted that the second mortgage is not the only form of an equitable mortgage. Under the deed system, an equitable mortgage could be created by the deposit of title deeds with the lender,[1] by an informal attempt to create a legal mortgage and in certain other ways that need not concern us now. As will be seen, the importance of the equitable mortgage has been diminished by the introduction of the Torrens registration system, but it is by no means obsolete.

1 A form no longer possible in New Zealand: see s 77, Property Law Act 1952.

The Torrens system of land registration

23.31 The deficiencies of the deeds system led to the introduction into New Zealand of the Torrens system of land registration in 1870.

The two systems existed side by side until 1924 when it was made compulsory to bring all transferred land within the Torrens system.

23.32 The warning given earlier concerning the extent of the coverage of this section needs to be repeated here. The following material is the barest of outlines of the workings of the Torrens system. It is not intended and should not be used as a substitute for a textbook on the law relating to land tenure. The following descriptions focus on freehold property; certain property held on a lesser tenure from the Crown is also included in the Torrens system.

Indefeasibility of title

23.33 The touchstone of the Torrens system is indefeasibility of title: registration as the registered proprietor is conclusive evidence of ownership subject only to certain exceptions related to a person who becomes a registered owner by means of his or her own fraud.[1] It is not necessary for the registered owner to prove that previous transfers were valid.

1 S 183, Land Transfer Act 1952.

The certificate of title

23.34 Each parcel of land which is registered under the Torrens system is issued with a certificate of title. The original of this certificate is always retained by the Land Transfer Office in the district where the land is located and a copy of the certificate is issued either to the registered owner or to the first registered mortgagee. As will be seen, this copy of the certificate is important and can play a role similar in some respects to the old deeds of title.

The public register

23.35 Most major dealings with the land are required to be registered with the Land Transfer Office. These dealings are recorded on a public register by notations on the original certificate of title. Consequently, an inspection of the public register will reveal details about the previous dealings with the land as well as any existing outstanding interests in the land which require registration. This public register is considered so important that everyone is deemed in law to know the contents of it.

23.36 Dealings with the land are entered on the register together with the precise time of registration. As will be seen, mortgages over the land have priority determined not by the rules mentioned above, but by time of registration.[1] It is possible to change the priority of two registered mortgages by agreement among the interested parties which may then be registered.

1 S 37, Land Transfer Act 1952.

Compensation system

23.37 The Torrens system has a compensation system built into it for two reasons. First, the indefeasibility principle means that occasionally someone who would have remained the owner of land under the deeds system will lose ownership to an innocent registered owner. The system provides for a type of insurance payment to the deprived owner in such a circumstance. Secondly, it is possible that ownership of land could be lost through some error in the Land Transfer Office. The system provides for compensation to be made by the Crown in certain circumstances.

Torrens land mortgages

23.38 As noted above, when the deeds system was replaced with the registration system, the law relating to mortgages was also rationalised. It was no longer necessary that a mortgage should be a formal conveyance of the property, since the interest could be placed on the register and the rights and obligations of the parties defined in the legislation. The end result is a clarification and simplification of the relationships established when land is mortgaged.

23.39 Under s 100 of the Land Transfer Act, a mortgage has effect as a security but does not operate as a transfer of the land. A mortgage is a registrable instrument and should be registered for reasons which will become apparent. It should be noted, however, that an unregistered mortgage is not a legal nullity; it may affect not only the immediate parties but third parties as well.[1] Further note that the distinction between legal and equitable mortgages, although blurred, is still relevant. For example, a mortgage document which purports to create a mortgage over Torrens system land is a valid equitable mortgage from the time of its creation even though the mortgagee does not have the legal rights provided by the statute until such time as the mortgage is placed on the register.[2]

1 Since it may form an equitable mortgage: see 23.40ff.
2 Ss 33, 34, Land Transfer Act 1952.

Equitable mortgages

23.40 Under the old system of land transfer, an equitable mortgage could be created merely by the mortgagor depositing the title deeds with the mortgagee. Provided that the parties intended to create a security interest by these actions, the Court would hold that there was indeed an equitable mortgage created.[1] The nature of the transaction has been succinctly stated by Pape J:

> The nature of an equitable mortgage by deposit of title deeds is not in doubt. The deposit of title deeds as security for the payment of a debt is regarded as an imperfect mortgage which the mortgagor is entitled to have perfected, or as a contract for a legal mortgage which gives to the party entitled all such rights as he would have had if the contract had been completed. By the deposit the mortgagor contracts that his interest in the property comprised in the deeds shall be liable for the debt and binds himself to do all that is necessary to effect the vesting in the mortgagee of such interest as a mortgage should create.[2]

1 For a modern discussion, see *Re Moulton Finance Ltd* [1968] Ch 325; the mere deposit of title deeds cannot create an equitable mortgage: s 77, Property Law Act 1952.
2 Per Pape J, *Re Nairn* [1961] VR 26, 28.

23.41 Although s 77 of the Property Law Act 1952 makes impossible the creation of an equitable mortgage by the mere deposit of title deeds, the same effect may be achieved by giving an agreement to execute a mortgage if called upon to do so. This means that a mere indication of intention is inadequate; what is required is an enforceable contract.

23.42 It seems common for a lender to take a completed memorandum of mortgage together with the certificate of title. If the lender chooses not to register the mortgage, it has been held that there is an equitable mortgage created and that it is probably not necessary for the lender to enter a caveat on the title for the mortgage to remain good.[1] No change in ownership can take place without the production of the duplicate certificate of title except in extraordinary cases. If it becomes necessary for the lender to resort to the security for repayment of the loan, the mortgage may be registered at any time in order to take advantage of the powers of sale given to a registered mortgagee.[2]

1 There may be circumstances when a failure to lodge a caveat will be held against the equitable mortgagee: see *Abigail v Lapin* [1934] AC 491.
2 See 23.52 and *J & H Just (Holdings) Pty Ltd v Bank of New South Wales* (1971) 45 ALJR 625.

23.43 Although convenient because of the simplicity, unregistered equitable mortgages suffer from some disadvantages. They are liable to be defeated by any prior equitable interest, although such defeat is by no means certain. An unregistered equitable mortgage is also subject to defeat by fraudulent dealings by the owner provided it is possible for the owner to provide some plausible explanation for the absence of the duplicate certificate of title. Finally, the mortgagee has no general power of sale. This last is not overly important since in the common form the lender has taken the certificate and a memorandum of mortgage and there is no impediment to registration with its consequential statutory power of sale.

Registered mortgages

23.44 A registered mortgage may be either a legal or an equitable mortgage in form, but since registration amounts to notice and since the rights and powers of the parties are the same, the distinction is of no practical importance. The essential features of a registered mortgage are that certain rights and obligations are implied by the statute into all mortgages except in so far as they are expressly varied or negatived by the parties to the mortgage.[1] There are, in addition, statutory powers of sale given to the mortgagee and powers of redemption given to the mortgagor.

1 S 75, Property Law Act 1952.

Property Law Act 1952 (Fourth Schedule) — implied terms

23.45 The implied terms of every mortgage are set out in the Fourth Schedule of the Property Law Act 1952. However, as noted above, these may be varied and it is virtually universal that this occurs. As also noted previously, the forms in use by bankers tend to be long and detailed documents which are intended to cover as many contingencies as the banks' solicitors were able to imagine.

23.46 The document which must be completed is known as a memorandum of mortgage and in order to effect registration of the mortgage it must be certified as correct by the mortgagor. Registration requires both the memorandum and the duplicate certificate of title.

Remedies

23.47 The mortgagee has essentially three separate remedies in the event of the borrower defaulting on the loan. The course of action which the mortgagee takes will depend upon all of the circumstances of the case with particular attention given to the financial position of the borrower and the value of the security interest.

Suit on the personal covenant

23.48 If the amount of the default is small in comparison with the total value of the security or if the debtor has significant assets apart from the property which has been mortgaged, it is always possible for the lender to ignore the mortgage and to sue on the promise of repayment which is an essential part of every form of memorandum of mortgage. Successful suit places the lender in the same position as any other judgment creditor, so that if the debtor still refuses to pay then the creditor may proceed to move against any of the debtor's assets, not merely against the property which was mortgaged. Of course, if the debtor has no other assets, then such a course will be fruitless.

Enter and take possession: s 106, Land Transfer Act 1952

23.49 Section 106 of the Land Transfer Act 1952 allows the mortgagee to enter into possession of the mortgaged property upon default by the debtor. For reasons which will become apparent, this is not a course which will ordinarily appeal to the banker except in extraordinary circumstances.

23.50 It is important to recognise that taking possession does not necessarily mean taking physical possession of the property, although this is allowed by the statute. More common is that the mortgagee assumes management and control of the property, taking any rents or other income from it. This may be done, eg, by giving formal notice to any tenant to pay rent directly to the mortgagee.

23.51 The reason that this is not a popular option with mortgagees under normal conditions is that the mortgagee is required to account to the mortgagor and assumes a responsibility toward the mortgagor to manage the property reasonably. Although not allowed a free hand in the management of the property, the mortgagee in possession is nonetheless responsible for it and may under some circumstances be unable to quit the property when it suits.

Mortgagee sale on default

23.52 The mortgagee's power of sale is the most drastic and most effective remedy. In the usual case, the memorandum of mortgage will contain an express power of sale. In the case of a registered mortgage, this is not necessary, since there is a power of sale given to the mortgagee by the Property Law Act 1952, but in the case of an unregistered equitable mortgage, there would be no power of sale in the absence of an express contractual term. For reasons which will become clear, it is advisable for the holder of an unregistered equitable mortgage to register the mortgage before exercising any power of sale.

23.53 The power of sale granted by the statute is one of sale upon two months' default. It is for this reason that there is usually an express power inserted in the memorandum of mortgage, commonly to shorten the period to a month or less.

23.54 In no case may the power of sale be exercised without compliance with s 92 of the Property Law Act 1952. Under that section, no power of sale, whether expressed in the memorandum or given by the statute, may be exercised unless the mortgagee has served the mortgagor with a notice giving the details of the alleged default and allowing the mortgagor a period of at least one month from the receipt of notice to remedy the default. Failure to comply with s 92 invalidates the power of sale.

23.55 The precise scope of the mortgagee's duty to obtain a fair market price is not entirely clear. On the one hand, it has been said that the mortgagee is not like a trustee for the mortgagor, but the Privy Council has said that it is the duty of a mortgagee to behave "as a reasonable man would behave in the realisation of his own property".[1] It is certainly clear that the mortgagee may not act fraudulently or sacrifice the property at a patently low price.

1 *McHugh v Union Bank of Canada* [1913] AC 299, 311; *Alexandre v New Zealand Breweries Ltd* [1974] 1 NZLR 497.

23.56 On the other hand, it is also clear that the mortgagee may organise the sale in any manner which suits. The property may be sold as an entire entity or in lots; it may be sold by private treaty or by auction and the mortgagee may specify whatever terms of payment that he or she may desire.[1] However, it is not proper for the mortgagee to dispose of the mortgaged property by an exchange.[2]

1 See the Fourth Schedule, Property Law Act 1952; *Born v Turner* [1900] 2 Ch 211.
2 *Taylor v Parkinson* (1911) 31 NZLR 354.

Statutory procedure for sale: ss 99-102, Property Law Act

23.57 Because of this uncertainty in the duties of the mortgagee, most mortgagees who are contemplating the sale of the secured property do so by means of the statutory method authorised by ss 99-102 of the Property Law Act 1952.

23.58 This is particularly so when the mortgagee would like to become the owner of the mortgaged property. Under the deeds system, this was possible by a procedure known as foreclosure, whereby the mortgagor's equity of redemption was extinguished. The procedure was not simple. In general, foreclosure could only be obtained by Court order after a full accounting between the parties and after the mortgagor had been given an opportunity to redeem the mortgage. The procedure was expensive and uncertain.

23.59 Foreclosure has now been abolished in New Zealand and replaced by the statutory procedure for sale.[1] The procedure provides a simple alternative to the foreclosure proceedings, but even when the mortgagee does not wish to become the full owner of the property it offers a significant advantage to the mortgagee, namely protection from any action by the mortgagor in the event that the property is sold at a price which is alleged to be below the market price. Given the uncertainties in the law mentioned above, this is a valuable protection for the mortgagee.

1 S 89, Property Law Act 1952.

23.60 The procedure is as follows:[1] the mortgagee applies to the Registrar of the High Court to conduct the sale. The sale is conducted by auction, an auctioneer being appointed by the Registrar for this purpose. The sale is without a reserve price and the mortgagor is free to bid for the property.

1 Ss 99-103, Property Law Act 1952.

23.61 However, the mortgagee is not in the same position as other would-be buyers. At the time of application to the Registrar, the mortgagee is obliged to place an estimate of the price on the property. The value of this estimate is of importance to both the mortgagor and the mortgagee.

23.62 If the purchaser of the property is the mortgagee and if the price paid is less than the estimate given in the application, then the mortgagee must give credit to the mortgagor for the difference in the price paid and the estimate. In effect, the mortgagee cannot purchase the property at less than the estimated price.

23.63 But it is not possible for the mortgagee to place an unrealistically low value on the property, for the mortgagor is entitled, at any time after the application has been made and prior to the auction, to have the mortgage discharged by paying the estimated price (or, of course, the value still owing under the mortgage if that is lower) together with any expenses of sale which have already been incurred.[1] In effect, the mortgagor may discharge the mortgage by paying the estimated price. Note that if this is less than the amount owing under the mortgage that the mortgagor will remain personally liable for the difference, but the debt will no longer be secured by the mortgage.

1 S 100, Property Law Act 1952.

23.64 Consequently, the mortgagor is given protection against the possibility of the mortgagee purchasing the property at a completely unrealistic price, a price which could even leave the debtor still owing a considerable sum of money. The protection is not as great as may appear, however, since the common practice is to estimate the value at an amount approximately equal to that owing under the mortgage plus the expenses associated with the sale.

23.65 When the sale is completed, the mortgagee must account to the mortgagor. The sum obtained from the sale is applied first to pay for the costs of the sale, an amount which may be substantial in the sale of a substantial piece of property.[1] Secondly, the amount owing under the first mortgage is paid to the first mortgagee; this will include principal outstanding, interest and any other charges owing under the mortgage. Thirdly, the sum is applied to any subsequent mortgages in the same manner; the second mortgage will be completely paid out, then the third, etc. Finally, if there is any surplus, it will be paid to the mortgagor.

1 S 104, Property Law Act 1952.

23.66 If the sale is made not by the first mortgagee but by a subsequent one, then all prior mortgagees must be paid out in full before even the expenses of the sale may be addressed. It will be unusual for a sale by subsequent mortgagees to yield enough to be a complete return to them.

Priorities

23.67 The basic rules of priority among mortgages of various kinds have already been discussed. These rules apply, but need some amplification in situations where the security is taken over Torrens land.[1]

1 The general law of mortgages applies to Torrens land except where inconsistent with the provisions of the Land Transfer Act 1952.

Torrens system: priority by registration

23.68 Because of the importance of the register when the subject matter is Torrens land, the differences between a legal and an equitable interest are obscured if the competing interests are registered. In that case, since registration constitutes notice to the world of the interest, there can be no such thing as a later legal interest created without notice of a prior equitable one. In effect, then, the priority of interests is determined entirely by the time of registration.

Normal rules of priority

23.69 When one of the interests is unregistered, the registered interest will gain priority even if it is registered with notice of the existence of the unregistered interest.[1] If both interests are unregistered, then it would seem that the normal rules apply.

1 Ss 182, 183, Land Transfer Act 1952.

Second and subsequent mortgages

23.70 The possibility of a mortgagor giving subsequent mortgages has a special importance to the banker, for the operation of the rule in *Clayton's case* works, in this instance, against the interest of the banker unless some steps are taken to safeguard his or her interest.

23.71 The question which arises concerns the priority of the mortgagees when both have made advances to the debtor after the creation of the second security interest. If the first mortgagee has the right to claim priority for advances made after this time, it is said that the advances are "tacked" onto the first security interest. So, for example, A takes a security interest over B's property which is expressed to constitute a security for present and future advances. A lends B $1,000. Later, B grants a security interest to C in return for a loan of $500. Assuming that A has the security interest with the greater priority, then if the security must be realised A takes the first $1,000 and, if there is sufficient, B takes the next $500. But now suppose that A lends a further $500. Is A entitled to the first $1,500? Or is A entitled to the first $1,000, B the next $500 and then A the following $500?

23.72 The situation is illustrated in *Hopkinson v Rolt*.[1] A lender took a floating charge to secure advances already made to the debtor but also expressed to cover all future advances. The charge agreement also contained a clause by which the borrower agreed not to grant any further encumbrances on the property. In fact, the borrower did grant further charges over the same property and the question before the Court was whether the lender had the right to "tack" advances made to the borrower which were advanced after the creation of the second encumbrance.

1 (1861) 9 HL Cas 514.

23.73 The Court held that there was no right to tack future advances which were made after the first mortgagee had notice of the creation of the subsequent security interest, but that advances made before having such notice could be tacked. In terms of the above example, A is entitled to first claim for the entire $1,500 if and only if the $500 advanced by A to B was made without notice of C's security interest. The holding is known as the rule in *Hopkinson v Rolt*.[1]

1 *Hopkinson v Rolt* (1861) 9 HL Cas 514.

23.74 The rule applies to Torrens land.[1] In this context, registration of the second interest does not provide notice of that interest to the first mortgagee, for there is no duty on the registered first mortgagee to continually search the register.[2]

1 *Matzner v Clyde Securities* [1975] 2 NSWLR 293.
2 *Nioa v Bell* (1901) 27 VLR 82; *Queensland Trustee Ltd v Registrar of Titles* (1893) 5QLJ 46.

23.75 It might be thought that the situation would be different if A was under a contractual or other obligation to make the further advances to B, but a later case established firmly that this was not the situation. If the borrower does in fact grant a subsequent security over the same property, then the lender is relieved of any obligation to make the further advances.[1]

1 *West v Williams* [1899] 1 Ch 132.

23.76 The rule in *West v Williams*[1] is thought by some to be incorrect and it has been the subject of modifying legislation in New Zealand. Section 80A of the Property Law Act 1952 allows the lender to tack later advances in two situations. In the first, if the mortgage document purports to secure a specified sum, then the lender may advance the whole or any part of that sum at any time and still rank in priority over a subsequent mortgage notwithstanding that the first mortgagee has notice of the later mortgage. This section does not cover the overdraft type of loan, since there is no provision for "re-advancing" money which has been lent and subsequently repaid.

1 [1899] 1 Ch 132.

23.77 Section 80A(2) allows the lender to specify a maximum sum in the mortgage document. As long as the outstanding amount does not exceed this named maximum sum the first mortgagee will have priority over subsequent mortgages. Although this section does appear to cover overdraft lending, it is probably unwise to rely upon it due to some uncertainty in its precise scope.

23.78 The importance of this to the banker is that the interaction of the rule in *Hopkinson v Rolt* and the rule in *Clayton's case* may work to erode the priority of the first security entirely. If the first security is for a loan by way of overdraft, then payments into the account will discharge the earlier debt (which is the one which has priority) whereas later advances will rank behind the second security in priority. The result is that if the account is a normal working overdraft the banker gradually loses all priority to the subsequent security interest.

23.79 There is a simple remedy. Immediately upon receiving notice of the creation of the subsequent security, the banker should stop the overdraft account at once. If it is desired to continue making advances to the customer, then a new account must be opened, but understood to be on terms whereby the security for the advances is substantially inferior to the original arrangements. This course of action is the only way in which the banker may retain the priority for the advances made prior to the creation of the subsequent security interest.

23.80 There have been several Australian cases which have allowed tacking in certain circumstances. In *Matzner v Clyde Securities*[1] the first mortgagor made further advances after receiving notice of the subsequent mortgage. The subject matter of the securities was a building under construction and it was found as a fact that the advances were made for the purposes of completing the construction, a result which was to the benefit of all concerned. The Court allowed the further advances to be tacked to the first mortgage.[2]

1 [1975] 2 NSWLR 293.
2 See also *Network Finance Ltd v Deposit & Investment Co Ltd* [1972] QWN 19.

Some special cases

Unit titles

23.81 The Unit Titles Act 1972 gives certain advantages to registered mortgages when the subject matter is a unit which is covered by that Act. General practice seems to be that banks will take only first mortgages over units, although there is no reason in law why that should be so. The Act provides for a body corporate which is responsible for the common parts of the premises and each unit title holder is required to make certain contributions to this body corporate. Repairs and other work performed by the body corporate can also impose a liability on the owner. The body corporate is required to insure the buildings but may, by unanimous resolution, decide not to insure.

Leasehold

23.82 There is no legal difficulty with taking a mortgage, either legal or equitable, over a leasehold, but it is clear that the commercial value of such a security will depend upon the terms and the conditions of the lease. It is common to include a term in the mortgage which requires the mortgagor to obtain the consent of the lessor and to include terms which require the mortgagor to comply with the terms of the lease. The purpose of this is to ensure that any default under the lease will also constitute a default under the mortgage.

Building in the course of erection

23.83 The financing of construction work usually provides for "progress payments", advances which are made from time to time as the construction reaches predetermined satisfactory stages of completion. The mortgages which are taken over such property have little legal novelty about them, but since there is the prospect of regular advances, care must be taken that subsequent securities are not given over the same property so as to attract the rule in *Hopkinson v Rolt*.[1] Care should also be taken to ensure that the insurance cover for the project is adequate at all times.

1 See 23.70ff.

Mortgagor's right to demand discharge

23.84 In the earliest concept of a mortgage, the mortgagor had no right to have the property reconveyed prior to the time stipulated in the contract. There is a long history of decisions which gradually gave the mortgagor more rights, but the matter is now dealt with by the statutes.

23.85 The most important of these is the right to redeem the mortgage at any time prior to the exercise by the mortgagee of the power of sale.[1] Any term in the mortgage which purports to limit or to remove the mortgagor's right of redemption is void,[2] save that the mortgagee may stipulate for the payment of all outstanding principal together with all interest that would accrue up to the contractual date when the final payment would be due. Since this amounts to payment of interest after repayment of the principal, there is generally little incentive for the mortgagor to take advantage of this right. Many mortgages include a term which gives the mortgagor the right to obtain an early discharge by giving a specified length of notice and/or paying a relatively small amount of extra interest. Of course, even without the express term, the way is open to negotiate with the mortgagee for an early discharge.

1 S 81(2), Land Transfer Act 1952.
2 See *Kreglinger v New Patagonia Meat and Cold Storage Co Ltd* [1914] AC 25.

23.86 Of course, the mortgagor is entitled both contractually and under the statute to have the mortgage discharged provided that the payment is made on the due date.

23.87 If the due date for payment has come and gone, then the mortgagor may still demand the discharge of the mortgage upon payment of all outstanding money owed provided that he or she gives three months' notice or is willing to pay three months' interest in lieu of giving notice.[1]

1 S 81(3), Land Transfer Act 1952.

23.88 The procedure for obtaining a discharge of a registered mortgage is simple. On the production of any document signed by the mortgagee and duly attested which purports to discharge the mortgage, the Registrar is bound to enter upon the register a notation that the mortgage is discharged. The mortgage is discharged at the time of registration of the discharge.

Chapter 24

Securities II

Chattels — Choses in action — Limited companies

24.1 This chapter examines three topics in the law of securities which are of the utmost importance to the lending banker. They are the special and difficult problem of security interests in chattels, assignments of choses in action and the particular forms of security which may be taken only from limited companies.

Securities over chattels

24.2 A banker who is contemplating a loan to a modern business may find that the land belonging to or leased by the business represents a very small part of the total value of the business. If the business is one of manufacturing, for example, then the primary assets of the business are likely to consist of the raw materials used in the manufacturing process, the machinery used to manufacture the goods and the final product prior to sale. There may also be substantial assets in the form of debts owed to the manufacturer. Again, if the business is primarily one of retailing, it is likely that the major assets will consist of stock and debts owed to the business.

24.3 The point of this is that much commercial lending is to businesses which are able to offer substantial security over chattels, eg, the raw materials and machinery, and over choses in action, eg, debts owed to the business. Lenders must be familiar with the broad outlines of the law relating to security interests over chattels and choses in action.

24.4 Unfortunately, the law of both subjects is complex. Any real life legal problem in this area is likely to demand the attention of experts. What this chapter attempts to do is to identify the likely areas of difficulty so that problems may be avoided where possible and referred to the experts at the earliest available opportunity. The discussion begins with a consideration of security interests in chattels.

Historical problems of securities over chattels

24.5 It is possible today to create security interests in chattels which are conceptually identical to the mortgage of deed system land, but it was not always so. A consideration of the problems perceived by the early common law will assist in an understanding of the modern problem of chattel securities.

24.6 The early common law generally refused to allow the creation or transfer of an interest in chattels unless the interest created or transferred was accompanied by a transfer of possession. Since the mortgage is the transfer of the legal title to the lender while the borrower retains possession, it would have been prohibited under this rule of the early common law. The rule is at least as old as *Twyne's case,*[1] and may be considerably older.

1 (1600) 3 Co Rep 80b; 76 ER 809.

24.7 The justification for the rule was that to allow such transactions would be an invitation to fraud. Chattels, it was argued, are different from land in that there is no way to prove ownership. Whereas a would-be purchaser or mortgagee of land could rely upon the title deeds to find the true owner, there was no comparable method of establishing existing interests in chattels. Consequently, a person in possession of a chattel could mortgage it first to one then to another, always representing that the chattel was unencumbered.

24.8 The rule in *Twyne's case* survived for some 200 years. Since few legal rules survive intact for so long a period, it must be presumed that it worked well enough for the commercial necessities of the time. Indeed, some have speculated that it was only with the rise of the industrial revolution and the subsequent movement of wealth from land to other forms of assets that the rule in *Twyne's case* began to inhibit commercial transactions.[1] Whatever the cause, legislation was introduced all over the common law world at about the same time to allow the creation or transfer of interests in chattels without the need to also transfer the possession of the chattels.

1 See Gilmore, *Security Interests in Personal Property,* Boston, 1965.

The system of registration

24.9 The legislation, represented in New Zealand today by the Chattels Transfer Act 1924, sought to overcome the "fraud problem" by a system of registration. Interests could be created, but they must be registered or suffer from certain deficiencies. Some of the legislation made unregistered interests totally invalid, but more usual was that the interest would be invalid only in certain circumstances or against certain parties.

24.10 The aims of the legislation are clearly stated in the Bills of Sale Act 1882 (UK):

> . . . avoiding the social evil that resulted from an owner of chattels being able to present to those giving him credit a fictitious appearance of prosperity whereas all his property, though still in his possession, might be disposed of by secret dispositions . . . .[1]

1 Sykes, p 441.

24.11 It must be said at once that the legislation has not, from a commercial point of view, been very successful. Documents which are registered are published by various trade papers and the resulting publicity has been damaging to the credit of the borrower. Registration fees and various forms of stamp duty are sometimes onerous. The result is that many arrangements, some very artificial, have been devised to avoid the legislation. The system is uncertain and unpredictable as a result.

24.12 Further adding to the problem is that the legislation is very badly drafted, resulting in what one commentator has referred to as the "quagmire of chattel securities" in New Zealand.[1] As will be seen, one of the results of this is that chattel mortgages form only a fraction of the interests used when it is desired to take a security interest in chattels.

1 Risenfeld, *The Quagmire of Chattels Security in New Zealand*, Auckland, 1970.

Which instruments require registration?

24.13 The Chattels Transfer Act 1924 requires the registration of certain "instruments". The definition of "instrument" by s 2 of the Act is cumbersome, but it is thought that there are four main categories of written transaction which fall within the definition. First is the "assurance of chattels" by which is meant the transfer of the legal or equitable title to the chattel.

24.14 Second is the "declaration of trust", an expression which may not extend the definition much beyond the notion of an equitable assurance of the chattel. In any case, the term does not include the so-called letter of trust which is used by bankers in documentary letter of credit transactions.[1]

1 *Re David Allester Ltd* [1922] 2 Ch 211; and see the discussion in Ch 29.

24.15 The third part of the definition of "instrument" is described briefly as a power to seize. These are instruments which embody agreements to the effect that the creditor has the power to seize, and usually to sell, certain chattels belonging to the debtor in the event of default.

24.16 Finally:

> Any agreement, whether intended to be followed by the execution of any other instrument or not, by which a right in equity to any chattels, or to any charge or security thereon or thereover, is conferred.

24.17 An example of this type of instrument is found in *Shears & Sons Ltd v Jones*[1] where the debtor agreed in writing that he would execute an instrument at a later date if the debt had not been paid by that time. Such an agreement gives an immediate right in equity and so is an instrument.

1 [1922] 2 Ch 802.

24.18 There then follows a list of documents which are exempted from the definition, and hence from the requirement of registration. The most important of these are those which evidence the transfer of chattels in the ordinary course of business of any trade or calling, any mortgage or charge given by a company and certain types of hire purchase agreements.[1]

1 It is unlikely that hire purchase agreements would fall within the requirements for registration in any case; see Sykes, *The Law of Securities*, 3rd ed, Sydney, p 701.

Consequences of registration

24.19 It is fundamental to an understanding of the Act to recognise that registration of an instrument does not give the agreement any force greater than it could have had under the general law. Phrased another way, if the agreement itself does not confer either legal or equitable rights, then registration will be wholly irrelevant. Consequently, in order to solve any problem involving chattel securities, it is necessary to consider the rights of the parties just as though the Act did not exist, then consider what modifying influences the Act might have upon those rights.

24.20 If an instrument is registered, then s 4 deems that the whole world is given notice both of the instrument and of its contents except that grantees of previously registered instruments are not deemed to have had notice. The exception is very important for bankers who have a registered instrument which is serving as a security for a fluctuating overdraft, for the combined operation of the rule in *Hopkinson v Rolt*[1] and the rule in *Clayton's case*[2] allows the safe operation of the account until such time as the banker receives actual notice of a second instrument.[3]

1 (1861) 9 HL Cas 514.
2 *Devaynes v Noble, Clayton's Case* (1816) 1 Mer 529, 572.
3 See 23.70 for a discussion of the rule in *Hopkinson v Rolt*.

24.21 Registration may also have an effect on the priorities when two or more instruments are given over the same chattels. Section 22 gives the first registered instrument priority over a second instrument provided that the grantee had no notice of the existence of the second instrument at the time of registration.[1]

1 This section may result in contradictory priorities when there are three or more instruments; see Tyree, "Circular Priorities in Secured Transactions" (1980) 87 American Math Monthly 186.

Consequences of failure to register

24.22 A failure to register makes the security invalid against certain parties but it retains its full or partial validity against others. Section 18 lists three classes of persons against whom the security interest is invalid in so far as the chattels concerned are still in the possession or apparent possession of the grantor. The parties listed are the assignee in bankruptcy of the grantor, the assignee or trustee acting under an assignment for the benefit of creditors of the grantor, and any sheriff or similar person who is seizing the chattels on behalf of an execution creditor.

24.23 Section 19 of the Act makes the unregistered security void against a bona fide purchaser or mortgagee for value who takes the interest without actual notice of the unregistered instrument.

24.24 Section 8 requires registration within 21 days. During that time, the security has full effect even though it is not registered.[1] This leads to the possibility of "rolling over" instruments in order to avoid the registration requirements, ie, executing a new instrument every 20 days. In theory, the existing instrument should always have full force despite the lack of registration. Surprisingly, the practice was held to conform to that theory in an old New South Wales case,[2] but it is very much doubted that a New Zealand Court would come to the same conclusion today.

1 *Marples v Hartley* (1861) 30 LJ QB 92 (NS) 92.
2 *Lyons v Cohn* (1877) Knox 92.

24.25 The reader should note that declaring the instrument to be void does not necessarily mean that the grantee under the instrument loses his or her interest. As an example, if the secured creditor has already exercised the right of seizure granted by the instrument and sold the goods then it is no longer necessary to rely upon the instrument. One case has referred to the instrument as being "spent" so that the rights of the claimants to the chattels or to the proceeds thereof no longer depend upon the instrument.[1]

1 See *Price v Parsons* (1934) 54 CLR 332.

24.26 A similar result is thought to follow as regards hire purchase agreements. The argument is that if the hire purchase instrument is declared void then the result is not that the owner of the legal title loses his or her interest but rather that the debtor loses the right of possession which is granted by the instrument.[1]

1 See Goode, *Commercial Law*, London, 1982 and Sykes, *The Law of Securities*, Sydney, 1978.

24.27 Finally, the Act applies only to written instruments. An oral agreement to create a security interest may be perfectly valid and, provided there is no contemplation of executing an instrument at a later time, is untouched by the Act.[1]

1 *New Zealand Serpentine Ltd v Hoon Hay Quarries Ltd* [1925] NZLR 73.

Legal and equitable securities over chattels

24.28 Because of the registration requirements, there is often a desire to create security interests in chattels which do not fall within the definition of "instrument". The remainder of this section examines the major characteristics of the various security interests which are commonly used in commercial financing.

Chattel mortgages

24.29 A chattel mortgage is similar in concept to the mortgage of deeds system land. A legal mortgage is the transfer of the legal title to the mortgagee, possession of the chattel remaining with the mortgagor. No particular form is necessary to create a legal mortgage, a simple contract being sufficient to transfer the title. It is not necessary that the contract be in writing.[1]

1 *New Zealand Serpentine Ltd v Hoon Hay Quarries Ltd* [1925] NZLR 73.

24.30 It is also possible to grant an equitable mortgage over a chattel. One method of so doing is to contract to grant a legal mortgage.[1] Another is, as with the mortgage of land, to attempt to create a legal mortgage but to fail due to lack of compliance with some formality, an unusual occurrence since there are generally no formalities required.

1 *New Zealand Serpentine Ltd v Hoon Hay Quarries Ltd* [1925] NZLR 73.

24.31 In either case, if the transfer of title, be it legal or equitable, is reduced to writing, then the resulting document is an example of an instrument which requires registration.

24.32 It is a peculiarity of the Act, one of the consequences of the poor drafting, that the Act applies only to documents, not to transactions. Thus, a perfectly valid chattel mortgage may be granted orally and the Act has nothing to say about it.[1] It is valid against all third parties if it is a legal mortgage and against third parties who take a later legal interest with notice if it is an equitable mortgage.

1 *New Zealand Serpentine Ltd v Hoon Hay Quarries Ltd* [1925] NZLR 73.

24.33 This is not to suggest that the taking of oral chattel mortgages is to be condoned as good business practice, for the problems of evidence alone suggest that such a course would not be prudent. The vagaries of the Chattels Transfer Act, together with the aforementioned ill effect on the borrower's credit which may result from the registration of the document, dictate that the taking of chattel mortgages is not much favoured as a means of obtaining a security interest in commercial financing transactions.

Mortgages over future chattels

24.34 It is sometimes desirable for the lending banker to make a loan to a customer which is to be used specifically for the purchase of some chattel. In such a case, it would be desirable that the lender should have a security interest in the chattel when it is acquired. At common law, not surprisingly, such an arrangement was considered merely a contract whereby the borrower agreed to execute a mortgage in favour of the lender at some time after the chattel was acquired. If such a mortgage was never formally executed, then the lender had no proprietary interest in the chattel. The remedy, if any, lay in contract.

24.35 However, in the great case of *Holroyd v Marshall,*[1] the Court of equity argued that a purported mortgage of a "future" chattel, although it clearly could not have any immediate proprietary effect, operated as a contract to assign title when the chattel was in fact acquired by the borrower. As a result of that contract and the operation of equity, the equitable title passed to the lender at the instant that the chattel was acquired. This is summarised, inexactly, by saying that it is possible to give an equitable mortgage over future goods, but it must be remembered that no proprietary interest can be acquired by the lender until such time as the borrower/mortgagor actually acquires the chattel.

1 (1862) 11 ER 999.

24.36 Unfortunately, the Act appears to make the equitable mortgage over future chattels a very unattractive form of security. Section 24 invalidates an instrument to the same extent as if it were unregistered in respect of chattels which are acquired by the grantor after the time the instrument was executed.

24.37 The exception to this avoiding provision is where the money lent is for the express purpose of purchasing the chattels listed in the instrument. Such a security is known as a purchase money security and operates on the theory that the legal interest in the chattel never vested in the debtor at all.[1]

1 See *Re Connolly Bros (No 2)* [1912] 2 Ch 25.

24.38 The analysis of competing claims may be confusing. In *Broadlands Finance Ltd v Shand Miller Musical Supplies Ltd*[1] a person completed two separate security documents which related to the purchase of musical instruments. The first was an instrument by way of security with the appellant which specified that the money lent was to be used for the purchase of the musical instruments. This instrument was registered by Broadlands Finance. The second instrument was an agreement whereby it was provided that the respondent was to retain legal title in the instruments until such time as the full amount of the purchase price was paid. This document was not registered, although it was of a form which should have been registered under s 5 of the Act.

1 [1976] 2 NZLR 124.

24.39 Although much of the argument concerned the effects of s 24 and of purchase money securities, a moment's reflection should show that the Act has little to say concerning the rights of the parties. Since legal title at all times vested in the respondent musical company, the instrument which was completed with the finance company could never have had the effect contemplated by the parties, for the debtor never had any legal title to pass nor did the finance company ever acquire the legal title from any other source. Indeed, the debtor never had any rights in the chattels beyond a right to possession granted by the instrument executed between himself and Shand Miller.

Pledge

24.40 The pledge is, in a sense, the opposite of a mortgage. Whereas in a mortgage, the grantor assigns his or her title to the creditor while retaining possession, in a pledge the owner grants the creditor the right to possession while retaining title. The pledgee has the right to retain possession of the chattel until such time as the obligation secured is discharged. In the event of default, the pledgee has the right to sell the chattel pledged and to recover the debt from the proceeds. If there is a surplus from the sale then the pledgee must account to the debtor; if there is a deficiency then the debtor remains liable for the excess.

24.41 In order to create a pledge, there must be an actual transfer of possession from the pledgor to the pledgee which results in the exclusion of the pledgor's rights to deal with the chattel.[1] The delivery may be actual delivery, as when the pledgor hands jewellery to the pledgee, or it may be constructive as when the pledgor hands the pledgee keys to a warehouse where the goods are stored.

1 *Madras Official Assignee v Mercantile Bank of India Ltd* [1935] AC 53.

24.42 The pledge comes to an end when the pledgor returns possession to the pledgee unless the return is temporary and for a particular purpose. An example of this might be that the pledgor is to ship the goods or to sell them on behalf of the pledgee. This occurs so often in commercial transactions that it will be examined in more detail in Ch 29.

24.43 Since the debtor parts with the possession of the goods, it is clear that the pledge does not pose the "social evil" which was the concern of the Bills of Sale Acts. The pledge is not a transaction which is covered by the definitions in the various Acts;[1] no registration is required whether the pledge is created orally or in writing.

1 *Re Vital Learning Aids Pty Ltd* [1979] 2 NSWLR 442.

Use of the pledge as a commercial security

24.44 At first glance, the pledge seems ill suited as a security device for commercial dealings. While the pledge of some personal item for a personal loan might make some sense, both to the lender and the borrower, it is hard to imagine that a business borrowing commercial funds could part with possession of the chattels which form some of the major assets of the business.

24.45 Such a view overlooks both commercial ingenuity and legal adaptability. In the case of the pledge, there are two factors which make it a viable commercial security, namely, the role which may be played by constructive delivery and those situations, common in international trade, where there are documents of title to the chattels.

Constructive delivery

24.46 If the goods are lying in the warehouse of some third party, then the pledge is easily effected by constructive delivery. The usual method is for the customer to sign a transfer order addressed to the warehouse which directs the warehouse to hold the goods to the bank's order. This transfer order, together with the warehouse receipt which acknowledges that the goods are being held on behalf of the borrower, are handed to the lender who then produces them to the warehouse to have a new receipt issued. The process is called "attornment" and the warehouse is said to "attorn" to the lender.[1]

1 Paget, p 466.

24.47 This procedure is enough to create a pledge and to give the lender the right of sale in the event of default, but it is common for lending bankers to require that the borrowing customer also sign a further document which expressly authorises the lender to sell in the event of default. There is no harm in this provided that the proper order of execution is observed, for it has been held that if the memorandum giving the power of sale is executed first, then the document is a bill of sale and must be registered.[1] If the memorandum is executed after the constructive delivery, then the document merely evidences the transaction, the pledge, and does not require registration.[2]

1 *Ex parte Hubbard* (1886) 17 QBD 690; *Charlesworth v Mills* [1892] AC 231.
2 See *Ex parte Hubbard* (1886) 17 QBD 690.

24.48 When the goods are stored on the borrowing customer's own premises, the problem is more difficult. It seems that any document issued by the customer which purports to grant delivery or transfer to the lending banker is likely to be construed as falling within the Chattels Transfer Act and so require registration. In the leading case, *Dublin City Distillery Ltd v Doherty,*[1] the owners delivered documents of this sort to the pledgee, but the House of Lords held that it could not amount to a constructive delivery and that the documents were bills of sale. Their Lordships appeared to be of the view that the delivery orders, etc which are excepted from the definitions of a bill of sale only include those which operate through the intervention of a third party who is in the possession of the goods.

1 [1914] AC 823.

24.49 This attitude places a considerable obstacle in the path of those who would pledge goods in the circumstances. There are two solutions, neither entirely satisfactory. In the first, the goods are left in the customer's possession and hypothecated to the bank, a procedure to be discussed in 24.51ff. The second is for the customer to place the goods in a separate area of his or her premises which are then isolated in some way. The banker is then granted a lease over this area so that the goods are indeed in the possession of the banker. This method has been used frequently in the United States where a large body of case law has arisen which is concerned with the degree of control which the banker musthave over access to the area where the goods are kept.[1] Because of these uncertainties and because of the legal and practical problems which may arise due to the bank being a lessee of the isolated premises, the method has never gained great popularity in New Zealand.

1 See Peden, *Stock in Trade Financing*, Sydney, 1974.

24.50 These constructive delivery methods are appropriate for creating a pledge when the goods are "domestic" goods. However, possibly the greatest use of the pledge as a security for money advanced is in the area of international trade. In such a case, there will nearly always be a bill of lading which is, inter alia, a document of title to goods. When there is a bill of lading, the pledge of the document is the same as a pledge of the goods and is a device much used, particularly in connection with the operation of documentary letters of credit. This is discussed in detail in Ch 29.

Charge or hypothecation

24.51 Hypothecation is a method of granting an equitable charge over chattels. The essence of an equitable charge is that there is no intention that title, either legal or equitable, should pass to the creditor either immediately or at any time in the future. Nor is there any intention that possession should pass. An equitable charge is sometimes described as the "shadow cast upon the property by the debt"; although neither title nor possession passes, there is no doubt that the creditor receives a good equitable proprietary interest in the goods.[1]

1 McLauchlan, "The Concept of 'Charge' in the Law of Chattel Securities" (1975-77) 8 VUW L Rev 283.

24.52 In the case of hypothecation, the charge is created by a letter of hypothecation, sometimes also called a letter of lien. Since the effect of such a document is to create a security interest while leaving the debtor in possession of the chattels, there is a very real danger that such documents may be caught by the definition of a bill of sale, so that it is vital that standard wording be used. If properly worded, letters of hypothecation fall within the exception of documents "used in the ordinary course of business as proof of the possession or control of goods".[1]

1 See *Re Slee, ex parte North Western Bank* (1872) LR 15 Eq 69 and *Re Hamilton Young & Co* [1905] 2 KB 772.

24.53 Although hypothecation is often used, there are several warnings which should be mentioned. The first is to repeat that it is not easy to say when the wording of a document purporting to grant the charge will be held to be a bill of sale. The second is to note that the security obtained is an equitable one. Since the goods are left in the possession of the borrower, there is more opportunity for fraudulent dealing. In the event that some third party obtains a legal interest in the goods without notice of the hypothecation, then that interest would defeat the equitable charge. Such would not be the case if the banker were able to obtain a pledge of the goods.

Securities over choses in action

24.54 The early common law took the same attitude towards choses in action that it did toward chattels: it was not possible to give a security interest in choses in action. The reason, however, was slightly different. The common law treated that prototypical chose in action, the debt, as merely another form of contractual obligation. Since the general rule was that neither the benefit nor the obligation of a contract could be assigned,[1] it was not possible to created security interests in debts or other choses in action.

1 *Lampet's case* (1613) 10 Rep 40b; 77 ER 994.

24.55 As we have come to expect, equity took a different point of view and allowed the creation of interests in debts which were enforceable by an action in equity. There were, however, substantial procedural difficulties which made the equitable assignment of debts a less than satisfactory mechanism for the creation of security interests.[1]

1 *Fitzroy v Cave* [1905] 2 KB 364.

24.56 In order to illustrate the procedure, suppose that D owes C a sum of money by virtue of some contractual obligation. It may be that the sum is not immediately due but that C wishes to obtain some funds immediately. C borrows from E and wishes to use the sum owed him by D either as a security for the loan or, alternatively, it might be intended that E should obtain repayment directly from D. At common law, the assignment of the debt to E could not be made and, furthermore, if D did pay E, such a payment would not amount to the discharge of the debt owed to C.

24.57 In the equitable procedure to enforce the assignment, E must sue C in a Court of equity and obtain an order that C should sue D in a Court of law to recover the debt which would then be held in trust for E. This, aside from being an clumsy procedure, meant that E's claim was subject to any defences that D might be able to raise against C.

24.58 The procedure has been simplified in several ways. First, the Judicature Act 1873 (UK) introduced a statutory form of assignment of debts and other choses in action. In New Zealand, this has been incorporated in s 130 of the Property Law Act 1952. Secondly, the procedure for enforcement, even if the assignment does not comply with the statutory requirements and is therefore only an equitable assignment, now calls only for the original creditor, C in the above example, to be joined as a party to the proceedings. If C does not wish to proceed against D as a plaintiff, then E may join D as a defendant in the action.

Assignment of debts

Many enterprises have the majority of their assets not in land or in chattels but in choses in action. One common asset is the debt which is owed to the enterprise and any system of law which is to satisfy the demands of modern commerce must allow the use of these assets as security for loans. In our law, this is done by means of the assignment or by means of the bill of exchange. The use of the bill for this purpose is the subject of Ch 10. Here the use of the assignment is further discussed.

Legal assignment

24.59 As mentioned above, debts and other choses in action are now assignable at law. A mortgage of a debt takes the same form as an old style mortgage of land, that is, there is an assignment of the debt to the lender with provisions that the debt should be reassigned. In order to make a legal assignment, the Act requires the following:

1 The assignment must be for the whole of the debt; it was held from an early time that the statute did not apply to the attempted assignment of a part of a debt.[1]

2 The assignment must be absolute and not by way of charge only; this does not mean that there can be no provision for reassignment, only that the original assignment must be absolute.[2]

3 Express written notice must be given to the original debtor, D in the above example.

4 The assignment will be subject to all equities which would have taken priority over the rights of the assignor if the Judicature Act had not been enacted. That is, all defences available to the debtor against the assignor and all rights of set off which would be available to the debtor in respect of claims which arose prior to the debtor's receiving the notice which completes the statutory assignment.[3]

1 *Forster v Baker* [1910] 2 KB 636; *Re Steel Wing Co Ltd* [1921] 1 Ch 349.
2 See *Tancred v Delagoa Bay and East Africa Railway Co* (1889) 23 QBD 239.
3 *Roxburghe v Cox* (1881) 17 Ch D 520.

24.60 Perhaps the only requirement which requires further comment is the second. Consider two forms of purported assignment. First, "I hereby assign to Smith the debt due me from Jones until such time as the building is completed". Secondly, "I hereby assign to Smith the debt due me from Jones. When the building is completed, Jones promises to reassign the debt to me". The first is not an absolute assignment; the second is, even though it contains a provision for reassignment.[1]

1 *Durham Bros v Robertson* [1898] 1 QB 765.

24.61 The rights of the assignee are that he or she may sue in his or her own name and that upon payment of the debt by the original debtor to the assignee, the debt is duly discharged.

Equitable assignment

24.62 The statutory provisions have not replaced the procedures available for an equitable assignment of debts or other choses in action.[1] There may well be an equitable assignment where the subject matter is inappropriate for a legal assignment or where the procedures required by the statute have not been carried through. Thus, there would be an equitable assignment of a portion of a debt when made for valuable consideration.[2] Also, there could be an equitable assignment when the original debtor is not notified in writing,[3] but the assignee may find that priority is lost if some other party gives notice of a later assignment to the debtor.[4]

1 *William Brandt's Sons & Co v Dunlop Rubber Co* [1905] AC 454.
2 *Re Steel Wing Co Ltd* [1921] 1 Ch 349.
3 *Durham Bros v Robertson* [1898] 1 QB 765.
4 See the rule in *Dearle v Hall* and the discussion at 24.65.

24.63 As mentioned above, in order to enforce an equitable assignment of a legal chose in action against the original debtor, it is necessary to join the assignor as a party to the proceedings.[1]

1 *Durham Bros v Robertson* [1898] 1 QB 765.

24.64 In order to create a valid equitable assignment, no special form of words is required as long as the meaning is plain.[1] The assignment may be made orally except in those cases where writing is required by some special rule of law.

1 *Tailby v Official Receiver* (1888) 13 App Cas 523.

Priorities: the rule in Dearle v Hall

24.65 Although a legal assignment requires that notice be sent to the debtor, there is no such requirement for the valid creation of an equitable assignment. It is, however, desirable that such notice should be given for two reasons. First, if the debtor has no notice of the assignment, the debt may be discharged by the debtor making payment to the original creditor, ie, the assignor of the debt. Once notice has been given to the original debtor, he or she disregards the notice at their peril, for if payment is made to the original creditor after receiving notice of the assignment, then the debtor may still be liable to the assignee as well.[1]

1 See, for example, *Brice v Bannister* (1878) 3 QBD 569.

24.66 The second reason for giving notice to the debtor is to establish priority in the event that the creditor/assignor makes further assignments of the debt. As in the case of multiple mortgages of real or personal property, there is nothing necessarily improper in making several assignments. But priority amongst assignees is determined in a slightly different way. It is the assignee who first gives notice to the debtor, provided that at the time of taking his or her assignment has no notice of any assignment previously made, who has priority. The rule is based on the argument that "perfection" of a security interest in chattels requires the taking of possession (or the registration of documents) and that the closest analogy when dealing with debts is to give notice to the debtor. The rule is known as the rule in *Dearle v Hall*,[1] the case in which it was first clearly stated.

1 (1823) 3 Russ 1; 38 ER 475.

Charges on accounts

24.67 When the debt to be assigned consists of a bank account, the principles are the same as the assignment of any other debt. A problem only arises because sometimes the lending banker wishes to take a security interest in an account held by the customer with the lending bank. Since the lending banker is the debtor here, there can hardly be an assignment of the debt to the banker/debtor.

24.68 The usual way around the problem is for the customer to provide a written authority for the banker to hold the deposit against the moneys secured and to apply the account for the purposes of discharge, or partial discharge, of the loan in certain defined circumstances.

Stocks and shares

24.69 It is possible to take a legal mortgage over shares in companies, but often the transfer of title to the mortgagee is not suitable due to the expense, the restriction on the transferability of shares or for some other reason. It is far more usual to take an equitable mortgage.

24.70 The creation of the equitable mortgage is a very simple matter. The customer deposits the certificates with the bank and executes a memorandum of mortgage which contains the contractual terms of the arrangement. These terms would ordinarily include a power of sale and an irrevocable power of attorney which would enable the banker to transfer the shares in the event of a default.

24.71 The primary disadvantage of the equitable mortgage of shares is that common to most equitable interests, that it may be subject to some prior, and undiscoverable, equity. If, for example, the customer borrower is a trustee of the shares, then the deposit of them may constitute a breach of trust. If that is so, it is likely that the beneficiaries will have priority over the interest of the equitable mortgagee.[1]

1 See *Coleman v London County and Westminster Bank Ltd* [1916] 2 Ch 353.

Life policies

24.72 A policy of life insurance is a frequently used security, particularly for personal loans. A legal mortgage over the policy may be taken by complying with the forms specified in the Eleventh Schedule of the Life Insurance Act 1908. Bankers customarily use their own form of assignment which gives the bank the right to make premium payments and debit the customer's account in the event that the customer fails to maintain regular premium payments. There may also be other clauses permitting the bank to deal with the policy in a number of ways.

24.73 The Act requires that the insurance company be given a formal notice of the assignment. When the assignee complies with the terms of the Act he or she may sue in their own name and, in addition, acquire priority over any other assignees who have not given notice provided only that there is no notice of the prior assignments at the time of taking the assignment. This is merely a statutory version of the rule in *Dearle v Hall.*[1]

1 See 24.65.

24.74 The usual form of the equitable mortgage is by now familiar. A deposit of the policy with the banker is accompanied by a memorandum of mortgage whereby the banker is granted a power of attorney to deal with the policy in whatever ways might be thought suitable. The equitable mortgage suffers the usual deficiencies of an equitable security.

24.75 Holden[1] lists three disadvantages of life policies as securities. None is very likely to arise in the usual course of things, but the banker should be aware of them.

1 In *Chorley,* pp 316, 317.

24.76 First, if the customer failed to make complete disclosure to the insurance company at the time of application, then the insurance company may not be liable on the policy. This is due to the fact that insurance contracts are contracts of utmost good faith, *uberrimae fidei.* Such a contract may be avoided if the proposer failed to disclose material facts, and this is so even if the non-disclosure is innocent. Since the disclosures are made in the insurance proposal long before the policy is ever made and the banker will never see that proposal, it is a risk which the banker cannot possibly guard against.

24.77 Secondly, if the customer dies as a result of a criminal act committed by himself or if he dies by his own hand, then the policy may not be enforceable.[1] It should, however, be noted that the scope of this rule is by no means clear and that expert advice should be sought immediately in the event that the insurance company indicates that it does not intend to accept liability on the basis of any act of the insured.

1 See *Beresford v Royal Insurance Co Ltd* [1938] AC 586.

24.78 Finally, Holden suggests that there is a risk that the person who has taken out the policy has no insurable interest in the life insured. As Holden admits, it is difficult to see how such a circumstance could arise when a policy is offered to a banker as a security for a loan, but if there is any doubt whatsoever, the proper course is to request the insurance company to formally admit that such an interest exists. This would form the basis of an estoppel in the event of any dispute.

Book debts

24.79 When the borrower is engaged in a trade or business, it may be that there are regularly occurring debts owed which the banker would like to take as security. These are usually called "book debts"; although there is no completely satisfactory legal definition of the term, it clearly contemplates debts which arise in the course of the business being pursued by the borrower. *Halsbury* gives the following definition:[1]

> By "book debts" are meant all such debts accruing in the ordinary course of a man's trade as are usually entered in trade books, but to constitute a book debt it is not necessary that the debt should be entered in a book.[1]

1 *Halsbury's Laws of England*, 3rd ed vol 2 p 384; cf 4th ed vol 3 p 291 n 4.

24.80 There would appear to be no reason why future book debts cannot be assigned in the sense that future chattels may be under the doctrine in *Holroyd v Marshall*,[1] that is that a purported assignment of future debts operates as a contract to assign the debts when they come into existence. When they do so come into existence the equitable title in them is passed immediately provided only that they are sufficiently identifiable.[2]

1 (1862) 143 ER 567.
2 See *Sykes,* p 600 and *Tailby v Official Receiver* (1888) 13 App Cas 523.

24.81 Consequently, there appears to be nothing to prevent a banker from taking an assignment of all present and future book debts as a means of securing an advance.

24.82 Generally, the assignee banker will not bother to give notice to each individual debtor, and this is particularly so when the business is a trade in which the debts are individually small even though numerous. As long as the loan is being serviced satisfactorily, the debtors will pay the customer/borrower as usual as the debts fall due. There will usually be a term in the assignment which authorises the borrower to collect these debts and to hold the proceeds for the use of the banker.

24.83 There is one point that is relevant to the discussion below concerning the registration of such documents as bills of sale. In the event of default, the banker will need to gain access to the books of the borrower in order to determine those debts still outstanding which may be collected by the assignee banker. Consequently, the assignment document should contain a right for the banker to seize the books. But the books are chattels and there is then no doubt that the document is a bill of sale.

Company securities

24.84 When the borrowing customer is a company, different types of securities may be taken. It is still possible to take mortgages of real property and of chattels and assignments of debts. However, there is in addition a form of security which is peculiar to companies, namely the so called "floating charges".

Floating charges

24.85 A floating charge has been judicially defined in the following terms:

> A floating security is an equitable charge on the assets for the time being of a going concern. It attaches to the subject charged in the varying condition in which it happens to be from time to time. It is of the essence of such a charge that it remains dormant until the undertaking charged ceases to be a going concern, or until the person in whose favour the charge is created intervenes. His right to intervene may of course be suspended by agreement. But if there is no agreement for suspension, he may exercise his right whenever he pleases after default.[1]

1 Per Lord Macnaghten in *Governments Stock and Other Securities Investment Co v Manila Railway Co* [1897] AC 81.

24.86 Although the floating charge is described as an "equitable charge", it does not "attach" to any particular asset of the company. The company is free to deal with the assets in the ordinary course of business. When the company ceases to be a "going concern" or when certain other circumstances occur, the charge is said to "crystallise"; it then converts into a fixed charge which attaches to all of the assets which were previously under the umbrella of the floating charge.

24.87 Crystallisation will ordinarily occur when some event causes the de facto cessation of business. The most common such event is the appointment of a receiver or a liquidator or the intervention of the lender who holds the floating charge.

24.88 Sometimes clauses are inserted in floating charges which specify that the charge will crystallise upon the occurrence of certain other events. Such a clause is known as an "automatic crystallisation clause". It would appear that in New Zealand such a clause will be effective if it is properly worded.[1]

1 See *Re Manurewa Transport Ltd* [1971] NZLR 909.

24.89 The reason that automatic crystallisation clauses are included is to provide a greater degree of security for the lender. Until the charge is crystallised, an execution creditor may gain priority over some of the assets of the company; in a typical case, it would be the more valuable assets. Once the charge has crystallised, it is, of course, a fixed equitable charge and therefore protects the assets from execution creditors and all others with merely an equitable interest in the goods. However, automatic crystallisation clauses are somewhat uncertain in their operation and may have effects that neither of the parties desire.

24.90 As an example, it might be that only a minor default could trigger the crystallisation clause, perhaps without the parties even being aware of it. Such an example might be a short delay in furnishing information or documents which the charge requires to be produced. In such a circumstance, the charge holder has the choice of taking some steps to formally reverse the crystallisation or of simply ignoring it, leading to a "decrystallisation" by agreement or estoppel. As Goode points out,[1] such a course of action may have effects beyond what is expected since a Court may conclude that the entire clause should be ignored as failing to express the intention of the parties.

1 Goode, *Legal Problems of Credit and Security*, Sweet & Maxwell, 1982, at p 41.

24.91 It seems that the Courts have a tendency to reduce the effect of automatic crystallisation clauses. In particular, the standard clause which declares that all moneys secured shall become due and payable in the event of issue of execution against the company does not have the effect of causing automatic crystallisation.[1] On the other hand, it would appear that a clause which specifically stated that the charge would crystallise upon the issue of a writ of execution would have the effect, in New Zealand, of crystallising the charge and establishing the priority of the charge holder over the interests of the execution creditors.[2]

1 See *Heaton & Dugard Ltd v Cutting Brothers Ltd* [1925] 1 KB 655.
2 See *Re Manurewa Transport Ltd* [1971] NZLR 909.

24.92 Floating charges must be registered under the Companies Act 1955. Failure to do so renders them void against a wide range of other creditors.

Subsequent charges

24.93 The company is, in the absence of agreement to the contrary, free to create further floating charges. These will, in the ordinary course of things, rank in the order of their creation. A crystallisation of one of the charges would be an event which would mean that the business is no longer a going concern and would result in the simultaneous crystallisation of all.

24.94 The very nature of a floating charge is to leave the assets free for the company to use in the ordinary course of business. One activity which is very much in the ordinary course of business is the granting of mortgages, either legal or equitable, over various assets of the company. Subject to what is to be said in the following paragraphs, a fixed charge over the assets of a company will have priority over the interest of the floating charge holder, provided that the fixed charge is created prior to crystallisation. This is so whether the fixed charge assumes the form of a legal mortgage, an equitable mortgage or a fixed equitable charge. It is so whether or not the person taking the fixed charge has notice of the equitable interest, for it is based not on notions of notice, but on the basic nature of a floating charge.

24.95 This is not a situation which is dear to the heart of a lender who is contemplating the taking of a floating charge. Generally speaking, the risk of allowing the company to carry on business aside from the giving of securities is enough of a risk to the integrity of the security. For this reason, it has become common to insert a so-called "restrictive clause", also called a "negative pledge", in the document which evidences the floating charge. The restrictive clause purports to prohibit the creation of any mortgage or charge which ranks equal to or ahead of the floating charge.

24.96 The effect which has been given to these clauses is not entirely logical, but is well established. If the person taking the fixed charge, whether legal or equitable, has notice of the restrictive clause, then the attempt to create a prior ranking interest will fail. Notice that it is the restrictive clause itself, not the existence of the floating charge, which must be brought to the notice of the person.

24.97 Since in the ordinary course of events the floating charge will be registered, it must then be asked if registration is notice to the entire world. The question needs refinement, for the Courts have consistently held that registration is notice of the existence of the floating charge, but not of the restrictive clause.[1] However, if the charge is a fixed charge over chattels, then it seems that registration not only gives notice of the existence of the charge but also of its contents.[2]

1 See *Wilson v Kelland* [1910] 2 Ch 306; *Dempsey v Traders' Finance Corporation Ltd* [1933] NZLR 1258.
2 S 4(2), Chattels Transfer Act 1924; *Re Manurewa Transport Ltd* [1971] NZLR 909.

24.98 A lender who takes a "purchase money" security will gain priority over the floating charge even if the money is lent with notice of the restrictive clause. In this case, the money is lent specifically for the purchase of a particular item and the theory is that the debtor acquires the property with charge in favour of the lender already attached, ie, the only property which is ever acquired by the debtor is the property subject to the charge in favour of the lender of the purchase money security.[1]

1 _Re Connolly Bros (No 2)_ [1912] 2 Ch 25.

24.99 There is a further point about subsequent charges. One of the reasons for inserting automatic crystallisation clauses is to prevent subsequent charges from gaining priority over the floating charge. The argument is that a clause such as that in _Re Manurewa_ causes the charge to crystallise when there is an attempt to create the later charge. Since the later charge is then created after the crystallisation, it cannot, if it is equitable, have priority.

24.100 This analysis is challenged by Goode who argues that:

> In accordance with normal principles of agency law, a person who (i) had dealings with the company in relation to the charged assets prior to crystallisation or (ii) knew of the floating charge, is entitled to assume the continuance of the company's dealing powers, despite crystallisation, until he has notice that the charge has crystallised.[1]

1 Goode, _Legal Problems of Credit and Security_, Sweet & Maxwell, 1982, at p 37.

24.101 Speight J held that the subsequent chargee had notice not only of the prior floating charge, but also of the restrictive clause, so that the floating charge holder in _Re Manurewa_ would have had priority whether or not the automatic crystallisation clause was held to be effective. The clause would, however, protect the floating charge holder from subsequent actions by unsecured creditors attempting to levy execution on the assets of the company which were comprised in the floating charge.

"Debentures": usual form is fixed and floating charge

24.102 The modern company will often need to borrow more than may be comfortably supplied by a single borrower. One common approach to the problem is to find large numbers of small investors. The problem is to devise a security which will operate so as to provide equal protection for all of these small investors; it would be absurd that a small investor who lends on Monday should have priority over one who lends on Wednesday. The method used is the issue of "debenture stock". The word "debenture" is one of those legal words which seems to have a shifting meaning. At its widest, it can mean any document which creates or evidences a debt, but here its use will be restricted to the documents which are used in the way to be described.

24.103 The solution to the problem is to create a trustee who is granted the floating charge over the designated assets of the company. The beneficiaries of this trust are the smaller investors who share in proportion to the amount of their investment.

24.104 From the banker's point of view, the most difficult problems arise when he or she becomes one of the investors. The most likely situation is that the banker will be a significantly larger investor than members of the general public and would like to have substantial control over the manner in which the loan is supervised. If the banker is a party to the original trust deed, then this may be possible to arrange. Particular care is exercised in such cases to ensure that the banker may dictate to the trustee the precise limits of the bank's security interest.

24.105 Debenture deeds have become very long and complex documents and a banker considering investment where debenture stock is to be used as the security would be well advised to seek specialist advice.

Directors' guarantees

24.106 Except in the most unusual circumstances, when the banker is contemplating a loan to a small company, the taking of securities from the directors will also be contemplated. It is not unusual, in addition, to take personal guarantees from the directors of the company. There are certain difficulties here, even, or especially, when the company is a "one person" company.

24.107 The banker must have regard to the rules of law which are concerned with the effects of directors who have an interest in the transaction which is being undertaken by the company. Generally speaking, directors of a company have duties toward the company with are of a fiduciary nature. As in all such situations, the person who has such a duty to perform should never be allowed to enter into transactions in which he may have a personal interest which may conflict with the interests of the company.[1]

1 See *Spicer & Son Pty Ltd v Spicer* (1931) 47 CLR 151.

24.108 This potential conflict may arise when the director is negotiating a contract between the company and a third party. Since one of the consequences of such an interest may be that the contract is voidable at the company's option, it is necessary for the banker to take great care when negotiating loans to a company through the agency of a director.

24.109 In particular, it often happens that the articles of a company prohibit an interested director from voting.[1]

1 This is the case if the company has adopted the "standard" articles from the Companies Act 1955.

24.110 The kind of problem which may arise is illustrated in *Victors Ltd v Lingard*.[1] The directors had personally guaranteed a loan to the bank. They later resolved that the bank should be granted a floating charge to secure the loan. Since one effect of granting the floating charge was to reduce their own potential liability, the Court held that they were indeed interested in the transaction and, consequently, had no right to vote on the resolution which created the floating charge!

1 [1927] 1 Ch 323.

24.111 There are several ways around this rather unpleasant situation. There may be a sufficient number of directors who are not "interested" who may be able to validly pass the resolution. The resolution may be passed by the members of the company in a general meeting instead of by the directors at a meeting of directors.

24.112 It seems likely that where both the directors' guarantees and the giving of a company security are preconditions to the granting of a loan, that the directors could not be said to be interested in the transaction. This would be so even if there were some delay in the granting of the company's charge, but in such a case it is of the utmost importance that documentation be placed in the file which would confirm that the granting of the security was indeed a precondition.

24.113 It appears that the rule that interested directors are precluded from voting may be abrogated by express provisions in the articles or memorandum of association. This provides yet another situation where the banker who is intending to lend to a company must pay careful attention to the terms of the articles and memorandum of association.

Chapter 25

The banker's lien

25.1 The banker's lien is a right conferred by law on the banker to retain certain documents as security for debts due from the customer. It is a right which exists without the necessity for any express agreement, although it may be changed by expressed agreement. The right of lien exists even if the customer is unaware of such a right.

Main features

25.2 The main characteristics of the banker's lien flow from the law merchant and have been accepted into the existing law of banker and customer. The main case concerning the characteristics of the lien is *Brandao v Barnett*.[1]

1 (1846) 12 Cl & F 787; (1846) 8 ER 1622.

General lien

25.3 One exceptional characteristic of the banker's lien is that it is a general rather than a particular lien. The distinction may be most readily made by example. A mechanic's lien gives a repairer the right to hold the item repaired until the owner tenders the amount of the specific repairs for which the item was brought to the repairer. If the owner of the object also owes the repairer for work performed in the past, the repairer has no right to demand that those sums be paid before releasing the object. The mechanic's lien is a particular lien. By contrast, the documents held under a banker's lien may be retained until all sums owing the banker are repaid. This right to retain the documents as security for the whole of the customer's indebtedness is summarised by saying that the banker's lien is a general lien.

Pledge

25.4 The banker's lien has another unusual characteristic, namely that it carries with it the power of sale and recoupment from the proceeds. This is such an unusual characteristic of liens that the banker's lien has been described as in the nature of an implied pledge.[1]

1 See Holden, *Law and Practice of Banking, Vol II, Securities for Bankers' Advances* (6th ed, 1980).

25.5 This power of sale is not particularly important in the case of negotiable instruments which are encompassed by the lien since the banker will either be able to deal with these as holder or as agent for collection, but when the securities consist of other documents, the power of sale may become an important method of realisation.

Right of set off

25.6 It is generally thought that money cannot be the subject matter of a lien. That it was considered so at one time can be traced to a speech by Lord Hatherley in *Misa v Currie*.[1] This seems wrong in principle, for either the money would not be identifiable or, if it were, would be paid in for some specific purpose which would exclude the possibility of the banker's lien. The correct analysis is probably that Lord Hatherley was referring to the right of set off. As was noted in Ch 8, the terminology was often used rather carelessly prior to *National Westminster Bank Ltd v Halesowen Presswork and Assemblies Ltd*.[2]

1 (1876) 1 App Cas 554.
2 [1972] AC 785.

Documents encompassed by the lien

25.7 The banker is not entitled to a lien over all documents in his or her possession which belong to the customer. The precise scope of the documents to which the lien attaches is not entirely clear.

"All securities deposited with" the banker

25.8 In *Brandao*, the Court suggested that the lien could be exercised over "all securities deposited with" the banker. While it is generally agreed that this is far too wide, there is no consensus on precisely which class of documents are subject to the lien. On the most narrow view, the lien attaches only to instruments which are fully negotiable. On the widest view, the lien attaches to all securities which are ordinarily dealt with on behalf of the customer other than those which are deposited for safe keeping.

25.9 The correct view is almost certainly somewhere between, for the lien has been held to apply to share certificates and various other non-negotiable documents.[1] On the other hand, it seems quite clear that the lien does not attach to documents of title to land.[2] In any case, by far the most important application of the lien in practice is in the non-controversial case of negotiable instruments.

1 See *Re United Service Co; Johnston's Claim* (1870) LR 6 Ch App 212; *Misa v Currie* (1876) 1 App Cas 554.
2 This is in spite of a Victorian case to the contrary, *Dale v Bank of New South Wales* (1876) 2 VLR (L) 27; it was held that a banker may have a lien over title deeds which the customer had deposited in the ordinary course of business, but not over deeds deposited for safe custody only.

25.10 The lien extends only to securities which belong to the customer. Securities deposited with the banker for whatever reason which do not belong to the customer may not be retained by the banker.

Qua banker

25.11 The banker's lien only attaches to those documents which have been deposited with the banker in his or her capacity as banker. Thus, as mentioned above, the lien does not attach to those documents which are given to the banker for safe keeping, for safe keeping is not, strictly speaking, a part of the banker/customer relationship. The document must be some document which is ordinarily dealt with by bankers and it must have been left with the banker for the purpose of being dealt with in that way. Again, the main example is a bill of exchange which has been delivered to the banker for collection; the bill is a document with which bankers, in their role as bankers, deal and leaving it with a banker for collection is leaving it to be dealt with in the usual way.

Express agreement

25.12 The lien may be excluded by an express contract between the customer and banker or by circumstances which are inconsistent with a lien. Thus, for example, money paid in for the express purpose of meeting a bill which has been accepted by the customer payable at the bank is not subject to a lien even if money could be the subject matter of a lien; nor can it be subjected to the banker's right of set off. Again, a bill or other negotiable instrument which is handed to the banker solely for safe keeping is not subject to the banker's lien.

25.13 Perhaps the most difficult problem here is the situation where securities are handed to the banker as security for a particular liability but are allowed to remain in the banker's custody when that particular liability is discharged. There is little authority on the matter, but in *Re London and Globe Finance Corporation*[1] the Court held that in such a circumstance, in the absence of evidence to the contrary, the documents had become subject to a general lien.

1 [1902] 2 Ch 416.

25.14 However, there is no doubt that in the event that the security must be realised in order to recover the debt, any surplus proceeds are available to the banker, either by way of the banker's lien or, more correctly, the right of set off.[1] It is very peculiar that the immunity which attaches to the securities themselves does not extend to the proceeds, but the law is clear on the matter.

1 See *Jones v Peppercorne* (1858) John 430; *Re London & Globe Finance Co Ltd* [1902] 2 Ch 416.

Creation and termination of the lien

25.15 Although the lien may be excluded by agreement between the parties, it is not a consensual security. The fact and the time of its creation and duration are matters of law and not of agreement between the parties.

When the lien attaches

25.16 Whatever the range of documents to which the lien might attach, there is no doubt that the time of attachment is when the documents have come into the banker's hands in his or her capacity as banker, ie, in the course of the banker's business. The most common example of this is the cheque which has been paid in for collection by a customer who has an overdraft.

25.17 But the fact that the banker has a lien on a cheque or a bill deposited for collection does not affect the banker's duty of actually collecting the instrument. Of course, this is no disadvantage to the banker, for in the ordinary course of things, receiving the proceeds for the instrument will either go to reduce an overdraft or into an account over which the banker has the right of set off.

25.18 Where the banker is a holder of a cheque over which there is a banker's lien, then the banker is a holder for value to the extent of any such lien. In certain cases, therefore, the banker may be in a position to pursue remedies ordinarily available to a holder for value.[1]

1 As an example where the banker was able to take advantage of this status, see *Barclays Bank Ltd v Astley Industrial Trust Ltd* [1970] 2 QB 527.

Termination of the lien

25.19 Like any other lien, the rights of the creditor are determined when he or she parts with possession. However, as noted above, in the most important example of the banker's lien, negotiable instruments, the normal way in which the lien will be terminated is by the collection of the instrument by the banker, in which case the right of the lien is replaced by the right of set off.

Extent of the lien

25.20 In the absence of an express agreement to the contrary, the lien can only be exercised when the debt owing from the customer to the banker is one which has arisen out of the banker/customer relationship. An Australian example will illustrate the principle: a customer of the bank, A, had an overdraft with the bank which the bank wished to have reduced or secured. As a security for the overdraft, A gave the bank a bill of exchange which had been accepted by W. Later, A's overdraft was paid off. However, the bank had discounted another bill which had been accepted by A; since it was clear that A owed the bank the amount of the accepted bill, the bank claimed to be able to retain the bill accepted by W under the banker's lien. The Court held that the lien did not attach, for the debt did not arise from the banker/customer relationship.[1]

1 See *Commercial Bank of South Australia v Wake* (1880) 14 SALR 31.

Chapter 26

Guarantees

26.1 A guarantee is not a "security" in the same sense that the word has been used in this section of the book, for it is not an interest in property. Nevertheless, the need for a guarantee often arises in precisely those circumstances where a security interest might be taken instead, and bankers often speak informally of a guarantee being a security. For these reasons, it is customary in banking law texts to include guarantees in the discussion of security interests.

Nature of a guarantee

26.2 A guarantee is a promise by which one person, called the guarantor or the surety, undertakes to answer for the present or future debt of another, called the principal debtor. The promise is made to the creditor of the principal debtor. It is a conditional promise of the form "if the principal debtor defaults, then I will honour the obligation". There can be no guarantee if there is no principal debtor and if there is no cause of action which has accrued against the principal debtor, then there is none against the guarantor, although there may be circumstances where the principal debtor may escape liability even while the guarantor cannot.

26.3 It is important to distinguish a contract of guarantee from one of indemnity. This is unfortunate, for while the distinction is quite clear in theory, it may be very blurred when considering an individual case. The essence of a contract of indemnity is an unconditional promise by one person to another that the obligation of a third party will be discharged. It is a promise of the form "If you lend $1,000 to A, then I will see that you are paid". A guarantee, on the other hand, would have the form "If you lend $1,000 to A and A defaults, then I shall".

26.4 The difference between the guarantee and the indemnity is brought sharply into focus when the principal debtor has some defence which negates or reduces liability. If the agreement is a guarantee, then the surety also escapes liability for there is no liability on the guarantor until the principal debtor fails to meet his or her obligation. However, if the agreement is an indemnity, then the "surety" remains liable, for the liability under an indemnity is a primary liability which exists independently of the liability of the principal debtor.

26.5 The Court will look to the substance of a promise to determine if it is a contract of guarantee or one of indemnity. The words used are not in themselves conclusive as to the nature of the contract.

26.6 There is no reason why a guarantee cannot be made to cover a continuing series of transactions such as might be found when the principal debtor is a banker's customer operating an overdraft. In such a case, the sum being guaranteed is not only a fluctuating amount, but the debt itself is one which is constantly changing due to the rule in *Clayton's case*. For obvious reasons, guarantees taken by bankers are normally of the continuing type.

Requirements of a guarantee

Writing

26.7 A contract of guarantee is one of the exceptions to the general common law rule that legally enforceable contracts may be made orally. Section 2 of the Contract Enforcement Act 1956 recreates a requirement which was originally enacted by the Statute of Frauds of 1676:

> . . . no contract of guarantee, will be enforced by an action in the Court, unless the contract itself or a memorandum or note of it is in writing and signed by the person against whom it is to be enforced or his authorised agent.

26.8 The section is concerned with enforceability rather than the existence of the contract. The requirement of writing is one of the major reasons for distinguishing contracts of indemnity, for contracts of indemnity do not require writing to be enforceable. While it is unlikely that a banker would contemplate taking a guarantee without writing, such a result may follow from mistake or inadvertence. In such cases, it may be possible to argue that the contract should be enforceable as a contract of indemnity.[1]

1 See 2.61.

Consideration

26.9 A contract of guarantee, like all other contracts not under seal, must be supported by consideration. It is common to state in guarantees that the consideration is the continuation of financial accommodation already given or the present granting and subsequent continuation of financial accommodation by the bank to the principal debtor at the request of the guarantor.

26.10 If the formula used states that there was some form of request, then the banker should take care to see that the guarantor actually makes such a request. In *Reid Murray Holdings Ltd v David Murray Holdings Pty Ltd*[1] evidence was given that there was no such request and that there was no intention that the named consideration should exist. The guarantee was only saved by virtue of the fact that it was given in the form of a deed.

1 (1972) 5 SASR 386.

26.11 The problem of consideration becomes even more troublesome when the guarantee is only intended to cover existing advances and no other advances are contemplated or covered by the guarantee. In such cases, the proper consideration is that the banker gives the principal debtor extra time, or alternatively, defers suing the principal debtor on the debt at the request of the debtor.[1]

1 See, for example, *Colonial Bank of Australasia Ltd v Kerr* (1889) 15 VLR 314.

Avoidance of guarantees

26.12 There are a number of circumstances where the surety may escape liability under the guarantee. Some of these arise merely from general contractual principles and some due to the special nature of a guarantee.

Misrepresentation or non-disclosure

26.13 A contract of guarantee, like any other contract, is liable to be avoided by the misrepresentation of a material fact, even if the misrepresentation is made innocently.[1] But although misrepresentation may avoid the contract, a mere failure to disclose information which would obviously be relevant to the guarantor's decision will not avoid. The normal rule is that a contract of guarantee is not a contract uberrimae fidei, ie, one of the utmost good faith and that generally the creditor is not obliged to disclose information to the would-be guarantor.[2]

1 *MacKenzie v Royal Bank of Canada* [1934] AC 468, 475.
2 *Davies v London and Provincial Marine Insurance Co* (1878) 8 Ch D 469.

26.14 Thus, in *Cooper v National Provincial Bank Ltd*[1] the plaintiff had guaranteed an overdraft of Mrs R, a customer of the defendant bank. The plaintiff claimed to be released from the guarantees on the grounds that the bank had failed to inform him of several facts which, had they been known to the plaintiff, would have resulted in his refusal to enter into the guarantee. The relevant facts were that the principal debtor's husband was an undischarged bankrupt who had authority to draw upon the account and that there was information known to the bank that the husband had in fact used the account improperly in the recent past. The argument of the bank was that there was no legal requirement for them to disclose this information and that, indeed, to do so would be a breach of the banker's duty of secrecy concerning the affairs of the customer.

1 [1945] 2 All ER 641.

26.15 The Court in *Cooper's* case upheld the bank's argument concerning the duty to disclose, thereby reaffirming the principle that a guarantee is not a contract uberrimae fidei. The point as to the duty of secrecy is less certain. Paget suggests that the banker has an implied authority to answer any questions put by the proposed surety, but Holden sees that as a doubtful proposition.[1] Probably the correct approach is that the banker has such implied authority if the surety is one which has been proposed by the principal debtor, but not if the surety is one of which the debtor is unaware.

1 *Paget*, p 502, Holden in *Chorley*, p 335, fn 30.

26.16 In any case, it is clear that if the would-be guarantor does ask a direct question of the banker concerning the account, then it must be answered truthfully and accurately. The precise scope of the information which the proposed guarantor is entitled to receive, in the absence of express authority from the principal debtor, is by no means clear. It would seem that the guarantor may ask from time to time the amount for which he or she is liable, but again Holden argues that if the total debt of the principal debtor is larger than the amount of the liability of the guarantor, the guarantor should not be told the amount of the total debt but only the liability under the guarantee.[1]

1 Holden, *The Law and Practice of Banking* (1971) Vol 2, 206.

26.17 It is certainly the case that the surety is not entitled to examine the customer's account activity or to be given a copy of the statement.[1] In the event that the surety does demand information concerning the account or other matters which appear to infringe upon the customer's right of confidentiality, the banker should decline to answer unless the customer is present and/or gives his authority to disclose the information sought by the surety.

1 *Ross v Bank of New South Wales* (1928) 28 SR (NSW) 539.

Cases where disclosure required

26.18 Although the guarantee is not a contract uberrimae fidei, there are certain circumstances in which certain information should be brought to the attention of the proposed guarantor even if the banker is not explicitly asked. Lord Campbell set out the general rule:[1]

> I should think that this might be considered as the criterion whether the disclosure ought to be made voluntarily, namely, whether there is anything that might not naturally be expected to take place between the parties who are concerned in the transaction, that is, whether there be a contract between the debtor and the creditor, to the effect that his position shall be different from that which the surety might naturally expect; and, if so, the surety is to see whether that is disclosed to him. But if there be nothing which might not naturally take place between these parties, then, if the surety would guard against particular perils, he must put the question . . .

1 In *Hamilton v Watson* (1845) 12 Cl & Fin 109; (1845) 8 ER 1339.

26.19 It is not easy to find examples of situations where the banker has a duty to disclose under the rule in *Hamilton v Watson*. In one case, the Court indicated that there might be a duty to disclose where the account to be guaranteed was not really that of the person in whose name it appeared, but rather belonged to an undischarged bankrupt.[1] However, there have been cases where the banker suspected that the customer was defrauding the guarantor, yet non-disclosure was held not to invalidate the guarantee.[2] It seems difficult to imagine circumstances which would fit more precisely into the category of cases defined by Lord Campbell. At best, then, it can be said that the situation is a very uncertain and unhappy one for the banker, for in a case which appears to fall within the rule in *Hamilton v Watson*, a failure to disclose might invalidate the guarantee while disclosure of the customer's affairs might be a breach of the banker's duty of secrecy.

1 *Cooper v National Provincial Bank Ltd* [1946] KB 1.
2 *National Provincial Bank of England Ltd v Glanusk* [1913] 3 KB 335; *Royal Bank of Scotland v Greenshields* [1914] SC 259.

26.20 Disclosure may also be required when the banker is aware, or possibly should be aware, that the proposed guarantor is acting under a misapprehension as to the truth of a material fact. If the banker allows the contract of guarantee to be concluded in such circumstances, it may be that his silence will amount to a misrepresentation allowing the guarantor to escape liability.[1]

1 *Royal Bank of Scotland v Greenshields* [1914] SC 259.

Undue influence

26.21 Although contracts of guarantee are not contracts uberrimae fidei, it has been noted that there is a duty on the banker not actively to misrepresent facts to the guarantor. There is a line of cases which suggest that there are circumstances where it is incumbent on the banker to do much more. These cases suggest that it is sometimes necessary to see that the intending guarantor be capable of making a free and informed opinion concerning the advisability of proceeding with the guarantee. In the absence of doing so, there will be a presumption that the banker has exercised undue influence on the guarantor with the result that the guarantee may be set aside or the banker may be required to pay damages.

Where banker a beneficiary of protected transactions

26.22 There are some situations where the relationship between the parties is such that if a transaction occurs which confers a benefit on the "dominant" party, then the law will presume that that party exercised some undue influence on the other in order to effect the transaction. The precise list of relationships which fall into this category includes, among others, parent and child, solicitor and client, trustee and beneficiary. In such a circumstance, there is a burden of proof on the dominant party to show that he did not exercise undue influence.

26.23 The presumption of undue influence is of concern not only for the parties directly concerned, but also those third parties who might also benefit from the transaction. In *Bank of New South Wales v Rogers*,[1] a niece had resided with her uncle since the death of her father. She sought advice from the uncle on all matters related to business. She mortgaged virtually the whole of her property in order to secure advances made by the bank to the uncle.

1 (1941) 65 CLR 42.

26.24 The Court summarised the law relating to such situations as follows:

> ... creditors cannot improve their security ... by instigating or inducing [debtors] to obtain further security for their debts from near relations or persons under their influence and not in a situation to resist their importunity. The inference of undue influence operates not only "against the person who is able to exercise the influence", but "against ... every person who claimed under him with notice of the equity thereby created", or with notice of the circumstances from which the Court infers the equity. But ... it would not operate against a person who is not shown to have taken with such notice of the circumstances. ...[1]

1 Per Starke J, at pp 51, 52.

26.25 Since it was found that the bank had notice of the special relationship between the uncle and the niece, there was an onus on it to prove that the niece had given the security free from any undue influence, that she had given it freely and with a full understanding of the consequences of her actions. Since she had obtained no independent advice, it was virtually impossible for the bank to show this; the security was set aside.

26.26 The relationship of husband and wife requires some special mention. Generally speaking, there is no presumption of undue influence merely because the parties are married.[1] However, the relationship is such that it may require only a small amount of evidence to turn the tables and raise the presumption of undue influence. If it can be shown that the creditor requested the wife's guarantee of a debt owed by her husband, that there was not a proper explanation of the significance of the guarantee and that the husband insisted that she give the guarantee, then the guarantee may be set aside, but the burden of proof is on the person attempting to avoid the guarantee.[2] It would seem that the same principle would apply when the husband is guaranteeing the debt of the wife.

1 *Bank of Montreal v Stuart* [1911] AC 120; *MacKenzie v Royal Bank of Canada* [1934] AC 468.
2 *Dunlop New Zealand Ltd v Dumbleton* [1968] NZLR 1092.

Where the creditor exercises undue influence on the guarantor

26.27 The position of a banker who gains a benefit from a guarantee which has been made under circumstances where the principal debtor is in a special relationship with the guarantor has been discussed. The question to be examined now is whether the relationship of banker and prospective guarantor is ever such that a presumption exists that the banker has exercised undue influence over the guarantor. In other words, should the relationship of banker and prospective guarantor be added, at least in some circumstances, to the list of relationships which are fiduciary in nature.

26.28 The story begins with a decision of the English Court of Appeal in *Lloyd's Bank Ltd v Bundy.*[1] Bundy and his son both banked at the same branch of Lloyd's bank. The son was engaged in business and maintained some company accounts at the branch. He sought advances from the bank and it was suggested that his father could act as guarantor. At the time of making the first guarantee, the bank manager suggested that Bundy should take legal advice. This Bundy did and entered into a guarantee which was secured by a charge over his farm.

1 [1975] QB 326; [1974] 2 Lloyd's Rep 366.

26.29 Some years later, the son wished to obtain further advances and his father was again approached about the possibility of increasing his liability. On this occasion, the father did not seek independent advice, nor was it suggested that he do so.

26.30 Although it is possible that the case could have been placed in the category of case which has been discussed, the Court instead held that the bank had breached a duty of care owed directly to Bundy, namely the duty to ensure that he obtained independent advice so that he was able to make a free and informed decision. After reviewing the cases in which transactions had been set aside due to the exercise of undue influence, Denning MR explained the origin and scope of the duty in the following terms:

> . . . I would suggest that through all these instances there runs a simple thread. They rest on "inequality of bargaining power". By virtue of it the English law gives relief to one who, without independent advice, enters into a contract upon terms which are very unfair or transfers property for a consideration which is grossly inadequate, when his bargaining power is grievously impaired by reason of his own needs or desires or by his own ignorance or infirmity, coupled with undue influence or pressures brought to bear on him by or for the benefit of the other.[1]

1 [1975] QB 326, 339.

26.31 The result was that both the guarantee and the charge over the property were set aside. It is not entirely clear that the bank did in fact take advantage of Bundy or that he was significantly misled as to the state of his son's finances or the import of the documents which he was signing. It should be noted that although Lord Denning's formulation of the duty is very wide, Bundy was in fact a customer of the bank, not a stranger.

26.32 *Bundy's* case caused considerable consternation in banking circles, for it seemed to place a very heavy burden on the banker who would like to take a guarantee or some other form of security from a third party. The concern was not eased when *Morgan's* case came before the Court of Appeal.

26.33 In *National Westminster Bank plc v Morgan*[1] a wife signed a legal charge to a bank in order to secure a loan made to her husband.
She had full knowledge of the circumstances, in the sense that she understood the nature of the charge and that she was indeed guaranteeing the loan to the husband, but she hoped it was the way of saving her home from being taken from her as the result of proceedings for possession which were being brought by a previous mortgagee.

1 [1983] 3 All ER 85.

26.34 The Court of Appeal held that a relationship of confidentiality could exist where one party relied on the guidance or advice of the other party who stood to benefit by the transaction. If the transaction was not at arm's length, then a presumption of undue influence might be raised, whereupon the party giving the advice would have to rebut it by showing that the other party had formed an informed and free independent judgment. The party relying on the other's guidance did not have to show that the resulting transaction was manifestly disadvantageous to himself before the presumption could be invoked.

26.35 In this formulation there need be no special relationship between the parties. It was enough that the wife relied upon the advice of the bank and that the bank stood to benefit. Since that was enough to raise the presumption of undue influence it was over to the bank to prove that the wife had entered into the transaction freely and with a full understanding of her position. Since she had not received independent advice, the bank failed in discharging this burden. The Court of Appeal set aside the charge.

26.36 The case went on appeal to the House of Lords which reversed the findings of the Court of Appeal.[1] According to the House of Lords, in order to raise the presumption of undue influence when the parties are not in a special relationship, it is necessary to show that the transaction had itself been wrongful in that it amounted to one in which an actual unfair advantage had been taken of another person; it is not enough in this situation to argue that there might have been an unfair advantage taken. Since it was clear in *Morgan's* case that the bank had not in fact taken an unfair advantage and since there was no special relationship involved, the bank was able to rely upon the charge.

1 [1985] 1 All ER 821; [1985] 2 WLR 588.

26.37 The relief of banking community afterthe House of Lords decision in *Morgan's* case was short lived. Before the House of Lords decision in *Morgan*, the Court of Appeal considered *Cornish v Midland Bank plc*.[1] The plaintiff customer signed a second mortgage in favour of the bank without appreciating, and without being informed by the bank, that it was so worded as to secure not only a loan of £2,000 for renovations to a farmhouse jointly owned by the plaintiff and her husband, but also secured unlimited further advances made to the husband. The bank in fact made further advances to the husband which were secured under the mortgage. When the farmhouse was sold, the proceeds barely covered the first and second mortgagees and sale expenses.

1 [1985] 3 All ER 513.

26.38 At first instance, the Court held, on the basis of *Bundy* and the Court of Appeal decision in *Morgan*, that the bank had been negligent in explaining the effect of the mortgage and that the mortgage should be set aside on the ground of undue influence. The husband was held liable to indemnify the bank for an amount of over £11,000. This indemnity was on the basis that if the mortgage was set aside, then the debt owed by the husband still existed.

26.39 When the House of Lords reversed the *Morgan* decision, it was natural that the bank should appeal the *Cornish* decision. The Court of Appeal agreed that the decision could no longer be sustained on the *Bundy/Morgan* line of reasoning, but then went on to hold that when the bank undertook to advise as to the nature and effect of the mortgage there arose a duty to do it carefully. The bank here had been negligent in this explanation. However, setting aside the mortgage was an equitable remedy which was not available unless the plaintiff could show undue influence. Under the House of Lords test in *Morgan*, that meant that the customer must show, at the very least, that the bank had taken unfair advantage so that there was raised a presumption of undue influence. It was impossible for the customer to show that unfair advantage had in fact been taken, and therefore no presumption of undue influence.

26.40 This did not mean that the bank succeeded, only that the remedy of setting aside the mortgage was not available. The plaintiff was still entitled to damages for the harm which had been caused by the negligent explanation of her responsibility under the mortgage. These damages were assessed so that the plaintiff was in the same position as if the mortgage had been set aside.

26.41 However, since the mortgage had not been set aside, the debt owed by the husband was discharged. It could not be argued that the bank was entitled to be indemnified by the husband, since the losses were caused by its own negligence and he had had no part to play in that matter.

26.42 It might be thought that the bank could avoid the problem by declining to give any advice whatsoever, since it appeared to be the undertaking of this responsibility which gave rise to a duty of care. The question of whether the bank actually has a duty to undertake this explanation was argued during the case, but was clearly not necessary for the decision.

26.43 However, Kerr LJ addressed the problem of whether it is incumbent upon the bank to undertake to give advice in the first place, concluding:

> I think that I would have inclined to the view that in the circumstances of this case the bank owed a duty to the plaintiff, as the bank's customer, to proffer to her some adequate explanation of the nature and effect of the document which she had come to sign. If expert evidence had been called as to the standard practices of banks in situations such as the present, I think that this would have supported the conclusion that bankers themselves recognise that their proper professional standards would not be consistent with mere silence on their part in such situations.[1]

1 At pp 522, 523.

26.44 On a strict view, the statement must be considered as obiter, but representing as it does the carefully considered statement of a senior member of the Court, it seems likely to be an accurate statement of the law. Consequently, it seems safe to suppose that there is a duty to explain to a customer and that the explanation must be done without negligence. It is not clear to what extent the duty to explain might extend to a guarantor who is not a customer.

26.45 In *Commonwealth Bank of Australia v Amadio*[1] the bank knew that the business of the principal debtor was in financial difficulties and they sought a mortgage from his parents, the respondents in the case, as security for the debt owed to the bank. They were an elderly couple who read little English; they believed that their son's business was a going and profitable concern and that their liability under the proposed guarantee would be limited to $50,000. They signed the mortgage in the presence of the bank manager without reading it. The bank sought recovery under the mortgage of more than $200,000. The High Court of Australia set the mortgage aside. The Court considered that the respondents were under a special disability due to their age and restricted knowledge of the language. In such a case, the Court considered that it should look to the conduct of the party attempting to enforce the dealing, holding that the facts known to the bank were such as to raise in the mind of any reasonable person a very real question as to the respondents' ability to make a judgment in their own best interests. The bank had a duty in these circumstances to make inquiries.

1 [1983] 57 ALJR 358.

26.46 The lesson for the banker is clear. In any situation where there might be a possibility of undue influence or where there is a duty to explain the effects of a guarantee or similar security to a customer, the banker should ensure that independent advice is obtained by the party proposing to give the security. When the debtor is a person who might unduly influence the proposed giver of the security, then this advice should be given in the absence of the debtor. Since this merely amounts to good business practice as well as good law, it should cause little hardship to the banker.

Re-opening credit contracts: Credit Contracts Act 1981

26.47 The Court in New Zealand has for some time had the power to re-open contracts of loans under certain circumstances. The Moneylenders Act 1908 granted the Court the power to re-open loans when the rate of interest was "excessive" but there was no power to look to the pre-contract negotiations and conduct.

26.48 Aside from the equitable principles discussed above for the setting aside of contracts because of undue influence, the Credit Contracts Act 1981 provides for the re-opening of contracts which are covered by that Act. Part I of the Act begins with a statutory definition of oppressive:

9. Meaning of oppressive — In this Act, the term "oppressive" means oppressive, harsh, unjustly burdensome, unconscionable, or in contravention of reasonable standards of commercial practice.

10. Re-opening of credit contracts — (1) Where, in any proceedings (whether or not instituted pursuant to this Act), the Court considers that —

(a) A credit contract, or any term thereof, is oppressive; or
(b) A party under a credit contract has exercised, or intends to exercise, a right or power conferred by the contract in an oppressive manner; or
(c) A party under a credit contract has induced another party to enter into the contract by oppressive means —
the Court may re-open the contract.

(2) Where a party under a credit contract refuses to agree to the early termination of the contract, or to vary or waive any term of the contract, or imposes conditions on such agreement he shall, for the purposes of this Act, be deemed to be exercising a right or power under the contract.

(3) Where, with the knowledge of the creditor under a re-opened credit contract, —

(a) The credit provided pursuant to the contract was used (whether in whole or in part) to pay amounts owing under another credit contract or other credit contracts; or
(b) Amounts owing under the contract were paid from credit provided pursuant to another credit contract or other credit contracts —
and the creditors under the contracts are either the same person or related bodies corporate, the Court may re-open all or any of those other contracts (whether or not it considers that any of the paragraphs (a) to (c) of subsection (1) of this section apply in respect thereof.

26.49 It is also clear that contracts of guarantee will be subject to re-opening:

4. Collateral contracts and linked transactions — (1) Where it is a term of a credit contract that another contract or a deed be entered into, the following provisions shall apply:

(a) Any part of that other contract or deed that relates to the provision of credit to, or the payment of money by, a debtor under the credit contract shall be deemed to form part of the credit contract for the purposes of Part I of this Act:
(b) If the other contract of deed is to be entered into for the purpose of giving security for the credit provided under the credit contract —
(i) The whole of that other contract or deed shall be deemed to form part of the credit contract for the purposes of this Act (whether or not it is entered into at the same time as the credit contract is made;
. . . .

26.50 The rights to re-open the contract expressed in s 10(1)(a) and (c) are not surprising; indeed, they appear very like the situations where the Courts of equity have claimed a right to intervene. However, the power to intervene in circumstances defined in s 10(1)(b) and (2) is a very radical departure from the generally accepted view that a person with a contractual right need not exercise that right "reasonably". The traditional view was expressed in *White & Carter (Councils) Ltd v McGregor*[1] where Lord Reid said:

It might be, but it never has been, the law that a person is only entitled to enforce his contractual rights in a reasonable way, and that a Court will not support an attempt to enforce them in an unreasonable way.

One reason why that is not the law is, no doubt, because it was thought that it would create too much uncertainty to require the Court to decide whether it is reasonable or equitable to allow a party to enforce his full rights under a contract.[2]

1 [1962] AC 413, 430.
2 At p 430.

26.51 This extended power to re-open the contract may have several consequences for bankers. When lending on overdraft, it is customary to declare that the entire overdraft is repayable on demand, and this is true even when the parties are contemplating finance for projects which would obviously suffer if suitable time were not available for refinancing. Under the sections mentioned, it is now clear that the debtor may be able to seek a re-opening of the contract.[1]

1 Whether the debtor would succeed or not is another question; see 26.54ff.

26.52 Under s 10(2) it is possible for a debtor to request re-opening of a contract when the creditor demands the payment of interest for a period after early termination.

26.53 Other circumstances where the exercise of the banker's contractual rights might be called into question are the power to call in the entire balance owing in the event of a default, various powers of sale and appointment of receivers, and any other power which is designed to give the banker excessive control over the debtor's affairs.

26.54 Since s 14 of the Act essentially provides the Court with the power to rewrite the contract completely and/or unwind any transactions related to the contract which may already have occurred, it is vitally important to have guidelines which will assist in determining when the Court will in fact find that terms or contracts are "oppressive". The Act itself provides guidelines in s 11:

11. **Guidelines for re-opening credit contracts** — (1) No credit contract or term of a credit contract, or act performed pursuant to or in relation to a credit contract, shall be considered to be oppressive if the contract, term, or act would not have been considered oppressive at the time at which, and in the circumstances in which, it was made or performed.
(2) In deciding whether paragraphs (a) to (c) of section 10(1) of this Act apply in respect of a credit contract and whether to re-open the contract under that section, the Court shall have regard to —
(a) All the circumstances relating to the making of the contract, the exercise of the right or power conferred by the contract, or the inducement to enter the contract, as the case may be; and
(b) Such of the following matters as are applicable (if any):

(i) Whether the finance rate for the contract, or any amount payable by the debtor under the contract (whether or not on default by the debtor), is oppressive:
(ii) Where a debtor is in default under the contract, whether the time given to the debtor by or pursuant to the contract to remedy

the default is oppressive having regard to the likelihood of loss to the creditor:

(iii) Where the creditor has required, as a condition of early repayment of the credit outstanding under the contract, that the debtor pay interest for a period subsequent to the date of repayment, whether the amount of interest is oppressive having regard to the expenses of the creditor and the likelihood that the amount repaid can be reinvested on similar terms:

(iv) Where the creditor has refused to release part of any security relating to the contract or has agreed to such a release subject to conditions, whether the refusal is, or the conditions are, oppressive having regard to the amount of the credit and the extent of the security that would remain after the release; and

(v) Such other matters as the Court thinks fit.

26.55 There is as yet little case law available to determine the way in which these provisions will be applied, but it is thought that the Courts will continue to be reluctant to re-open contracts when the relative strength of the parties is approximately equal or when the weaker party has received independent advice prior to entering into the contract. Thus in *Italia Holdings (Properties) Ltd v Lonsdale Holdings (Auckland) Ltd*[1] the plaintiff company sought a loan from the defendant finance company for $120,000. The defendant would only grant the loan on the condition that the plaintiff purchase from the defendant two sections of land for a total price of more than $98,000. The deal was made and the time for repayment was 10 May 1983. The plaintiff claimed relief under s 9 of the Credit Contracts Act 1981. The plaintiff said that the price for the properties was grossly inflated and that the condition was "oppressive".

1 [1984] 2 NZLR 1.

26.56 The plaintiff's claim was rejected. Although the purchase of the properties had been imposed as a condition, it was nothing more than the ordinary give and take and bargaining inherent in commercial transactions. The Court noted that the plaintiff had been involved in extensive property dealings, that it had expertise available to it to assess the market and that it had independent legal advice available throughout. In these circumstances, neither the contract nor any term of it was oppressive.

26.57 Section 13 of the Act indicates that commercial practice at the time when the contract was made, the power exercised or the inducements offered will be admissible evidence. By implication, it would seem that these matters are relevant to the determination of whether the contract or the conduct was oppressive, but it is also clear that these matters may not be decisive.

Principal debtor under a disability

26.58 Subject to certain important qualifications, the basic rule appears to be that when the contract with the principal debtor is void or unenforceable, the guarantor cannot be held liable under the guarantee. This rule follows logically, if somewhat harshly, from the basic notion that there can be no guarantor if there is no principal debtor. Prior to the passing of the Minors' Contracts Act 1969, the rule could be applied to allow a guarantor to escape liability where the principal contract was void due to the infancy of the principal debtor even when all parties knew at the time of contracting that the principal debtor was under age.[1]

1 *Coutts & Co v Browne-Lecky* [1947] 1 KB 104 followed in *Robinson's Motor Vehicles Ltd v Graham* [1956] NZLR 545.

26.59 This rigid application of the principle is so harsh that it is not surprising that Courts have occasionally sought to circumvent the result. After all, presumably one of the reasons that the bank sought the guarantee was precisely because of the minority of the borrower, and one of the reasons that the guarantor was willing to guarantee was to assist the minor to obtain the loan.

26.60 The way around the problem is to construe the guarantee as being an indemnity, for as already noted, an indemnity places the primary obligation on the surety and the fact that the principal debtor is suffering from some contractual incapacity will not in any way assist the surety to escape liability. This approach seems to have gained some sympathy from the Courts. In *Yeoman Credit Ltd v Latter*[1] Harman LJ said:

> Where all concerned know that the first promisor is an infant, so that as against him the promise cannot be enforced, the Court should incline to construe the document signed by the adult (the second promisor) as an indemnity, for that must have been the intention of the promisee and the second promisor. Both know that the first promise has no legal validity; it may be that both hope that the first promisor will honour his engagement, but with the knowledge that he cannot be obliged to do so it must have been their intention that the promise of the adult promisor should have an independent validity. Otherwise the whole transaction is a sham.[2]

1 [1961] 1 WLR 828.
2 At p 835.

26.61 Bankers have sought to avoid the problem by including in their forms of guarantee a clause to the effect that even if the moneys guaranteed are not recoverable from the principal debtor by reason of that person's contractual incapacity, that nevertheless the guarantor shall be liable for the sum as a principal debtor on the basis of an indemnity. The efficacy of such a clause does not appear to have been tested in Court.[1]

1 The terms used by the parties are not conclusive; see *Total Oil Products (Aust) Pty Ltd v Robinson* [1970] 1 NSWR 701.

26.62 The problem with minors is now eliminated by s 10 of the Minors' Contracts Act 1969 which provides that a guarantee shall be enforceable against the surety to the extent that it would have been if the minor had at all material times been a person of full age. However, presumably the principle in all of the "minors' cases" applies to other forms of contractual incapacity, so the cases are by no means irrelevant.

Ultra vires

26.63 When the principal debtor is a company and the loan guaranteed is one which is ultra vires, somewhat different principles apply. There is a long line of cases which hold that the guarantor may be held liable on the debt so long as the loan was entered into in good faith and in the honest belief that the company had the power to make the contract.[1]

1 See *Yorkshire Railway Wagon Co v Maclure* (1881) 19 Ch D 478; (1882) 21 Ch D 309.

26.64 The precise foundation for the decisions is not at all clear, but they have not been based expressly on the notion that the "guarantee" was in fact an indemnity. The matter is unlikely to arise now due to the changes in the Companies Act discussed in Ch 22.

Implied power of a company to give guarantees

26.65 Limited companies which were incorporated before 1 January 1957 have no implied power to give guarantees. This is true irrespective of the type or general purposes of the company. Consequently, when taking a guarantee from a company formed before this date, it is imperative to sight the memorandum of association to determine if there is an express power to give the guarantee.

26.66 For companies formed after 1 January 1957, there is an implied power to give guarantees unless the power is expressly excluded by the memorandum of association. Again, it is imperative for the banker to sight the memorandum before taking a guarantee from a limited company.

Clauses commonly found in bank guarantees

26.67 The modern bank guarantee form is a very lengthy document. Part of the reason for this length is the necessity, from the banker's point of view, to include clauses which will define when the guarantor may or may not take action to terminate the guarantee.

As noted by Weaver and Cragie, many of the modern cases on the subject are of interest only to legal draftsmen since they turn entirely upon the wording of some clause in the particular document before the Court.

26.68 The law is generally very protective of guarantors, many of whom have little or nothing to gain by entering into the guarantee and everything to lose. Clauses which purport to detract from the rights which guarantors might otherwise enjoy are construed strictly against the bank (which is always the party responsible for the form of guarantee), particularly those clauses which attempt to deny the guarantor the rights to terminate the guarantee and so to limit his or her liability.[1]

1 *Dunlop New Zealand Ltd v Dumbleton* [1968] NZLR 1092.

26.69 In the following paragraphs, the main rights of the guarantor to terminate the guarantee and/or to escape from liability will be discussed. It cannot be emphasised too strongly that the actual rights enjoyed by the parties will depend upon the construction of the particular document.

Limitation of the guarantor's liability

26.70 There is no reason why a guarantee may not be limited either in duration or in amount. A limitation as to duration causes no difficulties beyond those of interpretation; it is necessary to spell out precisely the obligations of the parties. As an example,[1] what does it mean to say "this guarantee shall cease to have effect two years after the date thereof"?

1 See Goode, *Legal Problems of Credit and Security*, Sweet & Maxwell, 1982.

26.71 In the case of a limitation of amount, the problem is more difficult. It is understandable that the guarantor will wish to limit the amount of total liability. There are two separate ways in which this might be done. First, the guarantor may guarantee only a certain amount of the debt. Secondly, there may be a guarantee of the whole of the advance, but with a limit on the liability. As an example, the first form is "I hereby guarantee $5,000 of the $10,000 that you are to loan to D". The second form is "I hereby guarantee the entire amount that you are to loan to D, subject to my liability being limited to $5,000".

26.72 It may seem that there is little difference in these forms, but they have quite different legal consequences. Suppose that the banker does in fact lend D the amount of $10,000 and that D defaults. The banker may then turn to the guarantor under either of the above formulae and demand the payment of $5,000. However, under the second formula, the guarantor is not permitted to prove in the bankruptcy of the principal debtor in competition with the banker unless the guarantor has paid the full amount of the principal debtor's indebtedness, even though that amount is greater than the amount for which the guarantor agreed to be liable. Indeed, the banker is entitled to prove for the full amount of the principal debtor's debt even though having received a part of the sum from the guarantor. It is only if the total amount recovered by the banker, from both the guarantor and the dividend in the bankruptcy, exceeds the amount of the debt that the guarantor has any rights to recover.[1]

1 *Re Sass, ex parte National Provincial Bank of England Ltd* [1896] 2 QB 12.

26.73 The situation is similar with regard to the guarantor's right to have resort to any securities given to the banker to secure the debt. If the second form of guarantee is used, the guarantor has no right against the securities until the whole debt is paid. If the first form is used, then the guarantor is entitled to share in the benefit of the securities.

26.74 The form used by bankers is, of course, the second one. Weaver and Cragie give the following as an example:

> This guarantee is to be security for the whole of the moneys hereby secured but nevertheless the total amount payable hereunder by the guarantor shall not exceed the sum of $ . . . . together with interest for a period of twelve months and the costs charges and expenses of obtaining or attempting to obtain payment from the guarantor.[1]

1 *Weaver and Cragie*, p 691.

26.75 Where the upper limit was left blank, the Full Court of the Supreme Court of New South Wales has held that the guarantee was for an unlimited amount.[1]

1 *Caltex Oil (Australia) Pty Ltd v Alderton* (1964) 81 WN (NSW) (Pt I) 297.

26.76 It is also customary that the forms used by bankers contain a clause to the effect that a certificate signed by certain officials of the bank which states the balance of the principal and interest owed by the customer shall be conclusive evidence of the customer's indebtedness for the purposes of the guarantee. This "conclusive evidence clause" has been upheld by the High Court of Australia,[1] but it is possible that it could be challenged under the Credit Contracts Act 1981.

1 *Dobbs v National Bank of Australasia Ltd* (1935) 53 CLR 643.

Notice of determination

26.77 Most bank guarantees are, as previously noted, continuing guarantees. The guarantor is, under ordinary conditions, entitled to terminate the guarantee as to future advances at any time by notice to the banker.[1] Such a notice does not relieve the guarantor of any liability which existed at the time of notice and the terms of the guarantee may very well call upon the guarantor to pay what is then due under the guarantee.

1 *Beckett v Addyman* (1882) 9 QBD 783.

26.78 In the event that the guarantor gives such a notice of determination to the banker, the banker should stop the account immediately to prevent any possible erosion of rights against the guarantor through the operation of the rule in *Clayton's case*. It is possible to open a new account for the principal debtor on terms to be arranged. The important point is that payment into the new account will not reduce the advances which were secured by the guarantee.

26.79 Most forms of guarantee used by bankers specify that the guarantee may only be determined by a specific period of notice, typically three months. The object of such a clause is clearly to allow the banker and customer to make mutually satisfactory arrangements. It is not at all clear whether the banker may, after receipt of the notice, continue to make voluntary advances during the intervening period.

26.80 On the one hand, the point of giving notice is to allow the guarantor the opportunity to limit his or her losses, and it is hard to see how the banker is prejudiced by being unable to rely upon the guarantor. On the other hand, to allow the guarantor to withdraw from any further liability may prejudice the principal debtor who may already have made plans which will call for finance which was fully and fairly expected to be forthcoming. The only advice which may be given is to express the rights and obligations as clearly as possible in the form of guarantee.

26.81 The notice of determination may also cause a problem when there is more than one guarantor. In *Kalil v Standard Bank of South Africa Ltd*[1] the particular wording of the guarantee stated only that the guarantee was in force until the bank should receive notice "from us" terminating the arrangement. The Court held that one of the guarantors, acting alone, could give notice of termination in relation to his own liability.

1 [1967] 4 SA 550 (AD).

Payment

26.82 Payment of the debt by the principal debtor extinguishes any potential liability of the guarantor. The only problems that have arisen in these cases is where the payment is properly made, the guarantor discharged, but then the payment is set aside by the operation of some other law, most typically as being a preference under some equivalent of the Insolvency Act 1967. It has been held in Australia that, on the wording of the particular guarantee in question, the liability of the guarantor did not revive.[1] The Court did, however, note that it was a simple matter for the bank to include a clause which would have led to the opposite result. Most bank guarantee forms now include such a clause.

1 *Commercial Bank of Australia Ltd v Carruthers* (1964) 6 FLR 247.

Variation in the principal contract

26.83 It is a basic rule that a material variation of the contract between the banker and the principal debtor will result in the discharge of the guarantor from all liability, and it does not matter that the variation may have been beneficial to the guarantor unless it is patently obvious that the variation either is beneficial to him or immaterial.[1]

1 *Dunlop New Zealand Ltd v Dumbleton* [1968] NZLR 1092.

26.84 Since the basic rule is so strictly construed, once again we find that many forms of guarantee contain clauses designed to circumvent it. Such clauses must be carefully drawn if they are to be effective. In *National Bank of Nigeria Ltd v Oba M S Awolesi*[1] the Privy Council held a guarantor to be discharged when the banker opened a second account for the principal debtor through which all later transactions passed. The action was held to be a substantial variation of the principal contract which was unknown and detrimental to the surety, in spite of the fact that the guarantor had agreed to guarantee all advances, overdrafts and liabilities of the principal debtor. The case is solely one of construction, but shows the need for care in drafting the clauses which purport to limit the rights which the guarantor might otherwise enjoy.

1 [1964] 1 WLR 1311.

Extension of time to the debtor

26.85 At first sight, it may seem strange to argue that an extension of time to the principal debtor can possibly result in the discharge of the guarantor, yet upon reflection it will be seen that the result is correct. During the extended period of time, it is quite possible that the financial position of the principal debtor will deteriorate even further from the circumstances which forced the granting of extra time in the first place.[1] Since, as will be seen, the guarantor has a right of recourse against the debtor, it will be in the interest of the guarantor to pay while the principal debtor still has substantial assets rather than wait until the last minute when the principal debtor has no assets whatsoever.

1 *Nisbet v Smith* (1789) 2 Bro CC 579; *Bolton v Buckenham* [1891] 1 QB 278.

26.86 Since the guarantor also has rights against co-sureties, the same principle applies and a guarantor may be discharged when extensions of time are give to a co-surety.

26.87 In either case, it is of the utmost importance to the banker to include clauses which will allow the extension of time and any other indulgence which the banker believes to be in the best interests of both the bank and the customer. It is well known that such an extension is often the difference between successful recovery of a loan and the total or near total loss through the customer's insolvency.

Release of the debtor

26.88 It is clear that, in the absence of express provisions, the release of the principal debtor by the creditor has the additional effect of releasing the surety.[1] It may seem extraordinary to think of the banker releasing the debtor, but there are situations which amount to an implied release, the most common being that in which the customer enters into a voluntary composition with his or her creditors outside of bankruptcy. This would ordinarily discharge the surety,[2] but it seems that a proper clause in the guarantee will prevent this.

1 *Perry v National Provincial Bank of England Ltd* [1910] 1 Ch 464.
2 *Ex parte Smith* (1789) 3 Bro CC 1.

26.89 In *Perry v National Provincial Bank of England Ltd*[1] the efficacy of such a contractual term was precisely in point. During the course of the judgment, Cozens-Hardy MR said:

> It is said " . . . there can be no right as against the surety, because by reason of this arrangement with Perry Brothers you [the creditor] have released Perry Brothers, and there can be no suretyship after the release of the principal debtor". But I think the answer to that is that it is perfectly possible for a surety to contract with a creditor in the suretyship instrument that notwithstanding any composition, release, or arrangement the surety shall remain liable although the principal does not.[2]

1 [1910] 1 Ch 464.
2 At p 473.

Release of securities or co-sureties

26.90 It is common practice for the banker to take securities from the creditor in addition to the guarantee. It may be that from time to time the banker may wish to realise some of the securities, to exchange them for other more appropriate securities, or even to release some of them so that the principal debtor may deal with them free of encumbrance. Under the general law, many, perhaps most of these actions would result in a discharge in whole or in part of the guarantor.[1] This flows logically from the fact that the guarantor would be prejudiced by such actions, possibly losing rights against securities. The same result flows from the release of any co-sureties and for the same reason.[2]

1 *Carter v White* (1883) 25 Ch D 666; *Dale v Powell* (1911) 105 LT 191.
2 *Ward v National Bank of New Zealand* (1883) 8 App Cas 755.

26.91 The general law result may be avoided by the inclusion of an appropriate clause in the form of guarantee and such clauses are routinely found in bank guarantee forms.

Change in the constitution of the debtor

26.92 A change in the constitution of the debtor terminates the guarantee as to any future advances.[1] Consequently, when the principal debtor is a group which might change its legal identity by a change in its membership, the lender runs a risk of finding the guarantors inadvertently discharged. Once again, the difficulty is overcome by a standard clause to the effect that the guarantor remains bound notwithstanding any change in the constitution of the principal debtor.

1 *Wright v Russel* (1774) 3 Wils KB 530; *Myers v Edge* (1797) 7 TR 254.

Death of the debtor or guarantor

26.93 The death of the principal debtor causes the guarantee to crystallise. It is clear that the principal debtor will not be receiving any further advances from the banker. Any outstanding cheques should be returned unpaid. The Bills of Exchange Act 1908, s 75 gives the banker authority to pay cheques which were drawn prior to the customer's death and presented within ten days. However, unless there is an express clause in the guarantee, it is thought that the guarantor would not be liable for the amount of these payments.

26.94 The death of the guarantor does not automatically terminate the guarantee. If the banker makes advances after the guarantor's death but before receiving notice of it, it appears that the banker is entitled to call upon the estate for the additional sums.[1] Notice of the death of the guarantor does terminate the agreement and again "crystallises" the liability under the guarantee to the amount for which he or she was liable at the time when the banker received notice of the death.[2]

1 *Bradbury v Morgan* (1862) 1 H & C 249; (1862) 158 ER 877.
2 *Coulthart v Clementson* (1879) 5 QBD 42.

26.95 Again, clauses in the standard form of bank guarantee modify this position. The usual clause calls for continuing liability until the expiration of a fixed period of time, typically three months, following the receipt of a notice in writing of the personal representatives' intention to determine the guarantee.

26.96 It is thought that notice of mental illness of the guarantor operates in the same way as notice of his or her death, but there is little authority on the matter.[1]

1 *Bradford Old Bank Ltd v Sutcliffe* [1918] 2 KB 833.

Guarantor's rights against the other parties

Debtor

26.97 When the guarantor has paid any amount to the creditor, he or she acquires an immediate right of action against the principal debtor. The right of action does not arise until such time as the guarantor has actually paid.[1] The guarantor also has the right to prove in the principal debtor's bankruptcy for any amount which he or she has paid under the guarantee, but as noted above, this right is usually circumscribed by standard clauses in the contract of guarantee which prohibit the guarantor from proving in competition with the bank.

1 *Re Fenton; ex parte Fenton Textile Association Ltd* [1931] 1 Ch 85.

Co-sureties

26.98 Just as the guarantor is entitled to an indemnity from the principal debtor when obliged to pay the creditor, so he or she is also entitled to look to any other sureties in the event that he or she has paid more than his or her "fair" amount. What constitutes the "fair" amount is a matter of some complexity when there are multiple co-sureties, some of whom may have paid sums to the creditor, some of whom have different limits of liability, and some of whom may have taken advantage of the rights of subrogation to securities.[1]

1 See, for example, *In re Arcedeckne* (1883) 24 Ch D 709; *Knight v Hughes* (1828) 172 ER 504.

Rights to securities

26.99 In general, if the guarantor pays off the entirety of the debt, then he is entitled to be subrogated to all of the rights previously enjoyed by the bank in respect of the debt. As a natural consequence of this rule, the guarantor is entitled to the benefit of all securities for the debt which are held by the bank. This entitlement extends to all securities received from the customer whether received before or after the making of the guarantee and irrespective of whether the guarantor knew of the existence of the securities at the time of entering into the guarantee.[1] The right extends to securities given by third parties.[2]

1 *Forbes v Jackson* (1882) 10 Ch D 615.
2 *Duncan, Fox & Co v North & South Wales Bank* (1880) 6 App Cas 1.

26.100 This right of subrogation is usually restricted somewhat by the clause which ensures that the right of the guarantor does not come into existence until the entire debt owed by the principal debtor is paid, not the amount for which the guarantor might be liable.

26.101 When the creditor bank holds securities, it might be thought that the guarantor could force the banker to resort to those securities before calling on the guarantor, but such is not the case. In spite of some earlier confusion,[1] it is clear that the creditor has the right to sue the guarantor without resorting to the securities. In *Ewart v Latta*[2] it was said:

> Until the debtor [ie, the guarantor] has discharged himself of his liability, until he has fulfilled his own contract, he has no right to dictate any terms, to prescribe any duty, or to make any demand on his creditor. The creditor must be left in possession of the whole of the remedies which the original contract gave him, and he must be left unfettered and at liberty to exhaust those remedies, and he cannot be required to put any limitation upon the course of legal action given to him by his contract by any person who is still his debtor, except upon the terms of that debt being completely satisfied.

1 *Duncan, Fox & Co v North and South Wales Bank* (1880) 6 App Cas 1, dictum of Lord Watson at p 22.
2 (1865) 4 Macq 983.

26.102 Once again, it will be found that most bank guarantee forms contain clauses which are intended to put the matter beyond doubt.

Chapter 27

The Mareva injunction

Definition — Purpose — Requirements for — Effects of

27.1 The Mareva injuction[1] is not, strictly speaking, a security interest since it is not a proprietary interest granted to the creditor either consensually or by law.[2] This is clearly true despite an attempt by Denning MR to elevate the injunction to a proprietary interest in *Z Ltd v A* .[3] Further, it is not something which, like a guarantee, is sought as a collateral "security" at the time when the loan is made. The Mareva injunction is only sought when relationships have deteriorated so far that the debtor is being sued by the creditor.

1 The unusual name is derived from the name of the second case in which the injunction was granted: *Mareva Compania Naviera SA v International Bulkcarriers SA* [1975] 2 Lloyd's Rep 509. The first case was *Nippon Yusen Kaisha v Karageorgis* [1975] 3 All ER 282.
2 This discussion of the Mareva injunction is necessarily incomplete. For a more detailed treatment, see Hetherington (ed), *Mareva Injunctions*, Sydney, 1983.
3 [1982] 2 WLR 288. The injunction is one which operates in personam; 27.10.

27.2 The problem which arises is that between the time of the initiation of the suit to recover the debt and the time when final judgment is obtained and, if necessary, execution issued, the debtor may take steps to remove assets from the jurisdiction of the Court. Any resulting victory for the plaintiff will be a hollow one if there are no assets against which the judgment may be enforced. The Mareva injunction is a recent development in the law which is intended to prevent the removal of assets from the jurisdiction of a Court. Since part of the assets will often be in the form of a bank account, the operation of the Mareva injunction must be understood by bankers.

Definition

27.3 The Mareva injunction restrains a defendant by himself or by his agents or servants or otherwise from removing from the jurisdiction or disposing of or dealing with those of his assets that will or may be necessary to meet a plaintiff's pending claim. The order is ordinarily made in a very wide form, at least in the first instance, and has the effect of "freezing" the assets of the defendant pending the outcome of the litigation.

Purpose

27.4 The situation in which a Mareva injunction may be granted and the purpose of the injunction is well illustrated by the *Mareva* case itself. The action was brought by the owners of a ship against the charterers in respect of unpaid hire charges. Prior to obtaining judgment, the owners sought an injunction of the kind now known as the Mareva injunction. Lord Denning described the plight of the shipowners as follows:

> There is money in a bank in London which stands in the name of these time charterers. The time charterers have control of it. They may at any time dispose of it or remove it out of this country. If they do so, the ship owners may never get their charter hire. The ship is now on the high seas. It has passed Cape Town on its way to India. It will now complete the voyage and the cargo will be discharged. And the ship owners may not get their charter hire at all. In the face of this danger, I think this Court ought to grant an injunction to restrain the defendants from disposing of these moneys now in the bank in London until the trial and judgment in this action.[1]

1 *Mareva Compania Naviera SA v International Bulkcarriers SA* [1975] 2 Lloyd's Rep 509, 511.

27.5 Between 1975 and 1980, it was not entirely clear that the Courts of New Zealand and Australia would follow the lead given by the English Courts. However, the prolonged litigation between the American citizen Nelson Bunker Hunt and BP Exploration Company (Libya) Ltd raised the question in these jurisdictions. BP Explorations had obtained a judgment of some $A30 million against Hunt.[1] Hunt was resident in the American state of Texas but had assets in many parts of the world, including Australia and New Zealand. He indicated an unwillingness to satisfy the judgment or to provide security for its satisfactionBP instructed solicitors in various jurisdictions, including New Zealand, to seek injunctions restraining Hunt from removing or dealing with assets in those jurisdictions pending registration of the English judgment under the procedures available for enforcement under reciprocal enforcement legislation.

1 See *BP Exploration Co (Libya) Ltd v Hunt* [1976] 3 All ER 879; [1982] 1 All ER 986.

27.6 Although there was considerable argument concerning the source of the jurisdictional power to grant the injunction, Barker J in the New Zealand Court relied on s 16 of the Judicature Act 1908 which says:

> The Court shall . . . have . . . all the judicial jurisdiction which may be necessary to administer the laws of New Zealand.

27.7 Barker J granted the injunction and noted that:

> The Court has to approach modern problems with the flexibility of modern business. In former times . . . it would have been more difficult for a foreign debtor to take his assets out of the country. Today, vast sums of money can be transferred from one country to another in a matter of seconds as a result of a phone call or a telex message. Reputable foreign debtors of course have nothing to fear; the facts of the reported *Mareva* cases indicate that the jurisdiction is wholesome; the sheer number of Mareva injunctions granted in London indicates that the jurisdiction is fulfilling a need.[1]

1 *Hunt v BP Exploration Company (Libya) Ltd* [1980] 1 NZLR 104, 118.

Requirements for granting

27.8 The early cases seemed to put limits on the circumstances in which a Mareva injunction would be granted, but one by one the requirements seemed to have been relaxed. Thus, it seems that it is not necessary for the defendant to be foreign,[1] it is sufficient that there is a threat that the assets will be dissipated within the jurisdiction,[2] and it would appear that the applicant for the injunction need not even have an existing cause of action against the other party so long as it seems likely that there will eventually be such a cause of action.[3]

1 *Prince Abdul Rahman v Abu-Taha* [1980] 3 All ER 409.
2 *Z Ltd v A* [1982] 1 All ER 556.
3 *Turner v Sylvestre* [1981] NSWLR 295.

27.9 Concerning the circumstances in which a Mareva injunction should be granted, Kerr LJ has make the following suggestions:

> It follows that in my view Mareva injunctions should be granted, but granted only, when it appears to the Court that there is a combination of two circumstances. First, when it appears likely that the plaintiff will receive judgment against the defendant for a certain or approximate sum. Second, when there are also reasons to believe that the defendant has assets within the jurisdiction to meet the judgment, in whole or in part, but may well take steps designed to ensure that these are no longer available or traceable when judgment is given against him.[1]

1 *Z Ltd v A [1982] 1 All ER 556, 572.*

Effects of a Mareva injunction

27.10 The granting of a Mareva injunction affects all who know of it, for it would be a contempt of Court to assist in violating the terms of the injunction by dealing with the assets of the defendant in any way which is inconsistent with the terms of the injunction. This is obviously of importance to bankers and others who deal with or have a claim to the assets of the Mareva defendant.

Proprietary interest

27.11 The granting of a Mareva injunction does not give the creditor or anyone else a lien on the assets of the debtor. The point was directly in question in *The Cretan Harmony*.[1] The owners of a ship sought an injunction against the charterers. The charterers had only one asset within the jurisdiction, a certificate of deposit with the First Nation City Bank of London. This asset was property which was covered by a floating charge given by the charterers to the Ulster Bank prior to the time when the injunction was sought. After the injunction had been granted, the Ulster Bank appointed a receiver under the terms of the floating charge. The question for the Court was whether the terms of the injunction precluded the receiver from dealing with the certificate. The Court held in favour of the receiver. During the course of the judgment, Buckley LJ said:

> It seems to me . . . that it is not the case that any rights in the nature of a lien arise when a Mareva injunction is made. Under such an injunction, the plaintiff has no rights against the assets. He may later acquire such rights if he obtains judgment and can thereafter successfully levy execution upon them but until that event his only rights are against the defendant personally.[2]

1 [1978] 1 Lloyd's Rep 425.
2 At p 431.

27.12 This view was reaffirmed and extended in *Iraqi Ministry of Defence v Arcepey Shipping Co SA and Gillespie Brothers Ltd, The Angel Bell*.[1] In that case a Mareva injunction had been obtained which "froze" the assets of the defendant. The defendant applied to be permitted to use part of the funds to pay a debt which fell due during the currency of the injunction. The Court held that the defendant should be entitled to make the payment even though there was some argument that the debt might not be enforceable because of breaches of the Moneylenders Act. The decision is clearly correct if one accepts that the purpose of the injunction is to prevent the fraudulent removal or dissipation of the assets of the defendant. To hold otherwise would mean that the granting of the injunction would override the provisions of the Insolvency Act. If the payment was a preference then it could be unwound in the event of a bankruptcy or a liquidation. The fact that it was not enforceable was largely irrelevant, the Court observing that businessmen frequently pay debts which are technically unenforceable.

1 [1980] 1 All ER 480.

27.13 The same line of argument has resulted in the defendant being permitted to use assets for the purposes of meeting legal costs. This is important since the financial position of the defendant will often be such that the solicitors will require payment in advance.[1]

1 See the comments of Rogers J in *Riley McKay v McKay (No 2)* [1982] 1 NSWLR 264.

27.14 A Mareva injunction will not be granted when there would be a consequential unjust interference with the rights of third parties to carry on their normal business. This has most often arisen when the injunction applied for would, if granted, have the side effect of preventing ship's cargo or the ship itself from leaving the jurisdiction. Thus, in *Gilfoyle Shipping Services Ltd v Binosi Pty Ltd*[1] the plaintiff sought a Mareva injunction to prevent the defendant from dealing with fuel in the ship's bunkers. If the injunction had been granted, there would have been considerable hardship on the owner of the ship and the ship's crew, the latter being mainly of Greek nationality. Barker J refused the injunction even though it meant the the assets of the defendant would literally be "going up in smoke" as the ship sailed for Australia the next day.

1 [1984] 2 NZLR 742.

27.15 The *Gilfoyle* decision was a direct application of the English decision in *Galaxia Maritime SA v Mineralimportexport*[1] where the Court similarly considered the welfare of the crew of a ship to be a significant factor in refusing the injunction.

1 [1982] 1 All ER 796.

27.16 The effect of the injunction on third parties who may not be creditors of the defendant is obviously of importance to bankers and will be discussed in detail below.

Effect on third parties

27.17 The effect of a Mareva injunction on third parties, particularly third party bankers, was discussed in *Z Ltd v A*.[1] The case arose from an alleged fraud on a non-English company. Telex and cable orders were forged which resulted in the transfer of some £2 million to London banks and which then reached the hands of the conspirators. When the fraud was discovered, the company sought and obtained a Mareva injunction from Bingham J which prevented any dealings with the defendants' assets except in so far as they exceeded the disputed £2 million. By a prompt use of orders for specific discovery, interrogatories, injunctions and Anton Piller orders, the plaintiffs were able to recover £1 million; there then followed a settlement whereby a "good deal of the balance" was recovered.[2] In spite of this settlement, the five London clearing banks and one other defendant sought and obtained leave to appeal with a view toward clarifying the position of third parties when receiving notice of a Mareva injunction.

1 *Z Ltd v A* [1982] 1 All ER 556.
2 At p 560.

27.18 The Court of Appeal held that a third party will be liable if, having notice of the terms of the injunction, he knowingly assists in the disposal of any of the assets of the defendant whether or not the defendant has knowledge of the injunction. One obvious consequence of this view is that the banker should, upon receiving notice of the injunction, freeze all accounts known to belong to the defendant as well as other assets held on his or her behalf.[1] The basis for the liability is that the third party who

> knowingly assists in the disposal of [the assets] . . . will be guilty of a contempt of Court, for it is an act calculated to obstruct the course of justice.[2]

1 *Z Ltd v A* [1982] 1 All ER 556, 562, 567.
2 At p 563.

27.19 The banker's obligation to honour the defendant's cheques is discharged because to do so has now become an unenforceable illegal obligation or, alternatively, it must be taken that the customer has only authorised the banker to do that which is lawful.[1]

1 *Z Ltd v A* [1982] 1 All ER 556, 563, 572.

27.20 From these principles, the Court extracted a set of guidelines which is intended to assist in the drafting and the interpretation of Mareva injunctions. The guidelines proposed are divided into two groups, the first aimed at applicants who are seeking Mareva injunctions which might affect third parties and the second describing the obligations imposed on the third parties who have received notice of the injunction. Since the banker may often be in either position, both sets of guidelines are given here.

27.21 Matters to be considered at the time of seeking and making the injunction include:

1 The plaintiff should normally be required to give an undertaking to indemnify against any liability incurred and to pay any expenses reasonably incurred in complying with the terms of the injunction.

2 The plaintiff should identify third parties upon whom it is intended to serve notice of the injunction. This, presumably, will enable the Court to insert terms intended to protect the third parties from unreasonable obligation. It is not intended that this should preclude the giving of notice to other third parties if additional information is obtained.

3 If possible, the plaintiff should identify assets held in the hands of third parties. The ability to make such an identification will probably be the exception rather than the rule in the case of assets held by the bank, since the bank owes a duty of secrecy to its customer which should preclude it from voluntarily disclosing either the existence or the extent of the defendant's assets held.[1] In this circumstance, the power of the Court to order the defendant or the third party bank to make discovery in proper cases is of the utmost importance.[2]

4 If the injunction is intended only to restrain dealings with the defendant's assets up to a maximum amount, the order should contain terms which state clearly that the "maximum sum" part of the order does not include assets known or believed to be in the hands of a third party. This is a matter of particular concern to the banks, since without such a term they are left in the position of being in possible breach of the order if they allow dealings with the account (and those dealings involve assets which are within the terms of the injunction) and in possible breach of contract with the customer if they do not permit dealings (and the defendant has adequate assets elsewhere).

5 If it is thought desirable to allow the defendant normal living expenses or, presumably, an operating account for any reason whatsoever, the order should indicate the sum to be allowed, but should not state the purpose for which the sum is to be used. The bank should open a special account for the defendant, placing the account in funds in accordance with the amounts mentioned in the injunction. It is no concern of the bank to inquire as to the actual use of the account.

1 *Tournier v National Provincial and Union Bank of England* [1924] 1 KB 461.
2 See *A J Bekhor & Co Ltd v Bilton* [1981] 2 All ER 565.

27.22 The obligations on the bank when receiving notice of the injunction include:

1 All accounts known to belong to the defendant should be

frozen at once. All cheques should be dishonoured for the reasons mentioned above.

2 There are some payments which may be made and which may be debited to the defendant's account. These payments may be loosely described as those which the bank is under some independent obligation to make. Thus, payments under a letter of credit or a bank guarantee, credit card transactions, and cheques drawn by the defendant which are supported by a cheque guarantee card may all be paid and debited to the defendant's account.[1] However, it appears that the sums from any such commercial transaction which are paid into the defendant's account will then be covered by the injunction.[2]

3 Unless expressly stated in the injunction, certain assets held by the bank are not to be frozen by the bank. Specifically mentioned by the Court are

(a) shares or title deeds held by the bank as security,

(b) articles in a safe deposit in the name of the defendant,

(c) future assets, ie, any assets which come within the control of the bank subsequently to the date on which the bank is served with the order save in so far as any of these assets are specifically referred to in the injunction,

(d) money held in a joint account which is in the name of the defendant and any other person or persons.

1 *Z Ltd v A* [1982] 1 All ER 556, 563, 570, 576.
2 *Intraco Ltd v Notis Shipping Corp* [1981] 2 Lloyd's Rep 256.

27.23 Unfortunately, these guidelines may be safely relied upon only if the injunction is carefully drawn so as to include specific terms which conform to the first set of guidelines. Since the granting of the injunction and its terms fall within the discretion of the Judge and since the exercise of this discretion must inevitably be influenced by the specific facts before him, bankers and other third parties can by no means be assured that injunctions will necessarily be so favourably drawn.

Costs of enforcement

27.24 The concern for the interests of third parties is also shown in the practice of requiring the applicant to meet many of the costs of enforcement. In *Searose Ltd v Seatrain (UK) Ltd*,[1] the injunction was granted only on the basis that the plaintiff, who naturally wished to notify the bank of the existence of the injunction, undertake to pay costs incurred by the banker in searching for relevant accounts of the defendant. In the absence of a centralised computing system, the costs of such a search for the accounts may be substantial.

1 [1981] 1 Lloyd's Rep 556.

27.25 The perceived ability of the applicant to pay such costs may itself be a factor in the decision to grant a Mareva injunction. In the *Gilfoyle Shipping* case,[1] the applicant offered to meet the costs of requiring the ship and crew to remain in Timaru. The third party shipowner expressed doubts about the ability of the applicant to meet such costs; this appeared to be one of the factors considered by Barker J in refusing the injunction.

1 *Gilfoyle Shipping Services Ltd v Binosi Pty Ltd* [1984] 2 NZLR 742.

Chapter 28

Documentary credits I

Antecedents — Uses — Types of credit

28.1 The modern documentary letter of credit has been called the "crankshaft of modern commerce". Although its current form is primarily a product of the twentieth century, its antecedents lie in the earliest days of travel when communication was poor and carrying cash was even riskier than it is today. It is also interesting to note that some of the most recent developments in the letter of credit, the so called "standby credit" are closer in form to the old style of letter of credit than to the new.

Antecedents

Traveller's letters

28.2 A traveller's letter of credit was a letter addressed by a person with international connections to one of those overseas associates, requesting that the overseas associate provide the named bearer of the letter, the traveller, with certain financial accommodation. The writer of the letter is called the issuer, the bearer is known as the beneficiary. The addressee of the letter goes under different names depending upon the accommodation which he is to provide.

28.3 The benefit to the traveller is obvious, but there are other more far reaching benefits of such an arrangement. The issuer of letters is very likely to be the addressee of letters of credit issued by parties to whom letters have been addressed. In a perfect world, the financial accommodation provided by a given addressee could be precisely cancelled by accommodation provided by a reciprocal arrangement. In practice, of course, things do not balance out quite so nicely, but they do balance partially with the consequence that much of the settlement of debts between issuers and addressees of the letters of credit could be settled by adjustment in their respective books. There was a substantial reduction in the need to move money, which usually meant precious metal, from country to country.

Cash

28.4 The traveller's letter of credit was classified according to the type of accommodation' provided by the addressee. The earliest, and in some ways the most common, was a cash credit. By presentation of the letter of credit at the office of the addressee and establishing his or her identity, the beneficiary would be able to draw cash up to the limit which was stated in the letter.

Discount facility

28.5 There were a number of refinements on the simple cash credit. When the parties were bankers, it was often desirable that the advancement of cash be accompanied by some form of bill of exchange. In the simplest form, the customer would draw a demand bill payable to himself or to the addressee of the letter of credit. The equivalent today would be a letter which guaranteed the addressee that he or she would be reimbursed for cheques drawn by the beneficiary of the letter. Another form of the letter requested that the addressee discount bills drawn upon the issuer by the beneficiary of the letter.

28.6 In both of these cases, in order for the credit to be of the utmost value to the beneficiary, it could be stipulated that the addressee would discount the bills without recourse to the beneficiary.

Letter of introduction for security purposes

28.7 There was one further refinement which was added as the popularity of the traveller's letter of credit increased. A letter of introduction, called in some cases a "letter of indication" was drawn separately. This letter was either carried by the beneficiary or was sent directly to the addressee and contained personal information about the beneficiary which was intended to assist in the identification process. The letter of introduction would also carry a specimen signature.

28.8 It was clearly important that the letter of credit be carried separately from the letter of introduction, for otherwise a forger would have the best of both worlds. Indeed, the early letters were issued with stern warnings that the letter of credit should be carried separately from the letter of introduction. Traveller's letters of credit are seldom used today, but they have been replaced by mechanisms that clearly derive from the credit themselves, but are more suited to the larger number of people who travel in modern times. Thetwo most popular forms of modern travel facility are traveller's cheques and credit cards.

Modern replacements

˙aveller's cheques

2˙ .9 Traveller's cheques are a direct descendant of the traveller's letter of credit. In *Rhodes v London & County Bank*[1] the plaintiff had arrangements with the defendant bank whereby he was issued with "circular notes" and a letter of introduction. The "circular notes" appear to have been a kind of accounting device whereby the financial institution which made advances to the bearer of the notes and the letter of introduction could easily obtain reimbursemer⁺ from the issuer.

1 (1886) 1 LD˙˙

28.10 The modern traveller's cheque may or may not be a bill of exchange, since the form of many traveller's cheques does not satisfy the requirements of s 3 of the Bills of Exchange Act 1908. From a functional point of view, it will be noted that the issuer of the traveller's cheque usually charges a fee for issuing, typically 1%, but the issuer also has the use of the traveller's money from the time of issue of the cheques until such time as the issuer is called upon to pay.

Third party credit cards

28.11 The letter of credit has also been replaced by the third party credit card. Functionally, this seems very much like the letter of credit, for the cards are issued by banks and other large organisations whose credit is recognised as being reliable. However, instead of being primarily a means of obtaining cash from financial institutions, the cards are primarily a means of obtaining goods and services from merchants who have agreed to honour the cards. The legal aspects of third party credit cards are discussed in Ch 21.

Cheque guarantee cards

28.12 Whereas the third party credit card is somewhat similar to the letter of credit which asks the addressee to provide cash, the cheque guarantee card is very similar to the letter of credit which requests the addressee to negotiate the traveller's bills of exchange. The cards are issued to their customers by banks. The banks "guarantee" that the customer's cheque will be met by the bank provided it does not exceed a ceiling amount.

Modern uses

28.13 Although the letter of credit has been largely replaced as a financial facility for travellers, it has been adapted in a different form for commercial use, particularly when the transaction is international. In all cases, the motivation for the use of credits is the same. The credit of a major bank or other financial institution is substituted for that of the party to the transaction.

Safe measures of payment in international sales

28.14 This substitution may be illustrated by a consideration of the major use of letters of credit, facilitating the international sale of goods by the substitution of a reliable paymaster who will stand in the shoes of the buyer. An exporter in country A may know little about the financial standing of the importer in country B, or, even worse, the exporter may know enough to be concerned that payment may be delayed. Nor is concern about the solvency of the trading partner confined to the seller, for the buyer must also be certain that property in the goods is transferred from the seller before payment is made, for otherwise the financial collapse of the seller could leave the buyer without the money and without the goods.

28.15 The letter of credit serves the interests of both. The credit of the issuing bank is substituted for the credit of the buyer, so that the seller can be certain that payment will be made. On the other hand, the buyer can be certain that payment will not be made until such time as the goods are actually shipped, for the "documentary" part of the documentary letter of credit means that the seller must present certain documents to the bank before payment will be made.[1]

1 See Ch 29 for a discussion of the documents involved in a documentary letter of credit.

28.16 The entire operation has been summarised neatly by Denning LJ:

> The sale of goods across the world is now usually arranged by means of confirmed credits. The buyer requests his banker to open a credit in favour of the seller and in pursuance of that request the banker, or his foreign agent, issues a confirmed credit in favour of the seller. This credit is a promise by the banker to pay money to the seller in return for the shipping documents. Then the seller, when he presents the documents, gets paid the contract price. The conditions of the credit must be strictly fulfilled, otherwise the seller would not be entitled to draw on it.[1]

1 *Pavia & Co v Thurmann-Nielsen* [1952] 2 QB 84, 88; the use of the word "confirmed" in the quotation would no longer be considered proper; see 28.45.

28.17 It is important to understand that the promise by the bank is to the beneficiary/seller. It is a separate contract which calls for the banker to pay provided only that the seller tenders the documents called for by the terms of the credit. The contract between the banker and the seller is independent of the contract between the buyer and seller, an independence which is so important that it is given a name: the autonomy principle.[1]

1 See the discussion in Ch 29.

Standby credits

28.18 The use of the documentary credit to facilitate international trade has one salient characteristic. Its abuse is controlled by the fact that neither the buyer nor the seller is ever in possession of the documents and the money at the same time. Valuable goods, more precisely, document of title to the goods, must be tendered in exchange for payment. Not only are the buyer and the seller both protected, but the banker who has issued the credit also has a security interest in the goods by virtue of the documents of title.[1]

1 See Ch 29.

28.19 In recent years the letter of credit has been adapted to serve a quite different function, one which does not provide the mutual protection of the documentary credit used in trade.

28.20 The "standby credit" originated in the United States where banks were not permitted to give bank guarantees. Particularly in construction work, it may be that delays in the performance of the contract will be very costly to the person for whom the building is being constructed. As a guard against this possibility, it is common to call for "performance guarantees" from the builder. If the building falls behind schedule or is not completed within the contractual time, the guarantor may be called upon to pay a fixed sum to defray the expenses associated with the late completion.

28.21 It will be appreciated that it may be controversial to determine whether or not a large construction project is or is not on schedule. One solution is to provide that experienced builders should act as referees to determine if the project is or is not on schedule. This solution will protect both parties, but is expensive and time consuming. The other solution is to leave the decision solely in the hands of one of the contracting parties.

28.22 This is the solution that has led to the use of the standby credit. The credit is in the form of an ordinary documentary credit, but the only document called for is a written notice from the beneficiary that the project is not on schedule.

28.23 A similar arrangement is the so called "first demand guarantee" which is used in Commonwealth countries. The document is in the form of a guarantee that, say, the project will be on schedule, but there is a "conclusive evidence" clause which states that a written demand from the beneficiary shall be conclusive evidence that the guarantee is due and owing. The first demand guarantee and the standby letter of credit perform exactly the same function and it would seem that both are governed by the same law.[1]

1 See, for example, Denning MR in *Edward Owen Engineering Ltd v Barclays Bank International* [1978] QB 159.

Commercial documentary credits

28.24 Letters of credit are most often referred to as "documentary credits" in order to emphasise the modern reliance on documents. The obligation to the beneficiary is not absolute, but is conditional upon the presentation of documents in conformity with the terms of the credit. In the standby credit, it might be very easy for the beneficiary to obtain the required documents, but in the ordinary sale of goods, the documents are an essential feature of the commercial operation of the credit.

The Uniform Customs and Practice

28.25 If the documentary letter of credit is to fulfill its purpose of providing a reliable method of payment in international transactions, it is obviously important that there should be as few disputes as possible concerning their operation. One method of assuring this is to standardise the law relating to documentary credits.

28.26 The Uniform Customs and Practice for Commercial Documentary Credits is an attempt to standardise the terms and conditions on which bankers will issue and act on commercial credits. The original version was formulated in 1933 by the International Chamber of Commerce. While widely accepted in many countries, the London bankers decided not to follow, with the result that the United Kingdom and Commonwealth countries went their own way. Given the dominant position of these countries in world trade at the time, the UCP was generally considered to be unsuccessful in achieving a standardisation.

28.27 The situation changed with the revision of the UCP in 1962. Further revisions were made in 1974 and 1983, the final drafts being the result of co-operation of a number of international bodies, including representatives from the socialist trading countries.

28.28 The UCP is one of the most successful attempts at legal standardisation. At the current time, the terms of UCP are incorporated by reference into virtually every letter of credit. The UCP is not law, but the terms are, by virtue of express inclusion, binding on the parties as contractual terms. Of course, there will still be differences in interpretation of the terms in different legal systems, but an ongoing effort by the International Chamber of Commerce is combined with a general willingness of Courts to give effect to foreign decisions to yield a law which comes very close to being a truly international law of letters of credit.

28.29 Because of this universality, the articles of the UCP will be given close attention when discussing the law of credits, keeping in mind always that they act merely as contractual terms between the parties.

Definition of a letter of credit :1983 revision

28.30 The definition of a letter of credit has been expanded somewhat in the 1983 revision to make it clear that standby credits are included.

Article 2
For the purposes of these articles, the expressions "documentary credit(s)" and "standby letter(s) of credit" used herein (hereinafter referred to as "credit(s)"), mean any arrangement, however named or described, whereby a bank (the issuing bank), acting at the request and on the instructions of a customer (the applicant for the credit),
   (i) is to make a payment to or to the order of a third party (the beneficiary), or is to pay or accept bills of exchange (drafts) drawn by the beneficiary, or
   (ii) authorises another bank to effect such payment, or to pay, accept or negotiate such bills of exchange (drafts), against stipulated documents, provided that the terms and conditions of the credit are complied with.

28.31 The applicant for the credit is also called the "account party" in much of the literature on credits. In a credit which is used to facilitate an international sale of goods, the account party will be the buyer; in a standby credit, the account party will be the person who is in a position similar to the principal debtor in an ordinary guarantee.

28.32 The definition contemplates that the issuing party will be a bank. There is, of course, no reason why the basic mechanism of the letter of credit should not be used when the issuing party is a non-bank. If such a credit included the UCP by reference, then there is a fundamental contradiction. However, it is thought that, as a matter of construction, the UCP would be interpreted in a way which would permit its application in the obvious way. An American case has held that a bank may be a confirming bank when the credit has been issued by a mortgage broker;[1] although the decision was based on the Uniform Commercial Code, there seems no reason why the same result would not be reached by an application of general principles.[2]

1 *Barclays Bank DCO v Mercantile National Bank* [1973] 2 Lloyd's Rep 541.
2 See Gutteridge and Megrah, p 8.

28.33 In addition to the basic definition, there are certain requirements concerning every credit to which the UCP applies. Article 11 is new in the 1983 revision and introduces for the first time the concept of the "nominated bank":

Article 11
(a) All credits must clearly indicate whether they are available by sight payment, by deferred payment, by acceptance or by negotiation.
(b) All credits must nominate the bank (nominated bank) which is authorised to pay (paying bank), or to accept drafts (accepting bank), or to negotiate (negotiating bank), unless the credit allows negotiation by any bank (negotiating bank).
(c) Unless the nominated bank is the issuing bank or the confirming bank, its nomination by the issuing bank does not constitute any undertaking by the nominated bank to pay, to accept or to negotiate.
(d) By nominating a bank other than itself, or by allowing for negotiation by any bank, or by authorising or requesting a bank to add its confirmation, the issuing bank authorises such bank to pay, accept or negotiate, as the case may be, against documents which appear on their face to be in accordance with the terms and conditions of the credit, and undertakes to reimburse such bank in accordance with the provisions of these articles.

Types of credits

28.34 Letters of credit are classified according to various criteria, some of which appear in the UCP, some of which refer to legal consequences and some of which refer to various commercial consequences. Some of the more important classifications are discussed here.

Legal classifications

28.35 Certain of the classifications are made by reference to the differing legal effects of the credits, usually by reference to the obligations imposed on the banker.

Revocable or irrevocable

28.36 Perhaps the most important classification is that into revocable and irrevocable credits. It is the only classification which is expressly recognised by the UCP. Roughly speaking, a revocable credit may be cancelled or modified without notice to the beneficiary, although, as will be noted below, the issuing banker may be responsible for certain transactions which have been completed.

28.37 Since one of the commercial reasons for using credits is to be certain of payment arrangements, it will be appreciated that a revocable credit is almost useless to a seller of goods. Consequently, it is rather astonishing to find that the basic position is given in Article 7(c) as "In the absence of [a contrary] indication the credit shall be deemed to be revocable".

28.38 The precise position of an issuing bank under a revocable credit is given by Article 9:

(a) A revocable credit may be amended or cancelled by the issuing bank at any moment and without prior notice to the beneficiary.
(b) However, the issuing bank is bound to:
  (i)   reimburse a branch or bank with which a revocable credit has been made available for sight payment, acceptance or negotiation, for any payment, acceptance or negotiation made by such branch or bank prior to receipt by it of notice of amendment or cancellation, against documents which appear on their face to be in accordance with the terms and conditions of the credit.
  (ii) reimburse a branch or bank with which a revocable credit has been made available for deferred payment, if such branch or bank has, prior to receipt by it of notice of amendment or cancellation, taken up documents which appear on their face to be in accordance with the terms and conditions of the credit.

28.39 The article does not call for the issuing bank to assume any responsibility to the beneficiary no matter what steps the beneficiary may have taken in reliance on the existence of the credit. A seller of goods who has actually shipped the goods, which must be done before the standard credit may be drawn upon, will be placed in a very embarrassing position if the credit is cancelled without notice before the documents are presented. Yet, this not only can happen, but the Courts have held that the issuing banker is under no duty to inform the beneficiary of cancellation and is under no liability if there is some failure to notify the beneficiary.[1]

1 *Cape Asbestos Co v Lloyds Bank Ltd* [1921] WN 274.

28.40 The result of this is that a revocable credit has very little commercial value and, indeed, it would appear that there are few revocable credits in use.

28.41 The undertaking of a bank which issues an irrevocable credit is quite different. The banker promises the beneficiary that, provided the documents presented conform to the credit and are presented within the time specified by the credit, payment will be made in the manner stipulated by the credit. The precise obligations of the issuing bank are set out in Article 10(a):

> An irrevocable credit constitutes a definite undertaking of the issuing bank, provided that the stipulated documents are presented and that the terms and conditions of the credit are complied with:
> (i) if the credit provides for sight payment — to pay, or that payment will be made;
> (ii) if the credit provides for deferred payment — to pay, or that payment will be made, on the date(s) determinable in accordance with the stipulations of the credit;
> (iii) if the credit provides for acceptance — to accept drafts drawn by the beneficiary if the credit stipulates that they are to be drawn on the issuing bank, or to be responsible for their acceptance and payment at maturity if the credit stipulates that they are to be drawn on the applicant for the credit or any other drawee stipulated in the credit;
> (iv) if the credit provides for negotiation — to pay without recourse to drawers and/or bona fide holders, draft(s) drawn by the beneficiary, at sight or at a tenor, on the applicant for the credit or on any other drawee stipulated in the credit other than the issuing bank itself, or to provide for negotiation by another bank and to pay, as above, if such negotiation is not effected.

28.42 It is clear that an irrevocable credit should not be amended without the beneficiary's consent, but it is also clear that amendment cannot be made without also obtaining the consent of the banks concerned. Article 10(d):

> Such undertakings can neither be amended nor cancelled without the agreement of the issuing bank, the confirming bank (if any), and the beneficiary . . . .

28.43 Of course, if there is an amendment made without the consent of the account party, then the banker would no longer be entitled to be reimbursed after the credit is payed.

When does the credit become irrevocable?

28.44 The definition of irrevocable credit is defective in that it does not state when the credit becomes irrevocable. There are two opposing points of view. One is that the credit becomes irrevocable when it is communicated to the beneficiary and the beneficiary acts upon it.[1] The other view is that the credit becomes irrevocable from the time that it is communicated to the beneficiary, with no need for action.[2] The latter view seems preferable from a commercial point of view since it is impossible for the issuing bank to know when the beneficiary has "acted" or, indeed, to place a very precise meaning on "acted".[3]

1 See Rowlatt J in *Urquhart Lindsay & Co Ltd v Eastern Bank Ltd* [1922] 1 KB 318.
2 See Greer J in *Dexters Ltd v Schenker & Co* (1923) 14 Ll L Rep 586.
3 Ellinger, p 9, discusses the point in some detail.

Confirmed or unconfirmed

28.45 In the normal course of events, notice to the beneficiary of a credit opened by the issuing bank is communicated through an intermediate bank located in the place where the beneficiary carries on business. This intermediate bank may be merely an agent of the issuing bank whose sole duty is to notify the beneficiary, or it may be that the intermediary bank is to assume obligations directly to the beneficiary. In the first instance, the intermediary is an "advising bank", in the second a "confirming bank".

28.46 Some of the older cases use the expression "confirmed" in discussing a credit which is irrevocable.[1] In more recent times, however, the meanings of the two expressions have become separate and distinct. Today, a credit is "confirmed" only if an intermediary bank assumes a direct obligation to the beneficiary.[2] The advantage to the beneficiary is that he or she may look to a local bank for performance of the credit rather than a bank which is very likely to be in the place where the account party, the buyer in the case of a sale of goods, is located. This is particularly important if the issuing bank refuses to pay, for if the beneficiary has a case to argue, it will be very much cheaper to sue a local defendant than one which is located in a foreign country.[3]

1 That is clearly the case with Lord Denning's speech in *Pavia & Co v Thurmann-Nielson* [1952] 2 QB 84, 88 quoted above.
2 See the discussion in *Panoutsos v Raymond Hadley Corpn of New York* [1917] 2 KB 473.
3 See, for example, *Edward Owen Engineering Ltd v Barclays Bank International Ltd and Umma Bank* [1978] QB 159, where it appeared that the would-be plaintiff could not even obtain a visa to pursue a suit against Libyan buyers.

28.47 The UCP defines the obligations of a confirming bank in terms which are virtually identical with those which describe the obligations of a bank issuing an irrevocable credit.[1] By implication, it would seem that the UCP considers that only irrevocable credits are capable of confirmation. It may be theoretically possible for an irrevocable letter to be confirmed, but there does not seem to be a practice of so doing.

1 See Article 10(b).

By mode of realisation

28.48 As will be noted from the Articles of the UCP above, there are numerous ways in which a credit may be realised. It is common commercial terminology to refer to credits in these ways, although generally speaking there is no particular legal significance to be attached to the various choices.

Acceptance credits

28.49 Thus, in an "acceptance credit" the obligation of the issuing bank is to accept bills drawn on it, provided such bills are drawn in conformity with the terms of the credit and are presented together with the other required documentation. The purpose of such an arrangement is, of course, to allow the beneficiary to discount the accepted bill in the appropriate markets; the bank is essentially lending its credit to the beneficiary. From a functional point of view, the beneficiary is carrying more of the costs of the finance than in other arrangements.

Clean credits

28.50 A "clean" credit provides for payment against documents. Ordinarily, the documents required will include a sight draft drawn either on the issuing bank or on the account party by the beneficiary. In either case, when a bill is included, it is intended that the payment should be without recourse to the drawer of the instrument.

Discount credits

28.51 In a "discount credit" also called a "negotiation credit" the issuing bank promises to pay either to the holder or to the drawer bills drawn in conformity with the credit and accompanied by the appropriate documents.

28.52 It should be noted that these terms are not precise legal terms and that they may vary in meaning over time or between countries or even between banks in the same country.

Straight and negotiation credits

28.53 A further form of classification which is sometimes used is based on the identity of individuals who may rely on the promise made by the issuing bank in the credit. In a "straight credit" the issuing bank's commitment is to the beneficiary only, although the benefits of that might be extended to other banks by virtue of the issuing bank requesting them to participate in the realisation of the credit.

28.54 By contrast, a "negotiation credit" is an open ended engagement by the issuing bank. The promise is to all drawers, indorsers and bona fide holders of drafts drawn under the terms of the credit that the drafts will be paid without recourse. An example of the "negotiation credit" is found in *Banco Nacional Ultramarino v First National Bank of Boston*[1] where the letter contained the following words:

> We hereby agree with the drawers, indorsers, and bona fide holders of bills drawn and negotiated in compliance with the terms of this credit that said bills will be duly honoured on presentation at our counter in Boston.

1 289 F 169 (1923).

Transferable credit

28.55 There are many cases where the beneficiary of the credit would like to use the credit to finance the very deal for which the credit was issued. A seller of goods who is the beneficiary of a letter of credit opened at the request of the buyer might very well need to open a letter of credit in the capacity of buyer of the subject goods. It would be easier to manage if the credit itself were transferable.

28.56 Unfortunately, the UCP does not encourage the transferability of credits. The matter is governed by Article 54 of the 1983 revision:

> (a) A transferable credit is a credit under which the beneficiary has the right to request the bank called upon to effect payment or acceptance or any bank entitled to effect negotiation to make the credit available in whole or in part to one or more other parties (second beneficiaries).
> (b) A credit can be transferred only if it is expressly designated as "transferable" by the issuing bank . . . .
> (c) The bank requested to effect the transfer (transferring bank), whether it has confirmed the credit or not, shall be under no obligation to effect such transfer except to the extent and in the manner expressly consented to by such bank. . . .
> (d) A transferable credit can be transferred once only . . . .

28.57 Since the purpose of transfer is to facilitate the main transaction, the first beneficiary will usually not wish the ultimate buyer to know how much has been paid for the goods or services received from the second beneficiary. Article 54(g) recognises this elementary commercial fact of life by permitting the first beneficiary to exchange his own invoice and draft for that of the second beneficiary under circumstances set out in that section.

Non-legal classifications

28.58 There are a number of non-legal classifications which are commonly used when referring to credits. Since there is little uniformity in this usage, it is crucial for banker and lawyer alike to discover precisely what is being discussed when certain terms are used.

Back to back credits

28.59 For a number of reasons, the issue of a transferable credit may not be feasible. The demands of Article 54 are such that the first beneficiary must give information to the account party early enough for the credit to be opened in the manner required. This may not be commercially desirable or practically expedient.

28.60 Indeed, the beneficiary is in a position to keep his or her affairs much more confidential if a separate credit is opened in favour of the supplier. Consequently, an alternative method is more often used. The irrevocable credit established by the overseas buyer is held by the seller's bank. In turn, the seller's bank issues a credit in favour of the supplier in terms which are identical in so far as stipulating for the documentation required, the time for which the credit is to be available and in other details except, of course, for price. Such an arrangement is called "back to back credits".

28.61 The crucial problem with back to back credits is to ensure that the documents which will force payment on the second credit are adequate to guarantee that the primary credit may be realised.

28.62 When the credits are standby credits, other problems may arise. The case of *Commercial Banking Co of Sydney Ltd v Patrick Intermarine Acceptances Ltd*[1] shows the dangers inherent in attempting to use back to back credits. In this case, the credits were standby credits which were intended to secure some financing arrangements. PIAL, a large merchant bank, borrowed some $A 1.5 million from the State Electricity Commission of Victoria (SECV). The purpose of the borrowing was to make a loan to a finance house First Leasing. First Leasing was an Australian subsidiary of the First National Bank of Boston. In order to secure the loan from SECV, PIAL made arrangements whereby the Commercial Banking Company of Sydney opened a standby credit in favour of SECV. The credit could be drawn upon by means of a certificate from SECV to the effect that repayment of the loan to PIAL had been demanded but not received.

1 (1978) 52 ALJR 404.

28.63 PIAL also required security from the Boston bank in the form of a standby credit in favour of PIAL which could be operated by a statement from PIAL to the effect that the First Leasing loan repayment had been demanded but not received. There was an undertaking by PIAL that if it was necessary to call on the Boston credit then they would lodge with the CBC their draft and any documents called for by the Boston credit.

28.64 The arrangement was perfectly good security for the CBC in the event of the failure of First Leasing, but what happened in fact was that PIAL went into liquidation before the loans became due. SECV called on the credit which had been opened by CBC and were paid.

28.65 The CBC argued that by virtue of that payment they were entitled to an equitable charge on the debt owed to PIAL. This argument was dismissed by the Privy Council:

> Their Lordships find it impossible to imply, from the provision that in a certain event the Commercial Bank should have a proprietary interest in Boston's liability to PIAL, a provision that, if that liability should never arise, the Commercial Bank should have a proprietary interest in a different liability of a different person to PIAL.[1]

1 Per Lord Diplock at p 407.

28.66 The CBC could have protected themselves very easily by taking an assignment of the First Leasing debt. Even an equitable assignment would have protected them from the liquidation of PIAL. It appears that the failure of PIAL is the one event that the bank never considered.

Revolving credits

28.67 A "revolving credit" is generally for a fixed amount and has an expiry date as in the normal credit, but there is a clause which permits "automatic renewal" to the upper limit following each transaction on the credit. It is merely a device to obviate the necessity and expense of issuing new and identical credits when it is contemplated by the parties that there will be a series of similar transactions. The "automatic renewal" usually permits total outstanding drawings under the credit to be at a certain level.

Import and export credits

28.68 Credits are sometimes referred to as "import" or "export" credits depending upon whether their function is to facilitate an import or an export transaction. Similarly, credits may be referred to as "sterling" or "dollar" credits depending upon the currency in which they are payable.

Deferred payment credits

28.69 A fairly recent innovation is the "deferred payment" credit. It is in the same form as a standard credit which promises payment against documents, but rather than being required to pay immediately, the bank is to pay at some later time.

Red clause credits

28.70 A "red clause" credit has as its object the assistance a seller who needs periodic finance in order to acquire the goods which are the subject matter of the underlying contract. The credit authorises the intermediary bank to make advances to the seller prior to shipment. The credit derives its name from the fact that traditionally the clause authorising pre-shipment payment was printed in red ink.

Assignment of credits

28.71 The problem of transferability is made much more difficult by the possibility of assigning some or all of the benefits of the credit, a possibility which is governed by the law relating to the assignment of benefits under a contract. A contractual right is a chose in action and normally such rights may be assigned either legally under s 130 of the Property Law Act 1952 or equitably. In either case, the assignee is subject to any equity which may have attached to the assignor.[1] Generally speaking, only those contractual benefits which are essentially personal cannot be assigned. It has been said that the substitution of one person for another should be confined to those situations where it can make no difference to the person on whom the obligation lies to which of the two persons he is to discharge it.[2]

1 See Ch 24.
2 *Tolhurst v Associated Portland Cement Manufacturers (1900) Ltd* [1902] 2 KB 660 (CA); [1903] AC 414 (HL).

28.72 The general view appears to be that the benefit of credits can be assigned, but it seems that the precise question has never been litigated. Of course, when the credit is operated by means of a bill of exchange, then the drawer and drawee of the bill must be as specified in the credit. If the bill is a time draft, then payment will ultimately be made to the holder of the bill and it seems that assignment of the proceeds will have no effect, at least so far as the operation of the credit is concerned.

Dangers for the assignee

28.73 From the standpoint of the assignee, the procedure is fraught with uncertainty and difficulty. Nothing will be paid until such time as the beneficiary complies strictly with the terms of the credit; since the assignee is not usually in a position to know if the conditions have been fulfilled and is not usually in a position to influence that fulfilment, he will be uncertain as to the time or even the fact of payment.

28.74 Sometimes the assignee, in order to overcome these difficulties, will require the documents to be delivered for inspection so he may have the opportunity of correcting any deficiencies in the documentation. In such a circumstance, the assignee may also wish to tender the documents directly. Unfortunately, this may not be possible if the decision of an Austrian Commercial Court is correct.

The Singer & Friedlander case

28.75 In *Singer & Friedlander v Creditanstalt-Bankerein*[1] the defendants opened a letter of credit in favour of one Aronson to be payable against a commercial invoice and warehouse receipts. The letter was for nearly $10 million and was to pay for a consignment of drugs. The plaintiff bankers were supplying finance to Aronson and as part of the security arrangements the credit was to be assigned to them. This was done in the following terms: "I hereby irrevocably and unconditionally assign to you all my rights and benefits under documentary credit . . . ."

1 [1981] Com LR 69.

28.76 The documents were given to the plaintiffs, but when they were finally presented, payment was refused on several grounds including that the purported assignment could give the assignee no right to present the documents to the issuing bank. Fraud was alleged and it was said that Aronson could not himself have presented the documents and claimed payment.

28.77 The Court held that there had been no transfer of the letter of credit in accordance with the provisions of the UCP. The Court went on to argue that to allow the third party presentation of documents would violate the prohibition on transferability:

> It would contradict the nature of the non-transferable letter of credit if in addition to the proceeds the beneficiary could also transfer the right to realise his claim by presentation of documents in conformity with the letter of credit or to impede the paying out of the proceeds by not presenting the documents. If also the right to present (or not to present) the documents were declared transferable the non-transferable letter of credit would come close to the transferable letter of credit so that the two notions could hardly be distinguished.

28.78 The matter of assignment remains one on which the law is unsettled. The decision of the Austrian Court has not been entirely satisfactory, not the least because it failed to deal adequately with certain communications between the parties which occurred before the attempted presentation of the documents. It might have been hoped that the 1983 revision of the UCP could have dealt with the matter.

Assignment of proceeds

28.79 Of course, even if the whole of the benefit of the credit may not be assigned, it is still possible to assign the proceeds of the credit, a possibility which is expressly recognised by the UCP in Article 55:

> The fact that a credit is not stated to be transferable shall not affect the beneficiary's right to assign any proceeds to which he may be, or may become, entitled under such credit, in accordance with the provisions of the applicable law.

28.80 There is no reason why the assignment of the proceeds should cause any difficulty. If the paying banker is notified of the assignment, then he is required to pay the assignee, possibly after setting off any debt due from the assignor which may be owing.

The operation of documentary credits

Obligations of the parties

The contract: time for opening the credit

28.81 The buyer who is obliged to arrange for the opening of a credit in favour of a seller must do so a reasonable period of time before the beginning of the period allowed for shipment under the contract of sale. It is clear that the seller is entitled to ship at any time during the contractual period and the credit must be available early enough that shipping arrangements may be made with confidence that the payment by credit will be made.[1]

1 *Pavia & Co SPA v Thurmann-Nielsen* [1952] 2 QB 84; *Sinason-Teicher Inter-American Grain Corp v Oilcakes and Oilseeds Trading Co Ltd* [1954] 1 WLR 1394.

The buyer and issuing banker

28.82 When the account party instructs his or her banker to open a credit, there will usually be an express undertaking in the application that the account party will put the banker in funds to meet the obligations under the credit, but even if there is no express clause there is an implied undertaking to the same effect. In any case, the matter is put beyond doubt by Article 16(a) of the UCP.

28.83 There is a conflict of views as to the rights of the account party who has placed the banker in funds to meet a credit. On the one hand, it is clear that the banker must use the funds for the purpose of meeting the credit and no other.[1] On the other hand, there is an old case which has held that the account party has only a right to prove in the bankruptcy or liquidation in the event that the banker fails before the funds have been so applied.[2] It may be that the effect of more recent decisions such as *Barclays Bank Ltd v Quistclose Investments Ltd*[3] would have the effect of giving the account party a proprietary right in the funds.

1 *Farley v Turner* (1857) 26 LJ Ch 710.
2 *Re Barned's Banking Co, Massey's case* (1870) 39 LJ Ch 635.
3 [1970] AC 567.

28.84 The articles of the UCP which regulate the relationships between the account party and the issuing bank absolve the bank from most responsibility. There is an obligation on the bank to examine the documents with reasonable care to see that they appear on their face to be in accordance with the terms and conditions of the credit,[1] but the banker assumes no responsibility for the "form, sufficiency, accuracy, genuineness, falsification or legal effect" of any of the documents.[2] These articles are reasonable when it is recalled that the banker is not expected, indeed, not entitled to go behind the documents.

1 Article 15.
2 Article 17.

28.85 The remaining Articles which exempt the bank from liability are rather less understandable, for the banker assumes no liability for matters which are solely within the control of the banker, yet which are disastrous for the account party in the event that the banker performs his or her duty negligently. Thus,

Article 18
Banks assume no liability or responsibility for the consequences arising out of delay and/or loss in transit of any messages, letters or documents, or for delay, mutilation or other errors arising in the transmission of any telecommunication. Banks assume no liability or responsibility for errors in translation or interpretation of technical terms, and reserve the right to transmit credit terms without translating them.

28.86 Article 19 exempts bankers from any liability due to disruptions by any cause beyond their control. Finally, Article 20:

(a) Banks utilising the services of another bank or other banks for the purpose of giving effect to the instructions of the applicant for the credit do so for the account and at the risk of such applicant.
(b) Banks assume no liability or responsibility should the instructions they transmit not be carried out, even if they have themselves taken the initiative in the choice of such other bank(s).
(c) The applicant for the credit shall be bound by and liable to indemnify the banks against all obligations and responsibilities imposed by foreign laws and usages.

Cable or telex advice

28.87 At one time, it was common to advise credits by cable. Much more common today is the telex advice, and various forms of "electronic mail" are beginning to be used. The 1983 revision of the UCP has attempted to deal with the situation by Article 12:

(a) When an issuing bank instructs a bank (advising bank) by any teletransmission to advise a credit or an amendment to a credit, and intends the mail confirmation to be the operative credit instrument, or the operative amendment, the teletransmission must state "full details to follow" (or words to similar effect), or that the mail confirmation will be the operative credit instrument or the operative amendment. The issuing bank must forward the operative credit instrument or the operative amendment to such advising bank without delay.

(b) The teletransmission will be deemed to be the operative credit instrument or the operative amendment, and no mail confirmation should be sent, unless the teletransmission states "full details to follow" (or words of similar effect), or states that the mail confirmation is to be the operative credit instrument or the operative amendment.

(c) . . . .

(d) Banks shall be responsible for any consequences arising from their failure to follow the procedures set out in the preceding paragraphs.

Advising bank

28.88 The relationship between the issuing bank and the intermediary bank depends to some extent upon what it is that the intermediary is called upon to do. However, in the absence of any express agreement to the contrary, it seems that the relationship is one of principal and agent. Consequently, if the intermediary has complied with the instructions given to it by the issuing bank, then it is entitled to reimbursement of any payments properly made by it.

28.89 When the intermediary pays or negotiates the drafts of the beneficiary, he or she will ordinarily be acting as the agent of the issuing banker. Provided that the payment or negotiation is in complete conformity with the conditions of the credit, the intermediary will be entitled not only to reimbursement, but to the indemnity of an agent. Care must be taken here, however, for there can arise situations where it will be held that the intermediary bank is acting outside the terms of the credit.[1]

1 See 28.93ff.

28.90 It is not uncommon for the issuing bank to request the intermediary bank to claim reimbursement from a third bank. The UCP regulates the situation in some detail:

Article 21
(a) If an issuing bank intends that the reimbursement to which a paying, accepting or negotiating bank is entitled shall be obtained by such bank claiming on another branch or office of the issuing bank or on a third bank (all hereinafter referred to as the reimbursing bank) it shall provide such reimbursing bank in good time with the proper instructions or authorisation to honour such reimbursement claims and without making it a condition that the bank entitled to claim reimbursement must certify compliance with the terms and conditions of the credit to the reimbursing bank.
(b) An issuing bank will not be relieved from any of its obligations to provide reimbursement itself if and when reimbursement is not effected by the reimbursing bank.
(c) The issuing bank will be responsible to the paying, accepting or negotiating bank for any loss of interest if reimbursement is not provided on first demand made to the reimbursing bank, or as otherwise specified in the credit, or mutually agreed, as the case may be.

28.91 The beneficiary will generally have no rights to force the intermediary bank to fulfill any of its obligations unless the intermediary has become a confirming bank. Aside from the common law position of want of privity, the UCP provides:

Article 6
A beneficiary can in no case avail himself of the contractual relationships existing between the banks or between the applicant for the credit and the issuing bank.

28.92 There is a direct contract between the issuing bank and the beneficiary, but the issuing bank will, in an ordinary international sale of goods, be located in another country. This is one of the main reasons why beneficiaries require confirmation from a local bank.

28.93 If the local bank is only an advising bank, it is necessary for the banker to take some care in dealing with the letter of credit. In *Aotearoa International v Westpac Banking Co*[1] Aotearoa was the beneficiary of a letter of credit which had been issued by an overseas bank. The local Westpac Bank acted as an advising bank only; the letter was not confirmed. The letter of credit, which incorporated the terms of the UCP, called for the usual shipping documents and for a bill of exchange drawn on the issuing bank by the beneficiary.

1 [1984] 2 NZLR 34.

28.94 The parties had a rather unusual procedure which was customarily followed in these letter of credit transactions. The beneficiary would sign, as drawer, a blank form of a bill of exchange and leave it with the bank to be filled up when the precise figures were available. That procedure was followed on this occasion, but during the filling up of the form, a typing error was made. The form was destroyed and a new form was completed and "signed" by one of the bank officials per pro the name of the beneficiary.

28.95 The completed form was presented, together with the rest of the shipping documents, for payment under the letter of credit, but due to deficiencies in the documentation, payment was refused by the issuing bank. In the meantime, the advising bank had credited the account of the beneficiary, imposing no conditions on the crediting of the account. In the words of the Court, the bank "negotiated" the letter of credit.

28.96 The bank claimed to be able to recover from the beneficiary, either as a holder of the bill of exchange or by virtue of a general right of recourse which, it was said, an advising bank has against the beneficiary when the letter of credit is "negotiated" in the manner described here.

28.97 Although the bank clearly had the authority to fill in the original form of the bill of exchange, there was no authority to sign a new form even though it was filled up in the same way that the old one should have been. Consequently, the beneficiary was not liable on the bill as their signature had been placed there without their authority.

28.98 As to the general right of recourse, the Court held that there was no such right. In the course of the judgment, Tompkins J said:

> It is my conclusion that in the absence of a valid bill or any contractual agreement whereby the plaintiff agreed to indemnify the first defendant, the first defendant has no right of recourse against the plaintiff arising from the first defendant having negotiated the letter of credit when the United Commercial Bank as the issuing bank has failed to pay.[1]

1 At p 50.

28.99 The lesson for advising bankers is very clear. When crediting funds under a credit in which the bank is acting as an advising bank only, it should be made clear that it is a conditional crediting and that the letter is not being "negotiated". It will not always be sensible to rely upon the bill of exchange, for some letters of credit do not call for a bill and the customer may wish to draw the bill "without recourse" in any event.

Chapter 29

Documentary credits II

Presentation of documents — Security over documents or goods

The confirming bank

29.1 There seems to be no judicial consideration of the extent of the liability of a bank which confirms the issuing bank's credit. Most authors indicate that the matter will depend upon the precise wording used, but there seems to be agreement that in the absence of very clear wording to the contrary, there is no guarantee of the issuing bank's obligations.[1] So, for example, if the beneficiary chose to tender documents directly to the issuing bank and that bank were to fail before making actual payment, then the beneficiary could not look to the confirming bank. On the other hand, it is clear that there is a direct undertaking by the confirming bank to the beneficiary which is similar in terms to the undertaking of the issuing bank.[2]

1 *Paget*, p 546; Gutteridge and Megrah, *The Law of Bankers' Commercial Credits*, 7th ed, London, 1985 p 82.
2 Article 10(b).

29.2 Some credits call for time drafts to be drawn by the beneficiary seller on the buyer. It is sometimes argued that the bank's responsibility ends when the buyer has accepted the draft, an argument which has been generally discredited.[1] A recent case on the responsibility of a confirming bank has discredited a similar argument, namely that the confirming bank's responsibility to the beneficiary does not arise if the buyer refuses to accept the draft.

1 *Gutteridge and Megrah*, p 23.

29.3 In *Forestal Mimosa Ltd v Oriental Credit Ltd*[1] the defendant was a confirming bank of a letter of credit which contained a marginal note incorporating the UCP as part of the terms of the contract. The buyers refused to accept bills drawn upon them and the defendant bank claimed that they were only liable if the buyers in fact accepted the bills. If the terms of the credit were read without reference to the UCP, then this would be a reasonable construction, in spite of the fact that such a construction would nullify the usual commercial effects of a credit, since it would mean that the buyers could unilaterally render the credit ineffective.

1 [1986] 2 All ER 400.

29.4 At first instance the Court held that the defendant bank was justified in not paying. In reaching this conclusion, the Court approached the construction of the credit by ignoring the UCP; if the terms interpreted in such a fashion could solve the problem at hand, then there would be no need to resort to the UCP. In other words, the UCP was only to be consulted for the purpose of filling in any gaps which might remain.

29.5 The Court of Appeal held that this was the incorrect approach. The terms of the UCP must rank equally with the other express terms of the credit. It might be that if there was a conflict then the express terms of the credit might prevail, but the terms were to be construed so as to prevent such a contradiction if at all possible. The Court held that it was possible to read the credit in such a fashion and that in so doing, it was clear that Article 10(b)(iii) of the 1983 revision placed responsibility on the bank. That Article reads:

> When an issuing bank authorises or requests another bank to confirm its irrevocable credit and the latter has added its confirmation, such confirmation constitutes a definite undertaking of such bank (the confirming bank), in addition to that of the issuing bank, provided that the stipulated documents are presented and that the terms and conditions of the credit are complied with:
>
> . . . .
>
> (iii) if the credit provides for acceptance — to accept drafts drawn by the beneficiary if the credit stipulates that they are to be drawn on the confirming bank, or to be responsible for their acceptance and payment at maturity if the credit stipulates that they are to be drawn on the applicant for the credit or any other drawee stipulated in the credit.

29.6 The defendant bank also argued that there were discrepancies in the documents which were serious enough to cast doubts on their authenticity, but the Court held that there was no substance to the argument. As noted above, the interpretation argued by the bank would have had the effect of rendering the credit of little commercial value.

Presentation of documents

Obligation of the issuing/confirming bank

29.7 We have already noted the duty of the bank to examine documents with reasonable care. The question of the extent to which a banker must examine the documents has arisen on several occasions. Perhaps the strongest statement on the matter is the following:

> . . . to assume that . . . a bank is bound carefully to read through all bills of lading presented to it in ridiculously minute type and full of exceptions, to read through the policies and to exercise a judgment as to whether the legal effect of the bill of lading and the policy is, on the whole, favourable to their clients, is an obligation which I should require to investigate considerably before I accepted it in that unhesitating form.[1]

1 Per Scrutton LJ in *National Bank of Egypt v Hannevig's Bank* (1919) 3 LDAB 213.

Rejection of the documents

29.8 When the documents are rejected as not being in conformity with the terms of the credit, there is nothing to stop the beneficiary from attempting to rectify the documentary deficiency and presenting the documents again. This might be the case, for example, if the deficiency was merely an oversight in obtaining a certificate of quality. Again, it may be possible to get the issuer of an offending document to reissue the document in a form which complies with the terms of the credit. All such activity requires time, however, and it may be that the resubmission of the documents cannot be made within the time before the credit expires.

29.9 It has occasionally been alleged that the bank owes a duty to the beneficiary to discover all defects in the documents at the time of the first presentation, thus giving the beneficiary the optimum chance of correcting the deficiencies in time. The legal form of this argument is that the bank is estopped from raising new reasons for rejection after it has rejected the documents for some other reason. The argument was rejected firmly in *Skandinaviska Aktiebolaget v Barclays Bank Ltd*:[1]

> It is suggested . . . by the plaintiffs . . . that they have a grievance because the defendant bank did not in the first instance raise the objections that are now raised to the documents, but referred the matter to their customer in Hull and simply sent forward the customer's complaints, which were not in the first instance based upon the documents, but which were based on some untenable contention which he put forward; and it is suggested that by that means the defendants had either by estoppel or waiver, by some rule of law applicable in this country, deprived themselves of the right that they would otherwise have had of resisting the claim. I am clearly of opinion that they have not done so. They were in an intermediate position. They had the usual feelings

of banking courtesy towards the foreign bank with whom they had had dealings for a long time, and they desired, and the intention was, to see whether, notwithstanding those objections which were being raised by the customer, the transaction could not be carried through as it ought to have been. I do not think that by doing that and by leaving unstated until the later stage the valid objections — valid in law — to the documents which had been taken by the plaintiff bank, English law can deprive them of any right whatsoever.[2]

1 (1925) 22 Ll L Rep 523.
2 Per Greer J at 525.

29.10 If it is decided to reject the documents, then there is an obligation on the bank to notify the intermediary bank or the beneficiary promptly in accordance with Article 16(d). Failure to do so may result in the bank being precluded from rejecting the documents.[1]

1 Article 16(e).

Acceptance of documents "under reserve"

29.11 There are circumstances where the banker to whom the documents are presented believes that the documents do not strictly comply with the terms of the credit. In such a circumstance, the banker could reject the documents, but if the buyer and seller are known to each other or if one or the other has a particularly good relationship with the banker, it might be that the parties would wish for the deal to go ahead in spite of the discrepancies.

29.12 The solution that is often adopted is that the banker will accept the documents "under reserve", forward them to the issuing bank who will in turn consult with their customer concerning the acceptability of the documents. If the seller is known to the intermediary banker, payment may well be made, again, "under reserve". Until recently, the words "under reserve" had not been sufficiently tested in the Courts to be certain of their legal meaning.

29.13 The Court in *Banque de l'Indochine et de Suez SA v JH Rayner (Mincing Lane) Ltd*[1] was faced with precisely this problem. It was found by the Court that the remitting bank genuinely believed that there were discrepancies in the documents which would have justified non-payment, the beneficiary genuinely believed that the bank was wrong and that payment should have been made, and both parties hoped that notwithstanding the alleged discrepancies the issuing bank would, with the concurrence of the account party, take up the documents and reimburse the intermediary bank. The intermediary bank made the payment to the beneficiary "under reserve".

1 [1982] 2 Lloyd's Rep 476.

29.14 At first instance Parker J summed up the two possible interpretations of the phrase:

> The question which arises appears to me to be "did the parties, in such circumstances, by paying and accepting under reserve intend that the bank should be entitled to repayment notwithstanding that it was in law obliged to pay when it did; or was it merely intended that the position of the bank should be protected to the extent that the customer should not thereafter be entitled to resist a demand for repayment on the ground that the payment was unqualified and that he was therefore entitled to retain the payment even if one or more of the irregularities was in law valid".

29.15 Parker J thought that the correct interpretation was the first, but the Court of Appeal reversed the decision. According to Kerr MR, "under reserve" meant

> . . . that payment was to be made under reserve in the sense that the beneficiary would be bound to repay the money on demand if the issuing bank should reject the documents, whether on its own initiative or on the buyer's instructions.

29.16 If the intermediary bank was under a contractual obligation, then the beneficiary has rights against the bank for a breach of contract. However, a right of suit against the bank is very much less valuable than being able to retain the payment.

The documents

29.17 One of the most fundamental concepts in the law of documentary credits is that the parties deal only in documents, not in goods or whatever the underlying transaction is about. This principle is enshrined in the UCP:

> Article 4
> In credit operations all parties concerned deal in documents, and not in goods, services and/or other performances to which the documents may relate.

The principle of strict compliance

29.18 Since the parties are dealing in documents, and since the obligation of the bank to pay only arises "provided that the stipulated documents are presented and that the terms and conditions of the credit are complied with",[1] there are bound to be questions concerning the meaning of "stipulated documents" and of when there is "compliance".

1 Article 10, UCP.

29.19 It is clear that both terms relate only to conditions which are actually embodied in the credit and that no external factors will be considered. So, for example, in one case it was the custom of a bank to send a standard memorandum to all beneficiaries of credits which had been opened in the bank; the Court held that the contents of the memorandum were not part of the credit and could not be used to impose conditions on the beneficiary.[1]

1 *Banque de l'Indochine et de Suez SA v JH Rayner (Mincing Lane) Ltd* [1982] 2 Lloyd's Rep 476; of course, if the credit itself contained a clause which incorporated the memorandum as part of its terms, then the result would be different.

29.20 The basic position concerning the tender of documents is given in the following extract:

> A tender of documents which, properly read and understood, calls for further inquiry or is such as to invite litigation is clearly a bad tender. But the operative words are "properly read and understood". I fully accept that the clause on this bill of lading makes it unusual, but properly read and understood it calls for no inquiry and it casts no doubt at all upon the fact that the goods were shipped in apparent good order and condition or upon the protection which anyone is entitled to expect when taking up such a document whether as a purchaser or as a lender on the security of the bill.[1]

1 Per Donaldson J in [1979] 2 Ll 450, 451.

29.21 Perhaps more clearly and succinctly, Lord Sumner has said:

> These documents have to be handled by banks; they have to be taken up or rejected promptly and without any opportunity for prolonged inquiry; they have to be such as can be re-tendered to sub-purchasers, and it is essential that they should so conform to the accustomed shipping documents as to be reasonably and readily fit to pass current in commerce.[1]

1 *Hansson v Hamel & Horley* [1922] 2 AC 36, 46.

29.22 The kind of difficulties which might arise when the parties depart from the "dealing in documents" principle are illustrated in *Banque de l'Indochine et de Suez SA v JH Rayner (Mincing Lane) Ltd.*[1] The credit called for the goods to be shipped on a conference line vessel. Note that this is quite different from calling for a document which states that the goods are shipped on a conference line vessel. The defendants claimed that since no document was called for, the statement could be ignored. Both Parker J and the Court of Appeal rejected this argument, instead holding that the statement meant what it clearly did not say, namely that some documentary evidence must be tendered as part of the documentation which would attest to the fact that the carrying ship was a conference line vessel.

1 [1982] 2 Lloyd's Rep 476.

Description of the goods

29.23 A credit which is being used to facilitate an international sale of goods will call for a description of the goods in various documents. In virtually all cases, a commercial invoice will be required and there may be other documents which contain descriptions of more or less generality of the goods.

29.24 The UCP has relatively little to say about the description of the goods. Article 41(c) provides:

> The description of the goods in the commercial invoice must correspond with the description in the credit. In all other documents, the goods may be described in general terms not inconsistent with the description of the goods in the credit.

29.25 In *JH Rayner v Hambro's Bank*[1] the credit called for "Coromandel groundnuts in bags". Although this was the expression used in the commercial invoice, the bill of lading described the shipment as "machine shelled groundnut kernels". Hambro's Bank refused to pay, a decision which was upheld by the English Court of Appeal. The Court rejected the argument that the two descriptions meant the same thing, a fact which was, apparently, well known to anyone in the groundnut trade. A banker cannot be expected to have knowledge of the customs and terms of trade.

1 [1942] 2 All ER 699.

29.26 The decision has been criticised, but it seems likely that when a bill of lading contains terms and descriptions which are not in the credit, then such a document is "inconsistent with the description of the goods in the credit". So, if the bill of lading had merely said "groundnuts", it is thought that the tender would have been good.[1]

1 See Gutteridge and Megrah, *The Law of Bankers' Commercial Credits*, 7th ed, 1984, p 150.

29.27 Although the documents must necessarily be consistent among themselves, does the full description of the goods need to be found in one document only or is it possible to read the documents as a whole to find if the description meets the requirements of the credit? The matter arose in *Midland Bank v Seymour*[1] where Devlin J said:

> ... there are only two alternatives that are open to anyone endeavouring to construe the document. One is that each of the documents must contain all the particulars, and the other is that all the documents

between them — that is the set of documents — must contain all the particulars. That, of course, is subject to this obvious qualification, that each document (if it has not to contain all the particulars) must contain enough of the particulars to make it a valid document.[2]

1 [1955] 2 Lloyd's Rep 147.
2 At p 152.

29.28 The bill of lading did not contain any reference to the quality although such a reference was to be found in the other required documents. Devlin J held that under the above principle of construction the tender was good. However, if the credit expressly calls for a particular document to contain the description, then the document must do so.

29.29 In *Soproma SpA v Marine & Animal By-products Corporation*[1] the contract of sale and the letter of credit described the goods as "Chilean Fish Full Meal, steamdried, minimum 70% protein". The sellers' invoice referred to "Chilean Fish Full Meal, 70% protein". By an error, the shippers' invoice was also included in the documents. It described the goods as "Chilean Fishmeal minimum 67% protein" and the certificate of quality said "the analysis or composition of the goods is in accordance with the following analysis: Protein 67 per cent minimum" and a second certificate stated "Protein 69.7 per cent".

1 [1966] 1 Lloyd's Rep 367.

29.30 McNair J held that there was a sufficient general description of the goods in the bill of lading, but that the inconsistencies in the descriptions of the protein content made the documents an unacceptable tender under the letter of credit. He also noted that the shippers' invoice was probably irrelevant in law although it might have afforded the buyers a reason for doubting the true protein content of the goods.

Particular documents

29.31 The range of documentation called for will vary greatly from credit to credit, but there is a core of documents which will be included in virtually every credit which is being used to facilitate an international sale of goods. This core consists of a bill of lading, a commercial invoice and a policy of marine insurance. It is imperative that the banker dealing with international transactions be familiar with the basics of each of these documents.

29.32 In recent times, a document known as the combined transport bill has been used to facilitate the demands of container transport. The intent of the document has been to extend the bill of lading to cover transport by road or rail as well as sea carriage in those circumstances where the consignor of the goods packs the container, sends it by road or rail to a port where it is shipped and then perhaps carried by road or rail again before reaching its final destination. The legal effects of the CT document will be considered briefly after a discussion of the traditional documents.

Bill of lading

29.33 A bill of lading serves three purposes. First, it is a document of title to the goods; as such, it represents the goods and may be pledged or sold. Secondly, it is evidence of the contract of carriage between the consignor and the shipper. Thirdly, it is a receipt given by the carrier which acknowledges receipt of the goods. It is negotiable in the sense that the rights of the consignor may be transferred to another party, although these rights are not transferred free of existing equities.

29.34 It is its role as a document of title which makes the bill of lading so important to bankers who are engaged in financing international trade, for the use of the bill of lading means that the scheme of trading in documents instead of goods is feasible.

Clean or unclean

29.35 The carrier of goods may be responsible for damage to them which occurs during the course of carriage. In order to guard against this liability, carriers will put "clauses" on bills of lading which indicate any existing defects in the appearance or packaging of the goods. This seemingly harmless practice causes great difficulties in international trade, not the least of which is the operation of the UCP:

> Article 34
> (a) A clean transport document is one which bears no superimposed clause or notation which expressly declares a defective condition of the goods and/or the packaging.
> (b) Banks will refuse transport documents bearing such clauses or notations unless the credit expressly stipulates the clauses or notations which may be accepted.
> (c) . . . .

29.36 It is not always easy to decide if a superimposed clause has the effect of making the bill a claused rather than a clean bill. Paget argues that the question is broader than that suggested by the UCP since there may be clauses which do not relate to the condition of the goods or packaging but which nevertheless make the bill an unacceptable one. As an example, it is said that bills containing a clause "Freight paid by cheque" are refused by London bankers on the basis that there is a reasonable doubt that the credit authorises the banker to accept such a bill.[1]

1 *Paget*, p 551; *Gutteridge & Megrah*, p 141.

Shipped or received

29.37 A "shipped" bill of lading states that the goods have been loaded on board the named ship. Some bills of lading are "received" bills, that is they state only that the goods have been received for shipment. The received bill is a natural outgrowth of modern port facilities where the goods may be kept for several days pending their turn in the loading process.

29.38 Generally speaking, a "received" bill of lading is not a good tender under either a cif contract or a documentary credit which calls for a bill of lading.[1] Fortunately, received bills may be transformed into shipped bills by virtue of a notation on the bill itself which verifies that the goods have actually been shipped.

1 *Diamond Alkali Co v Bourgeois* [1921] 3 KB 443.

29.39 These matters are now the subject of the UCP. Article 26 of the UCP makes it clear that when the credit calls for a bill of lading, that the bill must be a shipped bill. Article 27(b) formalises the concept of converting the received bill into a shipped bill.

29.40 However, if the credit does not call for a bill of lading, then a received document may be acceptable under the credit:

> Article 27
> (a): Unless a credit specifically calls for an on board transport document, or unless inconsistent with other stipulation(s) in the credit, or with Article 26, banks will accept a transport document which indicates that the goods have been taken in charge or received for shipment.

Stale bills

29.41 A "stale" bill of lading is one which is tendered so late that it is not possible for the documents to reach the consignee before the arrival of the goods. For many years, bankers would refuse to pay against stale bills of lading, even though they were tendered within the time before the credit expired and even though the terms of the credit were fully met in all other respects. The practice seemed to have little to recommend it and the 1974 version of the UCP addressed the matter directly. The 1983 revision considers the matter in Article 47:

> (a) In addition to stipulating an expiry date for presentation of documents, every credit which calls for a transport document(s) should also stipulate a specified period of time after the date of issuance of the transport document(s) during which presentation of documents for payment, acceptance or negotiation must be made. If no such period of time is stipulated, banks will refuse documents presented to them later than 21 days after the date of issuance of the transport document(s). In every case, however, documents must be presented not later than the expiry date of the credit.

29.42 Since it is not always obvious what is meant by the "date of issuance", Article 47(b) lists a set of rules concerning various types of transport document.

The transhipment problem

29.43 The operation of documentary credits which are being used to facilitate international trade is influenced by the requirements of the most common form of international sale contract, namely the cif contract. The cif contract is essentially a sale of goods which is effected by a sale of documents. If the documents are in order, then the buyer must pay for the goods even if it is known that the goods have been lost before the presentation of the documents and before property in the goods has passed to the buyer.

29.44 The scheme which allows this contract to operate efficiently is the concept of continuous documentary cover. For example, in the situation mentioned above, the buyer's rights are against the policy of marine insurance. It is clear that this documentary coverage must be continuous in the sense that damage to or loss of the goods must, in so far as possible, provide the party at risk with rights of recovery against the carrier or against the insurance.

29.45 It is for this reason that the bill of lading, the document which gives rights against the carrier, must cover the carriage from the port of origin to the port of destination.[1]

1 *E Clemens Horst Co v Biddell Bros* [1912] AC 18; *Hansson v Hamel & Horley Ltd* [1922] 2 AC 36; *Holland Colombo Trading Society Ltd v Alawdeen* [1954] 2 Lloyd's Rep 45.

29.46 The problem is that of transshipment, that is, the unloading of the goods at some intermediate port and the reshipment on a new ship which will then carry the goods to the original destination. The second carrier will issue a bill of lading, but it will be issued to the original carrier. The first carrier will disclaim all responsibility for the ongoing carriage. One solution to this problem is the so-called "through bill of lading" which is issued by the first carrier but purports to cover the entire voyage. There is little authority on the legal effects of a through bill.[1]

1 For a discussion, see *Hansson v Hamel & Horley Ltd* [1922] 2 AC 36.

29.47 For these reasons, the general rule is that transshipment is prohibited in a cif contract. Furthermore, it is very common for a documentary credit to contain a term which prohibits transshipment.

29.48 Unfortunately, most bills of lading contain a printed clause which gives the carrier unlimited rights to transship. It has never been finally decided if the tender of such a bill of lading may be defective under a cif contract, but as regards credits, the point is now clear both as to the tender of through bills and bills which contain transshipment clauses by virtue of Article 29:

> (a) . . . .
> (b) Unless transhipment is prohibited by the terms of the credit, banks will accept transport documents which indicate that the goods will be transhipped, provided the entire carriage is covered by one and the same transport document.
> (c) Even if transhipment is prohibited by the terms of the credit, banks will accept transport documents which:
>> (i) incorporate printed clauses stating that the carrier has the right to tranship, or
>> (ii) state or indicate that transhipment will or may take place, when the credit stipulates a combined transport document, or indicates carriage from a place of taking in charge to a place of final destination by different modes of transport including a carriage by sea, provided that the entire carriage is covered by one and the same transport document, or . . . .

Marine insurance

29.49 It will be recalled that the insurance policy is a vital element in the operation of cif contracts. It is considered so fundamental that a buyer is entitled to receive a valid policy even if it is known that the goods have arrived safely and may repudiate the contract if a valid policy is not among the tendered documents.[1]

1 *Orient Co Ltd v Brekke & Howlid* [1913] 1 KB 531.

29.50 A policy is a document which actually embodies the contract between the insurer and the insured. The marine insurance policy is governed by the Marine Insurance Act 1908 and the benefits of the policy may be transferred.

29.51 There are two documentation problems related to insurance. The first is that when a policy of insurance is first negotiated, it will not usually be with an insurer directly but with a broker. The broker will issue a "cover note" which is legally binding so far as the initial insured is concerned, but which does not, of course, contain the terms of the contract of insurance, nor is it transferable. However, because of the delay which may occur between the issue of the cover note and the policy, sellers sometimes have wished to tender the cover note as the insurance documentation. If the credit does not explicitly authorise this, then the cover note is not an acceptable insurance document.[1]

1 Article 35(b). Similarly, unless expressly authorised by the contract, a cover note is not a good tender under a cif contract: *Manbre Saccharine Co v Corn Products Co* [1919] 1 KB 198. It has been suggested that a certificate which incorporates the terms of the contract might be good tender: *Donald H Scott & Co Ltd v Barclays Bank Ltd* [1923] 2 KB 1.

29.52 The second problem concerns the move to so called "open cover" policies. A large exporter who makes frequent shipment might arrange with an insurance company for a general cover of all exports. In practice, this means that there is only one policy which places certain ceilings on the amounts to be insured. When the exporter ships goods, the insurer is notified and the goods are covered. It is clearly impossible for the seller to include the policy, yet any certificate issued by the insurer or the insured suffers from the same legal deficiencies as the broker's cover note. Once again, unless the credit expressly provides for appropriate documentation, such a certificate is not good tender.

29.53 It is customary in cif contracts for the insurance to be the cif price of the goods plus 10% to allow the buyer a profit in the event of the loss of the goods. The UCP recognises this practice in Article 37(b):

> Unless otherwise stipulated in the credit, the minimum amount for which the insurance document must indicate the insurance cover to have been effected is the cif ... value of the goods ... plus 10%. However, if banks cannot determine the cif ... value ... from the documents on their face, they will accept as such minimum amount the amount for which payment, acceptance or negotiation is requested under the credit, or the amount of the commercial invoice, whichever is greater.

The invoice

29.54 The commercial invoice is the only one of the three basic documents which is likely to be able to provide a full description of the goods. It is important therefore that the description contained therein should be in terms identical with those called for in the credit.

29.55 The UCP deals with commercial invoices in Article 41:

> (a) Unless otherwise stipulated in the credit, commercial invoices must be made out in the name of the applicant for the credit.
> (b) Unless otherwise stipulated in the credit, banks may refuse commercial invoices issued for amounts in excess of the amount permitted by the credit. Nevertheless, if a bank authorised to pay, incur a deferred payment undertaking, accept, or negotiate under a credit accepts such invoices, its decision will be binding upon all parties, provided such bank has not paid, incurred a deferred payment undertaking, accepted or effected negotiation for an amount in excess of that permitted by the credit.
> (c) The description of the goods in the commercial invoice must correspond with the description in the credit. In all other documents, the goods may be described in general terms not inconsistent with the description of the goods in the credit.

29.56 The descriptions of quantity and quality are particularly important, and many disputes have concerned the conformity of descriptions which in other circumstances might seem to be of little importance. Thus, it has been suggested that an invoice which describes 1,000,000 kilograms (1,000 metric tons) would not be a good tender under a credit which calls for 1,000 tons.[1] Article 43 deals with quantity and amount:

(a) The words "about", "circa" or similar expressions used in connection with the amount of the credit or the quantity or the unit price stated in the credit are to be construed as allowing a difference not to exceed 10% more or 10% less than the amount or the quantity or the unit price to which they refer.

(b) Unless a credit stipulates that the quantity of the goods specified must not be exceeded or reduced, a tolerance of 5% more or 5% less will be permissible, even if partial shipments are not permitted, always provided that the amount of the drawings does not exceed the amount of the credit. This tolerance does not apply when the credit stipulates the quantity in terms of a stated number of packing units or individual items.

1 *Gutteridge and Megrah.*

Other documents

29.57 It is very common for contracts and credits to call for additional documents. The range of possible certificates and documents is so wide and the possibility of verifying their authenticity in any reasonable amount of time causes considerable difficulty. The UCP gives a wide licence to bankers to accept documents which appear to be what is called for; in view of the diversity of such documents, it would seem difficult to place a greater responsibility on banks, given the usual requirements of making a prompt decision without the need to make background investigations.

Article 23
When documents other than transport documents, insurance documents and commercial invoices are called for, the credit should stipulate by whom such documents are to be issued and their wording or data content. If the credit does not so stipulate, banks will accept such documents as presented, provided that their data content makes it possible to relate the goods and/or services referred to therein to those referred to in the commercial invoice(s) presented, or to those referred to in the credit if the credit does not stipulate presentation of a commercial invoice.

29.58 The reference in this article to being able to "relate" to the goods of the invoice or the credit is to prevent the inclusion of certificates which attest to quality but it is impossible to tell from the certificate if the goods inspected were the goods which are the subject of the credit. For example, a certificate which referred to "100 new, good, Chevrolet m.6 4X4 trucks" was not a good tender on two grounds. First, the credit stipulated new. Secondly, and more importantly, the certificate did not relate to any specific trucks.[1]

1 *Bank Melli Iran v Barclays Bank (Dominion Colonial and Overseas)* (1951) 2 TLR 1057.

29.59 Also relevant to the question of other documents is Article 42:

Article 42
If a credit calls for an attestation or certification of weight in the case of transport other than by sea, banks will accept a weight stamp or declaration of weight which appears to have been superimposed on the transport document by the carrier or his agent unless the credit specifically stipulates that the attestation or certification of weight must be by means of a separate document.

The effect of opening a credit

29.60 The method of payment may be completely specified in the contract between the buyer and the seller, but more often it is remarkably silent on the issue. Of course, the contract may call for the buyer to open a credit in favour of the seller, but the parties seldom contemplate the effect of opening the credit if the course of the transaction does not proceed as contemplated. What happens for example, if the issuing bank becomes insolvent? Is the buyer entitled to present the documents directly to the seller, even if the credit is still on foot? What happens if the bank wrongly refuses to pay?

29.61 Some of these questions may be answered on general principles. It seems that when the contract calls for the opening of a credit, then the seller must evidently attempt to be paid under the credit. Only if that attempt fails would he or she be justified in attempting to present the documents directly to the buyer.[1]

1 *Soproma SpA v Marine & Animal By-Products Corporation* [1966] 1 Lloyd's Rep 367.

29.62 But there have been arguments raised to the effect that the mere opening of the credit in conformity with the contract of sale is itself complete payment; if the credit fails, then that is the seller's bad luck for having been paid the goods must now be delivered.

29.63 This view received some support from the High Court of Australia in *Saffron v Societe Miniere Cafrika*.[1] The seller had tendered documents which were not in conformity with the credit and payment was refused. Ordinarily, as mentioned above, this would leave the seller in control of the goods, but in the *Saffron* case the buyer achieved control of the goods, then claiming that payment had been made by virtue of the credit being opened. The Court said:

It would . . . be wrong to consider the question without regard to the kind of letter of credit for which the contract provides. A provision for payment by revocable letter of credit could hardly be regarded in any circumstances as negativing payment in the event of revocation. At the other end of the scale a provision for payment by irrevocable and confirmed letter of credit . . . might perhaps not unreasonably be regarded as a stipulation for the liability of the confirming bank in place of that of the buyer. Where the stipulation is for an irrevocable but not

confirmed credit there would be less reason for regarding the provision
of the credit as being all that is required by the buyer in any
circumstances.[2]

1 (1958) 100 CLR 231.
2 At p 244.

29.64 It is perfectly possible for the seller to contract that the buyer's
obligation is extinguished by the mere opening of the credit, but
the consequences are so serious for the seller that it does not seem
reasonable to infer the result merely from the fact that the seller
has requested that the credit be confirmed even when the seller
names the confirming bank. The reason for such a term is not to
relieve the buyer of all liability, but rather to avoid problems by
having a reliable paymaster who is located in the country of the
seller.

29.65 This is the view that was taken by the English Court of Appeal
in *WJ Alan v El Nasr Export & Import Co.*[1] The Court approved the
statement of the trial Judge who said that it seems:

> wrong that the primary obligation of the buyer to pay the price should
> be treated as extinguished unless there is some clear indication that both
> parties so intended and it seems to me that the provision for payment
> by way of letter of credit which is an arrangement not for the benefit
> of the seller alone, but of both parties, falls far short of any such
> indication, and as far as authority goes, I think that on the whole the
> balance of such authority as there is favours the same view.[2]

1 [1972] QB 189.
2 Per Orr J [1971] 1 Lloyd's Rep 401.

29.66 These questions have been reformulated by Lord Denning
in terms of whether the credit is absolute payment, conditional
payment, or no payment at all. The consequences of each are as
follows:

> If the letter of credit is absolute payment of the price, the consequences
> are these: The seller can only look to the banker for payment. He can
> in no circumstances look to the buyer. The seller must present the
> documents to the banker and get payment from him in cash or get him
> to accept sight or time drafts. If the banker does not take up the
> documents, the seller will retain them, resell and sue the banker for
> damages. If the banker takes up the documents in exchange for time
> drafts, and the banker afterwards becomes insolvent, the seller must
> prove in the liquidation. He cannot sue the buyer . . . .
> If the letter of credit is conditional payment of the price, the
> consequences are these: the seller looks in the first instance to the
> banker for payment; but, if the banker does not meet his obligations
> when the time comes for him to do so, the seller can have recourse to
> the buyer. The seller must present the documents to the banker . . . .
> It may mean that the buyer (if he has already paid the bank) will have
> to pay twice over. So be it. He ought to have made sure that he employed
> a "reliable and solvent paymaster" . . . .
> If the letter of credit is no payment at all, but only a means by which
> payment may be obtained . . . the consequences are these: the seller
> ought to present the documents to the banker. If he does not do so, he

will be guilty of laches in enforcing his security and the buyer will be discharged . . . . But if on the presentation the banker fails or refuses to take up the documents then . . . the seller will be entitled to take the documents round to the buyer . . . and demand that he takes them up and pay the price . . . .

As a result of this analysis, I am of the opinion that . . . [the letter of credit] operates as conditional payment of the price.[1]

1 *WJ Alan & Co v El Nasr Export* [1972] 2 QB 189, 209, 210.

Security over documents or goods

29.67 When the credit is one which is used to facilitate an international sale of goods, the documents of title to the goods may be used as a security. It is very unlikely that a bank would rely entirely upon the goods as security, but there is no doubt that they provide a useful adjunct to any other securities that the bank may have taken from the account party.

29.68 It is customary that the form used for application will contain a clause which authorises the bank to take possession of and to sell the goods in the event of a non-payment, but even without such a clause, it seems likely that the banker would have an implied pledge of the documents. It has been said that the intermediary bank would have an implied pledge of the documents, although the comments were admittedly obiter.[1]

1 Per Scrutton LJ in *Guaranty Trust Co of New York v Hannay & Co* [1918] 2 KB 623.

29.69 When the documents include a bill of lading, there is little difficulty, for the bill of lading is a document of title to the goods so that a pledge of the document is equivalent to a pledge of the goods themselves. The goods may be pledged merely by the indorsement and delivery of the bill. Furthermore, the bill of lading does not cease to be a document of title when the carriage itself is completed. It has been held that the contract of carriage is a combined contract of transportation of the goods by sea and a contract of bailment, so that until the goods are released from the bailment the bill of lading remains a good document of title.[1]

1 Per Diplock LJ in *Barclays Bank Ltd v Commissioners of Customs and Excise* [1963] 1 Lloyd's Rep 81.

29.70 There is somewhat more difficulty when the documents do not include a document of title. This will be the case when the goods are shipped by air, in which case the shipping document is the air waybill, or when there is a combined transport which calls for a combined transport bill of lading or waybill. The waybill generally evidences the receipt of the goods by the carrier and names the consignee. The carrier should deliver the goods only to the named consignee. Consequently, these documents cannot be used to obtain a pledge, but there is no reason why the bank should not have a charge over the goods by means of a letter of hypothecation.[1] Further, if the waybill names the bank as consignee, it may be that the bank can obtain a pledge of the goods.

1 See Ch 24.

Trust receipts

29.71 If the applicant for the credit is able to place the banker in funds to meet the credit, then the documents may be delivered immediately. However, very often, the applicant/buyer will need to resell and/or reship the goods to a sub-purchaser in order to obtain the funds. If the issuing banker wishes to retain security over the goods, this presents something of a problem. The solution is the "letter of trust".

29.72 At common law parting with the possession of the goods will usually determine a pledge, but it has always been possible to part with them for a specific purpose. The specific purpose in this case, is to allow the account party to sell or ship the goods. The "letter of trust" embodies an agreement between the account party and the banker whereby the banker agrees to release the goods to the account party for the above limited purpose and the account party in return agrees that the documents, the goods, and the proceeds of the goods when resold will be held in trust for the bank. The validity of the arrangement was by the House of Lords in *North Western Bank v Poynter, Son, & Macdonalds.*[1]

1 [1895] AC 56.

29.73 That case also illustrates one way in which the arrangement may be very beneficial to the bank. The goods were released to the account party who shipped the goods to a sub-purchaser. Before all of the payments were made, the account party became insolvent. The question was whether the bank was entitled to receive the balance of the purchase price or if it must prove along with general creditors. The House upheld the arrangement with the consequence that the bank was entitled to the balance of the purchase price.

29.74 Releasing the documents to the customer is not without its risks, for whereas the pledge is a legal security, the security under the letter of trust is an equitable one.[1] Davis[2] argues that the letter of trust is not a true trust situation but is a combination of bailment, agency and trust. It is clear that the bank's interest is only equitable. If a purchaser of the goods has no notice of the banker's interest, then the rights of the banker will be defeated provided the purchase has been for value and in good faith.

1 The precise nature of the security is not entirely clear.
2 Davis, *The Law Relating to Commercial Letters of Credit*, 3rd ed, London, 1963.

29.75 The validity of letters of trust has been challenged on a number of occasions. It has been claimed that the arrangement constitutes an unregistered charge on book debts or an unregistered bill of sale. These attempts have all failed, the most comprehensive analysis being that in *Re David Allester Ltd*.[1]

1 [1922] 2 Ch 211.

The autonomy principle

29.76 In a typical letter of credit arrangement, there are at least three separate contracts. There is the underlying contract, usually of sale, which is the reason for the existence of the letter of credit, there is the contract between the issuing banker and the buyer (or other account party) and there is the contract between the issuing banker and the beneficiary.

29.77 These contracts are obviously not independent in the business sense, for the letter of credit would not ordinarily exist without the underlying contract of sale. The question to be addressed in this section is whether or not the contracts are independent in the legal sense. The problem most commonly arises when there is a dispute between the buyer and seller prior to payment. Since withholding of payment is one of the strongest bargaining chips that any buyer has, it is understandable that the buyer should wish to stop the bank from making payment under the letter of credit until such time as the dispute is resolved.

29.78 If the contracts between the banker and each of the parties are somehow subservient to the underlying contract, then it seems reasonable that the buyer might be able to stop payment. But if the buyer is to have a free hand to stop payment, then the letter of credit mechanism becomes much less attractive to sellers. Further, if the payment can only be stopped for "good" reasons, then who is to arbitrate on the particular dispute?

29.79 Perhaps for these reasons, it has long been recognised that the letter of credit is a separate contract. This is known as the "autonomy princile" and was firmly established judicially surprisingly late in the development of letter of credit law.

29.80 As if to put the matter beyond all doubt, the principle is now enshrined in the UCP:

Article 3
Credits, by their nature, are separate transactions from the sales or other contract(s) on which they may be based and banks are in no way concerned with or bound by such contract(s), even if any reference whatsoever to such contract(s) is included in the credit.

29.81 The principle is illustrated by *Urquhart Lindsay & Co v Eastern Bank Ltd.*[1] The plaintiff company had sold machinery under a contract which called for payment by an irrevocable documentary credit issued by the defendant bank. The contract of sale provided for several shipments of the machinery and also contained a clause which called for a variation in the contract price in certain circumstances, but there was no reference to such matters in the credit itself. After several shipments had been made, the buyers claimed that the price on the next shipment should be reduced under the variation clause. The sellers did not agree. The buyers instructed the defendant banker to refuse to make the payment under the letter of credit for any amount over the sum which the buyers claimed was the correct price.

1 [1922] 1 KB 318.

29.82 The bank carried out the instructions of its customer, the buyer, and refused payment when the documents were produced. The Court held that the bank was not entitled to do so, that far from the letter of credit being a contract that was subservient to the contract of sale, that it was a fully autonomous contract. Indeed, if there was a conflict between the contract of sale and the letter of credit, the Court appeared to say that it was the contract of sale which might need to be rewritten.

29.83 Explaining the obligations of the parties, Rowlatt J said:

. . . the defendants undertook to pay the amount of invoices for machinery without qualification, the basis of this form of banking facility being that the buyer is taken for the purpose of all questions between himself and his banker, or between his banker and the seller, to be content to accept the invoices of the seller as correct. It seems to me that, so far from the letter of credit being qualified by the contract of sale, the latter must accommodate itself to the letter of credit.[1]

1 [1922] 1 KB 318, 323.

29.84 Furthermore, the Court held that on the breach of the contract to pay under the letter of credit, the bank became liable to pay damages which were to be assessed as on the repudiation of the contract as a whole. The bank had argued that there was a mere failure to make a payment and that, analogous to debt, there could be no assessment of damages beyond the amount of the payment in question. The Court rejected the bank's argument, holding that the bank was liable for all damages which flowed from the breach and that the sellers were under no obligation to take action to obtain payment in some other way; in particular, they were not obliged to take the lesser amount offered by the buyers.

29.85 In the absence of fraud on the part of the seller, the issuing banker is not entitled to refuse payment by any reference to the underlying contract of sale and this is true even when the issuing banker is in a position to know that the seller is in breach of the contract with the buyer and that the breach is severe enough to entitle the buyer to reject the documents.[1]

1 As to the nature of fraud see *United City Merchants (Investments) Ltd and Glass Fibres and Equipment Ltd v Royal Bank of Canada* [1979] 2 Lloyd's Rep 498 and 29.97.

Application: preventing the operation of the credit by injunction

29.86 In *Hamzeh Malas & Sons v British Imex Industries*[1] the contract between buyer and seller called for the goods to be delivered in instalments. It was alleged that the first instalment was defective and the buyers sought an injunction which would restrain the sellers from drawing on the credit until the rights of the parties under the contract of sale had been determined. The case is noteworthy for the fact that the Court of Appeal held that the Court had the power to grant such an injunction, but refused to do so on the basis that the credit constituted a separate contract:

> . . . the opening of a confirmed letter of credit constitutes a bargain between the banker and the vendor of the goods, which imposes upon the banker an absolute obligation to pay . . . .

1 [1958] 2 QB 127.
2 Per Jenkins LJ [1957] 2 Lloyd's Rep 549, 550.

29.87 There have also been cases where the account party has sought to gain an injunction which will prevent the bank from paying. In *Discount Records Ltd v Barclays Bank Ltd*[1] the plaintiffs had ordered goods from a French company. When the first shipments arrived, many of the cartons were simply rubbish. Some of the cartons had shipping marks which appeared to have been changed or tampered with.

1 [1975] 1 WLR 315.

29.88 Once again, the Court affirmed its jurisdiction to grant an injunction which would prevent the operation of the credit, but once again refused to do so. Megarry J noted that the Courts should be slow to interfere with bankers' credits except in very grave circumstances since the importance of maintaining commercial confidence in such arrangements is of the utmost importance.

29.89 But the Judge also noted that an injunction was quite improper here for quite another reason. The contract between the bank and the account party was a contract which was separate from the contract of sale. If the banker did the wrong thing under that contract by paying when payment should not be made, then the remedy was in damages for the breach of contract. If, on the other hand, the banker did the correct thing in paying, where was the ground for an injunction? It appears that an injunction is in order only when to refuse one would result in an irretrievable injustice.

Fraud

29.90 The autonomy principle, important as it is, must necessarily yield in certain cases. It has already been noted that the Courts have repeatedly asserted that there is a power to grant an injunction to prevent the operation of credits when the circumstances so dictate.

29.91 The only circumstance in which injunctions have in fact been granted is where fraud is involved, and recent cases have narrowed even this exception considerably. Interestingly enough, it is an American case which is always cited as authority for the so-called fraud exception to the autonomy principle.

29.92 In *Sztejn v J Henry Schroder Banking Corp*[1] the plaintiff contracted to purchase a quantity of bristles from an Indian firm. As partial fulfilment of that contract the plaintiff arranged with the defendant to open an irrevocable letter of credit in favour of the Indian sellers. The complaint alleged that the seller filled some 50 crates with cowhair and other worthless material with an intent to defraud the plaintiff.

1 31 NYS (2d) 631 (1941).

29.93 The plaintiff was seeking a declaration that the letter of credit was void and an injunction preventing the defendant banking corporation from paying pursuant to the letter of credit. It is fundamental to the understanding of the case to recognise that it came before the Court under a motion for dismissal filed by the defendant and that the procedure called for the Court to assume that the facts alleged, in particular the fraud, had been proved by the plaintiff.

29.94 The Court held that the plaintiff would, under those assumptions, be entitled to injunctive relief. It emphasised that this was under the assumption of fraud, that the bill of exchange which would be presented for payment under the letter of credit was still in the hands of the seller, the bank has been given notice of the fraud and the banker is willing to postpone payment pending an adjudication of the rights and obligations of the other parties.

29.95 Since the qualifications mentioned by the Court are often overlooked, it is worth reflecting on the very clear words of Shientag J:

If it had appeared from the face of the complaint that the bank presenting the draft for payment was a holder in due course, its claim against the bank issuing the letter of credit would not be defeated even though the primary transaction was tainted with fraud.[1]

1 At p 635.

29.96 The English Court considered the *Sztejn* case in *Discount Records Ltd v Barclays Bank*.[1] It is worth noting that the Court found insufficient evidence of fraud in that case to justify an application of the fraud exception. Given the facts of that case, it is difficult to see how extrinsic, ie, non-documentary, fraud could be shown. The Court considered it very relevant that the bill of exchange might be in the hands of a holder in due course.

1 [1975] 1 Lloyd's Rep 444; discussed above at 29.87.

29.97 The scope of the fraud rule has received clarification by the House of Lords in *United City Merchants (Investments) Ltd v Royal Bank of Canada*.[1] The second plaintiff was an English company which sold manufacturing equipment to a Peruvian company. There was an agreement between them to double the invoice price as a means of circumventing Peruvian exchange control regulations, the excess to be deposited in an American bank on behalf of the Peruvian company. A Peruvian bank issued a letter of credit to cover the transaction and the defendant bank confirmed. The rights under the credit were assigned to the first plaintiff.

1 [1982] 2 All ER 720.

29.98 The credit expired on 15 December 1976 and shipment of the goods was not accomplished until the day after. The Court found that there was fraud in that an employee of the loading brokers had improperly dated the bill of lading in order to make it appear that loading was timely. However, the employee was not acting on behalf of the plaintiff beneficiary of the letter of credit.

29.99 When the documents were presented to the Royal Bank of Canada, the confirming bank, for payment, it came to the attention of the bankers that the ship had in fact not arrived in port on the day on which the bill of lading was dated. It was clear to the bank that the bill of lading was to some extent forged and that there was some fraud which resulted in the documentation. Note that it is a contractual term of a cif contract that the seller present the buyer with correct shipping documents, so that the seller was in breach of the cif obligations even though there was no fault on the part of the seller.

29.100 The bank refused to pay, claiming the fraud exception. There were further complications due to the conspiracy to avoid the Peruvian exchange control regulations, but those are separate to the issues in the fraud part of the case. The House of Lords held that the bank was obliged to pay. It is worth quoting Lord Diplock at some length:

If, on their face, the documents presented to the confirming bank by the seller conform with the requirements of the credit as notified to him by the confirming bank, that bank is under a contractual obligation to the seller to honour the credit, notwithstanding that the bank has knowledge that the seller at the time of presentation of the conforming documents is alleged by the buyer to have, and in fact has already, committed a breach of his contract with the buyer for the sale of the goods to which the documents appear on their face to relate, that would have entitled the buyer to treat the contract of sale as rescinded and to reject the goods and refuse to pay the seller the purchase price. The whole commercial purpose for which the system of confirmed irrevocable documentary credits has been developed in international trade is to give to the seller an assured right to be paid before he parts with control of the goods that does not permit of any dispute with the buyer as to the performance of the contract of sale being used as a ground for non-payment or reduction or deferment of payment.

To this general statement of principle as to the contractual obligations of the confirming bank to the seller, there is one established exception: that is, where the seller, for the purpose of drawing on the credit, fraudulently presents to the confirming bank documents that contain, expressly or by implication, material representations of fact that to his knowledge are untrue. Although there does not appear among the English authorities any case in which this exception has been applied, it is well established in the American cases of which the leading or "landmark" case is *Sztejn v J Henry Schroder Banking Corporation* (1941) 31 NYS 2d 631. This judgment of the New York Court of Appeals was referred to with approval by the English Court of Appeal in *Edward Owen Engineering Ltd v Barclays Bank International Ltd* [1978] QB 159.

29.101 It seems likely that the "one established exception" may be too narrowly stated. It is generally thought that there must be fraud on the part of the beneficiary in order to come within the exception, and that fraud may not necessarily be limited to statements in the documents required to be presented under the terms of the credit, although no doubt some consequence of the fraud will appear there.

Index

511